3/01

Encyclopedia of
the Haudenosaunee
(Iroquois Confederacy)

Encyclopedia of the Haudenosaunee (Iroquois Confederacy)

Edited by
BRUCE ELLIOTT JOHANSEN
and
BARBARA ALICE MANN

GREENWOOD PRESS
Westport, Connecticut • London

Library of Congress Cataloging-in-Publication Data

Encyclopedia of the Haudenosaunee (Iroquois Confederacy) / edited by Bruce
Elliott Johansen and Barbara Alice Mann.
　　p.　cm.
　　Includes bibliographical references (p.　) and index.
　　ISBN 0–313–30880–2 (alk. paper)
　　1. Iroquois Indians—Encyclopedias.　I. Title: Encyclopedia of the
Haudenosaunee.　II. Title: Encyclopedia of the Iroquois.　III. Johansen,
Bruce E. (Bruce Elliott), 1950–　IV. Mann, Barbara A., 1947–
E99.I7 E53　2000
974.7'0049755—dc21　　　　99–043508

British Library Cataloguing in Publication Data is available.

Library of Congress Catalog Card Number: 99–043508
ISBN: 0–313–30880–2

First published in 2000

Greenwood Press, 88 Post Road West, Westport, CT 06881
An imprint of Greenwood Publishing Group, Inc.
www.greenwood.com

Printed in the United States of America

The paper used in this book complies with the
Permanent Paper Standard issued by the National
Information Standards Organization (Z39.48–1984).

10 9 8 7 6 5 4 3 2 1

Contents

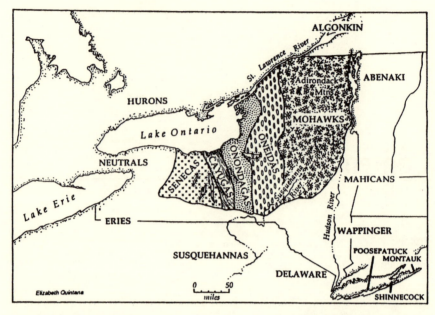

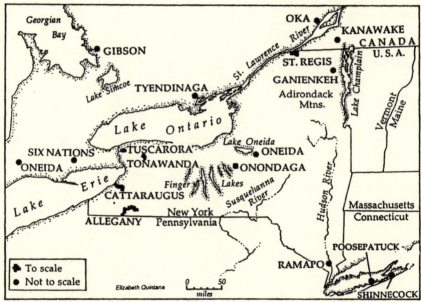

Haudenosaunee homelands, c. 1500 (top); Haudenosaunee reservations, 1999 (bottom).
© Elizabeth Quintana/Akwe:kon Press.

Preface

Lewis Henry Morgan's study of the Haudenosaunee Confederacy, *League of the Haudenosaunee, or Iroquois* (1851), founded the modern discipline of American anthropology and provided, in the words of John Wesley Powell, the founder of the Bureau of American Ethnology, the field's "first scientific account of an Indian tribe" (Morgan, *League*, v). A century and a half later, the book is still the most comprehensive single treatment of the Haudenosaunee, and one that, in its status as a virtual bible of anthropology, has ensured that the Haudenosaunee would become one of the most intensely studied aboriginal peoples on earth. In the intervening century and a half, the Haudenosaunee probably have been the subject of more anthropological study per capita than any other group of people on earth.

Examined critically, *League of the Haudenosaunee* reveals the intensity of Morgan's ethnocentricity. He seems enamored of the belief that the Iroquois League is dying, stating that it was "a shadow of its former self" when he was writing the book during the late 1840s (Morgan, *League*, 34). Morgan returns to this theme several times:

Their council fires, so far as they are emblematic of civil jurisdiction, have long since been extinguished, their empire terminated, and the shades of evening are now gathering thickly over the scattered and feeble remnants of this once-powerful league. Race has yielded to race, the inevitable result of the contact of the civilized with the hunter state. (Morgan, *League*, 145)

Morgan spends many pages doing his best to lock the Haudenosaunee into his own evolutionary schema for European political systems. He forgets, for the moment, that the Iroquois did not live primarily by hunting, but by growing corn and other agricultural products. At other points in his book, Morgan acknowledges that they maintained an agricultural estate that amazed many European observers. Morgan's remarks in *League of the Haudenosaunee* presaged his more organized schema in *Ancient Society* (1877), in which he engages in the social Darwinist exercise of separating all of humankind into three classes— savages, barbarians, and civilized peoples. It is cold comfort to many Haudenosaunee that he locked them into this scheme as "barbarians."

Ironically, as Morgan aged, he embraced notions of social Darwinism at the same time that many early Marxists, including Friederich Engels, embraced his ideas. Marx and Engels adhered to a schema of human development—slavery, capitalism, socialism, communism—that was not Darwinistic. "Survival of the fittest" evolved as a naturalistic, "scientific" metaphor for capitalism during the era many called "the Gilded Age."

Morgan believed that "a fatal deficiency in Indian society . . . the nonexistence of a progressive spirit" (Morgan, *League*, 142) doomed the Iroquois to his assumed state of decline, a belief that became one of the great unspoken assumptions of anthropology a century ago, in what some of the field's historiography still calls its "golden age." This may have been a golden age for anthropological professionals, but it was hardly a favorable time for their Native American "subjects." Some non-Indian historians still call the period "the era of the vanishing race," a time when a few hundred thousand survivors of a four-century holocaust struggled to survive against an onslaught that sought to remove their cultures from collective memory in America.

Morgan prepares his case that the Haudenosaunee are not "progressive," oddly enough, barely two pages after an enlightening discussion of how the Iroquois League changed by adopting the institution of the pine-tree chief, who is raised to the council outside the traditional hereditary structure. Such a practice would seem to indicate that this Native American polity could evolve or "progress." Morgan ignores the evidence that contradicts his assumption, and he never defines what he means by a "progressive spirit." Given Morgan's determination to consign the Iroquois to the past, he might be confounded by their revival (and that of many other Native American nations) almost a century and a half after his pioneering work was published.

Morgan thus planted in the seed ground of academic anthropology a paradoxical assumption that has shaped the practice of this social science for a century and a half. The assumption that the Haudenosaunee Confederacy is dying or is dead is an assertion that was no more true to living Haudenosaunee people in 1850 than it is today.

Morgan established an anthropological tone that seemed to prize Iroquois culture and people more dead than alive. Living Iroquois are dismissed as hardly artifactual enough to be worth considering—a set of assumptions that William N. Fenton, the non-Haudenosaunee world's "dean of Iroquois studies," repeated in his work to the end of the twentieth century.

Morgan ends his *League of the Haudenosaunee* with his own prescription for "the future destiny of the Indian," a blueprint heavily inked with the nostrums of missionaries, Anglo-American educators, and government officials who took it as their duty, in Morgan's time, to shape the futures of America's surviving

Native American peoples. There is no space in Morgan's work for the "authentic" Haudenosaunee to end up anywhere other than in museums under glass as quaint reminders of a dead past.

The effect of Morgan's work on the developing field of ethnology has been compared with that of his contemporary Charles Darwin on biology. Francis Sparkman, the historian, admired Morgan. Karl Marx read Morgan's *Ancient Society* and made copious notes. After Marx died, Engels inherited the notes and used them to produce *The Origin of the Family, Private Property, and the State*, which analyzes Iroquois political and social systems in light (as the book's subtitle states) of Lewis Henry Morgan's work. Engels was astounded by his discovery of a state with relative equality between men and women that did not have marked social classes.

One must know Morgan's work to understand why present-day Haudenosaunee people and non-Indian "Iroquois experts" find themselves so at odds. The imperialist arrogance of late-nineteenth-century views still informs the unspoken assumptions of old-guard ethnohistorians with regard to the Haudenosaunee. These unspoken assumptions allow some "experts" to joke among themselves that the Grand Council fire of the Iroquois is now fed by burning tires, another way of insisting that the confederacy no longer exists in a form that the non-Indian "experts" find "authentic." (The observation about burning tires is also a snide play on the fact that Leon Shenandoah, recent Tadadaho, or speaker, of the confederacy, made his living as operator of an automobile scrapyard.)

The academic establishment and modern Haudenosaunee people could not be more alienated from each other. The situation in Iroquois country is so well defined that I sometimes need to be reminded that this is not the state of affairs everywhere. I visited with Alfonso Ortiz, a Pueblo anthropologist, shortly before his death. My negative opinions of anthropology as a field of study were cut short by him. Ortiz, one of the best-known anthropologists of our time, reminded me that among his people, the best-regarded "anthros" are native and have been for many years. I am also reminded that Jay C. Fikes, who is trained as an academic anthropologist, wrote a culturally sensitive biography of the Winnebago (Ho-Chunk) leader and holy man Reuben Snake, avoiding nearly all the traps of assumption that plague the "experts" on the Haudenosaunee.

In Iroquois country, however, the "experts," so attached to Morgan's century-old ways of thinking, have been unprepared to realize that the confederacy is not only alive, but is expanding its sense of a self-defined voice that the observer-subject dichotomy of nineteenth-century anthropology denies. Some academics become uncomfortable when the "subjects" of research begin to demand a voice in the academic agenda.

In academia, Native American research agendas have been expressed increasingly through the development of curricula in Native American (or American Indian) studies. By the end of the 1990s, roughly ninety colleges and universities had organized Native American studies programs, from undergraduate minors to (in two cases, the University of Arizona and the University of California at

Los Angeles) doctoral programs. More than 350 professors across the United States, in more than one hundred colleges and universities, have identified themselves (for affirmative-action purposes) as American Indian or Alaska Natives (Lobo and Talbot, 2).

The basis of any academic field is the volume and quality of literature produced by those who teach in it. The shelf of books by and about American Indians has always been large, but never so large as it was late in the 1990s, when many colleges and universities adopted requirements that students take coursework in "ethnic diversity."

It may be surprising to today's students that attempts by non-Indians to see the world through Haudenosaunee and other Native American eyes are a recent innovation on a large educational scale. To illustrate changes in perceptions of the Iroquois and other Native American societies by non-Indians, let me take you back almost a century, to a lengthy entry on "Indians, North American," in *the Encyclopaedia Britannica*'s eleventh edition, published in 1911. The most prominent feature of this entry is a table on which every Native tribe or nation that the encyclopedia could find is listed according to its amenability to European ways of life (i.e., "condition, progress, etc."). The Mohawks of St. Regis are said to have been "practically all civilized and making fair progress" (*Encyclopaedia*, 461). Christian conversion seems to have been the major criterion for a good "grade." The Iroquois at Gibson are said to be "industrious and progressive [due to] influence of Methodist missions" (*Encyclopaedia*, 461).

The following statement describing the "temperance and morals" of the St. Regis (Akwesasne) Mohawks appeared in a U.S. Census Bureau bulletin published in 1891:

Ignorance is the key to much of their passivity, and the safeguards which religious forms have placed about their homes lack intelligent application to their outside relations through the unfortunate failure to combine religious teachings and observances in any language than their own. . . . The temptation to use spirits, which easily masters the unoccupied classes of any community, has had its effect here, as on other reservations. (Venables, 62)

This 1891 census report on the morality of the Akwesasne Mohawks concluded that "immorality among the St. Regis Indians, other than intemperance, is . . . rare," and that "the Saint Regis people . . . are better qualified for useful citizenship than several of the white races which seek America for a change of living" (Venables, 62).

G. Elmore Reaman, an Englishman, writing in the middle 1960s, reflected on Rudyard Kipling's poetic description, during the height of the British Empire, of "lesser breeds without the law." He then wondered how this description could ever be used to describe the Haudenosaunee, a "race of people that could furnish the prototype of the Constitution of the United States . . . and whose confederacy has many of the aspects of the present-day United Nations" (Reaman, xiv). During the same year, the American Society for Ethnohistory (ASE) defined its scholarly discipline as being devoted to "general culture history and process, and the specific history of all peoples on all levels of socio-cultural organization, emphasizing that of primitives and peasantries" (Axtell, 12). In 1971, in the midst of an upsurge in Native American activism that demanded acceptance of Indians as human beings rather than solely as objects of study, the reference to "primitives" was stricken from ASE's statement of purpose. The emphasis on levels of sociocultural organization (echoing Lewis Henry Morgan's gradations of cultures more than a century earlier) was retained.

In 1987, having been invited to Cornell University to take part in a conference on the Haudenosaunee influence on democracy, I met a traditional chief who told me lightheartedly that most Haudenosaunee were so tired of anthropologists that they usually told them tall tales about culture and history that brought chuckles to the faces of the anthro-wise. The laughter doubled when the chief said that most of the Anglo scholars seemed not to be able to tell the difference between real oral history and jokes meant to pull their metaphorical legs.

By the late 1980s, when the Haudenosaunee were locked in conflict with non-Indian "experts" over return of their wampum belts from New York State archives, the degree of Haudenosaunee alienation from anthropologists whom they believed to be intellectual strip miners of their culture had reached a palpable level. Scholars at the Cornell conference were introduced to large Iroquois audiences as "not anthropologists." The same year, William N. Fenton published his *False Faces of the Iroquois*, which may have been regarded as a seminal work in some circles. To many Haudenosaunee traditionalists, the publication of a book filled with photographs and drawings of their sacred Grandfather masks (photography of the ritual masks is strictly forbidden) was a supreme insult and a monument to cultural arrogance. Fenton should have known better after half a century of work with Haudenosaunee people.

The Haudenosaunee, who had been assigned by the intellectual heirs of Morgan to the subsidiary status of subjects in studies designed by non-Iroquois, have been working to find their own voice. In history, any complete description demands consideration of oral as well as written histories. I hope that this volume will help infuse a Haudenosaunee (Iroquois) voice into undergraduate library research.

Bruce E. Johansen

FURTHER READING

Axtell, James. "The Ethnohistory of Native America." In Donald L. Fixico, ed., *Rethinking American Indian History*. Albuquerque: University of New Mexico Press, 1997.

The Encyclopaedia Britannica. 11th ed. Vol. 13/14. New York: Encyclopaedia Britannica, 1911.

Fenton, William N. *The False Faces of the Iroquois*. Norman: University of Oklahoma Press, 1987.

Lobo, Susan, and Steve Talbot. *Native American Voices: A Reader*. New York: Longman, 1998.

Mann, Barbara A., and Jerry L. Fields. "A Sign in the Sky: Dating the League of the Haudenosaunee." *American Indian Culture and Research Journal* 21:2 (1997): 105–163.

Morgan, Lewis Henry. *Ancient Society*. New York: Henry Holt, 1877.

———. *Houses and House-Life of the American Aborigines*. With an introduction by Paul Bohannan. Chicago: University of Chicago Press, 1965.

———. *League of the Iroquois*. 1851. Secaucus, N.J.: Citadel Press, 1962.

———. *Systems of Consanguinity and Affinity of the Human Family*. Washington, D.C.: Smithsonian Institution, 1870.

Reaman, G. Elmore. *The Trail of the Iroquois Indians: How the Iroquois Indians Saved Canada for the British Empire*. New York: Barnes and Noble, 1967.

Venables, Robert W., ed. *The Six Nations of New York: The 1892 United States Extra Census Bulletin*. Ithaca, N.Y.: Cornell University Press, 1995.

Introduction

This is the first one-volume college- and university-library reference work on the Haudenosaunee (Iroquois Confederacy), containing about 200 entries describing their history, culture, present-day concerns, and historical contributions to general North American culture. This encyclopedia surveys the histories of the six constituent nations of the confederacy (Senecas, Cayugas, Onondagas, Oneidas, Mohawks, and Tuscaroras, who were adopted into the confederacy about 1725).

Study of the people who called themselves Haudenosaunee ("People of the Longhouse") has been central to the course of European-American scholarship and statecraft in eastern North America since Samuel de Champlain first fouled the reputation of the French with them. Champlain did not understand at the time that the people the French came to call "Iroquois" maintained alliances with other Native American peoples in much of northeastern North America, or that their territories stood astride the best trade route between the east coast of North America and the continent's interior, a matter of vital importance at a time when most trade (not to mention military forces) traveled by water. The utility of this route was illustrated abundantly after 1800 by the construction of the Erie Canal directly through the Haudenosaunee's traditional homelands in upstate New York. If Champlain had known how important the Haudenosaunee would become to the future of French and British rivalry in North America, he might have watched his diplomatic manners. Instead, he quickly engaged a band of Mohawks in armed conflict and killed a number of them.

Several entries in this volume also trace ways in which the practices of the Iroquois have filtered into general North American society. For example, the idea of "sleeping on it" comes directly from the debating practices of the Iroquois Grand Council, whose federal structure also provided a model for a federal system being developed by the founders of the United States. To "bury the hatchet" is also an Iroquois idiom, a reference to the founding of the confederacy, when the member nations threw their weapons of war into a large pit under the Great Tree of Peace.

Many of these Haudenosaunee contributions to general culture in the United States took place during a long history of trade, diplomacy, and occasional war at a time (roughly 1600 to 1800 on the Roman calendar) when the Haudeno-saunee were important players in the contest for North America that was being waged by European powers, principally Britain and France. The Haudenosaunee were a focal point for diplomacy by both the French and the British, a chain of events that allowed some of the people who would be influential in founding the United States (most notably Benjamin Franklin) to observe the Haudeno-saunee political system firsthand.

The history of the Haudenosaunee stresses the necessity of peacemaking, be-ginning with the peoples' national-origin story, in which the Peacemaker (De-ganawida) and his spokesman Hiawatha (also known as Aionwentha) waged an intellectual and spiritual battle of many years' duration to unite the Mohawks, Oneidas, Onondagas, Cayugas, and Senecas into a powerful federation that dom-inated commerce and diplomacy over a broad hinterland for several hundred years beginning, most probably, in 1142 of the "common era," as defined by modern European timekeeping. The unification accomplished by the Peacemaker and Hiawatha eliminated the blood feud among the Haudenosaunee and replaced bloody revenge with a formal legal system to deal with conflict and make po-litical decisions.

Looking back at this historical emphasis on peace, more than one observer has remarked on the irony attending the abundance of conflict in present-day Haudenosaunee communities over state taxation, the presence of gambling, and other issues. Occasionally—as in the bloody spring and summer of 1990 at Akwesasne and Kanesatake (Oka), Québec—these disputes have erupted in deadly gunfire in scenes some have compared to Northern Ireland or Beirut. This volume contains several entries describing the historical genesis of the League of Peace, as well as present-day controversies that have riven nearly all contemporary Iroquois communities. The contemporary emphasis of some of the entries that follow is new to reference literature.

This volume also broaches other new knowledge, or at least knowledge un-known or long ignored by European-Americans. Much of this new information, researched by Barbara A. Mann, describes in detail the roles and responsibilities of women, especially in governance and the management of day-to-day life, most notably in agriculture, the maintenance of knowledge, and the keeping of the home. Mann also contributes material that is new to the reference literature describing Haudenosaunee peoples who migrated westward into the Ohio River watershed during and after the American Revolution.

While traditional Haudenosaunee society maintains an intricate balance of gender roles, most of history has recorded men talking with men about men's business, notably trade, war, and diplomacy. Ethnohistorian James Axtell reminds us that "usually the record makers were explorers, colonists, or imperialists, who sought and often gained control over, or destruction of, native peoples. Invariably, their records and observations of the natives reflected their sociopolitical goals and their own cultural biases" (Axtell, 14).

The Encyclopedia of the Haudenosaunee (Iroquois Confederacy) also contributes to the reference literature new knowledge concerning the debate over the origin date of the confederacy as a political institution. The use to which a combination of oral and written sources may be put is illustrated by the work of Barbara Mann and Jerry Fields of the University of Toledo in dating the origins of the Haudenosaunee Confederacy. They began with oral history, which says that the Great Law of Peace was ratified by the Senecas after a "Sign in the Sky," a total eclipse of the sun. Knowing the site of the ratification (Ganondagan, in western New York State), Mann and Fields turned to European documents, namely eclipse tables, to date the event. The date they found, in late August 1142, is roughly three centuries earlier than the general scholarly consensus. Scholars who do not trust oral history have even argued that the confederacy was formed after contact with Europeans because no written records of it exist before that. None of them has taken such a Eurocentric set of assumptions to its logical conclusion, arguing, perhaps, that the sun did not rise and set on Turtle Island until someone arrived from Europe to write it down.

I have decided to use the term Iroquois interchangably with their own name for themselves, Haudenosaunee, to counter the assertions of some "experts" (the most notable being William A. Starna) who insist that use of "Haudenosaunee" should be avoided because "Iroquois" has become the commonly used term and thus a cultural and linguistic "marker." Such markers are socially and culturally defined (and the height of European-American arrogance). "Iroquois," a French name for the Haudenosaunee, has become popular in our time, eclipsing "Five Nations" ("Six Nations" after the addition of the Tuscaroras in the early eighteenth century), the term used by the English during Benjamin Franklin's day.

One cannot decipher the word map of Native American history without references to the politics of names. One must realize which names are Native American, which ones are European inventions, and what the names meant to the people who gave them, as well as to those who received them. Only then does one learn that "Huron" is a French reference to the head of a wild boar, an insult to peoples who called themselves "Wyandots." "Sioux" is archaic French slang for "snake" (or, by implication, "enemy"), applied to people who called themselves Lakotas, Dakotas, or Nakotas. The name "Dakota" in turn was expropriated by two of the states of the United States that bear names with Native American origins; roughly half of the states' names are derived from Native American origins.

Similarly, very few non-Iroquois know the name "Haudenosaunee" outside of scholars of their history. It means "People of the Longhouse," after the Haudenosaunee geographical metaphor that styles their confederacy as a traditional longhouse, with the Mohawks guarding the "Eastern Door," the Senecas at the "Western Door," and the Onondagas tending the central council fire. The use of the word "Haudenosaunee" in the title is one small attempt to supply a Native American viewpoint on subject matter that needs an indigenous voice.

NOTE

All unsigned entries were written by Bruce E. Johansen. Due to 400 years of transliteration into English by various authors, some terms may differ in spelling and diacritical marks from entry to entry, depending on the source material consulted.

FURTHER READING

Axtell, James. "The Ethnohistory of Native America." In Donald L. Fixico, ed., *Rethinking American Indian History*. Albuquerque: University of New Mexico Press, 1997: 11–28.

Mann, Barbara A., and Jerry L. Fields. "A Sign in the Sky: Dating the League of the Haudenosaunee." *American Indian Culture and Research Journal* 21:2 (1997): 105–163.

Encyclopedia of
the Haudenosaunee
(Iroquois Confederacy)

A

Adodaroh **(Tadadaho).** *Adadaroh* is the position title of the head chief of the men's Grand Council, also called *Tadadaho*. For a description of how the title evolved, see **The Second Epoch of Time.**

Adoption. Adoption is one of the legal provisions of the *Gayaněsshä''gowa* (**Great Law of Peace,** or Constitution of the Six Nations) of the League of the Haudenosaunee. Adoption allows an individual, a group, or an entire nation to be taken into the league, either as a full state of the league or as a member of a family, lineage, or state. Adoption is not a practice restricted to the Haudenosaunee, but is common among all the Native American nations of **Turtle Island** (North America). Each nation has its own rules surrounding the extension of citizenship.

Among the Iroquois, adoption is a function of naming and therefore the exclusive right of the *gantowisas*, or women acting in their official capacities. As heads of the family, clan, or nation, the women may induct person(s) into a family, clan, or nation of the league. In the past, if a population of a clan or nation seemed to be at a low ebb, the *gantowisas* had the right to call for a war to replenish the population. Daniel Richter has provided a fair discussion of this process under his term "mourning war" in *The Ordeal of the Longhouse.* In precontact and colonial times, adoptees were most often women and children taken during raids on enemy groups and brought back to the home towns of the various war parties. Male adoptees were secondary.

The treatment of male prisoners was quite different from that of female prisoners and their children. Unlike women, men were first forced to prove their bravery and general worthiness through tests of endurance. This not infrequently meant running the **gauntlet,** a severe trial in which the incumbent ran as many as a hundred yards between two rows of townsfolk who laid as many blows as possible upon him in passing. Any man unlucky enough to fall during the run was beaten to death on the spot. Survivors of the gauntlet were considered good prospects for adoption and tenderly nursed back to health, yet they were only adopted at the pleasure of the *gantowisas*, who might reject prospective adoptees for any reason. Those who were selected were named to replace dead relatives of their adoptive family, with the *gantowisas* bestowing the names. Those who were rejected often were killed.

Women and children did not run gauntlets, but were almost immediately adopted. Dickewamis (**Mary Jemison**, taken at age fifteen in 1758) remembered her adoption as being so quick that she did not realize what had happened until later. The *gantowisas* bathed her thoroughly, dressed her in their finest clothing, and then led her to the center of the adopting Clan Mother's **longhouse**, calling all the women of the town to view her. A **Condolence Ceremony** commenced, with great wailing on the part of the bereaved clan. At the ceremony, people sang and recited the words of consolation. Once the tears of the mourning family had been wiped from its members' faces, smiles went around the group as Jemison was clan-named Dickewamis ("A Pleasant Thing"), for a lost sister. She was greeted in a kindly manner on all sides and immediately took up her position as the newest member of her adoptive lineage (Seaver, 19–22).

The emotional ties of new adoptees were not naïvely assumed to transfer to their new identities with the ceremonies. Instead, host nations actively reeducated them as Iroquois, even when the adoptions occurred between Iroquoian groups. The **Senecas**, for example, maintained the town of Ganarqua (at what is currently Mud Creek in East Bloomfield, New York) as a reeducation camp. Members of the Neutral Nation, which had been overrun in war, were taken there. Other such camps existed in each nation. There, adoptees were taught the customs, language, rituals, rights, and duties of their new lives. After the adoptees had accustomed themselves to their Haudenosaunee identities, they were sent to their new homes.

Once the pace of invasion quickened, however, these leisurely reeducation programs were disrupted. By the eighteenth century, each adopting clan saw to the reeducation of its own recruits, keeping an eagle eye on its newest members. For example, soon after her adoption, the Seneca sisters of Dickewamis hurried her out of sight at a trading post when a party of settlers noticed her among their number. The Seneca women fled with Dickewamis in their canoe lest she desert her new Haudenosaunee relatives for the settlements (Seaver, 26–27).

Contrary to Western stereotypes, adoptees were not all "white prisoners" but were more frequently from other Native nations. It was not until the eighteenth century that it became common for the Iroquois, diminished in their own numbers by war and disease, to adopt prisoners from among the European invaders. Once the adoptions of Europeans began in earnest, however, they usually proved successful. One of the greatest scandals of the colonial, federal, and antebellum eras of American history was that the majority of those turned into "white savages" flatly refused to return to "civilization." So loyal to the league were they that their return was often forced by the terms of colonial and, later, U.S.

peace treaties. Even then, many, like the grown-up Dickewamis, went into fearful hiding rather than be compelled to return to the settlements (Seaver, 26–27, 43–46, 77–78). Accounts of such contented Euro-adoptees popped up often in travelogues and literature, including the writings of **Benjamin Franklin**. While rambling through Iroquoia, for instance, the French author Chateaubriand met a male Euro-adoptee who assured him that he had never been happy until he "became a savage" (Parker, *Analytical History*, 150).

In addition to individuals, whole groups and even nations could be adopted en masse, either at the petition of the adoptees or through military conquest by the league. The **Tuscaroras** were adopted as the sixth nation of the league in the early eighteenth century (dates differ, ranging from 1710 to 1735) at their own request. By contrast, the **Wyandot (Huron)** Nations of Canada were brought in through warfare during the so-called **Beaver Wars** of the seventeenth century. Nations adopted by involuntary means were considered incorporated states, as opposed to federally recognized member nations of the league. The speakers of incorporated states rose in council through the sponsorship of one of the recognized Six Nations. Indeed, these speakers were often born members of the sponsoring nation.

Upon being adopted, each nation was assigned its mentor nation and was given duties to fulfill. For example, upon adoption, first by the **Oneidas** and then by the **Cayugas**, the Delawares were given the position of "women," that is, they became federal judges. By the same token, upon adoption by the Senecas, the Ohio Wyandots were appointed adjunct guardians of the Western Door. These provisions of the Great Law allowed the league to expand indefinitely, yet they cemented goodwill by conferring full citizenship, rather than tributary status, on new nations.

The Great Law also allowed for other circumstances:

- Should any clan of the league become extinct, a sister clan was to be raised up in its place. This provision represented the only instance in which the men (members of the Grand Council) were responsible for an adoption.

- Should an individual of patrilineal Haudenosaunee descent wish to become legally Haudenosaunee, he or she might be adopted into a willing clan, lineage, or nation. This provision has confused many European-Americans who believe that any "Indian blood" makes one Haudenosaunee. Under the nonracist lineage laws of the league, however, only those born of a Haudenosaunee mother are considered Native, since descent is counted through the female line only. Thus did Gawaso Wahheh (**Arthur Parker**) and Katepakomen (**Simon Girty**), both born of Seneca fathers and European mothers, need to be adopted before they were considered to be Haudenosaunee under the Great Law.

- Should a clan seem to be depopulating, it might take in members from another clan. In modern times, Haudenosaunee individuals are frequently adopted into Tutelo clans in observance of an ancient promise made to the Tutelos when they first came into the league, that their nation would never be allowed to disappear.

- Should a member of one clan seem unwanted, another clan might ask to adopt that person into one of its lineages. Under these provisions, the sickly Sganyadaí:yoh (**Handsome Lake**) was cross-adopted into the Turtle Clan, although he had been born into the Wolf Clan of the Senecas.

- In other instances, if special clan knowledge seems in danger of disappearing due to a lack of talented individuals, a person of talent in another clan may be cross-adopted for training in the specialized skills of the adopting clan.

- Finally, there is an honorary form of "adoption" that is purely diplomatic and is used to facilitate political relations. A name may be given to a key individual from the outside on diplomatic occasions. This is not the same as a family, clan, or state adoption, although the distinction has been lost on many European-Americans granted such an honorary adoption. As Gawaso Wanneh warned in 1908, "Naming does not necessarily imply adoption, nor does family or clan adoption imply national adoption" (Converse, 19–20).

This last point is worth emphasizing. An honorary naming does not confer the rights and privileges of citizenship. It is not an adoption. Adoptions occur only when any one of three groups (family, clan, or nation) decides to name an individual ceremonially. Furthermore, adoptions are recognized within the adopting unit alone. Family adoptions remain a family affair. Clan adoptions are broader, conferring larger ceremonial rights and duties and leaving open the possibility that a clan title of office might be conferred at some future point. Clan adoptions are the commonest kind of individual adoption. National adoption is very rare. Yaiéwanoh (**Harriet Maxwell Converse**) was adopted by the entire Seneca Nation in an almost unique event. By the same token, the adoption of the Tuscaroras as a nation of the league marked the only time in history that this form of adoption occurred.

The flip side of adoption was disinheritance, also in the power of the *gantowisas*. Should any individual, group, or nation, adopted or otherwise, later prove itself unworthy of its status, the *gantowisas* were empowered by the Great Law to revoke its clan membership and/or national citizenship. Thereafter, the women (name holders) of the reviled group were to be "deemed buried and their family extinct" (Parker, *Constitution*, 43), a dire fate, not to be taken lightly.

Thus, contrary to the simplistic notion of adoption fostered by Hollywood—and even promoted in some academic texts—there are many forms of legal adoption under the Great Law, with each type carrying its own distinct duties and privileges. Honorary naming is not an adoption, nor is a family adoption to be confused with a clan or national adoption. National adoption of individuals is rare, while the adoption of a full nation is unique. Only the Tuscaroras were adopted as a nation. All other adopted nations have become incorporated states of one of the six existing nations.

FURTHER READING

Converse, Harriet Maxwell [Ya-ie-wa-noh]. *Myths and Legends of the New York State Iroquois*. Ed. Arthur Caswell Parker. New York State Museum Bulletin 125.

Education Department Bulletin No. 437. Albany: University of the State of New York, 1908.

Hewitt, J. N. B. "A Constitutional League of Peace in the Stone Age of America: The League of the Iroquois and Its Constitution." *Smithsonian Institution Series* (1920): 527–545.

Parker, Arthur C. *An Analytical History of the Seneca Indians*. 1926 Researches and Transactions of the New York State Archeological Association, Lewis H. Morgan Chapter. New York: Kraus Reprint Co., 1970.

————. *The Constitution of the Five Nations, or, The Iroquois Book of the Great Law*. Albany: University of the State of New York, 1916.

————. "Iroquois Adoption." In *The Life of General Ely S. Parker, Last Grand Sachem of the Iroquois and General Grant's Military Secretary*. Buffalo: Buffalo Historical Society, 1919: 329–333.

Powell, J. W. "Wyandot Government: A Short Study of Tribal Society." *Annual Report of the Bureau of Ethnology to the Secretary of the Smithsonian Institution* 1 (1879–1880): 57–69.

Richter, Daniel K. *The Ordeal of the Longhouse: The Peoples of the Iroquois League in the Era of European Colonization*. Chapel Hill: University of North Carolina Press, 1992.

Seaver, James E. *A Narrative of the Life of Mrs. Mary Jemison*. 1823. Syracuse, N.Y.: Syracuse University Press, 1990.

Shimony, Annemarie Anrod. *Conservatism among the Iroquois at the Six Nations Reserve*. 1961. Syracuse, N.Y.: Syracuse University Press, 1994.

Barbara A. Mann

Affiliated nations of the league. The Iroquois League was composed of numerous nations confederated for peace, security, and prosperity. When the league was originally formed, it contained only the founding nations of the **Oneidas, Mohawks, Onondagas, Cayugas**, and **Senecas**. Between 1710 and 1735, the **Tuscaroras** joined as the sixth full nation of the league.

In addition to these six nations, many more were adopted into the league as incorporated nations. Unlike the Tuscaroras, they did not experience full national adoption. This was for two reasons. First, when not all the citizens of a particular nation agreed to adoption, that nation could not be extended recognition as a full nation of the league. Thus, although a preponderance of Delawares entered the league, not all did. Consequently, the Delawares did not come in as a nation. Second, some nations such as the Attiwandaronks were brought in through military means, resulting in their adoption into clans as citizens of the Seneca Nation. Hence their identity became Seneca. League nations beyond the famous six included the following:

The Andastes. Also known as the Conestogas, the Andastes were the Susquehannock people with whom John Smith dealt in 1608. The Andastes joined in an unsuccessful French and Susquehannock war on the league in the early seventeenth century. Those not killed when a French invasion was repulsed in 1615 were scattered or adopted into the league as individuals.

The Attiwandaronks. The main nation of the so-called Neutrals, the Attiwandaronks were Canadian Wyandots living in Ontario. They were brought in through military action in 1651.

The Conestogas. See the Andastes.

The Conoys. Also called the Piscataways, the Conoys were closely associated with the Delawares and the Nanticokes. In 1765, the 150 Conoys who had survived the massacres perpetrated by the British against "the Delawares" during the French and Indian War (1754–1763) joined the league Delawares of Ohio, forming the Turkey (Foot) Clan of the league Delawares. The turkey was the symbol the Conoys presented as their signature at a treaty council in 1793.

The Delawares. Known to themselves as the Lenni Lenapes, they accepted the identifier "Delaware" when they discovered that it was the name of an honored European general. The Delawares were an important Algonkian nation absorbed by the league in 1720, first by the Oneidas and later, after the Oneidas had expelled them as troublemakers, by the Cayugas. In 1751, some of the league Delawares began to settle in Ohio at the invitation of the league Wyandots there. After the attempt by the so-called Paxton Boys of Pennsylvania to wipe them out during the French and Indian War, the league transferred a large number of Delawares to the safer territories of western Pennsylvania and eastern Ohio, again under the auspices of the Ohio Wyandots, themselves sponsored by the Ohio Senecas.

The Eries. Also called the Long-tailed Cat (or Lynx) Nation—the Iroquoian meaning of *erie*—the Eries were Seneca peoples whom geography and politics had split off as western Senecas in precontact times. Some oral traditions consider them to have been Seneca members of the league when it was originally formed. All traditions agree that hostilities eventually broke out between the Eries and the Senecas. In 1881, Chief Elias Johnson told one version of their fracas with the league, while in 1825, David Cusick told another, but both agreed that the original hostilities dated to well before European contact. The historical Eries, who lived along the southern shores of the Great Lake bearing their name, were (re)incorporated into the league militarily around 1656.

The Honniasonts. An Iroquoian-language group, the Honniasonts lived in western Pennsylvania and eastern Ohio, but were scattered by attacking Susquehannocks during their hostilities with the league. The Honniasonts turned to the Senecas for succor and were adopted into the league.

The Kah-Kwahs. Associated with the Eries, the Kah-Kwahs were also Seneca offshoots who might originally have been in the league as Senecas. They were pushed west and south around Lake Erie along with their Erie allies. They were later absorbed into the league during its westward expansion around 1656.

The Mahicans. An Algonkian people, the Mahicans (often mistakenly called Mohegans) were rivals of the Haudenosaunee who made war upon the league at least four times in the seventeenth century. Ill treated by their European allies, the Mahicans became a fragmented nation, many of whose members were individually taken into league clans. In 1772, 157 Mahican adoptees joined the league Delawares moved by the league to the relative safety of Ohio under the auspices of the Senecas and league Wyandots.

The Munsees. Mistaken in many Western texts for a separate nation, the Munsees were actually the Wolf Clan of the league Delawares in Ohio.

The Nanticokes. Escaping some of the first reservations set up in 1698, the Nanticokes, an Algonkian group, pushed into Pennsylvania, where they were taken in by the league in 1748. The Nanticokes moved into Ohio in 1784 and joined the league Delaware-Mahicans.

The Neutrals. The Wyandots of Canada (miscalled "**Hurons**," a French slur, in many Western texts). The Neutrals were so called because they remained neutral in the war between the league and the French and their Canadian Wyandot allies in the mid-seventeenth century. The Neutrals were actually a mini-league consisting of four nations under the leadership of the Attiwandaronks. All of the Neutral nations were brought into the league under Seneca adoption in 1651, consequent to military action.

The Piscataways. *See* the Conoys.

The Saponis. The Saponis were an Algonkian group originally from Virginia. Sometime after 1740, they moved to the major council grounds at Shamokin, Pennsylvania, under the auspices of **Shikellamy**, the league's chief liaison officer with the Europeans who were stationed there. In 1753, the Saponis were adopted into the league.

The Squawkihaws. Sometimes anglicized as the "Squawky Hill Indians," the Squawkihaws were Erie-affiliated peoples who also were originally Senecas and likely were league members at its founding. Allied with the Eries and Kah-Kwahs, they were later pushed west and south around Lake Erie by hostilities with the Senecas. They were adopted into the league with the Eries around 1656.

The Susquehannocks. The Susquehannocks, close relatives of the Andastes, allied themselves with the Canadian Wyandot supporters of the French invasion and were dispersed or adopted into the league upon the defeat of French forces in 1615.

The Tutelos. The Tutelos are a people of Catawba (Siouan) ancestry who took refuge at Shamokin under the care of Shikellamy. Closely associated with the Saponis, they were adopted into the league by the Cayugas in 1753. At the time of their adoption, the league pledged to them that they would never be allowed to die out as a people. To this day, naming ceremonies ensure that their numerical strength (fifty to sixty individuals) is maintained.

The Wappingers. An Algonkian group closely affiliated with the Mahicans, the Wappingers were pushed west by European invasion. After the Mahican-league wars, some were taken in by the league and emigrated into Ohio in 1784, where many joined the league Delaware-Mahicans. Eventually, some Wappingers moved on to Indiana.

The Wenros or Wenronhronons. Wyandots of Canada, the Wenros were closely affiliated with the Attiwandaronks (Neutrals) and the Eries. They were adopted into the league by the Senecas along with the Neutral Nations in 1651.

The Wyandots or Ywendats. The Wyandots originally included all of the nations of the Canadian Iroquois. Nearly all Wyandot nations were taken into the league en masse between 1649 and 1653, although some migrated into Ohio after the dispersal of 1649. The Ohio Wyandots had come into the league by 1700. Those Ohio Wyandots who did not accept adoption moved to the Ohio-Indiana border, where they were known as Potawatamies.

The Wyomings. A subdivision of the Susquehannocks, the Wyomings were apparently absorbed into the league along with the Susquehannocks in 1615.

FURTHER READING

Beauchamp, W[illiam] M[artin]. *The Iroquois Trail, or, Footprints of the Six Nations, in Customs, Traditions, and History.* Including David Cusick's "Sketches of Ancient History of the Six Nations." 1825. Fayetteville, N.Y.: H. C. Beauchamp, 1892.

Heckewelder, John. *Narrative of the Mission of the United Brethren among the Delaware and Mohegan Indians from Its Commencement, in the Year 1740, to the Close of the Year 1808.* 1820. New York: Arno Press, 1971.

Johnson, Chief Elias. *Legends, Traditions, and Laws of the Iroquois, or Six Nations.* 1881. New York: AMS Press, 1978.

Parker, A[rthur] C[aswell] [Gawaso Wanneh]. *An Analytical History of the Seneca Indians.* 1926. Researches and Transactions of the New York State Archeological Association, Lewis H. Morgan Chapter. New York: Kraus Reprint Co., 1970.

Shimony, Annemarie Anrod. *Conservatism among the Iroquois at the Six Nations Reserve.* 1961. Syracuse, N.Y.: Syracuse University Press, 1994.

Snow, Dean R. *The Iroquois.* Cambridge: Blackwell, 1994.

Swanton, John Reed. *The Indian Tribes of North America.* Smithsonian Institution, Bureau of American Ethnology Bulletin No. 145. Washington, D.C.: Smithsonian Institution Press, 1952.

Wallace, Anthony F. C. "Woman, Land, and Society: Three Aspects of Aboriginal Delaware Life." *Pennsylvania Archaeologist* 17:1–4 (1947): 1–36.

Barbara A. Mann

Akwesasne Freedom School. The Akwesasne Freedom School, an independent elementary and middle school (kindergarten through eighth grade), was founded during 1979 by **Mohawk** parents who were concerned that their language and culture was dying. In 1985, the Freedom School began a Mohawk-language immersion program, the only one of its type in the United States. The Mohawk **Thanksgiving** Prayer also is used as a curriculum base at the school, where students study reading, writing, math, science, history, and the Mohawk ceremonial cycle. The school's curriculum is designed to provide a solid academic education in a Mohawk cultural and historical context. During the mid-1990s, the school began construction of a new building because its former site was dangerously close to contaminated landfills run by a nearby General Motors foundry that had poisoned the school's drinking water.

During the years since the Freedom School was established at Akwesasne, a

Mohawk philosophy of education has had an impact on public school curricula at Akwesasne as well. Local elders are now teaching from the holistic perspective of their ancestors the knowledge that will enable young people to walk forward in this world with, on one hand, the Mohawk and Haudenosaunee teachings and wisdom and, on the other, an understanding of the Western way of knowing. Now young people can see the relevance of science and mathematics to their way of life. The Western world will need to be flexible enough to accept the validity of integrating its concepts and views into indigenous teachings and wisdom. Dominant-society students also have much to gain from this approach. They, too, can learn to understand others' world views and how cultures can be integrated into schooling to broaden educational experience.

For example, one educational science theme focuses on "trees" and acknowledges the living spirit of the tree, thus setting the stage for respect and interconnectedness; the importance of trees in the cycle of life is studied; students also study why certain trees in different indigenous cultures possess significance (geography); using Western techniques, students examine how trees live and why indigenous people worked with certain trees for various needs, such as basketmaking. This approach brings the trees into equality with man and recognizes their "aliveness."

For both cultures to flourish, it is necessary for indigenous people and Western educators not only to come to an understanding and acceptance of the validity of each other's beliefs but to work together for this educational "balance." For Haudenosaunee and Mohawk people, balance is one of the most basic teachings to grasp and comprehend. In achieving this, all things reach their rightful place.

At Akwesasne, a Science and Mathematics Pilot Project has been loosely integrated into the public school system under the domain of the Mohawk Council of Akwesasne. Initially, this project strove to define this educational balance for Mohawks. Culturally integrated curricula have been designed that incorporate Western ways of coming to know into Haudenosaunee ways of coming to know. Many projects have done the opposite; however, it is believed that for a local curriculum to be truly valid, it is important that the curriculum's primary approach be Haudenosaunee, with Western concepts serving to expand and reinforce learning.

The Haudenosaunee Thanksgiving Address forms the basis of the Akwesasne curriculum design. It contains the instructions for the conduct of human life on earth, to be grateful to all of creation and to announce that gratefulness every day. This address embraces the indigenous concept of the relatedness of all creation while exploring the internal and external environments of all living things. The indigenous concept of "ecology" examines and is compared to the dominant culture theories. Mother Earth is studied through the discovery of what constitutes "earth," or soils. Indigenous uses of soils are studied from an agricultural perspective as well as from an indigenous "potter's" perspective. Plant life is surveyed from a holistic indigenous perspective—its assistance to Mother Earth, people, and animals (ecology); medicinal characteristics; uses as natural dyes; the **Three Sisters** (**corn**, beans, and squash and the cultural significance they play.

Water is examined from an indigenous ecological perspective that incorporates study of its chemical composition and properties. Animals form the basis of the Haudenosaunee "clan system" or family organization. This significant practice is incorporated into the curriculum along with study of classification, characteristics, cells and cell functions. The study of "energy" includes components on the Haudenosaunee teachings of the Four Winds, Thunder, Lightning, Sun, and overall conservation, while also examining "Western" science. The cosmos is incorporated into the curriculum by providing experiential teaching in the indigenous and Haudenosaunee concept of "One with the Universe." The moon, stars, and other galaxies are intertwined with indigenous cosmos mythology to demonstrate the intricate thought of Haudenosaunee ancestors relative to cosmology.

Mathematics covers a survey of indigenous numbering systems, including those of the Haudenosaunee as well as other indigenous peoples, such as Mesoamerican geometry, the Mayan concept of zero, Inca and Mayan calendrics and computational techniques, the Inca counting board, and quipus. This holistic experiential program is designed to empower youth by bringing ancient aboriginal wisdom to life. Problem-solving and research skills are fostered in much the same way that ancestors developed their analytical skills.

FURTHER READING

LaFrance, Brenda. "Negotiating the Culture of Indigenous Schools." *Peabody Journal of Education* 69:2 (Winter, 1994): 19–25.

Brenda LaFrance and Bruce E. Johansen

Akwesasne Mohawks, historical sketch. While not a permanent settlement until about 1755, the site at the confluence of several rivers with the St. Lawrence River that **Mohawks** now call "Akwesasne" has been, perhaps for thousands of years, one of many locales used for hunting and fishing. About 1750, a faction of the Mohawks at **Kahnawake** moved south and west to the mouth of the St. Regis River, on the south shore of the St. Lawrence, because of internal disputes and the inability of the land at Kahnawake to support the entire community. This settlement became the core of the St. Regis Mohawk Reservation (called Akwesasne by the Mohawks), which today is the only Indian reservation with territory on both sides of the U.S.-Canadian border.

While St. Regis was predominantly Mohawk in its early days, a party of Abenakis was granted refuge there in 1759, during the French and Indian War. Some Onondagas also settled at St. Regis about 1760. In addition to Mohawks from Kahnawake, immigrants to St. Regis in the late eighteenth century included a number from the Mohawk Valley who had remained in the United States after the **American Revolution**. Most of the Mohawks from that region, who had supported the British, moved to Ontario.

While most Mohawks supported the British in the American Revolution, the Akwesasne Mohawks supported the new United States. Irregardless of this support, after the Revolution the Mohawks at St. Regis faced settlement pressures with no legal credentials to prove their ownership of the lands on which they had settled, despite the fact that their occupancy predated that of non-Indians in the area by half a century. Slowly, between 1800 and 1850, they assembled legal guarantees from the state of New York and Canada for the land that comprises the Akwesasne Reservation.

Because Mohawks at St. Regis and Kahnawake had supported the patriot cause, several Mohawks from the Montréal area migrated to the U.S. side of St. Regis to escape persecution by Tory supporters after the war. In 1783, the Treaty of Paris formally declared the border between the United States and Canada at forty-five degrees north, slicing the lands of the St. Regis Mohawks nearly in half. This boundary had little practical effect at first on the sparsely settled border. Later, the presence of the border (and a second border between English-speaking Ontario and French-speaking Québec, which also runs through St. Regis) would complicate governance there immeasurably. A series of treaties between the state of New York and the Haudenosaunee Confederacy (and later chiefs elected at St. Regis under a state-sanctioned government) legally defined the reservation between 1796 and roughly 1850.

Famine struck Akwesasne in 1813 and 1816, part of a global cooling precipitated by volcanic ash in the world's atmosphere. Agriculture failed both years in the face of snowstorms in April, May, and (in 1816) June. It is said that in 1813, potatoes grew no larger than walnuts. Between 1820 and 1850, a series of epidemics cut the population of St. Regis in half.

By 1850, the Canadian portions of Akwesasne were legally defined, and a separate Canadian-sanctioned government evolved there, with twelve chiefs. All during this time, the traditional Mohawk Nation Council, which drew representation from both sides of the border, continued to operate without legal sanction from Canada or the United States. Since the state of New York appointed three "trustees" to oversee its relations at St. Regis in 1802, tension between "elected" and traditional bodies has been a constant in Akwesasne politics.

In 1888, the Confederacy Council at Onondaga granted the St. Regis Mohawks use of the chieftainship titles that had been left vacant by the migration of Mohawks under **Joseph Brant** to Canada after the American Revolution. In 1898, the state of New York formalized the elective system, which was challenged by traditionals several times, most notably a year later when one Mohawk (**John Fire**, also known as John Ice or Jake Ice) was killed and several others were arrested as they resisted imposition of the "elective" system. In 1948, the Mohawks of Akwesasne supported a slate of tribal chiefs who dissolved the state-sanctioned council upon taking office. The state then staged an election in which the low number of Mohawks voting was a significant indication that the system lacked popular appeal at Akwesasne.

Mohawks from Akwesasne, Kanesatake, and Kahnawake have been mobile laborers for more than two centuries. Until the fur trade waned in the early nineteenth century, Mohawks from all three territories routinely journeyed into western Canada in the employ of the Hudson's Bay Company and Northwest Company as trappers and traders. Some of these Mohawks settled in Alberta; one group, called the Michel Band, established a reserve in the St. Albert region of Alberta that was originally slightly more than 25,000 acres. In 1913, the band's lands were reduced to about 10,000 acres, and in 1958, Canada ceased to legally define the area as a native reserve, although most of the families descended from the band still live in and near Edmonton, Alberta. Another band of Canadian Iroquois settled without legal status in the Jasper National Park on the Alberta–British Columbia border (Jennings et al., 71).

The Code of **Handsome Lake** began to acquire adherents at St. Regis during the 1930s, more than a century after it had become established in Seneca country. In 1935, one year after the Indian Reorganization Act was passed, the Mohawks of Akwesasne rejected it. Similarly, in 1953, Mohawks there flatly rejected termination, the sale of land base and obliteration of tribal identity. The Bureau of Indian Affairs (BIA) had little official contact with the Mohawks of St. Regis until the 1960s, when **Louis Bruce**, a Mohawk, became commissioner of Indian affairs. A BIA-funded social-service infrastructure was established after that.

Heavy industry has existed near Akwesasne since the early years of the twentieth century. The Aluminum Company of America, the area's first large industrial plant, opened in Massena, eight miles west of Akwesasne, during 1903. The opening of the **St. Lawrence Seaway** in 1959 caused large-scale industrialization and attendant pollution on and near the Akwesasne Reservation. Reynolds Metals built an aluminum-reduction plant less than a mile from Akwesasne the same year the seaway opened; by 1962, cattle on Cornwall Island were dying of fluoride poisoning. The effects of pollution at Akwesasne are evidenced by a decline in the number of people earning a living as farmers and fishermen in the area. In 1930, Akwesasne was the site of 129 commercial farms; in 1990, that figure was 19, according to figures maintained by the Mohawk Council at Akwesasne. The estimated number of fishermen declined from 104 to 11 during the same period.

During more than two centuries since the signing of the **Jay Treaty** in 1794 guaranteed Mohawk crossing rights on the U.S.-Canadian border, Akwesasne has been a prime location for Mohawk protests regarding restrictions of these rights. In 1968, Mohawks blockaded the International Bridge across Akwesasne to force redress of treaty violations by U.S. and Canadian customs officials. The permeable nature of the border at Akwesasne also has made it a favored crossing point for many types of smuggling between the United States and Canada, including liquor, various illegal drugs, tobacco products, and immigrants lacking legal papers.

Efforts to preserve Mohawk language and culture have been moderately successful at Akwesasne due in part to educational initiatives such as the **Akwes-**

asne Freedom School. About a third of the people at Akwesasne speak the Mohawk language with some degree of fluency. At the same time, the destruction of the Mohawk traditional economic base by pollution is evidenced by the fact that 58 percent of Akwesasne families lived below the poverty line in 1990, and 44 percent were dependent on welfare programs. The unemployment rate was 45 percent the same year, according to the Mohawk Council at Akwesasne. Many Mohawks work in industries near the reservation; sales of discount gasoline and cigarettes, as well as illegal smuggling across the border, are major sources of cash income.

FURTHER READING

Jennings, Francis, ed.; William N. Fenton, joint ed.; Mary A. Druke, associate ed.; David R. Miller, research ed. *The History and Culture of Iroquois Diplomacy: An Interdisciplinary Guide to the Treaties of the Six Nations and Their League.* Syracuse, N.Y.: Syracuse University Press, 1985.

Rarihokwats. *How Democracy Came to St. Regis.* Rooseveltown, N.Y.: Akwesasne Notes, 1971.

Richter, Daniel K. *The Ordeal of the Longhouse: The Peoples of the Iroquois League in the Era of European Colonization.* Chapel Hill: University of North Carolina Press, 1992.

Smith, Michael T., Leslie N. Gay, and James Thomas. "History of the Government of the St. Regis Indian Tribe." Report to John V. Meyers. Eastern Area Office, Bureau of Indian Affairs, February 1980.

Akwesasne Notes. Started in the late 1960s, at the time of American Indian activism's modern reassertion, *Akwesasne Notes* was one of the foremost Native-owned editorial voices for Native American rights in the United States and Canada. In a trade in which advertising pays most of the bills, it carried nearly none. At a time when newspapers came to resemble poor cousins of television, it rarely published in color, relying instead on pages dense with text. In a media world of megacorporations, *Akwesasne Notes* operated on a shoestring budget, rarely paying contributors or editors and fiercely maintaining its editorial independence.

Akwesasne Notes was first begun as a compilation of news on topics of concern to Native Americans from other sources. In December 1968, the idea for such a journal was born around the kitchen table of **Ernest Benedict** (Kaientaronkwen) at Akwesasne. The first editor of the newspaper was Jerry Gambill, a non-Native Canadian, who was given the Mohawk name Rarihokwats. Gambill was employed as a community-assistance worker in the Canadian Department of Indian Affairs when he first traveled to Akwesasne. He was fired from his government job in 1967, but remained at Akwesasne, living on Cornwall Island.

Coverage included a reunion of Native peoples who took part in the occupation of Alcatraz Island, reports on a heated intellectual debate over whether the Iroquois **Great Law of Peace** helped inspire the U.S. Constitution, a report from indigenous peoples in Australia contributed by a **Mohawk** family who visited there, the latest plans for coal mining on the Hopi reservation, and an account of negotiations between Nicaraguan native peoples and the government. Other articles reported on repression of Tibetan natives by the Chinese and the organization of U.S. chapters of the Green Party. *Akwesasne Notes* also has described native resistance to destruction of Brazil's rain forests, detailed accounts of human-rights violations in Guatemala, reported trade agreements between American Indian tribes and third-world nations, discussed a proposed world constitution, and editorially supported Greenpeace.

Akwesasne Notes' circulation averaged about 10,000 copies per issue by the 1970s. Most subscribers received the paper by mail. The publication had a geographic reach that few newspapers can match, with copies being mailed to indigenous people and their supporters around the world.

As a voice of Akwesasne's traditional government, the newspaper's content reflected its global approach to issues involving indigenous rights, but the focus of its coverage remained the Haudenosaunee ("People of the Longhouse"), the confederation of Indian nations that the French called the Iroquois and the English the Six Nations. Indeed, to read *Akwesasne Notes*, one has to lay aside any notions of the "noble savage." *Akwesasne Notes'* pages lay open accounts not only of internal dissension, but also of occasional murder and fraud, along with graphic descriptions of the abysmal living conditions on many reservations.

On January 9, 1988, a firebomb razed the newspaper's offices during **gambling**-related violence at Akwesasne. Installed in a new office with mostly donated equipment gathered from a worldwide network of supporters, *Akwesasne Notes* did not miss a bimonthly issue after it sustained $200,000 in uninsured losses from the midwinter fire. The fire gutted the Nation House that had been the newspaper's home for much of the previous two decades. In its first editorial after the fire during the spring of 1988, *Akwesasne Notes* wrote:

Our offices were torched by those amongst us here at Akwesasne who oppose our reporting on the conflicts that are plaguing the Haudenosaunee [Iroquois] nations. . . . With the gambling, the cigarette smuggling, the violence . . . it is understandable why those criminal elements amongst us are opposed to a free press disseminating information about the illegal and immoral activities around us. . . . They almost succeeded in putting us out of business . . . but we will survive. (Johansen, 26–27)

During 1991, following gambling-related turmoil at Akwesasne, the newspaper stopped publishing. It resumed in early 1995 in a glossy magazine format. For almost two years, the magazine provided a showcase for Native American issues and artwork. Unable to support the expenses of such a format, the publication reverted to tabloid newspaper format in 1997, then ceased publication again.

During almost three decades of publication, *Akwesasne Notes* incubated the talents of a number of notable Native American journalists and scholars, among them José Barreiro, editor of *Native Americas* at Cornell University, John C. Mohawk, **Seneca** professor of Native American studies at the State University of New York at Buffalo, and **Doug George-Kanentiio**, Mohawk activist and freelance writer.

FURTHER READING

Johansen, Bruce E. *Life and Death in Mohawk Country*. Golden, Colo.: North American Press/Fulcrum, 1993.

Akwesasne (St. Regis) Reservation, pollution of. Within the living memory of a middle-aged person in the 1990s, Akwesasne has become a toxic dumping ground riskier to health than many urban areas. These environmental circumstances have, in two generations, descended on a people whose whole way of life had been enmeshed with the natural world, a place where the Iroquois origin story says that the world took shape on a gigantic turtle's back. Today, environmental pathologists are finding turtles at Akwesasne that qualify as toxic waste.

The Akwesasne Reservation was abruply introduced to industrialism with the coming of the **St. Lawrence Seaway** in the middle 1950s. Soon after the seaway opened, industry began to proliferate around the reservation. A General Motors foundry opened, followed by aluminum plants and steel mills that provided raw materials and parts for the foundry. Akwesasne has been declared the most polluted Indian reserve in Canada and the largest nonmilitary contamination site in the United States (Lickers, 11). By the mid-1980s, the Mount Sinai School of Medicine, having studied pollution at Akwesasne, advised residents to eat no more than half a pound of locally caught fish per week. Women who were pregnant or nursing and children under fifteen years of age were told not to eat any local fish at all.

When Ward Stone, a wildlife pathologist for the New York State Department of Environmental Conservation, began examining animals at Akwesasne, he found that polychlorinated biphenyls (PCBs), insecticides, and other toxins were not being contained in designated dumps. After years of use, the dump sites had leaked, and the toxins had gotten into the food chain of human beings and nearly every other species of animal in the area. The **Mohawks'** traditional economy, based on hunting, fishing, and agriculture, had been literally poisoned out of existence.

The Mohawks started Stone's environmental tour of Akwesasne with a visit to one of the General Motors waste lagoons, a place called "un-named tributary cove" on some maps. Stone gave it the name "contaminant cove" because of the amount of toxic pollution in it. One day in 1985, at contaminant cove, the environmental crisis at Akwesasne assumed a whole new foreboding shape. The New York State Department of Environmental Conservation caught a female snapping turtle that contained 835 parts per million of PCBs. The turtle carries a special significance among the Iroquois, whose creation story describes how the world took shape on a turtle's back. To this day, many Iroquois call North America "**Turtle Island**."

While no federal standards exist for PCBs in turtles, the federal standard for edible poultry is 3 parts per million, or about 0.36 percent of the concentration in that snapping turtle. The federal standard for edible fish is 2 parts per million. In soil, on a dry-weight basis, 50 parts per million is considered hazardous waste, so that turtle contained more than fifteen times the concentration of PCBs necessary, by federal standards, to qualify its body as toxic waste.

During the fall of 1987, Stone found another snapping turtle, a male, containing 3,067 parts per million of PCBs in its body fat—a thousand times the concentration allowed in domestic chicken and sixty times the minimum standard for hazardous waste. Contamination was lower in female turtles because they shed some of their own contamination by laying eggs, while the males stored more of what they ingested.

In 1985, Stone, working in close cooperation with the Mohawks, found a masked shrew that somehow had managed to survive in spite of a PCB level of 11,522 parts per million in its body, the highest concentration that Stone had ever seen in a living creature, 230 times the minimum standard to qualify as hazardous waste. Using these samples and others, Stone and the Mohawks established Akwesasne as one of the worst PCB-pollution sites in North America.

In 1986, pregnant women were advised not to eat fish from the St. Lawrence River, historically the Mohawks' main source of protein. Until the 1950s, Akwesasne had been home to more than 100 commercial fishermen and about 120 farmers. By 1990, fewer than 10 commercial fishermen and 20 farmers remained.

The Environmental Protection Agency released its Superfund cleanup plan for the General Motors foundry during March 1990. The cleanup was estimated to cost $138 million, making the General Motors dumps near Akwesasne the costliest Superfund cleanup job in the United States, number one on the EPA's "most wanted" list as the worst toxic dump in the United States. By 1991, the cost was scaled down to $78 million, but the General Motors dumps were still ranked as the most expensive toxic cleanup.

"We can't try to meet the challenges with the meager resources we have," said Henry Lickers, a **Seneca** who is employed by the Mohawk Council at Akwesasne. Lickers has been a mentor to today's younger environmentalists at Akwesasne. He also has been a leader in the fight against fluoride emissions from the Reynolds plant. "The next ten years will be a cleanup time for us, even without the money," said Lickers (Johansen, 19).

The destruction of Akwesasne's environment is credited by Lickers with being the catalyst that spawned the Mohawks' deadly battle over high-stakes **gambling** and smuggling. "A desperation sets in when year after year you see the decimation of the philosophical center of your society," he said (Johansen, 19).

The Mohawks are not alone. Increasingly, restrictive environmental regulations enacted by states and cities are bringing polluters to Native reservations. "Indian tribes across America are grappling with some of the worst of its pollution: uranium tailings, chemical lagoons and illegal dumps. Nowhere has it been more troublesome than at . . . Akwesasne," wrote Rupert Tomsho, a reporter for the *Wall Street Journal* (Tomsho, 1).

At Akwesasne, Katsi Cook, a Mohawk midwife who has studied the degree to which mothers' breastmilk has been laced with PCBs at Akwesasne, said that "this means that there may be potential exposure to our future generations. The analysis of Mohawk mothers' milk shows that our bodies are, in effect, part of the [General Motors] landfill" (LaDuke, 45).

FURTHER READING

Johansen, Bruce E. *Life and Death in Mohawk Country*. Golden, Colo.: North American Press/Fulcrum, 1993.
LaDuke, Winona. "Breastmilk, PCBs, and Motherhood: An Interview with Katsi Cook, Mohawk." *Cultural Survival Quarterly* 17:4 (Winter 1994): 43–45.
Lickers, Henry. "Guest Essay: The Message Returns." *Akwesasne Notes*, n.s. 1:1 (1995): 10–11.
Tomsho, Rupert. "Reservations Bear the Brunt of New Pollution." *Wall Street Journal*, November 29, 1990, 1.

John Kahionhes Fadden and Bruce E. Johansen

Albany Congress (1754). Beginning nearly two generations before the **American Revolution**, the circumstances of diplomacy brought opinion leaders of the English colonies and the Haudenosaunee Confederacy together to discuss the politics of alliance. Beginning in the early 1740s, Iroquois leaders strongly urged the colonists to form a federation similar to their own. The Iroquois' immediate practical objective was unified management of the Indian trade and prevention of fraud. The Iroquois also stressed that the British colonies should unify against France.

This set of circumstances brought **Benjamin Franklin** into the diplomatic equation. He first read the Iroquois' urgings to unite as a printer of Indian treaties. By the early 1750s, Franklin was more directly involved in **treaty diplomacy** itself, at the same time that he became an early, forceful advocate of colonial union. All of these circumstantial strings were tied together in the summer of 1754 when colonial representatives, Franklin among them, met with Iroquois sachems at Albany to address issues of mutual concern, including protests of land fraud and the continued tenure of their ally **William Johnson** as a manager of British relations with the Haudenosaunee, notably the **Mohawks**. At the same time, colonial delegates debated and developed the Albany Plan of Union, a political design that echoes English and Iroquois precedents.

The Albany Congress convened on June 19, 1754. Most of the sessions of the congress took place at the Albany courthouse. On June 28, 1754, the day after **Hendrick** arrived with the Mohawks, New York governor James DeLancey met with him. The 200 Indians in attendance sat on ten rows of benches in front of the governor's residence, with colonial delegates facing them in a row of chairs, their backs to the building. Hendrick repeated the advice **Canassatego** had given colonial delegates a decade earlier to unite on an Iroquois model. This time, the advice came not at a treaty conference, but at a meeting devoted to drawing up a plan for the type of colonial union the Iroquois had been requesting. The same day, at the courthouse, the colonial delegates were in the early stages of debate over the plan of union.

DeLancey replied: "I hope that by this present Union, we shall grow up to a great height and be as powerful and famous as you were of old" (*Colonial Records*, 6:98). As Franklin formally proposed his plan of union before the congress, he wrote that the debates on the Albany Plan of Union "went on daily, hand in hand with the Indian business" (Bigelow, 295).

In drawing up his final draft, Franklin was meeting several diplomatic demands: the Crown's for control, the colonies' desires for autonomy in a loose confederation, and the Iroquois' stated advocacy of a colonial union similar (but not identical) to their own in form and function. For the Crown, the plan provided administration by a president-general to be appointed by England. The individual colonies were to be allowed to retain their own constitutions, except as the plan circumscribed them. The retention of internal sovereignty within the individual colonies closely resembled the Iroquois system.

Franklin chose the name "Grand Council" for the plan's deliberative body, the same name generally applied to the Iroquois central council. The number of delegates, forty-eight, was close to the Iroquois council's fifty, and each colony had a different number of delegates, just as each Haudenosaunee (Iroquois) nation sent a different number of sachems to Onondaga. The Albany plan was based in rough proportion to tax revenues, however, while the Iroquois system was based on tradition.

Basically, the plan provided that Parliament was to establish a general government in America that included all of the English colonies, each of which was to retain its own constitution except for certain powers (mainly mutual defense) that were to be given to the general government. The king was to appoint a president-general for the government. Each colonial assembly would elect representatives to the Grand Council. The Albany Plan of Union was defeated by the colonies' individual assemblies, but it provided a prototype for Franklin's Articles of Confederation twenty years later.

FURTHER READING

Colonial Records of Pennsylvania. Harrisburg, Penn.: Theo. Fenn & Co., 1851–1853.
Franklin, Benjamin. *Autobiography of Benjamin Franklin*. Ed. John Bigelow. Philadelphia: J. B. Lippincott, 1868.
Grinde, Donald A., Jr., and Bruce E. Johansen. *Exemplar of Liberty: Native America and the Evolution of Democracy*. Los Angeles: UCLA American Indian Studies Center, 1991.

Allegany Reservation (Seneca). The Allegany Reservation, seventy miles south of Buffalo, New York, occupies 30,190 acres, roughly 1.5 miles by 30 miles along the Allegheny River in southwesternmost New York State. The reservation, part of the **Seneca** Nation of Indians, was established by the **Canandaigua (Pickering) Treaty** of 1794. The reservation was sold to the Ogden Land Company under the **Buffalo Creek Treaty of 1838**, but was restored after Seneca protest in a second treaty four years later.

Major parts of the Allegany Reservation have been taken during the twentieth century for utility, highway, and railroad rights-of-way. More than 10,000 acres were taken during the 1950s for the right-of-way of the **Kinzua Dam** and reservoir, despite the fact that the land had been guaranteed to **Cornplanter** by George Washington's signature in the Canandaigua Treaty. When the land was flooded, some of Cornplanter's descendants asked wryly whether Washington had asked the Seneca leader if he knew how to swim. The Senecas were awarded $18 million by the federal government in 1964 for its negligence of their interests related to the construction of the dam, which created a thirty-five-mile-long lake.

The Allegany Senecas also have been involved in an ongoing controversy regarding the town of **Salamanca**, for which they were awarded $35 million in damages by the federal government in 1990 to help compensate for a century and a half of undermarket lease payments by non-Indians in violation of treaty rights. Some of this money was invested in a revolving loan fund for Seneca small businesses. In 1990, the reservation, which is governed by an elected tribal council under a constitution modeled on that of the United States (adopted by the Senecas in 1848), was home to 7,312 people.

American Revolution, Haudenosaunee involvement. Native American involvement was crucial to the course of the American Revolution. Native alliances, especially with the powerful Haudenosaunee (Iroquois or Six Nations) Confederacy, helped shape the outcome of the war. The war also was crucial for the Haudenosaunee Confederacy, which split for the first time in several hundred years over the issue of whether to support Great Britain or the new United States of America. The **Oneidas** allied with the Americans and assisted George Washington's army with crucial food supplies during its most difficult winter, at Valley Forge. On the other hand, most of the **Mohawks** and **Senecas** sided with the British and suffered from brutal raids principally by troops under the command of General **John Sullivan**. In the words of historian Richard Aquila, "The American revolution became an Iroquois civil war" (Aquila, 241).

The Seneca **Cornplanter** advocated neutrality, while **Joseph Brant**, a Mohawk leader, advocated alliance with the British, as did the Seneca **Red Jacket**. The name "Red Jacket" was a reference to a scarlet coat given to him by the British for fighting with them during the war. Cornplanter insisted that the quarrel was among the whites, and that to interfere in something that the Haudenosaunee did not fully understand would be a mistake. Brant contended that neutrality might cause the Senecas to be attacked by one side without allies on the other. Brant had visited England, had acquired a taste for English food and clothes, and had been told that land would be returned to the Mohawks by the British in exchange for alliance.

As one meeting broke up in a furor, Brant called Cornplanter a coward. Brant was influential in recruiting most of the Mohawks, Senecas, **Cayugas**, and **Onondagas** to support the British. Brant's ferocity as a warrior was legendary; many settlers who supported the Americans called him "Monster Brant." His sister, **Molly Brant**, had married **Sir William Johnson**, Britain's chief Indian agent in the Northeast and a lifelong friend of such Mohawk leaders as **Hendrick**, with whom he had fought side by side in the war with France two decades before his death in 1774.

Although **Skenandoah** asserted the Oneidas' official neutrality at the beginning of the American Revolution, he supplied warriors and intelligence to the patriots, as did the **Tuscaroras**. As Washington's army shivered in the snow at Valley Forge, Skenandoah's Oneidas carried **corn** to the starving troops. Washington later named the Shenandoah Valley of Virginia after the Oneida chief in appreciation of his support. During September 1778, the Oneidas supplied a key warning to residents of German Flats, near Herkimer, New York, that their settlements were about to be raided by the British and their Iroquois allies under Joseph Brant. The settlers were thus able to get out of the area in time, after which their homes and farms were burned and their livestock was captured.

Revolutionary forces often adopted a scorched-earth policy against Haudenosaunee who supported the British. George Washington's forces ended the battle for the Mohawk Valley by defeating the British and their Iroquois allies at the Battle of Johnstown. After the war, the Brant family and many of the other Mohawks who had supported the British in the Revolution moved to Canada to escape retribution by the victorious patriots. They founded the town of Brantford, Ontario, and established a new Haudenosaunee council fire there.

The Iroquois figured importantly in the Battle of Oriskany in 1777, the Battle of Wyoming Valley in 1778, and the Battle of Newtown in 1779. The war often was very brutal on both sides; Brant's forces torched farms owned by patriots as patriot armies, particularly (but not exclusively) those under Sullivan, systematically ransacked Iroquois villages and fields, meanwhile expressing astonishment at the size of Iroquois (especially Seneca) food stores. Because the Iroquois clan system cuts across national boundaries, relatives often found themselves fighting each other as the confederacy split its allegiance between the British and the patriots.

Cornwallis surrendered at Yorktown in 1781, but war parties continued to clash along the frontier for months after the British defeat became obvious. The Iroquois allies of the British sent out war parties as late as the early summer of 1782. The Iroquois allies of the British wanted to continue fighting, but their sponsors had given up. After the war, the efforts of the Iroquois went unrewarded by both sides. The British discarded their Mohawk, Onondaga, Cayuga, and Seneca allies at the earliest convenience.

The Americans did the same to their own allies, the Tuscaroras and Oneidas. At the conclusion of the Revolutionary War, the border between the new United States and Canada (which remained under British control) was drawn through Iroquois country in the Treaty of Paris (1783), without consultation. In 1784, during treaty councils held at **Fort Stanwix**, New York, many Iroquois realized that the new government was ignoring most of their land claims. Most of the negotiations were held at gunpoint, and the Iroquois were forced to give up claims to much of their ancestral territories.

Despite his reluctance to ally with the patriots, the Seneca leader Cornplanter became a close friend of George Washington after the war. He was given a strip of land in western New York for his people, whose descendants lived on the land until the mid-twentieth century, when it was flooded by water behind the **Kinzua Dam**, despite a two-centuries-old pledge by President Washington that the land would be protected.

In addition to their role as combatants in the American Revolution, American Indians played a key role in the contest of ideas that spurred the revolt. As early as 1744, the Onondaga sachem **Canassatego**, Tadadaho (speaker) of the Iroquois Confederacy at the time, urged the British colonists to unite on a federal model similar to the Iroquois political system. **Benjamin Franklin** printed Canassatego's advice at the 1744 **Lancaster Treaty Council** and later proposed an early plan for union at the **Albany Congress** of 1754. This plan, which included elements of both British and Iroquois political structures, was rejected by the colonies, but served as a model for Franklin's later Articles of Confederation.

During the early 1770s, before the American Revolution led to armed revolt, colonists adopted Mohawk disguises to dump British tea at Boston and at several other cities along the eastern seaboard. The American Indian, often portrayed as a woman, was used as a symbol of an emerging American nation long before Uncle Sam was adopted in that role.

FURTHER READING

Aquila, Richard. *The Iroquois Restoration: Iroquois Diplomacy on the Colonial Frontier, 1701–1754*. Detroit: Wayne State University Press, 1983.

Armstrong, Virginia Irving, comp. *I Have Spoken: American History through the Voices of the Indians*. Chicago: Sage Books, 1971.

Edmunds, R. David, ed. *American Indian Leaders: Studies in Diversity*. Lincoln: University of Nebraska Press, 1980.

Graymont, Barbara. *The Iroquois in the American Revolution*. Syracuse, N.Y.: Syracuse University Press, 1972.

Grinde, Donald A., Jr. *The Iroquois and the Founding of the American Nation*. San Francisco: Indian Historian Press, 1977.

Kelsay, Isabel Thompson. *Joseph Brant, 1743–1807, Man of Two Worlds*. Syracuse, N.Y.: Syracuse University Press, 1984.

Red Jacket. *A Long-Lost Speech of Red Jacket.* Ed. J. W. Sanborn. Friendship, N.Y.:
    N.p., 1912.
Stone, William L. *The Life and Times of Say-go-ye-wat-ha, or Red Jacket.* Albany, N.Y.:
    Munsell, 1866.
Waters, Frank. *Brave Are My People.* Santa Fe, N.M.: Clear Light, 1993.

Anderson, Wallace "Mad Bear" (Tuscarora), 1972–1985. Wallace "Mad
Bear" Anderson was a noted Native American–rights activist during the 1950s,
before a general upsurge in Native self-determination efforts a decade later.
Anderson later became a spokesman for Native American sovereignty in several
international forums.

Anderson was born in Buffalo, New York, and was raised on the **Tuscarora**
Reservation near Niagara Falls. The name "Mad Bear" was first used by An-
derson's grandmother in reference to his hotheadedness. He adopted it from her.
Anderson served in the U.S. Navy during World War II at Okinawa. He later
also served in Korea. Anderson became an activist after his request for a GI
Bill loan to build a house on the Tuscarora Reservation was rejected.

Mad Bear led protests against Iroquois payment of New York State income
taxes in 1957. Edmund Wilson recalled Anderson as "a young man in a lum-
berjack shirt and cap, broad of build, with a round face and lively black eyes"
(Wilson, 67). At the height of the protest, several hundred **Akwesasne** (St.
Regis) **Mohawks** marched to the Massena, New York, courthouse, where they
burned summonses issued for unpaid taxes.

In 1958, Anderson played a leading role in protests of a 1,383-acre seizure
of Tuscarora land by the New York Power Authority for construction of a dam
and reservoir. Anderson and other Iroquois deflated workers' tires and blocked
surveyors' transits. When the Tuscaroras refused to sell the land, a force of
about 100 state troopers and police invaded their reservation. Anderson met the
troopers and police with 150 nonviolent demonstrators who blocked their trucks
by lying in the road.

During March 1959, Anderson was involved in a declaration of sovereignty
at the Iroquois Six Nations Reserve in Brantford, Ontario, the settlement established by **Joseph Brant** and his followers after the **American Revolution**. The
declaration prompted an occupation of the reserve's council house by Royal
Canadian Mounted Police. During the same month, Mad Bear also attempted a
citizen's arrest of Indian Commissioner Glen L. Emmons in Washington, D.C.,
on allegations of misconduct in office. Emmons avoided the intended arrest, but
later resigned. During July 1959, Anderson traveled to Cuba with a delegation
of Iroquois and other Native Americans to exchange recognitions of sovereignty
with Fidel Castro, whose revolutionary army had seized power only months
earlier.

During 1967, Anderson formed the North American Indian Unity Caravan,
which traveled the United States for six years as the types of activism that he

had pioneered spread nationwide; Anderson also gathered opposition to termination legislation and carried it to Washington, D.C., from 133 Native American tribes and nations, effectively killing the last attempt to buy out reservations in the United States. In 1969, he helped initiate the takeover of Alcatraz Island. Anderson spent his later years advocating various Native American causes on a national and international level. He died in November 1985.

FURTHER READING

Anderson, Wallace (Mad Bear). "The Lost Brother: An Iroquois Prophecy of Serpents." In Shirley Hill Witt and Stan Steiner, eds., *The Way: An Anthology of American Indian Literature*. New York: Vintage, 1972.
Wilson, Edmund. *Apologies to the Iroquois*. New York: Farrar, Straus & Cudahy, 1960.

Antlers, as symbol. Antlers are used on the *Gus-tow-weh*, or ceremonial headdress of Haudenosaunee peace chiefs. A leader is presented with this headdress upon installation; if he is impeached, the antlers are removed, and he is said to have been "dehorned." A chief who is actively involved in the people's business is said to be "wearing antlers," which may be set aside if he must go to war or becomes mortally ill.

B

Beaver Wars. The term "Beaver Wars" has become a historical shorthand reference for the Haudenosaunee campaign against the Wyandots (Hurons), which culminated in their defeat and assimilation by the Haudenosaunee about 1650. Like most wars, this one had more than one initiating cause. The most prominent reason for the antipathy leading to the war, however, was competition over diminishing stocks of beaver and other fur-bearing animals. The Haudenosaunee cause during this conflict was aided immeasurably by their relatively recent acquisition of European firearms, which the Wyandots, for the most part, lacked. The Mohawks, situated near trading centers at Albany and Montréal, were among the first to acquire a stock of firearms; one French source estimated that they had close to 300 guns by 1643 (Richter, 62).

At the beginning of the seventeenth century, the Wyandots, who lived near Georgian Bay on Lake Huron, were a prosperous confederacy of 25,000 to 30,000 people, comparable to the Haudenosaunee. By 1642, the Wyandots had allied solidly with the French and also had entered an alliance with the Susquehannocks, south of the Iroquois, who felt as if a military vise was being closed around them. In 1642, 1645, and 1647, the Haudenosaunee tried to secure peace with the French, to no avail. After the third try, they decided to break the alliance. The Wyandots had built a confederacy similar in structure to that of the Haudenosaunee, although it was more geographically compact. The Haudenosaunee **Peacemaker** was a Wyandot.

By 1640, the Wyandots' economy was nearly totally dependent on trade with the French. At the same time, as they were weakened by disease, the Wyandots found themselves facing waves of raids by the Iroquois (principally **Mohawks** and **Senecas**), who were seeking to capture the Wyandots' share of the fur trade. The Mohawks had been exposed to European trade goods earlier than the Wyandots and may have been looking for furs to finance trade. The Wyandots' location at the center of several trade routes also made them an appealing point of attack at a time when demand was rising for beaver pelts, and available supply of the animals was declining.

For nearly a decade, the Mohawks and Senecas harassed the Wyandots. The Wyandots, fearing Iroquois attacks, sometimes curtailed their trade with the French during the 1640s. Between 1647 and 1650, a final Iroquois drive swept over the Wyandots' homeland, provoking the dissolution of their confederacy, as well as usurpation of the Wyandots' share of the fur trade by the Senecas and Mohawks.

Iroquois pressure against the Wyandots continued for several years after the conclusion of the "Beaver Wars" as Wyandot refugees sought new homes throughout the Great Lakes and the St. Lawrence Valley. Many of the Wyandot refugees experienced acute hunger, and a sizable number starved during this diaspora. Some Wyandots became so hungry that they ate human excrement; others dug up the bodies of the dead and ate them. This was done in desperation and with great shame, because cannibalism is directly contrary to Wyandot belief and custom.

Scattered communities of Wyandots gradually revived traditional economies after the hungry years of the 1650s. Many Wyandots settled in or near European communities (including Jesuit missions). Even those who became Christianized and Europeanized continued to live in **longhouses** during these years. They continued to hunt and trap as much as possible and to practice slash-and-burn agriculture.

A number of Wyandot refugees were adopted after the Beaver Wars by their former enemies, who, true to their own traditions, socialized Wyandot prisoners into the various Haudenosaunee families and clans. The Iroquois also were re-plenishing their societies, which had been hard hit by European diseases and the casualties of continual war.

FURTHER READING

Reaman, G. Elmore. *The Trail of the Iroquois Indians: How the Iroquois Nation Saved Canada for the British Empire*. London: Frederick Muller, 1967.

Richter, Daniel K. *The Ordeal of the Longhouse: The Peoples of the Iroquois League in the Era of European Colonization*. Chapel Hill: University of North Carolina Press, 1992.

Trigger, Bruce G. *The Children of Aataentsic: A History of the Huron People to 1660*. Montréal: McGill–Queen's University Press, 1976.

Bell, John Kim (Mohawk), b. 1953. John Kim Bell was born on the **Kahna-wake Mohawk** reserve near Montréal and became the first North American Indian to be employed as a professional orchestral conductor. Bell, a conductor with the National Ballet of Canada, also has been guest conductor of London's Royal Philharmonic Orchestra. In 1985, he founded the Canadian Native Arts Foundation in Toronto to promote the participation of Native Americans in the arts through scholarships and grants.

Benedict, Ernest (Kaientaronkwen) (Mohawk), b. 1918. Ernest Benedict is one of the **Akwesasne Mohawks'** most influential elders, a man who has lived on the territory since a time before large-scale pollution ruined most of its farming and fishing, before Akwesasne's major industries included **gambling** and smuggling. Benedict, who graduated from St. Lawrence College, fought proposals to terminate the Haudenosaunee nations. At one congressional hearing in 1948, he confronted Senator Arthur Watkins, the best-known advocate of termination legislation, after Watkins said that the federal government was tiring of its trust responsibilities to Indians and intended to divest itself of some of them. "What about solemn treaty commitments?" asked Benedict.

Can an honorable nation, just because it is tired, shrug off its responsibilities regardless of the wishes and conditions of the ward? . . . Perhaps Indians are tired too! Tired of poverty and ignorance and disease. They are weary of neglect and broken promises and fruitless hoping. (Hauptman, 49–50)

Akwesasne Notes was born around Benedict's kitchen table. Benedict also was a key founder of the **North American Indian Travelling College** at Akwesasne, which carried Haudenosaunee history and culture across Canada. Benedict quit his job at Reynolds Aluminum to develop the college.

Benedict was active during 1968 in protests of Canadian policies that curtailed **Mohawks'** freedom of movement across the international border, which is guaranteed under the **Jay Treaty** of 1794. From Benedict's home on Cornwall Island, the Mohawks of Akwesasne prepared to blockade the nearby International Bridge and force the issue of policies that required them to pay customs duties on anything worth more than $5, including food and other necessities of daily life. More than a hundred Mohawks imposed a wall of bodies that stopped traffic; then they let air out of the tires of many stalled vehicles. Police arrested forty-one Mohawks. After a second blockade in February 1969 and a long series of negotiations, Canadian officials agreed to abide by the terms of the Jay Treaty, which had been restated in Mohawk agreements with the St. Lawrence Power Authority during the 1950s.

In 1995, Benedict received one of fourteen Aboriginal Achievement Awards given to first-nations leaders across Canada by the Canadian Native Arts Foundation. Benedict, who has been elected to the Canadian Mohawk Council of Akwesasne several times, also has been a member of the Canadian Royal Commission on Aboriginal Peoples.

FURTHER READING

Hauptman, Laurence M. *The Iroquois Struggle for Survival: World War II to Red Power*. Syracuse, N.Y.: Syracuse University Press, 1986.

Bennett, Robert L. (Oneida), b. 1912. Robert L. Bennett, commissioner of the Bureau of Indian Affairs (BIA) under President Lyndon Johnson, was born on the Wisconsin **Oneida** reservation and was educated at the Haskell Institute. He later attended Southeastern University and earned an LL.B. degree in 1941. Bennett served in the Marine Corps during World War II. After the war, he held a number of posts in the BIA before becoming commissioner between 1966 and 1969.

As BIA director at the beginning of the self-determination era, Bennett tried to fashion programs that would hasten economic development on reservations. Bennett's administration also tried to extend the social-welfare policies of President Johnson's Great Society to reservation Indians, with various degrees of success. Bennett also fought off the last attempts to further termination—the buying out of Native titles to reservations—in Congress.

After his retirement from the BIA, Bennett directed the American Indian Law Center at the University of New Mexico Law School. He served on a number of boards of directors and garnered many awards working with Native groups across the United States.

Big Tree, John "Chief" (Seneca), fl. early twentieth century. Silent movies became popular within a generation after the final "closing" of the frontier at Wounded Knee. Until the 1920s, when sound replaced silent movies and non-Indians were hired to act as Indians, Native actors sometimes achieved stardom. One such star was the **Seneca** John Big Tree, who played major roles in sixteen movies filmed as early as 1922 and as late as 1950. Most of these movies, such as *Winners of the Wilderness* (1927) and *The Frontiersman* (1927), had western themes.

Blacksnake (Seneca), c. 1753–1859. Blacksnake was a nephew of both **Cornplanter** and **Handsome Lake**. Blacksnake also played a key role in publication of The Code of Handsome Lake in 1850, thirty-five years after Handsome Lake's death. The code combines elements of traditional Iroquois religion with Quakerism, which Handsome Lake had studied.

Blacksnake was born near Seneca Lake, probably in 1753 (some accounts say that he was born in 1749). His **Seneca** name was "Chainbreaker." Blacksnake aided the British in the **American Revolution**, fighting with notable Iroquois leaders such as Cornplanter and **Joseph Brant**. He participated in the Battle of Oriskany (1777), the raids in the Wyoming and Cherry valleys (1778), and the Battle of Newtown (1779).

After Handsome Lake pronounced his vision for reforming Iroquois society in 1799, Blacksnake became one of his most dedicated disciples. He fought with the Americans against the British in the War of 1812 and later became the Senecas' principal chief. He often was called "Governor Blacksnake" and was known for his desire to combine European-American educational practices with retention of Native traditions.

Blacksnake related memoirs late in his life that provide insight into the Iroquois role in the American Revolution, as well as the life and thoughts of Handsome Lake. Blacksnake died at Cold Spring, New York, in 1859 at the age of 106.

FURTHER READING

Abler, Thomas S., ed. *Chainbreaker: The Revolutionary War Memoirs of Governor Blacksnake As Told to Benjamin Williams*. Lincoln: University of Nebraska Press, 1989.
Wallace, Anthony F. C. *The Death and Rebirth of the Seneca*. New York: Knopf, 1970.
Wright, Ronald. *Stolen Continents*. Boston: Houghton Mifflin, 1992.

Blueye, Winona Esther (Seneca), b. 1903. Entering her ninth decade of life, Winona Esther Blueye, a **Tonawanda Seneca**, completed a thousand-page manuscript during the mid-1990s that translates orally spoken Seneca into written form. The book was based on a copy of the New Testament published in Seneca during the nineteenth century that was given to Blueye by her father. As a girl, she heard her grandfather preach in Seneca at the Baptist church in Tonawanda. Her great-great-uncle helped with the translation.

Blueye worked with a small circle of Seneca elders for thirty years to complete the translation out of concern that the language, left in its predominantly oral form, would die as the small number of fluent speakers passed away. "It is the most comprehensive Seneca language text that has ever been . . . written," according to **G. Peter Jemison**, director of the New York State historic site at **Ganondagan**.

FURTHER READING

Carter, Diane Louise. "Preserving the Language." Gannett News Service, October 9, 1995 (in LEXIS).

Brant, Joseph (Thayendanegea) (Mohawk), 1742–1807. Joseph Brant was a son of Aroghyiadecker (Nicklaus Brant), who was prominent on the New York frontier during the mid-1700s as an Iroquois leader and an ally of the British in the **American Revolution**. His grandfather Sagayeeanquarashtow (Sa Ga Yean Qua Prah Ton) was one of the four "American kings" who were invited to London to visit Queen Anne's court in 1710. Brant joined **William Johnson**, British Indian agent, at the age of thirteen and, with other **Mohawk** allies, was present at the Battle of Lake George when the elderly **Hendrick** was killed.

In 1758, Brant was one of the guides who led the Bradstreet Expedition to the French Fort Frontenac on the north shore of Lake Ontario. Two hundred and fifty Redcoats marched with the Mohawks, as well as 2,700 colonial volunteers. Fort Frontenac fell, and Brant began to appear more often at Johnson Hall, the center of British political and military affairs in Haudenosaunee country.

After the war with the French ended in 1763, Brant, who was still a young man, was tutored by Eleazer Wheelock at the Indian Charity School in Lebanon, Connecticut, which would later move to New Hampshire and become known as Dartmouth College. He was an able student but dropped out after a year. Brant was married for a time to Margaret, a daughter of the **Oneida** sachem **Skenandoah**. After Margaret's death, Brant married Catherine Croghan, a Mohawk daughter of George Croghan, a British Indian agent who was a close friend of William Johnson.

By 1765, Brant was married and settled in the Mohawk Valley. Brant translated the Gospel of Mark into Mohawk. He also accepted a job as a secretary to Johnson and acquired farmland, cattle, and an interest in a gristmill. As personal secretary to Johnson, Brant became known as the most able interpreter available to the British in northeastern North America. As a Mohawk leader, Brant attended meetings of the Iroquois Grand Council at Onondaga and provided firsthand intelligence to the British military.

After William Johnson died in 1774, Brant became secretary to his nephew **Guy Johnson**, who assumed the Indian superintendency for the British. In November 1775, Brant sailed for England with Johnson. "As a Pine Tree Chief of the Iroquois, he wore knee-high moccasins and a blanket draped over one shoulder. And as Col. Guy Johnson's secretary, he was equally at home in starched linen and broadcloth," wrote Frank Waters (Waters, 48).

Brant played a major role in rallying a majority of the Mohawks to the British cause during the American Revolution. Brant was told that some Mohawk lands would be returned to them if they allied with the British. A sketch of Brant appeared in the July 1776 edition of *London Magazine* just as (unknown to Londoners until mid-August) American revolutionaries were posting their Declaration of Independence in Philadelphia. On another visit to London in 1785, Brant dined with the Prince of Wales. Brant made a favorable impression upon high society in London. He fascinated the British because he spoke good English and had a European education. He also was a Mason, a staunch churchman, and a translator of the Bible into Mohawk. The British government provided him with personal guides to the sights of London.

By 1780, after Brant and Guy Johnson had crossed the Atlantic together several times and had worked closely together for half a dozen years, they had a falling-out over Johnson's dishonesty. Evidence mounted that Johnson was padding reports to the Crown to swindle large amounts of money in association with several traders at Niagara. For example, Johnson debited the king for 1,156 kettles when the actual number was 156.

After the American Revolution, Brant emigrated to British Canada with a number of Mohawks and other Iroquois, along with many other non-Indian British sympathizers. The British military maintained his rank at half pay and granted him land along the Grand River in Ontario, the site today of the **Grand River Iroquois** Reservation.

Brant visited England again in 1786, at the Court of St. James. He devoted many of his later years to translating the Bible and other religious works into Mohawk and to raising seven children by three wives. Brant died on November 24, 1807. A statue was erected in his memory at Brantford, Ontario, in 1866.

FURTHER READING

Edmunds, R. David, ed. *American Indian Leaders: Studies in Diversity.* Lincoln: University of Nebraska Press, 1980.

Graymont, Barbara. *The Iroquois in the American Revolution.* Syracuse, N.Y.: Syracuse University Press, 1972.

Grinde, Donald A., Jr. *The Iroquois and the Founding of the American Nation.* San Francisco: Indian Historian Press, 1977.

Kelsay, Isabel Thompson. *Joseph Brant, 1743–1807, Man of Two Worlds.* Syracuse, N.Y.: Syracuse University Press, 1984.

Stone, William L. *The Life of Joseph Brant Thayendanegea.* 1838. New York: Kraus, 1969.

Waters, Frank. *Brave Are My People.* Santa Fe, N.M.: Clear Light, 1993.

Brant, Mary (Molly, Degonwadonti) (Mohawk), c. 1735–c. 1795. Mary Brant, sister of **Joseph Brant**, married **Sir William Johnson** and wielded considerable influence on both sides of the frontier by bringing many Iroquois to the side of the British in the **American Revolution**. Born at **Canajoharie**, New York, of Nicklaus Brant, a Mohawk, and a mixed-blood Mohawk woman, Mary grew up with her brother Joseph at the family home in the Mohawk Valley. She first met Johnson in 1753, when she was about eighteen years of age. Between that year and Johnson's death in 1774, she bore him nine children.

The plundering of Mary Brant's home during 1777 by fellow Iroquois allied with the patriots provides a study in microcosm of the divisions that bedeviled the Iroquois Confederacy during the American Revolution. During the raid, the chairman of the Tryon County Committee of Safety enriched himself by carrying off wagonloads of goods. The patriots also urged the **Oneidas** of Oriska to make up their losses at the hands of the raiding Mohawks. Peter Deygart of the Committee of Safety urged the Oneidas to take two cows, horses, sheep, and hogs for every one that the Mohawks had earlier taken from them.

Before the American Revolution, many of the Mohawks had lived in greater comfort than the struggling white settlers. Thus the whites were only too pleased to loot Indian homes. A cursory glance at some of the articles taken in these raids reflects the wealth of these Indian communities. Agricultural products such as Indian corn, turnips, and potatoes were taken, as well as livestock, wagons, farm implements, and sleighs. Many Mohawk houses were sturdily built and had window glass, a rare item on the frontier. Among the things whites took were "several Gold Rings, Eight pair silver Buckels; a large quantity of Silver Brooches, Together with several silk Gowns" (Johansen and Grinde, 54).

Due to her position, Mary was actually more influential within the confederacy than her younger brother, Joseph. As a Clan Mother and consort of Sir William Johnson, she was a powerful figure within the traditional framework.

She also knew the ways of the white man. An observer commented that "one word from her goes farther with them than a thousand from any white Man." ("Molly Brant—Loyalist," 119). During the fall of 1777, Major John Butler invited Mary Brant to come to the frontier to live. The Iroquois Clan Mother hesitated, not wanting to alienate her friends and relatives at Cayuga. Later, however, she did move to Niagara. While there, she maintained an open house for all the leading men and women of the confederacy.

Mary Brant moved to Canada with the rest of Joseph Brant's band after the American Revolution, after which historical details of her life become sketchy. She probably died about 1795 in or near Brantford, Ontario.

FURTHER READING

Graymont, Barbara. *The Iroquois in the American Revolution*. Syracuse,: N.Y. Syracuse University Press, 1972.
Grinde, Donald A., Jr. *The Iroquois and the Founding of the American Nation*. San Francisco: Indian Historian Press, 1977.
Johansen, Bruce E., and Donald A. Grinde. *The Encyclopedia of Native American Biography*. New York: Henry Holt, 1997.
"Molly Brant—Loyalist." *Ontario History* 45:3 (Summer 1953).

Bruce, Louis R. (Dakota and Mohawk), 1906–1989. Louis R. Bruce, who was raised among the **Onondagas**, served as commissioner of the Bureau of Indian Affairs (BIA) during President Richard Nixon's first term. His tenure coincided with activist Native American political movements during the late 1960s and 1970s.

Bruce's father, Louis Bruce, a **Mohawk**, worked as a dentist, a major-league baseball player, and a Methodist missionary. His mother, Nellie Rooks, was Dakota (Sioux). Bruce attended Cazenovia Seminary, worked his way through Syracuse University, and became known as a star pole vaulter. After his graduation from college, Bruce worked as a clothing-store manager, as an official in the Works Progress Administration, and as a dairy farmer. He married Anna Wikoff, a former classmate at the Cazenovia Seminary, in 1930.

In 1957, Bruce played a major role in organizing the first Native American Youth Conference. He was a founder and executive secretary of the National Congress of American Indians. Bruce also was an unofficial advisor to New York governor Thomas Dewey and a friend of Eleanor Roosevelt. He worked on many New Deal programs during the 1930s to preserve Native American art, dance, music, and other oral traditions.

After Bruce was named BIA commissioner by President Nixon in 1969, he set out to "Indianize" the bureau by appointing a number of Native Americans to influential positions. He served as commissioner of Indian affairs from 1969 to 1972; his tenure in that office came to an abrupt end after the Bureau of Indian Affairs building was occupied by Indian activists a week before the 1972 election. Bruce was fired by President Nixon.

Bruce's policies at the BIA ran up against a considerable amount of opposition from interests that had benefited by keeping Native Americans in a subordinate position. In this respect, his ouster recalled that of the first BIA commissioner of Native American descent, **Ely Parker**, who had been drummed out of the office almost exactly a century earlier.

FURTHER READING

Ballantine, Betty, and Ian Ballantine. *The Native Americans Today*. Atlanta: Turner Publishing, 1993.

Buffalo Creek Treaties (1838, 1842). The Buffalo Creek Treaty of 1838 was one of the most blatant government-assisted land frauds in U.S. history. **Lewis Henry Morgan**, whose *League of the Haudenosaunee* was published barely more than a decade after the Buffalo Creek Treaty was executed, said that the treaty was carried out "with a degree of wickedness hardly to be paralleled in the history of human avarice" (Morgan, 33).

During January 1838, the **Senecas**, under protest, sold their four remaining reservations (at **Allegany, Cattaraugus, Tonawanda**, and Buffalo Creek) to the Ogden Land Company, with a representative of the United States in attendance.

Under the terms of the treaty, the Senecas relinquished title on their homelands to the Ogden Land Company for 500,000 acres in Wisconsin purchased on their behalf by the U.S. government. The United States, in exchange, granted the Iroquois as a whole (as well as the Stockbridge-Munsees) rights to 1.8 million acres in northeastern Kansas. For their 202,000 acres in New York State, the Indians (mostly Senecas) were paid $202,000, or about $1 an acre. Having compensated the Senecas, the government now urged them to march to Indian Territory (later Oklahoma) in a manner earlier experienced by the Cherokees on the Trail of Tears. The Senecas fought this plan bitterly. Despite revelations of fraud, forgery, and bribery on the part of Ogden Land Company's negotiators, Congress, pressured by President Andrew Jackson, who favored Indian removals, ratified the treaty.

In 1842, in another treaty negotiation, also at Buffalo Creek, the Allegany and Tonawanda reservations were returned to the Senecas, but Ogden Land Company retained preemption rights. In 1857, the Tonawanda Senecas were allowed to repurchase part of the land sold to Ogden Land Company almost two decades earlier.

FURTHER READING

Hauptman, Laurence M. *The Iroquois in the Civil War: From Battlefield to Reservation*. Syracuse, N.Y.: Syracuse University Press, 1993.
Morgan, Lewis Henry. *League of the Iroquois*. 1851. Secaucus, N.J.: Corinth Books, 1962.

The bundle of arrows was used by the Haudenosaunee as a symbol of the strength of union. Courtesy of John Kahionhes Fadden.

Bundle of Arrows, as symbol. A bundle of arrows, usually five or six in number, often was used as a symbol of unity by Haudenosaunee leaders, notably **Hendrick** and **Canassatego**, who advised the squabbling English colonies to adopt a federal political system on an Iroquois model. The bundle of arrows was eventually adopted on the U.S. Great Seal (along with the eagle, which is also an Iroquois symbol) as a bundle of thirteen arrows, one for each of the original states.

The first designs for the Great Seal represented the bundle with six arrows, directly from Haudenosaunee symbolism. Some anthropologists (a prominent example being Elisabeth Tooker) maintain that the bundle of arrows on the Great Seal is derived from the Roman fasces, which was adopted as a symbol (and root word) of fascism by the Mussolini regime. Tooker has yet to offer any historical support for such a derivation, however.

FURTHER READING

Grinde, Donald A., Jr., and Bruce E. Johansen. *Exemplar of Liberty: Native America and the Evolution of Democracy.* Los Angeles: UCLA American Indian Studies Center, 1991.
Tooker, Elisabeth. [Review of *Exemplar of Liberty*, by Donald A. Grinde, Jr., and Bruce E. Johansen.] *Northeast Anthropology* 46 (Fall 1993): 103–107.

"Bury the hatchet." "Bury the hatchet," a colloquialism in American English, is borrowed from the founding story of the Haudenosaunee Confederacy, during which the feuding clans of the **Mohawks, Oneidas, Onondagas, Cayugas,** and **Senecas** buried their weapons, including hatchets, under the Great Tree of Peace.

"Buttlegging." "Buttlegging," a wordplay on "bootlegging," is a slang term used at **Akwesasne,** a **Mohawk** reservation straddling the U.S. border in northern New York State, to describe the trade in smuggled cigarettes across the border. Under the **Jay Treaty** (1794), Mohawks are guaranteed the right to cross the border tax-free. U.S.-brand cigarettes manufactured in Canada are exported to the United States without tax stamps, purportedly for export. Smugglers at Akwesasne then ship them back into Canada, across the St. Lawrence River, by motorboat in the summer and automobile (across the frozen river) in winter, where the tax-free smokes are sold at shops on the **Kahnawake** Reserve, near Montréal, undercutting the taxed cigarettes of off-reservation retailers. In the middle 1990s, a carton of taxed cigarettes averaged $30 in Canada, with roughly $21 of that going toward taxes that are being used as social engineering to reduce smoking. Cigarettes on the Kahnawake Reservation averaged $12 a carton at about the same time. By 1990, Canadian authorities estimated that they were losing $25 million a year in tax revenues from cigarette smuggling. By the mid-1990s, estimates reached $30 million.

In June 1997, twenty-one Mohawks, most of them from Akwesasne, were arrested by federal officials in the largest bust of a smuggling ring in U.S. history. The indictment sought to recover $680 million in property allegedly purchased with profits from cigarette, liquor, and gun smuggling that crossed Akwesasne territory, including boats, cars, and real estate. Among those arrested was L. David Jacobs, former chief of the St. Regis Mohawk Council.

FURTHER READING

Johansen, Bruce E. *Life and Death in Mohawk Country*. Golden, Colo.: North American Press/Fulcrum, 1993.

C

Canajoharie (Kanatsiohareke). Canajoharie ("The Clean Pot") was an aboriginal **Mohawk** village near the village of the same name in the Mohawk Valley of eastern New York. In 1755, a fort was constructed there and named after **Hendrick** (Tiyanoga). In the early 1990s, Mohawks from **Akwesasne** purchased land in the same area with the intention of reestablishing a traditional Mohawk settlement there. The effort was led in large part by **Tom Porter**, who was soon to step down from a position as a Mohawk Nation Council subchief due to a heart condition.

The roughly 320 acres the Mohawks bought includes 200 to 250 acres of old-growth woodland, some of it 200 to 250 feet tall, near the Mohawk River. The land, once Montgomery Manor, a county home for the poor and aged, was purchased for $231,000 in 1993. About $200,000 of that amount was donated by a few close friends who asked to remain anonymous. The balance of the money was raised in bake sales, quilt auctions, and other community events at and near Akwesasne. The site purchased by the Mohawks, near the town of Palatine, was a Bear Clan village, Porter's clan. The area includes artesian springs from nearby hills. Porter said that he hoped to create a community "where we can preserve our language, our ceremonies, our philosophies, the way we look at the world . . . [with] no drugs, no alcohol, no gambling" (Reilly). Along this line, a Mohawk-language immersion program has been started on the site.

FURTHER READING

Reilly, Jim. "Group from St. Regis to Return to Land of Mohawk Ancestors; Indians Buy 322 Acres of Land for a Fresh Start." *Syracuse Herald-Journal*, September 12, 1993.

Canandaigua (Pickering) Treaty (1794). Timothy Pickering (soon to become U.S. secretary of war) negotiated the Canandaigua Treaty with the Haudenosaunee in 1794. Most of the representatives at this treaty council were **Senecas**. The treaty called for peace, as well as noninterference in the affairs of the Six Nations by the United States, quitclaims for lands already ceded, and an annuity of $4,500 a year. Hardly before the ink was dry on the guarantee of noninterference, the U.S. commissioners, having heard of General "Mad Anthony" Wayne's victory at Fallen Timbers (near Maumee and Toledo, Ohio), demanded portage rights at Niagara.

The Canandaigua Treaty is important today because it defines Seneca sovereignty specifically and Haudenosaunee sovereignty by implication. Specifically, the treaty says that the United States would "never claim the same [Seneca territory], nor disturb the Seneca nation . . . in the free use or enjoyment thereof; but it shall remain theirs until they choose to sell the same to the people of the United States" (Foster, Campisi, and Mithun, 117).

The invitation to a treaty council at Canandaigua reached the **Allegany** Senecas on August 23. The Senecas were adamant that they would take up the hatchet to prevent white settlement at Presque Isle and wanted no part of negotiations unless these were accompanied with an agreement that some lands already lost must be restored. Over the next few weeks, **Cornplanter** and other Senecas rebuffed the invitation to Canandaigua, stating that they had not requested a treaty meeting and that they did not want the presents that accompanied Pickering's invitation.

Cornplanter and some of the warriors continued to favor war, but at this moment the Seneca women began to intervene, insisting that custom provided them with a veto power over war. Iroquois custom did indeed provide such power to the Iroquois matrons. Cornplanter argued that the women should not have this power, that a decision to go to war should belong to the warriors, but he did not prevail. About one hundred Seneca warriors took part in the Battle of Fallen Timbers (Fenton, 658).

Cornplanter and others were at council when the first account of Anthony Wayne's victory in the Ohio country reached them. At Buffalo Creek the news was greeted by a stunned silence. Many, including Cornplanter, strongly believed that the western confederacy would crush Wayne's newly formed army.

Timothy Pickering had appeared at Canandaigua and had sent invitations to the Senecas to come to a treaty negotiation there, but the British were urging that the meeting be held at Buffalo Creek. Many of the Seneca chiefs blamed Cornplanter for their troubles. The following day, an elder rose in council and suggested that the best they could do would be to go to Canandaigua and make the best agreement possible. No one dissented, and most of the assembly soon set out for Canandaigua.

Treaty Proceedings

The Seneca and **Onondaga** contingents arrived and ceremoniously entered Canandaigua on October 14 (Fenton, 669). Altogether, about 1,600 members of the Six Nations attended (Fenton, 687), a number that represented a significant majority of the population. Some Seneca towns sent almost their entire populations.

Among the better-known Haudenosaunee at the Canandaigua Treaty council, which was held twenty-five miles southeast of present-day Rochester, New York, were Farmer's Brother (**Honayawas**), **Red Jacket**, and **Fish Carrier**, in addition to Cornplanter. George Washington sent Timothy Pickering as U.S. treaty commissioner; for this reason, the agreement is sometimes called the Pickering Treaty. Negotiations were undertaken at the north end of Canandaigua Lake in Seneca country.

A delegation of Quakers was present as observers, and their written accounts of the proceedings are an important part of the record. The Quakers were in attendance at the request of the Haudenosaunee, who had learned to distrust the whites' writing. They had long memories. A half-century earlier, colonial representatives had swindled **Canassatego** into giving up paper rights to much of the North American continent at the 1744 **Lancaster Treaty Council**. Most of the Haudenosaunee representatives could not read English, and so they had requested the help of the Quakers, whom they trusted to act as their eyes and ears in this regard.

The opening ceremonies of this negotiation adhered to Indian customs that required expressions of condolences for people who had passed away since the parties had last met. Following these formalities, Pickering announced that the commissioner representing the United States had offered to hear the the Iroquois' grievances. He introduced the Quakers who attended as witnesses to the proceedings, after which an Onondaga chief, Clear Sky, acknowledged the words that had been spoken and adjourned the meeting for the day. An evangelist, Jemima Wilkinson, asked to be heard and filled the time until dark praying and preaching at the center of the assembly. It was an embarrassing display to most of the participants but a historically significant event in the country that was to become New York's Burned-over District, the birthplace of numerous religious sects. Pickering proceeded to convene private meetings with selected individual Indians.

Red Jacket served as speaker on behalf of the sachems; this was to be as much his treaty as Pickering's. The first order of business involved Indian complaints about land cessions at three earlier treaties: **Fort Stanwix** (1784), Fort Harmar, and Fort McIntosh. There was a discussion about which lands the Six Nations claimed as their own. Pickering replied with seven points that recounted recent attempts to settle these claims, some of which had been frustrated by British agents (Fenton, 676). He went on to assure the Indians that the 1790 Non-intercourse Act was insurance against land frauds perpetrated by the states. He also suggested that land along Lake Erie south of Buffalo, ceded in the 1784 Fort Stanwix treaty, might be returned to Seneca hands.

When the British Indian interpreter Johnson arrived, Pickering denounced him as a British spy and accused the British of frustrating recent years' attempts at peace between the Indians and the Americans. Pickering complained that the

British had failed to relinquish forts inside U.S. territory in accordance with the treaty that ended the **American Revolution**. He said that he had orders from President Washington to refuse to allow any British agent to attend the negotiations and argued that the Six Nations, as a free and independent people, should decide whether to send Johnson away or to cover the council fire and go home themselves. Cornplanter took responsibility for inviting Johnson, but in this contest of wills Pickering was triumphant; Johnson left the meeting and returned to Canada. Despite his dismissal, Johnson had served another purpose: he had carried **Joseph Brant**'s affirmation of the defeat of the western Indians at Fallen Timbers to the Indians at the treaty council. He also returned to Canada with letters to Brant from people assembled at Canandaigua.

Pickering continued the strategy of holding private meetings with selected Senecas, most notably the war chief Cornplanter. This caused considerable distress among the sachem (peace) chiefs, who felt that Cornplanter had usurped the role of a sachem. Little Billy admonished him directly for this behavior (Fenton, 683). Pickering returned to discussing the terms of the treaty in public council. During the course of subsequent discussions, Cornplanter's role at the Fort Stanwix Treaty became more publicly known. It was discovered that he had received $800 from Pennsylvania and had in turn been granted 1,500 acres for a farm, information that cast Cornplanter in a negative light among the Senecas.

The Burning Issues

To the Indians, the burning issues at Canandaigua were familiar: the murders of Indians by whites were going unpunished; the land cessions at Fort Stanwix in 1784 had been unfair; the proposed settlement at Presque Isle was at issue as well. The Senecas insisted that the warrior chiefs who had negotiated the peace at Fort Stanwix had failed to submit the treaty to the Grand Council for ratification. Pickering proposed that the Senecas relinquish a strip of land four miles wide along the south of the Niagara River from Cayuga Creek to Buffalo Creek. Red Jacket replied that this was not acceptable because it would constitute a threat to their fisheries and their settlement at Buffalo Creek. Pickering dropped the issue and settled for construction of a road, to be owned by the Senecas, from Fort Schlosser to Buffalo (Fenton, 695).

The negotiations continued until there was a general consensus that both sides had achieved all they could. On November 9, however, Cornplanter complained of past dealings with the United States and offered that the sachems alone, and not the warriors, would sign the treaty. Pickering was unwilling to accept this. He felt that if the warriors did not sign, divisions would rise among the Indians that would undo the treaty (Fenton, 699).

Cornplanter's behavior significantly diminished his reputation as a friend of the United States in Pickering's eyes. The treaty was signed on November 11, 1794, and went into effect under U.S. law on January 21, 1795. The primary objective of the United States was to settle the question of the Six Nations' claims to lands in Ohio and the Erie Triangle and to embark on a policy of sincere negotiations and fair payment in land transactions. The day following the treaty signing, Pickering wrote to Secretary of War Henry Knox:

You will see the great object is obtained; an express renunciation, which takes in all of the lands in Pennsylvania, including the Triangle which comprehends Presu'Isle [*sic*]; and a pointed declaration that they will never disturb the people of the U. states in the free use and enjoyment of them, or any other lands not contained within the present described boundaries of the lands of the Six Nations. (Fenton, 705)

In return, Pickering relinquished lands earlier ceded along Lake Erie upon which the Six Nations had built settlements, and he abandoned for the time ambitions of securing the four-mile-wide strip along the Niagara River. He secured, however, a right of passage along that river from Fort Schlosser to Buffalo Creek.

The Text of the Treaty

The text of the treaty speaks to the issues that occupied the people who negotiated it. Article I establishes peace and friendship between the Six Nations and the United States. Article II guarantees to the **Oneida**, Onondaga, and **Cayuga** nations the lands they possessed on the day of the treaty, including words that guarantee that the United States will not claim these lands or disturb them "nor their Indian friends residing thereon and united with them, in the free use and enjoyment thereof." Article III describes the boundaries of the Seneca lands, a description that carefully omits and therefore disallows Six Nations claims to lands in the Ohio region. This article also includes recognition as belonging to the Senecas of a strip along the Niagara River "ceded" to **Sir William Johnson** (i.e., to the British) in 1764. In Article IV, the Six Nations promises never to claim lands outside these boundaries.

In the minds of the negotiations, most important, in the light of the history of the previous decade, were the lands in Pennsylvania and Ohio. Article V provides the United States the right to use a road along the Niagara River and to use the waterways, a right that was strongly desired by farmers and others in the Ohio-Kentucky region who needed an economical way to transport their goods to the markets.

In Article VI, the United States promises to pay goods valued at $10,000 and an annuity of $4,500, a considerable sum in 1794, evidence of the U.S. commitment to a policy of fair dealings with the Indians. In Article VII, both sides agree that no private, unofficial act of revenge will take place when a crime—murder, assault, robbery—is committed by either side against the other. Rather, the representative of the victim will submit a complaint to the representatives of the perpetrator. Should a white person commit such an offense against an Indian, the Six Nations will submit a complaint to the president or his appointed superintendent. If an Indian commits such a crime, the president will submit a complaint to the "principal chiefs" of the Six Nations, and "such prudent measures shall then be pursued as shall be necessary to preserve our peace . . . until the legislature . . . of the United States shall make other equitable provision for the purpose."

The Canandaigua Treaty was important because it provided the United States with security at a time when continued warfare with Britain and the Indians of the Great Lakes was not only possible but, as history would prove, inevitable. The treaty represents a historical moment when "fair treatment" of the Indians was not only the policy of the United States but was arguably the best policy for the survival of the country.

Unkept Promises

There are promises in this treaty that the people of the Six Nations believe that the United States has not kept. They believe that the United States recognized that the lands of the Six Nations belong to the Six Nations, not to the United States. They also believe that the termination era of the 1950s and its threat to assimilate the Iroquois into American society contradicted any reasonable interpretation of the promise not to claim the land or disturb the Six Nations in any way. It is not difficult to understand why many Iroquois believe that such a principle would preclude the United States, or New York State, from collecting taxes or enforcing a variety of laws and regulations on lands they have acknowledged have status as a sovereign domain distinct from their own.

Finally, many Iroquois believe that Article VII constitutes a promise of recognition of parallel legal jurisdictions far greater than they have enjoyed since 1794. The article states that in the event of a crime, the two parties will pursue prudent measures involving the president or his appointed superintendent until some other "equitable" provision shall be made. Some U.S. spokespersons claim that transferring jurisdiction to New York State fulfilled the requirement for equitable or equal provision that both parties would be involved in resolving the problem. Many Iroquois, most notably the traditional chiefs, have long complained that there was nothing equitable in either the spirit or practice of the U.S. legal system as it relates to this article.

The Canandaigua Treaty with the Six Nations of 1794 remains a seminal document in Iroquois-U.S. relations. It is also an important part of the history of both peoples because it marked a new and inevitable kind of relationship with the emerging United States and is evidence of one road in American Indian policy taken by the United States. In light of the history of other roads taken, some of which are among the most tragic and dishonorable in American history, the Canandaigua Treaty stands as a symbol of what might have been almost as much as it is a symbol of what came to be.

The treaty, signed by George Washington on January 21, 1795, is still in force today. After construction of the **Kinzua Dam**, the Senecas whom it displaced were compensated $18 million because the eviction violated the Canandaigua Treaty. The Canandaigua Treaty was being used in the late twentieth century to prod federal government bodies, such as the Environmental Protection Agency (EPA), to act on environmental problems that damage Haudenosaunee living conditions from sources in the United States. Pollution from off-reservation sources is most serious at **Akwesasne**, which has been ranked as the most expensive toxic cleanup in the United States by the EPA, and at the Senecas' **Tonawanda Reservation**, near Niagara Falls, which is close to Love Canal, one of North America's best-publicized toxic sites.

The Onondagas invoked sovereignty guaranteed under the Canandaigua Treaty in 1983 when they granted sanctuary to American Indian Movement leader Dennis Banks and his family as he was being pursued by federal law-enforcement authorities. At the time, the Grand Council at Onondaga issued a statement that read, in part:

Dennis Banks and his family now sit under the Long Leaves of the Tree of Peace. . . . [They] sit in the company of many nations and peoples who have at one time or another found shelter under the Great Tree of Peace. . . . "Treaties are made between nations, not men. . . ." This is a recent quote from the President of the United States. We believe this, and we remind the Government and the people of the United States that we, the Haudenosaunee, hold the first Treaty of Peace and Friendship with you as a new nation. . . . These are documents of commitment and now the responsibility of this generation. (Hill, 14)

FURTHER READING

Fenton, William N. *The Great Law and the Longhouse: A Political History of the Iroquois Confederacy*. Norman: University of Oklahoma Press, 1998.

Foster, Michael K., Jack Campisi, and Marianne Mithun, eds. *Extending the Rafters: Interdisciplinary Approaches to Iroquoian Studies*. Albany: State University of New York Press, 1984.

Hill, Rick. "Continuity of Haudenosaunee Government: Political Reality of the Grand Council." *Northeast Indian Quarterly*, 4:3 (Autumn 1987): 10–14.

Jemison, G. Peter. "Sovereignty and Treaty Rights: We Remember." *Akwesasne Notes*, N.S. 1:3–4 (Fall 1995): 10–15.

John C. Mohawk and Bruce E. Johansen

Canassatego (Onondaga), c. 1690–1750. Canassatego was *Tadadaho* (speaker) of the Iroquois Confederacy in the middle of the eighteenth century and a major figure in diplomacy with the French and English colonists. His advice that the colonies should form a union on a Haudenosaunee model influenced the plans of **Benjamin Franklin** for colonial union. Later in the century, a fictional Canassatego became a figure in English social satire in works such as John Shebbeare's *Lydia, or Filial Piety* (1755).

In 1744, Pennsylvania officials met with Iroquois sachems (peace chiefs) in council at Lancaster, Pennsylvania. This meeting was one of a number of significant diplomatic parleys between British colonists, the Iroquois, and their allies that preceded and helped shape the outcome of the French and Indian War. At the meeting, Canassatego and other Iroquois complained that the colonies, with no central authority, had been unable to restrain invasion of Indian lands by settlers. In that context, Canassatego advised the colonists to form a union emulating that of the Iroquois:

Our wise forefathers established Union and Amity between the Five Nations. This has made us formidable; this has given us great Weight and Authority with our neighboring Nations. We are a powerful Confederacy; *and by your observing the same methods, our wise forefathers have taken*, you will acquire such Strength and power. Therefore whatever befalls you, never fall out with one another. (Van Doren and Boyd, 75; emphasis added).

Richard Peters, a delegate from Pennsylvania, described Canassatego at Lancaster as "a tall, well-made man," with "a very full chest and brawny limbs, a manly countenance, with a good-natired [*sic*] smile. He was about 60 years of age, very active, strong, and had a surprising liveliness in his speech" (Boyd, 181, 244–245).

At the time of the **Lancaster Treaty Council**, Franklin, a Philadelphia printer, was publishing the transcripts of Indian treaty councils as small booklets that enjoyed a lively sale in the colonies and in England. The Lancaster Treaty was one of several dozen treaty accounts that he published between 1736 and 1762. Franklin probably read Canassatego's words as they issued from his press. Franklin became an advocate of colonial union by the early 1750s, when he began his diplomatic career as a Pennsylvania delegate to the Iroquois and their allies. Franklin urged the British colonies to unite in emulation of the Iroquois Confederacy in a letter to his printing partner James Parker in 1751 and as he drew up his Albany Plan of Union in 1754 (see **Albany Congress**).

In addition to advising the colonial representatives on political union at the Lancaster Treaty Council, Canassatego declined a colonial offer to educate Haudenosaunee young people. In an account written by Franklin, Canassatego said: "We are convinced therefore that you mean to do us good by your Proposal, and we thank you heartily." However, continued Canassatego,

Several of our Young People were formerly brought up at the Colleges of the Northern Provinces; they were instructed in all your sciences, but when they came back to us, they were bad Runners, ignorant of every means of living in the Woods, unable to bear either Cold or Hunger, knew neither how to build a Cabin, take a Deer, or kill an Enemy, spoke our Language imperfectly, therefore were neither fit for Hunters, Warriors, or Counsellors; they were totally good for nothing. (Franklin, 969–970)

Canassatego concluded his thought, according to Franklin: "To show our grateful sense of it [the offer], if the Gentlemen of Virginia will send us a dozen of their Sons, we will take Great Care of their Education, instruct them in all we know, and make Men of them" (Franklin, 970).

Canassatego died in 1750; a contemporary source says that he was poisoned by the French (Jennings, 363). Canassatego's words echoed to the eve of the **American Revolution**, amplified by Franklin's talents as author and publisher. In 1775, Canassatego's thirty-one-year-old advice was recalled at a treaty between colonial representatives and Iroquois leaders near Albany. The treaty commissioners told the sachems that they were heeding the advice their Iroquois forefathers had given to the colonial Americans at Lancaster, Pennsylvania, in 1744.

FURTHER READING

Boyd, Julian P. "Dr. Franklin, Friend of the Indian." In Roy N. Lokken, ed., *Meet Dr. Franklin*. Philadelphia: Franklin-Institute Press, 1981: 237–245.

Franklin, Benjamin. "Remarks Concerning the Savages of North America." In J. A. Leo Lemay, ed., *Benjamin Franklin: Writings*. New York: Library of America, 1987.

Grinde, Donald A., Jr., and Bruce E. Johansen. *Exemplar of Liberty: Native America and the Evolution of Democracy*. Los Angeles: UCLA American Indian Studies Center, 1991.

Jennings, Francis. *The Ambiguous Iroquois Empire: The Covenant Chain Confederation of Indian Tribes with English Colonies from Its Beginnings to the Lancaster Treaty of 1744*. New York: W. W. Norton, 1984.

Shebbeare, John. *Lydia, or, Filial Piety*, 1755 New York: Garland Publishing, 1974.

Van Doren, Carl, and Julian P. Boyd, eds. *Indian Treaties Printed by Benjamin Franklin, 1736–1762*. Philadelphia: Historical Society of Pennsylvania, 1938.

Wallace, Paul A. W. *Indians in Pennsylvania*. Harrisburg: Pennsylvania Historical and Museum Commission, 1961.

Cartier, Jacques (French), c. 1492–1557. Jacques Cartier, a French navigator, was born in Saint-Malo, Brittany, about 1492. He died in the same place on September 1, 1557. Cartier's three voyages (1534, 1535–1536, and 1541–1542) along the St. Lawrence River of **Turtle Island** (North America) were used by King Francis I of France to lay claim to large portions of northeastern North America.

By 1534, Cartier already had acquired some renown among his peers as an explorer. (He seems to have ventured as far west as Newfoundland and Brazil.) Francis I employed him on the recommendation of Jean Le Veneur, a French prelate who had attempted to negotiate with the pope for a relaxed interpretation of the papal bull of 1493 that had divided the "New World" between Spain and Portugal, cutting out all other (Catholic) colonial powers. This was a matter of some importance to Francis I, who believed that he was in heated competition with the Spanish and Portuguese for the wealth of America. Thus, as in the cases of so many other early explorers, Cartier's actual charter from the French Crown was to discover an Atlantic passage to Asia as well as "grandes quantités d'or 'et autres riches choses' " (great quantities of gold and other rich things), meaning precious metals and spices ("Cartier," 1829).

Cartier's charge took him into Iroquoia, the first recorded European to have interacted with people there. It is difficult to form a clear idea of Cartier's true reception at any of his stops along the St. Lawrence River because the only records of his voyages were penned by himself. In them, he freely presented conjectures as unassailable truth while Eurocentrically interpreting everything he experienced. In addition, he was wily and not above a lie, so that his accounts should be taken with a large dose of salt. It is necessary to read between the lines for Native American perceptions of events, a step too few historians or biographers have yet taken. Ramsay Cook and Marie-Christine Gomez-Géraud have led the way in attempting to peer beyond the veil of Cartier's self-interested words for a measured view of what really transpired between the Laurentian Iroquois and the first Frenchmen to meet members of the Haudenosaunee Confederacy.

His royal commission in hand, Cartier left France on April 20, 1534, with a crew of sixty-one men in two ships. He sailed up the St. Lawrence River, his candidate for the "Northwest Passage," but happened across the Iroquoian civilization instead. The first Americans to encounter him were a group living on Anticosti Island, part of a people now simply called "the Laurentians" because more precise records of their identity are lacking. All that is really known is that they were Iroquois.

On July 24 at the Bay of Gaspé, Cartier claimed North America for France by erecting a thirty-foot cross emblazoned with fleurs-de-lys and the words "Vive le Roi de France," something he did over the heated objections of the resident Iroquois. According to **Mohawk** tradition, they recited the roll call of the chiefs of the league by way of proving their prior claim to the land. Cartier himself recorded that their orator and primary chief, Donnaconna, "pointed to the land . . . as if he wished to say that all this region belonged to him, and that we ought not to have set up this cross without his permission." Cartier airily dismissed these passionate objections as a "harangue" (Cook, 26).

Finding neither gold nor spices, much less a Northwest Passage, Cartier made do by kidnapping two Iroquois at Gaspé—Dom Agaya and Taignoagny, sons of Donnaconna—and sailing back to France with his living proof that he had actually made landfall. (Some navigators attempted fraud, raising funds for a grand voyage and then pretending to have journeyed to the Americas when, in fact, they had only sailed out of view. After cooling their heels in Africa or the Azores, they sailed home again with wild stories and pocketed the proceeds. Such scams led financiers to demand proof that a voyage had actually occurred. Kidnapping unfortunate Natives became a standard "proof.")

Cartier arrived back home at Saint-Malo on September 5, 1534. The sight of the two unfortunate young men stirred great interest at the French court, for courtiers equated Dom Agaya and Taignoagny with the Aztecs, Mayas, and Incas kidnapped by the Spanish. This led them to entertain visions of vast, untapped wealth just awaiting French exploitation.

Hearing Cartier's fanciful claims of potential plunder, Francis I happily financed a second voyage to America. Cartier set sail for America once more on May 19, 1535, with Dom Agaya and Taignoagny in tow. Due to their total immersion in French during their captivity, they had learned to make do as translators and were consequently able to lead Cartier up the St. Lawrence as far as Québec, at the harbor of Sainte-Croix. Knowing that Cartier was after so-called precious metals (gold, silver, and copper) as well as spices, Dom Agaya and Taignoagny tried to divert Cartier away from Iroquoia with tales of the mysterious Kingdom of Saguenay, where, they assured him, such items were plentiful, along with Europeans like himself, dressed in wool.

Sailing up to the village of Stadacona—the homeland of Dom Agaya and Taignoagny, near modern-day Québec City—Cartier quickly set up a beachhead, with plans to press ahead to a great city he had also heard of, Hochelaga. The townspeople of Stadacona, overjoyed to see their young men home again and in good health, were reluctant to release them once more into Cartier's less-than-gentle custody. Thus, when Cartier tried to pressure the youths into guiding him on to Hochelaga, the French and the Stadaconas nearly came to blows. The youths clearly did not wish to continue with him—Cartier even accused them of conspiring against him—nor did Donnaconna wish Cartier to press any farther into Iroquoia. Somehow Cartier interpreted their resistance as ingratitude and disloyalty toward himself, although why abductees or their father should have felt gratitude toward a kidnapper seems inscrutable today.

In any case, muttering grimly to himself about treacherous heathens, Cartier left the bulk of his crew (now up to 110 men) at Stadacona, venturing ahead in two canoes to Hochelaga, a large Iroquoian city at the foot of the Lachine Rapids at modern-day Montréal. Greeted in the usual hospitable manner of Iroquoians (which he mistook for a gesture of personal worship), Cartier allowed the women and children to touch his strange metal clothing. He did not stay long, for the rapids above Hochelaga impeded him from traveling farther. The rapids did not discourage Cartier, however, but made him imagine that a Northwest Passage lay just beyond. Giddy illusions of ocean passages and untold wealth notwithstanding, one week later, Cartier returned empty-handed to winter at Stadacona.

Cartier found nothing of value to him at Stadacona, only seriously strained relations. The sailors he had left behind had been feeling so unsafe that they had barricaded themselves in a crude fort, whose standing artillery was aimed in all directions at just about anything capable of moving. Although Donnaconna welcomed Cartier back kindly, Dom Agaya and Taignoagny began agitating against him until Cartier himself retreated to the fort, posting twenty-four-hour guards.

The hostilities simmering just below the surface were stilled when, in December, both Stadaconas and Frenchmen came down violently ill en masse. Fifty Stadaconas died, along with twenty-five of Cartier's men. It seems very likely that the groups were suffering from different ills, however, since the Stadaconas had—and shared with Cartier—a cure for scurvy, the disease afflicting the French, whereas they were powerless against whatever was killing themselves.

His misfortunes simply exacerbated Cartier's ready paranoia about the Stadaconas. Despite the kindness they had shown him and his crew during their bout of scurvy, Cartier saw plots everywhere and retreated ever further into his own deceitfulness as he prepared for the major Laurentian attack he expected any day. When Laurentians began ingathering at Stadacona for a seasonal feast,

Cartier was sure that they were a war party and laid his own plans in earnest to take Donnaconna, Dom Agaya, Taignoagny, and two other chiefs prisoner. (Five more Laurentians, male and female, were taken later during his voyage home.)

Cartier's scheme was effected on May 3, 1536, but the Laurentians were so wroth at the abductions, while Cartier himself was so vulnerable, that he forced Donnaconna above decks just long enough to reassure everyone that he would return again, as had his sons the year before. Just how Cartier forced him to make such a speech is unclear, but it is not at all unlikely that the lives of his sons were at stake. Be that as it may, grudging ceremonies were called to seal the promise, and as the ice broke around his ships, on May 6, Cartier hightailed it down the St. Lawrence River with his ten prisoners. Arriving at Saint-Malo on July 16, Cartier palliated Francis I with wild tales of inland gold and spices, as well as a Northwest Passage whose location Cartier supposedly knew. Blinded by greed, Francis I accepted Cartier's report without the slightest proof.

Warfare in Europe prevented Cartier's return until 1541. By that time, Francis I was worried that the Spanish planned to claim the Northeast of Turtle Island and sought to forestall them by planting his own American colony along the St. Lawrence River. He therefore dispatched a colonization team headed by a French nobleman, Jean-François de La Rocque de Roberval, who was to direct the activities of Cartier. The fact that Francis I set Roberval up over Cartier suggests that by 1541, he might no longer have been taken in by Cartier's fabrications.

In the intervening time, nine of Cartier's ten prisoners, including Donnaconna, Dom Agaya, and Taignoagny, died in French captivity, having been baptized by Catholic priests, though whether this was forced—or, indeed, whether it happened post mortem—is unknown. The only other captive, a woman, remained in France when Cartier returned, though again, the reason (detention or choice) is a matter of speculation. When questioned by the Stadaconas concerning the fate of their friends and relatives, Cartier notified the new chief, Agona, that Donnaconna was dead (not unwelcome news for Agona's own status). Next, Cartier flatly lied, assuring the Stadaconas that the other nine had remained in France by choice, hale and hearty, enjoying life as wealthy chiefs.

Cartier arrived in America well ahead of Roberval and set up a base camp on August 23, 1541, at Québec. Once more, Cartier made it as far as Hochelaga, but only lingered a few hours, opting not to test himself against the rapids. Instead, he turned back and wintered in Québec, where the dissolute and even criminal behavior of his sailors against the Laurentians made the French even less welcome than they had been in 1535–1536.

Cartier had found some quartz and (probably) pyrite that he, incredibly, convinced himself were diamonds and gold. This "discovery" being as good an excuse as any to abandon his hot seat in Québec, he headed out for France the next spring, only to be intercepted at Newfoundland by Roberval (who was only just arriving, a whole year late). Roberval, an aristocrat who knew gold and diamonds when he saw them, angrily ordered Cartier back to his Canadian post, but, perhaps knowing the welcome that awaited him there, Cartier decided to chance fate by absconding in the middle of the night and sneaking back to France with his prize.

Once Cartier reached France, his prize was immediately revealed to be worthless, and Cartier never received another commission from the Crown. For his part, Roberval was summarily kicked out of "New France" by the thoroughly disgusted Iroquois, who, having had their fill of bad-mannered visitors, refused to allow him to establish a colony on their lands. A few historians have raised the possibility that Cartier made a fourth voyage in 1543 to bring Roberval back to France, but this is highly unlikely and unsubstantiated. Roberval certainly had not appreciated having been left in the lurch by Cartier the year before among a people Cartier had thoroughly alienated.

After his disgrace, Cartier lived out the remainder of his life on his estate outside of Saint-Malo, where he died fifteen years later. After the colonial reversals and the disillusionment over American "gold" that were attendant on Cartier's voyages, French enterprises on Turtle Island were put aside for a generation.

FURTHER READING

"Cartier (Jacques)." *Grand dictionnaire encyclopédique Larousse.* Vol. 2. Paris: Librarie Larousse, 1982: 1829–1830.

Cook, Ramsay, ed. *The Voyages of Jacques Cartier.* Toronto: University of Toronto Press, 1993.

Eccles, William John. *The Canadian Frontier, 1534–1760.* 1969. Rev. ed. Albuquerque: University of New Mexico Press, 1983.

Trigger, Bruce. *Natives and Newcomers: Canada's "Heroic Age" Reconsidered.* Kingston and Montreal: McGill–Queen's University Press, 1985.

Trudel, Marcel. *The Beginnings of New France, 1524–1663.* Trans. Patricia Claxton. Toronto: McClelland and Stewart, 1973.

Barbara A. Mann

Cattaraugus Reservation (Seneca). The Cattaraugus Seneca Reservation, home to 2,183 people in 1990, comprises 21,680 acres roughly thirty miles south of Buffalo, New York, along Cattaraugus Creek where it enters Lake Erie. The **Senecas** of the Cattaraugus and **Allegany** reservations make up the Seneca Nation, which selects chiefs through an elective system based on the Constitution of the United States and adopted in 1848. The tribal headquarters alternates every two years between Cattaraugus and Allegany. The Cattaraugus Reservation, like Allegany, was created under the **Canandaigua (Pickering) Treaty** (1794). The entire reservation was sold to the Ogden Land Company under the 1838 **Buffalo Creek Treaty**, and was restored four years later under the "compromise treaty" at the same location.

FURTHER READING

Tiller, Veronica E. Verlarde. *Tiller's Guide to Indian Country: Economic Profiles of American Indian Reservations.* Albuquerque, N.M.: Bow Arrow Publishing, 1994.

Cayuga. The Cayuga, one of the Haudenosaunee Confederacy's original members, is the only one of the five nations to lose its entire land base. Traditionally located in the Finger Lakes area of what is now New York State (west of the **Onondagas** and east of the **Senecas**), many Cayugas today live on Seneca reservations, in the state of Oklahoma, or at the Grand River reserve in Ontario.

Several derivations have been offered for the Cayugas' name, including "place where the locusts were taken out," "place where boats were taken out," and "mucky land" (Tower, 625). In the Grand Council of the Haudenosaunee Confederacy, the Cayugas are known as "those of the great pipe." They also have a role, with the **Oneidas**, as "younger brothers" in the debating protocol of the Grand Council.

Speculation places the Cayugas in west-central New York as early as 4,000 years ago; archaeological evidence places them in the area no later than 1300 C.E. After contact with Europeans, various sources report the Cayugas' numbers at about 2,000, which declined to about 1,100 by the mid-eighteenth century, due to warfare and disease. After that their population seems to have stabilized. By the early twentieth century, the Cayugas' dispersed numbers were growing, and may be more than 3,000 by the late 1990s. Estimating Cayuga population is vastly complicated by their wide geographic dispersal and mixture with other peoples.

With the other Haudenosaunee nations, the Cayugas took part in conflicts with the French during the seventeenth century and first two-thirds of the eighteenth century. Like other Haudenosaunee peoples, they took part in the depletion of beaver and other fur-bearing animals during this period as well.

Most Cayugas sided with the British during the **American Revolution**, which is a major reason they were nearly homeless in New York State by 1795. The punishing raids of the Continental Army under general **John Sullivan** targeted Cayuga as well as Seneca villages in 1779.

Despite their dispersal for more than two centuries, the Cayugas have a long tradition of operating as a group. They opposed the Indian Citizenship Act of 1924 with a unified voice, for example. The Cayugas' language is spoken widely, and taught within families. The Cayugas also have long maintained **Longhouse** religious ceremonies as a group.

Late in the twentieth century, the Cayugas were pursuing land claims (with the other Haudenosaunee nations). The Cayugas maintain an office under the leadership of Clint Halftown, a Cayuga of the Heron clan, who is recognized as a leader within the confederacy.

By the summer of 1999, negotiations were nearing completion on the Cayuga land claim, which has been in litigation since 1980. New York State has offered the Cayugas $110 million and 10,000 acres of land in Seneca and Cayuga counties, but the Cayuga County Legislature, a local body, has rejected the proposed settlement. The original Cayuaga lawsuit sought 64,000 acres and $350 million. If the case goes to court, as many as 7,000 non-Cayuga homeowners may face forced sale of their property.

FURTHER READING

Tower, Christopher B. "Cayuga." In Sharon Malinowski and Anna Sheets, ed., *The Gale Encyclopedia of Native American Tribes*, vol. I. Detroit: Gale Research, 1998: 25–30.

Central Trail. Haudenosaunee country, like the rest of eastern North America, was laced with trails, paths sometimes less than a foot wide, that were used by Native American peoples for trade and diplomacy, hunting, and war. One of the better-known pathways among the Iroquois was the Central Trail, which roughly follows the path of the present-day New York State Thruway east and west across upstate New York. This trail, which also roughly follows the path of the Erie Canal (which opened in 1825), connects all of the Haudenosaunee nations and provides access northward to Canada.

The Central Trail and others to which it was connected enhanced the pivotal position of the Haudenosaunee among Native peoples of the eastern seaboard, as well as between the competing commercial and diplomatic interests of French and English colonists. Other trails intersected this one, providing access southward to Pennsylvania and Virginia. Native American runners could carry messages as far as 100 miles a day on these trails. These runners sometimes carried messages stitched into **wampum** belts and strings between Haudenosaunee villages.

FURTHER READING

Aquila, Richard. *The Iroquois Restoration: Iroquois Diplomacy on the Colonial Frontier, 1701–1754.* Detroit: Wayne State University Press, 1983.

Ceremony, as Haudenosaunee way of life. For the Haudenosaunee, the traditional People of the Longhouse who have retained the ceremonies given to them by the Creator, ceremony is a way of life. The elders tell us that ceremony is a way of life that cannot be learned by reading a book. This way can only be learned through active participation in the ceremonies of the Longhouse and by living one's daily life according to the instructions given by the Creator.

The Creator, Sonkwaiatison, gave the Haudenosaunee, in the original instructions to them, ways to conduct their daily lives through the use of prayer and ceremony. The Creator gave the Haudenosaunee sacred songs, dances, and healing ceremonies to help them to live in harmony with the natural world.

There are many ceremonies among the Haudenosaunee. A **Condolence Ceremony** is performed when a *rotiiane* (chief) dies; another Condolence Ceremony is necessary to raise a new chief. Wedding and naming ceremonies provide two illustrations of the ceremonies that comprise the fabric of Haudenosaunee life. It is a way of life that recognizes no difference between what is spiritual and what is political.

The Creator has given to the Haudenosaunee many songs and dances; as a result, there are different societies, such as the Singing Society, the Corn Husk Society, and the False Face Society, that retain the knowledge and conduct the many different aspects of the ceremonies, including those connected with healing. The Creator gave the Haudenosaunee three major songs and dances: the **Great Feather Dance**, the Drum Dance, and the *Atonwa* or Personal Chant.

The Great Feather Dance is a song and dance that honors the Creator and the good mind of the people. The *Atonwa* is a song that is used to begin the ceremony when the children are being named, for it connects the natural world with the children being named. This is done so the named will be recognized and will be brought good luck throughout their lives. The Drum Dance song shows respect and appreciation to all the things the Creator has provided the *Onkwehshon:a*, the people, within their daily lives.

When the Creator gave the Haudenosaunee the sacred songs, dances, and ceremonies, the Haudenosaunee also were given the **Thanksgiving** Address, the *Ohen:ton Karihwatehkwen*, which literally translates to "Words before All Else." The Thanksgiving Address is recited at the opening and closing of all religious and other important events. The Thanksgiving Address is given to bring all minds together as one and to thank all life on earth and the universe for following the original instructions given to them by the Creator.

Mother Earth is thanked, along with the plants (with special notice to the medicine plants and the trees). The Thunderers, the waters, the birds, and the four-legged and two-legged animals also are thanked, along with the four winds, the fish, the stars, the sun, Grandmother Moon, the teachers, and the Creator. All are thanked for following the Creator's original instructions on how they should live, for by following the original instructions, the Great Circle of Life is continued in balance.

The songs and dances are performed in the **Longhouse** when the Faith Keepers, in keeping with their original instructions, announce that the time has arrived for a particular ceremony. Sometimes a ceremony is triggered by the phase of the moon or the alignment of the planets. Although the Faith Keepers may announce that it is time to perform a ceremony at various times within different months, the ceremonies generally follow the seasons and months outlined in the following paragraphs.

The Midwinter Ceremony is very important, for it signals a new solar cycle. The Midwinter Ceremony lasts for six days and is held in January, *Tsiothohrkó:wa*, which translates to "the Big Cold." Day one of the Midwinter Ceremony includes the Stirring of the Ashes, which represents the joining of community. Day two features the Great Feather Dance, which is performed for the Creator and to acknowledge the one mind of the people. The main event of day three is the **White Dog Sacrifice**. At one time, a white dog was actually sacrificed; however, today a decorated basket is used instead. The specific breed of white dog that once was used has since been lost to mixed breeding. On day four of the Midwinter Ceremony, the *Atonwa* is sung. The children are given their names on this day. On the fifth day, the Drum Dance is performed to show appreciation for the entire world. On the sixth day of the Midwinter Ceremony the Peach Bowl Game is played for the amusement of the Creator. The main reason to play the game is to help people remember that what they have around them is not theirs, for everything comes from another part of the Great Circle of Life and is never really theirs to own.

The Sap Ceremony is in February and is called *Enníska* (Lateness); in March it is called *Enniskó:wa* (Much Lateness). The Thunder Dance and Maple Ceremony are held in March and April, which is *Onerahtókha* (Budding Time). The Thunder Dance is held to honor the water life.

The Seed Ceremony is held in May, *Onerahtohkó:wa* (Time of the Big Leaf). The Seed Ceremony is held to honor the seeds that will germinate and feed the people.

The Moon Ceremony is held in early June, *Ohiaríha*, and in early fall during the month of October. The Moon Ceremony honors Grandmother Moon, women, and all female life that perpetuates the Great Circle of Life. The Strawberry Ceremony is held in June, as *Ohiaríha* (Ripening Time), to honor the medicine plants and other healing powers.

The Bean Ceremony is held in July, when it is called *Ohiarihkó:wa*, (Time of Much Ripening), and in August, as *Seskéha* (Time of Freshness). The **Green Corn Ceremony** also is held in August. The Bean and the Green Corn ceremonies honor these major food sources of the Haudenosaunee.

The Harvest Ceremony is held in October, *Kenténha* (Time of Poverty). The Harvest Ceremony is observed to be thankful for the good fortune of the year. Another Thunder Ceremony is held in November and is called *Kentenhkó:wa* (Time of Much Poverty), again, as in the spring, to honor water life. The last ceremony of the calendar year is the End of Season Ceremony, in December, *Tsiothkóhrha* (Time of Cold), to show thankfulness for the year that has passed and to prepare for the coming year.

The people who attend the ceremonies are asked to dress in their traditional clothing and to bring wild strawberries, which are made into a drink for all. Participants also bring food that is prepared by the elder women. The day usually begins early in the morning and ends at dusk. The Haudenosaunee ceremonies honor and thank the Creator and the natural world, which binds the community together as one heart, one body, and one mind.

NOTE

The information in this entry draws from Louise Konwaronhiawi (Martin) Serra (my maternal grandmother) and other elders and family members who orally passed traditional teachings to me.

FURTHER READING

"Faithkeepers of the Mohawk Nation." *Indian Time*, November 17, 1995, 14 (announce-
    ment of the End of Season Ceremony requesting strawberries for drink and food
    to share and asking for traditional clothing to be worn at the longhouse).
Jacobs, Carol. "United Nations Summit of the Elders." *Indian Time*, August 11, 1995,
    17 (discussing Thanksgiving Address).
"Mid-Winter Ceremonies." *Indian Time*, January 12, 1996, 6 (explaining the six days of
    the Midwinter Ceremony).
Mitchell, Michael K. "Origin of the Four Sacred Ceremonies." In Barbara K. Barnes,
    ed., *Traditional Teachings*. Akwesasne: North American Indian Travelling Col-
    lege, 1984.
Stokes, John D., ed. *Thanksgiving Address: Greetings to the Natural World*. Six Nations
    Indian Museum, Tracking Project, 1996.
———. "The Tracking Project." *Akwesasne Notes*. Winter 1996 (discussing how the
    Thanksgiving Address is used for opening and closing ceremonies as well as on
    the personal level to greet and thank each and every day and night).

Barbara A. Gray (Kanatiyosh)

Champlain, Samuel de, c. 1570–1635. Samuel de Champlain, exploring for
France, came into contact with the Haudenosaunee in 1609. Champlain led expeditions against the Haudenosaunee and allied with the Wyandots (Hurons) in
1609 and 1615. In addition, he was a geographer, mapmaker, and early ethnologist whose accounts of the Wyandots are still studied today.

During his first encounter with the Iroquois, Champlain's forces shot to death
two of their chiefs near the north shore of the lake that now bears Champlain's
name. Champlain continued the generally sour relationship between the French
and the Haudenosaunee initiated by Cartier, which continued until the French
were expelled from North America at the end of the French and Indian (Seven
Years') War in 1763. Despite popular myths that Champlain knew how to respect and get along with Native Americans, evidence indicates that he refused
wampum payments as ceremonial compensation for the murders of Frenchmen
by Indians, creating tension.

Champlain was an associate of Pierre du Gua, sieur de Monts, who was
granted by the French government the right to assign tracts of land in North
America, as well as a ten-year monopoly of the fur trade. In 1608, Champlain's
small expeditionary force built a fort on the site of present-day Québec City,
intending to participate in the fur trade. Twenty of 28 Frenchmen on the colonizing expedition died during the first winter. By 1620, only 60 people lived in
the fort (Dennis, 189). Even by 1650, fifteen years after Champlain died, New
France amounted to only about 2,000 people in a chain of isolated villages that
stretched for almost a thousand miles along the St. Lawrence River (Jennings,
85).

FURTHER READING

Champlain, Samuel de. *The Works of Samuel de Champlain*. Ed. H. P. Biggar. Trans.
    W. D. LeSuer and H. H. Langton. 7 vols. Toronto: Champlain Society, 1922–
    1936.

Dennis, Matthew. *Cultivating a Landscape of Peace*. Ithaca, N.Y.: Cornell University Press, 1993.

Jennings, Francis. *The Ambiguous Iroquois Empire: The Covenant Chain Confederation of Indian Tribes with English Colonies from Its Beginnings to the Lancaster Treaty of 1744*. New York: W. W. Norton, 1984.

Morison, Samuel Eliot. *Samuel de Champlain: Father of New France*. Boston: Little, Brown, 1972.

Child, Lydia Maria Francis, 1802–1880. Pressure to broaden the ambit of natural and civil rights to women arose early in the nineteenth century at roughly the same time as the abolitionist movement against slavery intensified. While the landmark Seneca Falls conference, which is usually credited with beginning the modern feminist movement in the United States, was not held until 1848, the ideological basis for the movement was set down by Lydia Maria Child in her *History of the Condition of Women, in Various Ages and Nations*, published in 1835. Child's book counterposed the Iroquois and Wyandot (Huron) cultures to notions of European patriarchy, and illustrated the importance of Native American women in political decision making.

Child's work was used extensively by later suffragists, including **Matilda Joslyn Gage** and **Elizabeth Cady Stanton**, both of whom used Iroquois society as an example of equality in gender relations. With Stanton and Susan B. Anthony, Gage coauthored the landmark *History of Woman Suffrage*.

FURTHER READING

Child, Lydia Maria. *Hobomok and Other Writings on Indian*. Ed. Carolyn L. Karcher. New Brunswick, N.J.: Rutgers University Press, 1986.

———. *Selected Letters, 1817–1880*. Ed. Milton Meltzer and Patricia G. Holland. Amherst: University of Massachusetts Press, 1982.

Circle Wampum. The Circle Wampum symbolizes the founding of the Iroquois Grand Council with fifty strings of **wampum** in a circle, one for each of the fifty titles of the leaders who make up the council. The fifty strings are joined to two circles, one at each end. One string is longer than the rest, reaching into the otherwise-empty center of the smaller circle. This string symbolizes the invitation of the Peacemaker to each of the forty-nine other chiefs of the league. A seat on the council is reserved for the Peacemaker, who is believed to be present in spirit. The equal length of the other Forty-nine strings reminds the chiefs that they are all of equal rank and are responsible to the people.

Colden, Cadwallander, 1688–1776. Cadwallader Colden was, in the words of historian Robert Waite, "the best-informed man in the New World on the affairs of the British-American colonies" (Colden, *History*, 1765, 2:v). He provided the first systematic English-language study of the Haudenosaunee Confederacy in 1727 and augmented it in 1747. In his *History of the Five Nations Depending on the Province of New York in America*, Colden, an adopted **Mohawk**, compared the Iroquois to the Romans because of their skills at oratory, warfare, and

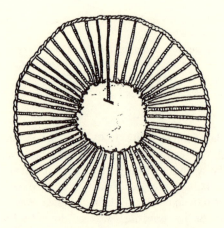

The Circle Wampum represents the fifty
seats of the Haudenosaunee Grand Council. The strand of wampum reaching into
the center of the inner circle represents the
seat that is forever reserved for the Peacemaker. Courtesy of John Kahionhes Fadden.

diplomacy, as well as the republican nature of their government. "When Life
and Liberty came in competition, indeed, I think our Indians have outdone the
Romans in this particular. . . . The Five Nations consisted of men whose courage
could not be shaken," Colden wrote (Colden, *History* 1747, vi).

Describing the Iroquois' form of government extensively, Colden wrote that
it had continued so long that European immigrants to America knew nothing of
its origins. "Each Nation is an Absolute Republick by its self, governed in all
Publick affairs of War and Peace by the Sachems of Old Men, whose Authority
and Power is gained by and consists wholly in the opinions of the rest of the
Nation in their Wisdom and Integrity," Colden wrote. "They never execute their
Resolutions by Compulsion or Force Upon any of their People." Colden stated
that "the Five Nations have such absolute Notions of Liberty that they allow no
Kind of Superiority of one over another, and banish all Servitude from their
Territories" (Colden, 17 *History*, 1747, xvii–xx).

Colden's *History of the Five Nations* was read by **Benjamin Franklin** before
he began his diplomatic career by representing Pennsylvania with the Iroquois
and their allies. In a letter to Colden on October 25, 1753, Franklin noted that
he had seen extracts of Colden's book in magazines. Upon his return to Philadelphia, Franklin promised Colden a copy of the 1744 Lancaster treaty and
stated that he had left his copy of Colden's book with a friend in Boston. Shortly
after attending the **Albany Congress** in 1754, Franklin made his first stop at
Colden's estate to thank him for the notes that Colden had sent to him at Albany.

Colden held several colonial offices, including lieutenant governor of New

York. He also carried on extensive research in various natural sciences. Colden's belief that the Indians, particularly the Iroquois, provided the new Americans with a window on their own antiquity was not unique to him. It was shared as well by Franklin, Thomas Jefferson, and **Thomas Paine** and, a century later, by the founders of modern feminism, as well as Karl Marx and **Friedrich Engels**. Such a belief provided a crucial link between Indian societies and their own, as well as a counterpoint by which two centuries of revolutionaries and reformers judged society's contemporary ills. "We are fond of searching into remote Antiquity to know the manners of our earliest progenitors; if I be not mistaken, the Indians are living images of them," Colden wrote (Colden, *History*, 1747, 49).

FURTHER READING

Colden, Cadwallader. *The History of the Five Indian Nations Depending on the Province of New-York in America.* 1747. Ithaca, N.Y.: Great Seal Books, 1958.
————. *The History of the Five Indian Nations of Canada Which Are Dependent on the Province of New York in America.* 1765. 2 vols. New York: New Amsterdam Book Company, 1902.

Concerning the League: The Iroquois League Tradition as Dictated in Onondaga by John Arthur Gibson. Partial transcriptions of the Haudenosaunee **Great Law of Peace** have been committed to written English and French since the late nineteenth century. Not until 1992, however, was the entire oral tradition published, in *Concerning the League: The Iroquois League Tradition as Dictated in Onondaga by John Arthur Gibson*, compiled by Hanni Woodbury, Reg Henry, and Harry Webster.

The 800-plus-page text of *Concerning the League* has three parts. It begins with an introduction outlining the history of the manuscript and a summary of the steps necessary to reconstitute it, as well as a summary of the Great Law and literature on it. The main part of the book (701 pages) comprises the text itself in English and in Onondaga. The third part of the book comprises linguistic appendices of interest to experts.

"All in all," wrote Iroquois specialist Michael K. Foster in a review of *Concerning the League*, "Woodbury has done a remarkable job of reconstituting a text of central importance to the Iroquois and students of the Iroquois. . . . I also want to congratulate her on the quality of the free English translation, which captures much of the rhetorical flavor of Iroquois oratory" (Foster, 118, 120). Woodbury faced some problems peculiar to translation of Iroquoian ritual language into English, such as the introduction of periods, which the original lacks. The book received one of two Society of the Indigenous Languages of the Americas Book Awards for 1994.

FURTHER READING

Foster, Michael K. [Review of *Concerning the League: The Iroquois League Tradition as Dictated in Onondaga by John Arthur Gibson*, comp. Hanni Woodbury, Reg

Henry, and Harry Webster on the basis of A. A. Golenweiser's manuscript.] *International Journal of American Linguistics* 62:1 (1996); 117–120.

Woodbury, Hanni, comp. *Concerning the League: The Iroquois League Tradition as Dictated in Onondaga by John Arthur Gibson.* Comp. Hanni Woodbury, Reg Henry, and Harry Webster on the basis of A. A. Goldenweiser's manuscript. Algonquian and Iroquoian Linguistics, Memoir No. 9. Winnipeg, Manitoba: University of Manitoba Press, 1992.

Condolence Cane. The Condolence Cane carries a graphic history of the chieftainship titles of the Haudenosaunee Grand Council. The cane contains fifty pegs, which are changed as new leaders assume office. The cane is used as an aid to memory for the record keepers of the council. It is what scholars call a "mnemonic device," that depicts symbols that trigger certain memories in the minds of speakers in an oral culture.

According to **Cayuga** elder **Jacob Thomas** (Barreiro, 80–81), the Elder Brothers (**Seneca** and **Mohawk**) are represented on one side of the cane, and the Younger Brothers (**Oneida** and Cayuga) on the other, illustrating the debate protocol of the Grand Council, in which the two "houses" attempt to reach **consensus** on an issue before referring it to the **Onondagas**, who act as executives. The cane also is arranged in the form of a symbolic **longhouse**, with the Mohawks' titles at the "Eastern Door," the Senecas at the "Western Door," and the Onondagas in the center (at the council fire), with the Oneidas to their east and the Cayugas to their west.

Each title has its own history, which is recalled during the "Roll Call of the Chiefs," part of the Haudenosaunee ritual of Condolence when it is used to "raise" chiefs to the council. According to Thomas, this type is called a "Big Condolence." Another ceremony, the "Small Condolence," is used to "elevate the minds of the bereaved family" of the chief who has died, necessitating the elevation of another man (Thomas, 83).

FURTHER READING:

Barreiro, José. "Chief Jacob Thomas and the Condolence Cane." *Northeast Indian Quarterly* 7:4 (Winter, 1990): 77–85.

Barreiro, José, and Carol Cornelius. *Knowledge of the Elders: The Iroquois Condolence Cane Tradition.* Special edition of *Northeast Indian Quarterly,* 1991.

Fenton, William N. *Roll Call of the Iroquois Chiefs: A Study of a Mnemonic Cane from the Six Nations Reserve.* Washington, D.C.: *Smithsonian Miscellaneous Collections* 111–15 (1950): 1–73.

Condolence Ceremony. After the Haudenosaunee adopted their **Great Law of Peace**, blood revenge as a means to justice among the various clans was replaced by a Condolence Ceremony, in which major crimes were atoned by payment of **wampum**, usually in strings or belts. In some ways, this payment is similar to the levying of a fine or jail term in European society, where the symbolic combat of court proceedings replaced blood revenge. By custom among the Haudenosaunee, ten strings of wampum atoned for the loss of a man, and twenty for the loss of a woman. The punishment was said to be doubled for a woman because she could bear life.

Condolence Ceremonies also were often used to open major diplomatic proceedings in which atonement was not at issue. In this case, condolence was expressed at the beginning of a treaty council (or other important meeting) to remember mutual acquaintances and loved ones who had passed away since the last meeting between the same parties. The first European account of a Condolence Ceremony for this purpose was recorded during the Treaty of Three Rivers in 1645. Certain verbal metaphors were used for this ceremony—the wiping away of tears, the dispelling of clouds, and the reappearance of the sun, among others.

Condolence rituals also play a role in consoling the relatives of council chiefs who have died and in installing leaders who replace them. In this case, as in other uses of the Condolence Ceremony, the purpose of the ritual is to assuage the minds of the living, including the *orenda* (mystical power) of the group, which is believed to have been diminished by death.

William Beauchamp, who observed Haudenosaunee condolence rituals early in the twentieth century, described the many metaphors that Haudenosaunee speakers used for the ceremony's healing functions:

The forest paths were symbolically cleared, thorns were taken out of the feet, tears were wiped away, the throat and ears were cleansed that all might speak and hear, the heart was restored to its right place, and clouds were removed from the sun in the sky. Blood was washed from the seat, [and] if anyone had died, graves were levelled or covered, the bones of the slain were gathered and hidden under the roots of some great tree. (Beauchamp, 393)

The Condolence Ceremony has roots in the founding epic of the Iroquois Confederacy, during which the **Peacemaker** performed the first such ritual for **Hiawatha**, who was grieving the loss of several members of his family at the hands of the evil Tadadaho. The Condolence Ceremony includes five related rituals and can take several hours to perform. Condolence Ceremonies undertaken by **Jacob Thomas** in the late twentieth century usually took six to eight hours over a two-day period (Barreiro and Cornelius 3). The first was usually called "Journeying on the Trail" or "Eulogy of the Roll Call of the Chiefs" and recalled the installation of the original fifty chiefs on the Grand Council. The second ritual in the sequence was called "Welcome at the Wood's Edge" and was preparatory for the third, "The Requickening Address," which was the heart of the ceremony. This was the extension of actual condolence, which was recited, in part, as follows:

Now then, we say, we wipe away
The falling tears, so that peacefully
you might look around. (Dennis, 102)

During October 1753, **Benjamin Franklin**, who was beginning a distinguished diplomatic career that would later take him to Europe as a U.S. envoy, attended a condolence council at Carlisle, Pennsylvania. On October 1, 1753, he watched the **Oneida** chief **Scarrooyady** and a **Mohawk**, Cayanguileguoa, condole the Ohio Indians for their losses against the French. Franklin listened while Scarrooyady recounted the origins of the Great Law to the Ohio Indians:

We must let you know, that there was a friendship established by our and your Grandfathers, and a mutual Council fire was kindled. In this friendship all those then under the ground, who had not yet obtained eyes or faces [that is, those unborn] were included; and it was then mutually promised to tell the same to their children and children's children. (Van Doren and Boyd, 128)

Franklin and the other colonial delegates were engaged in practical diplomacy, on one level; on another, they were absorbing Iroquois concepts of unity along with their urgings to confederate in a league similar to that of the Iroquois. Scarrooyady took for granted that the Pennsylvanians had some knowledge of the Great Law's workings. At the **Albany Congress** in 1754, New York governor James DeLancey's speech began with a condolence, using Haudenosaunee language: "I wipe away your tears, and take sorrow from your hearts, that you may open your minds and speak freely." Then Governor Delancey gave "A String of Wampum" in a ceremony similar to one Franklin had witnessed a year earlier at Carlisle (O'Callaghan, 6:567).

Lewis Henry Morgan wrote of the Condolence Ceremony during the mid-nineteenth century that "it was not uncommon to spend several days in these festivities; devoting the days in succession to athletic games, and the evenings to the feast, and to the social dance" (Morgan, 122). Jacob Thomas, the only person in the late twentieth century who could recite the entire Great Law of Peace and the condolence Ceremony from memory in the Haudenosaunee languages, explained the purpose of the Requickening Address:

The fifteen "sympathy strings" of wampum, the "Requickening Address," each carry a message "to lift the spirits of the bereaved nation." They are meant to calm the mind and reduce the pain and confusion of mourning. In the first one, speaking for the Younger Brothers (Oneida and **Cayuga**) . . . the speaker would say "We see across the fire that there is a death in the family. So we come to console, and we will shed tears with you because of your great loss. . . . String by string, the speeches describe the emotions of grief. (Barreiro, 84)

FURTHER READING

Barreiro, José. "Chief Jacob Thomas and the Condolence Cane." *Northeast Indian Quarterly* 7:4 (Winter 1990): 77–85.

Barreiro, José, and Carol Cornelius. *Knowledge of the Elders: The Iroquois Condolence Cane Tradition*. Ithaca, N.Y.: Northeast Indian Quarterly, 1991.

Beauchamp, William M. *Civil, Religious, and Mourning Councils and Ceremonies of Adoption of the New York Indians*. New York State Museum Bulletin No. 113. Albany, N.Y.: New York State Education Department, June 1907.

Dennis, Matthew. *Cultivating a Landscape of Peace*. Ithaca, N.Y.: Cornell University Press, 1993.

Fenton, William N. "An Iroquois Condolence Council for Installing Cayuga Chiefs in 1945." *Journal of the Washington Academy of Sciences* 36:4 (1946): 110–127.

———. "The Requickening Address of the Iroquois Condolence Council by J. N. B. Hewitt." *Journal of the Washington Academy of Sciences* 34:3 (1944): 65–85.

Morgan, Lewis Henry. *League of the Iroquois*. 1851. Secaucus, N.J.: Corinth Books, 1962.

O'Callaghan, Edmund B. *Documents Relative to the Colonial History of the State New-York*. Vol. 6. Albany: Weed, Parsons & Co., 1855.

Thwaites, Reuben Gold, ed. and trans. *The Jesuit Relations and Allied Documents: Travels and Explorations of the Jesuit Missionaries in New France, 1610–1791*. New York: Pageant Book Company, 1959.

Tooker, Elisabeth. "The League of the Iroquois: Its History, Politics, and Ritual." *Handbook of North American Indians*. Vol. 15, *Northeast*. Washington, D.C.: Smithsonian Institution, 1978: 418–441.

Van Doren, Carl, and Julian P. Boyd, eds. *Indian Treaties Printed by Benjamin Franklin, 1736–1762*. Philadelphia: Historical Society of Pennsylvania, 1938.

Consensus. Consensus is the primary mode of governance among the Haudenosaunee. It is one of three bedrock principles of the *Kayánerénhkowa* (**Great Law of Peace**, or Constitution of the Five Nations), coming in under the discussion of *Ne'' Găshasde''"sä'*, or popular sovereignty.

Consensus is a long process, designed neither for speed nor for efficiency, which are Western, not Iroquoian, values. Under Haudenosaunee law (and Iroquoian customs generally), the point of councilmanic discussion is not to "reach a decision" or "take action" (again, European values), but to achieve the One Mind of Consensus. Consensus building was, therefore, the essential political ingredient in the operation of the league and other Iroquoian governments.

Under traditional government, in order to arrive at consensus, all minds had first to be consulted. Consultation occurred through a set round of councils, each of which met to discuss the issue(s) at hand. The next council in line could not meet until its preceding council or subcommittee of council had come to an agreement on the matter. Both men and women had councils, with women's councils entertaining all issues first. Each council level, whether female or male, had to be in consensus before it sent a matter forward. If the **Adodaroh** (chairman of the federal men's Grand Council) or the **Jigonsaseh** (Head Clan Mother of the league) disagreed with a matter sent to him or her, he or she could "veto" or table it until a later time. Issues could be reintroduced as often as sponsors wished, and matters could always be revisited judicially, through the action of women's councils.

These rules exasperated Europeans who were accustomed to small, exclusive clusters of men making all decisions, whether or not others agreed. During the colonial era, various Crown forces attempted to push their own hierarchical styles onto the Iroquois, with little success. During the forced assimilation after the establishment of the United States, the women's councils were disbanded and Western-style government was foisted off on the people, but in the twentieth century, the old councilmanic styles have resumed. Although consensus is honored, women's councils have yet to reattain their formalized place.

FURTHER READING

Bonvillain, Nancy. "Iroquoian Women." In Nancy Bonvillain, ed., *Studies on Iroquoian Culture*. Occasional Publications in Northeastern Anthropology, No. 6. Rindge, NH: Department of Anthropology, Franklin Pierce College, 1980: 47–58.

Grinde, Donald A., Jr., and Bruce E. Johansen. *Exemplar of Liberty, Native America and The Evolution of Democracy*. Los Angeles: UCLA American Indian Studies Center, 1991.

Hewitt, J[ohn] N[apoleon] B[rinton]. "A Constitutional League of Peace in the Stone Age of America: The League of the Iroquois and Its Constitution." *Smithsonian Institution Series* (1920): 527–545.

———. "Some Esoteric Aspects of the League of the Iroquois." *Proceedings of the International Congress of Americanists* 19 (1915): 322–326.

Jacobs, Renée. "The Iroquois Great Law of Peace and the United States Constitution: How the Founding Fathers Ignored the Clan Mothers." *American Indian Law Review* 16:2 (1991): 497–531.

Mann, Barbara A. "The Lynx in Time: Haudenosaunee Women's Traditions and History." *American Indian Quarterly* 21:3 (1997): 423–450.

Powell, J. W. "Wyandot Government: A Short Study of Tribal Society." *Annual Report of the Bureau of Ethnology to the Secretary of the Smithsonian Institution* 1 (1879–1880): 57–69.

Thwaites, Reuben Gold, ed. and trans. *Jesuit Relations and Allied Documents: Travels and Explorations of the Jesuit Missionaries in New France, 1610–1791*. New York: Pageant Book Company, 1959.

Barbara A. Mann

Converse, Harriet Maxwell (Yaiéwanoh, Gayaneshaoh, "Bearer of the Law") (Seneca), 1836–1903. Harriet Maxwell Converse (Yaiéwanoh, Gayaneshaoh) was a beloved adoptee of the **Senecas**. As an adult, she collected traditions, songs, and stories of the old Haudenosaunee. She also was instrumental in defeating legislation that would have robbed the New York league peoples of their land.

Converse was born in Elmira, Ohio, during 1836, the youngest of seven children in a settler family with old ties of affection to the Senecas and Wyandots of the Ohio league. Her grandfather was known to them as Honest Trader, while her father, in some ways more Native than European, was named Brave Boy. Her mother was Marie Purdy, the second wife of Thomas Maxwell, who died nine years after his daughter's birth. This untoward event sent young Harriet off to school (probably boarding school) in Milan, Ohio. She showed great literary promise, writing poetry for publication even as a young woman.

Converse's first marriage was to a G. B. Clarke, but she was widowed at a young age. In 1861, she was married a second time, to the wealthy socialite Franklin Buchanan Converse of Westfield, Massachusetts, who took her on a five-year grand tour of Europe, Africa, and Asia, as well as to several tourist spots in the United States. Eventually, the couple settled in New York City. For years, Converse developed her literary talents, capturing much notice in her own time, particularly as a contributor to the *Ladies' Journal* (of Edinburgh), the *Scottish American*, the *British Advertiser*, and the *New York Independent*. Her strong Scottish nationalism, which she was not shy about articulating, could not be missed.

Converse's childhood connection to the League of the Haudenosaunee was revived when she met Donehogä´wa (**Ely S. Parker**); all her fond memories of her Native childhood playmates flooded back. The two became fast friends. Donehogä´wa escorted Yaiéwanoh to the **Tuscarora** Reservation, where he introduced her to his sister, Gähahno, the sitting *Jigonsaseh* of the league. Next, she visited the **Cattaraugus** (Seneca) **Reservation** in 1881, where she was introduced to the lineal descendants of Sagoyewatha (**Red Jacket**), the great Speaker of the Women during the revolutionary era.

Donehogä´wa stimulated more than childhood recollections, however. Converse was an educated woman who had read manuscript her own father had written about his league neighbors. She had also studied **Lewis Henry Morgan**'s *League of the Haudenosaunee*, which she knew that her friend Donehogä´wa had coauthored. The culture, traditions, and governmental organization of the league attracted her greatly at a time when women were significantly oppressed in the European-American culture. She devoted several pages of her private notes to the lofty legal, economic, religious, and social status of Iroquoian women, concluding that "as the woman of today stands advocate and petitioner of her own cause, should she not offer an oblation of gratitude to the memory of the Iroquois Indian who called the earth his 'mighty mother' and who, through a sense of justice, rendered to the mothers of his people the rights maternal, political, social, civil, religious and of land?" (Converse, 138).

Converse soon began openly throwing her prestige as an author and her upper-class social standing behind league causes in Albany and Washington, D.C. In consideration of her tireless labors in behalf of the league, individual Haudenosaunee presented her with gifts of increasing value, including precious heirlooms that later became part of the Converse Collection at the New York State Library.

Finally, the elders decided that it was only proper to adopt this woman who had shown such love of and loyalty to the league. Since her strongest connections were with the Senecas, the matter fell into the hands of Seneca Clan Mother Joondooh and her husband Thonasowah, a grand council chief of the Seneca. On June 15, 1885, at the Cattaraugus Seneca Reservation, Joondooh adopted Converse as a sister into the Snipe Clan of the Senecas under the traditional Faithkeeper's name of Gayaneshaoh, or "The Law Bearer," a name once worn by the daughter of Sagoyewatha (Red Jacket).

After her adoption, Converse continued living in New York City, where her home became something of a traveler's rest stop for lost or struggling Native Americans in that metropolis. She often wrote up and published their personal stories. At her death, several large scrapbooks containing these stories were found among her papers. Converse also was politically active, keeping an eye on both the state and federal legislatures and using her high social position in the European-American world to lauch preemptive countermeasures whenever any bill threatened the rights of the Haudenosaunee.

Late in 1885, Gayaneshaoh was initiated into the medicine society of the Little Waters. As an adjunct to this position, she became a member of the *Ganun ´dasē* lodge of the *Yeihdos*, or the Society of Mystic Animals. She was the first member known not to have been born a Haudenosaunee.

Gayaneshaoh soon became indispensable to the people, not for her legal or financial aid, which was to be had from many quarters, but for her special wisdom and careful knowledge of the Haudenosaunee people. The elders decided to adopt her not only into a family (as had happened in 1885), but into the *Owachira*, or lineage clan, a higher honor. Accordingly, in April 1890, Gayaneshaoh was adopted by the entire Snipe Clan under the name of Yaiéwanoh.

In 1891, Yaiéwanoh brought about the legislative defeat of a major state bill that would have wrought great hardship on the people. (The so-called "Whipple Bill" would have forcibly conferred U.S. citizenship on Native Americans, ending the reservation system and unleashing an orgy of land speculation of the sort that was stealing Oklahoma from the Removed Natives there.) In response to her monumental efforts and "by love and affection," the elders promoted her yet again, on April 8, 1891, by adopting her as a full, legal member of the Seneca Nation (Converse, 23).

Later in 1891, the state of New York began its "Indian museum," to which Yaiéwanoh presented many fine articles in what became known as the Maxwell-Converse Collection. At this point, she became active in the attempt (successful in 1898) to influence the Grand Council at Onondaga to deposit the wampum of the **Great Law of Peace** with the museum for safekeeping. Today, this transfer is controversial, but at the time, she was attempting to keep the belts of the Great Law from being destroyed by trophy-hunting tourists who had no qualms about helping themselves to "Indian artifacts."

On November 18, 1903, while she was getting ready to attend a dinner with Chief Tahamont of the Abenakis, Converse suffered what was probably a sudden stroke. Lying on the floor during her last few moments of consciousness before death, Converse managed to scribble a note entrusting all of her carefully collected papers to Gawaso Wanneh (**Arthur Parker**), thus ensuring that a fellow Seneca would be her literary executor. Though in shock at her death and himself barely more than a graduate student, Gawaso Wanneh took on the charge, laboring over her notes for the next five years until he was able to publish her work as *Myths and Legends of the New York State Iroquois*. The manuscript was prefaced by his detailed and loving biography of Yaiéwanoh, a study of her life and works.

FURTHER READING

Converse, Harriet Maxwell [Ya-ie-wa-noh]. *Myths and Legends of the New York State Iroquois.* Ed. Arthur Caswell Parker. New York State Museum Bulletin 125. Education Department Bulletin No. 437. Albany: University of the State of New York, 1908.

Parker, Arthur C. "Mrs. Harriet Maxwell Converse." *The Life of General Ely S. Parker Last Grand Sachem of the Iroquois and General Grant's Military Secretary.* Buffalo: Buffalo Historical Society, 1919: 323–324.

Barbara A. Mann

Cooper, Polly (Oneida), fl. 1770s. Polly Cooper became George Washington's cook during the Revolutionary War. Washington requested a Native American cook because of his preference for corn dishes. Polly Cooper may have been the wife of one of eight **Tuscarora** officers on Washington's staff. Through Polly Cooper, the **Oneida** sachem **Skenandoah** (Shenandoah) became aware that Washington's army was going hungry at Valley Forge. The Oneidas then used some of their stored food to assist Washington's troops.

The Oneidas who provided corn to Washington's troops also taught them how to cook it. Without Cooper's advice, the hungry soldiers might have eaten the corn uncooked and could have died when it expanded in their stomachs. At the end of the war, Martha Washington presented Cooper with a shawl in recognition of her efforts at Valley Forge. The shawl is displayed once a year to this day at the Oneidas' cultural center near Verona, New York.

Corlaer, as title. "Corlaer" was a title often used in treaty accounts by Haudenosaunee representatives as a reference to the governor of New York. The name is an Iroquois-language adaptation of Arent Van Curler, the Dutch founder of Schenectady, New York, who was regarded by the **Mohawks** as a trustworthy friend. He died in 1667, but his name survived as an honorary title in frontier diplomacy.

Historical records indicate that Van Curler curried favor with the Haudenosaunee by giving or trading liquor and guns that were sometimes forbidden by Dutch colonial law. Van Curler hid these transactions by evasive bookkeeping. It is likely that Van Curler supplied the Mohawks with many of the guns that helped them tip the military balance in the **Beaver Wars** against the Wyandots (Hurons).

FURTHER READING

Richter, Daniel K. *The Ordeal of the Longhouse: The Peoples of the Iroquois League in the Era of European Colonization.* Chapel Hill: University of North Carolina Press, 1992.

Corn and the Haudenosaunee. Corn enhanced the role of agriculture in many Native American economies. The Iroquois' oral history, for example, holds that corn had a key role in establishing agriculture as a major economic enterprise. The increasing role of agriculture had far-reaching sociopolitical, as well as economic, effects among the Iroquois, including support of matrilineal social structures and the establishment of a confederation based on the **Great Law of Peace**.

The Haudenosaunee (Iroquois) Confederacy adopted corn as a staple crop while its constituent nations developed large-scale political organization shortly after 1000 C.E. The Haudenosaunee's ability to produce a surplus of corn played a role in the political influence of the confederacy, which reached, through a chain of alliances, from their homelands in present-day upstate New York across much of New England and the Middle Atlantic regions.

The Iroquois' adoption of corn-based agriculture, along with cultivation of beans and squash (called "The **Three Sisters**"), played an important role in their adoption of a matrilineal social structure and a **consensus**-based political system. Before roughly the year 1000 C.E., the Iroquois were less prone to alliance and more frequently disposed to murder for revenge. An older confederacy to the north, possibly that of the Wyandots (Hurons), is said to have sent an emissary, the **Peacemaker**, to persuade the Haudenosaunee to make peace with each other and outlaw the blood feud, which was threatening social stability. The Peacemaker and **Hiawatha**, the **Mohawk** cofounder of the Haudenosaunee Confederacy, spent most of their adult lives persuading the feuding Haudenosaunee to accept their vision of peace. According to calculations by Barbara A. Mann and Jerry Fields, the confederacy was finally accepted in 1142 C.E., within living memory, perhaps, of the adoption of corn as a staple crop.

The size of the cornfields cultivated by the Haudenosaunee and their neighbors often surprised European-Americans. Among the Wyandots, who also cultivated corn for domestic consumption and export, the Recollect lay missionary Gabriel Sagard said that one could get lost as easily in their cornfields as in nearby woods (Dennis, 27). In 1669, a French visitor to **Seneca** country noted a village sitting at the center of an agricultural field (which apparently was fallow when he saw it) six miles around.

Early European observers indicated that the Haudenosaunee, particularly the Senecas, farmed corn in large fields. **Jacques Cartier**, exploring the St. Lawrence River during 1535, described such fields under cultivation around Haudenosaunee villages. Henry Hudson, exploring the river named after him, provided similar accounts. Large stores of grain also were reported.

The Frenchman Marquis de Denonville, in the course of his military expedition against the Haudenosaunee in 1687, reported that his forces destroyed more than 400,000 minots of corn (Mt. Pleasant, 33). A French minot, according to **Lewis Henry Morgan**, equals roughly three bushels, so the 400,000 minots of corn that Denonville's forces destroyed in 1687 equalled roughly 1.2 million bushels (Morgan, 199). While Denonville's estimate may have been inflated to please his superiors, even half that amount would have been a very large cache of corn.

French troops also found a granary that they estimated could hold at least three million bushels of corn at the Seneca town of **Ganondagan** when they destroyed it. This estimate (even subject to some self-aggrandizing statistical inflation) indicated that this site could have been a major source of winter sustenance for the entire Haudenosaunee Confederacy (Mohawk, 58). General **John Sullivan**, whose troops burned their way through Haudenosaunee corn stores roughly ninety years after Denonville's French forces, reported destroying 60,000 bushels of corn in a single town, Genesee (Mt. Pleasant, 33).

The Iroquois and other Native American peoples clearly possessed a command of corn-growing agriculture that exceeded the knowledge of early European and American non-Native observers. They also understood the principles of corn breeding. Many of the hybrid varieties of corn in use today stem from genetic types used long ago by the Iroquois and other Native American peoples (Mt. Pleasant, 37–38).

Corn was usually planted with squash and beans (together, the Iroquois called them "The Three Sisters") on small hills. This sort of planting promoted high yields because the beans fix nitrogen in their roots that fertilizes the corn and squash. Planting on hills also minimized soil erosion and leaching. Cornfields usually were tended by women, but were cleared by men. By the time of the first contacts with Europeans, slash-and-burn agriculture was being used, and most villages moved on an average of every twenty-five years, possibly because of soil exhaustion and population increases.

As in the rest of the United States, corn raising and other forms of agriculture have become a minority occupation on most Haudenosaunee territories during the last decades of the twentieth century. In 1990, a survey found that only seventy-five Iroquois families practiced agriculture full- or part-time, half of whom lived on the **Tuscarora Reservation**. Only 1,275 acres of Haudenosaunee territory were being used primarily for agriculture in 1990, more than half of that for the raising of hay (Quintana, 35–36).

FURTHER READING

Dennis, Matthew. *Cultivating a Landscape of Peace*. Ithaca, N.Y.: Cornell University Press, 1993.

Mohawk, John. "Economic Motivations: An Iroquoian Perspective." *Northeast Indian Quarterly* 6:1–2 (Spring/Summer 1989): 56–63.

Morgan, Lewis Henry. *League of the Iroquois*. 1851. Secaucus, N.J.: Corinth Books, 1962.

Mt. Pleasant, Jane. "The Iroquois Sustainers: Practices of a Longterm Agriculture in the Northeast." *Northeast Indian Quarterly* 6:1–2 (Spring/Summer 1989): 33–39.

Parker, Arthur C. *Iroquois Uses of Maize and Other Food Plants*. Albany: University of the State of New York, 1910.

Quintana, Jorge. "Agricultural Survey of New York State Iroquois Reservations, 1990." *Northeast Indian Quarterly* 8:1 (Spring 1991): 32–36.

Waugh, F. W. *Iroquois Foods and Food Preparation*. 1916. Ottawa: National Museum
of Canada, 1973.

Cornplanter (Gaianfẃaka, John O'Bail) (Seneca), c. 1735–1836. Cornplanter,
a half-brother of **Handsome Lake**, was a major Iroquois leader of the late
eighteenth century; he figured importantly in the shifting alliances that accompanied the **American Revolution** and became a personal friend of George
Washington through the Tammany Society, a group that observed the fusion of
European and Native American cultures in America.

Cornplanter's father was a white trader, John O'Bail (sometimes spelled
"Abeel"). Some sources contend that he was Irish; others say that he was Dutch.
All agree, however, that he was one of the biggest sellers of liquor to the
Senecas. O'Bail had been heard to boast that his trade had a profit margin of
1,000 percent. While many Englishmen detested O'Bail, they relied on his in-
telligence about the French, gathered from Indians with whom he did business.

Cornplanter was raised by his Seneca mother. He knew his father only
slightly, having met him a few times as a child. In 1780, Cornplanter led a
raiding party in the Schoharie Valley that took a number of prisoners, his father
included. Cornplanter released his father, who still made his living by bartering
guns, rum, and other things for furs. Cornplanter invited his father to join his
Senecas, but the elder O'Bail chose to return to his European-American family
at Fort Plain, New York.

As allies of the French in the French and Indian War (1754–1763), Cornplanter's warriors raided several British settlements. He may have been part of
the French force that defeated British General Edward Braddock and his aide
George Washington at Fort Duquesne (now Pittsburgh).

Cornplanter generally favored neutrality in the American Revolution. The
Iroquois Grand Council could not reach **consensus** on alliance in that war. **Joseph Brant** spoke eloquently about the necessity of taking up the hatchet, stating
that neutrality would lead to disaster and that the Americans or the British might
turn on the confederacy with a vengeance. **Red Jacket** and Cornplanter argued
against Brant. They insisted that this quarrel was among the whites; interfering
in something that they did not fully understand was a mistake. As the meeting
broke up in a furor, Brant called Cornplanter a coward. The people gathered at
Irondequoit divided into two camps and discussed the issue of going to war.

In general, the Senecas were disposed to neutrality. However, the words of
Brant stung the ears of the Senecas. They could not bear to be called cowards.
Finally, after lengthy discussion, the Senecas were swayed along with other
wavering groups to take up the king's cause. Of great importance was the consent of the Clan Mothers. The Senecas took this defeat gracefully and exhorted
the warriors to unite in the fight against the Americans. With this meeting, the
resolution was made unanimous. Thus did the majority of the Six Nations break
the league's neutrality and take up the British cause.

After the Revolution, Cornplanter secured for his people a tract of land on
both sides of the Allegheny River. He brought in Quaker teachers and helped

sustain a prosperous agricultural community that included large herds of cattle. Cornplanter signed several treaties on behalf of the Senecas, including those concluded at **Fort Stanwix** in 1784 and others at various locations in 1789, 1797, and 1802. Through his many associations with European-Americans (including a trip to England), Cornplanter picked up English clothes and mannerisms. On one occasion, fellow Senecas tore off Cornplanter's English clothes, dressed him in traditional attire, and greased his body.

During April 1786, the Tammany Society welcomed Cornplanter and five other Senecas to Philadelphia. In a remarkable ceremony, the Tammany sachems escorted the Senecas from their lodgings at the Indian Queen Tavern to Tammany's wigwam on the banks of the Schuylkill River for a conference. Within a few days, Cornplanter and the Senecas proceeded to New York City to address Congress.

In Philadelphia on May 1, 1786, St. Tammany's Day was marked with the usual celebrations and feasts, after which a portrait of Cornplanter was given to the Tammany Society. More than a dozen toasts were given, including the following: "The Great Council Fire of the United States—May the 13 fires glow in one blended blaze and illumine the Eagle in his flight to the stars," "Our great grand sachem George Washington, Esq.," "Our Brother Iontonkque or the Corn Plant—May we ever remember that he visited our wigwam and spoke a good talk from our great-grand-fathers," and "The Friendly Indian Nations— our warriors and young men who fought, bled and gave good council for our nation" (Grinde and Johansen, 184).

Later in his life, Cornplanter lost some of his prestige among the Senecas because of his agreement to land cessions. He retained enough influence to bring the Senecas to the American side in the War of 1812, however. Shortly before he died in 1836, Cornplanter had a dream that indicated that his friendship with all European-Americans had been mistaken. After the dream, Cornplanter destroyed all the presents that had been given him by non-Indians.

Cornplanter's people occupied the piece of land along the Allegheny River that had been given them by George Washington until the mid-twentieth century, when the Army Corps of Engineers decided that the land better suited the public convenience and necessity under water. The scope of the army's engineering projects had grown grandiosely since Washington himself helped survey the mountains that now comprise West Virginia, long before the pursuit of electricity became a legally valid reason for the state to seize land. In 1964, the bones of Cornplanter's people were moved from their land to make way for rising waters behind the **Kinzua Dam**. In the valleys at the Western Door, Senecas still ask sardonically if George Washington had ever asked Cornplanter if he knew how to swim.

FURTHER READING

Grinde, Donald A., Jr., and Bruce E. Johansen. *Exemplar of Liberty: Native America and the Evolution of Democracy*. Los Angeles: UCLA American Indian Studies Center, 1991.

Parker, Arthur Caswell. *Notes on the Ancestry of Cornplanter*. Rochester, N.Y.: Lewis H. Morgan Chapter, 1927.

Stone, William L. (William Leete). *Life and Times of Red-Jacket, or Sa-go-ye-wat-ha: Being the Sequel to the History of the Six Nations*. New York: Wiley and Putnam, 1841.

Cornplanter Grant. In 1795, George Washington, acting through the new federal government of the United States, together with the state of Pennsylvania, granted **Cornplanter** and his heirs 780 acres, to be held for them in perpetuity, on the west bank of the Allegheny River just south of the New York State line. This tract of land remained within the designated **Seneca** families until all but a few acres of it was inundated by an artificial lake created behind the **Kinzua Dam**.

Covenant Chain. The Covenant Chain was a diplomatic metaphor used by the British when they sought alliance with the Haudenosaunee against the French. The alliance was said to represent a chain, sometimes made of silver. When diplomacy was cordial, the chain was being "shined." If the two sides fell out in disagreement, the chain was said to be "rusting."

As with many Native American nations during the days of early contact with Europeans, Haudenosaunee trade and diplomacy were carried out in the context of the extended family. In **William N. Fenton**'s words, the Covenant Chain represented a "network of symbolic kinship" (Jennings, 12).

The image of the Covenant Chain was first used as a metaphor for alliance between the Haudenosaunee and the English at a treaty concluded in Albany during 1677. Before that, the most common metaphor for alliance had been a rope. For a brief period while the Dutch were active in trade, the rope became an iron chain, which was converted to an image of a silver chain under the British. For a time, Massachusetts Bay tried to gain an advantage in trade by calling its chain "golden," but the effort flopped.

The **Mohawk** leader **Hendrick** (Tiyanoga) was perhaps the most important individual link in the chain of alliance that saved the New York frontier and probably New England from the French in the initial stages of the Seven Years' War, which was called the French and Indian War in North America. Hendrick died maintaining the Covenant Chain at the Battle of Lake George in 1755, where **Sir William Johnson** defeated Baron Dieskau.

While Hendrick was alive, the Covenant Chain was a serious matter to him. During June 1753, for example, he led seventeen Mohawks in demanding an audience with Governor George Clinton in New York City. Hendrick angrily told Clinton that the English were not adequately protecting the Mohawks from the French, and that large areas of Mohawk land were being taken by English squatters. "The Covenant Chain is broken between you and us," Hendrick told Clinton as the Mohawks stormed out of his office (Aquila, 104–105). William Johnson, English Indian agent to the Iroquois and an adopted Mohawk, later reproved Hendrick for treating Clinton in an uncivil manner. At the same time, Johnson did his best to provide the English protection that Hendrick had sought. One of the results of his effort was the **Albany Congress** of 1754, at which Hendrick picked up a stick and threw it behind his back, lecturing the English: "You have thus thrown us behind your back, and disregarded us, whereas the French are a subtle and vigilant people, ever using their utmost endeavors to seduce and bring our people over to them" (Aquila, 108).

Benjamin Franklin, also a key figure at the Albany Congress, observed the diplomatic images evoked by the Covenant Chain early in his distinguished diplomatic career after he attended an Iroquois condolence council at Carlisle, Pennsylvania (See **Condolence Ceremony**). At this treaty meeting with the Iroquois and Ohio Indians (Twightees, Delawares, Shawnees, and Wyandots), Franklin watched the **Oneida** chief Scarrooyady and a Mohawk, Cayanguile-guoa, condole the Ohio Indians for their losses against the French. Having done this, Scarrooyady exhorted all assembled to "preserve this Union and Friendship, which has so long and happy continued among us. Let us keep the chain from rusting" (Van Doren and Boyd, 128). Franklin later used the Covenant Chain image in designs for early U.S. coins.

FURTHER READING

Aquila, Richard. *The Iroquois Restoration: Iroquois Diplomacy on the Colonial Frontier, 1701–1754*. Detroit: Wayne State University Press, 1983.

Jennings, Francis. *The Ambiguous Iroquois Empire: The Covenant Chain Confederation of Indian Tribes with English Colonies from its Beginnings to the Lancaster Treaty of 1744*. New York: W. W. Norton, 1984.

Jennings, Francis, ed.; William N. Fenton, joint ed.; Mary A. Druke, associate ed.; David R. Miller, research ed. *The History and Culture of Iroquois Diplomacy: An Interdisciplinary Guide to the Treaties of the Six Nations and Their League*. Syracuse, N.Y.: Syracuse University Press, 1985.

Richter, Daniel K., and James H. Merrell, eds. *Beyond the Covenant Chain: The Iroquois and Their Neighbors in Indian North America, 1600–1800*. Syracuse, N.Y.: Syracuse University Press, 1987.

Van Doren, Carl and Julian P. Boyd, eds. *Indian Treaties Printed by Benjamin Franklin, 1736–1762*. Philadelphia: Historical Society of Pennsylvania, 1938.

Cusick, Cornelius (Tuscarora), 1835–1904. Lieutenant Cornelius Cusick was the commander of Company D of the 132d New York State Volunteer Infantry during the Civil War. Cusick, a **Tuscarora** peace chief before the war, set aside the **antlers** of civil authority to assume an officer's role in the war. The detachment that Cusick commanded was sometimes known as the Tuscarora Company, although it was composed mainly of Germans and **Senecas**.

The Tuscarora Company took major casualties at the Battle of Fir Oaks (Seven Pines) on May 31 and June 1, 1862, in which 5,000 Union soldiers were killed or injured. The company's worst casualties were suffered as a result of "friendly fire"—the inadvertent explosion of a Union mine storehouse that killed thirty-five men of the 132d New York Volunteers. During the conflict, Cusick was known as "War Eagle," and the company he commanded was sometimes called "Cusick's Indians."

Cusick was born on August 2, 1835, of James and Mary Cusick on the Tuscarora Indian Reservation. Like the Seneca Parker family, the Cusicks had long been well known to their non-Indian neighbors.

D

Deganawida (The Peacemaker), fl. c. 1100s. Deganawida is the name of the **Peacemaker** who, during the great turmoil of the **Second Epoch of Time**, joined with *Jigonsaseh*, the leader of the Cultivators, and **Hiawatha**, the inventor of **wampum** and the **Condolence Ceremony**, to establish the *Gayanĕsshä''gowa*, or **Great Law of Peace**, also called the Constitution of the Five (later Six) Nations. For the full story of his place in the tradition of the league, see **Peacemaker** and **Second Epoch of Time**.

Dekanisora (Onondaga), c. 1650–1730. Dekanisora was a principal Haudenosaunee leader during the late seventeenth century. He also was an outstanding orator and a member of the Iroquois Grand Council, possibly holding the office of speaker, or Tadadaho. In 1688, he was among Iroquois who were traveling to Montréal for a peace parley when they were captured by the Wyandot (Huron) leader Adario, who was trying to instigate Iroquois-French conflict. Dekanisora and the other Iroquois led to believe that the French were responsible for the death of one warrior whom Adario did not release, and as a result they made war on Montréal, killing several French settlers.

Dekanisora's reputation as an orator reached **Cadwallader Colden**, who wrote that as a speaker Dekanisora could stand with the best in the world. Dekanisora was a frequent spokesman for the Iroquois at councils with both the English and the French, and he tried to maintain the Iroquois' distance from both. He died at Albany in 1730 during a treaty council.

FURTHER READING

Johansen, Bruce E., and Donald A. Grinde, Jr. *The Encyclopedia of Native American Biography*. New York: Henry Holt, 1997.

Deskaheh (Levi General) (Cayuga), 1873–1925. Deskaheh, a descendant of **Mary Jemison**, was Tadadaho (speaker) of the Iroquois Grand Council at

Grand River, Ontario. He presided during the early 1920s, when Canadian authorities closed the traditional **Longhouse**, which had been asserting independence from Canadian jurisdiction. Canadian authorities proposed to set up a governmental structure that would answer to its Indian-affairs bureaucracy. With Canadian police about to arrest him, Deskaheh traveled to the headquarters of the League of Nations in Geneva, Switzerland, carrying a Haudenosaunee passport, with an appeal for support from the international community.

Several months of effort did not win Deskaheh a hearing before the international body, in large part because of diplomatic manipulation by Great Britain and Canada, governments that were being embarrassed by Deskaheh's mission. Lacking a forum at the League of Nations, Deskaheh and his supporters held a privately organized meeting in Switzerland that drew several thousand people who supported Iroquois sovereignty.

In his last speech, March 10, 1925, Deskaheh had lost none of his distaste for forced acculturation. "Over in Ottawa, they call that policy 'Indian Advancement,' " he said. "Over in Washington, they call it 'Assimilation.' We who would be the helpless victims say it is tyranny. . . . If this must go on to the bitter end, we would rather that you come with your guns and poison gas and get rid of us that way. Do it openly and above board" (Johansen and Grinde, 111).

When he lay dying, relatives of Deskaheh who lived in the United States were refused entry into Canada to be at his bedside. Deskaheh died two and a half months after his last defiant speech. His notions of sovereignty have been maintained by many Iroquois into contemporary times. The Iroquois Grand Council at Onondaga issues its own passports, which are recognized by Switzerland and several other countries, but not by the United States or Canada.

FURTHER READING

Johansen, Bruce E., and Donald A. Grinde, Jr. *The Encyclopedia of Native American Biography*. New York: Henry Holt, 1997.
Tehanetorens [Ray Fadden]. *A Basic Call to Consciousness*. 1978. Rooseveltown, N.Y.: Akwesasne Notes, 1981 (1986 printing).

Dockstader, Frederick J. (Oneida/Navajo), b. 1919. Although he was born in Los Angeles, Frederick J. Dockstader spent many of his early years on the Navajo and Hopi reservations in Arizona. He became an outstanding anthropologist, author, and silversmith. Dockstader also became the staff ethnologist at the Cranbrook Institute in 1950. Later he became curator of anthropology at Dartmouth College.

In 1955, Dockstader became assistant director of the Museum of the American Indian (Heye Foundation) in New York City, and in 1960, he was named its director. Since his primary field of study was Indian art, Dockstader also was appointed commissioner of the Indian Arts and Crafts Board of the U.S. Department of the Interior in 1955. His books include *Indian Art in America,*

Indian Art in Middle America, Indian Art in South America, and *Pre-Columbian Art and Later Indian Tribal Arts.*

FURTHER READING

Dockstader, Frederick J. *Great North American Indians: Profiles in Life and Leadership.* New York: Van Nostrand Reinhold, 1977.

Donnaconna (Wyandot). *See* **Cartier, Jacques.**

E

Eagle, as Haudenosaunee political symbol. In the Haudenosaunee world view, the eagle hovers over the Great Tree of Peace, attentive to threats to the confederacy. The eagle has been adopted in a similar way as a prominent symbol on the Great Seal of the United States.

Engels, Friedrich, 1820–1895. Karl Marx and Friedrich Engels, the authors of *The Communist Manifesto*, became acquainted with the social and political system of the Iroquois late in their lives through the works of pioneer ethnologist **Lewis Henry Morgan**. When the *Manifesto* was originally published in 1848, Marx and Engels wrote that the history of all existing societies had been founded in a history of class struggles. In the 1888 edition of the *Manifesto*, Engels added a note qualifying that statement to take into account information on prehistorical societies with which he and the recently deceased Marx had become acquainted during the ensuing four decades.

Engels inherited Marx's copious notes on Morgan's *Ancient Society* (1877) after Marx's death in 1883 and authored *The Origin of the Family, Private Property, and the State*. Studying Morgan's account of "primitive" societies, with the Iroquois being his cornerstone, Engels provided what he believed to be an egalitarian, classless model of society that also provided justice between the sexes.

As prisoners of their own times and perceptions, Marx and Engels in 1848 had yet to shed their Eurocentric notions that history had begun with patriarchal, monarchial governments. One can imagine how the discovery of societies that operated differently must have fascinated them, much as it earlier had intrigued some of the major architects of the United States. Having rediscovered the "mother-right gens," Engels could scarcely contain himself: "It has the same significance for the history of primitive society as Darwin's theory of evolution has for biology, and Marx's theory of surplus value for political economy. . . .

The mother-right gens has become the pivot around which this entire science [of political economy] *turns*" (Engels, 3:201; emphasis added).

FURTHER READING

Engels, Friedrich. *The Origin of the Family, Private Property, and the State, in the Light of the Researches of Lewis H. Morgan.* 1886. In *Karl Marx and Friedrich Engels: Selected Works.* London: Lawrence and Wishart, 1968.

Grinde, Donald A., Jr., and Bruce E. Johansen. *Exemplar of Liberty: Native America and the Evolution of Democracy.* Los Angeles: UCLA American Indian Studies Center, 1991.

Morgan, Lewis Henry. *Ancient Society.* New York: Henry Holt, 1877.

———. *League of the Ho-de-no-sau-nee, or Iroquois.* 1851. New York: Dodd, Mead & Co., 1922.

F

Fadden, John Kahionhes (Mohawk), b. 1938. John Kahionhes Fadden, his father **Ray Fadden**, and their families have played a major role in preserving and reviving **Mohawk** language and culture though artistic and educational endeavors that have spanned much of the last half of the twentieth century. Their efforts have reached people across the United States and in many other countries through correspondence and books, while the Faddens' major impact in upstate New York has been through the family's Six Nations Indian Museum at Onchiota.

Born in Massena, New York, John Kahionhes Fadden earned a bachelor's degree in fine art at the Rochester Institute of Technology in 1961 and took graduate work at St. Lawrence University and the State University of New York at Plattsburgh. As his artistic talents developed, Fadden melded with them an intense political awareness of the changes taking place at **Akwesasne**, his homeland, where he often illustrated for the newspaper *Akwesasne Notes*. His art also portrays worldwide indigenous and ecological themes.

John Fadden's artwork had reached audiences around the world in more than sixty books by the late 1990s (including about twenty book covers), thirty exhibitions, eleven calendars, and other media. Fadden also has been a leader in efforts to provide Iroquois-produced materials for New York State schools. Until early 1994, he taught middle-school art for thirty-two years in the Saranac Central School system.

Fadden's work has been published by *Akwesasne Notes* for three decades; he also has created many posters and calendars for *Akwesasne Notes* depicting the Haudenosaunee creation and other traditions that have circulated worldwide. The Smithsonian Institution and National Zoological Park has commissioned Fadden to produce posters depicting Native American plants and medicines.

John Fadden's wife Eva is an accomplished carver in wood, soapstone, and other media. His son David is a graphic artist who by his early twenties had illustrated several books and magazines.

FURTHER READING

Whitaker, Robert. "Akwesasne Seeks to Rebuild a Nation." *Plattsburgh* [New York] *Press-Republican*, January 15, 1989.

Fadden, Ray Tehanetorens (Aren Akweks, Mohawk), b. 1910. Ray Tehanetorens Fadden has been a principal figure during most of the last half of the twentieth century in the preservation of **Mohawk** and other Iroquois language and culture. As founder of the Six Nations Indian Museum at Onchiota, New York, the Fadden family since the 1950s has been active in cultural affairs in New York State. With **Ernest Benedict**, another Mohawk, Fadden formed the Akwesasne Mohawk Counsellor's Organization, which took hundreds of Native American children across the United States to study history, paying for much of this work from his own pocket. He compiled histories, drew portraits and charts, and wove replicas of ancient Haudenosaunee story belts that line the walls of the Six Nations Indian Museum near his house in Onchiota, New York.

The Akwesasne Mohawk Counsellor's Organization provided more than 300 young Native Americans with training in bird and animal lore, camp craft, Indian ceremonials, Indian art, expression, and history, as well as Native American contributions to general U.S. culture. Fadden's students also learned first aid and physical culture. Fadden also has prepared twenty-six pamphlets and forty-two charts detailing Iroquois history as part of the Six Nations Museum Series.

Much of Ray Fadden's life and those of his wife and family has been dedicated to fighting degradation of the environment in the Adirondack Mountains, their home. Fadden says that acid rain and other pollutants are destroying the abundance and variety of life in the forest. "If you kill the forest life, you kill your own grandchildren," Fadden says (Ray Fadden, interview).

To many of his former students, Ray Fadden is a living legend. "He was father, grandfather, teacher [and] friend to three generations of Mohawks," said Ron LaFrance, a Mohawk and a former student of Fadden (LaFrance, interview). Stephen Fadden, a member of Ray Fadden's family, wrote:

The Indians, an average American knew, were silver-screen caricatures in John Wayne movies, knife in mouth, tomahawk in hand. Ray Fadden dared to rail against those images at a time when it was not chic to be Indian. . . . Visits by busloads of Indian and white children have been a common occurrence every summer [at the Six Nations Indian Museum] since 1953 [when it first opened]. Counted among the young children are grandparents who call Ray "uncle." His influence touches three generations of Haudenosaunee children. (Stephen Fadden, 43)

FURTHER READING

Fadden, Ray. Interview with Bruce Johansen. Onchiota, N.Y., June 2, 1990.
Fadden, Stephen. "Response." *Northeast Indian Quarterly* 7:1 (Spring 1990): 43–44.

LaFrance, Ron. Interview with Bruce Johansen. Albany, N.Y., October 4, 1993.
Whitaker, Robert. "Akwesasne Seek to Rebuild a Nation." *Plattsburgh* [New York]
     Press-Republican, January 15, 1989: 1.

Fenton, William N., b. 1908. William N. Fenton, who is called the "dean of
Iroquois studies" by many of his students, has had an influence that one observer
believes "has been felt by virtually every student of the Iroquois over the past
four decades" (Foster, Campisi, and Mithun, xiii). Fenton parlayed contacts with
Seneca informants into a career of federal employment, grants, books, and papers beginning during the 1930s. With the rise of Native American legal and
political assertion late in the twentieth century, however, Fenton lost his ties to
most contemporary Haudenosaunee, who thought that he had betrayed them by
publishing photos of sacred **Grandfather** (False Face) masks. Until political
context left him no other alternative, Fenton also opposed **repatriation** of Haudenosaunee **wampum** belts.

The Fenton family farm in New York's Conewango Valley lay between the
Cattaraugus and **Allegany** Seneca reservations. For many generations before
Fenton was born, his family had hosted Senecas passing through the area on
hunting expeditions. Fenton attended Dartmouth College, where he obtained a
bachelor's degree, and Yale University, where he earned his doctorate, studying
with Clark Wissler.

In 1935, Fenton became a Bureau of Indian Affairs fieldworker among the
Senecas during the administration of John Collier (director of the Bureau of
Indian Affairs under Franklin Delano Roosevelt), where he laid the basis of
personal relationships that supplied him access afforded few other non-Indians
at the time. Much of Fenton's life (excepting a few years of college teaching)
has been spent in government employment, including work with the BIA, the
Smithsonian Institution's Bureau of American Ethnology, and the National Research Council. During World War II, Fenton spent most of the war on the
home front as a gatherer of information for naval intelligence on the aboriginal
peoples of the South Pacific war zone. From 1954 to 1968, Fenton worked with
the New York State Museum in Albany; after that, he was appointed distinguished professor of anthropology at the State University of New York at Albany.

Many anthropologists, including Fenton, lost considerable political capital
with the Haudenosaunee by failing to recognize and respect their political and
social revival during the last half of the twentieth century. Fenton, acting as an
executive officer of the New York State Museum in Albany, argued that the
Iroquois would not be able to properly maintain or respect the wampum belts,
an opinion that angered many Haudenosaunee.

In 1971, Fenton lobbied actively to defeat a proposed New York State law
that would have returned twenty-six belts to the confederacy at Onondaga. The
bill passed one house of the New York State legislature before Fenton threw

his considerable professional influence against it. He argued that the confederacy was a historical dead letter, much to the chagrin of the peoples who still maintained its traditions. Fenton also argued, incorrectly, that the "chance of any Iroquois reading their original intent is nil" (Barreiro, 16). When the Haudenosaunee said that they needed their belts for religious reasons, Fenton criticized their "illusion of religiosity" (Barreiro, 16).

Fenton widened the gap between himself and living Iroquois by publishing photographs of False Face (Grandfather) masks in a book, violating a prohibition against photographing the ritual masks. Living Iroquois also scolded Fenton for acts of insensitivity such as naming a drinking session at the annual Iroquois Studies conference near Albany after one of their most important medicine societies, the Little Water Company. At the actual Little Water Ceremony, alcohol is strictly forbidden.

By 1990, the Iroquois were demanding return of their belts at the same time that a national clamor was beginning to rise from many Indian peoples over the return from museums of human remains and funeral objects. Fenton then stoked the coals of Haudenosaunee anger even hotter by criticizing the beloved Mohawk culture bearer **Ray Fadden**, founder of the Six Nations Indian Museum at Onchiota, New York. In a book review, Fenton paternalistically lectured Fadden and the Grand Council's chiefs on the proper treatment of their own history: "Iroquois do not take kindly to misuse of time-honored customs and rituals. Ray Fadden's use of the 'Fourteen Strings' of wampum as a vehicle for castigating writers about Indians violates the sensibilities of Longhouse people" (Fenton, Review, 59). At about the same time, Fenton added another log to the fire of Iroquois anger by taking credit for the return of the wampum belts that he had earlier tried to keep locked in the state archives.

The Ray Fadden essay to which Fenton reacted, "Fourteen Strings of Purple Wampum to Writers about Indians" (Bruchac, 97–98), did not name him. Fenton may have been reacting to the title of the essay or to the first two sentences: "We hold in our hand fourteen strings of purple wampum. These we hand, one by one, to you—authors of many American history books, writers of cheap, inaccurate, unauthentic, sensational novels, and other writers of fiction who have poisoned the minds of young Americans concerning our people" (Bruchac, 97).

During the 1990s, Fenton had a change of heart regarding his cache of Haudenosaunee cultural resources. In 1993, Oneida singer **Joanne Shenandoah** located a number of Iroquois songs archived under his copyright at the University of Indiana. When Shenandoah asked Fenton to obtain copies of these recordings, he refused. Shenandoah then asked to meet with him personally to explain why she wanted the recordings. Fenton agreed to meet with Shenandoah in May 1993. During that meeting, Shenandoah told Fenton that the Iroquois needed access to their traditional music for cultural survival. Fenton was impressed by Shenandoah's sincerity and agreed to consider the request. One week later, Shenandoah received written notice that Fenton had given her blanket permission to obtain any or all recordings of his material. Round Dance Productions, of which Shenandoah is a cofounder, has the largest collection of traditional Iroquois music today.

FURTHER READING

Barreiro, José. "Return of the Wampum." *Northeast Indian Quarterly* 7:1 (Spring 1990): 8–30.
Bruchac, Joseph, ed. *New Voices from the Longhouse*. Greenfield Center, N.Y.: Greenfield Review Press, 1989.
Fadden, Stephen. "Response." *Northeast Indian Quarterly* 7:1 (Spring 1990): 43–44.
Fenton, William N. *The False Faces of the Iroquois*. Norman: University of Oklahoma Press, 1987.
————. *The Great Law and the Longhouse: A Political History of the Iroquois Confederacy*. Norman: University of Oklahoma Press, 1998.
————. "The Hiawatha Wampum Belt of the Iroquois League for Peace." In *Men and Cultures: Selected Papers of the Fifth International Congress of Anthropological and Ethnological Sciences, Philadelphia, September 1–9, 1956*. Philadelphia: University of Pennsylvania Press, 1960.
————. "The New York State Wampum Collection: The Case for the Integrity of Cultural Treasures." *Proceedings of the American Philosophical Society* 115:6 (1971): 437–461.
————. [Review of *New Voices from the Longhouse*, by Joseph Bruchac.] *Northeast Indian Quarterly* 6:4 (Winter 1989): 59.
————. *Roll Call of the Iroquois Chiefs*. Washington, D.C.: Smithsonian Institution, 1950.
————. "Seth Newhouse's Traditional History and Constitution of the Iroquois Confederacy." *Proceedings of the American Philosophical Society* 93:2 (1949): 141–158.
————. ed. *Parker on the Iroquois*. Syracuse, N.Y.: Syracuse University Press, 1968.
Foster, Michael K., Jack Campisi, and Marianne Mithun, eds. *Extending the Rafters: Interdisciplinary Approaches to Iroquoian Studies*. Albany: State University of New York Press, 1984.

Fire [Ice], Jake [John] (Mohawk), d. 1899. The shooting deaths of Mathew Pyke and "Junior" Edwards at **Akwesasne** on May 1, 1990, created an ironic coincidence. May 1 had been declared a national **Mohawk** holiday in 1985 by the Canadian Mohawk Council of Akwesasne in memory of Jake Fire, who was shot and killed at 4 A.M., May 1, 1899, by a contingent of Canadian Dominion Police as Fire was protesting the imposition by Canada of the band system mandated by the Indian Advancement Act of 1884.

In 1898, the Clan Mothers of Akwesasne had written to Canada's governor general, contending that the Mohawks' traditional political system suited them, and that they did not wish to change it. In March 1899, a contingent of Royal Canadian Mounted Police arrived on the Canadian side of Akwesasne to enforce the change of governments. A crowd of 200 Mohawks caused them to retreat, but the police returned two months later. On May 1, 1899, the police occupied the traditionals' Council House and summoned the chiefs to a meeting. Seven who arrived were thrown to the ground and handcuffed.

Jake Fire, who was head chief, heard of the arrests and demanded the chiefs' release. When he arrived at the Council House, Fire was shot twice and killed. "This," observed Mohawk culture bearer **Ray Fadden**, "[was] the way Canada introduced our people to the principles of their democracy" (Fadden, interview).

Canadian records express some confusion over whether the man the Mounties killed was named Jake Fire or Jake Ice. According to Akwesasne historian Salli Benedict, Jake Fire was one of two brothers, Jacob and John Fire. John, who was often called Jake, had a Mohawk name that referred to ice, so he was sometimes called "Jake Ice" to distinguish him from his brother Jacob Fire (Wright, 374 n.10).

FURTHER READING

Fadden, Ray. Interview with Bruce Johansen. Onchiota, N.Y., June 2, 1990.
Wright, Ronald. *Stolen Continents*. Boston: Houghton Mifflin, 1992.

The First Epoch of Time: Creation Keepings. Iroquoian history falls into three main epochs: Creation, in the First Epoch; the **Great Law of Peace**, in the **Second Epoch**; and **Handsome Lake**, in the **Third Epoch of Time** (the present epoch). This entry concerns the First Epoch, whose main actors are the First Family: Sky Woman, her daughter, the Lynx, and her grandsons, Sapling and Flint. If the inceptions of the Second and Third Epochs can be dated to the twelfth and late eighteenth centuries, respectively, the Epoch of Creation began unimaginably long ago, well before the last ice age, a period mentioned in Creation tradition.

What Creation Was Not: Christian Interpolations

Recounting the tradition of Creation is no simple feat, and not merely due to its antiquity. The culturally destructive activities of the Christian missionaries suppressed or distorted much of its original content. They started tinkering with the tradition in the sixteenth century, believing that their call to proselytize justified bringing the Iroquoian Creation story into line with Christian theological themes that were alien to it. The heavy hand of European sexism also degraded the original.

The main warps were twofold. First, the important story of the strong female bond between the First Woman and her Daughter was downplayed or ignored, while the lengthy tradition of the First Woman's childhood, youth, and early adulthood in Sky World was excised. First Woman was eventually transformed from a strong female role model into a haggard old witch who dangerously favored her "evil" grandson. Some postmissionary versions omitted the story of the Daughter altogether, compressing her tale into First Woman's, so that it was she who bore the eventual male Twins (Converse, 33–34). It is possible that this slimming down was aided by missionary attempts to pull this cycle of the

Creation story into agreement with Christian fables, which could accommodate one, but not two, mother figures. Overall, much of the tampering worked to emphasize male over female content.

Second, the story of the male Twins (originally quadruplets) was exaggerated into the main body of the tradition, and its meaning was transformed to be theologically more useful to the missionaries. The original meaning of the twins/quadruplets—cosmic balance as displayed in the cardinal directions—was twisted into the dualistic brief for Christian Manicheanism, that is, the portrayal of two hostile spirits, one good and one evil, locked in eternal battle for control of the world.

The Twins, Sapling and Flint, were not, in fact, displaying good versus evil. They illustrate the cosmic balance of spirit elements. In their original context, the boys balanced one another out, *uki* (Sapling) to *otkon* (Flint). Sapling was more apparently beneficial to human beings because he was more solicitous of their comfort. By contrast, his little brother was likely to pull practical jokes on them. In the most ancient versions, Flint was what Western anthropologists like to call a "trickster figure," a powerful spirit with a sense of humor and an immature lack of patience. He often displayed childishly poor judgment, lack of foresight, and, at times, a mean streak. He might show up in times of crisis— indeed, he might well *be* the crisis—although he also might help out. Sapling was more predictably saccharine and therefore safer for human beings to deal with. In a way, the Twins embodied the certainty-uncertainty principle, but each was necessary to balance out the excesses of the other.

The missionaries bent all this to their own agenda. If Flint was soon cast as Satan, Sapling took a few centuries longer to transmute into *the* Creator. As **Arthur Parker** noted, "Strangely . . . it was the Thunder god," not Sapling, who first "metamorphosed" into the equivalent of the Christian God (Parker, *Myths*, 10). It was only with the relatively recent founding of the Longhouse Religion by Sganyadaí:yoh (Handsome Lake) that Sapling was transformed into "*the* Creator," a monodeity reminiscent of the Christian God. Although the Long-house Religious tradition has many modern adherents, some modern Iroquois believe that all such Christian interpolations should be identified and discarded from the Keepings (oral traditions).

Unfortunately, much of this alien content was accepted as authentic by nineteenth- and twentieth-century Euro-scholars, whose collected versions of the Creation tradition contained many blatantly Euro-Christian interpolations. In sorting through the record, then, it is important for the reader to remember that the "Native informants" who were willing to speak to Euro-scholars were usu-ally the most culturally assimilated people, and their versions of Creation re-flected this fact. For example, David Cusick, who came from a family infamous among the Haudenosaunee for converting to Christianity, backed the missionary terms of "Good Mind" and "Evil Mind" into his allusions to Sapling and Flint, respectively (Beauchamp, 2). A pure misrepresentation, this bald-faced interpolation was picked up by later Longhouse writers such as Jesse Cornplanter and is now widely circulated in scholarly lore as authentic.

On the level of stray detail, missionaries tweaked the story so that it seemed to accommodate their own teachings. For instance, they began Creation not with the courtship of First Woman's mother, but with the handy Fall of First Woman to earth, a revision that allowed for proselytizing discussions of *man's* supposed Fall, as told by Christians. Elsewhere, Sky World was reinterpreted as a crude version of Christian heaven, rather than a discrete, physical place traveling among the stars and inhabited by long-lived but not immortal Sky People. The missionaries created concepts from whole cloth whenever they felt it necessary. Thus was the concept of Hell, which had been completely absent from Iroquoian thought, engineered into the tradition by the missionaries. The Christian story of Adam's rib even made a brief appearance, as did the Eden story in some postmissionary versions of Creation (Hewitt, Part 1, 211, 321; Barbeau, 49).

What Creation Was

The actual tradition of Creation was largely a domestic tale of bonding and balance, featuring women and their children learning to survive by adapting to a new and puzzling environment. Much of Creation was very sad, speaking of great emotional loss and tragedy, with courage and perseverance ultimately prevailing.

The tradition also spoke eloquently of the special brand of Iroquoian spirituality that deals with the positive spirit energy of *uki* or *ugi* (called **orenda** by **J. N. B. Hewitt**), which is balanced out by the negative spirit energy of *otgont* or *otkon*. These spirit powers should be recognized as bonded pairs. They should not be separated from each other's influence and certainly not conflated with the Christian Manichean dichotomy. Creation involved accident, recklessness, and madness, but no satanic evil; there was also forethought, responsibility, and clarity, but no Jehovan godliness. Nothing that was done could not be undone. Everything was mediated. Creation was the cooperative effort of many spirits.

All of the Iroquoian nations, including the nonleague Iroquois, kept the Creation story. It varied somewhat in the telling, depending upon the nation and the Keeper, but the outlines of events were the same, moving from Sky World to Earth in a symphony of creative crescendos that bequeathed a functioning spirituality to the Iroquoian peoples.

Creation Keepings

The original ancestors of the Iroquois were the Sky People, denizens of Karionake, "The Place in the Sky," commonly called Sky World, a physical place that floated among the stars "on the farther side of the visible sky" ("Mohawk Creation Story," 32; Hewitt, Part 1, 141). Sky World was well populated, with a social order that greatly resembled later Iroquoian society. The people lived in close-knit, matrilineal clans. The Sky People were greatly gifted with *uki-otkon* power. In a **Mohawk** Keeping, it is said that the Sky People "had greatly developed what scientists call E.S.P." ("Mohawk Creation Story," 32), a talent later valued by their earth descendants, especially for tapping into dream knowledge. The geography of Sky World resembled that of Iroquoia too, with trees, crops, and **longhouses**. All of the flora and fauna later present in physical form on earth had spiritual counterparts (Elder Siblings) preexisting in Sky World. These animal spirit elders took part in Sky councils and performed creative tasks (Barbeau, 41–44; Hewitt, Part 2, 465).

In the center of Sky World grew a wonderful tree that, running the length of Sky World, held it together, from top to bottom. Some say that it was a wild cherry tree, others call it a crab-apple tree, while still others call it a pilar. The Tuscaroras call it a dogwood tree. An **Onondaga** version named the tree *Ono' 'djă* or "Tooth," presumably indicating the yellow dog-tooth violet. The tree itself was sacred, supplying food that the Sky People might gather—it sprouted from the sides and fell to the ground to be collected, just for the thinking. Tooth gave off a sweet odor. Some say that it was the fragrance of burning tobacco, while others describe it as the perfume of flowers. A bright orb sat at the top of Tooth. Its whiteness gave off the light of Sky World, a luminance that was never full or bright light but, instead, a perpetual half-light resembling the dawn or the dusk. The Councils of Sky World were held beneath the branches of Tooth (Hewitt, Part 1, 151, 282; "Mohawk Creation Story," 32; Converse, 32).

Several traditions speak of the conception, birth, childhood, and youth of the girl who was to become Sky Woman, also called Awenhai (Fertile Earth), Ataensic (Mature Flowers), Otsitsa (Corn), and, eventually, Iagentci (Ancient One, or Grandmother). Sky Woman's mother dallied with a man she did not actually love, enticing him daily by "disentangling" his hair. ("Combing out the hair" was a metaphor for interpreting dreams, part of making them true. It was a spiritual talent.) This unfortunate man, the father of Sky Woman, died before she was born and was "buried" high in the tree of Sky World. His was the first death ever to occur in Sky World, a spirit sign. Sky Woman grew up quickly (another sign of spirit power), in constant mourning for the father she never knew, prompting her grandmother to show her where her father had been buried (Hewitt, Part 1, 141–149, 256–265).

In another version, the deceased was not a sperm father, but the girl's maternal uncle (Hewitt, Part 2, 470). This cultural tidbit seems authentically old, since the mother's matrilineal brother, not an out-clan biological father, was traditionally the male authority figure of a longhouse and was often called "father."

As a girl, Sky Woman took to climbing high in the tree of Sky World to visit her father's coffin. Eventually, she learned how to hold spirit conversations with her deceased father. During one conversation, his spirit advised her on whom to marry, although the relationship did not seem very auspicious. The husband-to-be was a nasty, cruel, jealous, and (in many versions) very old man who put her through hard endurance tests to prove her worth. He made her carry extremely heavy burdens, which seemed light to her strength. In one particularly violent episode kept by both the Mohawks and the Onondagas, he forced her to cook **corn** mush and disrobe, after which he flung the scalding mush at her until it covered her naked flesh, then set his dogs on her to lick off her burnt skin. One Onondaga version stated that she "did fortify her mind against it, and so she did not flinch from it." In another version, her father's spirit had forewarned her of the corn-mush ordeal, cautioning her to endure it with courage and in silence (Hewitt, Part 1, 157–163, 276–279 [quote, 161]; Hewitt, Part 2, 474).

These tests proved her mettle. A woman of lesser stamina and mental composure could not have carried out the work before her. Although she did not yet know her destiny as the First Woman of Earth, Sky Woman completely trusted her father's spiritual foreknowledge of it and therefore, on his advice, married this cruel man. Converse recorded that it was Sky Woman's mission and fate, though unknown to her, to bring life to Earth (Converse, 33).

Sky Woman's husband is usually called the Ancient. She was soon with child through the sharing of breath with her husband (Hewitt, Part 1, 167). In one **Seneca** version, Sky Woman gave birth to her child in Sky World, but this seems anomalous (Hewitt, Part 1, 223). In nearly every other collected version, she was pregnant when she arrived on Earth, delivering her daughter there.

The Ancient was the presiding officer of Sky World and lodged in the shade of Tooth, thus earning the personal name of Hodä´'he' nä´ie' ne'´ Ono'´djä' or "He Who Has the Standing Tree Called Tooth" (Hewitt, Part 1, 165). The Ancient is also popularly called De'hao^n'hwěñdjiawä'´kho^n' or Te'hao^n'hwěñdjaiwä'´kho^n' meaning "He Holds the Earth" or "The Earth-Grasper" (Hewitt, Part 2, 464; Parker, *Myths*, 5). The Earth-Grasper had ultimate power over the Earth, although he did not often interfere with its operation.

Dreams were very important to the Sky People. It was necessary to reenact them, thus continually creating reality. One day, the Ancient had a troubling dream that rendered him ill. In a Seneca version, he had dreamed that a great "cloud sea" swam around under Tooth, the ocean of a restless and unlit world. Its spirit was calling out to the Sky People for aid in overcoming its extreme loneliness (Converse, 33). The Ancient needed his advisors to catch this dream. In an Onondaga version, he called a dream feast to do so. The feast was attended by many of the elder spirits of earth creatures, along with Aurora Borealis, a presence that often interacted with Sky People (Hewitt, Part 1, 173–176). In most versions, the Ancient's advisors saw what was needed to fulfill his dream: to pull up the great tree of Sky World, opening up the magnificent vista on the water world—Earth. "We will talk to it," said the Ancient, thus to relieve its loneliness. He ordered Tooth uprooted and, once this was done, its roots pointed to earth, showing the Sky People the way there. This is why the "floating island" (Earth) was said to have been created by the Ancient's dream (Converse, 31, 33).

All of the elders of the later plants and animals, as well as the heavenly bodies and elements associated with earth, came to peer over the edge at the water world. Deer, Spotted Fawn, Bear, Beaver, the Moving Wind, Daylight, Night,

Thick Night, the Sun, Spring Water, Corn, Beans, Squash, Sunflower, Fire Dragon, Meteor, Rattle, Otter, Wolf, Duck, Fresh Water, Medicine, Aurora Borealis, and, of course, the Great Turtle visited the window onto Earth (Hewitt, Part 1, 173–175). Some add that the Blue Sky, the Air, the Thunderers, the Tree, the Bush, the Grass, the Moon, the Star, and the Sun looked as well (Hewitt, Part 2, 473). The hole at the base of Tooth became a regular Sky World tourist destination.

Having uprooted the tree, the Ancient was thus able to fulfill the second part of his dream, that his wife was to fall through the hole in Sky World down to the water world below. Occasionally, it is said that she fell because of her own curiosity, having leaned too far over the edge for a better look at Earth (Parker, *Myths*, 6). Some Wyandot Keepings depict the illness as Sky Woman's, not the Ancient's, stating that to cure her, an aged shaman uprooted the tree and laid Sky Woman as near as possible to its medicinal roots—too near, as it turned out, for, the soil being unstable, the sick girl was sucked down into the hole and rolled into the void (Barbeau, 37). In yet another variant, this one Mohawk, her husband was considerate, not cruel, and gathered the living bark of Tooth for tea to calm the cravings of his pregnant wife. It was his kind deed that caused the Sky tree to collapse, opening the window onto Earth below and occasioning her slip ("Mohawk Creation Story," 32).

Most Haudenosaunee keep the version of the bad-tempered Ancient, however, attributing Sky Woman's tumble to his jealousy. In several versions, the Ancient was irrationally jealous of the Aurora Borealis, the Fire Dragon, and, especially, of Sky Woman, who was more gifted with *uki-otkon* than he. His obsession only grew with her pregnancy, which he doubted was his doing, "his bones having become dried" (Hewitt, Part 1, 178; quote, 221). In a fit of rage, he forced his wife to sit on the edge of the pit, with her legs dangling dangerously into it. Sometimes he is said to have grabbed her by one leg and tossed her over; other times he is said to have seized her by the nape of the neck and shoved; in an even more chilling account, as she sat peering into the abyss, he calmly pressed his two fingers onto the back of her neck and pushed (Hewitt, Part 1, 178, 223, 283–284).

Many traditions have Sky Woman grabbing wildly at the roots of the upended Tooth in a doomed effort to prevent her fall. Although she was unable to climb back up the ledge, she did get ahold of seeds from the munificent tree. In her right hand, she garnered the **Three Sisters**, Corn, Beans, and Squash. Some say that she also laid hold of Tobacco in her left hand. A Seneca version claimed that the white Fire Dragon or the Blue Panther—an *otkon* spirit jealously sought after by the Ancient—was at the root hole just as Sky Woman fell. In this version, it was the Blue Panther who gave her Corn, mortar, and pestle (Hewitt, Part 1, 224; Part 2, 481; Cornplanter, 9, 13). Jesse Cornplanter said that it was the Ancient himself who threw the Elder Plants—Corn, Beans, Squash, Sunflower, and Tobacco—along with the Elder Animals—Deer, Wolf, Bear, Beaver, and others—down the abyss after her in a final frenzy of rage (Cornplanter, 10).

In all versions, however, she slid down, down, down through space and into the atmosphere of Earth. (The suggestion of tradition is that the strong spirit of Sky Woman's father had foreseen all of these events, so necessary to the beginning of human life on Earth, and that this was why he had urged his daughter on to such an unfortunate marriage, with all of its character-building trials and tribulations.) Sick of the disruption in Sky World, upon her fall through the hole in Sky World, the Sky People set Tooth, the Tree of Light, back into its socket (Hewitt, Part 2, 480).

Now the Elder Creatures of Earth, alerted first by the farsighted Eagle, saw Sky Woman falling. For the first time, lightning (the Fire Dragon, or Meteor Man) streaked across the sky of Earth at her side as she hurtled through the atmosphere (Parker, *Seneca Myths*, 6). Sweeping into action, Heron and Loon caught and held the frightened Sky Woman aloft on their interlocking wings while, in an amusing portion of the tradition, the Great Tortoise sent around a moccasin, that is, he called an emergency council of Elder Animals to see what was to be done. (For a sprightly Wyandot version of the Elder Animals' Creation Council, see Barbeau, 38–44.) Knowing that she was a Sky Woman, unable to live on their watery planet, the Elder Spirits of Earth creatures all quickly agreed that she should not be dropped into the waters to die.

In one Seneca version, the Earth Elders were afraid that Sky Woman might injure Earth if she was allowed to fall unimpeded (Converse, 33). In another Seneca version, councilmanic discussion centered on who would be food for her, a pressing and unpleasant question. Bass volunteered his aid directly, leading the others to observe tartly that "thou hast no sense" (Hewitt, Part 1, 225). In a Wyandot version, Tooth itself had plummeted through its own hole ahead of Sky Woman, crashing into the ocean. This gave the animals the idea of diving down to the bottom of the sea for whatever dirt might have clung to its sacred roots (Barbeau, 38).

In every version, however, the great Snapping Turtle offered his carapace, vowing to carry the Earth above him forever as he swam. The idea gained ready assent, and the council of Earth Elders assembled its divers. Usually, the divers were said to have been Muskrat, Otter, Toad, and/or Beaver. In some versions, the Muskrat and Otter die in the attempt to bring up dirt in their mouths, with Beaver finally bringing it up on his tail, or Toad in his mouth. A Mohawk version has poor, dead Muskrat floating to the surface, his mouth smeared with the dirt that was to become Earth (Hewitt, Part 1, 287). A Seneca version says that it was Sky Woman herself who arrived with the dirt of Sky World on her hands and under her fingernails, gathered as she frantically clutched at the tree roots during her fall (Hewitt, Part 1, 226). Because a tad of dirt was now ready to accept her, the Birds were able to set Sky Woman down on her new abode, **Turtle Island**. Looking around forlornly, alone and torn from everything she had ever known, Sky Woman wept bitterly (Hewitt, Part 1, 225).

However the original dirt of Earth was garnered, in all versions it was spread rapidly and fluidly across the willing back of Turtle (a sign of spirit power). The animals first helped stamp the dirt out to the edges of Turtle's shell, but

Sky Woman also walked across the back of Turtle, the dirt racing ahead of her in plains and hills, as far as the eye could see. Sky Woman's *uki* talents helped the Earth increase in its size. She sang medicine chants as she walked in ever-increasing circles, spreading the dirt before her until it turned into the great land mass of Turtle Island ("Mohawk Creation Story," 29). Some versions add that at this point, Sky Woman also named the constellations, the sun, and the moon, as well as the wind, and anointed the animals of the Earth (Hewitt, Part 1, 227–228).

Wherever Sky Woman went, every kind of plant sprouted up before her. Now she planted the Three Sacred Sisters she had brought from Sky World. Some say that she found potatoes here (Hewitt, Part 1, 226), although potatoes are usually attributed to the little daughter soon born to her on Turtle Island. The land was full with the harvest, on which Sky Woman lived (although she occasionally took Bass up on his offer). As the land was full of growth, so was Sky Woman. She prepared her birthing hut and delivered herself of an infant daughter. They were at that time the only two human beings on Earth.

Like her mother before her, the Daughter, the Lynx (whom some call Hanging Flowers), grew quickly, showing that she, too, possessed a large measure of spirit power. Both Sky Woman and the Lynx communicated easily with the animals of Earth ("Mohawk Creation Story," 29). In those days, Sky Woman seated herself beneath a large tree and sent her daughter out daily to see the Earth and bring back news of what wonders it bore (Tooker, 38, 51). For all her travels, the daughter had never yet seen a man and yearned for a sort of companionship she had not known.

Her favorite playground was a large tree, with a heavy vine, on which she leaned in dreamy delight. A Seneca version showed her encountering the (North or West) Wind, which impregnated her with his breath (Hewitt, Part 1, 229). In Onondaga and other Seneca versions, she was successively courted by seductive, shape-shifting Earth Elder spirits proposing marriage to her. To each, the Lynx dutifully responded, "Not until I first ask my mother" (Cornplanter, 12–13; Hewitt, Part 2, 483–484).

Sky Woman continually refused the Earth Elders as consorts of her daughter until one day, the matter passed out of her hands. An engaging man-creature came along, his bark robe tossed rakishly over his shoulder, his black hair pulled up, and his handsome eyes gleaming. He was so gorgeous that the Lynx forgot to ask her mother, but lay with him immediately. Some assert that the two did not engage in coitus, but that the young man simply lay an arrow next to her body (Hewitt, Part 1, 291–292). In an Onondaga version, Sky Woman consented to, rather than resisted, this final match (Hewitt, Part 2, 384–385), but most versions showed Sky Woman to have been dismayed by the Lynx's unauthorized infatuation.

Young love won out, however, and soon the Lynx was pregnant, a fact that caused her mother to tremble. Sky Woman was fearful of the result of a pregnancy between two such different creatures as a Sky Girl and an Earth Man-

Being. In the very oldest Keepings of Creation, the Lynx was pregnant, not with twins (the common Keeping today), but with quadruplets, analogous to the four sacred messengers of the *Gaiwí:yo* (the Code of Handsome Lake) and connected with the Four Winds, or cardinal directions (Hewitt, Part 2, 468). An interesting potential echo of this ancient Keeping is found in a Seneca version that told the puzzling story of four children—two male and two female—who were Man-Beings (Hewitt, Part 1, 233). The story of the quadruplets, however, is almost completely lost today. The four children of the Lynx were eventually compressed down into two, with the personality traits of the four being redistributed between them.

As told in modern times, the Lynx overheard twin sons in her womb discussing their plans for the Earth life they were about to live. One already knew that he was to create game animals and new trees, but the other was more vague on specifics, merely announcing that he, too, would create, in one way or another (Hewitt, Part 2, 486). Labor pains overcame the Lynx a few days before her time, and she again overheard her sons holding forth, this time in a discussion over how best to be born, for neither of them precisely knew how to do it. In an Onondaga version, one infant pointed toward the birth canal and said, "I'll go that way"; and he did, being first born. The Elder Twin became known as Tharonhiawakon, Odendonnia, or Ioskaha ("Sapling"), meaning, roughly, the Spirit of Life (Hewitt, Part 1, 138). Sapling was perfectly formed, in the eyes of Sky Woman.

The Younger Twin protested his brother's path. "But this other way is so near," he said, pointing in some versions to the armpit and in others to the navel of his mother. "I shall leave that way," he said, and he did, killing his mother in parturition (Hewitt, Part 1, 185). Some Mohawks say that the second son, Tawiskaron[n] ("Flint") was born with a comb of flint on his head, by which means he had cut an exit path through his mother's armpit (Hewitt, Part 1, 185). Some Senecas say that he leapt forth from her navel, all covered with warts (Hewitt, Part 1, 231).

However it happened, by armpit or caesarian section, when Sky Woman saw that her beloved daughter was dead, she sat on the ground and wept inconsolably. She buried her daughter most tenderly, and from the Lynx's grave sprang all the plants of life: Corn, Beans, and Squash grew from her breasts, potatoes sprang from her toes, and tobacco grew from her head (Thomas). The Lynx had transmitted into Mother Earth, a living entity (Hewitt, Part 2, 542). Despite the continued spirit existence of her daughter, Sky Woman's grief almost undid her. It was then that Sky Woman grew suddenly old, becoming known in her turn as the Ancient, or Grandmother. Her grief soured into a bitterness of temperament that she had not possessed before. She became grumpy and impatient in her old age.

It finally came to Sky Woman that she was left alone to care for the infants of her deceased child. In some versions, she played favorites with the Twins, though the object of her affection altered. In Onondaga and Mohawk versions, also told by **Cayuga** chief **Jake Thomas**, Grandmother demanded of the Twins to know which of them had killed his mother. Flint immediately piped up with the lie that Sapling had done it, and, in the bitterness of her spirit, Grandmother threw Sapling away in the tall grass, keeping only Flint. It was only upon seeing the child still moving some time later that she took Sapling back in, although in some versions, he is doomed to live forever outside of her longhouse (Hewitt, Part 1, 186, 295). In other versions, however, Sky Woman was evenhanded with her grandsons (Hewitt, Part 2, 486; Barbeau, 44).

Like Sky Woman and the Lynx before them, the Twins grew rapidly, showing their great spirit power. They soon began to complete the process of Creation, although there were many disagreements between the brothers as to what final Creation should look like. While Sapling was bringing forth his trademark straw-berries, Flint was littering the landscape with brambles and briars. If Sapling created peaceful game animals, Flint responded with a spate of roaring, clawing, dangerous beasts.

At one point, in something of a snit, Flint trapped all of Sapling's sweet-natured animals in an underground cavern. Walking through the forest one day and noticing that all of his animals seemed to have gone, Sapling became concerned as to what might have befallen them. Finding their paw prints, he tracked them to the base of a mountain that Flint had put up. The tracks led inside the mountain. Annoyed, Sapling rolled aside the huge boulder with which Flint had sealed the entrance to his mountain cave and bid the animals to roam free again (Hewitt, Part 1, 195–197). As they passed before him out of their prison, Sapling was stunned to see some of the changes Flint had made in their forms, enlarging some, shrinking others, taking away legs here, or growing fangs there (Hewitt, Part 2, 525).

Interestingly, in one Seneca version, the Twins did not create the animals, but received them as a gift from their earthly father. Sapling brought them home in a knapsack and dumped its braying, noisy contents out on the longhouse floor. Grandmother came over to see what the commotion was. Upon spying the animals, she told the boys the names of each (Hewitt, Part 1, 235–238).

Flint is generally credited with calling down an ice age that brought with it dangerous, human-eating beasts. Sometimes he is said to have stamped his feet in a fit of pique, bringing on severe weather alerts. In a Mohawk version, Sapling found him one day fashioning a huge ice bridge that connected other land masses to Turtle Island. Sitting nearby, watching the progress of his work, was a gigantic bird with a human thigh dangling from its mouth. Suddenly noticing his annoyed elder brother bearing down upon him, Flint leapt up, dropped his work, and dashed across his ice bridge, with the vast carapace of ice and snow melting behind him as he ran (Hewitt, Part 1, 311–312; Part 2, 516).

Although most versions have Sky Woman bringing the vegetable food and creating the plants, some recent versions go so far as to give Sapling credit for bringing corn and inventing a way to pound it into meal and cook it (Hewitt, Part 1, 189–194). In a Seneca version, however, Sapling (or perhaps Flint) learned to cook by watching his grandmother. One morning, after she had gone outside, he cooked up his own mess of corn stew, having stolen his grand-mother's last store of corn meal to do so. His inconsiderate deed left her in want. When she saw what he had done, she began to cry, prompting his better nature to take over. He set out to repair the damage by looting the corn storage of a nearby family, thus resupplying his grandmother. Not yet easy over the matter, he went hunting early the next morning and bagged her a beaver (Hewitt, Part 1, 247–252).

Creation of the Sun, Moon, and Stars

The creation of the sun, moon, and stars is variously attributed to Sky Woman or Sapling. The oldest Wyandot and Onondaga versions give Sky Woman or the Elder Earth Animals credit for creating the sun, moon, and stars, especially the Milky Way (Barbeau, 41). A Seneca version has Sky Woman creating the heavens almost immediately after her arrival on Earth (Hewitt, Part 1, 226–227). Hewitt also recorded a Mohawk story of Grandmother using body parts of her dead Lynx as the material of the heavens (Hewitt, Part 1, 295–296), but the Lynx was emphatically Mother Earth in all versions, while the Moon is Grand-mother, leaving the origin of this version vague and questionable. Yet other versions, following the postmissionary trend of giving Sapling sole credit for Creation, showed him hanging the heavens, after the fashion of the Christian God (Hewitt, Part 1, 208; Part 2, 542–543).

One thing became immediately apparent in nearly every version of Creation: Flint was not nearly as skillful a creator as his brother. This was apparent not only in the animals that each brought forth, but in their attempts at creating humanity. Some say that whereas Sapling created humankind, Flint in a rival bout of creation only managed to bring forth monkeys (Barbeau, 51; Hewitt, Part 1, 214). Others contend that one day, Flint noticed that Sapling had made human beings. Marvelling at the feat, he sought to replicate it, going through inferior and unworkable models before he managed a viable version with the kindly advice of Sapling, who stopped by periodically to check on his little brother's progress.

Flint's first human was mostly made of water and therefore failed to breathe. On his second try, Flint added samples of his own mind, blood, spirit, and breath and finally succeeded in creating a living being, although his creation still lacked luster compared to Sapling's model. It is uncertain just what this creature was intended to have been in the older traditions—perhaps a bear—but after contact, the Iroquois quickly realized that Flint's water man was the European. By con-trast, Sapling had created the True Humans, or Native Americans (Hewitt, Part 2, 523–525; for a late version of Flint's creation of Europeans, see Parker, *Code*, 16–19).

In a story clearly showing missionary influence, Sapling took a rib from the male and inserted it into the female. This story nevertheless departed from the Christian story of Adam's rib in that Sapling also took a rib from the woman to insert into the man, thus making the two equal (Hewitt, Part 1, 211, 321). (The many tales of vision questers journeying to Sky World should be recalled here. The Sky People frequently took out the bones of questers, washed them, and returned them to their bodies in an improved condition. It is possible that the Keepers of the Adam's-rib version heard the missionary's own creation tale as a Sky Journey.)

Having created them, Sapling was greatly concerned for the comfort and ease of the Iroquoians. As a result, he created rivers with currents flowing in both directions, so that they might paddle easily in either direction. Flint, however, stopped by to correct his brother's overprotectiveness. He changed the river currents to flow in one direction only, so that people would always have to struggle in one direction, against the current (Hewitt, Part 1, 326–327). This story originally taught the principle of balance.

In older versions, De'hao^n'hwĕñdjiawă''kho$^{n'}$ (the Earth-Grasper), overseer of all, told Sapling that the good was maintained when Sapling and Flint "shall keep together, that continuously thou must watch him" (Hewitt, Part 2, 464, 554). The suggestion that Sapling stay close to Flint to spy on him was most probably a missionary interpolation. The two were to work together, like East and West, the respective directions with which Sapling and Flint are associated.

Numerous versions of Creation contain some version of the story of Hadu'´i'. As Sapling traveled about Turtle Island one day, he ran into a hunchbacked Earth spirit named Shagodiiwe$^{n'}$'gōwā or Hadu'´i' ("Whirlwind" or "Tornado"), who claimed to be the chief spirit of Earth (Parker, *Myths*, 6; Hewitt, Part 2, 468). The two fell into a dispute over who was the current "master" of the Earth. Hadu'´i' pointed out that he had arrived on Earth much earlier than the Sky People and had begun the project of Creation before they arrived. Sapling replied that although Hadu'´i' might have begun the job, he had finished it. To settle their dispute, the rivals staged a mountain-moving contest. Sapling won by bringing the mountain directly up behind Hadu'´i' while he was not looking. At that, Hadu'´i' capitulated to Sapling's greater mastery of Creation and agreed to be his assistant in the matter of managing humanity. He became closely connected with medicine. Because Hadu'´i' was simultaneously "full of orenda and even otgon," humanity would become afflicted with "mysterious ills" from which they could be cured by using medicine made from the spirit body of Hadu'´i' (Hewitt, Part 1, 197–200, 333–335; Part 2, 533–537). This became the founding story of the so-called False Face society.

Flint is often confused with Hadu'´i', and it is not impossible that the Hadu'´i' snippet represented a portion of one of the lost quadruplets' stories. Another possible quadruplet, complementary to the Wind, was the original Thunderer, Hï'´no$^{n'}$—not to be confused with the current Hawĕñi´o', the storm-related Thunderer of today. Hï'´no$^{n'}$ stood in *uki* relationship to the implied *otkon* of Hadu'´i', an *uki-otkon* relationship that paralleled the *uki-otkon* of Sapling and Flint (Parker, *Myths*, 8). This lost pair may well have been connected to the north-south axis. In what Keepings remain today, Hï'´no$^{n'}$ the

Thunderer, became an ally of Sapling. Like Hadu'´i', Hï'´no^n' possessed abilities similar to but lesser than Sapling's.

Some versions of Creation ended with a bowl game—sacred gambling with plum pits—to decide the fate of the creatures of the Earth. Originally, the game was only between the Twins, but later versions had Grandmother playing against Sapling along with Flint. As he had with Hadu'´i' and Hï'´no^n', Sapling won. In some versions, the victory allowed him to set up night and day (Hewitt, Part 2, 529–531; Parker, *Myths*, 9). The reference to the bowl game of fate is probably very old.

Perhaps as another result of having won the bowl game, some versions of the Creation tradition ended with Sapling sealing Flint into a cave in the bowels of the earth, resulting in Flint's being called Hanis'he´ono^n, meaning "He Who Dwells in the Earth" (Parker, *Myths*, 10; Converse, 36). Flint's final confinement in a cave was said to have come about in different ways. In one Seneca version, human beings of the *otkon* persuasion killed Flint. When Sapling found the body of his brother, he fell down and wept so piteously that the Sky itself seemed ready to crumble. The spirit of Flint, still very much on the scene, called out to his big brother not to grieve, for he had returned. Sapling told his brother's ghost that this could not be. It was time for Flint to "trail the tracks of her who was our mother," that is, to depart for the spirit realm (Hewitt, Part 1, 242–244).

More Missionary Influence

The influence of the missionaries becomes painfully obvious at the end of this otherwise-touching version, when Sapling described the afterlife to Flint as a split path. One road, he said, went to the God of the Christians—the "abode of His-word-is-master"—and the other, to their devil, "He-dwells-in-caves." Flint's "servants" were to dwell in caves forever. In another Christianized version from the Onondagas, the tradition ended when Sapling flung Flint down "to the bottom of the place where it is hot," binding him there by his hair (Hewitt, Part 1, quotes, 244; Part 2, 567). The trail in question was the Milky Way Trail, which splits visibly into two directions in the Sky. It was the missionaries who redefined the two destinations of the trail as the Christian heaven and hell, or the homes of His-word-is-master and He-dwells-in-caves, respectively. Originally, the Milky Way Trail, or spirit path to the stars, had no such connotations. It was viewed as the path home to Sky World (Hewitt, Part 1, 218).

An obviously older Mohawk version ended the tradition by showing the brothers engaged in a tit-for-tat spat that escalated into a lethal confrontation. The two lived together in a lean-to, one of whose sides was taller than the other. Flint dwelled at the shorter end, and Sapling, at the taller. One day, Sapling stoked their shared fire to perilous intensity, until it began to chip the chert from Flint's flinty legs. When his complaints did not persuade Sapling to lessen the flames, Flint saw that his brother meant him harm. He ran outside swiftly, looking for a cutting reed and a cattail spear, both of which he knew to be harmful to his brother. The fight then spiraled out of control, with the two furiously chasing each other all across Turtle Island, leaving huge chasms and water-filled depressions where their feet landed in their hurry. In this version, Sapling killed Flint, whose prone body transmuted into the Rocky Mountains. His spirit dwells to this day inside these mountains (Hewitt, Part 1, 328–332).

Flint was not permanently dead, however (Hewitt, Part 2, 547). All spirits continue to live, often in renewed bodies (Hewitt, Part 1, 218–219). Throughout Iroquoian history, Sapling continued reincarnating—most notably, as the Peacemaker in the Second Epoch—to aid his favorite creations, human beings, while the Lynx became Mother Earth and Grandmother became the smiling face of the Moon.

Flint runs in and out of history as well, most notably, whispering in the ear of Columbus and pointing out the way to Turtle Island. Flint did this out of boredom, thinking how funny it would be should the people run wild with rum, pursuing European trinkets and forgetting who they were. After he had brought the Europeans down upon the people, however, Flint repented, saying, "I think I have made an enormous mistake for I did not dream that these people would suffer so" (Parker, *Code*, 16–18).

FURTHER READING

Barbeau, C. M. *Huron and Wyandot Mythology with an Appendix Containing Earlier Published Records*. Canada, Geological Survey, Memoir 80; Anthropological Series, No. 11. Ottawa: Government Printing Bureau, 1915: 35–51.

Beauchamp, W[illiam] M[artin]. *The Iroquois Trail, or, Footprints of the Six Nations, in Customs, Traditions, and History*. Including David Cusick's "Sketches of Ancient History of the Six Nations." 1825. Fayetteville, N.Y.: H. C. Beauchamp, 1892.

Converse, Harriet Maxwell [Ya-ie-wa-noh]. *Myths and Legends of the New York State Iroquois*. Ed. Arthur Caswell Parker. New York State Museum Bulletin 125. Education Department Bulletin No. 437. Albany: University of the State of New York, 1908: 31–36.

Cornplanter, Jesse J. *Legends of the Longhouse*. 1938. Ed. William G. Spittal. Illust. J. J. Cornplanter. Ohsweken, Ontario: Iroqrafts, 1992.

Hewitt, John Napoleon Brinton. "Iroquoian Cosmology, First Part." In *Twenty-first Annual Report of the Bureau of American Ethnology to the Secretary of the Smithsonian Institution, 1899–1900*. Washington, D.C.: Government Printing Office, 1903: 127–339.

———. "Iroquoian Cosmology, Second Part." In *Forty-third Annual Report of the Bureau of American Ethnology to the Secretary of the Smithsonian Institution, 1925–1926*. Washington, D.C.: Government Printing Office, 1928: 453–819.

"The Mohawk Creation Story." *Akwesasne Notes* 21:5 (Spring 1989): 32–39.

Parker, Arthur C. *The Code of Handsome Lake, the Seneca Prophet*. New York State Museum Bulletin 163, Education Department Bulletin No. 530, November 1, 1912. Albany: University of the State of New York, 1913.

————. *Seneca Myths and Folk Tales*. Intro. William N. Fenton. Lincoln: University of
    Nebraska Press, 1989.
Thomas, Chief Jacob. "Creation." Pamphlet. Jake Thomas Learning Center.
Tooker, Elisabeth, ed. *Native North American Spirituality of the Eastern Woodlands:
    Sacred Myths, Dreams, Visions, Speeches, Healing Formulas, Rituals, and Cer-
    emonials*. New York: Paulist Press, 1979.

Fish Carrier (Ojageght) (Cayuga), fl. late 1700s. Fish Carrier was among a
minority of Iroquois chiefs who supported the patriot cause in the **American
Revolution**. He led forces that took part in the Wyoming Valley massacre
(1778) and the Battle of Newtown the following year. He worked during the
Revolutionary War to defuse tensions between the **Senecas**, who sided with the
British, and the **Oneidas**, allies of the Americans. In 1790, Fish Carrier signed
the Tioga Point Treaty in return for a tract of land and a peace medal from
George Washington. In 1794, he was present at the **Canandaigua Treaty** coun-
cil.

FURTHER READING

Johansen, Bruce E., and Donald A. Grinde, Jr. *The Encyclopedia of Native American
    Biography*. New York: Henry Holt, 1997.

Five Nations (and Six Nations), name derivation. The English colonists called
the Haudenosaunee Confederacy the Five Nations (Six Nations after the **Tuscaroras** joined between roughly 1700 and 1730). The term is derived from the
confederacy's federal structure, first of five nations (**Cayugas, Mohawks, Oneidas, Onondagas**, and **Senecas**), then six with the addition of the Tuscaroras.

Fort Stanwix Treaty (1768). During October and November of 1768, **Sir William Johnson** hosted a major treaty conference with the Haudenosaunee nations,
the Delawares, the Senecas of Ohio, the Shawnees, and others at Fort Stanwix,
near present-day Rome, New York. Substantial amounts of land were ceded by
the Six Nations, acting as agents for all the Indians, in negotiations with representatives of New Jersey, Pennsylvania, and Virginia. After the treaty was
negotiated, the British Crown told Johnson that he had taken too much land and
ordered some of it returned to the Indians. Boundaries were confirmed, and the
Coveneant Chain brightened.

Fort Stanwix Treaty (1784). The Treaty of Paris (1783), which contained the
terms of peace between Great Britain and the United States after the Revolutionary War, failed to mention the rights of the British government's Indian
allies. The Indian Committee of the Continental Congress submitted a report to
Congress in the fall of 1783 urging that the terms of peace include a demand
that the Indians surrender part of their country without compensation to the

United States (Fenton, 604). The New York Assembly proposed to expel all the **Mohawks, Onondagas, Cayugas**, and **Senecas**—the nations whose warriors had fought mostly for the British cause—from New York State (Fenton, 605). Even the **Tuscarora** and **Oneida** peoples, who had supported the American cause, were to be exiled to "vacant" Seneca lands in western New York under this plan.

U.S. officials met with representatives of the Six Nations at Fort Stanwix and concluded the war with a treaty. At these negotiations, the American representatives were very aggressive and insulting and even demanded hostages from the Indians. They insisted on land cessions that the delegates had not been empowered to grant and urged that the Indians were a conquered people and had thus forfeited their right to their lands (Fenton, 617–619).

Contrary to Haudenosaunee law and custom, the Indian representatives included very few peace chiefs. The Iroquois' side of the negotiations was conducted primarily by "warriors" who made land cessions that were not authorized by their national councils, including lands along Lake Erie, in Pennsylvania, and in Ohio (Fenton, 620). When the treaty was submitted to the Six Nations Grand Council, its terms were rejected. The treaty also was publicly rejected by the Six Nations council's spokespeople (Wallace, 152). At this treaty negotiation, **Cornplanter**, the spokesman for the warriors, separately negotiated a land cession with Pennsylvania that left him with land south of the New York border and a pension (Fenton, 820). **Red Jacket** later used this information to destroy Cornplanter's reputation.

The humiliation suffered by the Iroquois warriors at Fort Stanwix was not lost on the western Indians. The New York Iroquois were exposed to the expansionist ambitions of the new United States, but the Indians in the Ohio region were determined that they would not suffer the same fate as their Iroquois brethren. The United States pressed its conquest theory at the Treaty of Fort McIntosh with the Delawares and Wyandots in January 1785 and at the Treaty at the Mouth of the Great Miami with the Shawnees in February 1786 (Sword 41). The first meeting of the new western confederacy took place in Detroit in the autumn of 1785 (Wallace, 155). The United States ignored this new confederacy and now claimed to own the whole Ohio country. The western confederacy responded in the fall of 1786 with a four-point position denying the legitimacy of the conquest theory and repudiating land cessions in the three treaties of Fort Stanwix, Fort McIntosh, and Fort Finney (1786).

FURTHER READING

Fenton, William N. *The Great Law and the Longhouse: A Political History of the Iroquois Confederacy*. Norman: University of Oklahoma Press, 1998.

Sword, Wiley. *President Washington's Indian War: The Struggle for the Old Northwest, 1790–1795*. Norman: University of Oklahoma Press, 1985.

Wallace, Anthony F. C. *The Death and Rebirth of the Seneca*. New York: Knopf, 1970.

John C. Mohawk

Franklin, Benjamin, 1706–1790. Benjamin Franklin's life was frequently intertwined with the lives, societies, and affairs of Native Americans, especially the Haudenosaunee. As a printer, he published accounts of Indian treaties for more than two decades. Franklin began his diplomatic career by representing the colony of Pennsylvania at councils with the Iroquois and their allies. His designs for the Albany Plan of Union and later the Articles of Confederation contain elements of the Native American systems of confederation that he had come to know as a diplomat. Franklin also speculated liberally in Native American land.

Born in Boston, Franklin worked with his brother James as a printer until the age of seventeen. In 1723, he left Massachusetts for Philadelphia, where he became a successful printer and made his mark on history as an inventor, statesman, and philosopher.

Franklin's earliest contacts with the Iroquois occurred in Philadelphia, where his printing company published the Indian treaties entered into by the colonial Pennsylvania Assembly in small booklets that enjoyed a lively sale throughout the colonies. Beginning in 1736, Franklin published Indian treaty accounts on a regular basis until 1762. He was a delegate to the 1753 treaty with the Ohio Indians at Carlisle, Pennsylvania. In 1744, at the **Lancaster Treaty Council, Canassatego**, an **Onondaga** sachem, urged the colonies to unite in a manner similar to that of the Iroquois Confederacy. Franklin learned of Canassatego's words when he published the treaty proceedings.

At the **Albany Congress** in 1754, Franklin outlined a plan for colonial government and union that was the first blueprint for American government and intercolonial unity. The Albany Plan of Union contained elements of English political structure combined with Haudenosaunee precedents. When the French and Indian War erupted in western Pennsylvania in 1754, Franklin aided General Edward Braddock's unsuccessful attempt to retake Fort Duquesne from the French. He also took part in a campaign that built defensive positions at Gnaddenhütten, where Christianized Delaware Indians were located.

Franklin used his image of Indians and their societies as a critique of Europe: "The Care and Labour of providing for Artificial and fashionable Wants, the sight of so many Rich wallowing in superfluous plenty, while so many are kept poor and distress'd for want; the Insolence of Office . . . [and] restraints of Custom, all contrive to disgust them [Indians] with what we call civil Society" (Franklin, *Papers*, 17:381). Franklin described Indians' passion for liberty while making it a patriotic rallying cry; he admired Indians' notions of happiness while seeking a definition that would suit the new nation. Franklin wrote:

All the Indians of North America not under the dominion of the Spaniards are in that natural state, being restrained by no Laws, having no Courts, or Ministers of Justice, no Suits, no prisons, no governors vested with any Legal Authority. The persuasion of Men distinguished by Reputation of Wisdom is the only Means by which others are govern'd, or rather led—and the State of the Indians was probably the first State of all Nations. (Grinde and Johansen, 158–159)

As U.S. ambassador to France, among the French *philosophes*, Franklin was known as the "Philosopher as Savage." In his tract "Remarks Concerning the Savages of North America" (1784), Franklin asserted that Indians should not be termed "savages." Although he was sometimes paradoxical in his outlook, Franklin often compared the virtues and shortcomings of both Indian and white cultures, maintaining that Indian ideas and customs had great wisdom and value. Franklin died in 1790, shortly after the fashioning of the U.S. Constitution, which he had helped shape with his ideas of an amalgam between Native American and European cultures.

FURTHER READING

Aldridge, Alfred O. *Benjamin Franklin: Philosopher and Man*. Philadelphia: J. B. Lippincott, 1965.

————. "Franklin's Deistical Indians." *Proceedings of the American Philosophical Society* 94 (August 1950): 398–410.

Boorstin, Daniel. *The Lost World of Thomas Jefferson*. New York: Henry Holt, 1948.

Franklin, Benjamin. *Autobiography of Benjamin Franklin*. Ed. John Bigelow. Philadelphia: J. B. Lippincott, 1868.

————. *The Papers of Benjamin Franklin*. Ed. Leonard W. Labaree and Whitfield J. Bell. New Haven: Yale University Press, 1959.

Grinde, Donald A., Jr., and Bruce E. Johansen. *Exemplar of Liberty: Native America and the Evolution of Democracy*. Los Angeles: UCLA American Indian Studies Center, 1991.

Van Doren, Carl, and Julian P. Boyd, eds. *Indian Treaties Printed by Benjamin Franklin, 1736–1762*. Philadelphia: Historical Society of Pennsylvania, 1938.

G

Gage, Matilda Joslyn, 1826–1898. Matilda Joslyn Gage compared the status of women in Iroquois society with that of other women in nineteenth-century America in an important book in what Sally R. Wagner calls "the first wave of feminism," *Woman, Church, and State* (1893). In that book, Gage acknowledges, according to Wagner's research, that "the modern world [is] indebted to the Iroquois for its first conception of inherent rights, natural equality of condition, and the establishment of a civilized government upon this basis" (Gage, 10).

Gage was probably one of the three most influential feminist architects of the nineteenth-century women's movement, with **Elizabeth Cady Stanton** and Susan B. Anthony, according to Wagner, whose research was among the first to provide a scholarly basis for a resurgent feminist movement in the late twentieth century. Gage was later "read out" of the movement and its history because of her radical views, especially regarding oppression of women by organized religion.

Knowledge of the Iroquois' matrilineal system of society and government was widespread among early feminists, many of whom lived in upstate New York. The early feminists learned of the Iroquois not only through reading the works of **Lewis Henry Morgan**, Henry Schoolcraft, and others, but also through direct personal experience. With Stanton and Anthony, Gage coauthored the landmark *History of Woman Suffrage*, which was published in six volumes between 1881 and 1922. The six volumes cover history from 1848 (the Seneca Falls conference) to 1920 (the first national vote for women).

In her last book, *Women, Church, and State*, Gage opened with a chapter on "the matriarchate," a form of society she believed existed in a number of early societies, specifically the Iroquois. Gage discussed several Iroquois traditions that tended to create checks and balances between the sexes, including descent through the female line, the ability of women to nominate male leaders, the fact that women had a veto power over decisions to go to war, and the woman's supreme authority in the household. Gage also noted that Iroquois women had rights to their property and children after divorce.

Gage herself was admitted to the Iroquois Council of Matrons and was adopted into the Wolf Clan with the name Karonienhawi, "she who holds the sky." Wagner asserts that "nineteenth-century radical feminist theoreticians, such as Stanton and Gage, looked to the Iroquois for their vision of a transformed world" (Wagner, "Iroquois Confederacy," 32–33).

As contemporaries of Morgan, **Friedrich Engels**, and Karl Marx, Gage and the other founding mothers of modern feminism in the United States shared a chord of enthusiasm at finding functioning societies that incorporated notions of sexual equality. All seemed to believe that the Haudenosaunee model held promise for the future. Gage and Stanton looked to the Native model for a design of a regenerated world. "Never was justice more perfect, never civilization higher than under the Matriarchate," Gage wrote (Gage, 9–10). "Under [Iroquois] women the science of government reached the highest form known to the world," Gage believed. Writing in the *New York Evening Post*, Gage contended that "division of power between the sexes in this Indian republic was nearly equal" (Wagner, *Untold Story*, 26).

FURTHER READING

Allen, Paula Gunn. *The Sacred Hoop: Recovering the Feminine in American Indian Traditions*. Boston: Beacon Press, 1986.

Brown, Judith K. "Economic Organization and the Position of Women among the Iroquois." *Ethnohistory* 17:3–4 (Summer–Fall 1970): 151–167.

Carr, Lucien. *The Social and Political Position of Women among the Huron-Iroquois Tribes*. Salem, Mass.: Salem Press, 1884.

Gage, Matilda Joslyn. *Woman, Church, and State*. 1893. Watertown, Mass.: Persephone Press, 1980.

Landsman, Gail. "Portrayals of the Iroquois in the Woman Suffrage Movement." Paper presented at the Annual Conference on Iroquois Research, Rensselaerville, N.Y., October 8, 1988.

Stanton, Elizabeth Cady, Susan B. Anthony, and Matilda Joslyn Gage, eds. *History of Woman Suffrage*. Salem, N.H.: Ayer Co., 1985.

Wagner, Sally Roesch. "The Iroquois Confederacy: A Native American Model for Nonsexist Men." *Changing Men* (Spring–Summer, 1988): 32–33.

———. *The Untold Story of the Iroquois Influence on Early Feminists*. Aberdeen, S.D.: Sky Carrier Press, 1996.

Gambling in Haudenosaunee Country. Since the 1980s, commercial gambling has been a major source of controversy in many Haudenosaunee communities. Beginning with a strip of casinos at the **Mohawk** reservation of **Akwesasne** in the late 1980s, gambling spread to several other Iroquois territories during the 1990s. One of the New York casinos, the **Oneidas**' Turning Stone, near Syracuse, has been spectacularly profitable. Others lie in ashes.

"Civil War" at Akwesasne

Casino gambling was the immediate provocation of the "Mohawk Civil War" at Akwesasne that resulted in the shooting deaths of Mathew Pyke and "Junior" Edwards in 1990 (see **Warrior Society**). The problems at Akwesasne ran deeper than that, however. A gambling and smuggling economy developed there after the opening of the **St. Lawrence Seaway** and the construction of many large industrial plants in the 1950s and 1960s. By the 1970s, much of Akwesasne's hunting and agriculture had been poisoned out of existence. By the 1980s, some Akwesasne Mohawks were being warned not to eat produce from their own gardens and to avoid fish caught in local rivers because they contained toxic levels of several industrial chemicals. Several Mohawk women were told not to breast-feed their babies after toxic levels of polychlorinated biphenyls (PCBs) were found in their milk. In a poisoned land, some Mohawks turned to smuggling and gambling for income. Others sought to protect their homeland from these corrupting influences. The result was a tense war of nerves that exploded into armed conflict in 1989 and 1990.

For several years after the deaths at Akwesasne, casinos (except for bingo) were shut down. By the late 1990s, however, investors at Akwesasne negotiated a gambling compact with the state and began construction of a large new casino, which opened in 1999. In the late fall of 1998, wells being drilled for the casino disrupted the water table at Akwesasne, mixing local residents' well water with brackish salt water, as well as several industrial toxins left in the ground by prior dumping. Unusually warm winter weather expedited the spread of the pollution to wells supplying more than fifty homes.

Traditional Objections to Gambling

Many traditional leaders of the Haudenosaunee maintain that smuggling and gambling are not proper exercises of sovereignty, which is held collectively by a people, not individually by business owners. They believe that gambling promotes an unhealthy lifestyle that brings violence, drugs, and prostitution to reservation neighborhoods. The **Seneca** prophet **Handsome Lake** warned against the evils of gambling, as well as alcohol consumption. Many—but not all—adherents of the Code of Handsome Lake refuse to gamble for moral reasons. The Grand Council at Onondaga has long refused to allow gambling on its home territory near Nedrow, New York, south of Syracuse, despite offers of financial aid that would supplement meager income from lease and treaty payments (Hill, 6).

During the summer of 1987, over the objections of the **Tuscarora** Reservation's traditional council, a businessman on the reservation opened a small (construction cost: $400,000) bingo hall. The chiefs' council maintained that claims of exemption from state laws for personal gain (and not for the good of the people as a whole) were an invalid use of sovereignty. The U.S. Supreme Court ruled that the state could not shut down the Tuscarora bingo hall (and others in similar circumstances) in 1987. The conflict at Tuscarora became so sharp that business supporters for a time organized their own Warriors' Council. Within a few years, however, disputes developed over money within the bingo hall's management, and it closed. The owner's name was removed from the tribal roll by the Tuscarora Council of Chiefs (Hill, 7–9).

The Seneca Nation has operated a bingo hall since 1981 that generated $3 million a year in profits by the late 1980s, with very few internal problems. The operation has created about 100 new jobs and has helped fund day care, programs for senior citizens, a peacemaker court, and a dozen new tribal police positions, among other things. This bingo hall, unlike those at Tuscarora and Akwesasne, has been tribally, not privately, owned. Seneca leaders have warned that any attempt to start private gambling will be closed down by tribal police (Hill, 11).

Meanwhile, the Oneidas' Turning Stone Casino, twenty-five miles east of Syracuse, has produced 1,900 jobs and has become, according to Oneida Nation representative **Ray Halbritter**, the fifth most popular tourist attraction in New York State.

FURTHER READING

Hill, Richard. "Rattling the Rafters: High Stakes Gambling Threatens the Peace of the Longhouse." *Northeast Indian Quarterly* 6:3 (Fall 1989): 4–11.
Johansen, Bruce E. *Life and Death in Mohawk Country*. Golden, Colo.: North American Press/Fulcrum, 1993.

Ganienkeh. During the early 1970s, concurrent with the early development of the **Warrior Society** on the **Kahnawake** and **Akwesasne** (St. Regis) **Mohawk** reservations, a number of Mohawks began to discuss plans to establish a traditionally oriented settlement in the Adirondacks, in an area that the Ganienkeh ("People of the Flint," as the Mohawks call themselves) had occupied before contact with European-Americans. These Mohawks on May, 13, 1974, occupied a 612-acre tract of state land that had been a Girl Scout camp near Moss Lake, fifty miles north of Utica, within nine million acres of the Mohawks' traditional homeland. Unlike the occupation of Wounded Knee on the Pine Ridge Reservation a year earlier, this occupation was not temporary. Conflict developed with their non-Indian neighbors, especially after two non-Indians were shot in the area on October 28, 1974. After negotiations with state agencies, three years later the Mohawks who had taken the Moss Lake site migrated to another tract of land near Miner Lake, in Altona, northwest of Plattsburgh. Movement to the new tract of land was completed in mid-1978. Their settlement has remained on that site since.

FURTHER READING

Landsman, Gail. *Sovereignty and Symbol: Indian-White Conflict at Ganienkeh*. Albuquerque: University of New Mexico Press, 1988.

Ganondagan. Ganondagan, today a 250-acre New York State historical site twenty-five miles southeast of Rochester, New York, was once the **Senecas'** principal political and commercial center, populated by roughly 5,000 people. The state park was acquired in several parcels during the 1980s. The site, on lightly forested rolling hills, contains a model Seneca village and has five miles of hiking trails with seventy stainless-steel historic markers featuring the works of Seneca artists, with text by Seneca scholar John C. Mohawk. These educational signs are maintained by descendants of some of the area's original residents. The director of the site, which was opened in 1987, is Haudenosaunee artist and culture bearer **G. Peter Jemison**, an eighth-generation descendant of **Mary Jemison**.

Ganondagan (near Victor, New York) also was the site where the **Great Law of Peace** was debated for ratification by the Senecas during the Green Corn time (late August or early September) of 1142 C.E., according to Barbara A. Mann and Jerry Fields: "During a ratification council held at Ganondagan, the sky darkened in a total, or near total, eclipse" (Mann and Fields, 138). In 1687, 2,400 French soldiers under the command of the Marquis de Denonville descended on the town and burned it to the ground after escaping Senecas put their own longhouses to the torch rather than see them fall into French hands. French forces also destroyed large stores of **corn** and other foods.

FURTHER READING

Faber, Harold. "Indian History Alive at New York Site." *New York Times*, July 26, 1987, sec. 1, pt. 2, 36.

Mann, Barbara A., and Jerry L. Fields. "A Sign in the Sky: Dating the League of the Haudenosaunee." *American Indian Culture and Research Journal* 21:2 (1997): 105–163.

Gantowisas **(women acting in their official capacities).** The *gantowisas* were female officials among the Iroquois who enjoyed sweeping political, economic, religious, and social powers that their European counterparts could only envy. The earliest chronicles of European travelers (all men) remarked in astonishment regarding the rights, powers, and liberties of Iroquoian women. One of the chief goals of the early missionaries was to break the power of the *gantowisas*, a topic visited in chilling detail in Karen L. Anderson's *Chain Her by One Foot* (1991). Others, such as **Samuel de Champlain** and Joseph-François Lafitau, were content merely to wonder at the situation in print. In 1656–1657 a Jesuit Relation recorded that the *gantowisas* exercised *"beaucoup d'authorité parmi ces peuples,"* or great authority among their people (Thwaites, 44: 36), while in 1724, Father Lafitau stated directly that the *gantowisas* were "the souls of the councils" in whom was vested "all the real authority" (Lafitau, 1:69).

Politically, the *gantowisas* of the league, and Iroquoian *gantowisas* generally, had the right to confer or retract citizenship through **adoption**; call or end wars; appoint warriors and war chiefs; nominate all men to office; nominate all women to office; consider all matters in their own councils first; set the agenda of the league and the Wyandot Confederacy by deciding whether to send matters forward to the men's councils; name children and officers (including direction of funerals); and impeach errant officials, male or female. Women also were the judges, mediators, and keepers of the peace.

Economically, women owned all the land and the crops, as well as all the fruits of the men's hunts and the town's fishing. They owned the **longhouses**, all the household goods, the lineage names and titles to office, and all farming implements. In addition, the women oversaw all food and goods distribution, ensuring that the goods and services of life were equitably distributed to all. This included calling and managing the seasonal festivals.

Religiously, the majority of Iroquoian Faithkeepers were once women, and about half today remain women. Dream work was and remains the special province of women. At one time, the majority of the medical work using herbs, roots, and healing concoctions was in the hands of the women. Women also "cleaned the bones of the dead" during the Feast of the Dead (Bonvillain, "Iroquoian Women," 51), a religious extension of their naming and funerary rights.

Socially, the *gantowisas* had the right to arrange marriages and recognize divorces; control fertility; and name and rear all children until puberty (at which point the men took over with the boys). Despite some attempts by anthropologists to trace patrilineal descent patterns—what they are actually tracing is assimilation patterns—Iroquoian descent was and is counted solely through the mother. Among the **Senecas**, the *gantowisas* might take more than one husband. Nineteenth-century suffragists closely studied the *gantowisas* of the league for pointers on women's liberation (Wagner).

FURTHER READING

Anderson, Karen L. *Chain Her by One Foot: The Subjugation of Women in Seventeenth-Century New France.* New York: Routledge, 1991.

Bonvillain, Nancy. "Gender Relations in Native North America." *American Indian Culture and Research Journal* 13:2 (1989): 1–28.

———. "Iroquoian Women." In Nancy Bonvillain, ed., *Studies on Iroquoian Culture.* Occasional Publications in Northeastern Anthropology, No. 6. Rindge, N.H.: Department of Anthropology, Franklin Pierce College, 1980: 47–58.

Carr, Lucien. "On the Social and Political Position of Woman among the Huron-Iroquois Tribes." *Peabody Museum of American Archaeology and Ethnology, Reports* 16–17, 3:3–4 (1884): 207–232.

Champlain, Samuel de. *The Works of Samuel de Champlain.* Ed. H. P. Biggar. Trans. W. D. LeSuer and H. H. Langton. 7 vols. Toronto: Champlain Society, 1922–1936.

Jacobs, Renée. "The Iroquois Great Law of Peace and the United States Constitution: How the Founding Fathers Ignored the Clan Mothers." *American Indian Law Review* 16:2 (1991): 497–531.

Lafitau, Joseph-François. *Customs of the American Indians Compared with the Customs of Primitive Times.* 1724. Ed. and trans. William N. Fenton and Elizabeth L. Moore. 2 vols. Toronto: Champlain Society, 1974–1977.

Mann, Barbara A. "Haudenosaunee (Iroquois) Women, Legal and Political Status." In
    Bruce Elliott Johansen, ed., *The Encyclopedia of Native American Legal Tradi-
    tion.* Westport, Conn.: Greenwood Press, 1998: 112–131.
———. *Iroquoian Women: Gantowisas of the Haudenosaunee League.* New York: Peter
    Lang, 2000.
———. "The Lynx in Time: Haudenosaunee Women's Traditions and History." *Amer-
    ican Indian Quarterly* 21:3 (1997): 423–450.
Parker, Arthur C. *The Constitution of the Five Nations, or, The Iroquois Book of the
    Great Law.* Albany: University of the State of New York, 1916.
Powell, J. W. "Wyandot Government: A Short Study of Tribal Society." *Annual Report
    of the Bureau of Ethnology to the Secretary of the Smithsonian Institution* 1
    (1879–1880): 57–69.
Thwaites, Reuben Gold, ed. and trans. *The Jesuit Relations: Travels and Explorations
    of the Jesuit Missionaries in New France, 1610–1791.* 73 vols. New York: Pag-
    eant Book Company, 1959.
Wagner, Sally Roesch. "The Iroquois Confederacy: A Native American Model for Non-
    sexist Men." In William Guy Spittal, ed., *Iroquois Women: An Anthology.* Ohs-
    weken, Ontario, Canada: Iroquois Publishing and Craft Supplies, 1990: 217–221.
Wallace, Anthony F. C. "Woman, Land, and Society: Three Aspects of Aboriginal Del-
    aware Life." *Pennsylvania Archaeologist* 17:1–4 (1947): 1–36.

Barbara A. Mann

Garakontie, Daniel (Onondaga), c. 1600–1676. Daniel Garakontie ("Moving
Sun"), a lifelong ally of the French, was born at Onondaga in what is now New
York state. He spent some of his younger years in Montréal and made many
friends as he became known around the community as a person who could
redeem French captives from the Iroquois. In 1658, Garakontie also helped
Jesuit missionaries avoid a planned massacre by Iroquois. By 1661, he had
become one of the most influential leaders within the Iroquois Grand Council,
and he may have served as Tadadaho (speaker) of the confederacy.

Also in 1661, Garakontie welcomed the Jesuit Father Simon LeMoyne to his
community; he converted his cabin into a missionary chapel for religious services. A year later, he foiled an attempt to assassinate LeMoyne. Garakontie was
ridiculed at times for his passive acceptance of the whites and their religion, but
he replied that they were too strong to effectively resist. He also urged Indians
to reject alcohol and exhorted them on the benefits of schooling. All the while,
Garakontie continued to arrange freedom for French captives. He also sought
peace with the English. Garakontie was baptized in Québec in 1669, when he
was about seventy years of age, at which time he accepted the name "Daniel."
Garakontie died at Onondaga in 1676 and was buried with Christian services at
his request.

FURTHER READING

Johansen, Bruce E., and Donald A. Grinde, Jr. *The Encyclopedia of Native American
    Biography.* New York: Henry Holt, 1997.

Gauntlet, running the. As a figure of speech in American English, the Haudenosaunee custom of making prisoners of war "run the gauntlet" has come to
indicate endurance of an ordeal. Captives, some of whom later would be
adopted, were forced to walk between two parallel lines of their captors, en-
during slaps, kicks, and verbal insults. The gauntlet has been used in modern
times to express intense disapproval of a person's behavior, rather than to punish
war captives. This practice was used at **Akwesasne** during the **gambling**-related
crisis that peaked in deadly gun battles during the spring of 1990. Historic
Iroquois use of the gauntlet on war captives has been described by Daniel Richter: "[V]illagers holding clubs, sticks, and other weapons stood in two rows
outside the palisade entrance [of their village] to greet the victors and to make
the prisoners endure the gauntlet, an experience that occurred at far too agoniz-
ing a pace to be described as 'running.' Warriors might slowly lead prisoners
by a rope between lines of men, women, and children" (Richter, 67).

FURTHER READING

Richter, Daniel K. *The Ordeal of the Longhouse: The Peoples of the Iroquois League in
      the Era of European Colonization.* Chapel Hill: University of North Carolina
      Press, 1992.

George-Kanentiio, Douglas Mitchell (Mohawk), b. 1995. Doug George-
Kanentiio, a member of the Bear Clan, has been a key figure in **Akwesasne
Mohawk** political and cultural life in the late twentieth century. He has participated in **Mohawk** land-claims negotiations, was a member of the Mohawk
Nation Business Committee, was a founder of Radio CKON (at Akwesasne),
and was a founder of the Native American Journalists Association, from which
he received, in 1994, its highest kudo, the Wassaja Award for Journalism Ex-
cellence. George-Kanentiio also has been editor of *Akwesasne Notes* and *Indian
Time* news journals. He has served as a member of the Board of Trustees for
the National Museum of the American Indian, as a member of the Haudenosaunee Standing Committee on Burial Rules and Regulations (the **repatriation**
group of the Haudenosaunee Confederacy), and as a columnist for the *Syracuse
Herald-American* and *News from Indian Country*.

George-Kanentiio played a direct role in the Mohawk "civil war" at Akwesasne as a newspaper editor and ultimately as a participant in a four-day gun
battle in 1990 that resulted in the deaths of two Mohawk men. George-Kanentiio
identified the source of the violence at Akwesasne as illicit casino gaming, an
activity that began in 1986 and quickly expanded until the Mohawk reservation
became the fourth-largest gambling center in North America. His articles traced
the rise of gaming to the displacement of the Mohawks from their ancestral
lifestyles of fishing and farming beginning after World War II and accelerating
with the completion of the **St. Lawrence Seaway** and subsequent contamination
of the Akwesasne environment by industries built along that waterway.

George-Kanentiio also has written numerous articles and editorials about the political divisions at Akwesasne, which is governed by three Native councils and also is subject to the jurisdictions of Canada (Québec and Ontario) and the United States (New York State). He is an advocate for the revitalization of the ancestral Mohawk government called the Mohawk Nation Council of Chiefs. He also has attempted, with others, to create an economy based on ancestral values with attendant regulations.

George-Kanentiio has been critical of the smuggling of narcotics, tobacco, firearms, and illegal aliens through the Akwesasne territory. As a result, his newspapers were banned in some businesses, his offices were firebombed twice, and his personal residence was raked with machine-gun fire. He persisted in his opposition and received many threats against his life, yet he was given considerable encouragement by the Mohawk Nation Council and its supporters at Akwesasne.

In March 1990, the Akwesasne community split into two factions, resulting in an escalation of violence and terror serious enough to warrant evacuation of the reservation on April 26. Thousands fled the community, but there were a few isolated holdouts, one of whom was David George, Jr., a brother of George-Kanentiio. Rather than have his brother stand alone against the attacks of the progaming Mohawk Sovereignty Security Force (**Warrior Society**), George-Kanentiio elected to pick up a firearm and support his brother. He, along with eleven other Mohawk men, then withstood five days of intense fighting (April 27–May 1) against greatly superior forces until they were relieved with the occupation of Akwesasne by New York State police, the Royal Canadian Mounted Police, and a contingent of the Canadian army. Two men were killed during the fighting, and on May 13, 1990, George-Kanentiio was arrested by the Sûreté du Québec and charged with the shooting death of Harold "Junior" Edwards, one of the victims. He was cleared of the killing during the preliminary-hearing stage of the judicial proceedings for lack of evidence. George-Kanentiio maintained that his arrest was a political action resulting from his severe public criticisms of the U.S. and Canadian police.

George-Kanentiio resigned as editor of *Akwesasne Notes* and *Indian Time* in 1992 and moved to the **Oneida** Territory in central New York State. He secured a position as a columnist with the *Syracuse Herald-American* and, with his wife **Joanne Shenandoah**, formed Round Dance Productions, a nonprofit corporation dedicated to the preservation of Iroquois culture through music, art, and film. He assisted Mohawk spiritual leader **Tom Porter** in the relocation of Mohawks from Akwesasne to their ancient homes in the Mohawk Valley region.

George-Kanentiio also has worked with the Haudenosaunee Confederacy on economic issues, has played a key role in the repatriation of sacred items from the National Museum of the American Indian back to the Iroquois, and has been retained as a consultant to the Mohawk Nation Council on many issues. He has lectured on Iroquois issues throughout North America and Europe.

FURTHER READING

Johansen, Bruce E. *Life and Death in Mohawk Country*. Golden, Colo.: North American Press/Fulcrum, 1993.

German Flats Treaty Council (1775). Representatives of the Continental Congress met with Haudenosaunee leaders at German Flats (near present-day Herkimer, New York) in mid-August of 1775 to secure the Haudenosaunee's neutrality on the eve of their war for independence with Great Britain. This conference was so important to the rebellious American patriots that a delegate from the Continental Congress, **Philip Schuyler**, was among the colonial representatives.

After some preliminaries, the sachems and treaty commissioners decided to meet on August 24, 1775. According to protocol, the commissioners asked the sachems to appoint a speaker, but the sachems deferred to the commissioners, so the Americans picked Abraham, a Mohawk, adopted brother and successor to **Hendrick**. On the next day, the treaty commissioners, who had specific instructions from **John Hancock** and the Second Continental Congress, told the sachems that they were heeding the advice their Iroquois forefathers had given to the colonial Americans at the **Lancaster Treaty Council** at Lancaster, Pennsylvania, in 1744. At this point, the commissioners quoted **Canassatego**'s words:

Brethren, We the Six Nations heartily recommend Union and a good agreement between you our Brethren, never disagree but preserve a strict Friendship for one another and thereby you as well as we will become stronger. Our Wise Forefathers established Union and Amity between the **Five Nations**. . . . we are a powerful Confederacy, and if you observe the same methods . . . you will acquire fresh strength and power. ("Proceedings," August 25, 1775)

After quoting Canassatego, the Americans said that their forefathers had rejoiced to hear his words, and they had sunk

deep into their Hearts, the Advice was good, it was Kind. They said to one another, the Six Nations are a wise people, let us hearken to their Council and teach our children to follow it. Our old Men have done so. They have frequently taken a single Arrow and said, Children, see how easy it is broken, then they have tied twelve together with strong Cords—And our strongest Men could not break them—See said they—this is what the Six Nations mean. Divided a single Man may destroy you—United, you are a match for the whole World. ("Proceedings," August 25, 1775)

The Americans thanked the "great God that we are all united, that we have a strong Confederacy composed of twelve Provinces." The American delegates also pointed out that they had "lighted a Great Council Fire at Philadelphia and have sent Sixty five Counsellors to speak and act in the name of the whole" ("Proceedings," August 25, 1775).

FURTHER READING

Grinde, Donald A., Jr., and Bruce E. Johansen. *Exemplar of Liberty: Native America and the Evolution of Democracy.* Los Angeles: UCLA American Indian Studies Center, 1991.

"Proceedings of the Commissioners Appointed by the Continental Congress to Negotiate a Treaty with the Six Nations, 1775." Papers of the Continental Congress, 1774–89. National Archives, M247, Roll 144, Item No. 134. See Treaty Council at German Flats, New York, August 15, 1775.

Gibson (Wenta) Iroquois Reserve. Each fall, roughly 20,000 people visit the Gibson Reserve in Ontario, Canada, to witness the annual harvest of cranberries and to sample cranberry muffins, cranberry sauce, cookies, crepes, pancakes, and even cranberry fudge. Cranberries, which grow in a twenty-acre marsh, are harvested with a "punt," a specially designed paddleboat, or by the traditional **Mohawk** method: "walking the bog" behind a heavy wooden board that pushes the harvested berries across the bog to a conveyor belt. The cranberry harvest is held concurrently with a community fair that includes a farmers' market, an art exhibition, music, dance, sports competitions, and many culinary treats made from the "fruit of the bog." The Gibson Reserve includes one of only two cranberry bogs in Ontario; berries that are not consumed during the festival are sold to the Ocean Spray Company.

Girty, Simon (Katepakomen) (Seneca-Wyandot), 1741–1818. Katepakomen (Simon Girty) was the league Wyandot War Chief of Ohio during the **American Revolution** and defeated the revolutionary army under George Washington for control of the "Old Northwest." During his lifetime, he was also a scout, a British agent, and an interpreter.

Much nonsense has been written concerning the life, identity, and character of Katepakomen, who was born in 1741 at Chamber Mill, Pennsylvania, largely due to his status as the "*bête noir* of the frontier" (Richards, 3). Many of the factual mistakes concerning Katepakomen were cemented into the "official" record in 1890 by Consul Willshire Butterfield, Katepakomen's first well-credentialed biographer. Although Butterfield was highly regarded in his time, he was an unreliable and racist source, knowingly massaging his facts to fit his agenda. He unabashedly hated the subject of his study, writing what amounted to a smear while pretending that it was a scholarly biography.

Butterfield was not alone in this approach. The very existence of Katepakomen outraged eighteenth-, nineteenth-, and many twentieth-century historians, who almost uniformly denigrated him as a "white renegade." In consequence, for at least a hundred years after his death, he rivaled Benedict Arnold as the most hated man in U.S. history. Long after his demise, European-American historians continued choking out racist diatribes masquerading as biographical notes, for example, this 1917 sample from Nevin Winter:

Of all historic characters the name of the traitor to his race or to his country is buried deepest in the mire. His name becomes a byword and a reproach among the natives of the earth. . . . For him there remains only a pillar of historic infamy. He lives in the midst of the fiercest passions. . . . The white renegade who has abandoned his race and civilization for the company of the savages of the forest, is the most abhorred of all. For him there is no charity. . . . His name is inscribed with that of Brutus, of Benedict Arnold, and of Judas Iscariot. (Winter, 43)

Such partisan, skewed, and utterly bigoted perspectives continue to stand as the "historical" record on "Girty." Illiterate, Katepakomen was in no position to leave behind his own version of events.

Western sources are not the only records of his life, however. The Native oral tradition of Ohio tells quite a different story. To league peoples, Katepakomen was not a "race traitor," but the great war hero of the revolutionary era, who stood against settler terrorism and George Washington's invasions during the frightful years of the Revolution—and won. He is recalled as a clever, kind-hearted man and an able general who later assisted Tecumseh.

Following Butterfield's lead, all Western biographies of Katepakomen identify him as a Euro-settler by birth, whereas Ohio oral tradition has always maintained that he was of mixed Iroquois-European ancestry. Here, Butterfield muddied the record considerably, largely to cover up a fact that would otherwise have come out in the wash, to wit, that an Englishwoman, Mary (Crosby?) Newton Girty, mother of Katepakomen, enjoyed lusty relations with several men besides her husband, the hopeless drunk and self-styled Indian agent Simon Girty, Sr. At least one of her lovers was Native. Not only did Victorian conventions hamper Butterfield's full disclosure of the sexual facts in 1890, but they also inhibited his full disclosure of the racial facts. "White" women did not love "filthy Indians" in Jim Crow America.

Thus, despite the very clear evidence of his own primary sources (close relatives and longtime acquaintances of Katepakomen) and to steer clear of besmirching Mary's virtue, Butterfield gussied up the births of at least four of her sons (Simon, James, George, and John) while completely ignoring the evidence of a Native daughter. (By contrast, primary sources indicated that only her son Thomas had actually been sired by Girty, Sr.). In the whitewashing process, Butterfield remained silent on the tradition, well known to Ohio league peoples, that the true father of Katepakomen had been a **Seneca** man called Fish who had killed Simon, Sr., in 1751 during what was Westernly called "a frolic," or a liquor-facilitated festival. Fish remained with Mary (who seems to have been the subject of the men's quarrel) until 1753, when he was murdered by a settler. Ignoring this oral tradition of Katepakomen's parentage, Western biographers have simply repeated Butterfield's Euro-version of his genesis, assuming its truth (Mann, 610–613).

Biographers also tend to accept another Butterfield fiction, the age of fifteen as that of Katepakomen's first contact with his Native relatives. This error was based on the date 1756 when John Turner, then consort of Mary Girty, was taken as a league prisoner to the Seneca town of Kittanang, along with Mary and her children. Turner was immediately recognized by his league captors as the man who had murdered Fish, the better to possess Mary (and not, as rumored by Butterfield, in belated revenge for the death of Girty, Sr.). The league executed Turner for the murder of Fish. It is true that Katepakomen was about fifteen when all of this occurred, but it is not true that these events marked his entry into the league. He had by then long been a citizen of the league.

According to his granddaughter, Katepakomen had himself testified that he had been taken in by the Senecas at an early age. Katepakomen's grandson attested to the same story, adding that at the tender age of five, the Senecas had tested his grandfather for courage, a challenge that he had met with flying colors. The elders then predicted that he was to become a great leader. Katepakomen's documented fluency in all of the dialects of the league, as well as Delaware and Shawnee, support the testimony of an early-childhood induction (Mann 613, 614).

Some Westerners take the fact that Katepakomen had to be adopted into the league as evidence that he was fully European. This ignores Haudenosaunee law, which recognizes descent through the mother only. Since it was his father who had been Iroquois, his adoption was necessary under Iroquoian law before he could be counted as a citizen of the league. He was adopted first by the Senecas, the nation of his father, then by the Wyandots, the Seneca-sponsored Guardians of the Western Door in Ohio. In Ohio, the Senecas and Wyandots became almost indistinguishable.

By 1759, Katepakomen and his siblings were living full-time among the Iroquois League nations of Pennsylvania and Ohio. The French and Indian War was in full, nasty swing by then, and the British Crown needed proficient interpreters for its negotiations with Native nations. From 1959 until 1774, Katepakomen acted as one of those interpreters and was particularly affiliated with Fort Pitt (formerly the French Fort Dusquesne). His favored status did not go unnoticed, arousing the jealousy of many backwoods folk. In October 1773, settlers in Virginia and Pennsylvania, enraged against the "renegade," sought to arrest Katepakomen on trumped-up charges, but he escaped to his league relatives.

The British, already jousting with their restive colonists, refused to honor the settlers' charges against Katepakomen. Instead, they commissioned him as a second lieutenant at Fort Pitt in 1774, raising new colonial hackles. Crown officers such as Colonel Alexander McKee (whose mother had been Shawnee) and Katepakomen outraged the increasingly racist sensibilities of the colonists, who saw their "Indian" rivals for the land as "savages" to be "wiped out," not promoted.

In his new position, Katepakomen began negotiating for the British in ticklish situations with nonleague nations. In May 1776, he was named the interpreter to the British Middle Indian Department at Fort Pitt, although his Native resistance to British military discipline (a ferocious code) got him fired three months later. He continued to serve as a second lieutenant, however, until 1777, when he resigned in protest over having been ignored when a new round of promotions came through.

Angry at having been denied promotion, Katepakomen briefly considered fighting for the revolutionaries in the fall of 1777, but the Whig response to his overtures was to arrest him promptly on more trumped-up "conspiracy" charges. Galled, he broke out of jail the first evening of his incarceration. More interested in rubbing in the incompetence of his captors than in escaping, he spent the night in an apple tree just paces from the prison and returned the next morning, in his own words, "to show that they could not keep him" (Mann, 617). Meantime, miffed in their own turn by Katepakomen's offer to aid the revolutionaries, his Seneca relatives ratcheted up the ante, accusing him of conspiring against the league (Richards, 10). Caught between the fire on both sides, Katepakomen went into hiding until tempers had cooled all around. He finally threw his lot in with the league in 1778, after becoming thoroughly disgusted with a foray by the Pennsylvania militia under General Edward Hand against a village of Iroquoian women (the so-called Squaw Campaign).

His work from 1778 and 1779 has been characterized by all Western scholars as either interpreting for the British or attempting to rally Native nations to the British side. Although he did accept British pay and odd jobs, he is more accurately characterized as having been an agent of the league, organizing resistance in Ohio against Washington's and the settlers' planned use of the war as an excuse to grab the Old Northwest, a strategy the league was determined to thwart.

Katepakomen became key to the opposition, along with Alexander McKee and Matthew Elliott, a British officer. The three spied for the league and the British, in the process spreading as much disaffection as possible toward the Americans among the Native peoples of Ohio. This brought them into direct conflict with the Moravian missionaries of Ohio, especially **John Heckewelder**, who was unquestionably a spy for Washington's forces at Fort Pitt, and David Zeisberger, who was probably another American spy (Wallace, *Thirty Thousand Miles*, 133–134; Richards, 11).

By 1779, Katepakomen began taking on the duties of a league warrior, pushing back would-be invaders attempting to cross into Ohio from Kentucky. As his leadership abilities became more apparent to league elders, he was promoted by the **gantowisas** (women acting in their official capacities) to ever more responsible positions, eventually becoming the head war chief of the Wyandots in Ohio. In this position, he commanded up to 10,000 troops, fending off regular attempts at invasion by the revolutionary army.

He also participated in the courageous rescue of the league Delaware-Mahicans from a settler-planned genocide in 1781. The Delaware-Mahicans managed the league breadbasket in Ohio, along the Muskingum River. Their bountiful harvests were interfering with Washington's strategy of starving out the league through General **John Sullivan**'s and Colonel VanSchaik's synchronized destructions of the New York Seneca and **Onondaga** graneries and harvests in 1779 (Wallace, *Thirty Thousand Miles*, 409; Parker, 84). In 1781, Washington ordered Colonel Daniel Brodhead of Fort Pitt to destroy the Delaware-Mahican granaries and harvest. Accordingly, Brodhead rampaged through Goschochking, the Delaware capital in Ohio (Wallace, *Thirty Thousand Miles*, 400). He found the town empty, however. Having secured advance word of the plan, Katepakomen and the Delaware war chief **Hopocan** had spirited the entire Delaware-Mahican nation off to the safety of the Wyandot capital at Upper Sandusky between September 2 and 4, 1781.

Early in March 1782, the people returned for their harvest, but the Pennsylvania militia intercepted them on March 8, 1782, stealing the harvest and killing the Delaware-Mahican harvesters. (For the full story, see **Goschochking Genocide**.) Washington next sent in Colonel William Crawford, presumably (in the words of Paul Wallace) "to complete the work began at Gnadenhütten [Goschochking] by finishing off" all remaining league Delaware-Mahicans (Wallace, *Thirty Thousand Miles*, 199). Katepakomen was ready for him. Along with Hopocan, he entirely routed Crawford. Although Katepakomen and Hopocan had really wanted Colonel David Williamson, the leader of the genocide, they settled for taking Crawford prisoner when Williamson beat a cowardly retreat in the middle of the battle, stranding his superior officer in the field. On June 11, 1782, Crawford was tortured to death at the stake for the war crimes committed at Goschochking.

This league execution galvanized settler hatred of Katepakomen, who was viciously and quite wrongly demonized in settler propaganda and later "history" as having laughed manically at Crawford's agony (Seaver, 98; Roosevelt, 3:27). Based on this lurid characterization, for the next century and a half, Katepakomen was portrayed in Western literature and history as the savage murderer of the innocent Crawford. By contrast, oral tradition of the event consistently depicted Katepakomen as a compassionate man who had been so moved by Crawford's pleas for a "mercy shot" that he would have complied had others not restrained him, forbidding it (Marsh, 14). This tradition is confirmed by the recorded statement that Katepakomen himself made later, that "if Crawford had been his own father he could not have saved him" (Mann, 226).

After the 1783 Treaty of Paris, at which the British blithely ceded to the Americans the Northwest Territories that the league had won, Katepakomen became a man with a price on his head. He retreated to the safety of Amherstburg, Ontario, Canada, where he lived with his sister. Retirement, however, was hard for a man used to action, and when a Mrs. Mallott approached him about regaining custody of her daughter, Catherine, from the Shawnees, he agreed to help her. In late 1783, he walked down to the league-allied Shawnees of southern Ohio, among whom Catherine was residing, and petitioned for her release into his care. Thus began another chapter in his life that has been grossly misrepresented in historical literature.

The child of French settlers, Catherine (1766–1852) was captured in 1780 at the age of fourteen as she and her father were illegally traversing the Ohio River along with a party of settlers. At Wheeling, the Delawares and Shawnees halted their progress, taking her and nineteen others prisoner. Adopted by the Shawnees, she lived along the Mad River, marrying a Shawnee man in 1782 and giving birth to a child that died in 1783 during the years of league starvation.

The Shawnees agreed that Katepakomen might take Catherine north to "visit" her mother, but not before he had wintered with them. As the snow fell, Katepakomen "fell violently in love" with Catherine, a breathtaking beauty (Butterfield, 218). In 1784, she gave birth to her second child, John, who also died in infancy. This child had probably been sired by Katepakomen. Late in the summer of 1784, the couple trekked back north to Detroit, where Mrs. Mallott awaited the reunion with her daughter. Catherine did not remain with the mother who had sought her for so long, however, but continued on to Amherstburg with Katepakomen, for she returned his grand passion. Although they had probably been married according to Shawnee custom the previous winter, they were remarried by European rites in August 1784 in Canada.

Those historians who have dealt with this aspect of Katepakomen's career have been at pains to explain away Catherine's love for him. The general conjecture has been that Catherine married him to escape the savage clutches of the brutal Shawnees. Butterfield stated directly (without any evidence whatsoever) that "to her, a savage life was more terrible than death." He hinted that Katepakomen had extorted a promise of marriage from her in exchange for "her escape from captivity" (Butterfield, 214–215). Despite their popularity with Western historians, however, such arguments fly in the face of the fact that Catherine had been quite "safely" back among Europeans for several months when she took her Catholic marriage vows to Katepakomen, and indeed had left her mother, willingly following him to Canada, to do so.

However unsettling it might be to the racist imagination, the fact was that Catherine loved Katepakomen—nor was it any wonder. She had just spent four formative years in a culture that revered him as a great hero. His regard for her could only have been flattering, while his handsome features—family and acquaintances described him as tall, straight, and dark, "a fine looking man" with piercing eyes (Mann, 615)—would not have repulsed her. Together, the couple had four more children, resulting in numerous grandchildren.

In 1785, Katepakomen left his wedded bliss on a war mission to keep the Americans from taking Ohio in fact as well as in treaty. By June, he had rallied the Ohio league peoples to resist the onslaught of settlers looking for a way into that fertile land. In the fall, he was working to ensure a good Native turnout at the conference at the Great Miami (the Maumee River) at the major conference grounds (now in the heart of downtown Toledo). He spent considerable time at the Wyandot capital of Upper Sandusky among his relatives. For the next several years, he worked against American invasion, leading the attack on Dunlap's Station on the Maumee in 1791, before the Battle of Fallen Timbers (1794) made it decisively clear that the Native side had lost Ohio to the invaders. He then permanently retreated to Canada, supporting Tecumseh.

Throughout this period, Katepakomen returned home to visit his wife. His visits resulted in the births of Ann (in 1786), Thomas (in 1788), and Sarah (in 1791). Their final son, Prideaux, was not born until 1797. Around this time, the marriage became rocky as Katepakomen, depressed, turned to frequent drink and Catherine, in response, turned to morbid religiosity. Each spouse objected to the chief pastime of the other. Foes of Katepakomen circulated another vicious story dating from this time, that Katepakomen was physically abusive to Catherine, at one point (according to the story) hitting her on the head with a sabre. This was untrue. Actually, it had been Katepakomen who had been slashed in the head by Thayendanegea (**Joseph Brant**) during a personal imbroglio. Ultimately, however, unable to stand his drinking, Catherine did leave Katepakomen (Mann, 622, 623).

In 1813, when William Henry Harrison invaded Canada in pursuit of Tecumseh, Katepakomen knew that the American price on his head would lure bounty hunters to his doorstep. He therefore sought and received refuge at Thayendanegea's town at **Grand River**, Ontario, at least for the duration of the emergency. (Thayendanegea did not protest, having died in 1807.) After the War of 1812, Katepakomen returned to his home at Amherstburg. He lost his sight in 1816 from the old sabre wound inflicted by Thayendanegea so many years before. In his hour of blind need, Catherine returned to her once-beloved, nursing him fondly through his lingering, final illness. Two years later, on February 18, 1818, Katepakomen passed from life into legend when he died in Amherstburg. In recognition of his valuable services in life, the British government in Canada arranged a hero's funeral for him, dispatching a detachment of troops down from nearby Malden to give the old war chief a proper send-off, to the outrage of Revolutionary War veterans in the United States who only stiffened in their view of him as a "race traitor."

FURTHER READING

Butterfield, Consul Willshire. *History of the Girtys, Being a Concise Account of the Girty Brothers—Thomas, Simon, James, and George, and of Their Half-Brother John Turner—Also of the Part Taken by Them in Lord Dunmore's War, in the Western Border War of the Revolution, and in the Indian War of 1790–95.* Cincinnati: Robert Clarke & Co., 1890.

Heckewelder, John. *Narrative of the Mission of the United Brethren among the Delaware and Mohegan Indians from Its Commencement, in the Year 1740, to the Close of the Year 1808.* 1820. New York: Arno Press, 1971.

Mann, Barbara A. "Forbidden Ground: Racial Politics and Hidden Identity in James Fenimore Cooper's Leather-Stocking Tales." Ph.D. diss., University of Toledo, 1997.

Marsh, Thelma R. *Lest We Forget: A Brief Sketch of Wyandot County's History.* Upper Sandusky, Ohio: Wyandot County Historical Society, 1967.

Parker, Arthur C. "Sources and Range of Cooper's Indian Lore." In Mary E. Cunning-
    ham, ed., *James Fenimore Cooper: A Re-Appraisal.* Cooperstown: New York
    State Historical Society, 1954: 79–88.
Ranck, George W. "Girty, The White Indian." *Magazine of American History* 15 (March
    1886): 256–277.
Richards, James K. "A Clash of Cultures: Simon Girty and the Struggle for the Frontier."
    Timeline 2:3 (June–July 1985): 2–17.
Roosevelt, Theodore. *The Winning of the West: An Account of the Exploration and
    Settlement of Our Country from the Alleghanies to the Pacific.* 1889. 6 vols. New
    York and London: G. P. Putnam's Sons, 1903.
Seaver, James E. *A Narrative of the Life of Mrs. Mary Jemison.* 1823. Syracuse,: N.Y.
    Syracuse University Press, 1990.
Wallace, Paul A. W. *Conrad Weiser, 1696–1760: Friend of Colonist and Mohawk.* 1945.
    New York: Russell & Russell, 1971.
———. ed. *Thirty Thousand Miles with John Heckewelder.* Pittsburgh: University of
    Pittsburgh Press, 1958.
Winter, Nevin O. "The Renegades." In *A History of Northwest Ohio: A Narrative Ac-
    count of Its Historical Progress and Development from the First European Ex-
    ploration of the Maumee and Sandusky Valleys and the Adjacent Shore of Lake
    Erie, down to the Present Time.* Chicago and New York: Lewis Publishing Co.,
    1917: 43–53.

Barbara A. Mann

Goschochking Genocide, March 8, 1782. Goschochking (Gnadenhütten) was
the site of the most brutal of the many genocides that took place against Native
American peoples in Ohio during the eighteenth and nineteenth centuries. It was
conducted in 1782 by the Pennsylvania militia, 160 strong, commanded by Colonel David Williamson, who was acting under the authority of General George
Washington.

The militia murdered ninety-six league Delaware-Mahicans in Gnadenhütten,
a Moravian "praying town" within the territory of Goschochking, the Delaware
capital in Ohio. Another thirty Delaware-Mahicans taken prisoner during Williamson's hasty retreat to Fort Pitt were murdered along the way to silence
everyone with any knowledge of the war crime. Despite the militia's attempt to
eliminate all witnesses, some escaped: a young man who witnessed the opening
fire and two adolescent boys who fled Gnadenhütten in the midst of the murders.

The **American Revolution** was fought on two fronts, along the Atlantic sea-
coast and on the league lands. To break the back of the league, General Washington devised a plan to starve it out. He ordered the destruction of New York's
rich farmlands in 1779 and followed that up in 1781 (as soon as he could
penetrate Ohio) by ordering his commander at Fort Pitt, Colonel Daniel Brodhead, to destroy Goschochking, a task he finally accomplished in 1782. Goschochking was actually a trio of league Delaware towns, one for each Delaware
clan. It lay along the Muskingum River, whose bottomlands were quite fertile.
For two years after the ravaging of the league's breadbaskets in New York,

Goschochking had been sharing its harvests with the hungry leaguers of New York.

As part of his campaign, Brodhead was ordered to kill the league Delaware-Mahicans entirely. Learning of this plan, the league ordered the hasty removal of the Delaware-Mahicans from the Muskingum Valley to the league Wyandot capital at Upper Sandusky, in well-defended territory. Accordingly, from September 2 to 4, 1781, the Wyandots under Katepakomen (**Simon Girty**) and the Delawares under **Hopocan** ("Captain Pipe") secretly escorted the entire Delaware-Mahican nation to safety, thwarting the planned genocide for the time being.

The removal to Upper Sandusky was accomplished over the objections of the tiny faction of Delaware-Mahicans who had converted to the Moravian sect of Christianity. They believed themselves to be safe from the Americans because they were Christians and because the Moravian missionary **John Heckewelder** was an important spy against the league for General Washington. The league had better information, however, and knew that the Moravian Delaware-Mahicans were meant to have been killed along with all the rest.

The winter in Upper Sandusky was hungry, although safe from attack, since the Wyandots also had been dependent upon the Muskingum harvest. Unable to transport their harvest—a rich one in 1781—during their hasty withdrawal from Goschochking, the Delaware-Mahicans had buried it to prevent the American forces from looting it. Thus, when Brodhead finally attacked Goschochking, he found both the people and the harvest gone. After burning the deserted towns, he returned to Fort Pitt empty-handed.

By midwinter, the league peoples had been reduced to walking skeletons, many dying during 1781 and 1782 from starvation. Dangerous though it was for league peoples to venture back to Goschochking, now easily struck by forces out of Fort Pitt, the league had no choice. The famine had reached crisis proportions, so the buried food had to be recovered. Still believing themselves safe as "neutrals," the Christianized Delaware-Mahicans elected to return to the Muskingum fields as the bulk of the workers recovering the buried harvest. To reinforce the fact that they were a work crew and not a war party, the majority of those going were women and children. Accordingly, between 135 and 140 Delaware-Mahicans left Upper Sandusky on March 3, 1782, and headed back to Goschochking. Heckewelder promptly sent intelligence to Fort Pitt of their movements.

The revolutionary army, starving itself as an unintended result of their having destroyed the league fields, had every intention of resupplying itself by finding and plundering the Muskingum harvest. In a March 8 memorandum to General William Irvine, the new commander at Fort Pitt, Washington said that he had taken care of the provisioning problem, indicating that Williamson and the Pennsylvania militia had been dispatched to Goschochking anew under his orders (Mann, 166).

Arriving at Goschochking on March 8, 1782, the militia first murdered Shebosh, a leader, an act witnessed by a youth Heckewelder called "Jacob." Seeing what was afoot, "Jacob" instantly fled, his personal terror preventing him from warning anyone else. Next seeking out the bulk of the harvesters at Goschochking, Williamson and his men pretended to have been piously sent to aid fellow Christians retrieve their harvest. The militia had also brought along children to play with the Native children, to help lull the harvesters into a sense of well-being. Seeing both the apparent piety of the militia and the presence of settler children as proof that they were indeed "safe" as Christians, the Delaware-Mahicans even helped Williamson locate all but one of the work crews.

Once the harvest was unearthed, however, the militia dropped its pretense and brutally took the Delaware-Mahicans prisoner, shooting two young children in the process. The militia then confined its prisoners in two huts at Gnaden-hütten, the men and boys in one, the women and small children in the other. Williamson charged them with being a party of "Warriors" sent to attack the militia. They also charged the Delaware-Mahicans with horse theft. Both were capital crimes of which they were promptly convicted by Williamson's kangaroo court. The harvesters were sentenced to death.

The militia voted to club and scalp the Natives and then set the huts on fire to cover up the evidence of its crimes. Due to the heroics of the women, two children were hidden in a root cellar below the floorboards of the women's prison, but only one boy thereafter avoided death by smoke inhalation, escaping through a narrow vent to the outside. Unnamed by Heckewelder (because he was not a Christian convert), the boy later recalled that as he lay on his back in the crawl space, the blood from the murdered women fell so profusely through the floorboards that he feared being drowned in it.

In the men's hut, an adolescent boy (called "Thomas" by the missionaries) escaped by lying among the stacked bodies, playing dead, and then stealing out inches behind the armed guards, just before the hut was set afire. These two eyewitnesses to the crimes made it back to Upper Sandusky. Their stories were recorded by a remorseful Heckewelder in "Captivity and Murder" (1782) and again in his *Narrative* (1818). On the way back to Fort Pitt, the militia took thirty more league Delawares captive and murdered them all along the way. No one escaped this second massacre (Wallace, 197; Butterfield, 30).

When Katepakomen unmasked Heckewelder's treachery in a tense public scene at Upper Sandusky, Weshkahattees, a young Delaware, raced to Goschochking to rescue his relatives, arriving on March 8. At Welhik-Tuppeek (a field), he found a small group of harvesters who had not been discovered by Williamson. As the militia celebrated its kill into the evening, Weshkahattees stole into Gnadenhütten, floated away a canoe from under the eyes of the armed guards, and in several trips, silently ferried the survivors across the Muskingum, "west of death." With children and old folks on their backs, the party ran all the way back to Upper Sandusky, a nightlong journey. Upon unloading on the morning of March 9, they discovered that during their desperate flight, one child had died on its mother's back of hunger (Mann, 180–181).

The militia stole not only the harvest, but also eighty pack animals, furs, equipment, and the personal possessions of their victims (Marsh, 10; Mann, 222). Plundered items later sold by militiamen for personal profit at Pittsburgh also included "souvenir" shaving strops made from the skins of Delaware-Mahicans (Heckewelder, *History*, 342), indicating the fate of the thirty who had been murdered on the way back to Fort Pitt.

In a deceitful report printed in the *Philadelphia Gazette*, Williamson boasted of the genocide as a great victory in battle, presenting the harvesters as "warriors" and their goods as "provisions to supply their war parties" ("Notice" 2). Aware of the truth, Heckewelder spent the rest of his life atoning for what he had done. He went on a campaign to set the record straight, later recording that he was "ashamed of being a *white man*" (Heckewelder, *History*, 76; italics in the original). Heckewelder's most faithful reader, James Fenimore Cooper, later immortalized the phrase "The Last of the Mohicans," coined by settlers after the genocide. Though dramatic, it wrongly leaves the impression that all Delaware-Mahicans had perished on March 8, 1782.

After the details of the crime became clear to them, John Bull, the Euro-father of Shebosh, and the Moravians, David Zeisberger and John Heckewelder, raised a mighty ruckus, calling for justice. A halfhearted inquiry into the matter by revolutionary officials allowed the Pennsylvania militia to stonewall the investigation (Mann, 227). No one was ever indicted. In fact, Williamson became a public figure and mayor of Catfish, Pennsylvania (Mann, 220). Washington was pleased enough with him to send him back into Ohio two months later under Colonel William Crawford for an unsuccessful follow-up attack on the Delawares in May 1782.

The Goschochking genocide is commemorated by Ohio league and other Native peoples with annual powwows held on the old site of Goschochking, between the modern-day Ohio towns of Coshocton and New Philadelphia. The Moravians later raised a monument in a park in Gnadenhütten, inscribed "Here Triumphed in Death Ninety Christian Indians, March 8, 1782." This plaque ignores those victims who were not Christians, including six people murdered at the praying town and the thirty massacred along the road back to Fort Pitt.

FURTHER READING

Butterfield, Consul Willshire. *History of the Girtys, Being a Concise Account of the Girty Brothers—Thomas, Simon, James, and George, and of Their Half-Brother John Turner—Also of the Part Taken by Them in Lord Dunmore's War, in the Western Border War of the Revolution, and in the Indian War of 1790–95.* Cincinnati: Robert Clarke & Co., 1890.

Heckewelder, John. *History, Manners, and Customs of the Indian Nations Who Once Inhabited Pennsylvania and the Neighboring States.* 1820, 1876. The First American Frontier Series. New York: Arno Press and the New York Times, 1971.

———. *Narrative of the Mission of the United Brethren among the Delaware and Mohegan Indians from Its Commencement, in the Year 1740, to the Close of the Year 1808.* 1820. New York: Arno Press, 1971.

Howells, William D. "Gnadenhütten." In *Three Villages*. Boston: James R. Osgood and
    Company, 1884: 117–198.
Mann, Barbara A. "Forbidden Ground: Racial Politics and Hidden Identity in James
    Fenimore Cooper's Leather-Stocking Tales." Ph.D. diss., University of Toledo,
    1997.
Marsh, Thelma R. *Lest We Forget: A Brief Sketch of Wyandot County's History*. Upper
    Sandusky, Ohio: Wyandot County Historical Society, 1967.
"Notice." *Philadelphia Gazette*, No. 2705 (April 17, 1782): 2.
Wallace, Paul A. W., ed. "Captivity and Murder." In *Thirty Thousand Miles with John
    Heckewelder*. Pittsburgh: University of Pittsburgh Press, 1958: 170–207.

Barbara A. Mann

Governmental functioning and powers of the Haudenosaunee League. The
constitutional government of the Haudenosaunee League was set up by **Deganawida** (the **Peacemaker**), **Jigonsaseh**, and **Hiawatha** during the **Second Epoch
of Time**. It functioned through a set round of interfacing councils, both male
and female, that considered and decided the business of the league. These councils represented clans (the local level of government), on one hand, and nations
(the federal level of government), on the other, with the Clan Mothers' councils
meeting locally and the men's Grand Council meeting federally. The Head Clan
Mother of the league was the *Jigonsaseh*, while the chairman of the men's Grand
Council was the *Adodaroh*. The *Jigonsaseh*'s capital was located at Gaustauyea,
also called Kienuka ("The Fortress"), while the *Adodaroh*'s was at Onondaga.

Primary Concepts of Haudenosaunee Government

The government rested upon three primary concepts: *Ne" Skĕñ´no^n* (Health),
Ne" Gai´i·hwiio (Righteousness), and *Ne" Găshasde^n´´sä'* (Popular Sovereignty). Each of these three elements was split into its two complementary
halves, thus replicating the cosmic relationship of the Sacred Twins. *Ne"
Skĕñ´´no^n* (Health) meant physical and mental well-being, on one hand, and
peace, on the other. *Ne" Gai´i·hwiio* (Righteousness) meant ethical behavior,
complemented by social justice in implementing policies. *Ne" Găshasde^n´´sä'*
(Popular Sovereignty) meant bowing to the will of the people, but also public
safety, that is, national defense. All councils were responsible for seeing to it
that these principles were observed in governmental operations (Hewitt, "Some
Esoteric Aspects," 322; Hewitt, "Constitutional League," 541; Wallace, *White
Roots*, 13–14.)

The constitution of the league was variously recorded during the late nineteenth and early twentieth centuries, usually in connection with the tradition of
the *Gayanĕsshä´´gowa*, or "Great Binding Law." Detailed provisions of the *Gay-
anĕsshä´´gowa* identify qualifications for office, the lists of male and (in Dayodekane's "Traditional History and Constitution of the Iroquois Confederacy")
female position titles, and the powers and duties of each. The functions of
wampum are set forth, along with the official symbols of the league. Religious
ceremonies are protected as human rights. Installation rites are detailed.

Women's sections of the Great Law, generally the clans and consanguinity and **adoption** sections, gave the *gantowisas* (women acting in their official capacities) the ownership of the land and the power to keep and bestow lineage names, adopt or expel citizens, nominate officials to positions as chiefs, Clan Mothers, or warriors, impeach errant officials, and call wars. Men's sections dealt primarily with league relations with outside nations, federal councils, warfare, and national treason. Men's councils were specifically granted "the same rights as the council of the women" (Parker, *Constitution*, 55). For written versions of the full constitution, see Parker, *The Constitution of the Five Nations* (1916), containing one Newhouse version (another was composed in 1885), plus the chiefs' composite version; Gibson, *Concerning the League* (1912; Woodbury, 1992); and Dayodekane's "Traditional History and Constitution of the Iroquois Confederacy" (1885).

It is inappropriate to discuss the local and federal halves of the government in hierarchical terms or to assume that the men's federal council wielded executive power over nations and clans. These errors are all too common in Western descriptions of the league. There was no hierarchy, nor was the structure of government top-down. The structure was horizontal, with each half reciprocating the other in a circular process. No matter was ever closed as long as anyone in any council wanted to discuss it. The federal level held no power of fiat. If anything, the local councils were the more powerful of the two, but, on the whole, neither half was able to compel the other to do anything. The guiding precept of the league was **consensus**, not coercion.

It is also inappropriate to assume that the *Jigonsaseh* or the *Adodaroh* ruled over the women and men, respectively, after the fashion of European monarchs. They were first among equals, not executive or royal officers; their jobs were to facilitate consensus, not to issue directives. The only direct powers of the *Adodaroh* were to call meetings and to veto measures. On the women's side, the *Jigonsaseh* possessed these same powers, with the additional ability to call or end wars and to decide judicial questions. She took these latter steps in close consultation with the Clan Mothers.

Finally, it is wildly erroneous to focus on the operations of the men's councils while ignoring the operations of the women's councils. Unfortunately, this is the approach of nearly every Western treatment of league government, leaving the mistaken impression that women were secondary or subservient to men. In fact, some Western anthropologists, including Elisabeth Tooker, and ethnologists, including **Lewis Henry Morgan**, have actually gone so far as to state that this was the case (Tooker in Spittal, 199, 200; Morgan, 2:315). Such assertions are ahistorical, however, flying in the face of numerous, reliable primary sources, such as Joseph Lafitau, and documents that specifically listed women as speakers at various treaty councils. They also controvert the findings of primary anthropologists, such as Lucien Carr and J. W. Powell. The urge to sideline women in academic discussions of the league reflects European values that seriously distort a real understanding of the league (Mann, *Iroquoian Women*, Chapter 3).

The Principle of Twins

The principle of the Twins (originally quadruplets) is obvious in the structure of the councils, clans, and nations of the league. The Sacred Twins exist as the principle of reciprocating halves, whose usual metaphor is the east-west axis. East is meaningless without west, which is itself meaningless without east. Neither direction is more or less important than the other, and directionality exists only as long as both stand. This principle of collaborative halves guides every aspect of governmental organization.

The clans of the league exist in the reciprocating halves of Wolves and Turtles (called "moieties" by anthropologists after the French word *moitié*, meaning "half"). The Wolf half contains numerous clans, which sit opposite the Turtle clans. The actual clan lists differ, depending upon the nation and the stage of history at which they are named, but the central principle of mirror-image halves remains, historically guiding the halves of Clan Mothers' councils. All clans of the league (typically given in Euro-texts as Wolf, Bear, Beaver, Turtle, Deer, Snipe, Heron, and Hawk, although other minor clans exist) had Clan Mother representatives sitting in the Clan Mothers' councils on either the Wolf or the Turtle side.

By the same logic, the federal level was divided into reciprocating halves. Since the turn of the century, these halves have been referred to as the Elder and Younger Brotherhoods, but, as Hewitt showed, they were originally conceived of as Sisterhoods whose lineages represented the Mother and Father sides of the league (Hewitt, "Some Esoteric Aspects," 323; Hewitt, "Ethnological Studies," 240–241). The Elder Brotherhood (or Sisterhood) included the **Onondagas, Mohawks**, and **Senecas**, while the Younger Brotherhood (or Sisterhood) included the **Oneidas** and **Cayugas** (offshoots of the Mohawks and Senecas, respectively), as well as the **Tuscaroras**, who entered the league as a nation well after its founding. (Incorporated nations spoke locally through their adoptive clan councils and gained voice in the federal council through a sponsoring nation.)

This intricate interfacing of clans and nations, men and women, all operating councilmanically by halves, wove the league together in a web of interlocking citizenships and created a strong sense of identity and status. One was not merely a member of the Wolf Clan, but of the Wolf Clan of the Senecas whose female representatives sat in clan councils. One was not simply an Onondaga, but an Onondaga of the Deer Clan whose male representatives sat in the Grand Council. The latter-day habit of self-identification by nation only reflects Westernization. Traditionals know their clan as well as their nation.

The league was set up so that each clan, arranged by nation, held title to "names," or civic positions in governmental councils. Women alone held the rights over these titles of office, because women alone were the progenitors of the nation. Today, due to skewed methods of ethnographic collecting that greatly privileged male aspects of the culture, it is the names of fifty male grand councillors that are still known. Originally, however, there were women's titles to office as well, as noted by Dayodekane (Seth Newhouse) in his 1885 manuscript of the *Gayanĕsshä'ʹgowa*, the Great Law, or constitution, of the league (Fenton, 151, 152). Thus, while the men's titles have been preserved, the only woman's title still well known today is *Jigonsaseh*.

The order of deliberation in the councils was this: The Clan Mothers' councils considered all matters first, determining whether and when to forward them to the men's Grand Council (Bonvillain, "Iroquoian Women," 55; R. Jacobs, 503). The men could only consider matters sent to them by the women. Once a matter was forwarded to the men, they deliberated it according to their own judgment. Their consensus conclusion was not binding on clans or nations, however. Each nation might, through its clan councils, reconsider or reject the consensus of the Grand Council. Thus the clan councils performed judicial review of the matters coming out of the Grand Council.

The Three Courses of Action

Whether male or female, councils had only three possible courses of action on any matter: to accept, reject, or table a measure. Tabling meant that the matter might be taken up again for further deliberations at a succeeding convention of the council. Matters were not crudely debated by councils in body, however. Instead, councils operated according to a very involved and complex set of procedures (Parker, *Constitution*, 10–11). The two halves of councils were me-diated by Firekeepers. For men, Firekeepers were the Onondagas—the home identity of the *Adodaroh*. For women, the Firekeeper was the *Jigonsaseh* (Par-ker, *Life*, 42), with her titular clan lineage acting as the Firekeeping council-women.

First, to aid in their deliberations, councils immediately broke into their nat-ural halves upon convening, with agenda items evenly divided between the two. Second, each half formed subcommittees, one for each matter before it. Recon-vening by themselves, the subcommittees investigated and debated their assigned issues. When a subcommittee had itself come to a consensus, it brought its matter back before its half of the council, along with a recommendation, which again might be to discard, continue, or table an issue. At this point, the council half considered the report of its subcommittee, determining its own course of action, which might include sending it back to subcommittee for further study. When satisfied, the council half debated the issue in body, coming to its own consensus on the matter, that is, to accept, reject, or table.

If the half decided to accept the matter, the issue was passed to the Firekee-pers, who referred it to the other half of the council, which began the whole process over again, appointing its own subcommittee. Once the second half of the council had come to a consensus on the matter, its decision was announced to the other side. Often, by the end of the halved process, two different consen-suses had been reached. In that case, the two halves deliberated in body until they had come to a whole-council consensus to accept, reject, or table. If the decision was to accept, the matter was forwarded to the *Jigonsaseh* or *Adodaroh*, who could either accept or veto the matter. If the two halves could not agree, the Firekeepers debated and cast the deciding vote on the issue.

The men's and women's councils communicated their concerns to one another through speakers, whom Arthur Parker called "aboriginal public service commissioner[s]" whom, he said, were the appointed war chiefs of each group (Parker, *Constitution*, 11). This could not have always been true, since men sent female speakers to the women's councils. Although the *Jigonsaseh* could act as a military general in emergencies, few women took on a warrior's role. Thus the men's speaker to the *Jigonsaseh*'s council was almost certainly determined by another means.

Again, due to the skews in Western records, the names of women's male speakers to men's councils were recorded, whereas the names of the men's female speakers to the Clan Mothers' councils were overlooked. Well-known women's speakers to the men's Grand Council included Sagoyewatha (**Red Jacket**) and Seth Newhouse.

Because they kept the lineage titles and wampum, women nominated all officers (chiefs as well as Clan Mothers) to vacant titles of office. Titles of office stayed within the clan lineages of particular nations. In selecting Clan Mothers, there was no open voting on nominees. The women alone determined who was to succeed to office whenever there was an opening (Powell, 61). In selecting male chiefs, the women held the exclusive power to nominate, although the entire populace had the right to vote on their choice.

Democracy or Oligarchy?

It has been erroneously argued by some Western scholars that lineage titles resulted in the rule of oligarchies. This claim uses Western political structures to discuss Iroquoian political structures, damaging understanding. Assuming that such comparisons of distinct cultures are ever appropriate, the *owachira* (matrilineal clans) may be more properly viewed as political parties seeking qualified candidates for office. Nominations were just as likely to fall on adoptees as on clansfolk by birth, and sometimes an individual was adopted in precisely because she or he seemed a likely leader. Birth status was completely unimportant. Citizenship was the qualification.

In addition to naming individuals to office, women also could depose errant officers of the league through impeachment. Western scholars have mainly noted impeachments in connection with male offenders such as Sagonaquade (Albert Cusick), the sitting *Adodaroh* in 1874. However, the Clan Mothers did not hesitate to impeach any of their own who had committed treason (Bonvillain, "Iroquoian Women," 56). The primary impeachable offense historically was the one for which Cusick was deposed: converting to Christianity while in office. Conversion was seen as having accepted adoption by Europeans.

Barring impeachment, an office fell vacant only upon the death of the titleholder. This led to formalized funerary rituals—Requickenings—that ended with the naming of a new titleholder. Again, this process has been studied by Westerners solely in connection with men, but a process similar to the condolence council following the death of grand councillors also occurred after the death of Clan Mothers. Glimpses of it may be found in primary sources, including the bereavement council at which **Mary Jemison** received her adoption (Seaver, 19–22), as well as a Clan Mother's funeral described in detail by **John Heckewelder** (Heckewelder, 268–276). Powell also directly described the installation of new Clan Mothers (Powell, 61–62).

In addition to lineage offices, the Grand Council included positions for "pine-tree" chiefs. A pine-tree chief might not be entitled by lineage to a position in government, but had shown so much skill in statecraft as to merit recognition by the Clan Mothers. The pine-tree position died with the incumbent, however. It was not hereditary. It is unrecorded whether an equivalent provision was in place for exalting women on merit, but it was very likely to have existed, since the male and female councils operated as mirror-image institutions.

Types of Meetings

Business councils of elders, male and female, were called monthly (based on the lunar calendar) at the full moon, although they might be called more frequently if needed. Individual councillors who were concerned about an issue could approach Firekeepers to ask for a council to be called out of turn. Special situations or emergencies also might precipitate a quick council. The grand councils were, as the title indicates, large-scale affairs consisting of the top fifty officials of both genders. Called annually, the chiefs' Grand Council met at Onondaga, while the Clan Mothers' Grand Council met at Gaustauyea. Again, great attention has been paid in the ethnographic literature to the men's Grand Council, while the women's Grand Council has been studiously ignored, despite references in Lafitau, Dayodekane, and elsewhere that made its existence and importance obvious.

Special military councils also were convened at times of peril or war. Women appointed warriors and empowered war chiefs by giving them the black wampum of war. War councils had to run their decisions by the Clan Mothers' councils and the men's Grand Council. Either body might disagree with the war councillors, but military leaders had no rights over civic matters. The Clan Mothers had the ability to disband war councils and declare peace.

New citizens of the league were brought in by adoption, a process controlled by the Clan Mothers. For the most part, citizenship was granted through clan adoptions, which resulted in full citizenship for the adoptee. In only one instance was an entire nation granted adoption by the league proper. This was the case of the Tuscaroras. Following the Tuscarora War (1711), during which southern colonists attempted to press the nation into slavery, the Tuscaroras petitioned the Oneida Clan Mothers for admission to the league, a request that was approved. Between 1711 and 1735, when the last stragglers made it north to Ir-oquoia, the Tuscaroras came into the league, although the official date for their entry is usually set at 1722 or 1724.

All other new nations came in as clan adoptees, with rights in the clan and federal councils as determined by their adoptive clans and nations. Thus the Delawares (Lenni Lenapes) were originally taken in by the Oneida Clan Moth-ers, who later expelled them as uncooperative. The Cayuga Clan Mothers took pity on the refugees and adopted them into the league for the second time, at which point they gracefully accepted their positions along with their league land grant in Ohio. Thereafter, the Delawares held their own clan councils through their adoptive clans and spoke in the federal Grand Council through the Ca-yugas. By the same token, the Wyandots of Ohio came into the league under the sponsorship of the Senecas and spoke at Onondaga through their Seneca representatives. Both Delawares and Wyandots operated in the women's coun-cils of their adoptive clans.

Primary sources such as Heckewelder also make it appear that at least some adoptive nations such as the Delawares maintained their original clans for internal identity purposes, although the Great Law theoretically banned this practice. Nevertheless, Shimony documented the elaborate ceremonies still con-scientiously conducted by modern Haudenosaunee to maintain Tutelo names, based on an old promise the league made to the Tutelos upon their adoption that their nation would never be allowed to die out (Shimony, 253–256). It is very likely that similar promises were made—and kept—to other incorporated nations.

The Nature of Haudenosaunee Federalism

Because the league was based on the political reciprocity of the clans and nations, rather than on hierarchical order, there was no such thing as a federal directive or federal power. This fact has caused much confusion among Western scholars, leading several historians recently to deny that a coherent league, stretching from New York to Ohio, ever existed. Such scholars as Francis Jen-nings and Michael McConnell base their denials largely on the inability of the Grand Council at Onondaga to issue orders that Ohio was obliged to follow, yet this argument displays a serious misunderstanding of how the gendered league functioned.

Dictatorship, patriarchy, and authority are European forms of political defi-nition that have little relation to traditional Haudenosaunee values. The seat of power (i.e., the power to persuade) was the local Clan Mothers' councils, while Gaustauyea and Onondaga sought national and clanwide consensus, something that bubbled up as much from councils in the Land of the Three Miamis (Ohio) as from those in New York. Ohio was not a colony of New York, as these historians would have it, for the league did not colonize people; it adopted them. Ohio was, therefore, as much a part of the eighteenth-century league as was Seneca, a fact of which General George Washington was only too painfully aware in his dispatches, memos, and battle plans. It was not any internal revolt of Ohio against Onondaga that cut New York off from Ohio, as has been suggested. It was the deceitful Treaty of Paris (1783), in which the British ceded land they did not own to colonists who had not won it, treachery followed soon by the Battle of Fallen Timbers (1794) that conclusively stole Ohio from its Haudenosaunee League citizens.

The league survived the **American Revolution** and the forced assimilation that quickly followed. Despite the attempts by the U.S. government to foist new constitutions (which disempowered women) on league nations and to insist that the league no longer existed, the *Kayánerénhkowa*, or Great Binding Law, was preserved. Several versions of it from the late nineteenth and the early twentieth centuries were written down by elders determined to preserve the Haudenosaunee heritage. Today, although the great tradition of Clan Mothers' councils is only barely alive, two men's Grand Councils exist and function, one in Canada and the other in New York.

FURTHER READING

Bonvillain, Nancy. "Gender Relations in Native North America." *American Indian Culture and Research Journal* 13:2 (1989): 1–28.
———. "Iroquoian Women." In Nancy Bonvillain, ed., *Studies on Iroquoian Culture.* Occasional Publications in Northeastern Anthropology, No. 6. Rindge, N.H.: Department of Anthropology, Franklin Pierce College, 1980: 47–58.
Brown, Judith K. "Economic Organization and the Position of Women among the Iroquois." *Ethnohistory* 17:3–4 (Summer–Fall 1970): 151–167.
Campbell, Duncan Scott. "Traditional History of the Confederacy of the Six Nations." *Transactions of the Royal Society of Canada.* Series 3, vol. 5, no. section 2. Ottawa: Royal Society of Canada, 1912: 195–246.
Carr, Lucien. "On the Social and Political Position of Woman among the Huron-Iroquois Tribes." *Peabody Museum of American Archaeology and Ethnology, Reports* 16–17, 3:3–4 (1884): 207–232.
Colden, Cadwallader. *The History of the Five Indian Nations Depending on the Province of New-York in America.* 1747. Ithaca, N.Y.: Great Seal Books, 1958.
———. *The History of the Five Indian Nations of Canada Which Are Dependent on the Province of New York in America.* 1765. 2 vols. New York: New Amsterdam Book Company, 1902.
Dayodekane. *Cosmogony of De-ka-na-wi-da's Government: Cosmogony of the Iroquois Confederacy.* Oshweken [*sic*]: Six Nations Reserve, 1885.
Fenton, William N. "Seth Newhouse's [Dayodekane's] Traditional History and Constitution of the Iroquois Confederacy." *Proceedings of the American Philosophical Society* 93:2 (1949): 141–158.
Gibson, John Arthur. *Concerning the League: The Iroquois Tradition as Dictated in Onondaga by John Arthur Gibson.* 1912. Ed. and trans. Hanni Woodbury. Memoir 9. Winnipeg: Algonquian and Iroquoian Linguistics, 1992.
Grinde, Donald A., Jr. *The Iroquois and the Founding of the American Nation.* San Francisco: Indian Historian Press, 1977.
Grinde, Donald A., Jr., and Bruce E. Johansen. *Exemplar of Liberty: Native America and*

the Evolution of Democracy. Los Angeles: UCLA American Indian Studies Center, 1991.

Heckewelder, John. *History, Manners, and Customs of the Indian Nations Who Once Inhabited Pennsylvania and the Neighboring States.* 1820, 1876. The First American Frontier Series. New York: Arno Press and the New York Times, 1971.

Hewitt, J[ohn] N[apoleon] B[rinton]. "A Constitutional League of Peace in the Stone Age of America: The League of the Iroquois and Its Constitution." *Smithsonian Institution Series* (1920): 527–545.

———. "Ethnological Studies among the Iroquois Indians." *Smithsonian Miscellaneous Collections* 78 (1927): 237–247.

———. "The 'League of Nations' of the Iroquois Indians in Canada." *Explorations and Field-work of the Smithsonian Institution for 1929* (1930): 201–206.

———. "Some Esoteric Aspects of the League of the Iroquois." *Proceedings of the International Congress of Americanists* 19 (1915): 322–326.

"Iroquois (Haudenosaunee) Confederacy." In Bruce Elliott Johansen, ed., *The Encyclopedia of Native American Legal Tradition.* Westport, Conn.: Greenwood Press, 1998: 156–163.

Jacobs, Renée. "The Iroquois Great Law of Peace and the United States Constitution: How the Founding Fathers Ignored the Clan Mothers." *American Indian Law Review* 16:2 (1991): 497–531.

Jacobs, Wilbur R. "Wampum: The Protocol of Indian Diplomacy." *William and Mary Quarterly*, 3rd ser. 4:3 (October 1949): 596–604.

Johansen, Bruce E. *Forgotten Founders: Benjamin Franklin, the Iroquois, and the Rationale for the American Revolution.* Ipswich, Mass.: Gambit, 1982.

Lafitau, Joseph-François. *Customs of the American Indians Compared with the Customs of Primitive Times.* 1724. Ed. and trans. William N. Fenton and Elizabeth L. Moore. 2 vols. Toronto: Champlain Society, 1974–1977.

Mann, Barbara A. "Haudenosaunee (Iroquois) Women, Legal and Political Status." In Bruce Elliott Johansen, ed., *The Encyclopedia of Native American Legal Tradition.* Westport, Conn.: Greenwood Press, 1998: 112–131.

———. *Iroquoian Women: Gantowisas of the Haudenosaunee League.* New York: Peter Lang, 2000.

———. "The Lynx in Time: Haudenosaunee Women's Traditions and History." *American Indian Quarterly* 21:3 (Summer 1997): 423–450.

Mann, Barbara A., and Jerry L. Fields. "A Sign in the Sky: Dating the League of the Haudenosaunee." *American Indian Culture and Research Journal* 21:2 (1997): 105–163.

Morgan, Lewis Henry. *League of the Haudenosaunee, or Iroquois.* 1851. 2 vols. New York: Burt Franklin, 1964.

Parker, Arthur C. *The Constitution of the Five Nations, or, The Iroquois Book of the Great Law.* Albany: University of the State of New York, 1916.

———. *The Life of General Ely S. Parker, Last Grand Sachem of the Iroquois and General Grant's Military Secretary.* Buffalo: Buffalo Historical Society, 1919.

Powell, J. W. "Wyandot Government: A Short Study of Tribal Society." *Annual Report of the Bureau of Ethnology to the Secretary of the Smithsonian Institution* 1 (1879–1880): 57–69.

Seaver, James E. *A Narrative of the Life of Mrs. Mary Jemison.* 1823. Syracuse, N.Y.: Syracuse University Press, 1990.

Shimony, Annemarie Anrod. *Conservatism among the Iroquois at the Six Nations Reserve.* 1961. Syracuse, N.Y.: Syracuse University Press, 1994.

Spittal, William Guy, ed. *Iroquois Women: An Anthology.* Ohsweken, Ontario, Canada: Iroquois Publishing and Craft Supplies, 1990.

Wallace, Paul A. W. *Conrad Weiser, 1696–1760: Friend of Colonist and Mohawk.* 1945. New York: Russell & Russell, 1971.

———. *The White Roots of Peace.* Empire State Historical Publication Series No. 56. Port Washington, N.Y.: Ira J. Friedman, 1946.

Barbara A. Mann

Grand River (Ohsweken) Iroquois Reserve. During the **American Revolution**, the Haudenosaunee Confederacy split its support between the rebelling colonists and the British Crown. After the war, substantial numbers of Haudenosaunee who had supported the British moved (along with perhaps as many as 10 percent of the non-Indian colonists who had supported the Tories) to Ontario. A new community was established at Grand River, and a new Grand Council Fire was kindled there.

The British granted **Joseph Brant** 675,000 acres when the American Revolution ended; by the middle 1780s, about 1,450 Haudenosaunee and about 400 other allied people began moving from the United States to the Grand River Reserve. A substantial number of the **Mohawks** who moved to Grand River were related, in one way or another, to **Sir William Johnson**, who fathered several dozen children by an unknown number of Haudenosaunee women. For example, Chief G. H. M. Johnson, a grandson of Sir William, acquired property that became known as "Chiefswood" at Grand River on the Six Nations reserve. On this estate, **Emily Pauline Johnson**, the esteemed Mohawk poet, was born and grew up.

Most of the initial immigrants to Grand River were Mohawks under the leadership of Brant. During the 1780s, a band of Onondagas joined them, followed by two bands of **Cayugas** and a few **Senecas**. A number of **Oneidas** also moved from New York State to London, Ontario, at about the same time. By the middle 1780s, the Iroquois population in the Grand River area reached roughly 2,000. The Iroquois of Grand River readily accepted non-Indian settlement on their territories; some land was sold with the express purpose of supplying the Iroquois with cash income needed to meet the requirements of their daily lives.

The new Grand Council was the major governing body of the Six Nations Reserve at Grand River until 1924, when the Canadian Indian Act abolished it, according to Canadian law. The traditional **Longhouse** at Grand River persisted, however, as a governmental alternative to the chiefs sanctioned by Canada. In 1959, a traditionalist revolt began at Grand River in which the council house of the elective system at Ohsweken was occupied. Royal Canadian Mounted Police intervened to restore the elective system to power. Another similar revolt took place there a decade later.

In the middle 1950s, the Native population of the Grand River Reserve (mostly Mohawks and Cayugas) was about 6,500. By the middle 1990s, Native population there had risen to about 11,000 people (Oswalt, 421).

FURTHER READING

Oswalt, Wendell H. *This Land Was Theirs: A Study of North American Indians*, 5th ed. Mountain View, Calif.: Mayfield Publishing, 1996.
Parker, Arthur C. *The Life of General Ely S. Parker, Last Grand Sachem of the Iroquois and General Grant's Military Secretary.* Buffalo Historical Society Publications 23. Buffalo, N.Y.: Buffalo Historical Society, 1919.

Grandfathers (False Face masks). Grandfathers, masks that many non-Iroquois call False Faces, are vital parts of several Haudenosaunee **ceremonies**. These masks, when used properly, are said to be associated with healing physical illnesses, restoring mental health, and maintaining harmony between humankind and nature in Haudenosaunee society. The manner in which the masks are used is very important, and the Iroquois Grand Council is struggling to have masks returned to their proper uses from museums, merchants, private collectors, and other non-Iroquois.

Disagreement exists regarding the antiquity of the Grandfather (False Face) societies among the Haudenosaunee. William Beauchamp stated at the turn of the century that the ceremonies had been a relatively recent innovation (Beauchamp, 141), but **Arthur C. Parker**, writing at nearly the same time, believed that the ceremonies were much older, at least among the **Senecas**: "It is quite possible that the author of 'Van Curler's' Journal of 1634–35 mentions a false face when he writes: 'This chief showed me his idol; it is a head with the teeth sticking out; it is dressed in red cloth. Others have a snake, a turtle, a swan, a crane, a pigeon for their idols' " (Parker, 128). To Parker, the fact that very few non-Indian records mention the False Faces did not negate their existence: "Early explorers certainly could not have seen everything of Iroquois culture, especially some of the secret things, and their lack of description may be regarded as negative testimony rather than as positive evidence of the nonexistence of certain features which later students have found" (Parker, 128).

Present-day Iroquois often remark on the callousness with which some non-Indian "experts" on the Haudenosaunee have treated their Grandfathers and other ritual objects. These attitudes perhaps have their origins in a state of mind that values the masks for their market value (a very un-Haudenosaunee concept) while maintaining that present-day Iroquois people do not know how to "protect" their own ceremonial objects. **William N. Fenton**, who has often been called the "dean" of Iroquois studies in academic anthropology, has been sharply criticized by Haudenosaunee people for publishing a book filled with finely detailed color photographs of Grandfathers. Haudenosaunee traditionalists believe that the masks should not be photographed. Fenton has been largely ostracized from Iroquois communities, in part because he violated this rule.

Grandfathers in their proper context are used by Haudenosaunee medicine societies. They are not to be bought, sold, photographed, or placed on public display or used for any purpose other than their intended use in healing maladies and restoring balance in Iroquois societies. The masks, which may be made of wood (usually basswood) or cornhusks, represent the shared power of the original medicine beings. The masks' distorted features are sometimes characterized by a crooked nose and bent mouth, capped by a mane of long black hair. The "face" may be painted red, black, or white, or in a combination of these colors. The eyes are made of tin or copper, allowing space for the wearer's eyes. A mask is properly made after its creator has had a dream during which a spirit comes; the carver tries to replicate the face of this dream being on the mask. Having carved his mask, the creator becomes part of a medicine society.

All Grandfathers are regarded as sacred regardless of their size or age. The masks are believed to be empowered in the act of their creation. Any commercialization of the masks is regarded as damaging to the Haudenosaunee by the Grand Council and the medicine societies. The medicine societies operate privately, forbidding invasive inquiries by anyone who is not a member. The Grand Council at Onondaga has asked that all alienated Grandfathers be returned to their proper uses and has formed a committee that meets with museum personnel and other collectors to pursue this policy. "These masks were divorced from the people by museum collectors who let it be known they were willing to pay top dollar for the faces, regardless of how they were obtained. Many members of the healing societies were shocked to find that masks were stolen from their homes and sold by relatives in desperate need of cash," wrote **Doug George-Kanentiio**, a **Mohawk** and a columnist for the *Syracuse Herald-American* (George-Kanentiio, C-3).

FURTHER READING

Beauchamp, William M. *A History of the New York Iroquois, Now Commonly Called the Six Nations*. New York State Museum Bulletin No. 78. Albany: State of New York, 1905.

George-Kanentiio, Doug. "Iroquois Seek to End Outrage of Sacred Objects Being Sold." *Syracuse Herald-American*, September 17, 1995, C-3.

"Haudenosaunee Confederacy Announces Policy on False Face Masks." *Akwesasne Notes* 1:1 (Spring 1995): 39.

Parker, Arthur C. *The Code of Handsome Lake, the Seneca Prophet*. New York State Museum Bulletin No. 163, Education Department Bulletin No. 530, November 1, 1912. Albany: University of the State of New York, 1913.

Tooker, Elisabeth. *The Iroquois Ceremonial of Midwinter*. Syracuse, N.Y.: Syracuse University Press, 1970.

Grangula (Haaskouan, Big Mouth, La Grande Gueule) (Onondaga), fl. 1680s. The French gave Grangula this European name (*grande gueule* means "great mouth" in French) because of his oratorical abilities and his diplomatic skill. Grangula played the English against the French, maintaining Iroquois leverage, as he refused French demands that he quit trading with the English in

1684. In 1688, Grangula was a principal organizer of 1,200 warriors who marched to Montréal to arrange a truce. After a preliminary truce was signed, duplicity by the Huron chief Adario caused the Iroquois to mount an attack on Montréal.

Grangula was probably *Tadadaho* of the Iroquois Confederacy during meetings with the British and French in 1684. At these meetings, he denied both sides' demands for allegiance, saying that the Iroquois had been born free, and that they did not depend on the French or the British. "We may go where we please, and carry with us whom we please. If your allies be your slaves, treat them as such" (Armstrong, 7). Grangula warned against a buildup of armies in the area, saying that it would endanger the Great Tree of Peace, the security of the Iroquois Confederacy. Aggressive moves by either the French or the English could cause the Iroquois to "dig up the hatchet" from under the roots of the Iroquois Great Tree of Peace.

FURTHER READING

Armstrong, Virginia Irving, comp. *I Have Spoken: American History through the Voices of the Indians*. Chicago: Sage Books, 1971.

Great Feather Dance (*Ostowa'ko:wa*). The Great Feather Dance is the most sacred and powerful dance of the Haudenosaunee and is performed at all ceremonies with the exception of *Ohki:we* (the Feast of the Dead). It is done for Deganawida, the **Peacemaker**. When it is done, the participants think of his very special contribution to them, the *Kaienere:kowa* (the **Great Law of Peace**) and its importance as playing the major role in each of their lives. Both men and women take part in this dance; men dance in the outer circle and women in the inner circle. At the end of every verse, the singers ask the dancers if they want them to continue singing, and the dancers reply by yelling back, "Hio" (Yes).

The instrument used in this dance is the turtle rattle, which is a symbol of the world on the turtle's back, **Turtle Island** to the Haudenosaunee. The Creator is said to have loved the snapping turtle the best. When Mother Earth hears the sound of the turtle rattle, all of creation awakens and moves to its shaking beat.

Great Law of Peace. The Haudenosaunee Great Law of Peace (*Kaianerekowa*) is passed from generation to generation by the use of **wampum**, a form of written communication that outlines a complex system of checks and balances between nations and sexes. According to *A Basic Call to Consciousness*, published by **Mohawks** at **Akwesasne**, "Peace was to be defined not as the simple absence of war or strife, but as the active striving of humans for the purpose of establishing universal justice. Peace was defined as the product of a society which strives to establish concepts which correlate with the English words Power, Reason, and Righteousness" (Tehanetorens, 8). A complete oral recitation of the Great Law can take several days; encapsulated versions of it have been translated into English for more than a hundred years and provide one reason why the Iroquois are cited so often today in debates regarding the origins of U.S. fundamental law. While many other Native confederacies existed along the borders of the British colonies, most of the specific provisions of their governments have been lost.

To understand the provisions of the Great Law, one must understand the symbols it uses to represent the confederacy. One is the traditional **longhouse**. The confederacy itself is likened to a longhouse, with the Mohawks guarding the "Eastern Door," the **Senecas** at the "Western Door," and the **Onondagas** tending the ceremonial council fire in the middle. The primary national symbol of the Haudenosaunee is the **Great White Pine**, which serves throughout the Great Law as a metaphor for the confederacy. Its branches shelter the people of the nations, and its roots spread to the four directions, inviting other peoples, irregardless of race or nationality, to take shelter under the tree. The Haudenosaunee recognize no bars to dual citizenship; in fact, many influential figures in the English colonies and early United States, such as **Cadwallader Colden**, were adopted into Iroquois nations.

Each of the six nations maintained its own council, whose sachems were nominated by the Clan Mothers of families holding hereditary rights to office titles. The Grand Council at Onondaga was drawn from the individual national councils. The Grand Council also could nominate sachems outside the hereditary structure, based on merit alone. These sachems, called "pine-tree chiefs," were said to have sprung from the body of the people as the symbolic Great White Pine springs from the earth. The Grand Council seated fifty chiefs (one seat was included for the **Peacemaker**, who was said to be present in spirit). Each position on the council represented a matrilineal lineage (*owachira*). A chief for each lineage was "raised up" by **consensus** of the Clan Mothers holding the rights to that lineage, who were charged with polling the opinions of the people whom the chief would represent. The same Clan Mothers might impeach a sitting chief for any of a wide range of misbehaviors that undermined confidence in him. Chiefs enjoyed great prestige, but had very little coercive power.

The Great Law also included provisions guaranteeing freedom of religion and the right of redress before the Grand Council. It also forbade unauthorized entry of homes. All these measures sound familiar to U.S. citizens through the Bill of Rights.

If the Grand Council would not act on the will of the people, sachems faced removal under other provisions. Through public opinion and debate, the Great Law gave the Iroquois people basic rights within a distinctive and representative governmental framework. The Great Law resolved disputes by giving all parties an equal hearing. The Grand Council often functioned like a think tank. Above all, thinking was the activity that went on underneath the Great Tree. For the Iroquois, the more thinkers who were beneath the tree, the better. This process is in marked contrast to European hierarchical political and educational traditions.

The League of the Iroquois is a family-oriented government that has a constitution with a fixed corpus of laws concerned with mutual defense. Through the elimination of the clan blood feud, the state was given a monopoly on legally sanctioned violence. This process brought peace through a fundamental social contract. The Iroquois were not inclined to give much power to authorities because of the basic psychological attitudes instilled in Iroquois people. Thus unity, peace, and brotherhood were balanced off against the natural rights of all people and the necessity of sharing resources equitably. Unity for mutual defense was an abiding concept within the league. The Iroquois imagery of unity was a **bundle of arrows**, usually five or six, tied together to symbolize the complete union of the nations and the unbroken strength that such a unity portrays.

The Iroquois also have built-in checks and balances through the processes of consensus, removal, and public opinion. The notion of federalism was strictly adhered to by the Iroquois. The hereditary (hereditary is used here in the Iroquois sense because the Clan Mothers "inherited the right" to appoint and remove peace chiefs to the confederacy) Haudenosaunee sachems were interested only in external matters such as war, peace, and treaty making. The Grand Council cannot interfere with the internal affairs of the individual nations. Each nation has its own sachems, but they are limited in that they may deal only with their nation's relations with others in the confederacy.

FURTHER READING

Dennis, Matthew. *Cultivating a Landscape of Peace.* Ithaca, N.Y.: Cornell University Press, 1993.

Tehanetorens [Ray Fadden]. *A Basic Call to Consciousness.* 1978. Rooseveltown, N.Y.: Akwesasne Notes, 1981 (1986 printing).

Wallace, Anthony F. C. "Political Organization and Land Tenure among the Northeastern Indians, 1600–1830." *Southwestern Journal of Anthropology* 13 (1957): 301–321.

White Roots of Peace. *The Great Law of the Longhouse People.* Rooseveltown, N.Y.: Akwesasne Notes, 1977.

Woodbury, Hanni, comp. *Concerning the League: The Iroquois League Tradition as Dictated in Onondaga by John Arthur Gibson.* Comp. Hanni Woodbury, Reg Henry, and Harry Webster on the basis of A. A. Goldenweiser's manuscript. Algonquian and Iroquoian Linguistics, Memoir No. 9. Winnipeg, Manitoba: University of Manitoba Press, 1992.

Great White Pine. The primary national symbol of the Haudenosaunee is the Great White Pine (the Great Tree of Peace), which serves throughout the **Great Law of Peace** as a metaphor for the confederacy. Its branches are said to shelter the people of the confederated nations, and its roots spread to the four directions, inviting other peoples, irregardless of race or nationality, to take shelter under the tree. The Haudenosaunee recognized no bars to dual citizenship; in fact, many influential figures in the English colonies and early United States, such as **Cadwallader Colden**, were adopted into Iroquois nations.

In his vision that united the Haudenosaunee, the **Peacemaker** saw a giant white pine reaching to the sky and gaining strength from three counterbalancing principles of life. The first axiom was that a stable mind and healthy body should be in balance so that peace between individuals and groups could occur. Second, the Peacemaker stated that humane conduct, thought, and speech were a requirement for equity and justice among peoples. Finally, he foresaw a society in which physical strength and civil authority would reinforce the power of the clan system.

The Peacemaker's tree had four white roots that stretched to the four directions of the earth. From the base of the tree, a snow-white carpet of thistledown would cover the surrounding countryside. The white carpet protected the peoples that embraced the three principles. On top of the symbolic white pine, an **eagle** is perched. The Peacemaker explained that the tree was humanity, living within the principles governing relations among human beings. The eagle was humanity's lookout against enemies who would disturb the peace, a symbol that has since been adopted into the national imagery of the United States of America. The Peacemaker postulated that the white carpet could be spread to the four corners of the earth to provide a shelter of peace and brotherhood for all mankind. The Peacemaker's vision was a message from the Creator to bring harmony into human existence and unite all peoples into a single family guided by his three dual principles.

FURTHER READING

Wallace, Paul A. W. *The White Roots of Peace*. Santa Fe, N.M.: Clear Light Publishers, 1994.

Green Corn Ceremony. The Green Corn Ceremony is part of a yearlong Haudenosaunee **Thanksgiving** cycle; it is celebrated in late August or early September at the time that the **Three Sisters (corn**, beans, and squash), the vegetable staples of the Iroquois diet, reach maturity. The **ceremony** is dedicated to the food spirits, the Creator, and the people. The Green Corn Ceremony is performed to thank the food spirits for producing the harvest and to thank the Creator for making possible the completion of another cycle of growth for the harvest to come. The Haudenosaunee share the Green Corn Ceremony with several other Native American peoples in the eastern woodlands.

Several sacred ceremonies are usually performed during the Green Corn observances, all of which are expressions of thanks to the Creator for the privilege of life and sustenance. These ceremonies include the naming of infants and the elevation of newly appointed Faithkeepers. The **Great Feather Dance** and the Skin Dance (also called the Drum Dance) are performed, and the Peach Stone and Bowl Game is played between the various clans.

FURTHER READING

Fenton, William N. *The Seneca Green Corn Ceremony*. Albany: New York State Conservation Department, 1963.

Greene, Graham (Oneida), b. 1955. Graham Greene has become a well-known actor who has played Native American roles in some of the late twentieth century's most popular movies. He was nominated for an Oscar as best supporting actor in *Dances with Wolves* (1991), in which he worked with Rodney A. Grant, an Omaha. Greene also played major roles in *Clearcut* (1992), *Last of His Tribe* (1992), and *Cooperstown* (1993).

Greene was born on the Six Nations Reserve at **Grand River**, near Brantford, Ontario. He began his acting career in 1974 after having worked as a carpenter, welder, rock-music roadie, band manager, and music-studio owner. Greene's acting career did not become his major avocation until after he had lived in England during the early 1980s and had become known for his stage performances there. After returning to Canada, Greene was cast in the British film *Revolution*, starring Al Pacino. In addition to his many movie roles, Greene played in several television series in the United States and Canada and was active in several theatrical productions in Toronto, where he was residing in the 1990s.

Made famous by his role in *Dances with Wolves*, Greene also had a leading role in the Canadian television series *Outer Limits*, for which he was nominated for a Gemini, a Canadian "Oscar." In 1996, the First Americans in the Arts recognized Greene's role in Twentieth Century Fox's *Die Hard with a Vengeance* as the best nontraditional role by an actor or actress.

FURTHER READING

Johnson, Brian D. "Dances with Oscar: Canadian Actor Graham Greene Tastes Stardom." *Maclean's*, March 25, 1991, 60–61.
Wickens, Barbara, ed. "On the Case with Greene." *Maclean's*, October 20, 1997, 74.

The Gus-tow-weh is a traditional Haudenosaunee leader's headdress. Courtesy of John Kahionhes Fadden.

Gus-tow-weh. The *Gus-tow-weh* is the traditional Haudenosaunee chief's headdress, containing the "**antlers** of authority," which are removed upon death or
removal from council.

Guyasuta (Seneca), c. 1722–1794. Born along the Genesee River shortly after
1720, Guyasuta opposed European-American encroachment into the Ohio
Valley. His record was inconsistent, however, because at one point, in 1753, he
served as a guide for George Washington in his first military campaign.

As the British drove the French from North America shortly after 1760, Native nations also struggled to free themselves from British influence. The **Senecas** were the first to act. As early as 1761, a group of Senecas including
Guyasuta, the maternal uncle of **Handsome Lake**, carried a red **wampum** belt
(a declaration of war) from the Onondaga council to Fort Detroit. Pontiac did
not follow the Seneca plan in detail, but it was certainly a factor in fostering
his surprise frontier assaults in the spring of 1763. The prior circulation of the
Seneca plan suggested the method of the campaign.

In his later years, Guyasuta became known more as an orator than a warrior.
He tried to maintain Seneca neutrality in the **American Revolution**, but reluctantly joined the majority of Senecas who allied with the British. He fought in
only one Revolutionary War battle, at Hannastown, Pennsylvania, in 1782. Guyasuta died of smallpox in 1794.

FURTHER READING

Wallace, Anthony F. C. *The Death and Rebirth of the Seneca.* New York: Knopf, 1970.

H

Halbritter, Ray (Oneida), b. 1950. Ray Halbritter was among a handful of **Oneidas** who returned, during the 1970s, to the then-vacant thirty-two acres left to the Oneidas in the Verona, New York, area, about forty miles east of Syracuse. By the middle 1990s, about 300 Oneidas lived in the Verona area, out of 1,100 on the tribal roll.

Many of the Oneidas who first migrated to the Verona area lived at first in trailers, including Halbritter's aunt and uncle. One day in 1976, their trailer caught fire and burned both to death, as the local fire department refused to answer the call. Halbritter found himself organizing his neighbors to assemble a fire department of their own. "I can still smell the flesh burning," Halbritter said two decades later (Saul, A-6).

Halbritter, a graduate of Harvard Law School, became a leader among the Oneidas after that, applying his business acumen to the development of the Turning Stone Casino (opened in 1993) and other economic enterprises that, by the middle 1990s, had allowed the Oneidas to repurchase about 3,000 acres of formerly alienated land in the Verona area. By 1995, the Turning Stone was drawing an estimated $200 million a year in revenues. The Oneidas do not disclose financial data, but profits are estimated to be in the area of $60 million a year (Glaberson, "Struggle," A-1).

Halbritter's leadership also sparked controversy. Several Oneidas accused him of acting in a dictatorial fashion. In 1995, opponents held a "March for Democracy." Differences of opinion were especially acute between Halbritter and the Oneida Men's Council and Clan Mothers, who act as directors of the tribe, with Halbritter as chief executive officer. The traditional leadership of the Oneidas has impeached Halbritter, an action unrecognized by state and federal legal authorities. Maisie Shenandoah, a Clan Mother of the Wolf Clan who supported Halbritter's selection as chairman in 1977, said in 1995 that he "has turned against our people" (Glaberson, " 'Indian Gold,' " 12). Controversy developed, for example, over Halbritter's hiring of more than forty police officers to patrol the thirty-two-acre reservation.

FURTHER READING

Glaberson, William. " 'Indian Gold' Splits Tribe; Casinos Have Made One Native American Tribe Rich But the Fight for Spoils Has Divided Families." *Guardian* [London], June 18, 1996, 12.
———. "Struggle for Oneidas' Leadership Grows Bitter As Casino Succeeds." *New York Times*, June 17, 1996, A-1.
Saul, Stephanie. "Oneida Casino a Boon, But Not to the Tax Base." *Newsday*, September 24, 1996, A-6.

Half-King (Dunquat, Petawontakas) (Wyandot [Ohio Huron], fl. late 1700s. Dunquat was a leader of Wyandots (Hurons) who moved to the Ohio country; he was allied with the British in the **American Revolution** and led several raids on American settlements in the Ohio country during the war. He negotiated alliances with several bands, including other Wyandots, Shawnees, Delawares, Ottawas, and Chippewas. He also acted as a peace chief in intratribal conflicts, on one occasion protecting Christianized Delawares from attacks by a more traditional faction of the same tribe.

After the Revolution, Dunquat and his allies joined Little Turtle, the Miami chief, in his war against European-American expansion into the Ohio country, which had been ceded to the United States by the 1783 Treaty of Paris. By about 1800, a flood of immigrants was rolling over the Allegheny Mountains. Dunquat was a signer of the Treaty of Greenville (1795), which effectively ended the insurgency and surrendered much of present-day Ohio to the United States.

Dunquat was one of several leaders of Haudenosaunee peoples who lived in the upper Ohio Valley. These leaders were called "Half-Kings" by the English because they were believed to be emissaries of the Grand Council. "Half-King" was more an informal title than a personal name. As time passed, however, the Ohio Iroquois (sometimes called **Mingos** in contemporary records) became independent to the point of kindling their own central council fire for a time. The "half-kings" were vital links in the **Covenant Chain**.

Half-King (Scaroudy) (Oneida), fl. 1750s. Scaroudy was military successor to **Half-King (Tanacharison)** as an ally of the British in the war with the French during the 1750s and early 1760s. When Tanacharison died in 1754, shortly after the war began at the Battle of Great Meadows, Scaroudy, who was known as a great orator, maintained an alliance between the Ohio Valley Iroquois (whom the whites often called **Mingos**) and the British. Scaroudy was allied with British General Edward Braddock and George Washington, an aide to Braddock. During 1755, they suffered defeat at the hands of the French near Fort Duquesne (now Pittsburgh).

In October 1753, **Benjamin Franklin** began his distinguished diplomatic career by watching Scaroudy and a **Mohawk**, Cayanguileguoa, condole the Ohio Indians for their losses against the French. Franklin listened as Scaroudy recounted the origins of the Iroquois **Great Law of Peace** to the Ohio Indians at a treaty council in Carlisle, Pennsylvania. At this treaty council with the Iroquois and Ohio Indians (Twightees, Delawares, Shawnees, and Wyandots), Franklin absorbed the rich imagery and ideas of the Six Nations at close range.

The next day, the Pennsylvania commissioners (including Franklin) presented a **wampum** belt that portrayed the union between the Iroquois and Pennsylvania. The speech to the assembled Indians echoed the words of **Canassatego** spoken a decade earlier at Lancaster and recalled the need for unity and a strong defense:

Cast your eyes towards this belt, whereon six figures are . . . holding one another by the hands. This is a just resemblance of our present union. The first five figures representing the Five Nations . . . [and] the sixth . . . the government of Pennsylvania; with whom you are linked in a close and firm union. In whatever part the belt is broke, all the wampum runs off, and renders the whole of no strength or consistency. In like manner, should you break faith with one another, or with this government, the union is dissolved. We would therefore hereby place before you the necessity of preserving your faith entire to one another, as well as to this government. Do not separate; Do not part of any score. Let no differences nor jealousies subsist a moment between Nation and Nation, but join together as one man. (Grinde and Johansen, 198–199)

FURTHER READING

Grinde, Donald A., Jr., and Bruce E. Johansen. *Exemplar of Liberty: Native America and the Evolution of Democracy*. Los Angeles: UCLA American Indian Studies Center, 1991.

Half-King (Tanacharison) (Oneida/Seneca), c. 1700–1754. Tanacharison was born a Catawba, but was captured at an early age and raised as Haudenosaunee near the eastern shore of Lake Erie. Tanacharison was a valued ally of the British in the French and Indian War and held councils with several officials, including **Conrad Weiser**, George Croghan, and young George Washington, who was serving in his first combat situation.

Tanacharison fought as an ally of Washington in the Battle of Great Meadows (1754), the opening salvo of the final British war with the French in North America, which ended in 1763. As a result of this battle, in which Tanacharison killed at least one French officer, Washington surrendered Fort Necessity to the French.

In May 1754, as Washington was trying to find a small party of French in western Pennsylvania, the Virginia commander was completely dependent upon his Indian guides. Before they reached the Indian encampment, the English party was "frequently tumbling over one another, and so often lost that fifteen or twenty minutes search would not find the path again" (Johansen and Grinde,

157). But when Half-King and Monacatoocha joined the English, the French hiding place was found in little time. Tanacharison later moved to Aughwick (now Harrisburg), Pennsylvania, where he died of pneumonia in 1754.

FURTHER READING

Aquila, Richard. *The Iroquois Restoration: Iroquois Diplomacy on the Colonial Frontier, 1701–1754.* Detroit: Wayne State University Press, 1983.
Brock, R. A., ed. *The Official Records of Robert Dinwiddie, Lieutenant-Governor of the Colony of Virginia, 1751–1758.* Collections of the Virginia Historical Society 3.
Johansen, Bruce E., and Donald A. Grinde, Jr. *The Encyclopedia of Native American Biography.* New York: Henry Holt, 1997.

Hall, Louis (Karoniaktajeh) (Mohawk), c. 1920–1993. Louis Hall, whose **Mohawk** name is Karoniaktajeh (meaning "near the sky"), is regarded as the ideological founder of the **Warrior Society** in Mohawk country. The Warriors have played an important role in the Mohawk reserves of **Akwesasne**, in upstate New York, **Kahnawake**, near Montréal, and Kanesatake, near the Québec hamlet of **Oka**, beginning in the 1970s. Warrior advocacy of armed insurrection on the three reserves played a major role in firefights at Akwesasne that killed two Mohawk men on May 1, 1990, and in the standoff with Canadian police and troops at Oka later the same summer, in which Québec police officer **Marcel Lemay** was killed.

Hall was a member of the Kahnawake Reserve's traditional council in 1971 when it decided to sanction a group of young men who said that they wanted to revive a warrior society there. As "keeper of the well," Hall took the young men's request for sanction under advisement and placed it on the council's agenda.

Unlike the Mohawk Nation Council at Akwesasne, the Longhouse at Kahnawake became an advocate of the Warrior cause, so much so that in 1973 its members sought to have non-Indian families evicted from their reserve, a move opposed by the tribal council that Canada recognizes. After that split at Kahnawake, a group of Mohawks inspired by Hall's beliefs started the settlement at **Ganienkeh** to carry out their nationalistic vision of Mohawk tradition, including farms, a sawmill, cigarette sales, and high-stakes bingo.

During 1990, Hall's ideology helped provoke a rising, often-emotional debate over the future of the Haudenosaunee Confederacy. At the heart of this debate are two interpretations of history. One is that of the members of the Iroquois Grand Council at Onondaga, the Mohawk Nation Council, and many of the other national councils that comprise the Iroquois' original political structure. These people reject violence and look at the Warriors as illegitimate usurpers of a thousand-year-old history. The other interpretation, synthesized by Hall and espoused by the Warriors, rejects the governing structure as a creation of white-influenced religion (especially the Quakers) and advocates a revolution from within to overthrow it.

While some Iroquois have compared him to Adolf Hitler, Hall claimed that he admired Jewish people, saying that they had suffered persecution much as American Indians had. Hall was manifestly homophobic, but he was an Indian supremacist who stood the skin-deep aspect of Hitler's ideology on its head, believing that white men have hairy chests because they were born in biological union with monkeys. He was fond of pointing out that jackasses, like white men, have hair on their chests.

While Hall was hardly a cardboard cutout of Hitler, many of his adversaries in Mohawk country believe that his ideology is fundamentally fascist. An article in *Indian Time*, a newspaper serving Akwesasne that analyzed Hall's ideology in June 1991, carried a small drawing of Hitler, with one difference. One has to look closely to see two Native-style braids dangling from the back of his head.

Hall maintained that the Warriors hold the true heritage of the Haudenosaunee, and that today's traditional council and chiefs at Akwesasne have sold out to elitism, the Quakers, **Handsome Lake**, and white interests in general. Hall regarded the religion of Handsome Lake as a bastardized form of Christianity grafted onto Native traditions and considered its followers traitors or "Tontos." Hall called Handsome Lake's prophecies the hallucinations of a drunk.

"What can warrior societies do?" he asked, then answered: "Dump bridges into rivers—which are now sewers—and into the [St. Lawrence] Seaway, canceling all traffic, knock out powerhouses, high-tension power lines, punch holes in the reactors of nuclear power houses" (Hall). By such measures, Hall measured the ascendancy of Native national liberation. "Legal extermination of the Indians as a distinct people is an act of aggression," Hall wrote. "Oppression is an act of war against the people. Legislating Indians into extinction by way of assimilation is an act of war" (Hall).

Any Iroquois who did not subscribe to Hall's ideology was a racial traitor in his eyes, a sellout to Handsome Lake and the Quakers. For following the peace-oriented path, many of the Iroquois chiefs (including the entire Onondaga council) should be executed, Mafia-style, by hit men. "They should be executing the traitors," Hall said in 1990. "But they will have to do it the way the Mafia do it, in secret and never see the victim again. No body. No case." A year later, Hall backed off from the death threat, saying that the Warriors would replace the existing Grand Council by peaceful means (Johansen, 160).

FURTHER READING

Hall, Louis. "Rebuilding the Iroquois Confederacy." Unpaginated manuscript copy in author's files.

Hornung, Rick. *One Nation under the Gun: Inside the Mohawk Civil War*. New York: Pantheon, 1991.

Johansen, Bruce E. *Life and Death in Mohawk Country*. Golden, Colo.: North American Press/Fulcrum, 1993.

Hancock, John, 1737–1793. In the midst of the debates over independence in the Continental Congress, twenty-one Iroquois Indians came to meet with the Continental Congress in May 1776. The Indians lodged on the second floor of Independence Hall (then called the Pennsylvania State House) and observed the debates at the invitation of the delegates. On June 11, 1776, while Independence was being debated, the visiting Iroquois chiefs were invited formally into the hall of the Continental Congress, and a speech was delivered calling them "Brothers" and wishing that the "friendship . . . between us . . . will . . . continue as long as the sun shall shine . . . and the waters run." The speech also declared that the Americans and the Iroquois should be "as one people, and have but one heart" (Grinde and Johansen, 145). After this speech, an **Onondaga** chief asked to give John Hancock, president of the Continental Congress an Indian name. The Congress graciously consented, and the Onondaga chief gave the "president the name of *Karanduawn*, or the Great Tree" (Grinde and Johansen, 145).

FURTHER READING

Grinde, Donald A., Jr., and Bruce E. Johansen. *Exemplar of Liberty: Native America and the Evolution of Democracy.* Los Angeles: UCLA American Indian Studies Center, 1991.

Handsome Lake (Sganyadaí:yoh, Skaniadario) (Seneca), c. 1734–1815. Sganyadaí:yoh means "beautiful" (i.e., handsome) "lake," a reference to Lake Ontario. The term is not a personal name, but a position title of one of the Haudenosaunee Grand Council lineage (hereditary) chiefs of the **Senecas**. It authorizes the titleholder to take a seat in the men's Grand Council. Many chiefs have used this position title down through Iroquoian history.

The first man known to have borne this name was a founding member of the League of the Haudenosaunee in the twelfth century. This Sganyadaí:yoh gained a prestigious mention in the tradition of the *Gayaněsshä' 'gowa* (Great Law) for being (along with his speaker) the first—and for a long time, the only—Seneca to support the **Peacemaker** in his mission to establish the League of Peace. As with many names of great individuals, that of Sganyadaí:yoh transmuted into a position title for later generations to be kept and bestowed on succeeding chiefs by the Seneca Clan Mothers.

The second Sganyadaí:yoh recalled in tradition was the Handsome Lake found in Western chronicles, a visionary and spiritual leader who established the Longhouse Religion among the New York Iroquois in the early nineteenth century. Based on the *Gaiwí:yo*, also called the Code of Handsome Lake, the repository of his visions and ethical teachings, the Longhouse Religion actually borrowed heavily from Christianity in an attempt to conserve traditional ways then being suppressed by the European-American government that allowed church officials to run the New York reservations.

Handsome Lake's Early Life

Before he became a visionary, Handsome Lake led the life of a typical well-born Seneca man with family connections to other high-status individuals. His brother (called his "half-brother" by Euro-scholars) was the Seneca Gaiant'waka (Chief **Cornplanter**), while his nephew was Sagoyewatha (**Red Jacket**), the famed Seneca women's speaker to the men's Grand Council. Tradition states that Sganyadaí:yoh was born into the Wolf Clan at Conawagas, a Seneca town on the Genesee River in New York located outside of modern-day Avon. A sickly child, he was unlikely to have been nominated to any lineage title due to his poor health. However, the women of the Turtle Clan took pity on him and adopted him into their clan, promising titles.

As a youth, he became beloved of all, especially the women, whom he tirelessly protected, and the children, for whom he always had a story and a pouch filled with nuts bathed in maple syrup. A young woman quickly singled him out as husband material and asked her mother to arrange their marriage. As a responsible married man, he became even more popular, renowned for his good heart and strength of character. When a lineage sachem of the Wolf Clan died, the Wolf Clan Mothers quickly nominated him as successor, with the joyful permission of the Turtle Clan Mothers. To the astonishment of the Wolf and Turtle men, Handsome Lake assumed the title of the fabled sachem Sganyadaí-:yoh.

Before this stunning promotion, however, Sganyadaí:yoh was a "young man" (mistermed "warrior" in Euro-texts), also a position to which men were appointed by the women. Sganyadaí:yoh was selected to participate in the French and Indian War (1754–1763) and fought with the British-league alliance against the French. Immediately after this war, he took part in Pontiac's resistance movement, opposing the British. As more Europeans poured onto the continent, squeezing the original inhabitants, the crowding led to internecine Native strife over who was to occupy the ever-dwindling lands of the East. Sganyadaí:yoh fought with his Seneca brothers against the Cherokees and Choctaws of the South when the Haudenosaunee and the Algonkins were forced to compete for land by the Europeans' invasion.

Handsome Lake in the American Revolution

When the **American Revolution** broke out in 1776, the Continental army, knowing that it would not be able to fight on two fronts, urgently courted all eastern Native nations, begging them to remain neutral in this "family fight" with their "bad father," King George III. In the summer of 1777, at the annual meeting of the men's Grand Council in Oswego, Sganyadaí:yoh sided with his brother Gaiant'waka in calling for neutrality. Eventually, however, after numerous lethal and unprovoked depredations against them by the colonial militias, the Senecas decided to go to war against the colonists. Sganyadaí:yoh submitted to the **consensus** and fought once more for his people.

After the war and the British betrayal of their league allies at the Treaty of

Paris in 1783, Sganyadaí:yoh took part in the ongoing, fractious, and frustrating negotiations with the newly created European-American governments. The Haudenosaunee were defrauded of great amounts of land. Now Sganyadaí:yoh began drinking. In 1794, he stood silent and glum at the **Canandaigua Treaty**, which effectively stripped the New York league of its remaining lands. At the same time, his beloved wife died, followed quickly to the grave by two of his daughters. Sganyadaí:yoh began drinking heavily.

The Treaty of Big Tree in 1797, attended by Sganyadaí:yoh, continued the process of land "concessions." A grievous period of disillusionment and extensive alcoholism followed for Sganyadaí:yoh. Indeed, even before the Treaty of Big Tree, he was basically an invalid, spending most of his time lying alone in a miserable hut, unable to take the slightest care of himself. It is possible that he went to Big Tree simply for the alcohol that the U.S. side always provided the Native counselors. A shadow of his former self, he was no longer looked upon by the people as a great chief, but as a disgrace, a broken-down drunk. His stories were all sad, and his pouch was full of sand. The women considered impeaching him to wake his spirit up.

Grieved to see her father thus, his remaining daughter came to him with kind words and brought him to live in her **longhouse**. In his sixty-fifth year, she breathed new life into him, and he began to tell her of the strange things he had thought to have seen during those four years in a near coma in his own hut. New visions came to him in the far more comfortable (and sober) longhouse of his daughter. From his pallet, he saw sunlight streaking through the rafters, and his Grandmother, the Moon, smiling down. The birds called to him, and the seasons wafted their wonderful odors through the door to his nostrils. His spirit was stirred by the spirits around him, and he looked for wisdom.

One morning in 1799, listening to his daughter sing a medicine song as she shelled the beans, Sganyadaí:yoh felt his consciousness slipping away. Staggering to the longhouse door, he collapsed into the arms of his relatives as his spirit wandered out of his body, floating out of the cabin and on to Sky World. Thinking her father dead, his daughter called her uncle Gaiant'waka and the rest of the village. Everyone was saddened by the news; just as the old Sganyadaí:yoh they remembered seemed to have been coming back to them, he had died. His daughter dressed him in his burial robes, and notice went abroad that he was to be raised up (i.e., his lineage title was to be conferred upon a successor). Just then, a sachem and nephew of Sganyadaí:yoh, Taa'wonyas (the Awl Breaker), examined the body and refused to believe that Sganyadaí:yoh's spirit had departed for good. "Grieve not," he told the people, "he still lives."

Handsome Lake as Visionary

Around noon the next day, Sganyadaí:yoh came out of his coma and told his rejoicing relatives that his spirit had been visited by the Four Messengers of Sky World bringing to him the "Four Words" (or "Matters"): *onega, gutgont, onoityeyende*, and *yondwiniyas swayas*. These four matters became the cornerstone of the *Gaiwí:yo* and consisted of prohibitions upon the people. *Onega* means alcohol, the use of which was forbidden. *Gutgont* (*okton*) was the use of the negative spirit power, which, in the hands of the inept, did harm. (It is commonly, though inaccurately, given in English as "witchcraft.") It, too, was outlawed. *Onoityeyende* was said by some to be the practice of poisoning enemies in secret, although others more benignly rendered it "love medicine," while *yondwiniyas swayas* was "cutting the child off in the womb," or the use of birth-control techniques, including abortion. These, too, were prohibited by the *Gaiwí: yo*.

In addition to this foundation, many more teachings came to Sganyadaí:yoh, including the condemnation of Christian missionaries. Notwithstanding this overt unfriendliness to Christian missions, Sganyadaí:yoh incorporated many Christian precepts, values, and attitudes into his *Gaiwí:yo*, including monotheism, sins and public confession, and the submission of wives to husbands. How many of these borrowings were consciously made is unknown, although it is known that *Sganyadaí:yoh* had learned the mores and precepts of Christianity from his nephew, Henry Obail (Abeel), who had studied the Christian Bible under the Quakers in Philadelphia. However, unlike the Christian cultural hero, Jesus, *Sganyadaí:yoh* made no pretense of being a messiah or "son of God," but simply claimed to be the speaker of "the Creator."

Given the oppressive nature of his message for Haudenosaunee women—who had always controlled their own fertility, had been their own bosses, had held their own councils, had filled the majority of the positions as shamans, had owned all the fields, and had run the clans—it is not surprising that the Clan Mothers blocked consideration of the *Gaiwí:yo* by the men's council for almost fifty years. Its initial reception by the people in general was quite negative.

Handsome Lake was opposed by Sagoyewatha (the women's speaker) and by his brother, Gaiant'waka, who heckled his tellings and put as many obstacles in his way as possible. Sagoyewatha, speaking for the Clan Mothers, denounced Sganyadaí:yoh as an imposter passing off assimilation as tradition. Stung, Sganyadaí:yoh replied that the Four Messengers had just revealed to him that Sagoyewatha was scheming to sell off more Iroquoian land (an attack on the Clan Mothers, who owned the land). Tensions escalated from there between the Clan Mothers and the followers of Sganyadaí:yoh.

Around this same time, the federal government of the United States granted the Quakers the de facto power to run the New York reservations in an early program of forced assimilation. Under this program, some people gradually became so culturally desensitized to Christian proselytizing that they stopped recognizing it as the base of the *Gaiwí:yo* and accepted the teachings as familiar. Others regarded the *Gaiwí:yo* as the lesser of two evils. It was clear that the missionaries and the occupying government would forcibly prevent the older religions from being practiced, whereas the *Gaiwí:yo* did retain numerous traditional elements that would otherwise have been lost: the annual round of **ceremonies**; many of the older oral traditions; a masculinized version of the

clan kinship; the old marriage rites; the principle, although vitiated, of reciprocity; and ecological concepts with their attendant respect for nature.

As anticipated by many, the Quakers did not attempt to crush Sganyadaí:
yoh's religion, but smiled upon it as a primitive attempt by "the savages" to
modernize themselves. In 1809, they wrote testimonials to Sganyadaí:yoh's ef-
ficacy in proscribing drink among his followers and seemed to view him as a
Seneca temperance leader. Still, many traditionals rejected the Longhouse Religion altogether. It was never accepted by the Ohio league peoples, for instance,
where older religious practices were still alive and vigorous for almost two
generations after New York was occupied by a hostile power.

The U.S. government had reorganized the councils, installing a new system
so that new elections took place. Sganyadaí:yoh was (re)elected to his position
on the Seneca council in 1801. His election emboldening him, Sganyadaí:yoh
set out to destroy his critics, actually accusing Sagoyewatha (and, by implication,
the Clan Mothers) of witchcraft. This foolhardly accusation quickly dashed
much of his growing popularity. Along with his anti-birth-control stance, this
tactic greatly outraged the women and their male supporters, who were numerous. Sganyadaí:yoh began losing face among the people. The strength of the
reaction to his attack on Sagoyewatha caused Sganyadaí:yoh to backpeddle on
the issues of birth control and witchcraft, emphasizing land and alcohol issues
instead, that is, the issues that had popular support.

Handsome Lake Meets Thomas Jefferson

In 1802, Sganyadaí:yoh was among a delegation of **Onondaga** and Seneca
representatives who visited the capital and met President Thomas Jefferson. He
lobbied hard for an end to the sale of liquor to the Haudenosaunee, as well as
for an end to fraudulent land grabbing. He was far more successful with the
administration on temperance than on land retention. Jefferson prompted his
secretary of war (head of the department charged with "Indian affairs") to write
Sganyadaí:yoh a rather patronizing letter of support on behalf of the president
on the issue of his temperance work. Sganyadaí:yoh was clearly acceptable to
the Euro-overlords, if not to the Clan Mothers and their supporters.

One of the women's supporters was Gaiant'waka, at whose town (Cornplanter's Town) Sganyadaí:yoh had been living. The people at Cornplanter's Town
did not care how many letters of support he had from presidents and Quakers.
By 1810, his detractors had become so numerous and the situation so tense that
Sganyadaí:yoh was forced to move to Cold Spring, where he continued alien-
ating people. Early in 1812, he moved to Tonawanda, taking along his chief
supporters and his family, among whom was his grandson Sos´heowa, grandfather of **Ely S. Parker.** Sos´heowa was to become Sganyadaí:yoh's successor
on the Grand Council upon his death in 1815.

Handsome Lake's Final Years

After almost four years' residence at Tonawanda, Sganyadaí:yoh passed away.
During those years, he reflected upon the great hostility many had shown his

teachings; being kicked out of two towns in rapid succession preyed on his mind. Many say that in his final years at Tonawanda, he turned away from his own teachings. It is certain that he had grown quite reluctant to tell his visions or teach any more, distancing himself from and at times seeming to disclaim his own revelations.

In his fourth year at Tonawanda, Sganyadaí:yoh was invited by the Onondagas to come tell his third call. He was hesitant to comply with this invitation, as his third call was his quivering song, that is, his death song. His spirit guides returned to him, however, and advised him to go. Based on this vision, he predicted his death just as he set off for Onondaga. As word spread of his death vision, many joined his trek. Sganyadaí:yoh became increasingly depressed as he approached Onondaga; he seemed almost smitten by fear. Before the assembly he was to address, he broke down, unable to sing and denying that a spiritual meeting was in progress at all. "We are just sitting around the fire," he said (meaning that it was just a family gathering), and refused to teach. To cheer him up, the people played **lacrosse**, but Sganyadaí:yoh declined to watch and, again insisting that he was about to die, left the field.

His supporters took him to an Onondaga longhouse, forbidding all others to enter and swearing themselves to secrecy concerning events that took place within the longhouse. However, an Onondaga was hiding within and reported that once inside, Sganyadaí:yoh fell into terrible distress, accusing himself of having been laggard in spreading his message and wishing that he had dared to tell all of the visions he had been given. (What those untold visions were, he did not reveal.) His spirit then fell quiet, leaving him once more; four days later, on August 10, 1815, his body-soul followed. At about eighty-two, Sganyadaí:yoh was dead.

The Longhouse Religion after Handsome Lake's Death

A half-century after his death, Sganyadaí:yoh's legend outstripped his critics' complaints. Elders called a council to gather up his words, which Keepers (oral traditionalists) then committed to memory and knotted into **wampum**. (Sganyadaí:yoh had himself knotted wampum of his *Gaiwí:yo*.) He began to be called Sedwa'gowa'ne, meaning "our great teacher." In 1848, a recital of the *Gaiwí:yo* by Sos´heowa was taken down on paper for the first time at a mourning council in Tonawanda and translated for **Lewis Henry Morgan** by Donehogä´wa (Ely S. Parker). In 1851, it was published in *The League of the Haudenosaunee*. In 1861, the Grand Council heard (accepted) the *Gaiwí:yo* as legitimate. At the turn of the twentieth century, Gawaso Wanneh (**Arthur Parker**), himself a descendant of Sganyadaí:yoh, published another transcription. In 1994, Chief **Jacob Thomas** provided yet another version of the Code.

Between the death of Sganyadaí:yoh in 1815 and 1900, the Longhouse Religion flowered, garnering many supporters. By the turn of the twentieth century—a real nadir for all Native groups—Gawaso Wanneh observed that the teachings of Sganyadaí:yoh were on the wane and that "true believers" numbered only a few hundred (Parker, "Handsome Lake," 251). By the mid-twentieth century, however, the *Gaiwí:yo* was being recited with great frequency on the New York reservations, and during the general Native renaissance of the 1970s, many young New York Haudenosaunee began looking into it as a way back to their roots.

FURTHER READING

Morgan, Lewis Henry. *League of the Haudenosaunee, or Iroquois.* 1851. 2 vols. New York: Burt Franklin, 1901.

Parker, Arthur C. [Gawaso Wanneh]. *The Code of Handsome Lake, the Seneca Prophet.* New York State Museum Bulletin 163, Education Department Bulletin No. 530, November 1, 1912. Albany: University of the State of New York, 1913.

————. "Handsome Lake the Peace Prophet." Speech, 1916. In *The Life, of General Ely S. Parker, Last Grand Sachem of the Iroquois and General Grant's Military Secretary.* Buffalo: Buffalo Historical Society, 1919: 244–251.

Shimony, Annemarie Anrod. *Conservatism among the Iroquois at the Six Nations Reserve.* 1961. Syracuse, N.Y.: Syracuse University Press, 1994.

Thomas, Chief Jacob, with Terry Boyle. *Teachings from the Longhouse.* Toronto: Stoddart, 1994.

Wallace, Anthony F. C. *The Death and Rebirth of the Seneca.* New York: Knopf, 1970.

Barbara A. Mann

Haudenosaunee (Iroquois) League, origin date. European-American scholars and Haudenosaunee Keepers (oral traditionalists) have always been at wide variance over the founding date of the League of the Haudenosaunee. By and large, Euro-scholars seek to present the league as a recent invention, with those on the conservative end adding that it came about in response to European invasion. The dates presented by Euro-scholars ranges from a date just barely before contact, 1451, as argued by Dean Snow, to a more amorphous claim of some time in the mid-sixteenth century (i.e., about 1550).

Keepers of Haudenosaunee oral history, on the other hand, have always maintained the absolute antiquity of the league. The range of dates they offer starts at 3,000 years ago (Chief **Jacob Thomas, Cayuga**), includes a date between 1,000 and 2,000 years ago (Chief **Jake Swamp, Mohawk**), and ends at the year 1390, a date offered by a chiefs' council that, around the turn of the twentieth century, back-counted the estimated lifespans of the *Adodarohs*, or chairmen of the men's Grand Council. References in *The Jesuit Relations* from 1654 (Thwaites, 41:86–87) and 1691 (Thwaites, 64:100–101) quote the Haudenosaunee as telling the Jesuit missionaries that the league was quite ancient.

In 1997, Barbara A. Mann and Jerry L. Fields presented a compelling case for dating the founding of the league to August 31, 1142, thus confirming the Keepers. Mann and Fields regarded oral tradition as historical evidence, arguing that the Keepers were competent witnesses to their own history. Accordingly, the authors closely examined the entirety of oral tradition surrounding the founding of the league and insisted that all elements be accounted for by those proposing later dates. They held that events of the magnitude that led to the **Great Law of Peace**, as well as figures of the importance of the founders of the league, would have been recorded in European records had the league been a postcontact event. Conversely, since Europeans are mentioned nowhere in tradition, while the participants in the warfare of the time are clearly named (Mohawks, **Oneidas, Onondagas, Senecas**, and Cayugas), the authors concluded that the league was not founded in response to European pressures.

Considering the elements of tradition one by one, Mann and Fields showed that the Euro-colonial records of mid-sixteenth-century date simply cannot account for any of the elements clearly described in tradition. In particular, no written records exist regarding two of the revered leaders who brought the great law, **Deganawida** and **Hiawatha** (Ayonwantha). Of the third leader, **Jigonsaseh**, they showed that the one extant record of a seventeenth-century *Jigonsaseh* could not possibly have been speaking of the same *Jigonsaseh*, which in any case was a position title held by all Head Clan Mothers of the league, and not a personal name, as many scholars had assumed.

Mann and Fields also examined what they called "the archeology of tradition," matching up points in the Keepings to findings by archaeologists. Unlike the mismatch of tradition and evidence found for the mid-sixteenth-century claim, they showed that archaeological findings from the Owasco period (1100–1300) closely paralleled artifacts mentioned in tradition. In addition, Mann and Fields back-counted the *Adodarohs*, as had the earlier chiefs, but using modern actuarial methods. They came up with a time spread that allowed their 1142 date, but ruled out both the 1451 and the 1550 dates.

The precise date of August 31, 1142, offered by Mann and Fields was based on astronomical records. The Keepers speak of a Black Sun (total eclipse) that occurred immediately before the league was founded. This tradition was the same one cited by Dean Snow, who recently attempted to use it to date the league to the year 1451, after an eclipse date first put forward by Paul A. W. Wallace in 1948. This eclipse is the only basis for the 1451 claim. Mann and Fields showed that the eclipse track (or path of darkness caused by the eclipse) of the 1451 event fell far to the southeast of New York and would not have been visible to any of the Iroquoian nations. The eclipse of 1142, on the other hand, was not only spectacular and of long duration, but covered the entire geographical area inhabited by the early Iroquoian nations. It would have been eminently visible to all. Thus, unlike either the 1451 or the 1550 dates, the 1142 date offered by Mann and Fields dovetails neatly with the combined evidence of the Keepings, archaeology, historical records, actuarial calculations, and astronomy.

FURTHER READING

Hale, Horatio, ed. *The Iroquois Book of Rites*. Philadelphia: D. G. Brinton, 1883.
Mann, Barbara A., and Jerry L. Fields. "A Sign in the Sky: Dating the League of the

Haudenosaunee." *American Indian Culture and Research Journal* 21:2 (1997): 105–163.

Snow, Dean. "Dating the Emergence of the League of the Iroquois: A Reconsideration of the Documentary Evidence." In Nancy Anne McClure Zeller, ed., *A Beautiful and Fruitful Place: Selected Rensselaerswijck Seminar Papers*. Albany, N.Y.: New Netherland Publishing, 1991: 139–143.

Thwaites, Reuben Gold, ed. and trans. *The Jesuit Relations and Allied Documents: Travels and Explorations of the Jesuit Missionaries in New France, 1610–1791*. New York: Pageant Book Company, 1959.

Tooker, Elisabeth. "The League of the Iroquois: Its History, Politics, and Ritual." In *Handbook of North American Indians*. Vol. 15, *Northeast*. Washington, D.C.: Smithsonian Institution, 1978: 418–441.

Wallace, Paul A. W. "The Return of Hiawatha." *New York History: Quarterly Journal of the New York State Historical Association* 29:4 (1948): 385–403.

Barbara A. Mann

Heckewelder, Johann [John] Gottlieb Ernestus (Piselatulpe) (Moravian, German, adopted Delaware), 1743–1823.

John Heckewelder was a Moravian missionary to the league Delawares from 1761 until his retirement in 1810, but much more than that, he was an early ethnographer and historical actor of great consequence to the Ohio league. In the words of league historian Paul A. W. Wallace, "As a reporter of Indian life during his time and in his vicinity, [Heckewelder] has no superior" (Wallace, viii).

Heckewelder's Early Life

Born on March 12, 1743, of German parents exiled to England for practicing the "dangerous" Moravian faith—a Protestant sect of Christianity founded by the medieval Hussites in 1457—an adolescent Heckewelder set off for America alone, arriving at the Moravian settlement of Bethlehem, Pennsylvania, on April 20, 1754, just in time to witness the atrocities perpetrated against both the Moravians and the Delawares during the French and Indian War (1754–1763), which was in fact a war between the two imperial powers of Great Britain and France for control (according to European law) of eastern North America. In 1758, Heckewelder was apprenticed out as a barrel maker, to the dismay of this youth with a yen for adventure. He volunteered to go west as a missionary, but it was not until 1761, when he was eighteen years old, that he was tapped to go into the field with Frederick Post, a Moravian missionary and agent of the British Crown.

Post took the youth deep into Iroquoia, along the Muskingum River in Ohio, where, in 1762, he deserted the inexperienced lad to attend to Crown business. Had the **Senecas** not taken pity on the boy and helped feed him, Heckewelder would have starved to death. The forced immersion in the Seneca language that resulted from his abandonment began his career as a linguist. Heckewelder eventually spoke all six Iroquoian dialects, plus Lenni Lenape (Delaware), quite fluently.

Adoption by the Delawares

When he finally understood that Post was not coming back, Heckewelder retreated to Bethlehem to await reassignment. There he witnessed and recorded the attempt by the "Paxton Boys" to murder the Delawares and the heroic actions of Scottish colonel James Robertson that saved them against all odds (Mann, 148–155). Immediately after the war, Heckewelder was assigned to work under Moravian missionary David Zeisberger, who was taking 84 Delaware converts, now joined by some 157 Mahican converts, west to safety. In 1764 in Pennsylvania, Heckewelder was adopted by the Turtle Clan of the Delawares under the name Piselatulpe (Turtle). After residing awhile in western Pennsylvania, in 1772, the missionaries accompanied the league Delaware-Mahicans into southeastern Ohio along the Muskingum River, where they set up their tiny "praying towns" for their converts—Salem, Gnadenhütten, and Friedenshütten—around larger Goschochking, the capital city of the league Delawares of Ohio.

Aggressive settlers already had begun their attempt to seize Ohio, in flagrant violation of the **Fort Stanwix Treaty** of 1768, which had guaranteed all land north of the Ohio River to "the Indians." In 1774, these actions culminated in Lord Dunmore's War, in which, according to Heckewelder, "it became well known, the white people were the aggressors" (Heckewelder, *Narrative*, 130). Lord Dunmore's War was really a dress rehearsal for a massive assault on Ohio during the **American Revolution** by settlers intent upon grabbing the fertile farmland for themselves. The American Revolution was at least as much about seizing land from the Natives as about expelling the British Crown from it.

The Delawares began the war as neutrals, but the Moravians quickly showed their covert loyalties to the rebels. In 1778, when a sneak attack was launched against the peaceful Delawares of Ohio, league sachems realized that the revolutionary army had a spy in their midst. At first, Zeisberger was thought to be the agent, but soon enough, the league realized that it was Heckewelder, an accusation corroborated in 1958 when Paul Wallace turned up written evidence of its truth (Wallace, 133–134). Heckewelder was, however, well—and even fondly—regarded by the Delawares, who forbore to take action against him until September 1781, when the great war chief and spiritual leader **Hopocan** discovered that the revolutionary army out of Fort Pitt was planning genocide against all the Delawares in Ohio, whether league allied or neutral Christian. Hopocan took swift action, evacuating the entire nation north to the safety of Upper Sandusky, Ohio.

In that same action, Hopocan took all the Moravians prisoner during September 3 and 4 to stand trial for espionage in the British stronghold at Detroit. Despite his treachery, Heckewelder was unharmed by the Delawares and was even gently treated. Hopocan allowed Heckewelder's Delaware friends to take good care of his wife and infant daughter, while others clothed and fed him. After an arduous march (which included walking directly into a sudden tornado) and an October layover for the **Green Corn Ceremony** at the council grounds at the site of modern-day Toledo, Ohio, the prisoners arrived in Detroit around the first of November. The treason trial (spying for George Washington was a capital offense against the Crown) opened on November 9, 1781. Due to the extraordinary eloquence, political astuteness, and generosity of Hopocan, however, Heckewelder and his party were acquitted and returned to Upper Sandusky, Ohio. Arriving on November 22, they were put under the strict supervision of the league Delawares and their Wyandot hosts.

Incredibly, despite the surveillance and the strong warning to desist from his spying, Heckewelder immediately resumed his espionage activities, reestablishing contact with Fort Pitt. George Washington was planning a major action against "Canada" (in which category he included Ohio) and desperately needed Heckewelder's dispatches, which were sent out with clocklike regularity every ten days.

Heckewelder and the Goschochking Genocide (1782)

Instantly when he discovered this new treachery on March 13, 1782, the league Wyandot war chief Katepakomen (**Simon Girty**), took Heckewelder prisoner and arranged to send him back to Detroit on new charges. Unfortunately, Katepakomen was five days too late: Washington had used Heckewelder's news that 140 starving Delaware-Mahican farmers, primarily women and children, had returned to Goschochking to recover their harvest. Washington dispatched the Pennsylvania militia under Colonel David Williamson to seize their harvest; the result was the horrifying **Goschochking Genocide** of 1782, referred to in most Euro-texts as "Gnadenhütten."

Because Heckewelder personally knew and counted as friends 90 of the 126 killed and was acquainted with the rest, it is unlikely that he understood beforehand the use to which his information would be put. His probable deal with the revolutionary army was that he would supply Washington with intelligence in return for a promise that "his" Delawares (i.e., the Moravian converts) would be spared in the war. Betrayed, he suffered acute remorse over the Goschochking murders.

For the rest of his life, Heckewelder dedicated himself to exposing the genocide. His *Narrative* was primarily focused on telling the lethal truth of Goschochking and of Native-European contact generally, at least as it concerned the Delawares. The trauma he felt over Goschochking leapt back to life forty years after the event when he came to document the crime in his *Narrative*. Breaking down over his text, he lamented his lost friends: "Here they were now murdered! together with the children!—the loving children!" (Heckewelder, *Narrative*, 322). In his *History*, he dwelt upon the heinous nature of settler crimes, admitting that he was "ashamed of being a *white man*" (Heckewelder, History, 76; italics in the original).

After the genocide, the Moravians lost all credibility with the Delawares, including most of their former converts, who deserted their "teachers." Nor were Heckewelder's personal woes confined to the deaths of his friends. Once the awful news of the massacre arrived in Upper Sandusky on March 15, an enraged Katepakomen could scarcely be restrained by Heckewelder's friends from killing him on the spot. Heckewelder was detained in Detroit for the remainder of the war. It was probably only the Crown's knowledge that its cause was already lost that allowed him to live.

On behalf of the tiny number of remaining converts straggling into Detroit, Heckewelder and Zeisberger negotiated one year of sanctuary with the Michigan Chippewas, setting up a new "Gnadenhütten" village where modern-day Mt. Clemens, Michigan, is located. After three years, the Chippewas lost patience and kicked Heckewelder and the others out. Thus in 1785, Heckewelder began a long trek back to the Moravian stronghold of Bethlehem, Pennsylvania.

Heckewelder now dedicated himself to making restitution to the Delawares. He managed to secure a series of appointments to governmental commissions and committees in the effort to recover a homeland for the Delawares, leaning on a promise made to them in 1778 by the Continental Congress that they could secure actual statehood after the Revolution if they would remain neutral. After Mad Anthony Wayne's murderous rampage through Ohio and Indiana, with settlers set to begin pouring into the newly "opened" lands, Heckewelder got himself appointed to the surveying committee mopping up after Wayne and steered its 1797 recommendation that a tract of land in Ohio be apportioned to the remnants of the league Delaware-Mahicans. Heckewelder himself surveyed the 12,000-acre land grant in modern Delaware County, Ohio, which became one of the first reservations in the United States. It was run by the Moravian missionaries until 1806, when illegal settlers began pouring in and the Moravians struck camp, returned to Bethlehem, and left the Ohio Delaware-Mahicans high and dry.

Heckewelder's Later Years

After his retirement from missionary work in 1810, Heckewelder devoted the remainder of his life to writing his memoirs and histories, as well as composing language manuals for the various Iroquoian and Delaware dialects he spoke so well. Major philosophical societies commissioned his work and found it to be excellent. He brought out both his *Narrative* and his *History* to widespread acclaim, both popular and academic, becoming the acknowledged and valued source of James Fenimore Cooper's *Leather-Stocking Tales*.

In 1826, three years after his death—that is, when he could no longer defend himself—Heckewelder was subjected to a critical attack that amounted to a frontal assault by racist scholars. Leading the charge was General Lewis Cass, who ridiculed Heckewelder's knowledge of Native American cultures and sneered at his pro-Native perspectives as "naive." A determined racist and "Indian hater" who is recalled in the oral traditions of Ohio and Michigan as a butcher, Cass became the architect of the **removal** policy as President Jackson's secretary of war (Mann, 272–291).

Despite a vigorous defense of Heckewelder's reputation by scholars of his

own time, Cass's attacks became the last word in the increasingly racist atmosphere of Euro-America, which had declared its "manifest destiny" vis-à-vis the
conquest of North America. Sympathy for Natives' sufferings could not be tol-
erated in view of this imperial goal. Heckewelder was thus set aside as a source
in the interests of politics and was soon forgotten by the triumphalist historians
of nineteenth- and early-twentieth-century Euro-America. Although Francis
Parkman regarded Heckewelder as important, it was not until the 1950s that
Paul Wallace resurrected Heckewelder as a respectable primary source, compil-
ing his extant writings in 1958.

FURTHER READING

Heckewelder, John. *History, Manners, and Customs of the Indian Nations Who Once
    Inhabited Pennsylvania and the Neighboring States.* 1820, 1876. The First Amer-
    ican Frontier Series. New York: Arno Press and the New York Times, 1971.
———. *Narrative of the Mission of the United Brethren among the Delaware and Mo-
    hegan Indians from Its Commencement, in the Year 1740, to the Close of the
    Year 1808.* 1820. New York: Arno Press, 1971.
Mann, Barbara A. "Forbidden Ground: Racial Politics and Hidden Identity in James
    Fenimore Cooper's Leather-Stocking Tales." Ph.D. diss., University of Toledo,
    1997.
Rondthaler, Rev. Edward. *Life of John Heckewelder.* Ed. B. H. Coates, M.D. Philadel-
    phia: Townsend Ward, 1847.
Stockton, Edwin L., Jr. "The Influence of the Moravians upon the Leather-Stocking
    Tales." *Transactions of the Moravian Historical Society* 20 (1964): 1–191.
Wallace, Paul A. W., ed. and annot. *Thirty Thousand Miles with John Heckewelder.*
    Pittsburgh: University of Pittsburgh Press, 1958.

Barbara A. Mann

Hendrick (Tiyanoga) (Mohawk), c. 1680–1755. Tiyanoga, a member of the
Wolf Clan who was called Hendrick by the English, was a major figure in
colonial affairs between 1710, when he was one of four **Mohawks** invited to
England by Queen Anne, and 1755, when he died in battle with the French as
an ally of the British. Hendrick advised **Benjamin Franklin** and other colonial
representatives on the principles of Iroquois government at the **Albany Congress** of 1754.

Hendrick knew both Iroquois and English cultures well. He converted to
Christianity and became a Mohawk preacher shortly after 1700. In England, he
was painted by John Verelst and called the "Emperor of the Five Nations."
Hendrick was perhaps the most important individual link in a chain of alliance
that saved the New York frontier and probably New England from the French
in the initial stages of the Seven Years' War, which was called the French and
Indian War (1754–1763) in North America.

Well known as a man of distinction in his manners and dress, Hendrick visited
England again in 1740. At that time, King George II presented him with an

ornate green coat of satin, fringed in gold, which Hendrick was fond of wearing in combination with his traditional Mohawk ceremonial clothing.

A lifelong friend of **Sir William Johnson**, Hendrick appeared often at Johnson Hall, near Albany, and had copious opportunities to rub elbows with visiting English nobles, sometimes as he arrived in war paint, fresh from battle. Thomas Pownall, a shrewd observer of colonial Indian affairs, described Hendrick as "a bold artful, intriguing Fellow and has learnt no small share of European Politics, [who] obstructs and opposes all [business] where he has not been talked to first" (Jacobs, 77). Hector St. Jean de Crevecoeur, himself an adopted Haudenosaunee who had participated in sessions of the Grand Council at Onondaga, described Hendrick in late middle age, preparing for dinner at the Johnson estate, within a few years of the Albany Congress:

[He] wished to appear at his very best. . . . His head was shaved, with the exception of a little tuft of hair in the back, to which he attached a piece of silver. To the cartilage of his ears . . . he attached a little brass wire twisted into very tight spirals. . . . A girondole was hung from his nose. Wearing a wide silver neckpiece, a crimson vest and a blue cloak adorned with sparkling gold, Hendrick, as was his custom, shunned European breeches for a loincloth fringed with glass beads. On his feet, Hendrick wore moccasins of tanned elk, embroidered with porcupine quills, fringed with tiny silver bells. (Crevecoeur, 170)

In 1754, Hendrick attended the conference at Albany that framed a colonial plan of union. By the time Hendrick was invited to address colonial delegates at the Albany Congress, he was well known on both sides of the Atlantic, among Iroquois and Europeans alike. Hendrick had played a major role in convening the Albany Congress in large part because he wished to see his friend Johnson reinstated as the English superintendent of affairs with the Six Nations. Hendrick maintained that without Johnson's aid, the **Covenant Chain** would rust. It was Johnson himself who conducted most of the day-to-day business with the Indians at Albany.

At the Albany Congress, Hendrick repeated the advice that **Canassatego** had given colonial delegates at Lancaster a decade earlier. Unlike the **Lancaster Treaty Council** of 1744, the Albany Congress was devoted not only to diplomacy, but also to drawing up a plan for the type of British colonial union the Iroquois had been requesting. The same day, at the courthouse, the colonial delegates were in the early stages of debate over the plan of union.

Hendrick was openly critical of the British at the Albany Congress and hinted that the Iroquois would not ally with the English colonies unless a suitable form of unity was established among them. In talking of the proposed union of the colonies and the Six Nations on July 9, 1754, Hendrick stated, "We wish this Tree of Friendship may grow up to a great height and then we shall be a powerful people." Hendrick followed that admonition with an analysis of Iroquois and colonial unity in which he said, "We the United Nations shall rejoice of our strength . . . and . . . we have now made so strong a Confederacy." In reply to Hendrick's speech, New York governor James DeLancey said: "I hope that by this present Union, we shall grow up to a great height and be as powerful and famous as you were of old." Benjamin Franklin was commissioned to compose the final draft of the Albany Plan of Union the same day (Grinde and Johansen, 107).

Hendrick died at the Battle of Lake George in the late summer of 1755, when Sir William Johnson defeated Baron Dieskau. The elderly Mohawk was shot from his horse and bayoneted to death while on a scouting party on September 8.

FURTHER READING

Crevecoeur, J. Hector St. Jean de. *Letters from an American Farmer.* New York: E. P. Dutton, 1926.

Grinde, Donald A., Jr., and Bruce E. Johansen. *Exemplar of Liberty: Native America and the Evolution of Democracy.* Los Angeles: UCLA American Indian Studies Center, 1991.

Jacobs, Wilbur R. *Wilderness Politics and Indian Gifts.* Lincoln: University of Nebraska Press, 1966.

Wallace, Paul A. W. *The White Roots of Peace.* Philadelphia: University of Pennsylvania Press, 1946.

Hewitt, John Napoleon Brinton (Tuscarora), 1859–1937. J. N. B. Hewitt was a noted ethnologist who worked for fifty years in the Smithsonian Institution's Bureau of American Ethnology. He was regarded by Euro-scholars as an expert in Iroquoian language, history, tradition, **ceremonies**, and social/political structure. Because of his partial descent from the **Tuscaroras**, he was thought by Euro-scholars to have "inherited" a "natural" understanding of the Haudenosaunee, a view rooted in the eugenics craze, a racist philosophy that swept the so-called Western world during his lifetime. Among the Haudenosaunee, Hewitt was regarded as someone looking to (re)learn things his family had forgotten.

Hewitt was born on the Tuscarora Reservation outside of Lewiston in Niagara County, New York, on December 16, 1859, to a mother of partial Tuscarora descent and a Scottish father. Since his father was a physician, Hewitt grew up in a predominantly middle-class European-American environment, although he did learn something of the Tuscarora dialect as a child. His parents sent Hewitt to public and private schools in Wilson and Lockport. As a teenager, he spent some time as a farmer and a journalist. His original intention was to follow in his father's footsteps and become a Western doctor. When he was twenty-one in 1880, however, on the strength of his "Tuscarora" credentials, Hewitt received a job offer from Erminie A. Smith, an anthropologist with the Smithsonian Institution, who needed him to help collect Iroquoian "legends." Hewitt worked closely with Smith between 1880 and 1884. On her death in June 1886, Hewitt was offered her position with the Smithsonian's Bureau of American Ethnology

(BAE). He went to Washington, D.C., and worked for the Smithsonian until his death on October 14, 1937.

Hewitt became particularly interested in the social and political organization of the League of the Haudenosaunee. Convinced that the tradition of the **Great Law of Peace** contained as much fact as fiction, he spent considerable time trying to disentangle the two. In pursuit of his goal, Hewitt gathered a mass of oral history on **Deganawida** and **Hiawatha**. Although he seemed to realize the importance of the Clan Mother *Jigonsaseh* to the original tradition and did some work to revive knowledge of her, he had imbibed a sexist bias from living in a Euro-culture that led him to treat *Jigonsaseh* as a minor figure in the epic. Nor did Hewitt understand that men kept men's traditions and women kept women's traditions. He was "collecting" information on *Jigonsaseh* only from men. In the course of his "collecting," he became perforce a linguist of some ability and translated some of the traditions he learned into English.

Although Hewitt was a prolific writer—the author of some 12,000 manuscript pages—his publications were limited to contributions to Frederick Webb Hodge's *Handbook of American Indians North of Mexico* (1907–1910) and his own three works on the league and on the cosmology of the Iroquois generally, along with stray ethnographic notes, obscurely published. Of particular note was "A Constitutional League of Peace in the Stone Age of America" (1920).

Why Hewitt did not publish more and for a larger audience is a mystery. The official story is that his own excruciating conscientiousness over detail prevented it, but that in itself is probably a clue to the underlying reason. His scrupulousness came about in response to the racist thinking of the time that identified him as "an Indian" and therefore concluded that he was necessarily less competent than his European-American colleagues. It is notable that even today, Hewitt's work is more severely criticized than that of his contemporaries, despite the racist flaws and wild inaccuracies so readily apparent in their work.

In addition to his work on the Iroquois, Hewitt looked into Native linguistics, especially the relationship between Iroquoian dialects and the Cherokee (Algonkin) language. Interestingly, modern linguists have since established that Cherokee and Iroquois diverged into separate languages about 5,000 years ago. Hewitt also was a founding member of the American Anthropological Association.

FURTHER READING

Fenton, William N. "The Requickening Address of the Iroquois Condolence Council by J. N. B. Hewitt." *Journal of the Washington Academy of Sciences* 34:3 (1944): 65–85.

Hewitt, J[ohn] N[apoleon] B[rinton]. "A Constitutional League of Peace in the Stone Age of America: The League of the Iroquois and Its Constitution." *Smithsonian Institution Series* (1920): 527–545.

———. "The Culture of the Indians of Eastern Canada." *Explorations and Field-work of the Smithsonian Institution for 1928* (1929): 179–182.

———. "Era of the Formation of the Historic League of the Iroquois." *American Anthropologist* (old series) 7 (January 1894): 61–67.

———. "Ethnological Studies among the Iroquois Indians." *Smithsonian Miscellaneous Collections* 78 (1927): 237–247.

———. "Field Studies among the Iroquois Tribes." *Explorations and Field-work of the Smithsonian Institution* (1931): 175–178.

———. "Field Studies of the Iroquois in New York State and in Ontario, Canada." *Explorations and Field-work of the Smithsonian Institution for 1936* (1937): 83–86.

———. "Iroquoian Cosmology, First Part." In *Twenty-first Annual Report of the Bureau of American Ethnology to the Secretary of the Smithsonian Institution, 1899–1900.* Washington, D.C.: Government Printing Office, 1903: 127–339.

———. "Iroquoian Cosmology, Second Part." In *Forty-third Annual Report of the Bureau of American Ethnology to the Secretary of the Smithsonian Institution, 1925–1926.* Washington, D.C.: Government Printing Office, 1928: 453–819.

———. "The 'League of Nations' of the Iroquois Indians in Canada." *Explorations and Field-work of the Smithsonian Institution for 1929* (1930): 201–206.

———. "Legend of the Founding of the Iroquois League." *American Anthropologist* (old series) 5 (April 1892): 131–148.

———. "The Requickening Address of the League of the Iroquois." In *Holmes Anniversary Volume: Anthropological Essays.* 1916. New York: AMS Press, 1977: 163–179.

———. "Some Esoteric Aspects of the League of the Iroquois." *Proceedings of the International Congress of Americanists* 19 (1915): 322–326.

Hodge, Frederick Webb, ed. *Handbook of American Indians North of Mexico.* Bureau of Bureau of American Ethnology, Smithsonian Institution, Bulletin No. 30. Washington, D.C.: Government Printing Office, 1912.

Powers, Mabel. *The Indian as Peacemaker.* New York: Fleming H. Revell Co., 1932.

Barbara A. Mann

Hiawatha (Ayonwantha) (Mohawk), c. 1100–c. 1180. As a historical figure, Hiawatha was a **Mohawk** living at a time of great turmoil among the Iroquoian peoples. A brutal civil war had split the Five Nations (**Senecas, Cayugas, Onondagas**, Mohawks, and **Oneidas**) into polarized factions. Along with the **Peacemaker (Deganawida)** and **Jigonsaseh**, the Head Clan Mother of the Cultivators, Hiawatha helped establish the *Gayaněsshä'ʹgowa*, or **Great Law of Peace**. Hiawatha is particularly credited with inventing **wampum** and the **Condolence Ceremony**. (See also **The Second Epoch of Time: The Great Law Keepings**.)

Hiawatha's special message was one of compassion for human suffering and, as such, was an essential complement to the Peacemaker's message of the nonviolent resolution of disputes. The beautiful Condolence Ceremony, which wipes the tears from the eyes of the bereaved, makes daylight for them, and covers the graves, was his creation.

Hiawatha also invented wampum, which became vitally important to the day-to-day operations of the Iroquois League. Evolving from the strings of the Condolence Ceremony into larger and more complex "belts," and using Hiawatha's original vision of wampum as a container of messages that could be passed meaningfully from person to person, wampum knotting became a form of writing essential to the administration and recordkeeping of the Five, and later Six, Nations.

Hiawatha's wampum was long kept as a sacred item. Indeed, a wide belt said to have been made by Hiawatha himself became the symbol of league unity. Everything was connected to everything else by white lines of wampum (white signifying *uki*, peace and goodness). Called the **Hiawatha Belt**, it was purchased by John Boyd Thatcher of Albany and deposited in the Library of Congress around the turn of the twentieth century (Parker, 47 n. 1).

In the nineteenth century, European-American ethnographers started "collecting" various Native oral traditions that, for the most part, they did not understand. Standards of scholarship were much lower at the time, and little heed was paid to the large cultural distinctions among Native American groups. Some very questionable material thus made its way into the Western chronicles, not the least of it from the fallible pen of Henry Rowe Schoolcraft, who was as much a fraud as a scholar. He freely made up, interpolated, and gutted traditions, mixing and matching them as he saw fit. Native sensibilities mattered little to him. One of his most fanciful and least grounded works, his *Algic Researches* (1839, 1856), contained a fractured "Myth of Hiawatha." ("Algic" was Schoolcraft's invented word for woodland cultures.)

Schoolcraft's Hiawatha bore no resemblance to the historical figure cherished in Haudenosaunee tradition. Schoolcraft turned him into an Annissinabe (Chippewa) and confused him with the Annissinabe (Ojibway, also known as Chippewa) cultural hero Nanapush ("Manabozho"). Ignorance was not to blame here, but a raging disrespect for Native cultures: Schoolcraft knew the difference, but simply liked the sound of "Manabozho." In addition—and this probably was ignorance—Schoolcraft confused Hiawatha with Tarachiawagon, one name for the Peacemaker. Finally, Schoolcraft plagiarized Joshua Clark's *Onondaga, or, Reminiscences of Earlier and Later Times* (1849), pretending that the research was his own.

The issue was only confounded further when Henry Wadsworth Longfellow used Schoolcraft's mangled version of tradition as the basis of his epic poem *The Song of Hiawatha* (1855). Longfellow himself plagiarized the Finnish poem *Kalevala* and lifted lore from the Icelandic epic *Edda* to write his dubious *Song*, creating an Iroquoian nightmare that not only cast Hiawatha as an Annissinabe-Finnish-Icelander, but also turned him into a Christian philosopher, as well. Knowing nothing of the true Hiawatha and hopelessly confusing him with the Peacemaker, Longfellow presented Hiawatha as a fey, imitation Jesus. Longfellow's *Song of Hiawatha* became wildly popular with nineteenth-century European-American readers.

Although these Western versions of the Hiawatha story are completely without foundation in Haudenosaunee oral tradition, some modern west-of-the-

Mississippi Algonkins reenact Longfellow's version of *The Song of Hiawatha* at powwows, to the extreme discomfort of Haudenosaunee onlookers. The Iroquoian Hiawatha of history needs to be firmly disengaged from these fantastic nineteenth-century misrepresentations. Hiawatha's unflagging speakership for the Peacemaker, his message of compassion, his creation of the Condolence Ceremony, his invention of the Iroquoian writing system, and his combing the snakes from the hair of *Adodaroh* are what should be told about him.

FURTHER READING

Howard, Helen A. "Hiawatha: Co-founder of an Indian United Nations." *Journal of the West* 10:3 (1971): 428–438.
Mann, Barbara A. "The Fire at Onondaga: Wampum as Proto-writing." *Akwesasne Notes*, n. s. 1:1 (Spring 1995): 40–48.
Osborn, Chase S., and Stellanova Osborn. *Schoolcraft, Longfellow, Hiawatha*. Lancaster, PA: Jaques Cattell Press, 1942.
Parker, A[rthur] C[aswell]. *The Constitution of the Five Nations, or, The Iroquois Book of the Great Law*. Albany: University of the State of New York, 1916.
Wallace, Paul A. W. "The Return of Hiawatha." *New York History: Quarterly Journal of the New York State Historical Association* 29:4 (1948): 385–403.

Barbara A. Mann

Hiawatha (Five Nations) Wampum Belt. The Hiawatha **Wampum** Belt symbolizes the structure of the Haudenosaunee Confederacy, with four connected squares representing the **Senecas, Cayugas, Oneidas**, and **Mohawks**. The symbol of the tree of peace in the center (an elongated triangle) represents the **Onondagas**, who tend the central council fire.

The Hiawatha Belt is presently 10.5 inches wide and 21.5 inches long, but its frayed edges suggest that it may have been longer in the past. The white squares and tree-of-peace symbol are made of purple wampum against a background of white wampum.

The Hiawatha Belt symbolizes Haudenosaunee unity. Courtesy of John Kahionhes Fadden.

The Hiawatha Belt has been dated by **William N. Fenton** to the mid-eighteenth century, but this is probably not an origin date. Belts were repaired and thus replaced bead by bead over time, so they may be several centuries older than scientific dating of existing belts indicates. A belt may have been repaired several times over the centuries, gradually changing as bead-making technology (such as the introduction of glass beads by Europeans) evolved. The belt is now held by the Grand Council.

FURTHER READING

Fadden, Stephen. "Beaded History: The Hiawatha Belt Is the Founding Document and Symbolizes the 'Constitution' of the Iroquois Confederacy." *Northeast Indian Quarterly* 4:3 (Autumn 1987) 17–20.

Hill, Charlie (Oneida), b. 1951. Charlie Hill, a nationally known comedian, was raised on the Wisconsin Oneida Reservation. Hill honed his talents at the Comedy Shop in Los Angeles, which he calls "the fastest [comedy] track in the world" (Brixey, 1-F). He also has performed in avant-garde theater in Seattle, New York, and other cities.

Hill has released a comedy album titled *Born Again Savage*. He credits Dick Gregory, Lenny Bruce, and Richard Pryor for inspiring his comedic talents. "They call us 'vanishing Americans,' " Hill says. "But when was the last time you saw a Pilgrim?" (Haga, 1-R). Hill has appeared before many large audiences, including those for television shows hosted by David Letterman, Merv Griffin and Mike Douglas, and Jay Leno. While Hill was performing at the La Mama Experimental Theatre in New York City, he worked with the budding Jay Leno on comedic technique. Hill says that he was inspired by Gregory because his humor had humane goals and a political dimension that "talked about the humanness of all of us" (Koch, 39-P).

Hill's comedy sometimes has a serious political edge: "They talk about the American holocaust, but they just call it Manifest Destiny." Hill jokes that he watched the movie *1492* backward so it would have a happy ending. "It's my job to get people to laugh with us [Native Americans] instead of at us" (Koch, 39-P). In the 1990s, Hill and his Navajo wife were living with four children in a traditional manner on the Navajo Nation's Big Mountain area.

FURTHER READING

Brixey, Elizabeth. "Laugh It Up for Indians." *Wisconsin State Journal* (Madison), February 26, 1993, 1-F.
Haga, Chuck. "How Many Comedians Does It Take to Battle Oppression?" *Minneapolis Star-Tribune*, February 26, 1993, 1-R.
Koch, John. "Comic Stands Up for Native Americans." *Boston Globe*, November 21, 1990, 39-P.

Hill, Richard W. "Rick" (Tuscarora), b. 1950. Richard W. Hill was born in Buffalo, New York, after his father migrated there in search of employment as a worker in construction and iron. Hill is a former director of the Institute for American Indian Arts in Santa Fe; he also has directed exhibits at the Heye Museum in New York City and is a pioneer in arranging for American Indians to define which art and artifacts will be displayed there. In 1992, Hill used this approach in designing the art show titled "Pathways of Tradition: Indian Insights into Indian Worlds," from which Native American consultants picked for display 900 items from the Heye Museum's inventory comprising hundreds of thousands of objects. "Now the process is reversed," Hill said in 1992. "The Indians are the selectors and the professional curators are the advisors" (Reif, 43). He also has taught Native American Studies at the State University of New York (Buffalo).

Hill is a founder of the Association for the Advancement of Native North American Arts and Crafts. He also has played a leading role in evolving plans for the National Museum of the American Indian, to be constructed on the Washington Mall about the year 2002.

FURTHER READING

Reif, Rita. "Museum Displays Indian Artifacts." *New York Times*, November 15, 1992, 43.

Hiokatoo (Seneca), c. 1708–1811. Hiokatoo, husband of **Mary Jemison**, became known for his merciless handling of enemies during the French and Indian War. He led a force of Indians who massacred settlers at Cherry Valley on November 11, 1778. Jemison, a white captive who had been adopted by Hiokatoo and the **Senecas** at age thirteen, recalled him as unusually cruel:

He was a man of tender feelings for his friends . . . yet, as a warrior, his cruelties to his enemies perhaps were unparalleled. . . . In [his] early life, Hiokatoo showed signs of thirst for blood . . . [by] practicing cruelties upon every thing that chanced to fall into his hands, which was susceptible to pain. . . . He could inflict the most excruciating tortures upon his enemies. (Heard, 153)

Hiokatoo died of consumption (probably a cancerous tumor) in 1811, at the reported age of 103. He is reputed to have been a practicing warrior for three-quarters of a century.

FURTHER READING

Heard, J. Norman. *Handbook of the American Frontier*. Vol. 2, *The Northeastern Woodlands*. Metuchen, N.J.: Scarecrow Press, 1990.

Honayawas (Farmer's Brother) (Seneca), c. 1724–1815. Honayawas was one of the **Senecas'** principal war chiefs at the turn of the nineteenth century. He acquired the name "Farmer's Brother" from whites in the neighborhood of his

Buffalo Creek, New York, home after he forged a friendship with George Washington, a farmer himself. Honayawas signed treaties at Big Tree (1797) and Buffalo (1801). During the War of 1812, he supported the Americans against the British. When Honayawas died, he was buried in Buffalo with U.S. military honors.

FURTHER READING

Johansen, Bruce E., and Donald A. Grinde, Jr. *The Encyclopedia of Native American Biography*. New York: Henry Holt, 1997.

Hopocan (league Delaware), c. 1725–1794. Hopocan was a great eighteenth-century spiritual leader and war chief of the league Delawares in Pennsylvania and Ohio. It is unknown where or even exactly when he was born. Hopocan belonged to the Munsee (Wolf) Clan of the Delawares, a nation that had been incorporated into the League of the Haudenosaunee. Hopocan's eventual movement into southeastern Ohio indicated that he had originally come from modern-day Pennsylvania, where Delaware refugees had initially secured refuge from the European invaders by accepting adoption into the Iroquois League.

Hopocan's Allies and Enemies

During the French and Indian War (1754–1763), an English-settler death squad calling itself "the Paxton Boys" attempted to murder all Native Americans within its reach, the Delawares being chief among its targets. Hopocan was radicalized by the viciousness of the Paxton Boys' actions and fought with the French against the British colonizers. Like many woodlanders given the choice between an exploiter who had come to America to trade (the French) and one who had come to stay (the British), he chose the lesser of two evils, but it is incorrect to characterize him as having fought for the French. A dedicated foe of invasion throughout his life, Hopocan is more properly characterized as having fought for the Delawares; his "enemy" was consistently the land-grabbing settler, of whatever national origin.

After the French and Indian War drew to an unsatisfactory close (from the Delaware point of view), Hopocan joined Pontiac's resistance of 1763. His objective was to take Fort Pitt (formerly Fort Duquesne) for the league, which recognized the strategic location and importance of the fort for the British in holding the league lands of western Pennsylvania and Ohio. Hopocan was unsuccessful in this bid. At this period of his life, it is likely that he lived in Goschochking, near modern-day West Hickory, Pennsylvania, which was established as the Delaware capital in Pennsylvania in 1765. When Pontiac's resistance also failed to stop European encroachment, Hopocan joined the Delaware-Mahicans traveling yet farther west, once more under the auspices of the Iroquois League, which had reserved rich bottomlands along the Muskingum River in southeastern Ohio for their use.

Hopocan played an important role during the French and Indian War that was recognized and honored by his people. Although the Clan Mothers had already conferred their lineage title of war chief upon him, in 1763 he was given the name Konieschquanoheel (also given as Konieshguanokee), meaning "The Dawn Maker" or "The Maker of Daylight" (sometimes erroneously given as "The Maker of Delight," after a mistaken transcription). Konieschquanoheel was an important spiritual designation, as was Hopocan itself, which means "Calumet" or "Tobacco Pipe," symbolizing the peacekeeping function of the Delawares within the league. From a clumsy translation of the name Hopocan, he came to be known as "Captain Pipe" among the Europeans, a trivialization by which he is still named in some historical texts.

Hopocan as a Leader

As a leader of the league Delawares in Ohio, Hopocan inherited the pesky presence of Moravian missionaries whom his predecessor, Chief Pakanke, had invited in as a courtesy to his speaker, Glickhican, a convert to the Moravian religion. The Moravian missionaries proved quite troublesome to Hopocan and the league throughout the **American Revolution**. Although theoretically neutral, as were the Delawares at first, the missionaries covertly sided with the rebels. **John Heckewelder**, the missionary stationed at the village of Salem, just outside of Goschochking, began actively spying on the league for George Washington's forces at Fort Pitt.

In 1778, pursuant to the Delawares' neutrality, Hopocan signed a peace treaty at Fort Pitt. Soon thereafter, in spectacular violation of the treaty, a "patriot" militia made a sneak attack on his lineage village near the Shenango River, during which his mother was wounded and his brother was killed. At first, Katepakomen (**Simon Girty**), the war chief of the league Wyandots, misidentified David Zeisberger, the lead Moravian missionary in Ohio, as the culprit who had sent intelligence to the patriots at Fort Pitt, but in fact, documentation turned up in 1958 proving that Heckewelder had been the spy (Wallace, 133–134).

The treachery of the attack and the complicity of the Moravians galvanized Hopocan and led him and the Ohio Delawares into the war on the side of the league (often misrepresented as "the British side"). The league was fighting to retain its rights to western Pennsylvania and Ohio, lands General George Washington often called "Canada" in his memos and dispatches. Washington assumed, quite wrongly, that this was "British" territory, although it was still occupied and de facto controlled by the Haudenosaunee League.

In the late summer of 1781, Hopocan caught wind of a genocidal plot against the Delaware-Mahicans in their Muskingum breadbasket. On one hand, Washington wanted their food to provision his own haggard troops; on the other, the rich farms of Ohio were interfering with the success of Washington's earlier strategy literally to starve out the league in a series of concerted campaigns that had destroyed the harvests and granaries of the Senecas and Onondagas in 1779.

Alerted to the plan, Hopocan acted swiftly. To end the flow of intelligence, he took the Moravians prisoner on September 3–4, 1781. Heckewelder secretly sent an appeal for help to Fort Pitt. His messenger was Glickhican's niece, who tipped Heckewelder's hand by stealing Hopocan's own war horse to make her ride to Fort Pitt. Realizing that time was of the essence if he was to save the Delaware-Mahicans, Hopocan spirited them en masse to the safety of Upper Sandusky, the league Wyandot capital in Ohio, where they all arrived on October 11. Before they left Goschochking, however, the Delaware-Mahican women buried their lush harvests in secret pits to keep them out of enemy hands.

Shortly thereafter, Colonel Daniel Brodhead, commander of Fort Pitt, destroyed Goschochking and surrounding league Delaware fields, leaving intact, however, the small, but now-empty, Moravian villages of Salem, Gnadenhütten, and Friedenshütten on its outskirts. He did not find the food.

Hopocan escorted the Moravians, particularly Heckewelder, to Detroit, the British headquarters of its western theater, for trial on capital charges of espionage. Along the way, Hopocan lay over for a **Green Corn Ceremony** at the major council grounds at the far Western Door of the league, the point where Swan Creek meets the Maumee River in modern-day downtown Toledo, Ohio. There—to the intense dismay of the missionaries in his charge—Hopocan went liquor questing and remained thoroughly inebriated from October 25 to 27. In fact, he was preparing his words for the great council in Detroit, where he knew that the life of his sometime friend Heckewelder would be on the line.

Hopocan before a British Court

The trial opened on November 9, 1781. In the words of historian Paul Wallace, Hopocan "st[ole] the show" (Wallace, *Thirty Thousand Miles*, 186), delivering a magnificent address to the British court. In a surprise move, Hopocan defended the Moravians, who, he said, had been acting out of fear and could not, after all, have been in Ohio in the first place had his people not allowed them to be. Thus he took the blame for the intelligence leak on himself. Hopocan also pointedly questioned the right of the Crown to demand that he address George III as "Father," a term he then ironically employed throughout the rest of the speech. Next, he skillfully placed the blame for the war on British cupidity and European bloodlust.

Finally, Hopocan bluntly informed the British of his lack of confidence in their good faith: "Think not that I want sense to convince me," he chided the presiding Crown officers, "that although you *now* pretend to keep up a perpetual enmity to the long knives [i.e., the revolutionaries], you may, before long, conclude a peace with them" (Heckewelder, 135). These were prescient words. Before two years were out, this was precisely what had occurred, with the British blithely handing over Ohio and the whole "Old Northwest" to the new United States of America at the Treaty of Paris in 1783, despite the fact that the Haudenosaunee League had won the war in the west.

Thus the British commandant prudently gave in to Hopocan's plea that the Moravians be released unharmed. He even allowed them to return to Ohio in

Hopocan's custody. Hopocan trusted in a chastised Heckewelder to improve his trustworthiness, but this proved to be a grave mistake, for as soon as the Moravians arrived "home," Heckewelder renewed his intelligence link to Fort Pitt, eventually providing the crucial information that led to the genocide of March 8, 1782.

The Goschochking Genocide

Washington and his Fort Pitt commanders were still intent upon seizing the Delawares' food stores. Hearing from Heckewelder on March 3 that between 135 and 140 Delaware-Mahican men, women, and children, all unarmed farmers, had returned to Goschochking to pull their food out of hiding, he dispatched Colonel David Williamson and the Pennsylvania militia to steal their provisions. While they were at it, the militia voted to murder, plunder, and scalp in the most hideous way the 96 people they trapped at Goschochking, plus 30 more Delawares taken prisoner on the militia's way back to Fort Pitt. Although the league blamed Heckewelder and the Moravians for this disaster, Hopocan blamed himself.

Emboldened by the "success" of the **Goschochking Genocide**, Washington ordered another "ethnic cleansing," a new expedition into Ohio on a mop-up mission against the remaining Delaware-Mahicans (Mann, 166, 227–228). Roused to profound emotion by the murder, plundering, and desecration of the Delaware-Mahicans of Ohio, Hopocan and Katepakomen mounted an overwhelming resistance to Colonel William Crawford's invasion, which was launched in June 1782. In the battle that followed, the patriots were routed. Williamson beat a cowardly retreat, knowingly abandoning Crawford to capture in the process. Hopocan had really wanted Williamson, who was known to have led the Goschochking Genocide, but he settled for taking Crawford prisoner instead to stand trial for the crime. On June 11, 1782, Hopocan led Crawford into Old Town, a Wyandot village, where the women condemned him to death for the revolutionary army's crimes against humanity. Crawford was accordingly tortured to death at the stake in retribution. Even though the Treaty of Paris (from which the league had been excluded) handed over the "Old Northwest" to the new European-American country, Native Americans remained in control of the Ohio country for another twenty years, until Mad Anthony Wayne, known as Sukachgook, the Black Snake, to the league, seized it in a series of murderous campaigns.

Hopocan's Last Years

During this period and into old age, Hopocan remained a staunch foe of European-American invasion, although he signed a peace treaty at Fort McIntosh, Ohio, in 1785, and another at Fort Harmar in 1789. Both treaties were broken by the settlers. By 1791, when the United States was gearing up to take over Ohio militarily, Hopocan was too worn out to relish the thought of another punishing war and thus cautioned against the stand that was being planned for the summer of 1794. He closed his eyes for the last time that year, just three days before the cataclysm known as the Battle of Fallen Timbers, which was fought on August 20, 1794. Hopocan was thereby spared the devastating outcome, brought on once more by the treachery of the British he had never trusted: They promised aid to the allied Native nations, but then slammed the gates of their fort shut in the faces of the retreating Natives in the heat of battle, thus sealing their loss.

In 1794, Hopocan was living in his lineage village on the Sandusky River in Ohio, called "Captain Pipe's village" in European-American sources. This has led Euro-scholars to assert that he died there. A strong Wyandot tradition contradicts this, however, stating that he died on his way to the 1794 Green Corn Ceremony at the major council grounds in modern-day Toledo. Never quite making it to the council, he laid down for the last time beside the Maumee River at Grand Rapids, Ohio (the site of a modern park), just before the Battle of Fallen Timbers (1794), a few miles away. Heckewelder, who knew him, also recorded that Hopocan had died "near the rapids of the Maumee" just "days before the defeat of the confederated Indians by Wayne" (Heckewelder, n. 3). A statue was later erected in Hopocan's honor at Barberton, Ohio.

FURTHER READING

Heckewelder, John. *History, Manners, and Customs of the Indian Nations Who Once Inhabited Pennsylvania and the Neighboring States*. 1820. 1876. The First American Frontier Series. New York: Arno Press, 1971.

Mann, Barbara A. "Forbidden Ground: Racial Politics and Hidden Identity in James Fenimore Cooper's Leather-Stocking Tales." Ph.D. diss., University of Toledo, 1997.

Wallace, Paul A. W. "John Heckewelder's Indians and the Fenimore Cooper Tradition." *Proceedings of the American Philosophical Society* 96:4 (August 1952): 496–504.

———, ed. and annot. *Thirty Thousand Miles with John Heckewelder*. Pittsburgh: University of Pittsburgh Press, 1958.

Barbara A. Mann

Huron (Wyandot), name derivation. For all its pseudoexotic sound and regular use today by European-American scholars, the term "Huron" is European and is unconnected with any Iroquoian word. As Thelma Marsh (Ohio Wyandot) stated emphatically in 1974, the "people call themselves 'Yendots' " (Marsh, 13). "Ywendat" is popularly transcribed as "Wyandot."

Marsh also noted that " 'Huron' is a derogatory term meaning 'bristly haired' " (Marsh, 13). She was essentially correct: *Huron* is from the French *hure*, which means "prickly boar's head," alluding to the spiky hairs on the heads of wild pigs. The French particle *on* that was affixed to *hure* was a denigrating suffix indicating a group of people (Swanton, 233). Importantly, the term *huron* was not invented to describe Native Americans, but came into use in precontact Europe. In the medieval to early modern French vernacular, *huron* meant any uncouth person or a ruffian. The French aristocracy had hurled the slur "huron" at their own peasantry since at least 1358 (Cranston, 48–49).

The term was applied to the Laurentian Iroquois of America by sixteenth-century French sailors, most probably under **Jacques Cartier**. Seeing Iroquoian men standing on the shores wearing their distinctive "Mohawk" hairdos, the sailors laughed and pointed, crying out, "Quelles hures!" (What louts!). Succeeding French invaders picked up and perpetuated use of this "funny" term.

Modern Euro-scholars claim that "Huron" is a common identity marker, but this is only so because they make it so. Since the correct and respectful term, Wyandot, is available and is just as commonly known, Native Americans believe that there is no excuse for not using it.

FURTHER READING

Cranston, James Herbert. *Étienne Brûlé: Immortal Scoundrel*. Toronto: Ryerson Press, 1949.

Marsh, Thelma R. *Moccasin Trails to the Cross: A History of the Mission to the Wyandott Indians on the Sandusky Plains*. Sandusky, Ohio: United Methodist Historical Society of Ohio, 1974.

Swanton, John Reed. *The Indian Tribes of North America*. Smithsonian Institution, Bureau of American Ethnology, Bulletin 145. Washington, D.C.: Smithsonian Institution Press, 1952.

Barbara A. Mann

I

Iroquois Arts: A Directory of a People and Their Work. *Iroquois Arts: A Directory of a People and Their Work* is the most comprehensive collection of information on Iroquois creative activity. The 400-page book, published in 1983 by the Association for the Advancement of Native North American Arts and Crafts, contains capsule descriptions and photographs of 560 Iroquois artists who practice in basketry, beadwork, bone and antler work, clothing, cornhusk work, featherwork, leatherwork, painting, pottery, silverwork, stonecarving, textiles, and woodworking. The book also contains a listing of Iroquois-run arts and crafts outlets.

FURTHER READING

Johannsen, Christina B., and John P. Ferguson, eds. *Iroquois Arts: A Directory of a People and Their Work.* Warnerville, N.Y.: Association for the Advancement of Native North American Arts and Crafts, 1983.

Iroquois Nationals Lacrosse Club. The Iroquois Nationals **Lacrosse** Club in 1990 became the first Native American sports team to compete as a national entity. Coached by **Oren Lyons**, who was well known in his youth as an all-American lacrosse goalie at Syracuse University, the Iroquois Nationals were formed in 1983. During ensuing years, they traveled to such venues as Australia and England to compete under their own flag as an exercise in national sovereignty. In 1990, the World Lacrosse Federation granted the Nationals' request for membership as a nation.

The club also maintains a youth team, the Junior Nationals, which in 1996 traveled to Japan to compete in the sport's junior-league world championships. The Haudenosaunee Grand Council recognizes lacrosse as "one of our most revered traditions, spiritually, and as a celebration of health, strength, courage, and fair play" (George-Kanentiio, 95). Lacrosse, which was originally a Haudenosaunee sport, by the 1990s was being played on a worldwide basis.

FURTHER READING

George-Kanentiio, Doug. "The Iroquois Nationals: Creating a Sports Revolution for American Indians." *Akwesasne Notes*, n.s. 1:2 (Summer 1995): 94–95.

J

Jay Treaty (1794). The major purpose of the Jay Treaty of 1794 was the establishment of a commission to formalize the border between the United States and Canada. Part of the treaty upholds the right of the **Mohawks** and other Haudenosaunee peoples to pass freely between the United States and Canada. Because officials on the Canadian side failed to observe the treaty, **Akwesasne Mohawks**, whose home straddles the border, initiated protest actions in 1968. Akwesasne leader Mike Mitchell was arrested during the same year for transporting a number of household goods across the border, a case that was later reopened with another border crossing in 1988. From **Ernest Benedict**'s home on Cornwall Island, the Mohawks of Akwesasne prepared to blockade the nearby International Bridge and force the issue of policies that required them to pay customs duties on anything worth more than $5 that crossed the border, including food and other necessities of daily life. More than a hundred Mohawks imposed a wall of bodies that stopped traffic; then they let air out of the tires of many stalled vehicles. Police arrested forty-one Mohawks. After a second blockade in February 1969 and a long series of negotiations, Canadian officials agreed to abide by the terms of the Jay Treaty.

Mitchell's legal battle regarding interpretation of Iroquois border-crossing rights under the Jay Treaty was still alive in 1997, more than 200 years after the treaty was signed. The Canadian federal government during September 1997 decided to appeal a court ruling that affirmed the Mohawks' border-crossing rights. At issue was the right of the Mohawks to cross the border without paying duty on goods meant to be traded with other Native Americans. During November 1998, the appeals court upheld the original ruling in support of the Mohawks, who now waited to see whether the government would appeal to the Supreme Court of Canada.

FURTHER READING

Johansen, Bruce E. *Life and Death in Mohawk Country*. Golden, Colo.: North American Press/Fulcrum, 1993.

Jemison, G. Peter (Seneca), b. 1945. G. Peter Jemison, an eighth-generation descendant of **Mary Jemison**, is a Heron Clan **Seneca** from **Cattauraugus**. An artist who formerly directed the American Indian Community House Gallery in New York City, Jemison has been the longtime manager of **Ganondagan**, a historic Seneca village site designated as a state and federal historic site twenty-five miles southeast of Rochester, New York. Jemison also has been active in national efforts to advocate the **repatriation** from museums and other non-Indian archives of Native American remains and funerary objects.

Jemison has served as chairman of the Haudenosaunee Standing Committee on Burial Rules and Regulations. "What we see objectively is when you ask a museum like the New York State Museum what remains could be identified as Caucasian, that number is zero, or very close to zero," he has said. "When you ask about Native American [remains], that's all there is. Isn't there something strange about this?" (Crowe, A-3).

Jemison, whose media as an artist include acrylics, pen and ink, charcoal, and colored pencils, began drawing as a boy. Encouraged by his parents and art teachers, he attended the State University of New York at Buffalo in art (1962–1967). He also studied art at the University of Siena, Italy, during 1964.

In addition to his reputation as an artist, Jemison is well known in Haudenosaunee country as an organizer of shows for other artists. One example of many such shows that Jemison has curated was "Where We Stand: Contemporary Haudenosaunee Artists," which showed August 15–December 21, 1997, at the New York State Historical Association Fenimore House Museum. This show featured a number of Haudenosaunee artists active in a wide array of forms, from painting to basketweaving, silversmithing, prints, and sculpture.

FURTHER READING

Crowe, Kenneth C. "Museums Work to Restore Tribal Heritage." *Albany Times Union*, December 10, 1995, A-3.

Jemison, Mary, 1742 [or 1743]–1833. Mary Jemison, a white woman, was abducted in 1758 from a frontier settlement in Pennsylvania by a party of Shawnees and French at the age of fifteen. Mary's parents, who were captured with her, later were killed at Fort Pitt, but Mary and her brother were spared and later ransomed to the **Senecas**. In her biography, published in 1823, Jemison recalled that she had been adopted by two Iroquois women who had lost a brother in the **American Revolution**.

Once she was assimilated by the Senecas, Jemison married Sheninjee, a Delaware warrior, in an arranged union. Jemison balked at first, but appreciated Seninjee's warmth and humor and came to love him. Sheninjee died at an unknown date thereafter; later, Jemison and her three-year-old daughter hid in the woods when colonists came calling, demanding their return to European-American society.

Jemison later married the Seneca war chief **Hiokatoo**, to whom she bore six children. Hiokatoo treated Jemison kindly, but was notorious for his cruelty against enemies. Jemison was mother to eight Seneca children, three of whom died at young ages because of alcoholism or alcohol-incited incidents.

The Senecas gave Jemison a tract of land two miles by one mile near the Genesee River, which she farmed. She died at the age of ninety, a Seneca grandmother in all but blood, on the Buffalo Creek Reservation in New York.

A large number of Senecas and **Cayugas** are descended from Mary Jemison's family. **Deskaheh** (Levi General), the Haudenosaunee leader who took the confederacy's case for sovereignty to the League of Nations during the 1920s, was a descendant of Mary Jemison (Akwesasne Notes, 13). **G. Peter Jemison**, director of the New York State historical site at **Ganondagan**, is also related to her.

FURTHER READING

Gangi, Rayna M. *Mary Jemison: White Woman of the Senecas: A Novel*. Santa Fe, N.M.: Clear Light, 1996.

Reaman, G. Elmore. *The Trail of the Iroquois Indians: How the Iroquois Nation Saved Canada for the British Empire*. London: Frederick Muller, 1967.

Seaver, James, ed. *A Narrative of the Life of Mrs. Mary Jemison*. 1823. Foreward by George Abrams. Syracuse, N.Y.: Syracuse University Press, 1990.

Tehanetorens [Ray Fadden]. *A Basic Call to Consciousness*. 1978 Rooseveltown, N.Y.: Akwesasne Notes, 1981 (1986 printing).

Jigonsaseh, Jikonsaseh, Yegowaneh, Gekeasawsa, Djigoⁿ'sl''s̲ⁿ ("The Fat-faced Lynx" or "Wildcat," also "The New Face") (Seneca/Attiwandaronk ["Neutral"]). *Jigonsaseh* was the position title of the Head Clan Mother of the Haudenosaunee League. Her many titles include "The Mother of Nations," "The Peace Queen," "The Great Woman," "The Fire Woman," and "The Maize Maiden." She was a direct, lineal descendant of Sky Woman through her daughter, the Lynx (see **The First Epoch of Time** for further information on the First Family). The *Jigonsaseh*'s traditional headquarters was at Gaustauyea or Kienuka ("The Fortress"), a site that later fell inside the boundaries of the Tuscarora Reservation in New York.

Duties of the *Jigonsaseh*

The *Jigonsaseh*'s traditional obligations included feeding all visitors, including war parties, regardless of their national loyalties, and discovering their business in Iroquoia. All visitors were safe within the precincts of Gaustauyea, her home town; her **longhouse** was a place of absolute sanctuary. She was charged with making and keeping the peace among individuals, clans, and nations, using mediation and negotiation. In circumstances when the use of force became unavoidable, she had the right to raise and command armies. She also convened all the meetings of the Clan Mothers' councils to discuss the business of the people and to forward the Clan Mothers' **consensus** agenda to the men's Grand Council, sitting at Onondaga. The civil chiefs could not consider any matter that had not been sent forward by the *Jigonsaseh* on behalf of the **gantowisas**, or women acting in their official, councilmanic capacity.

The original *Jigonsaseh* was an "astute stateswoman" who cofounded the league along with the **Peacemaker** and **Hiawatha** (Hewitt, "Some Esoteric Aspects," 322). In most traditions of the *Gayaněsshä'´gowa*, or **Great Law of Peace**, the Peacemaker sought her out early in his career to form an alliance with her. She was herself the leader of the faction Elizabeth Parker (the daughter of a late-eighteenth- and early-nineteenth-century *Jigonsaseh*) termed "the Cultivators" (Parker, *Life*, 44), a group the Peacemaker desperately needed to succeed in his peace quest. Most sources identify this first *Jigonsaseh* as a Wyandot Attiwandaronk, or so-called Neutral. (See also **The Second Epoch of Time: The Great Law Keepings**.)

When this original Peace Woman died, her name passed through the generations as the title indicating Head Clan Mother, the position she had held in life. Early in the twentieth century, Gawaso Wanneh (**Arthur C. Parker**) claimed to have found the grave of this twelfth-century *Jigonsaseh*. It was laden with freshwater pearls (Jemison, 69).

Records of the *Jigonsaseh*

Although the traditional record has been greatly distorted and partially destroyed by invasion, missionizing, forced assimilation, and Euro-ethnography, traditions and historical records exist telling of later *Jigonsasehs*. In 1881, Chief Elias Johnson (**Tuscarora**) told of an unworthy *Jigonsaseh* who, through personal treachery, instigated a war between the **Senecas** and their offshoot nations, the Eries (also called the Cat Nation), the Squawkihaws, and the Kah-Kwahs. In Johnson's Keeping, this *Jigonsaseh* allowed some Mississauga scouts to kill enemy Seneca scouts as they slept peacefully at Gaustauyea in what should have been complete safety. This act of treachery brought on a massive war between the Senecas and their league allies and the Eries, the Squawkihaws, and the Kah-Kwahs, resulting in the destruction of the New York towns of the latter.

As a result of this war, the Eries and their affiliated peoples were driven into the Ohio country, where they laid the basis of the league's later claim to that area. According to Johnson, as a result of the treachery of this *Jigonsaseh*, the position was abolished until the nineteenth century (Johnson, 173–185; Mann, *Iroquoian Women*, Chapter 3). This last claim does not, however, square with other sources, either traditional or historical, which maintain that *Jigonsasehs* continued to serve from the founding of the league through the nineteenth century.

In 1825, David Cusick told quite another version of this same tradition, one in which the *Jigonsaseh* behaved honorably against the treachery of others.

Cusick placed her in the time of the ninth **Adodaroh** of the league, making her about the ninth *Jigonsaseh* of the league. In his telling, the *Jigonsaseh* exercised direct control over twelve precincts and was in the process of negotiating a peace between the Mississaugas and the Senecas. Underhanded machinations of the Mississaugas placed her in a difficult position, which was only exacerbated by the antics of a Haudenosaunee rival for the position of *Jigonsaseh*, a woman who attempted to politick at Onondaga for the removal of the sitting *Jigonsaseh* in favor of herself. In the end, however, the sitting *Jigonsaseh* triumphed, not only halting the war, but retaining her seat (Beauchamp, 32–34; Mann, *Iroquoian Women*, Chapter 3).

Seneca tradition holds that during the ferocious **Beaver Wars** of the seventeenth century, a time when the league was busily incorporating the Northern Wyandots into the league, the Senecas took the entire nation of Attiwandaronks captive, including its *Jigonsaseh*. This was a moment of great rejoicing for the Haudenosaunee, as it allowed the then-vacant position of *Jigonsaseh* to be filled. The former Seneca lineage of the league *Jigonsaseh* probably had been wiped out by disease, triggering the constitutional ability of the Grand Council to raise up a sister branch of her line and to grant it Keepership of the titles held by the extinct lineage. Since the Attiwandaronks were the people who had given birth to the first *Jigonsaseh*, sister lineages were still available to revive the Seneca line that had died out. From this new blood arose at least two more great *Jigonsasehs*, one in the seventeenth and another in the nineteenth century. Both women appear in Western historical records.

The *Jigonsaseh* and the Marquis de Denonville

Early in 1687, the French Crown attempted to seize the Senecas' territory, a breadbasket as well as a formidable barrier to French incursions into **Turtle Island** (North America). King Louis XIV of France ordered Jacques René de Brisay, the Marquis de Denonville, one of his most seasoned war leaders, to take the Seneca territory and demolish the Haudenosaunee resistance to French invasion. Unscrupulous and contemptuous of the Senecas, Denonville began by inviting the men's Grand Council and several Clan Mothers to a peace conference. He then summarily took all of them prisoner and sent them to France as slaves. Denonville believed that by wiping out the Haudenosaunee government at one stroke, he could wipe out the resistance. What he did not realize was that he had left the powerful *Jigonsaseh* untouched, for, in accordance with custom, she had not left Gaustauyea, but had only sent her speaker to the distant council.

This *Jigonsaseh* rose to the occasion, rallying the remaining chiefs and Clan Mothers, appointing war chiefs, and assembling an army (including women warriors), which she personally led against Denonville. She proved to be a brilliant tactician. The deciding battle occurred at **Ganondagan** (called La Chine in French documents), near modern-day Victor, New York. There the *Jigonsaseh* conclusively routed Denonville. By the end of 1687, the *Jigonsaseh* not only had driven Denonville out of Seneca territory, inflicting on him the most ignominious defeat of his life in the process, but had chased his army all the way back to the gates of Montréal, to the consternation of the French. In June 1688, Denonville sued for peace and capitulated to the *Jigonsaseh*'s demands that he dismantle the French fort at Niagara, which was done on September 15, 1688, by order of Denonville himself (O'Callaghan, 1: 68–69). She also demanded and won the return of the Grand Council, but only thirteen had survived life as galley slaves in the king's navy (Mann, *Iroquoian Women*, Chapter 3).

There are indications in the records of yet other prominent *Jigonsasehs*, including the mother of the Keeper Elizabeth Parker. There was also a "Queen" Aliquippiso, the mother of Gaiant'waka ("Exalted Name"), called Chief **Cornplanter** by the Europeans (Parker, "Notes," 10). The next *Jigonsaseh* about whom much information exists was also the last known *Jigonsaseh* of the league, Gähahno (**Caroline Parker Mountpleasant**). In defiance of the U.S. government, which had abolished the older league government, she secretly held councils at Gaustauyea from 1853 till 1878, when the U.S. government rerecognized her position. She continued as *Jigonsaseh* until her death in 1892. No later *Jigonsaseh* was named, although her lineage and title continued to exist in abeyance among the Wolf Clan of the Senecas.

FURTHER READING

Beauchamp, W[illiam] M[artin]. *The Iroquois Trail, or, Footprints of the Six Nations, in Customs, Traditions, and History.* Including David Cusick's "Sketches of Ancient History of the Six Nations." 1825. Fayetteville, NY: H. C. Beauchamp, 1892.

Hewitt, J. N. B. "A Constitutional League of Peace in the Stone Age of America: The League of the Iroquois and Its Constitution." *Smithsonian Institution Series* (1920): 527–545.

———. "Ethnological Studies among the Iroquois Indians." *Smithsonian Miscellaneous Collections* 78 (1927): 237–247.

———. "Field Studies among the Iroquois Tribes." *Explorations and Field-work of the Smithsonian Institution in 1930* (1931): 175–178.

———. "Some Esoteric Aspects of the League of the Iroquois." *Proceedings of the International Congress of Americanists* 19 (1915): 322–326.

Jemison, Pete. "Mother of Nations: The Peace Queen, a Neglected Tradition." *Akwe:kon* 5 (1988): 68–70.

Johnson, Chief Elias. *Legends, Traditions, and Laws of the Iroquois, or Six Nations.* 1881. New York: AMS Press, 1978.

Mann, Barbara A. *Iroquoian Women: Gantowisas of the Haudenosaunee League.* New York: Peter Lang, 2000.

———. "The Lynx in Time: Haudenosaunee Women's Tradition and History." *American Indian Quarterly* 21:3 (1997): 423–450.

O'Callaghan, E. B., ed. *The Documentary History of the State of New-York.* 4 vols. Albany: Weed, Parsons & Co., 1849–1851.

Parker, A[rthur] C[aswell] [Gawaso Wanneh]. *An Analytical History of the Seneca Indians.* 1926. Researches and Transactions of the New York State Archeological Association, Lewis H. Morgan Chapter. New York: Kraus Reprint Co., 1970.

———. *The Constitution of the Five Nations, or, The Iroquois Book of the Great Law.* Albany: University of the State of New York, 1916.

———. *The Life of General Ely S. Parker, Last Grand Sachem of the Iroquois and General Grant's Military Secretary.* Buffalo: Buffalo Historical Society, 1919.

———. "The Maize Maiden." In *Rumbling Wings and Other Indian Tales.* Garden City, N.Y.: Doubleday, Doran & Company, 1928: 179–191.

———. *Notes on the Ancestry of Cornplanter.* 1927. Researches and Transactions of the New York State Archaeological Association, Lewis H. Morgan Chapter. New York: Kraus Reprint Co., 1970.

Powell, J. W. "Wyandot Government: A Short Study of Tribal Society." *Annual Report of the Bureau of Ethnology to the Secretary of the Smithsonian Institution* 1 (1879–1880): 57–69.

Wallace, Paul A. W. *The White Roots of Peace.* Empire State Historical Publication Series No. 56. Port Washington, N.Y.: Ira J. Friedman, 1946.

Barbara A. Mann

Johnson, Emily Pauline (Tekahionwake, "Double Wampum") (Mohawk), 1861–1913. Emily Johnson, a well-known **Mohawk** poet, was one of four children born to George Henry Martin Johnson, head chief of the Six Nations at **Grand River**, and Emily Howells of Bristol, England. Johnson, a descendant of **Sir William Johnson**, was born on the Six Nations Reserve, Brantford, Ontario. Johnson wrote poetry from a young age, despite her lack of formal education (she attended Central High School in Brantford for two years). She was largely self-taught and an avid reader.

Johnson wrote largely in obscurity until 1892, when a recitation of *Cry from an Indian Wife* and other poems she recited before the Young Liberals' Club of Toronto brought her fame across Canada. *The Song My Paddle Sings* became her best-known poem as she toured Canada. In 1894, Johnson published a book of poems, *The White Wampum*, from which she recited during a visit to London, England. Her second book of poems, *Canadian Born*, was published in 1903 and sold out in less than a year.

Johnson gave dramatic performances of her poetry in Native regalia across Canada and the United States and in England until failing health forced her retirement from touring. At that time, she settled in Vancouver, British Columbia, and lived there until her death. Her works also include *Flint and Feather* and *Legends of Vancouver*. The following excerpt is from one of her earliest published poems, *A Cry from an Indian Wife*:

> They but forgot we Indians owned the land
> From ocean unto ocean: that they stand
> Upon soil that centuries agone
> Was our sole kingdom and
> Our right alone.
> They never think how they would feel today,
> If some great nation came from far away,

Wresting their country from their hapless braves,
Giving what they gave us—but wars and graves. (Reaman, ii)

FURTHER READING

Johnson, E. Pauline. *Flint and Feather: The Complete Poems of E. Pauline Johnson (Tekahionwake)*. Toronto: Musson Book Co., 1969.
————. *Legends of Vancouver*. 1911. Toronto: McClelland & Stewart, 1922.
Reaman, G. Elmore. *The Trail of the Iroquois Indians: How the Iroquois Nation Saved Canada for the British Empire*. London: Frederick Muller, 1967.

Johnson, Guy, 1741–1788. Guy Johnson, **William Johnson**'s nephew, helped direct British campaigns against American revolutionary forces in the Mohawk and Wyoming valleys as an ally of the **Mohawk Joseph Brant**. He was at Fort Niagara from 1777 to 1779. He also was present at the Battle of Newtown against forces led by General **John Sullivan**.

Before the **American Revolution**, he had built a large mansion at Amsterdam, New York, called "Guy Park." Guy Johnson became a British Indian agent with the Iroquois and their allies after the elder Johnson's death in 1774. He played a key role in swinging many Iroquois, particularly Mohawks, to the British interest during the American Revolution. After the Revolution, a number of Johnson's Mohawk supporters moved to Canada; today, many of their descendants live at Kanesatake (**Oka**), **Grand River**, Ontario, and **Kahnasatake**, Québec, as well as in many of Canada's eastern urban areas.

Guy Johnson was well known within the Haudenosaunee Confederacy and had served an ample apprenticeship under Sir William. Guy Johnson inherited from his uncle a problematic policy among the Six Nations. Quintock (Kentucky) was filling with non-Indians. Harrisburg, Ohio, and Louisville already were firmly established as white settlements on the Ohio in 1773. The Iroquois were alarmed, since many of the people from the Six Nations were resettling in the Ohio region to escape the encroachments of non-Indians in their traditional territories further east.

Talk of war grew within the confederacy as Johnson sought to soften this injury by promising that the king would punish these lawless individuals. Johnson reminded the Iroquois of their covenant with the Crown and asked that they refrain from reprisals. He knew that if the Iroquois joined the Shawnees in resisting the whites in Kentucky, other western tribes would join the resistance movement, just as they had done during the rebellion led by Pontiac during the early 1760s.

Guy Johnson retained the services of Joseph Brant as his secretary. In July 1776, Brant and Johnson returned to America from England just as the spirit of independence was beginning to sweep the eastern seaboard. With the passage of the Declaration of Independence by the Continental Congress, the English felt compelled to press for Iroquois support.

Johnson was largely responsible for holding most of the Mohawks with the

British interest throughout the American Revolution. By 1779, however, the British cause was lost in Iroquois country, as General John Sullivan's troops raped the countryside and pillaged Iroquois villages. The same year, the New York Assembly confiscated Guy Park and the rest of Johnson's property in America. After the Revolution, Johnson returned to England, where he engaged in several futile attempts to regain his property.

By 1780, after Brant and Johnson had crossed the Atlantic together several times and had worked closely together for half a dozen years, they had a falling-out over Johnson's dishonesty. Evidence mounted that Johnson was padding reports to the Crown to swindle large amounts of money in league with several traders at Niagara. For example, Johnson debited the king for 1,156 kettles when the actual number was 156. Guy Johnson died in London, England, on March 5, 1788.

FURTHER READING

Edmunds, R. David, ed. *American Indian Leaders: Studies in Diversity*. Lincoln: University of Nebraska Press, 1980.

Graymont, Barbara. *The Iroquois in the American Revolution*. Syracuse, N.Y.: Syracuse University Press, 1972.

Grinde, Donald A., Jr. *The Iroquois and the Founding of the American Nation*. San Francisco: Indian Historian Press, 1977.

Johnson, Sir William, 1715–1774. Sir William Johnson was probably the most influential single Englishman in relations with the Haudenosaunee and their allies during the French and Indian War (1754–1763). From Johnson Hall, his mansion near Albany, Johnson forayed on Indian war parties, painting himself like an Iroquois and taking part in ceremonial dances. He was a close friend of the elderly **Hendrick**, with whom he often traveled as a warrior. **Joseph Brant** fought beside Johnson from the age of thirteen. Hendrick was killed making war on the French with Johnson against Baron Dieskau's forces at Lake George in 1755.

Johnson emigrated to America from Ireland in 1738 and established a plantation from which he traded with the Haudenosaunee, especially the **Mohawks**, gaining their trust. At the beginning of the French and Indian War, Johnson was commissioned as British superintendent of Indian affairs for the northern district, making him the main British liaison with the Haudenosaunee and many of their allies. Johnson kept the post until he died in 1774, steering the Mohawks successfully into an alliance with the British Crown against French interests that persisted through the **American Revolution** under the direction of his nephew, **Guy Johnson**.

Because he successfully recruited a sizable number of Iroquois to the British interest, Johnson was made a baronet, Sir William Johnson, with a 5,000-pound-sterling award. From his home near Albany, Johnson learned the customs and language of the Mohawks. He had a number of children by Mohawk women and acknowledged them as such. He had several other children by his wife, **Mary (Molly) Brant**, a Mohawk Clan Mother and granddaughter of Hendrick. Johnson was well liked, particularly among the Mohawks. Hendrick had a high regard for the Englishman. One of the main agenda items at the **Albany Congress** in 1754 was Hendrick's demand that Johnson be maintained as British Indian agent.

In June 1760, in the final thrust to defeat the French in North America, Johnson called for an attack on Montréal. About 600 warriors responded. Many Native Americans living in the Montréal area also responded to his call. Johnson reported that he was sending gifts to "foreign Indians" who were switching their allegiance from the sinking French Empire. By August 5, 1760, the Native contingent had reached 1,330.

The defeat of the French and their departure from Canada at the end of the war upset the balance of power that the Haudenosaunee had sought to maintain. They could no longer play one European power against another. The English now occupied all the forts surrounding Iroquois country. Johnson played a key role in pressing the Crown to limit immigration west of the Appalachians, but land-hungry settlers ignored royal edicts such as the Royal Proclamation of 1763, intensifying conflicts over land. In the meantime, Johnson became one of the richest men in the colonies through his land transactions and trade with Indians.

The aging Sir William, his face pockmarked with signs of advancing syphilis, died at a meeting with the Iroquois on July 11, 1774, at his mansion near Albany. For two hours, Johnson addressed the Iroquois in the oratorical style he had learned from them, summoning them to the British cause in the coming American Revolution. Suddenly, Johnson collapsed. He was carried to bed, where he died two hours later. The assembly of chiefs was stunned by his sudden death.

FURTHER READING

Flexner, James Thomas. *Mohawk Baronet*. New York: Harper & Row, 1959.

Graymont, Barbara. *The Iroquois in the American Revolution*. Syracuse,: N.Y. Syracuse University Press, 1972.

Grinde, Donald A., Jr. *The Iroquois and the Founding of the American Nation*. San Francisco: Indian Historian Press, 1977.

Hamilton, Milton W. *Sir William Johnson: Colonial American, 1715–1763*. Port Washington, N.Y.: Kennikat Press, 1976.

Sullivan, James, ed. *The Papers of Sir William Johnson*. Albany, N.Y.: University of the State of New York, 1921–1965.

K

Kahnawake Mohawks. Kahnawake, a **Mohawk** settlement near Montréal, was first begun as a Jesuit mission. In 1711, Joseph Germain, a Jesuit, described a mission of 500 to 600 Iroquois (mainly Mohawks), "families who have left their own country, because they were not free to form a Church and to live a Christian life there, on account of the insults offered by their infidel countrymen and the English" (Aquila, 75).

About 1750, a faction of the Mohawks at Kahnawake moved south and west to the mouth of the St. Regis River, on the south shore of the St. Lawrence River, because of internal disputes and the inability of the land at Kahnawake to support the entire community. This settlement became the core of the St. Regis Mohawk Reservation, called **Akwesasne** by many of its residents, which today is the only Indian reservation with territory on both sides of the U.S.-Canadian border.

During the early decades of the twentieth century, many of Kahnawake's residents, the fabled "**Mohawks in high steel,**" built bridges and skyscrapers in Montréal, Toronto, and the urban areas of the northeastern United States, especially New York City. After construction of the **St. Lawrence Seaway** in the 1950s, traditional Native ways of making a living, such as hunting and trapping, were destroyed. Many Kahnawake Mohawks found work smuggling tobacco products, alcohol, and firearms from the United States into Canada to evade high taxes and legal restrictions there. By 1990, provincial police routinely raided Kahnawake's seventy smoke shops for contraband cigarettes.

At Kahnawake, a movement in support of an indigenous school began in 1971 after two students were involved in a snowball fight at a Québec high school attended by 400 Native Americans and 2,300 non-Indians. The Indian participant in the snowball fight was disciplined, but the white student was not, leading to a three-day occupation of the school's auditorium and demands for Mohawk history and language classes. At the time, the only Native American employee at the school was the janitor. Mohawk parents and students won some concessions from the government of Québec: some Mohawk history and language classes were taught, and some Indian staff were hired. The Mohawks thought that the efforts were halfhearted, so in 1978, they held a referendum on starting a Native American high school at Kahnawake. The Kahnawake Survival School was established in the fall of 1978, mainly with volunteer teachers and community donations.

Kahnawake also is the birthplace of the Mohawk **Warrior Society**, under the ideological direction of **Louis Hall**. The Warrior Society, which was prominent in **gambling**-related violence at Akwesasne and the occupation at Kanesatake (**Oka**) was started at Kahnawake in the early 1970s and has been strong in Kahnawake since its inception. The tradition Mohawk Council there (unlike the Mohawk Nation Council at Akwesasne) has been strongly influenced by the Warrior Society ideology. Hall was a longtime member of the Kahnawake Longhouse.

Following the confrontation at Kanesatake (Oka) in 1990, Warriors at Kahnawake blockaded the Mercier Bridge, which bisects the reserve and connects Montréal with a suburb, Chateauguay. Residents of the French-speaking suburb responded with several nights of anti-Mohawk rioting that included the stoning of Mohawk cars leaving the reserve and the burning of Mohawks in effigy. The blockade tightened an economic vise on French Canadian towns in Canada's largest urban area. The Mohawks pledged that after the blockade ended, they would no longer patronize businesses in Chateauguay; the roughly 6,000 people who live at Kahnawake had been spending an estimated $45 million a year in the town.

In September 1997, Royal Canadian Mounted Police (RCMP) arrested a Kahnawake Mohawk, Mathew Watio Lazare, in connection with the illegal manufacture and sale of smuggled liquor, cigarettes, and stolen goods. The Kahnawake government created considerable controversy by refusing the RCMP's request to search Lazare's warehouse, called South Texas Ranch. Undercover operatives for the RCMP had infiltrated Lazare's operation and lured him and Brian Jacobs, an associate, to an off-reserve location where they were arrested. Police reports alleged that Lazare had been manufacturing alcoholic beverages that could cause blindness or death. It also was alleged that his warehouse trafficked in several types of stolen goods, including liquor, cigarettes (which were stamped with bogus British Columbia tax seals), fine cutlery, winter boots, canned food, and lawn tractors.

Also during 1997, residents of the Kahnawake Reserve mobilized in opposition to the proposed construction of four grain elevators near a school after the band council and Canadian government had given approval to Archer Daniels Midland (ADM) for the project. The Mohawks said that their children would be exposed to gases, vermin infestation, grain dust, and the potential for fire and explosion in the elevators. On October 9, 1997, several hundred people, many of them students and staff at the Kahnawake Survival School, marched four miles to deliver a petition to the offices of the band council demanding that the grain elevators not be built. Band chief Joe Norton was sharply criticized at a large community meeting on October 20 because he had allowed ADM to obtain a permit without the approval of residents. The grain elevators are yet another industrial legacy of the St. Lawrence Seaway, which runs adjacent to the twenty-six acres obtained for construction. Opponents of the elevators say that no more than four acres are actually necessary for the project. As of 1999, the project was on hold.

FURTHER READING

Alfred, Gerald R. *Heeding the Voices of Our Ancestors: Kahnawake Mohawk Politics and the Rise of Native Nationalism.* Toronto: Oxford University Press, 1995.
Aquila, Richard. *The Iroquois Restoration: Iroquois Diplomacy on the Colonial Frontier, 1701–1754.* Detroit: Wayne State University Press, 1983.
Deer, Kenneth. "RCMP Carry Out Sting Operation." *Eastern Door* (Kahnawake), September 19, 1997, 1.

Kateri Takawita (Mohawk), 1656–1680. Kateri Takawita was born in Caughnawaga, New York (now called Auriesville), of a Mohawk father and a Christian Algonquian woman who had been captured by the Mohawks and who died of smallpox when Kateri was four years of age. Shortly after her mother's death, smallpox also killed Kateri's father and left her eyes so sensitive to light that she had to spend much of her life inside and alone. Ostracized by some of her Mohawk relatives, Kateri spent much of her time with missionaries.

She was raised by an uncle, a Mohawk, who abused Kateri. Later, she moved to a community of Christian Indians near Montréal, where she served the people as the first Native American nun. She was baptized in 1676. Kateri's health always had been frail, and she died at the age of twenty-four, after which she became an example of Catholic devotion so strong that many people claimed to have been cured of physical ailments after receiving visions of her. She was recommended for canonization in 1844 and beatified in 1980. In the late twentieth century, an effort was being mounted inside the Vatican to raise her to sainthood.

FURTHER READING

Johansen, Bruce E., and Donald A. Grinde, Jr. *The Encyclopedia of Native American Biography.* New York: Henry Holt, 1997.

Kenny, Maurice (Mohawk), b. 1929. One of Native America's best-known contemporary poets, **Mohawk** Maurice Kenny was born in Watertown, New York, in 1929 and raised in New York's north country, in the Adirondacks and along the St. Lawrence River. He was educated at Butler University, St. Lawrence University, and New York University, where he studied with the renowned American poet Louise Bogan. He lived in New York City for several years during the 1950s. During the 1960s, Kenny lived in Mexico, the Virgin Islands, and Chicago. Later he returned to his home in the Adirondacks of upstate New York.

Kenny has worked as a poet in residence or visiting scholar at several colleges and universities, including North Country Community College, the University of Oklahoma, Paul Smith's College, the University of California at Berkeley, Gettysburg College, the American Indian Community House in New York City, and the University of Victoria, British Columbia. His poetry has been included in more than a hundred books and journals, including *Trends*, a Scottish journal, as well as *World Literature Today, American Indian Quarterly, Blue Cloud Quarterly, Wicazo Sa Review, Saturday Review*, and the *New York Times*. Kenny was awarded an honorary doctorate by St. Lawrence University in 1995.

Kenny's collections include *North: Poems of Home* (1977), *Dancing Back Strong the Nation* (1979), *I Am the Sun* (1979), *Blackrobe: Isaac Jogues* (1982), *Boston Tea Party* (1982), *Is Summer This Bear?* (1985), *Rain and Other Fictions* (1985), *Between Two Rivers* (1987), and *Last Mornings in Brooklyn* (1991). Portions of his work have been translated into several languages, including Russian, Dutch, French, Polish, Italian, and German.

Kenny's *Blackrobe* (1982), a collection of poems, was nominated for a Pulitzer Prize in poetry. His *Mama Poems* received the American Book Award in 1984. Joseph Bruchac has written that Kenny is "achieving recognition as a major figure among American writers. Already seen by some critics as one of the four or five most significant Native American poets ... [as] a distinctive voice, one shaped by the rhythms of Mohawk life and speech, yet one which defines and moves beyond cultural boundaries" (Bruchac, 161). Literary critic Craig Womack has written that "contemporary poet Maurice Kenny's unique combination of historic and poetic faculties is an excellent addition to ... tribal histories as well as to American poetry in general" (Womack, 95).

FURTHER READING

Bruchac, Joseph, ed. *New Voices from the Longhouse*. Greenfield Center, N.Y.: Greenfield Review Press, 1989.

Kenny, Maurice. *On Second Thought: A Compilation*. Norman: University of Oklahoma Press, 1995.

Womack, Craig. "The Spirit of Independence: Maurice Kenny's *Tekonwatonti/Molly Brant: Poems of War*." *American Indian Culture and Research Journal* 18:4 (1994): 95–118.

Kinzua Dam. The construction of the Kinzua Dam flooded one-third of the **Allegany Seneca Reservation**, 9,000 acres of **Seneca** land, in violation of the **Canandaigua Treaty** of 1794. The flooding required the removal of about 160 families, or about 600 people, from the valley in which many of them had lived for several generations (Bilharz, xx). Seneca **G. Peter Jemison** recalls that "our elders wept openly, and as a result of that, we lost many of them [to death] in the succeeding years" (Jemison, 12).

Plans to build a giant flood-control project to protect the growing city of Pittsburgh had surfaced as early as 1908. For two decades, the Army Corps of Engineers had compiled studies of the idea without informing the Native Americans living on the land that would be flooded. In August 1941, the Allegheny Reservoir Project was authorized by Congress. World War II intervened, so the project was not officially taken up again until 1956. The dam was to be constructed at the Kinzua Narrows along the Allegheny River just to the south of New York's border with Pennsylvania. The Senecas' reservation was twelve miles downstream.

The dam, which cost $125 million during the late 1950s, flooded all Seneca land below 1,365 feet in elevation, including the entire Cornplanter Tract, land that had been set aside for **Cornplanter**'s band by George Washington (see **Cornplanter Grant**). The Cornplanter Tract also had special meaning to the Senecas as the site on which **Handsome Lake** had many of his visions (Wilson, 191).

The Senecas had fought proposals to build a dam since 1927 using the Canandaigua Treaty as a defense, only to find themselves told by the federal courts in 1958 that the "plenary power" of Congress allowed it to abrogate treaties unilaterally. The U.S. Supreme Court validated that point of view in June 1959 by denying the Senecas a writ of certiorari. In 1984, the Seneca Nation of Indians declared September 24 "Removal Day" in observance of resistance to the Kinzua Dam; ten years later, the Senecas marked the thirtieth anniversary of their removal from the Kinzua Dam site.

FURTHER READING

Bilharz, Joy A. *The Allegany Senecas and Kinzua Dam: Forced Relocation through Two Generations*. Lincoln: University of Nebraska Press, 1998.

Hauptman, Laurence M. *The Iroquois Struggle for Survival: World War II to Red Power*. Syracuse, N.Y.: Syracuse University Press, 1986.

Jemison, G. Peter. "Sovereignty and Treaty Rights: We Remember." *Akwesasne Notes*, n.s. 1:3–4 (Fall 1995): 10–15.

Wilson, Edmund. *Apologies to the Iroquois*. New York: Vintage Books, 1960.

L

Lacrosse. Haudenosaunee people often call lacrosse "the Creator's Game." According to Robert W. Venables, "Lacrosse is more than a game. It includes religious meanings, purpose, and even ceremony" (Venables, 13). The playing of lacrosse is said to promote life. A sick person may have a game organized in his or her honor in the belief that the person's health may be improved "simply by seeing that the whole community cared enough to turn out for a game in the sick person's honor" (Venables, 14). Some traditional lacrosse games are played with a ball laced with herbs and other medicines to help a specific person who is ill.

The spiritual aspects of lacrosse are taught to Iroquois young people at a young age. The ball used in lacrosse has been said to represent the moon, which is believed to have been formed long ago when a lacrosse ball was thrown into the sky. During historic times, the game of lacrosse also functioned to keep warriors in physical shape and to sharpen their skills at teamwork between battles. One Iroquois name for the game is *Tewaarathon*, meaning "Little Brother of War" (Swezey, D-12).

Lacrosse players are expected to be role models in their communities, and they may be taken off a team by traditional chiefs if they misbehave. Prior to the 1994 World Games in Manchester, England, for example, two players on the **Iroquois Nationals** were barred from the team after they shoved a **Tuscarora** woman in a dispute over reservation **gambling** (Swezey, D-12).

"When you talk about lacrosse, you talk about the lifeblood of the Six Nations," says **Oren Lyons**, Faithkeeper of the Haudenosaunee Grand Council at Onondaga and an all-American lacrosse player as a goalkeeper when he was a student at Syracuse University in the late 1950s (Lipsyte, 28). On the 1957 Syracuse University team, Lyons played alongside Jim Brown, later a celebrated professional football player. Lyons's father also was a well-known lacrosse goalkeeper.

The object of the game is to catch a five-ounce hard-rubber ball and carry it, with the assistance of teammates and webbed sticks, to a goal. Today, lacrosse is played on an area a little larger than a football field. A smaller version, "box lacrosse," is played indoors on a field the size of an ice-hockey rink. Teams usually play ten to a side in "a spectacular, thundering game of flowing patterns [that] requires great stamina and a head for tactics and technicalities" (Lipsyte, 28).

European explorers, many of them French, observed the Iroquois and other Native Americans playing lacrosse in the seventeenth century. The Jesuits called the game "le jeu de la crosse" because, they said, the game stick resembled a bishop's crosier. While some anthropologists have theorized that the game was played as a surrogate for war or to prepare for it, a history of the game compiled by the North American Indian Travelling College says that "Natives played lacrosse for fun, physical fitness, and spiritual development" (Lipsyte, 28).

Before Europeans started playing the game in the mid-nineteenth century, lacrosse matches sometimes involved hundreds of players playing for several days at a time. Goals could be several miles apart in different villages. When white Canadians started playing the game, rules were regularized and sanctions were invoked against payment of players. During 1867, a **Mohawk** lacrosse team toured England and France, spurring establishment of lacrosse teams there.

In 1880, the Iroquois were barred from playing in international competition because the keepers of the rules said that they were "professional." The Iroquois also were barred from the Canadian championships. Lyons says that most Native American players did not have the income to play without being paid enough to get them to the next match. He believes that the Iroquois were exiled from international play because they were beating white teams at a time when Indians were presumed to be an inferior race.

In 1983, a century after their exile from a game that now was played world-wide, Native American teams were again allowed into international matches. By 1985, the Iroquois Nationals Lacrosse Club was touring England and winning three of five matches, including a tie with the English national team. By the late 1990s, the Iroquois Nationals had become a world-class lacrosse team, as evidenced by their July 1998 victory over England's national team by a score of 10 to 9 at the World Games in Manchester, England. The team's player who scored the winning goal in the match with England was Rex Lyons, son of Oren, who is carrying his family's lacrosse tradition into another generation.

FURTHER READING

Lipsyte, Robert. "Lacrosse: All-American Game." *New York Times Sunday Magazine*, June 15, 1986, 28.
Swezey, Carl. "For Iroquois Nation, Lacrosse Is Spiritual." *Washington Post*, July 20, 1998, D-12.
Venables, Robert W. "More Than a Game." *Northeast Indian Quarterly* 6:3 (Fall 1989): 12–15.

Vennum, Thomas, Jr. *American Indian Lacrosse: Little Brother of War.* Washington, D.C.: Smithsonian Institution Press, 1994.

Lancaster Treaty Council (1744). One of the more important treaty councils between the Haudenosaunee, their Native American allies, and delegates of the Middle Atlantic colonies, including Pennsylvania and Virginia, took place at Lancaster, Pennsylvania, during the summer of 1744. Lancaster was a frontier settlement at the time.

According to one observer, the Iroquois and their *Tadadaho* (speaker of the confederacy) **Canassatego** "[s]trode into town . . . [and] ran the show. . . . He dined and drank and joked with the colonial gentlemen, and he collected a quite satisfactory payment for the lands . . . to which the Iroquois claimed a right of conquest" (Jennings et al., 46). At the same time, Virginia delegates got Canassatego's consent for their own version of empire building. Canassatego signed a deed of cession that obtained for Virginia, at least on paper, settlement rights according to the colony's charter. The charter had no well-defined western or northern boundary at the time, so Canassatego was, again in theory, signing away all of the present-day United States north of Virginia's southern boundary except the lands explicitly claimed by the Haudenosaunee. Canassatego clearly did not understand the import of the agreement (Jennings et al., 46).

At Lancaster in 1744, Canassatego also advised the assembled colonial governors on Iroquois concepts of unity and urged the colonists to form a federal union on an Iroquois model. **Benjamin Franklin** probably first learned of Canassatego's advice when he set his words in type. It was Franklin's press that issued Indian treaties in small booklets that enjoyed a lively sale throughout the colonies. Beginning in 1736, Franklin published Indian treaty accounts on a regular basis until the early 1760s, when his defense of Indians under assault by frontier settlers cost him his seat in the Pennsylvania Assembly. Franklin subsequently served the colonial government in England.

FURTHER READING

Jennings, Francis, ed.; William N. Fenton, joint ed., Mary A. Druke, associate ed.; David R. Miller, research ed. *The History and Culture of Iroquois Diplomacy: An Interdisciplinary Guide to the Treaties of the Six Nations and Their League.* Syracuse, N.Y.: Syracuse University Press, 1985.

Marshe, Witham. *Lancaster in 1744: Journal of the Treaty at Lancaster in 1744, with the Six Nations.* Annotated by William H. Egle, M.D. Lancaster, Penn.: New Era Steam and Job Print Press, 1884.

Van Doren, Carl, Julian P. Boyd, eds. *Indian Treaties Printed by Benjamin Franklin, 1736–1762.* Philadelphia: Historical Society of Pennsylvania, 1938.

Land Area of the Haudenosaunee in New York State. The aboriginal homeland of the Haudenosaunee stretched from Lake Champlain and the Hudson River in the east to the Niagara River and Lake Erie in the west and from the St. Lawrence River in the north to the Delaware River and the central Pennsylvania mountains in the south. Included in this region are not only large sections of New York but parts of Ontario, Québec, Pennsylvania, and Ohio. Within this area dwelt many tens of thousands of Iroquois along with refugees from dozens of other nations. Pequots, Nanticokes, French, English, Africans, Conestogas, Lenni Lenapes, **Wyandots**, Abenakis, Tutelos, and many others built their communities within Haudenosaunee territory or immigrated to the Confederacy as families or individuals. Within the actual borders of present-day New York State, the confederacy held active jurisdiction over 80 percent of the state's current area, or over 39,000 of its 49,576 square miles.

As defined by the Haudenosaunee, each member nation was given custodial responsibility over specific territories. Within this region, the nations were to provide food, shelter, clothing, and medicine for their citizens and visitors while living in a state of ecological balance with other species of life. The Haudenosaunee believed that their territory was like a **longhouse**, the ancestral housing style used by the Iroquois. Inside this long, rectangular building lived each nation, as a family. Each "family" had its own hearth and gathered its own food but was bound to respond to the needs of its relatives while living in a state of tolerance and respect. No single nation had the right to breach the peace of the longhouse by disruptive behavior.

The longhouse was built on an east-west axis. Those who lived at its eastern entrance were the **Mohawks**, or the Keepers of the Eastern Door. They are also known as the People of the Flint. Indigenous Mohawk land reached north to the St. Lawrence River (including the Isle of Mont Royal, now the city of Montréal) and south to the Delaware River. Its boundaries were the Oswegatchie and Unadilla rivers in the west and Lake Champlain and the Hudson River in the east. The total acreage within New York State is 9,941,760 acres or 15,534 square miles. This figure is arrived at, as are all others, by totaling the land area of each county within the ancestral regions of the nations, then adding to that number the area of towns and districts adjacent to the ancient boundary lines when a county straddles such borders. In all instances, oral traditions are the basis for determining the boundary lines, which in turn use rivers, lakes, or natural land formations in defining territory.

Immediately west of the Mohawk Nation were the **Oneidas**. Their principal communities were clustered southeast of Oneida Lake, with smaller towns to the north and south. The Oneidas are known as the "younger brothers" to the Mohawks. They are also called the "People of the Standing Stone." Their homeland went from the St. Lawrence River in the north to the Susquehanna River in the south and from West Canada Creek in the east to the middle of Lake Oneida and the Chittenango Creek in the west. The land area of the Oneidas consisted of 3,724,160 acres or 5,819 square miles.

Adjacent to the Oneidas were the "People of the Hills," the **Onondagas**. Their natural borders were Oneida Lake and Chittenango Creek in the east, Lake Ontario and the St. Lawrence River to the north, the Susquehanna River to the south, and Skaneateles Lake to the west. They retain aboriginal title to 2,670,720 acres or 4,173 square miles.

Along the great wetlands now called the Montezuma National Wildlife Refuge lived the "People of the Pipe," the **Cayuga** Nation. Their homelands contained some of the most fertile land of all the Haudenosaunee territory. The Cayugas had 1,998,720 acres (3,123 square miles) from Skaneateles Lake in the east to Seneca Lake in the west and from Lake Ontario in the north to Pennsylvania in the south.

The "People of the Great Hill" are commonly known as the **Seneca** Nation. Their territory extended from Seneca Lake to the Niagara River and from Lake Ontario to the Pennsylvania border and far beyond. Within New York they have 6,558,720 acres or 10,248 square miles of homeland.

The **Tuscarora** Nation, also called "The Shirtwearers," returned to Iroquois territory beginning during the first decade of the eighteenth century, about 1710. They had villages on Oneida-Mohawk land along the Susquehanna and Delaware rivers and south of Oneida Lake. They were compelled to move to the Niagara region during the **American Revolution**.

It is important to note that these figures include only that area currently within the boundaries of New York State and not land in other U.S. jurisdictions. As of 1998, the Iroquois land base in New York consisted of the following: The Mohawks had 14,460 acres along the St. Lawrence River in Franklin County. The Oneidas had begun the decade with 32 acres and had expanded to an estimated 5,000 in Oneida and Madison counties. The Onondaga Nation had 7,300 acres south of Syracuse in Onondaga County. The Cayugas had no land base in New York State as of April 1998. The Tuscaroras had a land area of 5,778 acres next to the city of Niagara Falls. East of their reservation is **Tonawanda Seneca Reservation** territory with its 7,317 acres straddling Erie, Genesee, and Niagara counties. South of Buffalo is the **Cattaraugus** Seneca territory of 17,025 acres and nearby **Allegany** consisting of 30,984 acres. Northeast of Allegany is the Oil Springs reservation of 640 acres (1 square mile). The total land holdings for the Iroquois are 88,504 acres of the original 25,000,000, about .034 percent of the ancestral Haudenosaunee territory in New York State.

Between 1784 and 1850, much of the Haudenosaunee nations' land holdings was taken through fraudulent treaty claims; many of these were illegal because they violated the various Non-intercourse Acts passed by Congress during that period. These acts required congressional approval of Indian land cessions to prevent fraud. As a result of these land cessions, many Haudenosaunee moved to Canada (to **Grand River** and other communities), Wisconsin, Kansas, and Indian Territory (later Oklahoma). None of these treaties were approved by the Haudenosaunee Grand Council.

Usually, a wealthy land speculator would ask the state legislature to authorize a treaty or agreement with an Indian nation from which the speculator wished to extract land. The legislature would then authorize the agreement and find some members of the nation (who usually were not authorized to act by its people as a whole) to sign a treaty. These "treaty chiefs" would then be bribed to concede property. All of this was done legally under the U.S. legal system, usually for a fraction of what the land would have been worth on the open market.

Another device was the lease-as-sale. The Indians would be told that they were signing a lease when actually they were signing to sell their land. Most of western New York State changed hands by one of these two methods. Such land transfers probably were in violation of the **Fort Stanwix Treaty of 1784**, which recognizes the Haudenosaunee's interest in their aboriginal lands. These devices also were almost certainly violations of the federal Non-intercourse Acts passed between 1790 and 1834, which were meant to prevent just this kind of fraud.

During the 1950s, the Haudenosaunee lost several thousand acres of land to dams, reservoirs, and highways, as well as electrical and gas lines and water-ways. The best-known example of such land seizures (usually under governmental-agency powers allowing seizure of land for "eminent domain," or public uses) was the **Kinzua Dam**, which flooded land promised to the Senecas by agreement between George Washington and **Cornplanter**. Some of Corn-planter's descendants were forced from their homes, and they asked bitterly whether Washington had asked the old chief if he knew how to swim.

Today, most of the confederacy's member nations are pursuing land claims through the courts. The Onondagas have a claim to much of the Syracuse urban area, for example. The Onondagas have refrained from pursuing land claims against private owners, while the neighboring Oneidas have announced their intention to sue for return of private land.

FURTHER READING

Berkey, Curtis. "The Legal Basis for Iroquois Land Claims." *Akwe:kon Journal* 10:1 (Spring 1993): 23–25.

George-Kanentiio, Doug. "How Much Land Did the Iroquois Possess?" *Akwesasne Notes*, n.s. 1:3–4 (Fall 1995): 60.

Tehanetorens [Ray Fadden]. *A Basic Call to Consciousness*. 1978. Rooseveltown, N.Y.; Akwesasne Notes, 1981 (1986 printing).

Vecsey, Christopher, and William A. Starna, eds. *Iroquois Land Claims*. Syracuse, N.Y.: Syracuse University Press, 1988.

Wallace, Anthony F. C. "Political Organization and Land Tenure among the Northeastern Indians, 1600–1830." *Southwestern Journal of Anthropology* 13 (1957): 301–321.

Doug George-Kanentiio and Bruce E. Johansen

Laughing, Tony (Mohawk), b. 1947. Mohawk Tony Laughing opened the first Las Vegas–style casino at **Akwesasne**, Tony Vegas International, with $500,000 of his own money, most of which was earned from smuggling. The new casino, which opened in 1988, employing 240 people, was opened without state, federal, or tribal approval. Laughing told the press that armed guards would defend it from the police raids that had plagued earlier attempts to install slot machines on the reservation. At one point, the elected St. Regis Tribal Council shut off Tony Vegas's water supply, along with that of Hart's Palace, another casino. The **gambling** promoters brought in bottled water for their employees and customers.

The $375,000 building housing Tony Vegas International was constructed with thick brick walls, no windows, and only one entrance, so that it could be easily defended. Laughing began with 24 slot machines, planning to expand to 500, along with blackjack, craps, and other games of chance. Laughing was seen driving around the reservation in his late-model Cadillac, contacting people on its cellular phone. "Gambling is a viable way of making a living for me and my family. It's a way for us to get into the mainstream of society," he told reporters (Johansen, 28).

On March 6, 1989, a brawl between gambling supporters and opponents at Tony Vegas International escalated into a fight that injured Mohawk Eric Sunday. At its height, the scuffle involved about 400 people, including gambling opponents, casino employees, and members of the **Warrior Society**. After state police waded into the crowd, gambling opponents told them to remove TVI's slot machines, or they would do it on their own. Police seized one machine for evidence and arrested Laughing as the crowd streamed into the casino and wrecked 50 other one-armed bandits.

Laughing, who still was listed as a fugitive from a federal arrest warrant, frequently used his office at TVI. He even granted interviews against a backdrop of ten AK-47 rifles lined against a wall. He showed a reporter a bullet hole above his desk. Laughing said, "They [opponents of gambling] can picket all they want. But if they attack my property, we will defend it." (Johansen, 41). The casino owner described how he feeds the casino's daily transaction records into a paper shredder he called his "Ollie North machine."

Laughing estimated that he had recouped his initial $700,000 investment in his casino (earned from smuggling cigarettes) and had tripled it for a net profit of about $2.1 million. In another interview, Laughing defended his casino as a source of jobs. "These are good-paying jobs," he said. "And that is clear money. There is no income tax," (Johansen, 41). Laughing said that he employed 280 people at Tony Vegas International, 240 of them **Mohawks**. Security personnel earned $5 to $12 an hour, and poker dealers up to $1,200 a week.

On September 21, 1989, Laughing was arrested following a thirty-minute high-speed chase off the reservation. State troopers found $87,000 in cash in his car. Laughing had been spotted about 6:20 P.M. in a car driven by Brenda Jock through Fort Covington, New York, outside reservation borders. State troopers gave chase after Jock refused to stop. Police chased the car to the Canadian National Railway tracks in Brasher, where the car stalled. Laughing shoved the front passenger door open and fled into nearby woods, where police finally arrested him. Jock was charged with hindering prosecution, reckless endangerment, and several motor-vehicle violations. Laughing said that he was on his way to dinner when police arrested him. "Seriously, I figured that if I did get caught I'd have my bail money," said Laughing (Johansen, 41). After gambling-related violence killed two Mohawks on May 1, 1990, Tony Vegas International and other casinos at Akwesasne were closed. Laughing continued to be active in the **Warrior Society**.

FURTHER READING

Johansen, Bruce E. *Life and Death in Mohawk Country.* Golden, Colo.: North American Press/Fulcrum, 1993.

Lemay, Marcel, 1959–1990. The Sûreté du Québec (SQ), the provincial police, massed roughly 100 officers around the **Mohawk** barricade at Kanesatake (**Oka**) before sunrise on July 11, 1990, a Wednesday. Wearing olive-green fatigues and gas masks, the officers apparently hoped that they could bring the barricade down with a show of force, without actually moving against the people behind it. The Mohawks at Kanesatake had barricaded a seldom-used road near their reserve to protest proposals to turn land they claimed into nine extra holes for the hamlet of Oka's municipal golf course.

At 8:45 A.M., about 100 police attacked the barricade and roughly 200 Indian men and 100 women and children, unleashing tear gas that a sudden switch in wind direction blew back into their faces. Apparently surprised by the Mohawks' fire, the police retreated in such pell-mell fashion that they left behind an assortment of vehicles, including two vans, four patrol cars, and a large front-loader brought in to dismantle the blockade. Instead, the Mohawks and their supporters used the machine to dump the other abandoned vehicles onto a new barricade across Highway 344, which was built as an obstacle course, with vehicles tilted on their sides across the road.

In the ensuing melee, Marcel Lemay, one of the officers, was killed. Lemay, who held the rank of corporal in the SQ, was fatally injured under conditions so chaotic that after a year of forensic testing, Canadian officials still were not sure from which side of the conflict the bullet that killed him had come.

Livingston, Robert, 1654–1728. Robert Livingston was one of the best known of several secretaries of Indian affairs at Albany who were responsible for recording the proceedings of treaty councils. Such a position demanded acute knowledge of Haudenosaunee diplomatic protocol, by which treaty councils usually were conducted. The "Indian Records" maintained by Livingston are studied nearly three centuries later as some of the most complete records of what occurred at important treaty councils.

FURTHER READING

Livingston, Robert. *The Livingston Indian Records, 1666–1723.* Stanfordville, N.Y.: E. M. Coleman, 1979.

Logan, James (Tahgahjute) (Cayuga), c. 1728–1780. The son of a **Cayuga** mother and a French father, Tahgahjute took the name "Logan" after James Logan, secretary to William Penn. The **Cayuga** Logan was born at Shamokin, Pennsylvania, and supported the colonists throughout his adult life, rallying to the English cause in the war with the French and in Pontiac's rebellion. His friendship was strained severely in 1774 when at least one of Logan's relatives was murdered in an unprovoked attack.

A gang of white squatters massacred a camp of peaceful Indians at the mouth of Yellow Creek, Ohio, in the spring of 1774. According to contemporary reports, the victims included Logan's entire family. The Indians retaliated with a number of attacks after the massacre. After that, Logan refused to attend a peace conference, but sent a speech via an interpreter that Thomas Jefferson later compared to the great orations of ancient Greece and Rome: "I may challenge the whole orations of Demosthenes and Cicero, and of any more eminent orator, if Europe has furnished more eminent, to produce a single passage, superior to the speech of Logan" (Hamilton, 139). Logan's speech was popularized during the nineteenth century in millions of copies of *McGuffey's Reader*.

According to the speech's most popular rendition, Logan said, in part:

I appeal to any white man to say, if he ever entered Logan's cabin hungry, and he gave him not meat; if he ever came cold and naked, and he clothed him not. During the course of the last long and bloody war, Logan remained idle in his cabin, an advocate for peace. Such was my love for the whites, that my countrymen pointed as they passed, and said, "Logan is the friend of white men." I had even thought to have lived with you, but for the injuries of one man. Colonel Cresap, the last spring, in cold blood, and unprovoked, murdered all the relations of Logan, not sparing even my women and children. There runs not a drop of my blood in the veins of any living creature. . . . Who is there to mourn for Logan?—Not one. (Hamilton, 139–140)

According to Charles Hamilton in *Cry of the Thunderbird: The American Indian's Own Story* (259), Logan's speech contained some factual errors. It was a man named Greathouse, not Cresap, who initiated the massacre. Logan had no wife or children, but his sister was killed.

Logan was infuriated and stricken with grief. That summer he attacked several white families located on Indian land and killed several people. By late summer, border raids increased, and the Ohio frontier was raging in conflict. Virginia called out its militia to punish Logan. Several thousand Indians and whites met at the Battle of Point Pleasant. The Indians (Shawnees, Mingos, Delawares, **Wyandots**, Cayugas, and **Senecas**) were outnumbered and were defeated by the militia. The Iroquois League at Onondaga refused to sanction the war and chose to ignore the Shawnees, who were trying to form their own western confederacy. As the revolution waned, Logan became increasingly addicted to alcohol and may have lost his sanity. He was murdered by his nephew in 1780 as they returned from a trip to Detroit.

FURTHER READING

Hamilton, Charles, ed. *Cry of the Thunderbird*. Norman: University of Oklahoma Press, 1972.

Jefferson, Thomas. *Notes on the State of Virginia*. 1784. Ed. William Peden. Chapel Hill: University of North Carolina Press, 1955.

Seeber, Edward D. "Critical Views on Logan's Speech." *Journal of American Folklore* 60 (1947): 130–146.

Wallace, Anthony F. C. *The Death and Rebirth of the Seneca*. New York: Knopf, 1970.

Longhouse, as Haudenosaunee national symbol. The Haudenosaunee often characterized their confederacy as a longhouse, with the **Mohawks** at the "Eastern Door," the **Senecas** at the "Western Door," and the **Onondagas** in the middle, tending the fire of the Grand Council. In this characterization, the Haudenosaunee are seen as one large extended family living in the symbolic national longhouse, with its roof along the St. Lawrence River and Lake Ontario and its floor along the present-day border between New York and Pennsylvania, embracing most of upstate New York. The name of the people, "Haudenosaunee," may be translated as "people of the longhouse" or "people who build [longhouses]."

As early as 1654, European sources describe Haudenosaunee leaders characterizing their confederacy as a longhouse, "completed cabin," or "extended house." A Mohawk whom Europeans called "the Flemish Bastard" (he had mixed parentage) was noted in the *Jesuit Relations* during that year as describing the confederacy:

We, the five nations, compose but one cabin; we maintain but one fire; and we have, from time immemorial, dwelt under one and the same roof.... From the earliest times, these five Iroquois Nations have been called in their language ... "The completed cabin," as if to express that they constituted but one family. (Thwaites, 27:137)

FURTHER READING

Reaman, G. Elmore. *The Trail of the Iroquois Indians: How the Iroquois Nation Saved Canada for the British Empire*. London: Frederick Muller, 1967.

Thwaites, Reuben Gold, ed. and trans. *The Jesuit Relations and Allied Documents: Travels and Explorations of the Jesuit Missionaries in New France, 1610–1791*. 73 vols. Cleveland: Burrows Brothers Co., 1896–1901.

Longhouse, as Haudenosaunee residence. **Samuel de Champlain** described the Haudenosaunee longhouse as

a kind of arbor or bower covered with bark approximately fifty or sixty yards long by twelve wide with a passage ten or twelve feet broad down the middle from one end to the other. Along each side runs a bench four feet above the ground where the inmates [*sic*] sleep in summer to avoid the innumerable fleas. In winter, they sleep closer to the fire on mats underneath the benches where it is warmer; and they fill the hut with a supply of dry wood to burn at that season. A space is left at one end of the cabin for

The longhouse is a traditional Haudenosaunee family dwelling. Courtesy of John Kahionhes Fadden.

storing their maize, which they place in large barrels in the middle of the floor; boards suspended overhead preserve their clothing, food, and other things from numerous mice. (Reaman, 18)

Champlain wrote that the average longhouse contained two dozen nuclear families clustered around a dozen council fires. Smoke "concentrates at will, causing much eye trouble" and sometimes blindness in old age (Reaman, 18).

Lewis Henry Morgan described a typical Haudenosaunee longhouse as being "generally from fifty to 130 feet in length, by about sixteen in width, with partitions at intervals of about ten or twelve feet, or two lengths of the body. Each apartment was, in fact, a separate house, having a fire in the centre, and accommodating two families, one upon each side of the fire. Thus a house of 120 feet long would contain ten fires and twenty families" (Morgan, 315). Food was stored, according to Morgan, "upon cross-poles, near the roof [**corn** was] braided together by the husks. . . . Charred and dried corn and beans were generally stored in bark barrels, and laid away in corners" (Morgan, 318). Surplus corn also was stored underground in caches. Because it was charred and then dried in the sun, the stored corn was nearly immune to diseases of rot brought on by excess moisture underground. When the corn was exhumed for travel, it was only half as heavy as it had been when fresh.

FURTHER READING

Morgan, Lewis Henry. *League of the Iroquois.* 1851. Secaucus, N.J.: Corinth Books, 1962.
Reaman, G. Elmore. *The Trail of the Iroquois Indians: How the Iroquois Nation Saved Canada for the British Empire.* London: Frederick Muller, 1967.

Longhouse Religion. *See* **Handsome Lake**.

Lyons, Oren (Joagquisho) (Onondaga), b. 1930. Oren Lyons, a Turtle Clan **Onondaga**, became known worldwide during the last half of the twentieth century as an author, publisher, and crisis negotiator, as well as a spokesman for the Haudenosaunee in several world forums. He is also an accomplished graphic artist as well as **lacrosse** player and coach. In addition, Lyons is a professor of Native American studies at the State University of New York at Buffalo.

Lyons was educated in art at Syracuse University between 1954 and 1958, where he played lacrosse at a level that earned him a berth in the Syracuse Sports Hall of Fame, as well as all-American status. Lyons has played or coached lacrosse most of his life. In 1990, Orens coached an Iroquois national team that played in the world lacrosse championships in Australia. He enjoyed a successful career as a commercial artist at Norcross Greeting Cards in New York City for more than a decade, from 1959 to 1970. Lyons began as a pasteup artist at Norcross; in a dozen years at the firm, he worked his way up to head planning director for seasonal lines. In 1970, Lyons returned home to the Onondaga territory, where he was condoled (selected) as Faithkeeper of the Iroquois Grand Council. He also edited the Native American newspaper *Daybreak*, published in the early 1990s.

Lyons was part of a negotiating team from the Iroquois Confederacy that helped resolve the 1990 standoff between **Mohawks** and authorities at Kanesatake (**Oka**), Québec. The confederacy's negotiators came to occupy a crucial middle ground between the **Warrior Society** and Canadian officials during the months of negotiations that preceded the use of armed force by the Canadian army and police at Kanesatake and **Kahnawake**. The Iroquois negotiators urged both sides to concentrate on long-term solutions to problems brought to light by the summer's violence. They recommended a fair land-rights process, the creation of viable economic bases for the communities involved in the crisis, and the recognition of long-standing (but often-ignored) treaty rights, including border rights.

Lyons also has been involved in a number of other Iroquois-rights issues, most notably the return of **wampum** belts to the confederacy by the state of New York. He has spoken on behalf of the Haudenosaunee in several international forums, including the United Nations. Lyons also is known as an author, notably as a coauthor of *Exiled in the Land of the Free* (1992).

FURTHER READING

Lyons, Oren, John Mohawk, Vine Deloria, Jr., Laurence Hauptman, Howard Berman, Donald A. Grinde, Jr., Curtis Berkey, and Robert Venables. *Exiled in the Land of the Free: Democracy, Indian Nations, and the Constitution*. Santa Fe,: N.M. Clear Light Publishers, 1992.
Nabokov, Peter, ed. *Native American Testimony*. New York: Viking, 1991.

M

"Mingo," linguistic derivation. "Mingo" is a slur term taken from the Lenni Lenape (Delaware) word *mengwe*, meaning "sneaky" or "stealthy." Applied to a group, it means "the sneaky people" (Wallace, 425).

"Mingo" was first used against the Haudenosaunee in the mid-eighteenth century by a tiny faction of league Delaware-Mahicans in Ohio (241 people) who had converted to the Moravian sect of Christianity. Politically dissatisfied with their status as incorporated peoples of the league and mistaking their conversion to Christianity for adoption by Europeans, these Moravian converts believed that they would be able to secede from the league and return to their mid-Atlantic homelands through their connection with the Moravians, headquartered in Bethlehem, Pennsylvania. When this proved not to be the case, the disaffected Moravian Delaware-Mahicans flung the epithet *mengwe* at the Haudenosaunee.

The Moravian missionaries picked up the denigrating term as "Mingo" and used it in their writings to smear all league peoples in Pennsylvania and Ohio. "Mingo" came into use by settlers as a popular racial slur against the Haudenosaunee, especially during the **American Revolution** when the league proved to be formidable in defending its Ohio and Pennsylvania territories from invasion. Later Western historians picked up this slur from biased primary sources and, without understanding its origin or meaning, began applying it exclusively to the league peoples of Ohio.

By the twentieth century, scholars had come to act as if the league peoples of Ohio were somehow separate from the league and had called themselves "Mingos." This is completely false. Not only were the Haudenosaunee of Ohio part of the league, but they called themselves **Senecas**, Wyandots, Delawares, **Onondagas**, Mahicans, **Tuscaroras**, and so on (Miller, 51). Ohio league peoples of today resist the free use of the term "Mingo" in historical texts and are trying to raise awareness in academia about its impropriety. For historians to continue writing histories of Ohio in which they habitually refer to the Haudenosaunee as "Mingos" is on a par with their writing histories of Europe in which they consistently refer to the Jews as "the sneaky people."

FURTHER READING

Mann, Barbara A. "Forbidden Ground: Racial Politics and Hidden Identity in James Fenimore Cooper's Leather-Stocking Tales." Ph.D. diss., University of Toledo, 1997.
———. *Iroquoian Women: Gantowisas of the Haudenosaunee League.* New York: Peter Lang, 2000.
Miller, Susan. "Licensed Trafficking and Ethnogenetic Engineering." *American Indian Quarterly* 20:1 (1996): 49–55.
Wallace, Paul A. W., ed. *Thirty Thousand Miles with John Heckewelder.* Pittsburgh: University of Pittsburgh Press, 1958.

Barbara A. Mann

Mohawk ceremonial cycle. Attendance and participation in Mohawk ceremonies are restricted to Iroquois people and carefully selected Native American guests. A generation ago, such rituals were partially open to non-Indian observers, but were closed when the activities within the **Longhouse** were used by a few social scientists for research purposes. The Iroquois, and particularly the **Mohawks**, were upset with this practice of being analyzed and exploited by academics and closed the doors of their longhouses to all non-Natives.

In addition, the Mohawks believe that these rituals have spiritual and communal significance only when the thoughts and prayers of the people are in harmony. This act, the Mohawks believe, is difficult to achieve when the efforts to secure collective mind are disrupted by the analytical behavior of any one person. In addition, the Mohawks believe that it is vital for the people in attendance to feel at ease with the rituals, something they cannot do if they feel that they are being observed by individuals they do not know.

Midwinter Ceremony

Midwinter ceremonies are held four days after the first new moon following the winter solstice, when the Pleiades constellation is almost overhead. They last five to eight days. During this time, the Mohawks sing the **Great Feather Dances**, Women's Dance, and the sacred Drum Songs and join in the Stirring of the Ashes ritual. The longhouse is divided into two sides after the first day: the Wolf and Turtle clans on one end of the building and the Bear Clan on the other. Also a part of the Midwinter Ceremony is the Peach Stone Game between the two sides and the Tobacco Burning (formerly the **White Dog Sacrifice**).

Maple Ceremony

The Maple Ceremony is held in late February or March when the sap begins to rise with the coming of the first warm days of an approaching spring. It is usually observed in one day, in which the sacred Great Feather Dance is sung, along with the Women's Dance. This day is given to the trees and all they mean to the Mohawk people, with the maple as the representative of all trees. Maple sap is passed among the people to drink.

Thunder Dance

When spring arrives, usually in March, the Thunder Beings return. The Faith-keepers of the nation listen to the first rumble of thunder and then call on the people to assemble at the Longhouse. The Thunderers are believed to be sky dwellers with the power to replenish the earth while also keeping the creatures of destruction beneath the earth. During this one-day ceremony, the Thunder Dance is performed in honor of the sky dwellers to thank them for bringing the rains back to the land.

Ohki:we

The *Ohki:we* is the ceremony for the dead. It takes place over one night and is meant to encourage the departed to continue their journey back to the Creator. It is held in early spring, March or April, by members of the *Ohki:we* Society and lasts from dusk to dawn. After the ritual is completed, a social dance is held to entertain the spirits as well as the people.

Hatowi

Hatowi is a ceremony that concerns the healing society the Mohawks call **Grandfathers** or *Hatowis* (referred to as the False Faces by anthropologists). Those who are members of the society or have been healed by it go to the Longhouse on a March evening set aside by the *Hatowis* to renew their medicines.

Sun and Moon Dance

The ritual of the Sun and Moon Dance lasts for one day in April or early May. It is meant to give thanks for the growing power of the sun and the influence of the moon on the waters of the earth. Special dances are held for the Eldest Brother (the sun) and Grandmother (the moon), and sun bread and moon bread are passed among the people.

Seed Ceremony

The Seed Ceremony is a one-day event that takes place in early May, before the seeds are placed into the ground. Special prayers are said to encourage the seeds to grow; the Great Feather Dance also is held.

Planting Ceremony

The Planting Ceremony is held just before the fields are planted. A special **Thanksgiving** ceremony is held at the Longhouse, during which the Peach Stone Game is played between the men and women so they may know who will have the honor of watching over the crops as they grow. This ritual takes place in May and lasts for at least one day.

Strawberry Ceremony

The Strawberry Ceremony takes place in one day, after the ripening of the first berries. The Faithkeepers watch for the correct time, at which they summon the people to the Longhouse to give thanks for the strawberry as a sign of renewal and to acknowledge the birth of children and other living things. Strawberries are said to be the food consumed by the spirits as they journey to the Creator's land.

Stringbean Ceremony

In late July or early August, when the stringbeans ripen, the Faithkeepers set a day for the people to give thanks for this plant. They share beans during the ceremony and hold a Great Feather Dance in celebration.

Corn Ceremony

The one-day Corn Ceremony is meant to give thanks for the most important of Mohawk foods. Again, the Faithkeepers are instructed to watch for the **corn** to ripen, at which time they call the people to the Longhouse to express their collective gratitude to the Creator for the corn. This ceremony takes place in August.

Harvest Ceremony

The Harvest Ceremony is a three-or-four-day event that takes place in late September or early October, after the fields have been harvested. It celebrates the food that the people have gathered throughout the past four months. Children are named at the Harvest Ceremony, and Drum Dances and the Great Feather Dance are held. A Peach Stone Game is also enjoyed between the men and the women to entertain the Creator and decide who will oversee the Longhouse rituals. Food is prepared and shared among the people.

Thunder Ceremony

The Thunder Ceremony is a one-day ritual to thank the Thunder Beings for the rain and to release them back to their dwelling places in the west. The autumn Thunder Ceremony is held in late October or early November, with all the rituals, including a Thunder Dance, held in one day.

End of Seasons

The one-day End of Seasons ritual releases the men of the community to go on hunting expeditions for the animals used by the Mohawks as primary sources of food. This ceremony, held usually in late October or early November, is meant to give the men good luck so that they will return to their families with sufficient catch to take them through the winter.

Doug George-Kanentiio

Mohawk lunar calendar.

Roman Month	In Mohawk	Mohawk Meaning in English
January/February	*Tsiothohrkó:wa*	Coldest time
February/March	*Enníska*	Days getting longer
March/April	*Enniskó:wa*	Time of more sunlight
April/May	*Onerahtókha*	Trees leaking
May/June	*Onerahtohkó:wa*	Leaves in full bloom
June/July	*Ohiaríha*	Fruits ripen
July/August	*Ohiarihkó:wa*	Great ripening time
August/September	*Seskéha*	Leaves start change
September/October	*Saekehkó:wa*	Leaves not green
October/November	*Kenténha*	Lean time
November/December	*Kentenhkó:wa*	Great lean time
December/January	*Tsiothkóhrha*	Time of cold weather

Mohawks, as symbol at Boston Tea Party. The American patriots who dumped tea into Boston Harbor to protest taxation without representation dressed as **Mohawks** as a symbol of American independence opposed to the tea, which was taken to be a symbol of British oppression. The Mohawk disguise at the Tea Party was part of a general trend in revolutionary art and other propaganda that portrayed Indians as a symbol of America and of freedom in the patriots' eyes. Paul Revere, who helped popularize these symbols as a visual artist, also portrayed a Native American woman as the first national symbol of the new United States before Uncle Sam was invented.

On the evening of December 16, 1773, three vessels lay at anchor in Boston Harbor. All told, they carried 342 chests containing over 90,000 pounds of dutiable tea worth about 9,000 pounds sterling. Shortly after 6 P.M., between thirty and sixty men roughly disguised as Indians and calling themselves "Mohawks" boarded the ships. Hundreds of silent onlookers at the wharf saw the "Mohawks," organized into three groups, swiftly and systematically break open the tea chests and pour their contents into the sea. Since the water was only two or three feet deep, the tea began to pile up, forcing the men to rake it aside to allow room for the rest. In less than three hours they had completed their work and had disappeared into the darkness; to this day the identities of most remain unknown. Eighteen months later, the colonists were locked in military combat with Great Britain. The Boston Tea Party had ushered in a series of events that led directly to war and eventually independence.

The Tea Party was a form of symbolic protest—one step beyond random violence, one step short of organized, armed rebellion. The tea dumpers chose their symbols with utmost care. As the imported tea symbolized British tyranny and taxation, so the image of the Indian and the Mohawk disguise represented its antithesis: a "trademark" of an emerging American identity and a voice for liberty in a new land. The image of the Indian was figured into tea dumpers' disguises not only in Boston, but also in cities the length of the Atlantic seaboard. The image of the Indian, particularly the Mohawk, also appeared at about the same time and in the same context in revolutionary songs, slogans, and engravings.

Boston's patriots were not known for their civility in the face of British authority. Boston's "Mohawks" sparked physical confrontation over the tea tax. As they dumped the tea, the "Mohawks" exchanged words in a secret sign language using Indian hand symbols and sang:

> Rally Mohawks, and bring your axes
> And tell King George we'll pay no taxes
> on his foreign tea;

> His threats are vain, and vain to think
> To force our girls and wives to drink
> his vile Bohea!
> Then rally, boys, and hasten on
> To meet our chiefs at the Green Dragon!

> Our Warren's here, and bold Revere
> With hands to do and words to cheer,
> for liberty and laws;
> Our country's "braves" and firm defenders
> shall ne'er be left by true North Enders
> fighting freedom's cause!
> Then rally, boys, and hasten on
> To meet our chiefs at the Green Dragon. (See Goss, 128)

After the Tea Party, the British passed the Coercive Acts in an attempt to bring rebellious Massachusetts to its knees. The acts closed the port of Boston. The Coercive Acts also provided for the quartering of troops once more in the town of Boston, stoking resentment of its citizens once again. The Boston Tea Party is regarded by some as the first "battle" of the **American Revolution**. In 1773, Britain exported 738,083 pounds of tea to the colonies. In 1774, the figure fell to 69,830. Imports of tea fell all along the Atlantic seaboard: from 206,312 pounds to 30,161 in New England; from 208,385 pounds to 1,304 in New York; and from 208,191 pounds to none in Pennsylvania (Labaree, 331).

FURTHER READING

Brant, Irving. *James Madison: The Virginia Revolutionist*. Indianapolis: Bobbs-Merrill, 1941.

Goss, Elbridge Henry. *The Life of Colonel Paul Revere*. Boston: Gregg Press, 1972.

Grinde, Donald A., Jr., and Bruce E. Johansen. *Exemplar of Liberty: Native America and the Evolution of Democracy*. Los Angeles: UCLA American Indian Studies Center, 1991.

Griswold, Wesley S. *The Night the Revolution Began: The Boston Tea Party, 1773*. Brattleboro, Vt.: S. Greene Press, 1972.

Labaree, Benjamin W. *The Boston Tea Party.* New York: Oxford University Press, 1964.

Thomas, Peter David Garner. *Tea Party to Independence: The Third Phase of the American Revolution, 1773–1776,* Oxford: Clarendon Press, 1991.

Mohawks, historical sketch. According to the journalist Edmund Wilson (who is sometimes disputed), "Mohawk" is an Algonquian name for the enemies they called "man eaters." The people who are known as Mohawks call themselves "Ganienkeh," "The People of the Flint." They are one of the five original nations of the Iroquois Confederacy (along with the **Senecas**, the **Onondagas**, the **Cayugas**, and the **Oneidas**). The confederacy, which played a pivotal role in colonial history, likened itself to a traditional Iroquois **longhouse**, in which the Senecas were said to live at the "Western Door," and the Mohawks at the "Eastern Door."

The Mohawks also played an important role in the creation of the Iroquois Confederacy. Their oral history relates that both the **Peacemaker** and **Hiawatha** were adopted Mohawks, and that the Mohawks were the first of the five nations to embrace a vision of peace and reason to end bloodshed.

Like many other Native American peoples, the Mohawks' first widespread contacts with Europeans were followed by devastating epidemics of several imported diseases, the deadliest of which was smallpox. Traveling in the area during the winter of 1634–1635, the Dutch trader Harmen Meyndertsz van den Bogaert observed, while in Mohawk country, that "I could see nothing but graves" (Gehring and Starna, 4–5). Between 1640 and 1670, the Mohawks lost roughly half their population (Dennis, 263).

There is sharp disagreement among historians regarding the historical temper of the Mohawks. Richard Aquila cites a Jesuit who told the governor of New France in 1684 that "the French man who came here told me that whilst you were at La Famine a false alarm reached Montreal that the Iroquois were coming; that there was nothing but horror, flight, and weeping at Montreal" (Aquila, 38). Francis Jennings disagrees vehemently about the reputation of the Mohawks: "There is little substance in the old myth, so sedulouly cultivated by **[Cadwallader] Colden** and **[Lewis Henry] Morgan**, that the name of Mohawk was so dreaded that other tribes would flee upon a mere rumor of Iroquois approach" (Jennings, 43).

Mohawks also have played a central role in American popular literature, from James Fenimore Cooper's *Last of the Mohicans* to popular Hollywood movies. A Mohawk disguise was adopted by colonists who participated in the Boston Tea Party.

Today, major Mohawk settlements include **Akwesasne** (also called St. Regis), which straddles the U.S.-Canadian border near Massena, New York, and Cornwall, Ontario; **Kahnawake**, near Montréal; and Kanesatake, near the village of **Oka**, Québec. The aboriginal homelands of the Mohawks covered much of northeastern New York State and areas of southern Québec. Land claims have been filed for a small portion of that area. Some Mohawks also have established a community in the Mohawk Valley, **Canajoharie**, by purchasing private land.

During the early 1990s, several armed confrontations at all three reserves caused considerable controversy and violence. Two men, Mathew Pyke and "Junior" Edwards, were shot to death on May 1, 1990, at the peak of confrontations over smuggling and **gambling**.

The seeds of social disorder were sown in Mohawk country during the 1950s with the construction of the **St. Lawrence Seaway**. The Mohawks' homelands (and other areas) became sites for heavy industry and pollution. Since the 1960s, pollution has eliminated most farming at Akwesasne, and people may no longer eat fish or garden produce from the area. A group of General Motors toxic dumps near Akwesasne is the most expensive cleanup job on the Environmental Protection Agency's "Superfund" list.

After traditional means of making a living were destroyed, the geographical area of Akwesasne, straddling the U.S.-Canadian border, became a site of large-scale smuggling of alcohol and tobacco, as well as other drugs and weapons, from the United States into Canada. A nationalistic **Warrior Society** spread at Akwesasne, Kahnawake, and Kanesatake during the 1980s, a reaction to the brutalization of life at all three reserves.

As traditional ways of life have become unworkable in Mohawk country, many people have moved away, especially to urban areas such as Montréal and New York City, two of many metropolitan areas where Mohawks have become well known as builders of skyscrapers and bridges as the **Mohawks in high steel**.

In the midst of environmental contamination, smuggling, and gambling, a revival movement also has been taking place in Mohawk country late in the twentieth century. Traditional Mohawks have established their own schools (such as the **Akwesasne Freedom School**) and museums (such as the **Fadden** family's Six Nations Indian Museum at Onchiota, New York). Today, at least a third of Mohawks are able to speak at least some of their native language.

FURTHER READING

Aquila, Richard. *The Iroquois Restoration: Iroquois Diplomacy on the Colonial Frontier, 1701–1754*. Detroit: Wayne State University Press, 1983.

Colden, Cadwallader. *The History of the Five Nations Depending on the Province of New York in America*. 1747. Ithaca, N.Y.: Great Seal Books, 1958.

Dennis, Matthew. *Cultivating a Landscape of Peace*. Ithaca, N.Y.: Cornell University Press, 1993.

Gehring, Charles T., and William A. Starna, trans. and eds. *A Journey into Mohawk and Oneida Country, 1634–1635: The Journal of Harmen Meyndertsz van den Bogaert*. Syracuse, N.Y.: Syracuse University Press, 1988.

Jennings, Francis. *The Ambiguous Iroquois Empire: The Covenant Chain Confederation of Indian Tribes with English Colonies from Its Beginnings to the Lancaster Treaty of 1744*. New York: W. W. Norton, 1984.

Johansen, Bruce E. *Life and Death in Mohawk Country*. Golden, Colo.: North American Press/Fulcrum, 1993.

Morgan, Lewis Henry. *League of the Ho-de-no-sau-nee, or Iroquois.* 1851. New York: Corinth Books, 1972.

Snow, Dean R., Charles T. Gehring and William A. Starna, eds. *In Mohawk Country: Early Narratives about a Native People.* Syracuse, N.Y.: Syracuse University Press, 1996.

Tehanetorens [Ray Fadden]. *Tales of the Iroquois.* Rooseveltown, N.Y.: Akwesasne Notes, 1976.

———. *A Basic Call to Consciousness.* Rooseveltown, N.Y.: Akwesasne Notes, 1986.

Wallace, Paul A. W. *The White Roots of Peace.* Santa Fe, N.M.: Clear Light Publishers, 1994.

Wilson, Edmund. *Apologies to the Iroquois.* New York: Farrar, Straus & Cudahy, 1960.

Mohawks in high steel. The destruction of the natural world, along with erosion of the **Mohawk** land base, at **Akwesasne** made living by the old ways nearly impossible and prompted many Mohawks to look for other ways to survive in the cash economy. During the first half of the twentieth century, some took up work as the legendary "Mohawks in high steel," the men who constructed large parts of the urban skylines from Montréal to New York City.

The first Mohawks to work "high steel" came from the **Kahnawake** Reserve near Montréal. In 1886, the Dominion Bridge Company, the largest builder of steel structures in Canada, erected a railroad bridge across the St. Lawrence River that passed through the Kahnawake Reserve. The company agreed to hire Mohawks on the project. Later, Mohawks were hired to work on steel superstructures across Canada.

The work required athletic skills, including climbing and balancing during heavy labor. It was dangerous for Mohawks and white workers alike. On August 29, 1907, the entire steel superstructure of the Québec Bridge (nine miles from Québec City) collapsed while it was under construction, killing ninety-six men, of whom thirty-five were Kahnawake Mohawks.

In 1915 and 1916, a Kahnawake resident named John Diabo became the first Mohawk to work the high steel in New York City. He got a job on the Hell Gate Bridge and was known as "Indian Joe." Diabo worked for a while on an Irish gang until several other Mohawks joined him, and as they formed their own team. After a few months of work, Diabo, who was a superb athlete, slipped off a high beam, fell into the river below the bridge, and drowned. The rest of the work gang took his body back to Kahnawake and never returned.

A decade later, in 1925 and 1926, a large number of Mohawk steelworkers migrated to New York City again because of a building boom of skyscrapers. Over the ensuing decades, the Mohawks became legendary as high-beam steelworkers on Manhattan Island; their families established a community in the Gowanus neighborhood of Brooklyn.

FURTHER READING

Blanchard, David. "High Steel! The Kahnawake Mohawk and the High Construction Trade." *Journal of Ethnic Studies* 11:2 (1983): 41–60.

Hill, Richard. *Skywalkers: The History of Indian Ironworkers.* Brantford, Ontario: Woodland Indian Cultural Educational Centre, 1987.

Katzer, Bruce. "The Caughnawaga Mohawks: The Other Side of Ironwork." *Journal of Ethnic Studies* 15:4 (1988): 39–55.

Wilson, Edmund. *Apologies to the Iroquois*. New York: Farrar, Straus & Cudahy, 1960.

Morgan, Lewis Henry, 1818–1881. A pioneer ethnologist who is regarded as the "father" of American anthropology, Lewis Henry Morgan provided an early detailed ethnographic account of the Iroquois in his *League of the Ho-de-no-sau-nee, or Iroquois* (1851). While Morgan's was not the first detailed account of the Iroquois—**Cadwallader Colden** had published one more than a century before him—Morgan's studies have informed several generations of scholars. Morgan's writings also inspired **Friedrich Engels** in his authorship of *The Origin of the Family, Private Property, and the State* (1883).

Morgan was born at Aurora on Cayuga Lake. He attended Union College and later became wealthy as a corporate lawyer in Rochester, New York. Morgan was elected to the New York State legislature while he developed his interest in the Iroquois and his friendship with **Ely Parker**, the Seneca who later would serve as Ulysses S. Grant's secretary and the first Native American commissioner of Indian affairs. Together with other citizens of upstate New York, Parker and Morgan participated in the Gordian Knot, later known as the Grand Order of the Iroquois, an intellectual and social club.

Parker became the major informant for Morgan and made for Morgan the contacts that enabled him to write his pioneering book on the Iroquois. In the middle 1840s, Morgan began publishing his research under the pen name "Skenandoah" in the *American Review*. Between the publication of his *League of the Iroquois* in 1851 and *Ancient Society* in 1877, Morgan became one of the most important social scientists in nineteenth-century North America.

Ironically, as Morgan aged, he embraced notions of social Darwinism at the same time that the early Marxists embraced him. Karl Marx read Morgan's *Ancient Society* a few years before he died and made copious notes. Friedrich Engels inherited the notes and used them to produce *The Origin of the Family, Private Property, and the State*, which analyzes Iroquois political and social systems. Engels also held out hope that future societies based on a communist model would embrace Iroquois notions of social and economic equality.

Morgan also commented frequently on newsworthy events of his time that involved Native Americans. After the Battle of the Little Bighorn in 1876, the elderly Morgan wrote in the *Nation* that the Sioux and Cheyennes who had obliterated Custer's troops at the Little Bighorn were defending their birthright. Morgan's point of view was not popular among whites, however. Retaliation against the Lakotas, Cheyennes, and others by progressively larger army units followed.

FURTHER READING

Morgan, Lewis Henry. *Ancient Society, or Researches in the Line of Human Progress from Savagery through Barbarism to Civilization*. Chicago: C. H. Kerr, 1877.

————. *Houses and House-life of the American Aborigines.* With an introduction by Paul Bohannan. Chicago: University of Chicago Press, 1965.

————. *League of the Haudenosaunee, or Iroquois.* 1851. Secaucus, N.J.: Corinth Books, 1962.

Resek, Carl. *Lewis Henry Morgan: American Scholar.* Chicago: University of Chicago Press, 1960.

Tooker, Elisabeth. *Lewis H. Morgan on Iroquois Material Culture.* Tucson: University of Arizona Press, 1994.

Trautmann, Thomas R. *Lewis Henry Morgan and the Invention of Kinship.* Berkeley: University of California Press, 1987.

Mountpleasant, Caroline Parker (Gähahno, *Jigonsaseh*) (Seneca), 1824– 1892. Gähahno (Caroline Parker Mountpleasant) was the last *Jigonsaseh* (Head Clan Mother) of the league. She was born on the **Tonawanda Seneca Reservation** in New York, the daughter of Gaontgwutwus and her husband, Jonoesdowa (William Parker), the chief at Tonawanda. A sister of Donehogä´wa (**Ely S. Parker**) and paternal aunt of the scholar Gawaso Wanneh (**Arthur C. Parker**), she was born into the same distinguished family that had produced the prophet Sganyadaí:yoh (**Handsome Lake**) and the orator Sagoyewatha (**Red Jacket**). Her grandmather had been the *Jigonsaseh* during the late eighteenth century.

As a girl, Gähahno attended school at Pembroke in Genesee County. A former playmate recalled that although she "was away at school a good deal," she frequently returned to Tonawanda with gifts for the children (Parker, 1919, 235). Although she was forced to do schoolwork in English, her first language was Seneca. Seeing a promising and ambitious pupil, the Quakers chose her for further education at the State Normal School (teacher's college) at Albany. For all her Westernized learning, Gähahno also practiced and excelled at traditional arts. She was a moose-hair, quill, and bead worker of the first order. In fact, her work was so fine that **Lewis Henry Morgan** used samples of it to illustrate his *League of the Haudenosaunee* (1851). Gähahno married Dagayahdont ("Falling Wood," John Mountpleasant), who was a chief of the **Tuscaroras**.

Soon after the United States came into being, Quakers went onto league reservations in New York to impose the first round of "Christianizing and civilizing" on the Haudenosaunee. This cultural tinkering continued throughout the nineteenth century as the United States saw fit to impose its alternative constitutions of 1848 and 1868 on the people in its effort to make them forget their so-called savage ways. The **Senecas** were placed under particular stress by a constitution that summarily dissolved their league form of government and disenfranchised the *gantowisas*, or female officials of the league, women who had traditionally played a strong role in government.

The Clan Mothers did not submit easily to these profound changes in their culture. Due to heavy internal resistance, the office of *Jigonsaseh* was openly reinstated in 1878, and Gähahno was consensually appointed to the position.

Yet it was known to the Haudenosaunee that she had actually taken up the position in 1853, some twenty-five years before the open "reinstatement" of 1878. The Clan Mothers had obviously continued to meet and work secretly during the years of oppression. As the restored *Jigonsaseh* in 1878, Gähahno located her headquarters at the ancient, revered site of Kienkua ("The Stronghold"), a significant selection. Although it was then located on the Tuscarora Reservation, it was traditionally held to have been the seat of the first *Jigonsaseh*, she of the founding of the League (Johnson, 173, 184–185).

Three pictures of Gähahno are known to exist. The first acted as the frontispiece of the second volume of Lewis Henry Morgan's *League of the Haudenosaunee* in 1851. It continued to stand as the frontispiece in the 1901 revised edition. A young woman in 1851, Gähahno was still two years away from her appointment to the lofty office of *Jigonsaseh*, a position regarding which Morgan was silent and probably ignorant. The caption beneath this full-length portrait of Gähahno simply read, "a Seneca Indian Girl in the costume of the Irequois [*sic*]" (Morgan, 2:ii). The second picture was an early photo or daguerreotype taken of her about the same time as the Morgan portrait. She was wearing the same closely embroidered outfit (Parker, *Life*, facing 88). The exquisitely embroidered skirt she wore in both portraits was probably an example of her own work, but the skirt went out of her possession and into the Morgan Collection, later passing into the hands of the New York State Museum.

The third portrait, obviously cut out from a larger, perhaps family, photograph, appeared as Plate 20 in *An Analytical History of the Seneca Indians* by her nephew, Gawaso Wanneh. In his caption, he noted that Gähahno was "a Tonawanda Seneca" who had "inherited the title of 'the Mother of Nations' or 'Peace Queen' " through her clan lineage (Parker, *Analytical History*, 136).

FURTHER READING

Johnson, Chief Elias. *Legends, Traditions, and Laws of the Iroquois, or Six Nations.* 1881. New York: AMS Press, 1978.

Morgan, Lewis Henry. *League of the Haudenosaunee, or Iroquois.* 1851. 2 vols. New York: Burt Franklin, 1964.

Parker, A[rthur] C[aswell] [Gawaso Wanneh]. *An Analytical History of the Seneca Indians.* 1926. Researches and Transactions of the New York State Archeological Association, Lewis H. Morgan Chapter. New York: Kraus Reprint Co., 1970.

———. *The Life of General Ely S. Parker, Last Grand Sachem of the Iroquois and General Grant's Military Secretary.* Buffalo: Buffalo Historical Society, 1919.

Rothenberg, Diane. "Erosion of Power: An Economic Basis for the Selective Conservatism of Seneca Women in the Nineteenth Century." *Western Canadian Journal of Anthropology* 6:3 (1978): 106–122.

———. "The Mothers of the Nation: Seneca Resistance to Quaker Intervention." In M. Etienne and E. Leacock, eds., *Women and Colonization.* New York: Praeger, 1980: 63–87.

Barbara A. Mann

N

Newhouse, Seth (Dayodekane) (Mohawk and Onondaga), 1842–1921. Seth Newhouse, who was of **Mohawk** and **Onondaga** parentage, transcribed the Haudenosaunee **Great Law of Peace** into manuscript form during 1885 at the **Grand River** Reserve in Ontario. Newhouse's version of the Great Law has been examined by scholars for more than a century. Disagreements have arisen regarding how true Newhouse's version is to Haudenosaunee traditions, and how much his version was influenced by political conditions (such as the dominance of Mohawks at Grand River) during the middle and late nineteenth century. On his own initiative, Newhouse traveled widely among Iroquois communities in New York and Ontario to compile a history of the Haudenosaunee as well as his written version of the Great Law.

Newhouse's telling of the Great Law may be compared with another version written by the Seneca chief John Arthur Gibson, which has been published. Gibson's version has been officially endorsed by the Grand River Council. Newhouse tried and failed to achieve the endorsement of the Grand River Council several times until 1899. Otherwise, he traveled and farmed forty-five acres at Ohsweken, and he and his wife, Lucy Sero, a Mohawk from Tyendinaga, raised three daughters and one son (Weaver, 179). Newhouse worked with **J. N. B. Hewitt** at the Smithsonian Institution, where his manuscript of the Great Law is archived, to translate his manuscript into Mohawk.

FURTHER READING

Fenton, William N. "Seth Newhouse's Traditional History and Constitution of the Iroquois Confederacy." *Proceedings of the American Philosophical Society* 93:2 (1949): 141–158.

Grinde, Donald A., Jr. [Review of *Concerning the League*, Hanni Woodbury, Comp.] *American Indian Culture and Research Journal* 18:1 (1994): 175–177.

Weaver, Sally M. "Seth Newhouse and the Grand River Confederacy in the Mid-

Nineteenth Century." In Michael K. Foster, Jack Campisi, and Marianne Mithun, eds., *Extending the Rafters: Interdisciplinary Approaches to Iroquoian Studies.* Albany: State University of New York Press, 1984: 165–182.

Woodbury, Hanni, trans. *Concerning the League: The Iroquois League Tradition as Dictated in Onondaga by John Arthur Gibson.* Syracuse, N.Y.: Syracuse University Press, 1992.

North American Indian Travelling College. Beginning during the 1960s, the North American Indian Travelling College, which has its home offices at **Akwesasne Mohawk** territory, became known to people across the United States through the activities of its traveling troupe, the White Roots of Peace. The college also houses a museum, gift shop, book shop, tours, and a model Mohawk village. Each July, the college also hosts an annual festival of Native American song, dance, and crafts called "Friendship Days."

O

Oakes, Richard (Mohawk), 1942–1972. Richard Oakes was among the leaders of the occupation of Alcatraz Island in 1969 and was murdered shortly thereafter under mysterious circumstances. His death helped inspire plans for the 1972 cross-country Native American march called the Trail of Broken Treaties.

Before Oakes became involved with the Alcatraz occupation, he had lived most of his life in upstate New York or in New York City, where he had been an ironworker for eleven years. He recalled his upbringing on the **Akwesasne** (St. Regis) **Mohawk** Reservation:

I grew up on the St. Regis Reservation in New York, near the Canadian border. It's a big reservation, six miles square, with three thousand people and three thousand problems. My growing up was hard, as it was for most Indians. The hopes were there, the promises were there, but the means for achieving them weren't forthcoming. I couldn't adjust. I went to the schools, went to the high school until I was sixteen, but the system never offered me anything that had to do with being an Indian. . . . All they wanted me to do was to become part of the machinery, to make me into what they wanted, a *white* Indian. I wanted to do something for my people. (Oakes, 35; italics in the original)

Oakes was a leader of the Iroquois traveling troupe White Roots of Peace in the late 1960s. His visit to San Francisco with the group in 1969 had an electrifying effect on local Native Americans, out of which developed plans to occupy Alcatraz Island. The occupation was staged as a claim under a century-old federal law that gives Indians first option on U.S. government land that has been declared surplus. Oakes also played an important role in establishing early Native American studies programs at several California colleges and universities and worked to restore ancestral lands to the Pitt River and Pomo Indians of California.

Oakes was shot to death while walking along a dirt road near a YMCA camp outside Santa Rosa, California. Michael Oliver Morgan, a caretaker at the camp, was charged with manslaughter in Oakes's death, but was acquitted by a district-court jury on March 16, 1973. Defenders of Oakes asserted that he was murdered for his advocacy of treaty rights, while Morgan's attorney said that Oakes had jumped his client from a bush.

A week after Oakes's unexplained murder sent shock waves through Native American activist circles, in late September 1972, about fifty people met in Denver to formulate plans for the cross-country trek they named the Trail of Broken Treaties, which reached Washington, D.C., in early November and occupied the head office of the Bureau of Indian Affairs within days of the 1972 national election.

FURTHER READING

Johansen, Bruce E., and Roberto F. Maestas. *Wasi'chu: The Continuing Indian Wars.* New York: Monthly Review Press, 1979.
Oakes, Richard. "Alcatraz Is Not an Island." *Ramparts*, December 1972, 35–38.

Ohio League. The League of the Haudenosaunee once encompassed large portions of what is now the northeastern United States, stretching from New York through the western half of Pennsylvania and across most of Ohio. The Iroquoian claim to the Land of the Three Miamis (Ohio) is ancient and twofold. In the first instance, it is based on traditions that go back to the Alligewi (Mound Builders of Ohio). Tuscaroras and **Senacas**, as well as some **Onondagas**, maintain that the Alligewi were ancestors of the Iroquois. Other traditions, such as those maintained by the Tuscarora David Cusick, stated that Ohio had been taken from the Alligewi in a ferocious war. Both traditions may be true, since defeated nations were traditionally adopted in by the Iroquois.

In the second instance, the claim to Ohio was based on the fact that Ohio was indisputably the homeland of the Eries (the Cat People, or Lynx Nation), whom all traditionalists state were Iroquois. The Eries settled south of the lake that bears their name, from its southern shoreline down to central Ohio. According to tradition, this happened thousands of years before contact with Europeans. Cusick stated in his 1825 tradition that as early as 2,200 years before Columbus, the Iroquois held Ohio against an invasion by the "Emperor" of a southern people who lived in a "Golden City." This war lasted a century, with the Iroquois victorious (Beauchamp, 10–11).

The Ohio clans of the Iroquois included the Eries, Squakihaws, and Kah-Kwahs, some of whom also lived for a time in the extreme western portions of New York, near the eastern shore of Lake Erie. The Squakihaws, closely connected to the Eries and perhaps a clan of them, were lineage Senecas (Johnson, 44, 51). According to some traditional evidence, the Eries, Squakihaws, and Kah-Kwahs were members of the league at its founding through their connection with the Senecas.

These three Seneca groups moved east for a time, living in New York, but retreated west to the old lands of Ohio after a series of fracases with the Senecas.

The dating of these hostilities is uncertain. According to Cusick, the earliest squabble occurred between the Squakihaws and Senecas about 1,000 years before Columbus or about 500 C.E., eventually culminating in more extensive strife in the twelfth century that conclusively drove the three clans westward (Beauchamp, 16–17, 31–34). Elias Johnson, however, placed this last event more recently, about the year 1200 C.E. (Johnson, 184).

Ignoring this traditional evidence of a long Iroquoian tenure in Ohio, Euro-historians have insisted that the Haudenosaunee only claimed Ohio during the seventeenth-century **Beaver Wars** after defeating the Eries, whom historians have not properly understood to have been Senecas themselves. In particular, historians, including Francis Jennings, Richard White, and Michael McConnell, have assumed that Ohio was colonized by the league in some temporary and relatively new alliance with Ohio peoples. In *Empires of Fortune* (1988), for example, Jennings quite falsely presented Ohio leaguers as "Seneca and Cayuga tribesmen" who "migrated there [Ohio] as individuals" and who "acquired an identity distinct from their parent tribes" (Jennings, 26). Richard White joined the chorus in 1991, arguing that the "Mingos"—a slur terms for Ohio leaguers— were "offshoots of the Iroquois," a fragmented and isolated faction rather than league members (White, 201). McConnell also improperly segregated the Ohio from the New York Leaguers, calling his artificial group the "Ohio Valley Iroquois" and depicting it as a temporary "alliance" of "Ohio Indians," rather than a duly constituted segment of the league (McConnell, 67).

This argument overlooks the antiquity of the Iroquoian presence in Ohio. Just because Europeans only became aware of Ohio in the seventeenth century does not mean that the league was unaware of Ohio until that time. Worse, it freely interpolates the European concept of "colonization," and its associated economic exploitation of subject peoples into its discussion of Haudenosaunee history. On all fronts, the argument shows a stunning misapprehension of the political and economic structure of the league.

First, the league did not colonize people, it made full citizens of them. The Wyandots of Ohio, along with the Eries and their lineages, were adopted in as affiliated nations of the league. Second, the land was not exploited as hunting grounds for the benefit of New York. Both traditional and historical evidence makes it clear that the league peoples of Ohio were settled and permanent farmers, similar to the league peoples in New York.

Ohio and western Pennsylvania proved to be crucial areas of resistance during the late eighteenth century. During the **American Revolution**, the league actually won the war in the west (Ohio and western Pennsylvania) against General George Washington, particularly under the leadership of the league Wyandot war chief Katepakomen (**Simon Girty**). It was only the treachery of the British at the Treaty of Paris (1783) that signed over Ohio to the revolutionaries without so much as consulting their league "allies."

After the Revolutionary War, the new United States did its best to alienate Iroquois interests in New York from those in Ohio, where the league was still well organized, armed, and strong. Leaders who had held back the revolutionary army continued to fight—and win—important battles against furious assaults on Ohio by forces of the United States. Katepakomen fought along with Tecumseh (who was presented the war belt of the league by the Ohio league peoples). After Tecumseh's death, the old league alliance sided with Little Turtle of the Miamis, who prosecuted the unsuccessful war against Sukachgook, the Black Snake (Anthony Wayne). The Native American loss at the Battle of Fallen Timbers (1794) resulted in the Treaty of Greenville, which, on August 5, 1795, ceded not only the old league portions of Ohio to the United States, but also portions of Michigan, Indiana, and Illinois, which had never been league land.

Once Ohio had been seized for settlement by Europeans, the former league peoples found themselves pressed onto preserves, such as the Delaware Reservation set up in 1797. The names of counties in modern-day Ohio (Wyandot, Seneca, Huron, Miami) still serve as rough indicators of where those reservations were located. Admitted as a state in 1803, Ohio began pressing for the Christianization and/or **removal** of Native American populations, moves that were heavily resisted, accounting for the fact that Ohio removal did not occur until 1845. Even then, one-third to one-fourth of the people hid out, refusing to go, so that only the most assimilated (especially Christianized) elements were forced west of the Mississippi. During allotment, when Native nations were split up, many Ohio league survivors managed to obtain allotments in their old Ohio homeland.

Throughout this period, the federal government was interested in breaking all league contact between Ohio and New York. Redefining the Ohio members of the league as "**Wyandots**" and/or "**Mingos**" (a slur), the federal government refused to recognize any connection. The New York league did not so quickly forget Ohio, however, with Senecas, in particular, agitating to aid their Ohio relatives in the various wars of resistance. The **Fort Stanwix Treaty of 1784**, which forced the league to cede much Seneca territory, was hotly resisted by Sagoyewatha (**Red Jacket**), while the Senecas as a whole never accepted the loss of their Ohio lands. At the **Canandaigua Treaty** of 1794, even as the news of Little Turtle's defeat arrived, Sagoyewatha still fervently opposed relinquishing league land (Parker, 130–131, 136). Gradually, however, between forced assimilation and land grabs in New York, the eastern portion of the league lost sight of Ohio, wrapped up as it was in its own mighty struggles. Today, it comes as a surprise to many New York and Canadian league peoples to learn that their relatives still survive in Ohio and Pennsylvania.

FURTHER READING

Beauchamp, W[illiam] M[artin]. *The Iroquois Trail, or, Footprints of the Six Nations, in Customs, Traditions, and History.* Including David Cusick's "Sketches of Ancient History of the Six Nations." 1825. Fayetteville, NY: H. C. Beauchamp, 1892.

Calloway, Colin G. *Crown and Calumet: British Indian Relations, 1783–1815.* Norman: University of Oklahoma Press, 1987.

Hale, Horatio, ed. *The Iroquois Book of Rites*. 1883. Intro. William N. Fenton. Scholarly Reprint Series. Toronto: University of Toronto Press, 1978.

Jennings, Francis. *Empire of Fortune: Crowns, Colonies, and Tribes in the Seven Years' War in America*. New York: W. W. Norton & Company, 1988.

Johnson, Chief Elias. *Legends, Traditions, and Laws of the Iroquois, or Six Nations*. 1881. New York: AMS Press, 1978.

Mann, Barbara A. "Forbidden Ground: Racial Politics and Hidden Identity in James Fenimore Cooper's Leather-Stocking Tales." Ph.D., diss., University of Toledo, 1997.

———. *Iroquoian Women: Gantowisas of the Haudenosaunee League*. New York: Peter Lang, 2000.

McConnell, Michael N. *A Country Between: The Upper Ohio Valley and Its Peoples, 1724–1774*. Lincoln: University of Nebraska Press, 1992.

Parker, A[rthur] C[aswell] [Gawaso Wanneh]. *An Analytical History of the Seneca Indians*. 1926. Researches and Transactions of the New York State Archeological Association, Lewis H. Morgan Chapter. New York: Kraus Reprint Co., 1970.

Swanton, John Reed. *The Indian Tribes of North America*. Smithsonian Institution, Bureau of American Ethnology, Bulletin 145. Washington, D.C.: Smithsonian Institution Press, 1952.

Wallace, Paul A. W., ed. *Thirty Thousand Miles with John Heckewelder*. Pittsburgh: University of Pittsburgh Press, 1958.

White, Richard. *The Middle Ground: Indians, Empires, and Republics in the Great Lakes Region, 1650–1815*. Cambridge: Cambridge University Press, 1991.

Barbara A. Mann

Oil Springs Seneca Reservation. Near Cuba, New York, on the border between Cattaraugus and Allegany counties, the **Senecas** hold title to a one-square-mile tract of land that encloses a natural flow of petroleum that was used in the past as a liniment to treat rheumatic pains and ulcers. The tract was included as a Seneca landholding in the Big Tree Treaty of 1797 at the special request of **Handsome Lake**. In the late twentieth century, no Senecas lived on the tract; it was leased entirely to non-Indians.

Oka, Québec, standoff with Mohawks, 1990. The **Mohawks** of Kanesatake changed the face of Canadian Indian affairs in 1990 during a standoff with Québec police and Canadian army troops that lasted almost three months. The standoff was sparked by an effort by the municipality of Oka, a hamlet in Québec, to extend its nine-hole gold course to eighteen holes on land claimed by the Mohawks. The standoffs at Kanesatake and **Kahnawake** made national headlines in Canada and occupied the airwaves there in a way and to a degree unprecedented in the United States for a Native American issue. Not even Wounded Knee in 1973 attracted as much press coverage.

The confrontation began with a Mohawk blockade of a rarely used country road. Québec police ordered the Mohawks to disperse pending use of force. The Sûreté du Québec (SQ) massed roughly 100 officers around the Mohawk barricade at Oka before sunrise on July 11, 1990, a Wednesday. Wearing olive-green fatigues and gas masks, the Sûreté officers apparently hoped that they could bring the barricade down by a show of force, without actually moving against the people behind it.

The Confrontation Begins

At 8:45 A.M. on July 11, about 100 Québec provincial police attacked the barricade and roughly 200 Indian men and 100 women and children, unleashing tear gas that a sudden switch in wind direction blew back into their faces. Apparently surprised by return fire from the Mohawks, the police retreated in such pell-mell fashion that they left behind an assortment of vehicles, including two vans, four patrol cars, and a large front-loader that had been brought in to dismantle the barricades. During the fifteen-minute gunfight, SQ corporal **Marcel Lemay** was fatally injured under conditions so chaotic that after a year of forensic testing, Canadian officials still were not sure from which side of the conflict the bullet that killed him had come. After the bloodshed of July 11, both sides dug in at Oka and settled into a protracted standoff. Mohawks patrolled the manicured golf course in golf carts and fashioned impromptu clubs out of nine-irons taken from the pro shop.

Blockade of the Mercier Bridge

Within minutes of the July 11 police raid at Oka, Québec police faced a second confrontation closer to Montréal. Mohawks at Kahnawake used concrete barriers to block two highways that cross their reserve leading to the Mercier Bridge, a major commuting route connecting the island occupied by downtown Montréal with its southern suburbs that usually carries about 60,000 vehicles a day into and out of the city center.

The Sûreté du Québec quickly deployed about 2,000 officers around the blockade on the Mercier Bridge. With 2,000 other officers deployed around the barricade at Oka, the Sûreté du Québec at one point in mid-July had only about 440 officers left to conduct routine business and react to any emergencies that might arise in the rest of provincial Québec, an area roughly one-sixth the size of the continental United States. After that, the Royal Canadian Mounted Police and Canadian army troops began planning to replace the police.

In Chateauguay, a town of 40,000 near Kahnawake, local residents called for military action to end the blockade of the Mercier Bridge within a day of its erection. Crowds of several hundred townspeople who use the bridge to commute to Montréal chanted, "We want the Army! We want the Army!" By night, residents of the town, who were being forced to drive into Montréal by lengthy alternative routes, carried cameras, binoculars, and snacks to the bridge's on-ramps behind the police blockades to watch the confrontation. Vendors sold junk food from trucks to people in the crowd, some of whom carried signs urging police to "give the Indians what they want—a war."

During the days after the bridge blockade began, impromptu marches of 1,000 to 2,000 people wound through streets lined with fast-food restaurants and muffler shops, burning Mohawks in effigy. They bragged about fistfights with Indians in local bars and rumbles in community schools. Some of the residents demanded a new bridge that would bypass the Mohawk reserve. About a week and a half after the bridge was blockaded for the second time in two years, the Québec government agreed to study a commuter-train route from the area to central Montréal. Townspeople also fretted over a possible decline in property values because of the blockade.

Before the Mercier Bridge had been blockaded for a week, a crowd of angry French Canadians had strung up a life-sized effigy of a Native man clad in army fatigues. They had painted a large red target on its chest and had stuffed a pack of cigarettes into the pocket of its shirt. As one man slipped a noose around the strawman's head, another hoisted the rope around a traffic light.

On August 12, a Sunday, at least 75 people, 16 of them police officers, were injured in Chateauguay as a crowd estimated by Reuters at 7,000 people surged into police lines, throwing rocks and bottles at them. The police sprayed the demonstrators with tear gas and beat them with nightsticks. During a four-hour pitched battle, they arrested 18, only to release them a few hours later.

On July 25, with the standoff at Oka about to enter its third week, the *Toronto Star* reported that while many grocery-store shelves had emptied at Kanesatake, the Mohawks seemed to be getting some food that was being smuggled past police barricades; reports circulated that the Québec Native Women's Association was secretly ferrying food onto the reserve by boat. While police had been unclear regarding whether they would allow food past their barricades, the Red Cross said that there had been no deliberate effort to starve the Indians into submission. Instead, the government was forcing charities that wanted to bring food into the blockaded area to get five or six signatures on a permission form before they could do so.

More than 3,000 people from across Canada and several other countries converged in Oka's Parc Paul Sauve during the afternoon of Sunday, July 29, to support the Mohawks and to pray for a peaceful settlement of the confrontation. Some of the people at the peace rally, organized by Canada's Assembly of First Nations, offered flowers to police. The people at the rally also had planned to deliver truckloads of food to the besieged Mohawks during a procession, but they canceled the public event after angry Oka residents threw up a protest blockade along their route.

Within days of the shootout at Kanesatake and the blockading of the Mercier Bridge, Canada's summer of Mohawk discontent tapped a large number of long-smouldering grievances among Native people across the country. Sympathy blockades rose across the sparsely settled plains and mountains of this vast country. There was a wave of fear that summer among some white Canadians that if Canada's Natives became organized and angry enough, they could cripple the country's infrastructure. They could block train tracks, blockade bridges, and topple power lines from remote regions to urban areas, thus hobbling commerce. All during the summer, **Louis Hall**'s warning that the **Warrior Society** could shut down Canada spread through the nation's communication media.

Killing the Meech Lake Accord

Natives already had thrown a political monkey wrench into the works of the Meech Lake Accord during 1990. The accord was meant to satisfy Québec's demands for autonomy within the Canadian federation. Konrad Sioui, head chief of the Assembly of First Nations, indicated that the raid at Oka had been in direct retaliation for the fact that Elijah Harper, the only Native member of Manitoba's legislature, had led an effort against ratification of the Meech Lake Accord by its deadline of June 23. Harper's vote started a chain of procedural circumstances that kept the accord from going into effect.

If it had been ratified, the accord would have given Québec a "special status" designation in the Canadian confederation while, at the same time, refusing to acknowledge Native peoples' original occupancy of Québec and the rest of Canada. Harper, who had first been elected to Manitoba's legislature in 1981 from the northern riding (district) of Rupertsland, which includes his home of Red Sucker Lake, obstructed the accord precisely because Canadian Natives were angered by their omission in it. Sioui also said that the entire Canadian governmental system for negotiating land claims ought to be revamped.

Eighty-five percent of Québec never has been signed away by treaty. While leaders of the Québec independence movement had at least paid lip service to the idea that any constitution for an independent Québec should respect Native land claims as an issue of minority-group justice, probably very few French Canadians were prepared to meet the Natives' assertion that their claim to the province did not extend much beyond the Montréal and Québec City urban areas.

The Confrontation Dissolves

By September 25, the Warriors and others inside the treatment center at Kanesatake that had been the center of Warrior activity since the confrontation first began were visibly tired of living under siege conditions. They were tired of constant confrontation and of dealing with an overflowing septic tank they called "the monster." At one point, fatigue dissolved into hilarious comic opera when the Mohawks lobbed water-filled condoms at the soldiers. As the condoms splattered on razor wire and the ground, the Mohawks inside the army's barricades burst out laughing, and so did the soldiers.

On September 26, at 6:53 P.M., after seventy-eight days (five more than the 1973 siege at Wounded Knee, South Dakota), the fifty men, women, and children occupying the treatment center surrendered. Most of them emerged wearing camouflage clothing and waving a Warrior flag. As they filed out of the treatment center that had been their home for more than two and a half months, some of them claimed victory and scuffled briefly with troops and police. Sixteen women and twenty-four men were arrested and taken to Farnham, an army base about forty-five miles east of Montréal. The six children in the group were released to family members. During the next few days, troops and police began rolling up razor-wire fences and removing sandbags before they rolled away in their armored personnel carriers and other vehicles. Residents of both the Mohawk settlement and the town began to trickle back into their homes.

FURTHER READING

Hornung, Rick. *One Nation under the Gun: Inside the Mohawk Civil War.* New York: Pantheon, 1992.

Johansen, Bruce E. *Life and Death in Mohawk Country.* Golden, Colo. North American Press/Fulcrum, 1993.

Morrison, Andrea P., and Irwin Cotler, eds. *Justice for Natives: Searching for Common Ground.* Montréal: McGill–Queen's University Press, 1997: 298–312.

"Onas." "Onas," the title used by the Iroquois as a reference to the proprietor of Pennsylvania, is an Iroquoian word for "feather" or "quill," both of which were used as writing instruments during the seventeenth and eighteenth centuries. Thus "Onas" is an Iroquoian pun on William Penn's name (Calloway, 114).

FURTHER READING

Calloway, Colin, ed. *The World Turned Upside Down: Indian Voices from Early America.* Boston: Bedford Books/St. Martin's Press, 1994.

Oneidas, historical sketch. Like other peoples of the Haudenosaunee (Iroquois) Confederacy, the Oneidas adopted **corn** as a staple crop around the year 1000 C.E., a change that probably was followed within a few generations by the formation of the Iroquois Confederacy. By the time European-Americans encountered the Oneidas and other Iroquois, this confederacy was a trading and diplomatic power among the Native American peoples of eastern North America. The Oneidas enjoyed a commanding position astride the only relatively flat passage between the Hudson River and the Great Lakes; in the nineteenth century, this country would be traversed by the Erie Canal, a major economic lifeline before the spread of railroads a few decades later.

"Oneida" is probably an anglicization of this people's own name for themselves, *Ona yote ka o no*, meaning "Granite People" or "People of the Standing Stone." The Oneidas, one of the five original nations of the Iroquois Confederacy (with the **Mohawks, Onondagas, Cayugas**, and **Senecas**), occupied an area in upstate New York near present-day Syracuse, adjacent to the Mohawks on their east and the Onondagas on the west.

Before contact with Europeans, the Oneidas were a semisedentary people whose main sustenance was derived from corn, squash, and beans, supplemented by animal protein from hunting. They lived in communal **longhouses** that contained extended families of matrilineal descent. The Oneidas belonged to three clans. They were the smallest, in terms of population, of the five nations in the

Iroquois Confederacy. In the 1600s, the Oneidas had one principal town that included about eighty longhouses. The town was destroyed by a French Canadian expedition in 1696.

The first European to visit Oneida country who left a historical record was a Dutch surgeon, Harmen Meyndertsz van den Bogaert, who traveled westward from Fort Orange (Albany) in 1634 and 1635. The Oneidas sheltered the Dutchman during the deepening winter and fed him venison, salmon, bear meat, cornbread baked with beans, baked squash, and beaver meat. The fact that the Oneidas could bring such a feast out of winter storage speaks volumes about the abundance of their economy at the time. Van den Bogaert described storehouses of beans and maize; he estimated that one of these contained 300 bushels of corn stored for the winter.

According to van den Bogaert's accounts, the Oneidas traded salmon to the Mohawks, perhaps for bear meat. Traveling Mohawk traders passed through Oneida settlements while van den Bogaert lived there. To reciprocate for the Oneidas' hospitality, he gave them salt, tobacco, knives, needles, axes, cloth, ham, and beer, but he discovered that he was not the first to introduce them to European trade goods. The French had arrived earlier, leaving some of the Oneidas with French clothing and razors. Van den Bogaert wrote of seeing the "Kanosoni" or the "extended House" while visiting the Oneidas. He also gave good descriptions of the fabric of Iroquois life, including the use of **wampum**, social life, town construction, and customs.

During the early 1660s and continuing into the 1690s, Oneida and other Iroquois populations were sharply reduced by a series of epidemics, principally smallpox. By the late 1660s, according to French observers (Richards, 25), two-thirds of the Oneida population was comprised of adopted Wyandot (Huron) and Algonquian captives. Alcohol was already taking a toll on the Oneidas as well. At about the same time, the European-religion frontier reached Oneida territory with the arrival of the Jesuits. By 1690, the new English government at Albany was approving purchases of Native land in Iroquois country. The Oneidas' population and economic base continued a protracted decline, mitigated somewhat by **adoption** of war captives.

The Oneidas, unlike a majority of other Iroquois, supported the patriots during the **American Revolution**. The Oneidas' corn surplus, an asset in peacetime trade, was put to use in 1777 feeding General George Washington's hungry troops during their desperate winter at Valley Forge. An Oneida, **Polly Cooper** (also called Polly Cook), served as Washington's cook for much of the war at his specific request. Washington asked his staff to employ a Native American cook because of the commander's fondness for meals made with corn.

General Washington also came to know the Oneida chief **Skenandoah** (sometimes anglicized as "Shenandoah"), who lived to an age of about 110, an anomaly at a time when the average life span was between 35 and 40. The Oneidas also supported George Washington's troops with military aid at the Battle of Oriskany (1777), which prevented the British from advancing to a position that would have allowed them free access across New York State and up the Hudson River and would have divided the colonies in half.

The Iroquois League split after some Oneidas took part in the patriots' scorched-earth march under General **John Sullivan** in 1779, which destroyed the homes and economic base of many other Haudenosaunee people who had sided with British interests. Many Oneidas were hounded into abandoning their homes and taking shelter at patriot forts, while another 800 fled their homeland. The Oneidas often were targets of raids by the Mohawks under **Joseph Brant**, who supported the British in the Revolution. The American Revolution was the first time that members of the Iroquois Confederacy had gone to war with each other. After the Revolution, some of the Oneidas moved to Thames River, Ontario. Others moved to Green Bay, Wisconsin.

Despite the Oneidas' aid in the Revolution, New York Oneida lands were steadily eroded after U.S. independence was formalized in the Treaty of Paris (1783). During the mid-nineteenth century, within less than twenty years, Oneida landholdings were reduced from several hundred thousand acres to 60,000.

In the mid-eighteenth century, the Oneidas lived on roughly 5.3 million acres in central New York. Two treaties in 1785 and 1788 sharply reduced the Oneida territory. These treaties were written to the advantage of several land companies with the assistance of New York State. In 1821, the Oneidas purchased a tract of fertile land from the Menominees and Winnebagos of Wisconsin; about 700 Oneidas emigrated there in three parties over two decades. During roughly 150 years, lands owned by the Oneidas of New York were reduced to a few hundred acres.

The Oneidas of Wisconsin, like their ancestors of Washington's time, became known for their abundant corn crops. The Wisconsin Oneida reservation at this time had a sawmill, a gristmill, and a blacksmith's shop, all owned by Oneidas (Richards, 70). The Wisconsin Oneidas sent between 110 and 145 men to serve in the Union army during the Civil War (out of a total population of about 1,400). Between 46 and 65 of them died as a result of enemy action or disease (Hauptman, 67). At about the same time, the Oneidas' reservation was being denuded of large forest tracts by non-Indian commercial timber cutters, some of whom were aided by destitute Oneida families that needed cash income after their main wage earners had been killed in the war. The same destitution had compelled many young men to join the Union army to take advantage of war bounties that ranged up to $300 per man by 1864, a substantial amount of money at the time.

By 1930, New York Oneida landholdings were down to about 1,000 acres. By the late twentieth century, the Oneida reservation in New York was down to 32 acres east of Syracuse. Some investment capital was provided in 1974 by a $1.2-million award (including accrued interest) from the Indian Claims Commission. Economic stimulus was provided late in the 1980s by construction of casinos in both New York and Wisconsin. By the late 1990s, Oneida landholdings in New York State had been increased to about 4,000 acres, largely through the investment of casino profits (Kates, 25).

On January 21, 1974, the U.S. Supreme Court sustained the Oneidas' position that the Non-intercourse Acts applied to takings of their lands by New York State. This decision opened the way for other New England tribes, most notably the Passomoquoddy and Penobscots of Maine, to sue for recovery of lands lost in violation of the Non-intercourse Acts, passed between 1790 and 1834, which required that all sales of Native American lands be approved by the federal government.

Many Oneidas have been prominent from early U.S. history to the present in addition to Skenandoah. The Oneida chief Grasshopper was a confidant of James Madison. **Frederick J. Dockstader**, the anthropologist and historian, was of Oneida and Navajo descent. In our own time, Oneida **Joanne Shenandoah** has earned a national reputation as a folk singer, and **Graham Greene** has become a well-known actor, especially for his leading role in *Dances with Wolves*. About 5,000 Oneidas lived in the United States late in the twentieth century.

The Turning Stone Casino, twenty-five miles east of Syracuse, has produced 1,900 jobs and has become, according to Oneida Nation representative **Ray Halbritter**, the fifth most popular tourist attraction in New York State. By 1997, the casino and other Oneida businesses were employing 2,400 people, making the Oneida Nation the second-largest employer in central New York. By the fall of 1997, 2.5 million people were visiting the Turning Stone annually.

Eighty-five percent of the Turning Stone's employees are non-Indian. An expansion of the Oneidas' casino and hotel accommodations during the late 1990s was expected to increase the Oneida payroll to 2,600, making it the largest single employer in the region. While Halbritter points to the economic benefits of the Oneidas' growing payroll, local public officials complain that the Oneidas' business ventures pay no sales or excise taxes to cities, counties, or the state. Additionally, land purchased by the Oneidas has been taken off the property-tax rolls.

In September 1997, the Oneidas attempted to assuage these criticisms by paying Oneida County $71,080 and Verona County (in which the casino is located) $55,230 in lieu of property taxes. The payments, which have been pledged on an annual basis (Kates, 25), are called Oneida Nation Silver Covenant Chain Grants after the **Covenant Chain** image that was utilized in early treaty councils. The grant program actually began in a limited way during 1996 with Oneida Nation gifts to local schools. The grants will be made on land that the Oneidas of New York have repurchased inside the 270,000-acre area in central New York that was designated as Oneida Territory under the **Canandaigua Treaty** of 1794. The Oneida Nation says that the grants, on average, will replace nearly 200 percent of lost tax revenue. The program has a political aim, as well: to illustrate to local non-Indian governments that the Oneidas are a sovereign nation that should be dealt with in a peer relationship.

In addition to land purchases, the Oneidas have used some of their gambling profits to start other businesses, such as the Oneida Textile Printing Facility in Canastota, their first effort at diversification outside of gambling. Oneida Textile, located in a renovated 6,000-foot structure, prints and markets T-shirts, sweatshirts, and other items of clothing. A 285-room luxury hotel was opened in September 1997, adding 450 jobs. Casino profits also have been used to build a council house, a health-services center, a cultural center and museum, a recreational center (with a swimming pool, gymnasium, and **lacrosse** box, and other facilities), and medical, dental, and optical facilities and to fund scholarship programs, job training, legal assistance, Oneida language and music classes, elder meals, and day care. A convention center–arena and golf course are planned.

Most of the Oneidas' economic development has taken place since 1985, when 90 percent of Oneidas in central New York lived in poverty. Oneida County executive Ralph Eannance believes that the Oneidas' business boom has been the single biggest factor in central New York's economic recovery during the late 1990s, following the closure of a major U.S. Air Force base and large layoffs at major defense contractors such as Lockheed Martin (Kates, 22).

By the late 1990s, the Oneidas were negotiating with New York State for authority to open a second casino in the Catskills, a location closer to the urban market of New York City than the Pequots' Foxwoods Casino, the largest Indian gaming operation in the United States. Tribal Chairman Ray Halbritter hinted that the Oneidas might be willing to trim a land claim for 250,000 acres in exchange for permission to build the casino. The Oneidas' claim that the land was taken from them illegally between 1785 and 1846 has been upheld by the U.S. Supreme Court.

For the Oneidas of Wisconsin, gambling has been the key to a quarter-century of economic development that reduced reservation unemployment from 75 percent in 1970 to 5 percent in 1995. In 1969, the Oneida government in Wisconsin employed 9 people; by 1995, the payroll was 3,389—1,611 tribal members, 357 Native Americans who are not Oneidas, and 1,421 non-Indians. Officials in central New York estimate that the job growth in Oneida businesses has been matched roughly one-to-one in other businesses (Kates, 25).

The Oneida Nation of Wisconsin's annual budget in 1969 was about $50,000, nearly all of which came from federal funds. In 1995, the tribe's budget was $158 million, of which 80 percent was generated on the reservation (Johnson, 17–18). The Oneida Nation has become one of the largest employers in metropolitan Green Bay, bringing more than a billion dollars a year in economic activity to the area (Johnson, 17). Tim Johnson writes that the Oneidas have used Indian gaming to develop reservation infrastructure, including education, in a way that has "merged Indian culture with corporate practices and left the Oneidas in a position to protect, preserve, and strengthen their identity far into the future" (Johnson, 17). Prosperity has come to the Oneidas of Wisconsin at the same time as a revival of the traditional Longhouse Religion. Gambling revenues have played a major role in the recovery of several thousand acres of land sold during the lean years.

Non-Indians flock to the Oneidas' casino from a radius of 200 miles, arriving by the busloads to play 5,000 slot machines that can pay off as high as $1 million. Prizes at the bingo tables can be as high as $250,000. "When I walk into that casino, I'm overwhelmed," said Dr. Carol Cornelius, a Wisconsin Oneida. "I think, 'My people did all this.' " Cornelius recalls, "Twenty-five years ago when I graduated from high school there were no jobs. As young folks we went to Milwaukee and found out we couldn't handle city life. There just wasn't a future. Now I see all of these young people working and I think, 'all of these people now have job skills' " (Johnson, 20).

FURTHER READING

Hauptman, Laurence M. *The Iroquois in the Civil War: From Battlefield to Reservation.* Syracuse, N.Y.: Syracuse University Press, 1993.
Johnson, Tim. "The Dealer's Edge: Gaming in the Path of Native America." *Native Americas* 12:2 (Spring/Summer 1995): 16–25.
Kates, William. "Oneidas' Enterprises Bolster Struggling Central New York." Associated Press in *Omaha World-Herald*, November 5, 1997, pp. 22, 25.
Richards, Cara E. *The Oneida People.* Phoenix: Indian Tribal Series, 1974.

Oneidas, Thames River, Ontario. The Oneidas of Thames River, Ontario, moved from New York to Ontario during the late 1700s and settled near London, Ontario. A band of slightly more than 400 people departed New York State in 1840 under the leadership of Moses Schuyler and William T. Doxtator. With their accumulated savings, they purchased 5,400 acres near Caradoc. The Oneidas of Thames River later sought and obtained membership in the Canadian central council of the Iroquois at **Grand River**, Ontario.

Onondagas, historical sketch. The Onondagas are one of the five original nations of the Iroquois Confederacy (along with the **Mokawks, Cayugas, Oneidas**, and **Senecas**). Located in central upstate New York near present-day Syracuse, the Onondagas act as keepers of the Iroquois' traditional central council fire and as executives in the Iroquois Confederacy. "Onondaga" is a slightly anglicized version of their self-given name, *o-nun-da-ga-o-no*, meaning "people of the hills," after their earliest villages, which, like those of the Senecas, were located on hills overlooking valleys.

According to Iroquois legend, the Onondagas and the Senecas were the last of the five nations to agree to the **Great Law of Peace** proposed by **Hiawatha** and the **Peacemaker**. The evil wizard Tadadaho, who long frustrated the plans of the Peacemaker and Hiawatha, was an Onondaga who obstructed the establishment of the confederacy. The origin story of the Iroquois League describes a years-long struggle during which Tadadaho, with his snake-encrusted head, his crooked body, and his wildly enlarged sexual organs, frustrated attempts to bring peace to the Haudenosaunee. When Tadadaho finally agreed to recognize the Great Law of Peace, his name was given to the council's chief executive officer as proof, to the Iroquois, of the triumph of peace over war and of good over evil.

Late in the twentieth century, one of two Haudenosaunee Grand Councils (the other is at **Grand River**, Ontario) meets in a simple log structure near Nedrow, south of Syracuse, on what remains of Onondaga ancestral territory. Every five years in that cabin until his death in 1998, **Jake Thomas** recited the entire Great Law of Peace in the Onondaga language. Thomas was the only person alive in the late twentieth century who could recite the whole story from memory, with aid from several **wampum** belts that record history for the Onondagas and other Iroquois. He could recite the law in all five Haudenosaunee languages. Thomas's recitation of the Great Law usually took him three or four eight-hour days.

Lake Onondaga, which figures prominently in the origin story of the Iroquois League, today is surrounded by Syracuse and its suburbs. The lake is badly polluted, and most fish taken from it may not be safely eaten. Syracuse and its suburbs also figure in one of the more dramatic of many Iroquois land claims in upstate New York. By the middle 1990s, the Onondagas were considering a court test of a land claim to Syracuse and many of its suburbs, based on fraudulent practices by land speculators and the state of New York two centuries earlier.

In the late twentieth century, the Onondagas' territory comprised 7,300 acres. An estimated 600 people live on the territory, but the number is not exact because census takers are not allowed on the territory. The Onondaga tribal roll included about 1,600 people in 1990. The Onondaga territory was described by Robert Lipsyte in the middle 1980s as "a reservation nestled in a lovely valley among the low, rounded hills that gave its residents the name 'Onondaga'— People of the Hills" (Lipsyte, 28).

During the 1990s, conflict on the Onondaga territory intensified over whether Onondaga businesspeople should be allowed to sell tax-free gasoline and tobacco products. The Grand Council denied permission and sought to shut such businesses down.

FURTHER READING

Bradley, James W. *Evolution of the Onondaga Iroquois: Accommodating Change, 1500–1655*. Syracuse, N.Y.: Syracuse University Press, 1987.
Lipsyte, Robert. "Lacrosse: All-American Game." *New York Times Sunday Magazine*, June 15, 1986, 28.
Tuck, James A. *Onondaga Iroquois Prehistory*. Syracuse,: N.Y. Syracuse University Press, 1971.

Orehaoue (Cayuga), fl. late 1600s. Early in his life, Orehaoue was violently opposed to the conversion of Indians by missionaries and kept them out of

Cayuga territory while he was influential there. In 1687, Orehaoue was captured by the French Denonville expedition and sold into slavery. He traveled to France as a galley slave and remained there two years. Returning to America in 1689, Orehaoue became a strong French ally and a Christian, a belief he then held so strongly that he was fond of saying that if he had witnessed the crucifixion of Christ, he would have sought the scalps of those who killed him.

FURTHER READING

Johansen, Bruce E., and Donald A. Grinde, Jr. *The Encyclopedia of Native American Biography*. New York: Henry Holt, 1997.

Orenda (uki). *Orenda* was the word coined by **J. N. B. Hewitt** to discuss what he deemed the "magic power" concepts of the Iroquoian peoples (Hewitt, "Constitutional League," 537). Although the word *orenda* is of questionable authenticity, it is in common use today by most scholars. This is unfortunate, for it distorts the actual concept.

First, the more proper term for *orenda* is *ughi* or *uki*. Second, as Gawaso Wanneh (**Arthur Parker**) observed, the "term 'medicine' means a mystic potence" (Converse, 22), not "magic." Third, and most importantly, *uki* is only one of two halves of spirit force. It must be counterbalanced by its natural twin, *otgont* or *otkon*. Only taken together do *uki* and *otkon* form the universe of "medicine."

Uki is predictable and human-friendly. *Otkon*, on the other hand, animates the West-called "trickster" element, that is, it operates on its own, nonhuman agenda that does not formulate its actions based on their usefulness to humanity. *Otkon* only incidentally confers benefits or harm on human beings.

Each medicine half possesses the same amount of daylight and darkness. *Uki*'s half of the day runs from midnight to noon, while *otkon*'s runs from noon to midnight. Both halves of medicine are portals into spirit consciousness, although those who are new to or inexperienced in spirit work should avoid *otkon* until they have a solid relationship with the spirits. *Uki*, on the other hand, is never dangerous to humans. Today, the medicine pair is usually associated with the Sacred Twins, Sapling (*uki*) and Flint (*otkon*).

By artificially singling out *uki* for elevation as *orenda* and then presenting it as the totality of spirit access, ignoring *otkon*, Hewitt helped obfuscate the meaning of Iroquoian medicine for Westerners. The mistake is now widespread, permeating modern academic texts, so that *orenda* is considered in complete isolation from *otkon*, while *otkon* is now freely translated in standard linguistic handbooks as "evil power" (see Chafe, 59).

These errors originated with the missionaries, who played their usual havoc with non-Western cultural concepts. Christians immediately superimposed their own Manichean dichotomy (i.e., "good" and "evil" as competing, polar opposites) on the twinship principle. In the process, they recast the spirit-access portals in the image of their own concepts of good (*uki*) and evil (*otkon*), locked in an eternal struggle for human souls.

Ironically, the missionaries had not meant to do this, for they condemned all Native spirit work as consorting with the devil and tended themselves to confuse *uki* with *otkon*, pronouncing both "evil." Most missionaries were, in fact, unable to distinguish between *uki* and *otkon*, as illustrated in this passage from Gabriel Sagard's 1632 relation: "this word Oki [*sic*] means a great devil just as much as a great angel, a raging devilish disposition as well as a great, wise, understanding or efficient intelligence, which does and knows something out of the ordinary" (Sagard, 170).

Over time, Westernized Iroquoian individuals lost track of authentic tradition and began accepting these Christianized formulations. In the nineteenth century, especially, with its forced assimilation, many Iroquoians came to associate *otkon* with evildoing "witchcraft"—a Christian concept—although no Native ever accepted that *uki* was evil. This Christianized definition of the *uki-otkon* unit was carried over into the Longhouse Religion by Sganyadaí:yoh (**Handsome Lake**), who outlawed the use of *otkon* and attempted to smear the numerous Clan Mothers who fiercely opposed the patriarchal aspects of his *Gaiwí:yo* (Code) as "witches." Due to the level of resistance he met in this last endeavor, he soon dropped his persecution of these women, but his proscriptions against *otkon* remained in the *Gaiwí:yo*. Because of the *Gaiwí:yo*'s heavy emphasis on Sapling as a solitary Creator, it also became customary among Longhouse religionists to do all their spirit work during the *uki* half of the day.

Not all modern Iroquois are Longhouse religionists, however. Some, especially the Ohio league peoples and many "removed" to Oklahoma (as "Wyandots"), continued the older concepts and practices associated with the *uki-otkon* unit.

FURTHER READING

Chafe, Wallace. *Handbook of the Seneca Language*. New York State Museum and Science Service, Bulletin No. 388. Albany: University of the State of New York, State Education Department, 1963.

Converse, Harriet Maxwell [Ya-ie-wa-noh]. *Myths and Legends of the New York State Iroquois*. Ed. Arthur Caswell Parker. New York State Museum Bulletin 125, Education Department Bulletin No. 437. Albany: University of the State of New York, 1908.

Hewitt, J. N. B. "A Constitutional League of Peace in the Stone Age of America: The League of the Iroquois and Its Constitution." *Smithsonian Institution Series* (1920): 527–545.

———. "Iroquoian Cosmology, First Part." *Twenty-first Annual Report of the Bureau of American Ethnology to the Secretary of the Smithsonian Institution, 1899–1900*. Washington, D.C.: Government Printing Office, 1903: 127–339.

———. "Iroquoian Cosmology, Second Part." In *Forty-third Annual Report of the Bureau of American Ethnology to the Secretary of the Smithsonian Institution, 1925–1926*. Washington, D.C.: Government Printing Office, 1928: 453–819.

Parker, Arthur C. *The Code of Handsome Lake, the Seneca Prophet.* New York State Museum Bulletin 163, Education Department Bulletin No. 530, November 1, 1912. Albany: University of the State of New York, 1913.

Sagard, Gabriel. *The Long Journey to the Country of the Hurons.* 1632. Ed. George M. Wrong. Trans. H. H. Langton. Toronto: Champlain Society, 1939.

Thomas, Chief Jacob, with Terry Boyle. *Teachings from the Longhouse.* Toronto: Stoddart, 1994.

Barbara A. Mann

Oronhyatekha (Mohawk), 1841–1907. One of the earliest Native Americans to practice European-style medicine, Oronhyatekha began his education at a mission school near Brantford, Ontario, near his birthplace on the Six Nations Reserve. He studied at Wesleyan Academy in Wilbraham, Massachusetts, Kenyon College, and the University of Toronto, often paying his educational expenses by organizing "wild west" shows in which he recruited whites to depict Indians.

In 1860, Oronhyatekha delivered an address on behalf of the Canadian Six Nations to the Prince of Wales (later King Edward VII). The prince invited Oronhyatekha to continue his education at Oxford University. Oronhyatekha studied medicine at Oxford and returned to Toronto to practice, having acquired not only medical knowledge, but also an upper-class English affectation in his clothes and manners. Oronhyatekha married a granddaughter of the Mohawk leader **Joseph Brant**, another Mohawk who had traveled to England and had returned home changed.

FURTHER READING

Johansen, Bruce E., and Donald A. Grinde, Jr. *The Encyclopedia of Native American Biography.* New York: Henry Holt, 1997.

P

Paine, Thomas, 1737–1809. Thomas Paine displayed a fascination with Native American societies after arriving in America from England shortly before the Revolutionary War. Paine worked examples of Native American societies into his writings on occasion; Paine's image of the Indians helped to shape some of the ideas in his famous revolutionary tract *Common Sense* (1776).

Paine attended a treaty council at Easton, Pennsylvania, in 1777, in order to negotiate the Iroquois' alliance, or at least neutrality, in the **American Revolution**. According to Samuel Edwards, a biographer of Paine, he was "fascinated by them" (Edwards, 49). Paine quickly learned some Mohawk and was soon comparing Native American societies to Europe's in his writing. "Among the Indians," wrote Paine, "there are not any of those spectacles of misery that poverty and want present to our eyes in the towns and streets of Europe" (Foner, 1:610). To Paine, poverty was a creation "of what is called civilized life. It exists not in the natural state. . . . The life of an Indian is a continual holiday compared to the poor of Europe" (Foner, 1:610). As one who sought to mold the future in the image of the natural state, Paine admired the Indians' relatively equal distribution of property, but he realized that it was impossible "to go from the civilized to the natural state" (Conway, 1:70).

Benjamin Franklin sponsored the Englishman Paine's visit to America in 1774. Paine's ideas are a good example of the transference of New World ideas to the Old. Paine's *Common Sense* illustrated how imbued Americans were with the "self-evident" truths of natural rights. *Common Sense* captured the essence of the American spirit by saying that civil and religious liberties stemmed from governments in a natural state.

During the few years that Paine lived in America, he spent considerable time with American Indians, especially the Iroquois. On January 21, 1777, Paine was appointed by Philadelphia's Council of Safety as a commissioner to negotiate a treaty with the Iroquois and allied Indian nations at Easton. The commissioners toted a thousand dollars worth of presents with them to the Dutch Reformed Church in Easton, where, by Paine's account, "after shaking hands, drinking rum, while the organ played, we proceeded to business" (Conway, 1:88). Paine with his prominent nose, lofty forehead, ruddy complexion, and eyes that Paine's compatriot Charles Lee said shone genius, was particularly well known among the Senecas. John Hall, who emigrated from Leicester, England, to Philadelphia in 1785, recorded in his journal for April 15, 1786:

> Mr. Paine asked me to go and see the Indian chiefs of the Sennaka Nation. I gladly assented. . . . Mr. Paine . . . made himself known . . . as Common Sense and was introduced into the room, addressed them as "brothers," and shook hands cordially[.] Mr. Paine treated them with 2s. bowl of punch. (Conway, 2:462)

FURTHER READING

Conway, Moncure Daniel. *The Life of Thomas Paine.* 2 vols. New York: J. P. Putnam's Sons, 1908.

Edwards, Samuel. *Rebel: A Biography of Tom Paine.* New York: Praeger, 1974.

Foner, Philip S., ed. *The Complete Writings of Thomas Paine.* New York: Citadel Press, 1945.

Grinde, Donald A., Jr., and Bruce E. Johansen. *Exemplar of Liberty: Native America and the Evolution of Democracy.* Los Angeles: UCLA American Indian Studies Center, 1991.

Paine, Thomas. "Common Sense." In *The Complete Political Works of Thomas Paine.* New York: Peter Eckler, 1892.

Parker, Arthur Caswell (Gawaso Wanneh or Gáwaowaneh, "Big Snowsnake") (Seneca), 1881–1955. A well-known anthropologist, ethnologist, folklorist, museum curator, and historian of his people, Gawaso Wanneh (Arthur C. Parker) was born on April 5, 1881, on the **Cattaraugus Reservation** in New York. He came from a distinguished lineage that included the prophet Sganyadaí:yoh (**Handsome Lake**), the orator Sagoyewatha (**Red Jacket**), the Grand Sachem Donehogä'wa (**Ely S. Parker**), and at least two *Jigonsasehs*, his great-great-grandmother, Aliquippiso, and Gähahno (**Caroline Parker Mountpleasant**), his paternal aunt. Arthur Parker's father was Frederick Ely Parker, a **Seneca**, and his mother was Geneva Griswold, a European-American.

English is sometimes characterized as having been Gawaso Wanneh's first language, but this is questionable. He certainly learned fluent Seneca in early childhood from living among Seneca speakers on the reservation. It is more correct to say that he had two "first" languages, English and Seneca.

Parker's Education

Gawaso Wanneh's Western education was a bit haphazard until 1899, when he entered the Dickinson Seminary at Williamsport, Pennsylvania. From there, he went on to graduate work in anthropology at Harvard University under Professor F. W. Putnam. Later, at the University of Rochester, Gawaso Wanneh stated that no matter how far he went in his Western education, "each year I slipped back [to the reservation] for a month or longer and listened to the wisdom of the tribal sages, the medicine men, and the chiefs" (Parker, *Rumbling Wings*, xi). It was their knowledge that he sought to preserve in *Rumbling Wings* and *Skunny Wundy*, works intended to convey to the youth of his people traditional knowledge that was rapidly eroding under the onslaught of "Christianization and civilization."

Little is known of his college career other than that Gawaso Wanneh changed majors from divinity, a staunchly European-American field, to anthropology, the field that his great-uncle, Donehogä´wa, jointly founded in America with **Lewis Henry Morgan**, before finally winding up in what would today be called Native American studies. Graduate school did not improve the impression that Western education had so far made on Parker. Under the tutelage of F. W. Putnam of Harvard, he worked essentially as an "ethnic ringer," a student valued for his racial "admission ticket" into the Iroquoian culture rather than as an aspiring scholar in his own right (Mann, 179). Under such bigoted mismanagement, Gawaso Wanneh chose not to complete his graduate studies.

Parker's Museum Employment

Leaving without the final degree, Parker became the special assistant archaeologist for the American Museum of Natural History during 1901 and 1902. Putnam, the temporary curator of the museum at this time, encouraged his students to supply the museum with their own artifactual collections in return for paid positions. Gawaso Wanneh accepted the offer. During the following summers of 1903 and 1904, Gawaso Wanneh worked as a field archaeologist for the Peabody Museum of American Archaeology and Ethnology and the American Museum of Natural History. His personal friend Yaiéwanoh (**Harriet Maxwell Converse**) had named Gawaso Wanneh the literary executor of her estate. Thus, after her sudden death in 1903, he also edited and organized her materials, which were published in 1908 as *Myths and Legends of the New York State Iroquois*.

In need of income in 1904, Gawaso Wanneh took odd jobs as a journalist for the *New York Sun* and as an archaeologist for the New York State Library. Later in 1904, he was hired by the State Education Department of New York to secure as much ethnographic information as possible on the Haudenosaunee. Once more, he was being used as an ethnic ringer, for it was specifically his Seneca descent that seemed to have landed him the job.

Seneca elders were not necessarily as impressed by Parker's biological credentials as academics, however. Before the elders entrusted Parker with deep traditional knowledge, they tested his intentions and loyalties. After a probationary period of several months, during which he proved himself, the elders decided to adopt him. The Haudenosaunee determine descent through the maternal line. Since Parker's mother was not Seneca, by Iroquoian law, Parker was not a member of the nation until he had been properly adopted. Parker was taken into the Bear Clan of the Seneca under the distinguished name of Gawaso Wanneh, or "Big Snowsnake." This marked the turning point in his life. Thereafter, he sought to preserve traditional lore.

Gawaso Wanneh also was impressing the European-American scholarly world. He soon made a name for himself in his field and found that jobs were no longer so difficult to come by. In 1906, he was conditionally offered the position of archaeologist for the Science Division of the New York State Museum. His record alone was considered insufficient to secure him the appointment. The museum board also demanded that he pass a rigorous civil-service examination, which he did, landing a permanent appointment at $900 a year. Parker quickly discovered that his superiors felt that the main contribution he could make was in the acquisition of Haudenosaunee artifacts for display. Not content merely to have the Morgan, Converse, and Maxwell collections, the museum's director pressured Gawaso Wanneh to pull out his spade and begin digging.

Parker and Gravesite Excavations

It was now that Gawaso Wanneh first undertook what is today the most controversial aspect of his career: he excavated gravesites. At the turn of the twentieth century, this was the hottest craze in the fields of anthropology and archaeology. According to **G. Peter Jemison**, J. Sheldon Fisher, who personally knew Gawaso Wanneh at this period, said that he "meant no disrespect to his ancestors" but, instead, was motivated by the belief that "he was entitled to know about them" (Jemison, 69). Gawaso Wanneh was particularly interested in resurrecting the traditions of the *Jigonsasehs*, or Head Clan Mothers of the league. He was, therefore, intrigued by a gravesite he believed to have been that of the first Peace Queen, the ally of the **Peacemaker**, who, along with **Hiawatha**, established the Iroquois League. However grisly to modern sensibilities, the first *Jigonsaseh* was his most important discovery, although it was disputed by Euro-scholars who assumed an incorrect date for the first *Jigonsaseh*. To his museum superiors, the "important objects of ceremonial equipment" that he spaded up were his signal finds (Fenton, 17).

Gawaso Wanneh also worked to keep the **wampum** of the league that had been transferred by the elders to New York State for safekeeping during the worst years of freewheeling plunder by European-American "tourists." Although it is no recommendation to the Iroquois today, this effort impressed his museum superiors and, incidentally, probably saved some of the most sacred wampum belts from being broken up and sold, bead by bead, as "souvenirs."

In 1911, in an event that some Haudenosaunee believe was spiritually initiated, a fire destroyed the better part of the State Library collection Gawaso Wanneh had amassed, including the Morgan and Converse collections. Despite his personal heroics—he ran into the burning building to rescue what he could—the majority of the collections was destroyed.

Financial Hardship

About this time, Gawaso Wanneh also began to experience financial hardship. The museum was unwilling to grant a Native American a living wage, having raised his annual salary to only $1,200—half of the salaries paid to European-Americans doing similar work. To make up the difference, Gawaso Wanneh began lecturing and writing for profit. At the same time, Parker produced an extraordinary number of unremunerated scholarly articles as part of his museum duties. His dissatisfaction with his post notwithstanding, professional jobs for "Indians" were still scarce. He thus remained with the New York State Museum until 1924.

In 1925, Gawaso Wanneh left the Department of Education to found the Rochester Municipal Museum of Arts and Sciences, acting as its director until 1946, when he retired. In this capacity, he devoted his many talents to exploring and writing about issues he considered important, whether or not European-American scholars agreed. In view of his own extraordinary contributions to Native American studies, Gawaso Wanneh felt—properly, many argue—that he deserved the scholarly recognition that institutionalized racism had denied him. Although he did not have a doctorate, from roughly the 1930s on, whenever people addressed him as "Doctor," he did not demur. In 1940, Union College finally rectified the slight, bestowing an honorary doctorate on him for his lifetime achievements. The honor was not gratuitous. In retrospect, Gawaso Wanneh's work has only grown in significance and now forms the modern backbone of primary studies on Haudenosaunee traditional culture and lore.

Mainstream Anthropologists' Attacks on Parker

In 1916, when his *Constitution of the Five Nations* (one of his most significant works) first appeared, it was savagely attacked by mainstream anthropologists, with A. A. Goldenweiser and **J. N. B. Hewitt** leading the charge. Goldenweiser was the first to articulate in print a claim that the league was but a figment of the Iroquoian imagination. It had only been set down as a blueprint for constitutional government in the late nineteenth century, Goldenweiser contended in an argument since taken over by modern conservative anthropologists intent on proving that the league did not influence the U.S. Constitution, despite a wealth of historical primary sources to the contrary.

Although it might be supposed that anyone who had himself been devalued as a scholar based on his Native descent might temper his remarks, Hewitt also purported to have found damning mistakes in Parker's *Constitution*, all of which in retrospect were arguably nitpicking. More important, Hewitt implied that Gawaso Wanneh had lied about how he had come across his sources, although this insinuation was based entirely on Hewitt's own speculations regarding the antiquity of desperate traditions. It is worth mentioning that the **Seth Newhouse** tradition so despised by Hewitt—a version of which appeared in the *Constitution*—was and still is regarded as "the canon" by many traditional Haudenosaunee (Wallace, 74).

Over the course of his long career, Gawaso Wanneh did not forget his Native American identity, nor did anyone else. In 1914, he founded American Indian Day. In 1916, he was honored with the Cornplanter Medal and, in 1939, with the Indian Achievement Medal. In addition, he worked tirelessly in many leadership positions, serving as president of numerous organizations, including the Society of American Indians, the New York State Archaeological Association, the New York State Historical Association, the Society of Colonial History, and the New York State Indian Welfare Society. During the "reorganization" of Native America in the 1930s, Gawaso Wanneh set up the Indian Arts Project. In 1954, just before he died, he was recognized with the Guggenheim Award.

Parker as Author

Gawaso Wanneh was a prolific author, producing some 350 articles and 14 books. In addition to his scholarly works, he also produced two volumes of traditional lore aimed at his own people, *Skunny Wundy and Other Indian Tales* (1926) and *Rumbling Wings and Other Indian Tales* (1928). He also acted as the editor of the *American Indian Magazine* from 1913 to 1916. Primary among his published articles and books are *Excavations in an Erie Indian Village* (1907), *Myths and Legends of the New York State Iroquois* (edition, 1908), *Iroquois Uses of Maize and Other Food Plants* (1910), *The Code of Handsome Lake* (1912), "The Legal Status of the American Indian" (1915), *The Constitution of the Five Nations, or, The Iroquois Book of the Great Law* (1916), *General Grant's Military Secretary* (1919), *The Archaeological History of New York* (1922), *Seneca Myths and Folk Tales* (1923), *An Analytical History of the Seneca Indians* (1926), *Notes on the Ancestry of Cornplanter* (1927), *A Manual for History Museums* (1935), *Red Jacket: Last of the Seneca* (1952), and "Sources and Range of Cooper's Indian Lore" (1954). Parker died on January 1, 1955.

FURTHER READING

Dockstader, Frederick J. *Great North American Indians*. New York: Van Nostrand Reinhold, 1977.

Fenton, William N. "Editor's Introduction." In *Parker on the Iroquois*. Ed. William N. Fenton. Syracuse,: N.Y. Syracuse University Press, 1968: 1–47.

Jemison, Pete. "Mother of Nations: The Peace Queen, Neglected Tradition." *Akwe:kon* 5 (1988): 68–70.

Mann, Barbara A. "Epilogue: Euro-forming the Data." In Bruce E. Johansen, Donald A. Grinde, Jr., and Barbara A. Mann, *Debating Democracy: Native American Legacy of Freedom*. Santa Fe, N.M.: Clear Light Publishers, 1998: 160–190.

Parker, Arthur C. [Gawaso Wanneh]. *The Life of General Ely S. Parker, Last Grand Sachem of the Iroquois and General Grant's Military Secretary*. Buffalo: Buffalo Historical Society, 1919.

———. *Notes on the Ancestry of Cornplanter*. 1927. Researches and Transactions of the New York State Archaeological Association, Lewis H. Morgan Chapter. New York: Times Presses, 1970.

————. *Rumbling Wings and Other Indian Tales.* Garden City, NY: Doubleday, Doran & Company, 1928.

————. "Sources and Range of Cooper's Indian Lore." In Mary E. Cunningham, ed., *James Fenimore Cooper: A Re-Appraisal.* Cooperstown: New York State Historical Society, 1954: 79–88.

Thomas, W. Stephen. "Arthur Caswell Parker: 1881–1955: Anthropologist, Historian, and Museum Pioneer." *Rochester History* 18:3 (1955): 1–20.

Wallace, Paul A. W. "Cooper's Indians." In Mary E. Cunningham, ed. *James Fenimore Cooper: A Re-appraisal.* Cooperstown, NY: New York State Historical Society, 1954: 55–78.

Barbara A. Mann

Parker, Ely S. (Donehogä´wa, "He Holds the Door Open," also known as Häsanoan'da, "The Reader") (Seneca), 1828–1895. Donehogä´wa (Ely S. Parker) was a lawyer, engineer, ethnologist, author, and a grand sachem of the Iroquois League. Born at Indian Falls near modern-day Pembroke, New York, he was the son of the **Seneca** Gaontgwutwus and her husband, Jonoesdowa. Also known as William Parker, Jonoesdowa was the chief at the Seneca **Tonawanda Reservation**. Donehogä´wa's grandfather was Sagoyewatha, "He Causes Them To Be Awake" (**Red Jacket**), the famed speaker of the Clan Mothers during and immediately after the colonial era. His sister was Gähahno (**Caroline Parker Mountpleasant**), the last *Jigonsaseh* of the league.

Parker's Early Life

As a boy Donehogä´wa attended a Baptist missionary school near Tonawanda and then was sent to Canada for a more traditional education in hunting and fishing. Working as a stablehand on a military base, he was harassed by British soldiers for being unable to understand their language. This seeded in Parker a determination to learn perfect English. At the age of twelve, Parker entered the Yates Academy in New York before going on to the Cayuga Academy in Aurora. At Rensselaer Polytechnic Institute in Troy, New York, Parker studied civil engineering. Along the way, he picked up ethnology. Donehogä´wa also studied law and, had he been of European extraction, would certainly have been admitted to the New York bar, for he passed the examination. Being an "Indian," however, he was forbidden a law career on the grounds that he was not a citizen of the United States. This was the first of many racist barriers to his career ambitions, denying him his due.

The Senecas, knowing Parker's skill as a lawyer, made good use of his services. They sent him to Albany, New York, and Washington, D.C., to advocate land claims after the Senecas were defrauded of nearly all of their New York lands by unscrupulous speculators in flagrant violation of treaties negotiated with the U.S. government. Donehogä´wa proved such an able lawyer in resecuring titles that prominent European-Americans, including President James K. Polk, took notice.

Parker Meets Lewis Henry Morgan

In 1844, while he was among a Seneca delegation to the New York State capital of Albany, Donehogä´wa stirred the notice of the ethnographer **Lewis Henry Morgan**, who seized the opportunity of a chance meeting in a bookstore to establish an acquaintance with the famous Seneca lawyer. The friendship that blossomed between the two men led to their collaboration on *The League of the Haudenosaunee, Iroquois* (1851), the landmark study that established anthropology as a discipline in America. When the work was published, however, the title page bore only the name of Morgan, its European-American author, omitting that of Donehogä´wa, whose status was reduced to that of Native informant, a tactic used to privilege and overcredit Euro-anthropologists until quite recently.

Although the tactic preferred that the "informant" remain anonymous, Morgan's conscience moved him to dedicate the study of Häsanoan'da (Donehogä´wa), "A Seneca Indian," acknowledging that the book was actually "the fruit of our joint researches." He thus inscribed the work to his partner "in acknowledgement of the obligations, and in testimony of the friendship of the author." Oddly enough, even though Morgan was frankly admitting that without the "intelligence and accurate knowledge" that Donehogä´wa had lavished on the project, it could not have been produced, Morgan continued to present himself as the only scholar involved. Following this questionable lead, Western scholars since generally have attributed sole authorship of *The League of the Haudenosaunee* to Morgan (Morgan, 1: vii, xii).

This latest racist slight notwithstanding, it was Donehogä´wa's intimate knowledge of the culture, language, and history of his people that made the work the classic it remains today, despite what Gawaso Wanneh (**Arthur Caswell Parker**) characterized as "a number of errors both in statement of fact and in the viewpoint of certain matters" resulting from Morgan's interpolated misperceptions (Parker, 88). Any who would like to assess the real value of Donehogä´wa's contributions to *The League of the Haudenosaunee* should compare it with *Ancient Society, or, Researches in the Line of Human Progress from Savagery through Barbarism to Civilization* (1877), a work of eugenics that showed Morgan's mettle when he operated on his own.

Parker Becomes a Seneca Chief

In 1852, Donehogä´wa became a chief of the Senecas. In 1853, he was elevated to the position of a grand sachem of the league (Adodaroh) under the name Denehogawa. He spent the next several years (until 1857) fighting for the preservation of the Tonawanda Reservation, which surrounding European-Americans were still attempting to parcel out among themselves. Due largely to Donehogä´wa's legal savvy, the Tonawanda Reservation was retained by the Senecas.

Because of his engineering background, Donehogä´wa was next able to land several governmental jobs, including work on the Erie Canal. From 1858 to 1861, Donehogä´wa held the position of superintendent of construction in Galena, Illinois, where he formed another historically instrumental friendship, this time with Ulysses S. Grant.

Parker in the Civil War

The Haudenosaunee had always actively opposed southern slavery. In 1862, soon after the Civil War broke out, Donehogä´wa resigned his engineering position and attempted to join the Union army; in fact, he offered to raise a regiment of league soldiers. His efforts, however, were spurned by the racist establishment, which was even loath to allow escaped slaves to fight in their own behalf. (Besides, the thought of a rearmed league gave many members of Congress shudders.) Undaunted, a short time later, Donehogä´wa applied for a position with the U.S. Army Corps of Engineers. Again, rampant racism dashed his hopes. Finally, in May 1863, he applied to his friend Grant, who had since become a man of some importance to the Union army.

Grant came through for his friend, appointing him engineering captain of the Seventh Corps of Volunteers, just in time for Parker to join Grant's brilliant campaign against the southern stronghold of Vicksburg. Grant soon discovered Donehogä´wa's legal abilities and transferred him to the post of his own military secretary in August 1864, at the rank of lieutenant colonel of the Volunteer Army.

Donehogä´wa wrote the articles of surrender signed at Appomattox on April 9, 1865. Incredibly, many historians still record that all he did was copy them out in their final version, a task he was purportedly given because of his excellent penmanship. This ridiculous cover story needs to be reevaluated in light of the superb legal abilities that Grant knew his high-ranking aide Donehogä´wa possessed. General Grant wanted a skilled lawyer to compose the terms of surrender. Immediately afterwards, Grant promoted Donehogä´wa to the rank of brigadier general of the Volunteer Army—in recognition of his services, not his penmanship.

After the war, Grant saw to it that his right-hand man was properly promoted through the more prestigious ranks of the U.S. Army, commissioning him up from the rank of lieutenant to that of brigadier general. In this capacity, Donehogä´wa traveled widely on special commissions dealing with "Indian affairs" west of the Mississippi. Of particular note were his 1866–1868 negotiations with Spotted Tail and Red Cloud following Red Cloud's successful military bid to force the U.S. Army to dismantle its forts along the Powder River. Donehogä´wa's negotiations ultimately led to the Treaty of Fort Laramie (April 29, 1868) with Red Cloud, which ceded the Black Hills to the Lakotas in return for Red Cloud's confinement on a reservation in Nebraska.

Parker's Marriage Stuns High Society

Also after the war, Donehogä´wa met and married Minnie Sackett, a European-American woman of some status in the refined classes of Washington, D.C. In the fall of 1867, Washington society was stunned by the announcement of their interracial engagement, with the marriage set for December 17, 1867.

In an attempt to prevent the marriage, a European-American "friend" of Do-
nehogä´wa drugged him surreptitiously the night before the wedding so that he
could not appear at the Church of the Epiphany on time. Indeed, he did not;
the plot succeeded, causing something of a scandal as Donehogä´wa was accused
of abandoning his bride at the altar.

Knowing better, however, the couple reset the date for December 25, but
once more, when the guests arrived, the church doors were bolted and the wedding was apparently called off. Donehogä´wa's nephew, Gawaso Wanneh, supplied the reason in his biography: There had been a "sinister threat" made against
the life of Donehogä´wa should he show up for the wedding (Parker, 146). On
this second occasion, the couple decided to take no chances. Mindful of the
danger, instead of appearing at the planned event, they slipped around the corner
to a small chapel where they were wed privately. The couple had only one child,
a daughter, Maud.

Parker Appointed Commissioner of Indian Affairs

In 1868, Donehogä´wa's old friend, Ulysses Grant, was elected president of
the United States. He did not forget his astute aide, but appointed him the U.S.
commissioner of Indian affairs in 1869. Donehogä´wa's position with European-
American officialdom has distressed some modern Natives who regard his work
for the Indian Bureau as treachery to Native causes, particularly since one of
his main jobs was to help Grant set up what turned out to be a murderous policy
of pacification (the "Peace Policy") aimed at the western Native American
nations. It is, however, all too easy to take potshots from the safe distance of
nearly a century and a half. Donehogä´wa used his position to emplace—over
considerable opposition—what were for their time enlightened policies, however
the bullets might have continued to fly out west.

In the end, Grant had done Donehogä´wa no favor by appointing him to head
the Indian Bureau. The work was demoralizing and unnerving, due partly to the
genocidal "Peace Policy" aimed at west-of-the-Mississippi Native American
nations, but also due to the profound level of corruption extant in the bureau.
Just prior to Donehogä´wa's appointment, Senator James B. Doolittle had completed a congressional investigation of the "Indian Ring," a circle of corrupt
Indian agents who had been openly pocketing governmental money meant to
have bought food and supplies for reservation inmates. Donehogä´wa came into
office on the crest of a reformist wave that dumped in his lap the job of quelling
those powerful and dishonest, yet well-heeled, "business" lobbies surrounding
the bureau.

Donehogä´wa did his best to clean up the massive corruption that had been
legendary in "Indian agencies" since the time of the British colonies. He worked
on behalf of the Lakotas, forcing the Big Horn Association to cease its illegal
mining operations on Lakota lands, thus creating yet more enemies among prominent European-Americans. He replaced the grifters in the bureau with his own
handpicked people, many of them Quakers, and set up a watchdog group, the

Board of Indian Commissioners, to root out corruption at the Indian Bureau. Parker's original plan called for Native Americans to sit on this board alongside European-Americans, but once more, ingrained racism in high places prevented this from happening.

Racism was not done with Donehogä´wa, however. Many of the highly placed "Indian Ring" profiteers whom Donehogä´wa had just put out of business lusted for revenge, as well as a return of their former graft-friendly stations. They plotted to remove Donehogä´wa from office and saw their opportunity in the pacification programs out west. Together, they conspired to withhold food shipments to the new Lakota reservations by using their social and economic influence to prevent Congress from appropriating the promised funds, in complete violation of federal treaty agreements. People on these reservation lands began, literally, to starve. Donehogä´wa's handpicked agents pleaded with him to send relief. Desperate to correct the situation, Donehogä´wa acquired food on credit without first taking any bids from suppliers, both of which actions were against the law. He was promptly impeached by Congress for his high crime of compassion, the end his enemies had been plotting to bring about.

The impeachment hearings did not quite go as the "Indian Ring" had planned, however, for when the extenuating circumstances were disclosed to the public, Donehogä´wa's initiative in keeping the government's promises emerged as noble, while the determined opposition and greedy motives of the profiteers appeared debased. All charges were dropped; in fact, Congress wound up applauding Donehogä´wa, but in the end, the "Indian Ring" won after all. Disgusted, frustrated, and emotionally shattered by the entrenched racism and deeply rooted corruption of Washington, Donehogä´wa resigned in 1871 and went home.

Parker's Later Years

It was around this time that Donehogä´wa met and became close to **Harriet Maxwell Converse**, who was to be adopted by the Seneca Nations as Yaié-wanoh. She became a prominent ally of his in the fight to keep reservation lands in Native American hands. Parker showed Converse the various Haudenosaunee reservations in New York and introduced her to his sister, Gähahno, the sitting *Jigonsaseh* of the league, as well as the lineal descendants of Sagoyewatha (Red Jacket).

Back in New York, Donehogä´wa turned his hand to several business enterprises, some of which worked, and some of which did not. In need of a job, he took the position of superintendent for buildings and supplies with the New York City Police Department in 1876 and remained in this position for the rest of his life. Parker died on August 31, 1895, at Green Corn Time on his estate in Fairfield, Connecticut. In 1897, two years after his death, Parker's remains were transported to Buffalo, New York, by his close friend Yaiéwanoh and his wife. He was reburied in the same plot as his grandfather, Sagoyewatha. On Decoration Day 1905, a grave marker was placed on the site by Reno Post, No.

44, of the Grand Army of the Republic, which was honored to have had Do-
nehogä´wa on its rolls.

FURTHER READING

Armstrong, William N. *Warrior in Two Camps: Ely S. Parker, Union General and
    Seneca Chief.* Syracuse, N.Y.: Syracuse University Press, 1978.
Morgan, Lewis Henry. *League of the Haudenosaunee, Or Iroquois.* 1851. 2 vols. New
    York: Burt Franklin, 1901.
Parker, Arthur C. *The Life of General Ely S. Parker, Last Grand Sachem of the Iroquois
    and General Grant's Military Secretary.* Buffalo: Buffalo Historical Society,
    1919.
Prucha, Francis Paul, ed. *Documents of United States Indian Policy.* Lincoln: University
    of Nebraska Press, 1975.

Barbara A. Mann

Peacemaker, the (Deganawida) (Wyandot), fl. 1100s c.e. Before the Europeans came to North America, during the **Second Epoch of Time**, when the
Haudenosaunee (People of the Longhouse), the **Senecas, Oneidas. Onondagas,
Cayugas**, and **Mohawks**, had not yet accepted the **Great Law of Peace**, *Kai-
aneraserakowa*, there was much conflict and turmoil among the *Onkwehonwe*,
the people. It was a civil war. The old ones always said that when there was
much trouble, a messenger would come from the home of the Creator to help
the people.

Soon the Peacemaker came to the *Onkwehonwe*. He was born to a Huron
woman near the Bay of Quinte. It is said that during his birth, there were very
unusual circumstances that were a sign to the *Onkwehonwe* that this baby was
special and had special spiritual powers. It is believed that his very being was
imbued with the Creator's message of Peace, *Skennen*, Power, *Kashastensera*,
and Righteousness, *Ne'' Gai´i·hwiio*. (Shenandoah, 9).

When the Peacemaker was very young, he spoke of bringing the people together in Great Peace, *Skennenkowa*. The Peacemaker's own people did not
accept his message of Great Peace, so he traveled to the *Kanienkahake*, the
People of the Flint, which is what the Mohawk people prefer to call themselves
(Shenandoah, 10). On his journey to the Mohawks, the Peacemaker arrived at
a waterfall where, on the eastern side of the river, lived a woman. This woman's
name was Tsikonsase. Tsikonsase promoted the warring of the *Onkwehonwe* by
feeding the warriors and allowing them to rest in her house as they traveled
from the east and the west along the warpath. The Peacemaker sat down and
spoke to her: "I know what you have been doing by feeding the warriors. You
have been aiding the warring, and continuing to do so is wrong. You must
stop!" He then told her that he was sent to spread the message of Great Peace,
and that she must listen to him ("Women's Nomination Belt," 3).

The Peacemaker told her the message that all people are to love each other.
They are to live in Peace and Unity with each other and with all the natural

world that surrounds them. He said that there are three parts of his good message: Peace, *Skennen*, Strength/Power, *Kasastensera*, and Righteousness, *Ne"Gai'i·hwiio*. Peace, *Skennen*, would unite the nations, and the Peace would follow the *Onkwehonwe* wherever they went. Strength/Power, *Kasastensera*, would bring all the nations together under the Great Law of Peace to become one extended family. Righteousness would stop the warring and bloodshed and would allow Peace to flourish. After the woman heard the message, she knew it to be right, and she vowed to stop promoting war and accepted the Great Law of Peace, *Kaianaraserakowa*. Tsikonsase (*Jigonsaseh*) was the first woman to accept the Peacemaker's message of Peace, and she was very influential in promoting peace among the *Onkwehonwe*. Today she is known as the Mother of the Nations, for "it is said her blood line originates from the first woman on earth" ("Women's Nomination Belt," 3).

The Peacemaker told her that women will always have an important role among the Haudenosaunee and in this Peace (Jemison, 68). The Haudenosaunee are a matrilineal society. In other words, clans are passed on from mother to child. The Peacemaker told Tsikonsase that each Chief, *Royaner*, which literally translates to "nice" or "good," would be selected and put into his position by the Clan Mother. The *Iotiianehshon*, Clan Mothers, would hold the title; therefore, if a chief goes astray, then it is the duty of the Clan Mother to remove him from his position (Jemison, 68–69).

While among the Mohawks the Peacemaker found leaders who were willing to accept his teachings of the Great Law of Peace, the warrior leaders were causing much unrest and violence. These warrior leaders were sometimes said to have committed cannibalism upon their enemies. It was a horrible time for the *Onkwehonwe* (Shenandoah, 10).

The Peacemaker sought out the war leaders, for he wanted them to listen to his good message of Peace, Power, and Righteousness, and he wanted them to accept the message, to become of sane mind, and to abandon warring and bloodshed. The nine Mohawk men who accepted the message, the Great Law of Peace, were given the title of chief. The Mohawk were the first to accept the Peacemaker's message. Today, the original names of these nine chiefs who first accepted the Great Law of Peace are preserved, and when a chief is condoled (raised to office) through the **Condolence Ceremony**, the newly raised chief relinquishes his old name and takes the original name of the title that he now holds (Buck, 34).

While he was among the Mohawks, the Peacemaker called for Ayowenta, an Onondaga, who later became a Mohawk by adoption, to come and stand by his side. Ayowenta is the Onondaga spelling; in Mohawk his name is written as **Hiawatha**, which may be more familiar to the reader, but has nothing to do with Longfellow's poetic creation (Johansen, 22). Ayowenta had isolated himself from his people and had sought solace in the woods after his daughters had been murdered. Ayowenta was an excellent orator. He stood by the side of the

Peacemaker. Ayowenta was a loyal friend and helper in promoting the Great Law of Peace (Shenandoah, 11).

The Peacemaker then traveled to the Oneidas to spread his message. The Peacemaker, as he had done with the Mohawks, sought out the violent leaders who were fighting and killing and told them of his good message from the Creator. These leaders listened to the Peacemaker's good message and, as had the Mohawks, agreed to replace their negative thinking and actions. The Oneidas agreed to accept the Great Law of Peace if the other nations would be bound and live by the law also, which required them to live in Peace and Unity. As with the Mohawks, there were nine leaders who agreed to follow the Great Law of Peace, and they became chiefs (Shenandoah, 11).

The Peacemaker then traveled to the Onondagas and, as he had done with the Mohawks and the Oneidas, sought out the leaders who were causing havoc and told them of the good message. Most of the leaders accepted the Great Law of Peace, except one very twisted man who dealt in bad medicine. His name was *Tadadaho*. *Tadadaho* was very strong and wicked, and he refused to listen to the Great Law of Peace. The Peacemaker tried to reach *Tadadaho* with the good message, but *Tadadaho* refused, so the Peacemaker moved on to spread his message to the Cayugas (Shenandoah, 11).

Ten of the Cayuga leaders accepted the Peacemaker's message and agreed to be bound by the articles of the Great Law of Peace. The Peacemaker then traveled on to the Senecas. The Senecas had a large number of warriors, but after a while, eight of the leaders agreed to accept the Great Law of Peace. All of the nations had agreed to accept the Great Law of Peace, all but the Onondaga leader *Tadadaho*. All efforts to talk with Tadadaho and get him to accept the Great Law had failed (Shenandoah, 11).

Tsikonsase, the Mother of All Nations, also known as the Peace Queen, called the Peacemaker and Ayowenta into her house, for she had a plan to bring *Tadadaho* under the Great Law of Peace (Shenandoah, 12). She said, "Go find *Tadadaho*, and when you do, you shall sing him a special song and his mind will be transformed and he will be able to hear the good message." The Peacemaker and his followers went to find *Tadadaho*. After a long time, they found the *Tadadaho* in a swamp. His body was dirty and twisted, and he had snakes woven into his hair that gave him a frightful look. His face bore the look of the cruelty that was in him (Shenandoah, 12).

The Cayugas had learned the song that Tsikonsase had suggested, and they began to sing the song to *Tadadaho*. However, the Cayugas made a mistake in singing the song, so it did not work. The Peacemaker then sang the song in a strong, clear voice, without mistakes. The Peacemaker's singing worked, for *Tadadaho* was able to hear the Peacemaker's good message, and his twisted mind and body became straightened. Then Ayonwenta was able to comb the snakes from the hair of *Tadadaho*. Although *Tadadaho* was wicked and was often thought to be so evil that he appeared not human, the singing released

him from the evilness, and he accepted the Peacemaker's message of the Great
Law of Peace. Tsikonsase said that the songs and words would heal his mind,
and they did.

When *Tadadaho* accepted the Great Law of Peace, he become the Firekeeper
of the Grand Council. The job of the *Tadadaho*, from that day on, is to promote
Peace, Power, and Righteousness (Shenandoah, 12). After *Tadadaho* accepted
the Good Message, the Onondagas were then represented by fourteen chiefs,
and the nations became bound together in Unity, Peace, and Strength under the
Great Law of Peace.

Interestingly, although I have not been able to find confirmation, it appears
that the number of feathers that are worn in the feathered ***Gus-tow-wehs*** (hats)
of each nation of the Haudenosaunee coincides with the order in which they
accepted the Great Law of Peace from the Peacemaker. For example, the Mohawks were the first to accept the Great Law of Peace, and they wear three
eagle feathers standing straight up in their *gus-tow-wehs*. The Oneidas, second
to accept the Great Law of Peace, wear one three eagle feathers also but two
of the feathers are worn straight up and one is tilted downward. The Onondagas,
next to accept the Great Law, all but *Tadadaho*, who accepted later, wear two
eagle feathers in their *gus-tow-wehs*, one up and one tilted downward. The
Cayugas, the fourth to accept the Great Law of Peace, wear one eagle feather
tilted slightly downward, while the Senecas, who accepted the Great law last,
wear one single eagle feather straight up in their *gus-tow-wehs*. The feathers
worn also allow the Haudenosaunee to recognize each other easily. The **Tuscaroras** do not wear any eagle feathers in their *gus-tow-wehs* because they did
not originally accept the Great Law of Peace from the Peacemaker. The Tuscaroras joined the confederacy and accepted the Great Law of Peace between
1710 and 1730 (Johansen, 21; Caduto, 139).

NOTE

As Chief **Jacob Thomas** elegantly stated during his reading of the Great Law of Peace
in 1992, "All the English terms we use are not really right." In other words, what Chief
Thomas is saying is that the Haudenosaunee languages are very descriptive, for the words
paint a picture in the mind of the listener. Many of the Haudenosaunee terms cannot be
adequately reproduced in the English language. Therefore, the English words used in this
entry can only give the reader a basic understanding. For example, my own name, Kanatiyosh, cannot be translated adequately into English because it explains a reaction, a
feeling. Picture walking through the woods and coming upon a clearing that contains the
most beautiful waterfall and flowers ever seen. While most non-Haudenosaunee would
be awed by such a site and utter the words "How awesome," a Mohawk coming upon
such a site would say, "Kanatiyosh."

FURTHER READING

Buck, Roy. "The Great Law." In Barbara K. Barnes, ed., *Traditional Teachings*. Corn-
     wall, Ont.: North American Indian Travelling College, 1984.

Caduto, Michael J., and Joseph Bruchac. *Keepers of the Night*. Golden, Colo.: Fulcrum Publishing, 1994.

Jemison, Pete. "Mother of Nations: The Peace Queen, a Neglected Tradition." *Akwe:kon* 5 (1988): 68–70.

Johansen, Bruce E. *Forgotten Founders: Benjamin Franklin, the Iroquois, and the Rationale for the American Revolution*. Ipswich, Mass.: Gambit, 1982.

"Leon Shenandoah, Fire Keeper for the Haudenosaunee, Dies at 81 after Serving as Tadodaho for More Than a Quarter of a Century." *Indian Time*, July 26, 1996, 1.

Mitchell, Mike Kanentakeron. "The Birth of the Peacemaker." In Barbara K. Barnes, eds., *Traditional Teachings*. Cornwall, Ont.: North American Indian Travelling College, 1984.

Shenandoah, Leon. "Forward." In Paul A. W. Wallace, *The White Roots of Peace*. Santa Fe, N.M.: Clear Light Publishes, 1994.

Thomas, Jacob. *The White Roots of Peace: Reading of the Great Law of Peace, Iroquoian Institution*. Video series, 10 tapes. 1992.

"The Women's Nomination Belt." *Indian Time* 14:28 (July 19, 1996): 3.

Barbara A. Gray (Kanatiyosh)

Pierce, Maris Bryant (Ha-dya-no-doh, Swift Runner) (Seneca), 1811–1874. After the **American Revolution**, the **Senecas** who remained in the United States were faced with reconstructing lives shattered by the punitive raids of **John Sullivan** in 1779. The destitution of the area contributed to the rise of **Handsome Lake**'s prophecy and to the land-rights activities of Maris Bryant Pierce. Pierce fought efforts to convince Senecas to cede all of their lands in New York and move westward. His primary focus was the 1838 **Buffalo Creek Treaty**.

Pierce was born on the **Allegany Seneca Reservation**, a tract of forty-two square miles left from Seneca landholdings that had once covered much of present-day western New York State. He was converted to Christianity as a teenager and attended Dartmouth College, entering as a freshman in 1836. While a college student, Pierce spent much of his time researching and speaking on issues affecting Seneca land tenure. Pierce explained why the Senecas should oppose emigration from New York to Missouri or Kansas:

The right of possession of our lands is undisputed, so with us it is a question dealing directly to our interest. . . . Our lands are fertile, and as well situated for agricultural pursuits as any we shall get by a removal. The graves of our fathers and mothers and kin are here, and about them still cling our affections and memories. . . . We are situated in the midst of facilities for physical, intellectual, and moral improvement. . . . In this view of facts surely there is no inducement for removing. (Johansen and Grinde, 290)

Pierce joined with fourteen other Seneca chiefs in opposition to removal as stipulated in the Buffalo Creek Treaty of 1838, which the Senecas had signed after considerable coercion. The federal government had paid for 750 gallons of whiskey meant to keep the Senecas inebriated during the negotiations.

Pierce mobilized opposition to the Buffalo Creek Treaty among Senecas and

some non-Indians that led to a renegotiation in 1842. The Senecas had hoped
to have their property reinstated on lines existing before 1838; instead, they
were left with even smaller reservations. Pierce's birthplace was slated to be
turned over to non-Indian settlers. Pierce and his wife Mary Jane Carroll were
forced to move from Buffalo Creek in 1845. Reluctantly, the Senecas agreed to
the terms because they could stay in New York State. During his later years,
Pierce acted as secretary of the Seneca Nation; he also played a role in bringing
an elective form of government to the Senecas in 1848.

FURTHER READING

Johansen, Bruce E., and Donald A. Grinde, Jr. *The Encyclopedia of Native American
     Biography.* New York: Henry Holt, 1997.
Pierce, Maris Bryant. *Address on the Present Condition and Prospects of the Aboriginal
     Inhabitants of North America.* Philadelphia: J. Richards, 1839.
Vernon, H. A. "Maris Bryant Pierce: The Making of a Seneca Leader." in L. G. Moses
     and Raymond Wilson, ed., *Indian Lives: Essays on Nineteenth- and Twentieth-
     Century Native American Leaders.* Albuquerque: University of New Mexico
     Press, 1985: 19–42.

Porter, Tom (Mohawk), b. 1944. A **Mohawk** and member of the Bear Clan,
Tom Porter was a longtime subchief on the Mohawk Council of **Akwesasne**
until heart problems forced his retirement in the middle 1990s. Many at Akwesasne regard Porter as a spiritually gifted person. He has been involved actively in the **Akwesasne Freedom School, North American Indian Travelling
College**, and *Akwesasne Notes*. Porter had been invited to speak to various
audiences around the world on Haudenosaunee history and culture. In the middle
1990s, he moved with a number of Haudenosaunee (mainly Akwesasne Mohawks leaving disorder there) to **Canajoharie**, a site in the Mohawk Valley.

Porter played a central role in the Akwesasne Mohawks' traditional council,
the Mohawk Nation Council, before and during the violence that led to the
deaths of Mathew Pyke and "Junior" Edwards there on May 1, 1990. Porter
also was a leader in the spiritual and cultural revival of Akwesasne and an
advocate of environmental cleanup there.

In the early 1990s, Porter played a major role in acquiring land in the Mohawk
Valley that would host Mohawks migrating from Akwesasne, people who have
been made refugees by pollution, smuggling, and **gambling**. Proposals for a
migration to the Mohawk Valley were being aired when violence hit its height
in 1990. Porter was one of the moving forces behind the proposals, which called
the settlement Canajoharie (Kanatsiohareke) ("The Clean Pot" in Mohawk). He
envisioned it as an agriculturally based settlement that also would offer traditional spiritual teaching and combine the old ways with modern energy-
conservation technology.

FURTHER READING

Porter, Tom. New York State Assembly hearings, "Crisis at Akwesasne." Day 1 (Ft.
     Covington, N.Y.), July 24, 1990.

R

Red Jacket (Sagoyewatha) (Seneca), c. 1755–1830. Red Jacket, a nephew of **Handsome Lake**, was a major Iroquois leader during the late eighteenth and early nineteenth centuries. He was probably best known as an ally of the British in the **American Revolution**. Red Jacket's name as a young man was Otetiani, meaning "he is prepared." Later he took the name Sagoyewatha, meaning "he causes them to be awake." The name "Red Jacket" came from a scarlet coat given to him by the British for fighting with them during the American Revolutionary War.

Red Jacket's skills lay more in diplomacy than in the waging of war. After he fled the Battle of Oriskany in 1777, avoided battle at Wyoming Valley in 1778, and made an early exit at the Battle of Newtown in 1779, Red Jacket got a reputation as a coward. At another point during the American Revolution, Red Jacket killed a cow and smeared his tomahawk with blood to convince other Iroquois that he had killed a white man. Instead, **Joseph Brant** and **Cornplanter** ridiculed Red Jacket as a "cow killer."

After the war, Red Jacket reconciled his differences with the Americans, unlike Joseph Brant, who moved to Canada with a sizable number of **Mohawks** and other Haudenosaunee. In 1792, Red Jacket was among a number of Iroquois chiefs invited to Philadelphia to parley with George Washington. In the War of 1812, he fought with the United States against the British.

Regardless of his political allegiances, Red Jacket believed that Indians should retain their own lands and cultures. He sought and sometimes won extensive legal protection for reservation lands. Red Jacket's speeches in defense of native rights have been cited by generations of Haudenosaunee. One famous speech, given in 1828, was addressed to a representative of the Boston Missionary Society named Mr. Cram, who was requesting approval to recruit Iroquois to his faith.

Brother, listen to what we say. There was a time when our forefathers owned this great island. Their seats extended from the rising to the setting sun. The Great Spirit had made it for the use of Indians. He had created the buffalo, the deer, and other animals for food. He had made the bear and the beaver. Their skins served us for clothing. He had caused the earth to produce **corn** bread. All this he had done for his red children because he loved them. If we had some disputes . . . they were generally settled without shedding much blood.

But an evil day came upon us. Your forefathers crossed the great water and landed on this island. Their numbers were small. They found friends and not enemies. They told us they had fled from their own country for fear of wicked men. . . . They asked us for a small seat. We took pity on them, granted their request, and they sat down among us. We gave them corn and meat; they gave us poison in return. . . . they wanted more land; they wanted our country. . . . Wars took place. . . . You have got our country, but you are not satisfied. You want to force your religion upon us. . . . [But] we also have a religion which has been given to our forefathers and handed down to us, their children. . . . Brother, we do not wish to destroy your religion or take it from you. We only want to enjoy our own. (Waters, 54)

On another occasion, Red Jacket sarcastically told a "black-coat" (clergyman): "If you white people murdered 'The Savior,' make it up yourselves. We had nothing to do with it. If he had come among us, we would have treated him better" (Johansen and Grinde, 316).

In 1821, Red Jacket sent a letter to De Witt Clinton, governor of New York, enumerating the problems that the Iroquois were having with white settlers, including illegal cutting of timber on Indian lands, poaching of livestock, the death of fishing stocks because of dam building, and the decrease in hunting animals. "The greatest source of all our grievances is, that the white men are among us," Red Jacket concluded (Johansen and Grinde, 316).

In his last years, Red Jacket became alcoholic and was deposed as an Iroquois leader in 1827. The **antlers** of leadership were restored to Red Jacket shortly before he died on January 20, 1830, in Seneca Village, New York. He was memorialized with a statue erected in 1891 by the Buffalo Historical Society near the grave of Cornplanter. His grandson, **Ely S. Parker**, was buried in the same plot in 1897.

FURTHER READING

Armstrong, Virginia Irving, comp. *I Have Spoken: American History through the Voices of the Indians*. Chicago: Sage Books, 1971.

Hamilton, Charles, ed. *Cry of the Thunderbird*. Norman: University of Oklahoma Press, 1972.

Johansen, Bruce E., and Donald A. Grinde, Jr. *The Encyclopedia of Native American Biography*. New York: Henry Holt, 1997.

Red Jacket. *A Long-Lost Speech of Red Jacket*. Ed. J. W. Sanborn. Friendship, N.Y.: N.P., 1912.

Stone, William L. *The Life and Times of Say-go-ye-wat-ha, or Red Jacket*. Albany, N.Y.: Munsell, 1866.

Waters, Frank. *Brave Are My People*. Sante Fe, N.M.: Clear Light, 1993.

Removal and the Haudenosaunee. Unlike the Cherokees and other southeastern Native American nations, most of the Haudenosaunee successfully resisted
pressure to move to Indian territory (later Oklahoma) or Kansas when removal
became official U.S. government policy, beginning in 1830. Several hundred
Haudenosaunee did emigrate; many of them suffered the same degree of dep-
rivation experienced on a much larger scale by the Cherokees and others.

Beginning during the late fall of 1831, roughly 400 **Senecas** from the Sandusky, Ohio, area marched for eight months to lands assigned them in northeastern Indian Territory along the Cowskin River. The band marched during the
worst of an unusually cold winter and suffered many (officially uncounted)
deaths before arriving on July 4, 1832, only to find that some of the land they
believed that they would occupy had been assigned to Cherokees. Another band
of about 300, mostly Senecas and Shawnees from the Ohio country, arrived six
months later, having suffered more than 40 deaths along the way (Hauptman,
88).

Between 1846 and 1852, a smaller group, including 44 **Cayugas**, was moved
to assigned reservation land in Kansas after its members ceded their lands in
upstate New York to the Ogden Land Company in connection with the **Buffalo
Creek Treaty** of 1838. Most of them died within a few years of cholera, starvation, exposure to the cold, or a combination.

FURTHER READING

Hauptman, Laurence M. *The Iroquois in the Civil War: From Battlefield to Reservation.*
    Syracuse, N.Y.: Syracuse University Press, 1993.

Repatriation and the Haudenosaunee. Accompanied by members of a **Tonawanda Seneca** family to the National Museum of the American Indian (NMAI)
in the early 1990s, **G. Peter Jemison** realized one more reason to push for the
return of traditional medicine masks. "One of the masks had been identified by
a family member," said Jemison, chair of the Haudenosaunee Standing Committee on Burial Rules and Regulations (Jemison). The identified mask, along
with 462 others belonging to the Haudenosaunee, had been obtained by a number of collectors who at one time or another were trustees of or collectors for
the Museum of the American Indian (MAI) between 1898 and 1970. The major
collectors included Joseph Keppler, William Stiles, W. C. Bernard, George
Gustav Heye, Alanson B. Skinner, and Frank G. Speck. Keppler, who worked
with **Harriet Maxwell Converse**, bequeathed her collection of masks and **wampum** belts after her death in 1903 (NMAI, 22). Converse, who was adopted by
the **Senecas** in the late 1880s, also collected many cultural artifacts, much like
Lewis Henry Morgan, for the New York State Museum during the 1880s and
1890s.

In some cases, "the masks were sold by family members who had no right
to sell them," said **Doug George-Kanentiio (Mohawk)**, a member of the Board
of Directors of NMAI and chair of its Collections Committee (George-

Kanentiio). "Other masks were carved specifically for sale," added George-Kanentiio. "The physical proximity of the Iroquois and the cultural significance of the masks to the Iroquois were two reasons why George Gustav Heye collected them," said Richard West, Jr., director of the NMAI (West).

Asked why so many of the returned masks belonged to the Senecas, **Rick Hill (Tuscarora)** said, "The Senecas had no form of traditional governance to prevent the sale of them" (Hill). During the 1840s, some Senecas chose to adopt an elected form of government after having their traditional chiefs experience deceit and corruption at the hands of land companies. The Tonawanda Band of Senecas is the only Seneca community that maintains a traditional form of government with Clan Mothers and appointed chiefs. "At the turn of the century, the Haudenosaunee were in a state of transition," said George-Kanentiio, alluding to the flux many Haudenosaunee communities experienced with regard to religion, education, and adoption of Western lifestyles (George-Kanentiio).

"**William Fenton** also collected masks, and focused his study of them at **Allegany** and **Cattaraugus**, both Seneca communities," said Hill, a professor or American studies at the State University of New York (SUNY) at Buffalo (Hill). Fenton was affiliated with the New York State Museum and SUNY Albany's Department of Anthropology and was consulted regularly by the Board of Trustees of the MAI.

In 1981, when the Haudenosaunee first requested the return of all the masks held by the museum, the MAI held the largest collection of Haudenosaunee medicine masks in the United States (NMAI, 35). In November 1998, seventeen years after its initial request, and after five years of repeated visits and meetings with NMAI officials in New York City, the Haudenosaunee leadership, including Jemison's committee, welcomed home the 463 masks held by the museum.

"The masks were given to us by the Creator for our protection," said Jemison. "We have an obligation to bring them back and release them from where they are to help us" (Jemison). Jemison's committee took its lead from Haudenosaunee leaders and elders who in 1974 issued its policy on the status, sale, exhibition, and return of medicine masks and then began a concerted effort in 1975 to have the masks returned from the then Museum of the American Indian and what is now the NMAI.

The repatriation of the masks, including one that was used by **Joseph Brant**, was made possible by the federal law that created the NMAI in 1989 and recent amendments to the Native American Graves Protection and Repatriation Act (NAGPRA) initially passed by Congress in 1990. NAGPRA allows tribal officials, chiefs, and elders to inspect tribally affiliated items held in museums across the country. Once the objects are determined to be significant to tribal sacred rituals, museums have little recourse but to return the items.

The documentation process has proven to be a test of patience. "The burden of proof is on us," said Jemison. "How do we prove we were here, especially with a history that is oral?" (Jemison). It was the knowledge held by elders and family members able to recall family histories and events that provided the proof in this case. The museum's acquisition records helped further identify specific Iroquois Nation origins. That the Haudenosaunee were the only indigenous groups to use medicine masks in New York State further solidified the documentation.

An integral part of NAGPRA requires a museum to conduct an independent search of historical records to document the rituals of a tribe in order to justify a repatriation. If the rituals are deemed sacred and ceremonial and museum-held objects are required for ongoing religious practices, then typically a repatriation follows. The independent research also ensures that the cultural patrimony is returned to the proper tribal group.

The Haudenosaunee have had some success in using NAGPRA, but have also had to appeal to the ethical senses of museum directors during repatriation efforts. A case in point is the New York State Museum, which held a large collection of Haudenosaunee wampum belts. Beginning with Henry Carrington, a special agent for the 1890 federal census, the State Museum collected wampum belts that were used for the recitation of the **Great Law of Peace**. The museum also held wampum recording the first treaty between the United States and the Iroquois Confederacy at the end of the Revolutionary War (Sullivan, 9; Wolcott, 26). In 1899, the New York State legislature passed a law authorizing the State Education Department's Board of Regents, which oversees the State Museum, to obtain "by purchase, suit or otherwise any wampums in the possession of the Ho-de-no-sau-nee or any preceding wampum keeper" ("A Century Ago," A-1). This state law gave the State Museum the official title of "wampum keeper" (Sullivan, 9). "The Confederacy was under the impression that it gave only temporary custody of the wampum belts to the State Museum," said Ray Gonyea, a former curator of the State Museum (Gonyea). Changes in legislation and thus title to the wampum did not take place until the late 1980s.

Those changes began under the tenure of Martin Sullivan as director of the State Museum when he realized in 1983 that as director he was also the wampum keeper. Through the cooperative efforts of his office and the leaders of the Haudenosaunee, twelve of the twenty-six wampum belts held by the museum were returned to the Haudenosaunee in October 1989. Four of the most significant belts returned were the **Hiawatha Belt**, tracing the formation of the confederacy, the **Tadadaho Belt**, signifying the principal leader of the Haudenosaunee, the **Wing or Dust Fan Belt**, used in convening the council of chiefs, and the **Washington Covenant Belt**, which recorded the first treaty between the United States and the Haudenosaunee (Sullivan, 9). At present, the Haudenosaunee leaders continue to request from the State Museum the return of the remaining belts.

After its first request to the MAI in 1968 for the return of wampum, the Haudenosaunee in 1996 welcomed home the wampum held by that museum. Included in the collection were seventy-three pieces of wampum and wampum strings used to convey specific announcements or events, and a small number of wampum belts (Gonyea). The very first wampum return took place in Six Nations at Ohsweken in Ontario in 1988 from the Royal Ontario Museum.

"There is still some skepticism among museums," said Jemison. "With repatriation looked upon positively by most, museums now wonder how they are going to tell our story" (Jemison). With the burden of proof on Native peoples, it is their history and recollections via oral-history accounts that have given many museums a new understanding of specific tribal groups. One could conclude, at a practical level, that both parties benefit under the cloak of NAGPRA.

Cultural and/or sacred objects, such as masks, held by private collectors do not have to be returned under present law. In some instances, particularly with estate sales, such items are put up for auction. This was the case with a small collection of Haudenosaunee medicine masks in 1993. Alerted to the auction by the American Indian Ritual Object Repatriation Foundation (AIRORF), which monitors the two major auction houses in New York City (Sotheby's and Christie's), the confederacy sent delegates to Sotheby's. "When the masks were put on the auction block," said Jemison, "four Confederacy Chiefs walked into the auction room and sat down. No one bid on the masks after that" (Jemison). With the help of the AIRORF, the owner of the masks donated them to the AIRORF, which then returned them to their original owners, the Tonawanda Band of Senecas (Martin, 27). The AIRORF, considered controversial by some in the repatriation field, offers anonymity and a tax deduction to private owners as incentives for the return of sacred objects.

There are, however, anthropologists and museums across the United States that refuse to remove from display or return indigenous human remains, despite the fact that the study of human remains has not resulted in any new understanding of indigenous people in many decades (Mihesuah, "American Indians," 230). While the return of remains is a contentious issue even among tribal groups across the country, the Haudenosaunee have agreed to rebury in their traditional territory the human remains of tribes whose customs prohibit acceptance of their deceased members (George-Kanentiio). In the fall of 1998, the Mohawk Nation at **Akwesasne** culminated a few years of work with the Museum of Civilization in Hull, Québec, to repatriate eighty-five Mohawk human remains. Found near Prescott, Ontario, and dated to be at least 500 years old, the remains were buried in Akwesasne territory (Mitchell).

"The amount of human remains in museums is staggering," said Jemison about deceased Haudenosaunee members. Across the country, approximately one million Indian remains, with a diversity of tribal affiliations, are currently held in public and private institutions (Mihesuah, "Introduction," 153). Human remains are the next priority for Jemison's committee, a priority that will force Jemison and others to further confront stereotypes and institutional racism. "It's difficult to not be emotional," said Jemison, "but you have to contain that to be effective. You have to go with a good mind" (Jemison).

Among the human remains that Jemison's committee hopes to repatriate is a

Bureau of Indian Affairs collection containing 438 Haudenosaunee remains and the 110 associated funerary objects found with the remains. With each repatriation, the Haudenosaunee clearly are gaining new avenues to relearn and practice traditional customs. "The return of the masks and the wampum allows people to hold on, to understand the culture even more," said George-Kanentiio (George-Kanentiio). Certainly, with the restoration of ceremonies and rituals, each community has an opportunity to spiritually strengthen itself.

Jemison and members of his committee clearly took pride in their work as the truck carrying the masks and escorted by federal marshals rolled up to the Onondaga Nation Longhouse. "When I deliver the mask belonging to the Tonawanda family which identified it, then I will feel as if I have accomplished something," said Jemison (Jemison). The return of the masks also is viewed as a harbinger of greater objectives. "The long range plan is for the NMAI to return major things and hope that other museums see the positive impact repatriation has on the people," said Gonyea (Gonyea).

FURTHER READING

"A Century Ago: Call to Preserve All Wampums." *Post-Standard* (Syracuse, N.Y.), January 30, 1999, A-1.

George-Kanentiio, Doug. Personal communication, November 12, 1998.

Gonyea, Ray. Personal communication, July 5, 1996.

Hill, Rick. Personal communication, July 5, 1996.

Jemison, G. Peter. Personal communication, July 5, 1996.

Martin, Kallen M. "The Beginning of Respect." *Native Americas* 14:3 (1997): 24–29.

Mihesuah, Devon A. "American Indians, Anthropologists, Pothunters, and Repatriation: Ethical, Religious, and Political Differences." *American Indian Quarterly* 20:2 (Spring 1996): 229–237.

———. "Introduction, Issue on Repatriation." *American Indian Quarterly* 20:2 (Spring 1996): 153–164.

Mitchell, Joyce. Personal communication, November 20, 1998.

National Museum of the American Indian, Smithsonian Institution, Repatriation Office. Haudenosaunee (Iroquois) Medicine Mask Repatriation Request, May 5, 1998.

Sullivan, Martin. "Return of the Sacred Wampum Belts of the Iroquois." *History Teacher* 26:1 (1992): 7–14.

West, Rick, Jr. Personal communication, July 5, 1996.

Wolcott, Fred R. *Onondaga: Portrait of a Native People.* Syracuse, N.Y.: Syracuse University Press, 1986.

Kallen Martin

Rickard, Clinton (Rowadagahrade) (Tuscarora), 1882–1971. Clinton Rickard, a **Tuscarora** sachem and elder, was best known nationally as a founder of the Indian Defense League of America in 1926. This group, which based its work on the inspiration of **Deskaheh**, the **Cayuga** chief who took the Iroquois Confederacy's assertions of sovereignty to the League of Nations during the 1920s, was formed to resist erosion of Native American lands and rights. At a time when American Indians were being told that they were members of a "vanishing race," Rickard, in the words of Barbara Graymont, "taught Indians to be proud of being Indian, to honor their traditions and appreciate their culture" (Graymont 48.)

Rickard was born on the Tuscarora Reservation near Niagara Falls, the third son of George and Lucy Rickard. He joined the U.S. Army as a young man and saw service in the Philippines between 1902 and 1904; he sailed around the world going to and from this duty base. While in the Philippines, Rickard contracted malaria, attacks of which recurred during the rest of his life.

Returning to his homeland, Rickard married his first wife, Ivy, in 1904. He worked as a farm laborer and at a limestone quarry, where he became a foreman. He also was inducted into the Masonic Order. Ivy died in 1913, after which Rickard married his second wife, Elizabeth, who sometimes handled his correspondence as Rickard became more deeply involved in the affairs of the Tuscarora Nation as a chief after 1920. Rickard became a chief of the Beaver Clan on Tuscarora's national council, where he was called Rowadagahrade, meaning "Loud Voice." He also became a student of the U.S. Code and treaties. At this time, Rickard was especially active in efforts to reduce non-Indian poaching of Tuscarora timber and to enforce border-crossing rights guaranteed under the **Jay Treaty** of 1794.

In 1926, Rickard and several associates formed the Indian Defense League of America (IDLA), a group advocating Indian rights mainly by legal means. Rickard was instrumental in winning recognition of Haudenosaunee border-crossing rights, along with exemption from an immigration fee that had made cross-border trade almost impossible for many Haudenosaunee people. Rickard and the IDLA organized letter-writing campaigns and political demonstrations in the United States for rights based on the Jay Treaty. He also became a close friend of the Six Nations *Tadadaho* Deskaheh.

Rickard's second wife, Elizabeth, died in 1929 at age thirty-two of a stroke after giving birth. During the 1930s, his health suffered from grieving, recurring malaria, and health problems brought on by rough treatment by Canadian authorities while he was jailed there. During the depression, much of Rickard's energies went into providing emergency relief for Tuscaroras and other Native peoples who were devastated by the depression. Rickard also married a third time.

After World War II, Rickard was active in opposition to termination proposals and provided leadership to Tuscaroras against the New York Power Authority's proposals to flood part of the reservation under a reservoir that was part of expanded power-producing facilities at Niagara Falls. He continued to be active in legal issues, often aided by his son and ally William, who died in 1964 of acute emphysema. In his later years, Rickard paid special attention to the preservation of the Tuscarora language.

The IDLA was among the first Indian defense groups to use treaties as a defense of Native American lands and cultural integrity, presaging renewed activism that began in the 1950s with **Wallace "Mad Bear" Anderson** (who also was active in the IDLA) and in the 1960s with fishing-rights protests in Washington State, the occupation of Alcatraz Island, and the formation of the American Indian Movement. Rickard's activism was conducted in a context of official assimilationist policies that attempted to dissolve traditional Iroquois governments in both the United States and Canada. Like the chiefs of the Haudenosaunee Confederacy's Grand Council, Rickard asserted nationhood for American Indian peoples to the point of refusing to accept U.S. (or Canadian) citizenship and voting rights. "How can you be a sovereign nation and be forced to be a citizen of a foreign government?" Rickard asked after the United States enacted American Indian citizenship in 1924 (Rickard, 50).

FURTHER READING

Graymont, Barbara, ed. *Fighting Tuscarora: The Autobiography of Chief Clinton Rickard.* Syracuse, N.Y.: Syracuse University Press, 1973.

Rickard, Jolene. "The Indian Defense League of America." *Akwesasne Notes*, n.s. 1:2 (Summer 1995): 48–53.

S

Sadeganaktie (Onondaga), c. 1640–1701. Sadeganaktie was probably Tada-daho of the Iroquois Grand Council late in the seventeenth century. He was known in Iroquois, British, and French circles as a spellbinding orator. On one occasion, in 1693, he became ill on the eve of an important conference in Albany; he was carried bodily from Onondaga (near contemporary Syracuse, New York) to Albany by his people on whose behalf he would speak. Upon Sadeganaktie's death in 1701, the **antlers** of office were bestowed on Sadegan-aktie's son, who shared the same name.

FURTHER READING

Johansen, Bruce E., and Donald A. Grinde, Jr., *The Encyclopedia of Native American Biography*. New York: Henry Holt, 1997.

St. Lawrence Seaway, effects on Mohawks. While the St. Lawrence Seaway brought economic prosperity to the non-Indian urban areas and industries that grew along its path, Native American peoples, mainly **Mohawks**, were devas-tated. The destruction of the Mohawks' lands and resources by construction along the St. Lawrence River was not new. As early as 1834, Mohawk chiefs told Canadian officials that control structures built to channel the flow of the St. Lawrence River near Barnhart Island were destroying important fish-spawning grounds. Environmental degradation in the Mohawk communities of **Akwesasne** and **Kahnawake** took a quantum leap after the late 1950s, however, when the St. Lawrence Seaway opened access to bountiful cheap power. Access to power drew heavy industry that soon turned some segments of this magnif-icent river into open sewers.

Construction of the seaway was begun during the summer of 1954. It was among the largest earth-moving projects in the history of humankind. More than 200 million cubic yards of earth were moved, and 6.2 million cubic yards of concrete were poured. Nine thousand people were relocated as 22,000 workers attended to the project at the height of construction (Hauptman, 133). July 1, 1958 is called "The Day of Inundation" by many Mohawks who were in the path of rising waters that flooded 40,000 acres of land, including ancestral cemeteries and twelve villages. The water level was raised eighty feet in some places, and the area's entire ecology was reshaped.

The Akwesasne area was home to many trappers before construction of the seaway devastated trapping areas and wetlands. To speed the melting of ice in the spring, the level of the river is raised and dropped very quickly so that air pockets caught in the water will pulverize the ice. The swirling, crushing action of water, ice, and air also floods muskrat and beaver hutches, killing their occupants. The animals drowned en masse, destroying the traditional trapping industry in the area.

The seeds of frustration among Mohawks and other Iroquois that gave rise to the **Warrior Society** were sown during the 1950s, when the governments of the United States and Canada ignored Native American protests against construction of the seaway. John C. Mohawk, a professor of Native American studies at the State University of New York at Buffalo, who is a **Seneca**, traces Mohawk frustrations from the time of first contact with Europeans intent on imposing their languages, cultures, and religions as they usurped Native lands. Ignoring Native complaints about the seaway fit finely during the 1950s with an official policy of "termination," under which Native reservations were to be broken down as Indians were absorbed into the "American mainstream" in both the United States and Canada.

Had the construction of the St. Lawrence Seaway shortly after World War II and subsequent industrialization of the area not destroyed traditional ways of making a living in Mohawk country, **gambling** and smuggling might never have emerged as avenues of economic survival there. The gambling and smuggling economy that grew up after the construction of the seaway produced armed conflict that resulted in the deaths of two Mohawks, Mathew Pyke and Harold Edwards, Jr., on May 1, 1990.

FURTHER READING

Alfred, Gerald R. *Heeding the Voices of Our Ancestors: Kahnawake Mohawk Politics and the Rise of Native Nationalism.* Toronto: Oxford University Press, 1995.

Andersen, Diana. "Toxics in the St. Lawrence: An Examination of the Problem." *Northeast Indian Quarterly* 5:3 (Autumn 1988): 16–18.

Gefell, Ann M. "River Recollections: Portraits of Life along the St. Lawrence River in the Twentieth Century." *Northeast Indian Quarterly* 5:3 (Fall 1988): 4–15.

Ghobashy, Omar Z. *The Caughnawaga Indians and the St. Lawrence Seaway.* New York: Devin-Adair, 1961.

Hauptman, Laurence M. *The Iroquois Struggle for Survival: World War II to Red Power.* Syracuse, N.Y.: Syracuse University Press, 1986.

Johansen, Bruce E. *Life and Death in Mohawk Country.* Golden, Colo.: North American Press/Fulcrum, 1993.

Ransom, James, and Henry Lickers. "Appraisals of Toxic Contamination at the St. Regis
    Mohawk Reservation." *Northeast Indian Quarterly* 5:3 (Fall 1988): 22–34.

Sakarissa (Tuscarora), c. 1730–1810. Sakarissa (meaning "Spear Dragger")
represented the **Tuscaroras** in several treaty negotiations following their migration from the Carolina country to western New York, where they were taken in
as the sixth nation of the Haudenosaunee Confederacy. He was a signatory on
the **Fort Stanwix Treaty** of 1768. As an elderly man, in 1805, Sakarissa helped
found the Tuscarora Congregational Church.

FURTHER READING

Johansen, Bruce E., and Donald A. Grinde, Jr. *The Encyclopedia of Native American
    Biography.* New York: Henry Holt, 1997.

Salamanca, New York, lease controversy. Between 1850 and 1870, expansion
of railroads in western New York caused a number of non-Indians to establish
homes in the town of Salamanca, more than 90 percent of which is on **Seneca**
land. The controversy over non-Indian leases in the town began in June 1850,
when the newly formed Seneca Nation of Indians leased a 145-acre right-of-
way along 11.66 miles of track of the New York and Erie Railroad for $3,000
(Hauptman, 117). The issue was not resolved legally until 1990 by an act of
Congress.

The village's first name was Hemlock. It was renamed for the Spanish duke
of Salamanca, who brought a large amount of stock in a local railroad. During
the 1860s, while many Seneca men were serving in the Union army during the
Civil War, their families raised necessary cash by leasing property in Salamanca
to immigrant whites. By 1870, the non-Indian population of the town was nearly
2,000 people. In addition to the New York and Erie, expansion of the Atlantic
and Great Western Railroad at about the same time made Salamanca a major
rail hub and brought non-Indian settlement and industry to the area.

In 1871, Judge George Baker of the New York Supreme Court ruled all of
these leases legally invalid because they violated the Trade and Intercourse Acts
(Non-intercourse Acts), passed by Congress between 1790 and 1834, which
stipulated that Indian land could not be alienated without the approval of the
federal government. By 1874, non-Indians in Salamanca were lobbying for such
action by Congress. As a result, Congress extended the original leases (many
of them at very low rental rates) in 1875 and 1890. In 1892, the same leases,
now more than 3,000 in number, were extended again, this time for ninety-nine
years. Because the leases were not adjusted for inflation, by the 1980s many of
them paid practically nothing in current dollars.

In 1942, the U.S. Supreme Court ruled against 800 non-Indian leaseholders
at Salamanca who had been delinquent in payments to the Senecas in *United
States v. Forness*. The defendants, Fred and Jessie Forness, had not paid the
token $4 a year required by their lease on property in downtown Salamanca for

eleven years, putting them $44 in arrears. The Court found that the Senecas did indeed have a right, like any other landlord, to cancel a lease that was several years in arrears.

In 1990, a year before the leases were set to expire, President George Bush signed the Seneca Nation Settlement Act, which provided the Senecas some compensation for past breaches of U.S. trust responsibility and adjusted lease rates closer to market values, with adjustments for inflation. By 1995, only 16 of roughly 3,000 non-Indian residents of Salamanca had not agreed to new lease terms. That year, federal prosecutors prepared eviction cases against the 16 people who refused to pay. Most ultimately paid the rent.

FURTHER READING

Hauptman, Laurence M. *The Iroquois in the Civil War: From Battlefield to Reservation.* Syracuse, N.Y.: Syracuse University Press, 1993.

Sayenqueraghta (Old Smoke) (Seneca), c. 1707–1786. During the French and Indian War and the **American Revolution**, Sayenqueraghta was one of the most respected of all the chiefs in the Haudenosaunee Confederacy. He also was said to have presented a commanding physical presence that complemented his booming voice. In council, Sayenqueraghta had voiced his doubts about **Joseph Brant**'s alliance with the British.

Sayenqueraghta spoke for the Six Nations at several treaty councils with the English between 1758 and 1775; he signed the Treaty of Easton in 1758 and treaties at Johnson Hall in 1759 and 1764, as well as at Fort Stanwix (1759). Although he was nearly seventy years of age during the American Revolution, Sayenqueraghta led **Seneca** forces during several battles, including Oriskany, Wyoming Valley, and Newtown.

FURTHER READING

Wallace, Anthony F. C. *The Death and Rebirth of the Seneca,* New York: Knopf, 1970.

Schuyler, Peter (Quider), 1657–1724. Peter Schuyler was one of Britain's foremost Indian agents. "Quider," the name used to recognize him among the Iroquois, also was an Iroquois name used for the British government in Albany. It was based on a **Mohawk** pronunciation of "Peter."

In 1678, Schuyler was appointed British representative to the Iroquois Confederacy. He kept the Iroquois from uniting against the English in support of the French in King William's War (1689–1697). Schuyler was Albany's first mayor after it was incorporated in 1686. He also served as acting governor of New York in 1719 and 1720, shortly before his death.

In 1710, Schuyler invited four Mohawks, including **Hendrick**, to the court of Queen Anne in London as part of a diplomatic offense to win Iroquois alliance from the French. The fact that all four were Mohawks was not coincidental, for the Mohawks were the best known of the five Iroquois nations to the English, the keepers of the Eastern Door of the longhouse, which opened at the British trading post of Albany.

FURTHER READING

Bond, Richmond P. *Queen Anne's American Kings*. Oxford: Clarendon Press, 1952.

Schuyler, Philip, 1733–1804. Grandnephew of **Peter Schuyler**, one of the first British Indian agents to the Iroquois, Philip Schuyler was born into a family that had become one of the wealthiest in America and probably the richest in Albany after Peter Schuyler was appointed the city's first mayor in 1686. Philip Schuyler fought in the French and Indian War (1754–1763) and became a major general in the Continental army during the **American Revolution**. He was a member of the Board of Indian Commissioners.

Schuyler was present on August 15, 1775, at an important meeting between colonial representatives and Iroquois leaders at **German Flats**. He attended this meeting as part of a delegation from the Continental Congress that was seeking Iroquois alliance during the coming American Revolution.

After the Battle of Saratoga, General Schuyler sent a **wampum** belt to the Six Nations, telling them of the great victory over Burgoyne and asking them to make peace with Congress. As the wampum belt made its way westward, pro-American Iroquois rejoiced and pro-English factions began to waver. At Cayuga, the Widow McGinnis seized the belt and had another one made that read more favorably for the British cause.

Under the Treaty of Paris (1783), Great Britain ceded to the United States a large area of land west of the Appalachians that was still largely occupied by Native American peoples, many of them expatriated Haudenosaunee. Schuyler argued (agreeing with George Washington) that a pell-mell rush of settlement should be restrained to forestall problems with the Native peoples in the area. This policy led to the negotiation of several treaties that were subsequently broken, the most famous being the **Fort Stanwix Treaty** of 1784 with the Iroquois. Schuyler served as U.S. representative from New York in 1789–1791 and 1797–1798; his daughter Elizabeth married Alexander Hamilton.

FURTHER READING

Gerlach, Don R. *Philip Schuyler and the American Revolution in New York, 1733–1777*. Lincoln: University of Nebraska Press, 1964.
Graymont, Barbara. *The Iroquois in the American Revolution*. Syracuse, N.Y.: Syracuse University Press, 1972.
"Proceedings of the Commissioners Appointed by the Continental Congress to Negotiate a Treaty with the Six Nations, 1775." Papers of the Continental Congress, 1774–89. National Archives, M247, Roll 144, Item No. 134. See Treaty Council at German Flats, New York, August 15, 1775.

The Second Epoch of Time: The Great Law Keeping. Iroquoian history falls into three main epochs: Creation, in the **First Epoch**; the **Great Law of Peace**, in the Second Epoch; and **Handsome Lake**, in the Third and Present Epoch of Time. The main figures of the Second Epoch were **Deganawida**, the hero of tradition, hereafter called the **Peacemaker**; *Jigonsaseh*, the Head Clan Mother; **Hiawatha**, the inventor of the condolence **wampum; and** *Adodaroh* (*Tadadaho*), the leader of the "enemy" faction.

During the Second Epoch, the *Kayánerénhkowa, Kayaněñsäko′ně* or *Gayaněsshä′′gowa* (Mohawk, Onondaga, and Seneca, respectively, for the Great Binding Law of Peace) was set in place to create the Five (later Six) Nation Confederacy. The original five nations founding the league were the **Senecas, Mohawks, Onondagas, Oneidas**, and **Cayugas**. These were later joined by the **Tuscaroras**, whose entry (a process) has been variously presented in Western texts as occurring in 1711, 1724, and 1735. In addition to the six full-member nations, many other nations, such as the Wyandots and the Delawares, were later incorporated in whole or in part through the process of **adoption**, sometimes militarily forced.

Antiquity of the League

The Keepers (oral traditionalists) have always maintained the great antiquity of the league, in stark contrast to Euro-scholars, a majority of whom have long tried to attribute the formation of the league to the pressures of European invasion and, consequently, have dated the founding of the league to the mid-fifteenth or mid-sixteenth centuries. Some European-American scholars, including Paul A. W. Wallace, have placed the founding of the league in the fifteenth century before the landfall of Columbus, that is, within a few years of contact with Europeans. In fact, the foundation of the league occurred much earlier and was caused entirely by Iroquoian internal pressures.

The *Jesuit Relations* of 1654 and 1691 recorded the Haudenosaunee telling the Catholic missionaries that the league had existed "de tout temps [from the earliest times]" (Thwaites, 41:86–87) and "de toute ancienneté [from all antiquity]" (Thwaites, 64:100–101). Chief **Jake Thomas**, a modern Keeper, claimed that the league was 3,000 years old, while Chief **Jake Swamp**, another modern Keeper, did not think that a founding date 2,000 years ago was out of bounds, although he placed it at 1,000 years ago (Mann and Fields, 114). In 1825, Keeper David Cusick dated the founding of the league to 1,000 years before the arrival of Columbus (Beauchamp, 16). In 1885, Keeper **Seth Newhouse** declared that the league predated the arrival of Columbus (Vecsey, 81). In 1997, Barbara Mann and Jerry Fields published a scholarly article, "A Sign in the Sky," that used Keepings, archaeology, history, and astronomy to date the league to the year 1142.

Conflicting Contents of Tradition

Many different—and sometimes profoundly different—Keepings exist concerning the identities, behavior, and deeds of the key individuals of the epoch.

Each Keeping has its modern adherents, and the contradictions in the versions they know sometimes lead to intense debate. Censorship is, however, a European invention. The Iroquois have never sought to dictate what people may hear or must believe; hence all versions are traditionally "correct." A spread of extant versions of the Keepings is therefore included in the presentation here. Although telling one overall story, this recital identifies the different versions, and who kept them, as it goes along.

The "collecting" methods of nineteenth- and many twentieth-century European-American ethnographers built a considerable skew into the written record. It should be kept in mind that nearly every extant Keeping that has come down to us in writing has been a men's story. The women's traditions were slighted by Western ethnographers, who did not realize that men and women kept their own traditions. Much of the women's version of what transpired has therefore been lost. Consequently, the story of the *Jigonsaseh* is much less well recorded today than the stories of either Hiawatha or the Peacemaker, although there are indications in works of **Arthur C. Parker** and **J. N. B. Hewitt** that hers was once a vibrant tradition.

There is also evidence that older traditions did not necessarily look like those that are recorded and/or maintained orally today. The most stunning departures from the standard modern traditions of the Great Law—and one of the strongest indications that many more versions once existed than were ever "collected"— are found in David Cusick's 1825 "Sketches of Ancient History of the Six Nations," one of the oldest written versions of the tradition of the law, as well as in Elias Johnson's 1881 rendition.

There is also strong evidence that the Haudenosaunee actively refrained from telling the tradition of the law to Europeans until the late nineteenth century. The names of the Peacemaker and Hiawatha might have been recorded as early as 1801 and 1816 (Vecsey, 91), but their importance to the league was not understood by Europeans until the twentieth century. **Cadwallader Colden** (1688–1776), who was well acquainted with the colonial history and structure of the league, was ignorant of its tradition. **John Heckewelder** (1743–1823), likewise well versed in the laws of the league and other traditions, never mentioned the story of its founding. **Lewis Henry Morgan** (1818–1881) made only one buried reference to the Peacemaker, whose importance he clearly did not comprehend, and otherwise demonstrated his total ignorance of the tradition of the Great Law (Morgan, 1:96). Since Morgan's ghost-writer for *The League of the Haudenosaunee* was the knowledgeable Seneca Häsanoan´da (**Ely S. Parker**), these omissions and distortions bespoke an Iroquoian intention of keeping the tradition from the Europeans.

Indeed, the identities, interrelationships, and actions of the figures of league tradition were so completely unknown to nineteenth-century European-Americans that Henry Wadsworth Longfellow, using execrable research by Henry Rowe Schoolcraft (Wallace, 1948, 396), wildly misconstrued Hiawatha not only as the Peacemaker, but as an Algonkin to boot, in his *Song of Hiawatha*

(1855). As late as 1892, the runaway popularity of *The Song of Hiawatha* among middle-class European-Americans led ethnographer William Beauchamp to note in some wonderment, "It is rather odd that what is now the most famous of Iroquois names"—he meant Hiawatha—"was almost unknown until little over half a century ago" (Beauchamp, 137). The true name and nature of the Peacemaker remained unknown to academics until scholars J. N. B. Hewitt (Tuscarora ancestry) and Arthur C. Parker (Seneca) brought them forward at the turn of the twentieth century.

The Traditions of the Great Law

Despite the great variety of extant league traditions, they all contain two sections: first, the story of the founders and their struggles to bring the league about; and second, a recital of the provisions of the Great Law, or Constitution, that resulted. Only the tradition of the struggle is presented here. For the provisions of the Great Law, see Fenton, "Seth Newhouse's [Dayodekane's] Traditional History and Constitution of the Iroquois Confederacy" (1949); Gibson, *Concerning the League* (Woodbury, 1992); and Parker, *The Constitution of the Five Nations* (1916). For a summary, see the entries **Governmental Functioning and Powers of the Haudenosaunee League** and *Gantowisas*.

The Struggle

All versions of the Second Epoch agree that it opened onto the tangled and ferocious landscape of war, although the nature of the war differs depending on the tradition. Some of the Keepings hold that the league was formed in self-protection against an outside military threat, while others state that a former unified identity had been forgotten, and the people had become fragmented, engaging in hostilities against those they no longer recognized as kin (Johnson, 45–52; Beauchamp, 16–17).

On the other hand, the women's Keepings retained by Arthur C. Parker, especially in "The Maize Maiden," indicate a war over subsistence methods in which agriculture, which had been brought from another nation (most likely the Wyandots), was being attacked by an older hunting culture. The farming culture of what Elizabeth Parker called "the Cultivators" eventually won a leading place in culture. Indeed, this tradition traced the establishment of the Green Corn Festival to the triumph of "the Maize Maiden" (*Jigonsaseh*) and "Corn Tassel" (the Peacemaker) over Black Lynx (*Adodaroh*) (Parker, "Maize Maiden," 191; Mann and Fields, 122–126).

Yet another explanation—typically the only explanation known to European-American academics—speaks of "blood feuding," or wars of revenge spiraling out of control, with no ideological component beyond the presumed bloodthirstiness of the combatants. The people as mindlessly "lustful for war" can be found in the Newhouse version, among others (Parker, *Constitution*, 16).

There are indications in the older recorded traditions that a confederation of some sort antedated the Haudenosaunee League as it is known today, and that this earlier confederation crumbled to bits during the bloody civil war of the

Second Epoch. Cusick stated that 2,200 years before Columbus (1,200 years before the present league), an older league had formed to promulgate a war of resistance against the "Emperor" of a "Golden City" that held a vast empire to the south. The Emperor was attempting to invade Iroquoia, igniting a defensive war that lasted a full century and finally ended favorably for the Iroquois (Beauchamp, 10–11). Elias Johnson (Tuscarora) recounted an early, rather weak confederacy, as well, among the "first six families" (nations), under the direction of Tarachiawagon (Johnson, 43).

These traditions may help explain the vast differences in league dating, especially Thomas's assertion of a 3,000-year-old league. The traditions also seem to fit in with the Earth-Grasper tradition that closed out the First Epoch by showing the people drawing together into councilmanically ordained clans for the preservation of peace (Hewitt, "Iroquoian Cosmology," 594–607).

Anomalous Traditions

In Cusick's version of the tradition of the Great Law, the only Second Epoch figure mentioned was *Adodaroh*, and he was the hero of the tale. According to Cusick, the Five Families (Nations) each began igniting their own council fires, without much regard to the others. Eventually, a war broke out among them, for reasons unspecified by Cusick. He did, however, note that *Adodaroh*, an Onondaga, was "the most hostile chief" active in this war, adorned, on head and body, by "black snakes." His eating bowls were made from the skulls of his enemies, and his spoons, from their bones. In the course of time, however, *Adodaroh* desired a change in his lifestyle, and this desire led him to ask the people to change his adornment. With white wampum (a peace emblem), they drove away the black (war) snakes and clothed him instead in the wampum. At that point, *Adodaroh* emerged as "a law giver, and renewed the chain of alliance of the Five Nations and framed their internal government, which took five years in accomplishing it [*sic*]" (Beauchamp, 16–17).

If all actors but *Adodaroh* were absent from Cusick's tradition, only Hiawatha appeared in Johnson's 1881 version, with the *Jigonsaseh* and *Adodaroh* appearing only at the end as bit players operating at Hiawatha's behest. According to Johnson, Hiawatha (whose name, he stated, meant "a wise man") was the reincarnation of Tarachiawagon into a human being, an Onondaga man. In Johnson's version, he married an Onondaga woman and fathered one greatly loved daughter. Hiawatha also set up governmental councils among the Five Nations, which were at peace with one another (Johnson, 45–46).

In Johnson's telling, the threat came from outside the Iroquoian world. A horde, previously unknown, but a "furious and powerful enemy from north of the great lakes," fell upon the Iroquois (as opposed to Cusick's "emperor" pushing up from the south). Hiawatha rallied a resistance force with the aid of his spiritually powerful "white stone canoe." Approaching a major war council in his canoe, Hiawatha and his daughter, who aided him in his labors, were stunned by the approach of an "immense" "Celestial" bird that, swooping down on the pair, seized the "Terrestrial and Celestial" daughter and bore her off to the skies, from whence she never returned (Johnson, 47–49).

In the Johnson version, Hiawatha, distraught by his loss, fell into a despair from which he was only roused by the dedicated labors of his Iroquoian friends. Ultimately, he came around and, resuming his role of political organizer, spoke the words that congealed the Five Nations into one league capable of fending off its northern enemies. The order given by Johnson made the Onondagas the "first nation," Fire Keepers; the Oneidas, the second nation and wise counsellors; the Senecas, the third and great speakers; the Cayugas, the fourth and shrewd hunters; and the Mohawks, the fifth and knowledgeable farmers and cabin builders. According to Johnson, Hiawatha then appointed the *Jigonsaseh*, or Head Clan Mother of the league, from a branch of the Senecas. The *Adodaroh*, "being considered next in wisdom" to Hiawatha, was appointed the Head Sachem of the league. The nations agreed to Hiawatha's terms, a confederacy was formed, and another great Sky Bird visited the assembly and rained snow-white feathers (emblems of peace) down on them (Johnson, 49–52). The Cusick and Johnson versions of the Great Law tradition are rather anomalous, at least as measured by today's better-known versions, which form the backbone of what follows.

The Peacemaker

Today's best-known traditions of the Great Law begin with the birth of the Peacemaker. On the pragmatic level, the Wyandots north of Iroquoia saw the vicious war that was raging to the south and were afraid that it might spread to them. On the spiritual level, Sapling, the Twin co-creator of the First Epoch, returned periodically to instruct and/or aid the people, often under the name Tarachiawagon, or Sky Holder. These two levels combined in the Second Epoch in the person of the league-era Peacemaker. He was a spiritual emissary who came to aid the Iroquois in their time of desperate need. "It is from the sky that he came with his mission," Gibson said (Gibson, 23).

The Peacemaker was absolutely not Hiawatha. He was, instead, a Wyandot who lived north of Lake Ontario and west of Iroquoia. He was later adopted by the Mohawks. Newhouse placed his homeland near the town of Kahanayenh (Tkahaánaye) on a nearby hill, Tironatharadadohn, on the Bay of Quinte, near the modern town of Kingston, Ontario (Parker, *Constitution*, 14, 65; Wallace, *White Roots*, 11).

All traditions present his birth as a spiritually guided event, often forecast in dream time. His Grandmother, Kahęto?ktha? ("End of the Field"), learned in a dream that he was to come through her daughter Kahętehsųk ("She Walks Ahead") on a great mission to the people (Gibson, 6–12; Parker, *Constitution*, 66; Wallace, *White Roots*, 11). In turn, Kahętehsųk learned through a dream of her son's mission to the tumultuous south, where he was to bring about a lasting peace among the *Ongwe Howeh* or Iroquois (Parker, *Constitution*, 14). In the Chiefs', Gibson's, and Newhouse's 1916 versions, the daughter and future mother of the Peacemaker was portrayed as a "virgin," a reference to certain versions of Iroquoian cosmology that presented the conception of the Twins as virginal. Some suspect that these references are evidence of missionary influence over traditional thought.

Newhouse said that despite their dreams, the women attempted to drown the infant. At the instigation of the grandmother, the daughter twice threw the baby into the lake through a hole in the ice. Both times, however, he was found comfortably at her breast in the morning. The third time, the grandmother herself attempted to dispatch the child, yet once more, he appeared on his mother's breast at morning's first light. It was at this point that the mother and daughter determined that their dream visions had been accurate and decided to nurture the child, in accordance with the instructions received in their dreams (Parker, *Constitution*, 14). Three was the traditional number of warnings, while the ability to overcome death, especially by water, was a sure sign of *uki*, or positive spirit power.

Gibson, however, in a version followed by Thomas, presented both Kaḥẹtoʔkthaʔ and Kaḥẹtehsųk as deeply loving and protective parents to the boy. At first, Kaḥẹtoʔkthaʔ was upset with her daughter for not naming the father of her child, and this made life miserable for both of them. A dream message soon set her straight, however, after which the two women anticipated the birth with happy expectation (Gibson, 3–13).

In due time, a healthy boy was born. He grew rapidly (another traditional sign of spirit power) and became a handsome youth who, as soon as he could speak, began telling people that it was not good to be unkind to one another (Gibson, 14). A Mohawk account stated that he had a double row of teeth that caused him to stutter badly and made him an object of derision (Howard, 431), although others claimed that his Wyandot dialect of Iroquois was only marginally comprehensible to the southern nations.

Newhouse said that the Peacemaker's own Wyandot relatives were abusive toward the young man out of jealousy "of his handsome face and good mind," but conceded that he was "a peculiar man" whose pacifistic philosophy the people did not understand (Parker, *Constitution*, 15). Gibson, on the other hand, showed the Wyandots as open to and appreciative of his messages, with the Clan Mothers calling assemblies specifically so that he might speak them (Gibson, 27–42).

When he came of an age to consider serious matters, the Peacemaker began his journey to the troubled Iroquois southeast of Lake Ontario in a traditional way, by paddling eastward across the lake in a "white stone canoe" (a reference to an ice floe hollowed out to navigate; Hewitt, "Constitutional League," 537). This was a particularly spiritual craft, modeled after one used by an earlier incarnation of Tarachiawagon (Johnson, 45). Although harboring her doubts that such a craft would float—"I love you, my child, but what are you doing in launching a stone boat?"—his grandmother and, in several accounts, his mother, as well, helped the Peacemaker launch his canoe and thus begin his great mission of peace to the south (Gibson, 54–59; quote, 55–56; Parker, *Constitution*, 67; Wallace, *White Roots*, 11). The fact that his stone canoe did not sink, but navigated, was taken as a sign that his words were spiritually inspired (Wallace, *White Roots*, 12).

When he alighted on the far shore of the lake, the Peacemaker was spotted by hunters, who were bedazzled by the light reflecting off his white stone canoe. For his part, the Peacemaker looked about at the desolate surroundings, taking the lack of fields as a sign that no settlements were nearby. The hunters said that they were refugees from the fighting. The Peacemaker immediately replied with his own message of Peace and then reentered his canoe in search of the settlements (Wallace, *White Roots*, 12).

Newhouse stated that the Peacemaker first approached the Mohawks, under whom he endured a physical trial to establish his credentials and his mission. Having explicated the cause of Peace, he offered to allow the Mohawks to attempt to kill him. If they succeeded, it would show that his mission was not spiritually guided. If they failed, it would prove that he was, as he claimed to be, a Sky emissary. Accordingly, the Peacemaker climbed a tall tree and sat amidst its top branches. The Mohawks cut the tree down and tumbled it over a cliff and into a body of water. No one believed that he could survive such a fall, but the next morning, the people saw the Peacemaker, hale and hearty, cooking his breakfast in his cabin. Ascertaining that the scouts had seen a living being and not a ghost, the Mohawks began whispering among themselves that he might indeed be able to bring forth the Great Peace (Parker, *Constitution*, 15–16).

Jigonsaseh

Many Seneca Keepers held that the Peacemaker's first dedicated stop was at the Peace House of That Great Woman, the Peace Queen, the Fire Woman, the Mother of Nations, Yegowaneh, whom Elizabeth Parker called the leader of "the Cultivators" (Parker, *Life*, 17, 46). Hewitt described her as a cofounder of the league, of the same rank as Hiawatha, an "equally astute stateswoman" (Hewitt, "Some Esoteric Aspects," 322). In many versions, including one kept by Corbett Sundown (Seneca), she was Seneca; in others, including one told by Jake Thomas, she was a Neutral, that is, a nation later adopted into the Senecas (Jemison, 69).

According to Elizabeth Parker, Yegowaneh's land had not yet been dragged into the great civil war then raging, but her territory, a neutral portion of Seneca land, was regularly crossed by soldiers from both sides of the dispute on their way to battle. Yegowaneh provided food for the war chiefs of both sides (an ancient obligation of the Peace Woman) and lectured them as they ate on their duty "to follow the paths of peace." She reminded the warmongers that everyone involved was, ultimately, Iroquoian and, therefore, kin (Parker, *Life*, 45).

When the Peacemaker entered her **longhouse**, she brought him food and then, after he had eaten, asked him his business, a customary duty of Clan Mothers in general and of the Peace Woman in particular. She listened intently as he replied with a long description of his peace mission and its three parts, *Ne"* *Skĕñ'no"*. (Health), *Ne" Gai'i·hwiio* (Righteousness), and *Ne" Găshasde"'sä'* (Popular Sovereignty). Each of these three elements was split into its two complementary halves. *Ne" Skĕñ'no"*. (Health) meant physical and mental well-being, on one hand, and peace among men and women, on the other. *Ne"* *Gai'i·hwiio* (Righteousness) meant behaving well while advocating goodness, as well as embedding social justice in the apportionment of civic rights and duties. *Ne" Găshasde"'sä'* (Popular Sovereignty) meant observing the sacred will of the people and also the organized civic and/or military power to enforce it (Hewitt, "Some Esoteric Aspect," 322); Hewitt, "Constitutional League," 541; Wallace, *White Roots*, 13–14).

Yegowaneh agreed that these were excellent principles, but asked how the Peacemaker intended to put them into political practice in real life. He answered that this should be done through the longhouse (i.e., through the ancient clan structure) under the direction of the Clan Mothers, who were to hold power over the elective male chiefs. The clan representatives of the Five Nations were to group together in one figurative *Kanonsiónni*, or Longhouse of the Nations, that would function through thought (councils), not war. Yegowaneh immediately accepted this plan, thus becoming the first influential person to enter into the Peace Plan. In recognition of her wisdom, the Peacemaker renamed her *Jigonsaseh* (Wallace, *White Roots*, 14).

In some versions, the *Jigonsaseh* volunteered of her own accord to stop feeding the passing war parties (Wallace, *White Roots*, 14; Parker, *Constitution*, 71). In others, the Peacemaker asked or gently told her to desist from feeding the soldiers, pointing out that because she fed them, they were able to go forth renewed in strength to commit future atrocities (Gibson, 91–92). Either way, upon her full commitment to the cause of Peace, the Peacemaker sent her on a mission to the east, that is, to the Mohawks and Oneidas (Parker, *Constitution*, 71). On the third day of her journey, she became a Peace Chief and a Speaker of the Good Message of Peace (Gibson, 93). She was a full partner in the cause of Peace, the Peacemaker's Speaker to the Women.

In "The Maize Maiden," *Jigonsaseh* taught the Peacemaker the farming ways of her people, explaining **corn** and its uses at length (Parker, "Maize Maiden," 189). Gibson also showed the Peacemaker closely questioning the guardians of the field concerning the crops, especially corn, and hearing, "Actually, it is our sustenance, the corn" (Gibson, 191–195; quote, 192). In the Chiefs' version, it was Hiawatha who was puzzled by the cornfields. He questioned a guardian of the fields as to their purpose. The guardian replied that he protected the fields from scavengers and enemies, "that our children might live from the harvest" (Parker, *Constitution*, 76). Throughout the traditions, Hiawatha and the Peacemaker are continually coming across guardians of the fields, who are always friendly to their message.

The *Jigonsaseh* was regarded in many traditions as the cosmic Mother, a reincarnation of the First Epoch Lynx, or mother of the Sacred Twins, who became Mother Earth. Chiefs Joseph Jacobs (Cayuga), David Skye (Onondaga), and David John (Onondaga) claimed that *Jigonsaseh* meant "She-Whose-Face-Is-Doubly-New," a reference to the pure face of a newborn babe, unsullied as yet by life (Hewitt, "Field Studies," 178). *Jigonsaseh* is also said to indicate the new leaves of corn emerging from the ground in the spring, another reference to rebirth, as the faces of spirits awaiting (re)birth are depicted as lying beneath the ground, in the womb of Mother Earth, smiling up at humanity.

Having joined the Peacemaker's cause, the *Jigonsaseh* worked tirelessly, often at peril of her life, to lobby for the cause of Peace among the warring factions. The Peacemaker would refuse to open meetings until she arrived (Parker, *Constitution*, 90; Gibson, 223, 229–230). Elizabeth Parker said that he consulted her "in every important detail" of their work and that, failing her approval, both Hiawatha's work and the principles of the league itself "could have been assailed." In short, she was "sacred to her people for her word was law and her sanction was necessary in all political measures" (Parker, *Life*, 46).

Hiawatha

The next important figure approached by the Peacemaker was Hiawatha. Numerous, often mutually exclusive, versions of Hiawatha's story cycle exist today, but not because any think him to be the Peacemaker. On the contrary, one set of versions introduces him as a cannibal and right-hand man of *Adodaroh*. Another set presents him as a wise and eager recruit to the Peacemaker's cause. The bulk of these traditions unite in presenting Hiawatha as the Peacemaker's handpicked Speaker to the men.

In the cannibal versions, most notably told by Gibson and Thomas, as well as by Paul Wallace in his version of tradition, Hiawatha was a dangerous man, to be approached gingerly. Hiawatha was said to have been born Onondaga; in other versions, he was merely said to have married into the Onondagas, becoming a valued chief himself. In some traditions, it was *Jigonsaseh* who advised the Peacemaker to approach Hiawatha. Most state that once he had determined to visit Hiawatha, the Peacemaker talked his intention over with *Jigonsaseh* before attempting this dangerous mission (Wallace, *White Roots*, 14).

Once sure of his purpose, the Peacemaker came upon the fearsome Hiawatha very cautiously, climbing up on the roof of his cabin and using it, first, as a good hiding spot, and second, as a good lookout point. After he had lain prone on his stomach, watching for hours, the Peacemaker's patience was finally rewarded when he spied Hiawatha in the dusk, dragging a human body home for dinner. He watched Hiawatha light the fire beneath his cooking pot. While waiting for it to boil, Hiawatha glanced into the pot from time to time, checking on its progress. At the same time, the Peacemaker was looking down through the smoke hole in Hiawatha's roof. Both of them looking into the pot simultaneously led to a comedy of errors, for the Peacemaker's face was reflected in the pot just as Hiawatha peered into it, causing Hiawatha to mistake the Peacemaker's reflection for his own (Gibson, 78–81; Thomas; Wallace, *White Roots*, 15; Vecsey, 84).

At this point, astonished by the physical beauty of the face staring back at him, Hiawatha staggered back, lingering momentarily to consider what he had just seen. It seemed to him to have been a vision. As a reality check, he reapproached the pot, peeked in again, and once more saw the magnificent face staring back at him, radiating deep wisdom. "It is an amazing thing that I am so handsome," he mused to himself (Gibson, 87). Hiawatha finally concluded that "this cannot be the face of a cannibal" (Thomas). He then put aside his former cannibalistic alliances, hauled his cooking pot out to an uprooted tree, and dumped its contents of butchered human meat out into the root hole (Thomas; Gibson, 87–88). At that point, the reformed cannibal felt very lonely and thought to himself, "Perhaps someone will come here, some stranger it may be, who will tell me what I must do to make amends for all the human beings I have made to suffer" (Wallace, *White Roots*, 15).

Sensing that the teachable moment had arrived, the Peacemaker jumped down from the roof, came around to the front of the cabin, and introduced himself. Hiawatha could hardly wait to tell his visitor of the transforming vision he had just had. Rather than explain the source of Hiawatha's vision, the Peacemaker launched instead into a discourse on his cause of Peace while the new friends went hunting, bagging a deer. Carrying the deer over his shoulders back to Hiawatha's lodge, the Peacemaker told him, "Deer is what humanity was meant to feed upon." Open to the message, Hiawatha was quickly enlisted in the Peacemaker's cause and was sent forth to the nations to call for an end to internecine warfare (Wallace, *White Roots*, 15–17; Gibson, 85–90). The Peacemaker foretold that Hiawatha would be the one to "comb the snakes out of Atotarho's hair" and that, for this reason, he would be called "Hiawatha, He Who Combs" (Wallace, *White Roots*, 17). In 1971, frustratingly unnamed "Mohawk informants" told Helen Addison Howard a much-abbreviated version of the same story that introduced Hiawatha briefly as "a man who eats humans," but who, upon meeting the Peacemaker, immediately went over to his side, becoming the "first convert and chief disciple" of Peace (Howard, 430).

The tale of how the Peacemaker and Hiawatha met is far less dramatic in those versions that do not recall Hiawatha as a cannibal. In the Newhouse version, Hiawatha and the Peacemaker did not encounter one another until near the end of the tradition, when they had to join forces to pacify *Adodaroh* and emplace the Great Law of Peace. Prior to that, each had been working independently for peace, with Hiawatha calling numerous councils among the Onondagas in hopes that his kinsfolk could help determine a way to calm down *Adodaroh*, who was causing great difficulty with his singular ways (Parker, *Constitution*, 17). In the Onondaga version told by Skanawati (John Buck), the Peacemaker did not encounter Hiawatha until after an angry *Adodaroh* had arranged for his family to be murdered. This telling likewise had the Peacemaker and Hiawatha working independently for peace long before they met (Hewitt, "Legend," 133–134).

In the Chiefs' 1900 version, the Peacemaker did not become acquainted with Hiawatha until after he had met both the *Jigonsaseh* and the *Adodaroh* (whom he reformed without the aid of either Hiawatha or the *Jigonsaseh*). Coming across a town he had not yet visited, the Peacemaker asked to meet the people's *Royaner* (or lineage chief) and found himself taken to the longhouse in which Hiawatha lived. Broaching the topic of his Peace cause, he discovered that the wise and beloved chief had already heard of it. In fact, from the moment Hiawatha had first heard the plan detailed, he had been unable to sleep for sheer excitement. At that moment, the Peacemaker named the chief Haiyo^{n}hwat'hǎ, meaning, it was said, "He has misplaced something but knows where to find it" (Parker, *Constitution*, 71).

The Chiefs continued that at this point, Hiawatha vouched for the Peacemaker, telling his people that the Peace plan was sound. The council was not entirely convinced, however. The main war chief asked how the plan would deal with the powerful nations east (Oneidas and Mohawks) and west (Senecas and Cayugas), who were not showing any signs of accepting the Peace. The Peacemaker stated that those nations had already accepted the plan. Still unconvinced, the war chief proposed the tree test of integrity, leading into the story earlier attributed by Newhouse to the Mohawks, and from which the Peacemaker escaped unscathed (Parker, *Constitution*, 72–73). Gibson repeated a similar story twice, since the triumph of the Peacemaker over death greatly guaranteed his credentials (Gibson, 109–21, 154–157). In one Gibson version, Hiawatha assumed the Peacemaker's place in the test (Vecsey, 84).

Hiawatha's Condolence Wampum

In all versions, Hiawatha lost his entire family, and this misfortune sent him into irretrievable, almost manic grief. The number of his daughters (one, three, or seven) and whether his wife was among the deceased depend upon the version at hand. The mysterious Tehyohrohnyohron, meaning the "high-flying bird which pierces the Skies" (Parker, *Constitution*, 75–76), figured prominently in most of the traditions of their deaths.

In the Buck version, *Adodaroh* wished to crimp the political opposition of Hiawatha so badly that he resorted to his usual murderous means. Spotting Hiawatha's best-loved and pregnant daughter out gathering firewood, *Adodaroh* directed the gathering council delegates' attention to the Sky, where they saw "a beautiful creature" coming in for a landing near to where the young woman stood. As the people raced past one another for a better look, they trampled the daughter to death. She was the last of Hiawatha's surviving children, and her loss threw him into deep mourning (Hewitt, "Legend," 133).

In Gibson's and the Chiefs' versions, the townsfolk noticed something in the Sky in the middle of a **lacrosse** game that had been called to lift Hiawatha's spirits, which were flagging due to the deaths of all but one of his daughters. As the teams watched, the Great Blue Bird came "down steadily from on high." (Blue was the color of Sky, hence sacred spirit, and was often tricky or selectively invisible.) In an attempt to capture the beautiful but unknown thing while it was flying very low, the excited crowd chased it, colliding with Hiawatha's remaining, pregnant daughter, who died shortly afterwards (Gibson, 137–138; Parker, *Constitution*, 75).

In Newhouse, the seven beloved daughters of Hiawatha were assassinated in a conspiracy hatched by the Peace camp. The plotters reasoned that cutting all of Hiawatha's emotional ties to Onondaga would push him out into the wider world to fulfill his larger destiny. They hired the powerful shaman Ohsinoh to work *uki/otkon* in their favor (Parker, *Constitution*, 18–19) (*Uki* is the positive aspect of medicine; *otkon*, the negative aspect. They are complements, not polar opposites.) In yet other versions, Hiawatha's three daughters died in quick succession of a mysterious illness, while it was his wife who was trampled to death in the panicked stampede to see what had come to land from Sky World (Wallace, *White Roots*, 20).

However he came to be so bereft, through the machinations of *Adodaroh*, the intervention of the Peace camp, or the spiritual presentation of a Sky sign, Hiawatha lost his bearings for some time, bowed down to the ground with unbearable grief. It was at this point that he "split the sky" (or "split the heavens"). **William Fenton**'s oft-cited gloss of "split the sky" to mean "I am deeply disturbed" is simply wrong. (Fenton was quoted by Woodbury in her translation of Gibson, 138 n.2.) The Split Sky is the north-south axis. When Hiawatha announced that he would "split the sky," he meant that he would travel the north-south axis, away from Onondaga and his anguish. Buck said that he traveled due south, as did Newhouse and others (Akweks, 10, 11; Hewitt, *Legend*, 133; Parker, *Constitution*, 19; Wallace, *White Roots*, 20).

Hiawatha was to languish in his profound despair for some time before realizing how to come to grips with such pain. No joy could penetrate his heart; tears fell continually from his eyes. As he plodded on, regardless of his surroundings, he passed the Tully Lakes. Seeing him coming, the ducks kindly responded to his request for aid by lifting the water above his head so that he might pass across the lake bed dry footed. It was then, as he crossed, that something caught his eye, sparkling in the sun—layers of shells. Stooping down, Hiawatha scooped them up and tucked them into his medicine bag. Once he had passed, the ducks replaced the water in the lake bed, while Hiawatha took and roasted three of their number for dinner. He named the place where he stayed Ohondogónwa, meaning "the Land of Rushes" (Parker, *Constitution*, 20; Wallace, *White Roots*, 20).

That evening, musing over his shells, Hiawatha took the handy rushes from around the lakeshore and made three strands of wampum, symbols of his sorrow. Each night, he would place a longer pole between two upright, notched sticks and drape the wampum over the horizontal bar. He cried aloud that should he ever meet anyone who was suffering the same depth of sorrow as himself, he would offer that person the condolence of the wampum, in which the words of comfort that accompanied each string would come true, sinking into the heart of the mourner to create a new and happier reality (Parker, *Constitution*, 21; Wallace, *White Roots*, 20–21).

In many versions, Hiawatha roamed the countryside for a long time camping, setting up his poles and wampum, and reciting his message. Hiawatha and his wampum became famous, but the people were not sure that his ceremony would work to comfort the bereaved. In the Chiefs' version, however, Hiawatha came rather quickly to a town where the Peacemaker was staying. Hiawatha sent a cornfield guardian to town with a message to his chief (the Peacemaker) that "the Good News of Peace and Power" had come. When the Peacemaker heard this message, he immediately went into the field to greet the stranger who spoke such words. Upon seeing that it was Hiawatha, the Peacemaker ordered him not to enter the town until he had been officially invited, by means of a woman, after he had cut and hung up his *o'go'rha* (Mohawk) or *o'tko'ä'* (Seneca)— strings of quills used as wampum (Parker, *Constitution*, 76–77).

The Chiefs' version continued that when the woman had identified Hiawatha the next morning, she hastened to tell the Peacemaker, who dispatched the war chief to escort Hiawatha into town. The war chief found Hiawatha sitting by his fire, staring at the three *o'tko'ä'* strings suspended from his pole. Three times (the traditional number of calls or warnings), the war chief summoned Hiawatha into town; three times, Hiawatha ignored him.

The Peacemaker was soon told of this puzzling behavior, but when he heard that Hiawatha sat mourning before his wampum, he understood the difficulty. Completing two more strings of wampum, he sent them to Hiawatha, who accepted his invitation wampum to enter town, where he delivered his Good Message of Peace. Their business in that town being finished, the pair left town suddenly, in the middle of the night, to travel to the next town. Some say that they departed in such haste because the townsfolk had not honored Hiawatha as they should have (Parker, *Constitution*, 77–79).

Gibson told a very similar version of this story, except that there was no rush to leave town, for Hiawatha was well received. Nor was the Peacemaker present at the town when he arrived. The chief issuing the invitation was not the Peacemaker. It was only after Hiawatha had spoken that the Peacemaker arrived. Thereafter, the two continued on their mission, journeying forth together (Gibson, 139–172).

Hiawatha's special mission of the condolence wampum was not yet completed, however, for having hung up his wampum for all to see, having explained its use, and having demonstrated its meaning, he had yet to be condoled himself on his great personal loss. The climactic moment of Hiawatha's story cycle arrived the day the Peacemaker went deliberately to the place where Hiawatha's smoke was seen to pierce the sky (a reference to prayer and tobacco smoke). Hesitating until he heard Hiawatha repeat his wonted plea, "This is what I would do if I found anyone burdened with grief," the Peacemaker stepped forward. Gently taking the wampum strings from his friend's pole and adding to them wampum he had made, the Peacemaker repeated, "string by string," the comforting words of the great **Condolence Ceremony**. He wiped the tears from Hiawatha's eyes; he made daylight for Hiawatha and covered the grave; he lifted the sorrow from Hiawatha's heart and cleared his mind (Wallace, *White Roots*, 21–22). This was the first Condolence Ceremony. The people nearby saw the Peacemaker perform the ceremony and the relief it afforded Hiawatha. Thereafter, they began using Hiawatha's condolence wampum to heal those in grief.

Adodaroh (Tadadaho)

In those versions in which Hiawatha accepted the Peacemaker's commissions, he dedicated himself to helping finalize the Peace. In a Mohawk version, Hiawatha sent out runners to call councils among all the Onondagas. The Adodaroh alone among the Onondagas remained unmoved by the Peace Plan. He even sought to impede Hiawatha's councils by making a habit of meeting canoeloads of delegates at the landing zones to stand imperiously in the way of the disembarking councillors. Three times, Hiawatha sent out runners, but after the first two delegations had been faced down by the *Adodaroh*, few councillors mustered the courage to respond to the third set of runners (Howard, 431). Other versions state that the runners had been sent by the Peacemaker himself, and that they went far beyond the borders of Onondaga, to the Adirondacks, Cherokees, Northern Wyandot Nations, Eries, Delawares, Shawnees, Miamis, Ottawas, and Sacs (Parker, *Constitution*, 80–81; Hewitt, "Legend," 146–147).

Well might the arriving delegates have feared *Adodaroh*. In those versions that are partially silent on the cannibals, he is merely presented as a bloodthirsty thug who did not hesitate to arrange for the assassination of his political enemies and/or members of their families (Howard, 431; Parker, *Constitution*, 19). In the more numerous versions that speak of cannibals, *Adodaroh* was frankly identified as one (Akweks, 15; Parker, *Constitution*, 17, 69). He was described by Newhouse and by Buck as "insane" or "mad," an "angry" man who "rage[d]" (Parker, *Constitution*, 17; Hewitt, "Legend," 134).

All traditions except Cusick's and Johnson's—and even they described him as fierce—presented *Adodaroh* as a horrifying presence, experienced in *otkon* (negative spirit power) and visually terrifying to look upon. The twisted convolutions of his mind were mirrored by the living snakes that he wove, writhing, into his hair. He wound yet more snakes around his body. His fingertips were mittens made of severed snake heads, their eyes still glaring at people as he gestured and pointed, his hands never still. His grossly enlongated, snakelike penis was wrapped around his waist like a python, in many loops (Thomas; Hewitt, "Legend," 136, 140; Gibson, 228; Parker, *Constitution*, 89; Wallace, *White Roots*, 18). Newhouse stated that for terror's sake, the Onondagas "satisfied his insane whims," hinting at his cannibalism (Parker, *Constitution*, 17).

Due to the obdurate recalcitrance of *Adodaroh*, who held out long after all others had agreed to the Peace, some (mostly Western ethnographers) say that the Onondagas were the last nation to come to the council. *Adodaroh*, however, was only one Onondaga and not the nation. Thus the traditional claim is that the Senecas were the last nation to ratify the Peace plan.

The Reluctant Senecas

Singly and together, the Peacemaker, Hiawatha, and *Jigonsaseh* traveled throughout Iroquoia, tirelessly carrying the message of Peace. They frequently commissioned runners from among their supporters to announce meetings they had called to press for Peace. These runners shape-shifted into swift and far-sighted hawks (Gibson, 203) or crows (Hewitt, "Legend," 135). At each meeting, more people came over to the cause of Peace, until a majority of the people favored it.

In many versions, the Senecas were the holdout nation, reluctant to come over to the Peace cause (Parker, *Constitution*, 25–26). In these versions, a place of great honor is reserved for a chief known as Sganyadaí:yoh, or **Handsome Lake**, the first—and, for a long time, along with his speaker, the only—Seneca to join the cause of Peace (Gibson, 213–221). In these versions, the Seneca Nation was convinced by a spectacular display of Sky *uki* arranged by the Peacemaker, who promised that he would deliver "a sign in the sky" to them. As kept by Aren Akweks (**Ray Fadden**, Mohawk) and Torewawaguhn (George Nash, Mohawk), the sign, a "black sun," or total eclipse, did occur, persuading all of the Senecas to join the cause of Peace (Wallace, "Return," 399; Mann and Fields, 135–149).

In an alternate version, the Senecas were enticed into the league by the *uki* power of the Peace Song, sung by the combined representatives of the Mohawks, Oneidas, Onondagas, and Cayugas as they crossed Canandaigua Lake, traveling to the recalcitrant Senecas. In this telling, it was the Peace Song (and the sight of numerous singers) that persuaded the Senecas to lay down their arms and agree to enter the league (Wallace, *White Roots*, 23).

The Transformation of Adodaroh

The final moment of tradition is usually presented as the dramatic transformation of *Adodaroh* from a dangerous madman into a valued member of the community, although not all traditions contain such a section. In the Chiefs' version, for instance, *Adodaroh*, not Hiawatha, was the fearsome cannibal re-formed when he mistook the Peacemaker's reflection in his cooking pot for his own handsome face, so that *Adodaroh*'s transformation happened early in the recital (Parker, *Constitution*, 69–70). As the Chiefs told it, the holdout at the end who made the lake fronting the final council impassable, was actually Odatc"'te', a principal Oneida chief (Parker, *Constitution*, 82). In the Johnson and Cusick versions mentioned previously, *Adodaroh* was never the main threat in the first place.

However, the best-known versions today all close with the three Peace leaders, Hiawatha, *Jigonsaseh*, and the Peacemaker, joining forces to reform the diehard Onondaga chief, *Adodaroh*, who continued resisting the message of Peace long after all the other representatives of the Five Nations had agreed to enter the league. In several versions, the Peacemaker and Hiawatha arrived at the final council before *Jigonsaseh*, whose tardiness worried them, the implication being that her safety was at stake. The two men knew that they could not conduct the final business of establishing the league without her, and presumably, so did *Adodaroh*. Thus the men feared that he had caused some great harm to befall her. However, her canoe was finally spotted paddling down the river to the council grounds (Gibson, 223–224; Parker, *Constitution*, 88, 90).

In some versions, before the final business could be conducted with *Adodaroh*, preliminary meetings had to take place to hammer out the final form and content of the Great Law. Buck said that constitutional "matters" were put into wampum as they were agreed upon (Hewitt, "Legend," 135). Newhouse stated that the Peacemaker proposed the form of corresponding chiefs and Clan Mothers, with Hiawatha approving it (Parker, *Constitution*, 27). However, Newhouse left something out: the women's part in the council. Elizabeth Parker supplied that. She was emphatic that the *Jigonsaseh* was consulted on the final form of the Great Law and that without her "sanction" of Hiawatha's "plans," neither the "integrity" nor the "principles of the confederacy" would have stood. With the Clan Mothers' rights fully guaranteed, she acceded to the plan (Parker, *Life*, 46; Jemison, 69). The Chiefs likewise agreed that the *Jigonsaseh*, "this great woman our mother," had approved the plans (Parker, *Constitution*, 91).

Having designed and voted on the form of the proposed league, the delegates still had to bring *Adodaroh* into the circle of **consensus** if the Great Law were to be legally emplaced. The challenge was to "straighten and reconstruct his mind, so that he m[ight] again have the mind of a human being" (Hewitt, "Legend," 135). Central to the success of this effort was the *Athahino^n'ke*, mentioned in several traditions. The Cayugas say that *Jigonsaseh* taught it to the Peace camp. Newhouse referred to it as "the Peace Hymn," although Buck called it "the Six Songs," that is, there were six verses (Parker, *Constitution*, 27, 28; Hewitt, "Legend," 137, 138). A song of **thanksgiving**, it expressed gratitude to the war chiefs, the Clan Mothers, the elders, the ancestors, Peace, and the people/league (Vecsey, 87; Hewitt, "Legend," 139). When it was sung properly, it had the power to calm the mind of *Adodaroh*, making him receptive to transformation (Parker, *Constitution*, 24).

Adodaroh may have been insane, but he was also clever and aware of his own best political interests. Therefore, it was necessary to draw him in with an offer worthy of his stature as primary chief of the Onondagas. Thomas said that it was the *Jigonsaseh* who designed the compromise package that was to prove acceptable to the statesman in *Adodaroh*. Under her terms, the Onondagas (his nation) were to be the Fire Keepers of the league. They were to have fourteen chiefs in the men's council, more than any other nation. Of course, since *Ado-*

daroh was the principal chief already, this offer meant that he would become the first Fire Keeper of the league (Gibson, 231).

Armed now with a song and a plan, the Peacemaker and Hiawatha sought to cross the lake to where *Adodaroh* sat glowering at them. The pair did not travel alone, but took with them the assembled delegates of the Five Nations to impress upon *Adodaroh* just how far out of consensus he stood—a powerful argument in Iroquoian culture (Gibson, 222; Parker, *Constitution*, 91). Getting physically close to *Adodaroh* was difficult, however, because he was able to command the elements. Ominously, the Peace delegates could hear *Adodaroh* shouting across the distance, taunting them. On the first and second approaches of the delegation, *Adodaroh* called the winds up to tornado force, but the Peacemaker cried, "Rest, wind!" and "Stop, wind!" Instantly, the air was becalmed (Gibson, 222–232; Wallace, *White Roots*, 24–25). Some versions dispense with the windy crossing and merely hold that the delegation came singing upon *Adodaroh*, instantly effecting "a radical change over his mind" (Hewitt, "Legend," 138).

At this juncture, the Peacemaker was growing truly anxious over the absence of *Jigonsaseh* and repeatedly asked those about him if she had yet arrived. He refused to continue the proceedings without her. Finally, it was reported to him that she had come. He personally went back in a canoe to ferry her across to the capstone council himself. The moment he beached his canoe, she "got in and stood up in front" while Hiawatha and other delegates paddled back to the place where *Adodaroh* sat (Gibson, 229–230; Parker, *Constitution*, 89–90).

Now the Peacemaker and Hiawatha set about retransforming *Adodaroh* into human shape. In both the Buck and the "Newhouse" (Dayodekane's "Cosmogony" attributed to Newhouse) versions, using his own *uki* powers and presenting wampum with each address, the Peacemaker first righted the misshapen body of *Adodaroh*, changing his feet from bear claws into human feet and his hands from turtle claws into human hands, before attempting to clip his elongated penis down to the span of one man's hand. In this final effort, the Peacemaker was unsuccessful, for even as he clipped the penis short, it grew back to its former length. After the Peacemaker's third, failed attempt to shorten the penis, the assembled chiefs intervened, taking away the "potency" of *Adodaroh*'s penis, that is, "its ability to kill persons." Turning to the Peacemaker, they assured him that it would "make no more trouble" (Hewitt, "Legend," 136, 139–140; Fenton, 149).

The Gibson version was far less graphic, however, merely describing the Peacemaker addressing *Adodaroh*, quieting the writhing fingers, smoothing down the moving hair, and resetting his face into human contours (Gibson, 233–235). In other versions, once the body of *Adodaroh* had been straightened by the Peacemaker, the mind of *Adodaroh* was smoothed by Hiawatha, who "combed the snakes out of his hair" (Wallace, *White Roots*, 25). "Combing out the hair" is an Iroquoian metaphor that means two different things: (1) to untangle the confused and hostile thoughts of someone who is in moral or mental chaos; or (2) to interpret the visions and/or dreams of another, combing out their spiritual meaning. In combing out *Adodaroh*'s hair, Hiawatha was doing both, for it was not only the ethical mind of *Adodaroh* that was twisted, but his spiritual faculties as well. Thus did Hiawatha earn the name "He Who Combs" (and not, as is sometimes erroneously written, "He Who Makes Rivers").

Once the mind and body of *Adodaroh* had been set straight, the Peacemaker asked *Jigonsaseh* to set the deer **antlers** of office on his head, a public demonstration of her approval of the proceedings. She did, and her act inaugurated the league (Gibson, 237; Parker, *Constitution*, 91). Gibson recorded that she then officially crowned the remaining chiefs of the new Grand Council one by one as the Peacemaker called each forward to receive his badge of office (Gibson, 241–250). With the *Jigonsaseh*'s consecration of the officials of the league, the Peacemaker recited the Great Law for all to hear.

The names *Adodaroh* and *Jigonsaseh* transformed into position titles that were transmitted in perpetuity through matrilineages of the Onondaga (*Adodaroh*) and Seneca (*Jigonsaseh*) nations. The Head Fire Keeper of the men became the *Adodaroh*, while the Head Fire Keeper of the women was the *Jigonsaseh*, or Head Clan Mother, of the league. The names of other notable leaders of the time, such as Saganyadaí:yoh (Seneca), likewise transmuted into the position titles of the offices they held in the new league. For a list of the titles of the men's Grand Council, see Morgan (1:60–61). Perhaps the only comparable list of Clan Mothers' titles that was ever collected exists on pages 139 and 190–191 of the as-yet-unpublished, handwritten Dayodekane manuscript, a microfilm version of which exists at the Smithsonian Institution (Fenton 150, 152). If Dayodekane was Newhouse, he was in a position to know those titles well, because Newhouse was the women's speaker to the Grand Council (Fenton, 157).

The Farewell Prophecy

His mission finally completed, the Peacemaker bade farewell to the people, leaving them with a frightening prophecy that warned them never to disagree heatedly with one another, for in a time yet long distant, the White Panther, that Fire Dragon of Discord, would fall upon the people and take away their "rights and privileges." In that grim time, he said, the people were to hold fast to one another, offering each other support, not opposition. Although the oppressor would mock them, saying, "You were a proud and haughty people once," and kick aside their "heads with scorn," the people of the league would avenge themselves before all was said and done (Parker, *Constitution*, 103–104).

In the end, the Peacemaker quietly returned home to Quint Bay to live out his remaining years. His Wyandot brothers had long waited to see him again. One day, to their surprise, they saw him peering around a tree at them. According to Jake Thomas, he was 120 years old when his mission ended (Thomas).

FURTHER READING

Akweks, Aren (Ray Fadden). *The Formation of the Ho-de-na-sau-ne or League of the Five Nations*. St. Regis Mohawk Reservation, Hogansburg, N.Y.: Akwesasne Counselor Organization, 1948.

Beauchamp, W[illiam] M[artin]. *The Iroquois Trail, or, Footprints of the Six Nations, in Customs, Traditions, and History*. Including David Cusick's "Sketches of Ancient History of the Six Nations." 1825. Fayetteville, NY: H. C. Beauchamp, 1892.

Buck, Roy. "The Great Law." In Barbara K. Barnes, ed., *Traditional Teachings*. Cornwall, Ont.: North American Indian Travelling College, 1984.

Colden, Cadwallader. *The History of the Five Nations Depending on the Province of New-York in America*. 1747. Ithaca, NY: Great Seal Books, 1958.

Dennis, Matthew. *Cultivating a Landscape of Peace*. Ithaca, N.Y.: Cornell University Press, 1993.

Fenton, William N. "Seth Newhouse's [Dayodekane's] Traditional History and Constitution of the Iroquois Confederacy." *Proceedings of the American Philosophical Society* 93:2 (1949): 141–158.

Gibson, John Arthur. *Concerning the League: The Iroquois League Tradition as Dictated in Onondaga by John Arthur Gibson*. 1912. Ed. and trans. Hanni Woodbury. Memoir 9. Winnipeg: Algonquian and Iroquoian Linguistics, 1992.

Griffin, Robert, and Donald A. Grinde, Jr., eds. *Apocalypse of Chiokoyhikoy*. Saint-Nicolas, Québec: Presses de l'Université Laval, 1997.

Hale, Horatio, ed. *The Iroquois Book of Rites*. 1883. Intro. by William N. Fenton. Toronto: University of Toronto Press, 1963.

Hewitt, J[ohn] N[apoleon] B[rinton]. "A Constitutional League of Peace in the Stone Age of America: The League of the Iroquois and Its Constitution." *Smithsonian Institution Series* (1920): 527–545.

———. "Era of the Formation of the Historic League of the Iroquois." *American Anthropologist* (old series) 7 (January 1894): 61–67.

———. "Ethnological Studies among the Iroquois Indians." *Smithsonian Miscellaneous Collections* 78 (1927): 237–247.

———. "Field Studies among the Iroquois Tribes." *Explorations and Field-work of the Smithsonian Institution* (1931): 175–178.

———. "Iroquoian Cosmology, Second Part." In *Forty-third Annual Report of the Bureau of American Ethnology to the Secretary of the Smithsonian Institution, 1925–1926*. Washington, D.C.: Government Printing Office, 1928: 453–819.

———. "The 'League of Nations' of the Iroquois Indians in Canada." *Explorations and Field-work of the Smithsonian Institution for 1929* (1930): 201–206.

———. "Legend of the Founding of the Iroquois League." *American Anthropologist* (old series) 5 (April 1892): 131–148.

———. "Some Esoteric Aspects of the League of the Iroquois." *Proceedings of the International Congress of Americanists* 19 (1915): 322–326.

Howard, Helen Addison. "Hiawatha: Co-founder of an Indian United Nations." *Journal of the West* 10:3 (1971): 428–438.

Jemison, Pete. "Mother of Nations: The Peace Queen, a Neglected Tradition." *Akwe:kon* 5 (1988): 68–70.

Johansen, Bruce Elliott. *Forgotten Founders: Benjamin Franklin, the Iroquois, and the Rationale for the American Revolution.* Ipswich, Mass.: Gambit, 1982.

Johnson, Chief Elias. *Legends, Traditions, and Laws of the Iroquois, or Six Nations.* 1881. New York: AMS Press, 1978.

Mann, Barbara A. "The Lynx in Time: Haudenosaunee Women's Traditions and History." *American Indian Quarterly* 21:3 (Summer 1997): 423–450.

Mann, Barbara A., and Jerry L. Fields. "A Sign in the Sky: Dating the League of the Haudenosaunee." *American Indian Culture and Research Journal* 21:2 (1997): 105–163.

Morgan, Lewis Henry. *League of the Haudenosaunee, or Iroquois.* 1851. 2 vols. New York: Burt Franklin, 1964.

Parker, A[rthur] C[aswell]. *The Constitution of the Five Nations, or, The Iroquois Book of the Great Law.* Albany: University of the State of New York, 1916.

———. *The Life of General Ely S. Parker, Last Grand Sachem of the Iroquois and General Grant's Military Secretary.* Buffalo: Buffalo Historical Society, 1919: 43–46 [Keepings of Elizabeth Parker].

———. "The Maize Maiden." In *Rumbling Wings and Other Indian Tales.* Garden City, NY: Doubleday, Doran & Company, 1928: 179–191.

Thomas, Chief Jake. Personal communication to Barbara A. Mann, April 5, 1997.

Thwaites, Reuben Gold, ed. and trans. *The Jesuit Relations and Allied Documents; Travels and Explorations of the Jesuit Missionaries in New France, 1610–1791.* New York: Pageant Book Company, 1959.

Vecsey, Christopher. "The Story and Structure of the Iroquois Confederacy." *Journal of the American Academy of Religion* 54:1 (1986): 79–106.

Wallace, Paul A. W. "The Return of Hiawatha." *New York History: Quarterly Journal of the New York State Historical Association* 29:4 (1948): 385–403.

———. *The White Roots of Peace.* Empire State Historical Publication Series No. 56. Port Washington, N.Y.: Ira J. Friedman, 1946.

Barbara A. Mann

Seneca-Cayuga Tribe of Oklahoma. The Seneca-Cayuga Tribe of Oklahoma occupies roughly 4,000 acres of prairie ninety miles northeast of Tulsa, Oklahoma. Like most other Native American settlements in Oklahoma, this one has roots in the **removal** policies of the 1830s.

Most of the Native people who live on this reservation are descended from the Sandusky (Ohio) **Senecas**, who were guaranteed a 40,000-acre reservation there by treaty in 1817. During 1832, however, at the same time that many other Native nations were being compelled to move to Indian Territory (now Oklahoma), the Sandusky Senecas were persuaded to sell their lands in Ohio and move west of the Missouri River. The Sandusky Senecas suffered great hardship on the journey and, once in Oklahoma, found that the land assigned to them was unfit for agriculture. A new reservation was negotiated in the northeastern corner of Indian Territory, adjacent to the Cherokee Nation.

During 1881, a band of roughly 100 **Cayugas** from New York and Ontario joined the Senecas in Oklahoma. Ten years later, the reservation was allotted, and much of its land was opened to non-Indian settlement. The tribe incorporated as the Seneca-Cayuga Tribe of Oklahoma in 1937 under the Oklahoma Indian Welfare Act.

In the middle 1990s, the Seneca-Cayugas of Oklahoma were governed by the Seneca-Cayuga Business Council, with six members, including a head chief. The tribe holds 1,093 acres in federal trust, with the balance (slightly less than 3,000 acres) in individual allotments. The tribe has enhanced its revenue through operation of a modest bingo hall, a restaurant, and a smoke shop. Roughly 800 of 2,500 enrolled tribal members live on the reservation.

FURTHER READING

Tiller, Veronica E. Velarde, ed. *Tiller's Guide to Indian Country: Economic Profiles of American Indian Reservations*. Albuquerque: BowArrow Publishing, 1996.

Senecas, historical sketch. The Senecas are located at the "Western Door" of the Haudenosaunee Confederacy, mainly, in historic times, between the Genesee River and Seneca Lake in the Finger Lakes area of present-day western New York State. "Seneca," derived from classical European history, is a term used by European colonists to describe a people who called themselves *Ge-nun-de-wah-ga*, "People of the Great Hill." The Senecas' account of their origins has them emerging from the underworld onto a great hill believed to be at the head of Canandaigua Lake.

The Senecas' first fleeting contact with Europeans occurred in 1534, during the explorations of **Jacques Cartier**. More sustained contact occurred shortly after 1600 with the arrival of **Samuel de Champlain**, who set the Senecas at odds with the French for much of the subsequent two centuries by allying with Wyandots (Hurons) who killed and cannibalized several Senecas during 1615. By roughly 1630, the Haudenosaunee Confederacy, with the Senecas and the **Mohawks** supplying most of the military muscle, decided to conquer the Indian allies of the French, including the beaver-rich Wyandots. Within a decade, by 1650, after a number of military campaigns that came to be known as the **Beaver Wars**, the Wyandots were obliterated as a nation. Their remnants (as many as 700 after one battle) were captured. A majority were adopted as Senecas, but a minority were tortured to death. By 1657, perhaps ten other Native groups had been defeated militarily and absorbed in this manner.

During the following decades, the Senecas were devastated by several epidemics of disease, the most severe being smallpox in 1660–1661. The Senecas and other Haudenosaunee peoples stepped up **adoptions** as their populations fell due to disease; they remained a formidable diplomatic balancing power between French and British interests in North America. The French, under Marquis de Denonville, savaged Seneca country in 1687, pillaging the Senecas' main population center at **Ganondagan**, twenty-five miles southeast of present-day Syracuse, and pushing the Senecas more adamantly toward the British in the last of the "French and Indian Wars," which expelled French political authority from North America during the early 1760s. In 1698, French soldiers raiding Seneca villages looked in awe at their stores of corn. One observer remarked that he had seen more than a million bushels of **corn** in storage, "which the owners had not had time to destroy" (Reaman, 35). Other reports at about the same time described Haudenosaunee cornfields up to two miles in length.

The Senecas split sharply (reflecting discord in the confederacy at large) over whether to support patriots or Tories during the **American Revolution**. Ultimately, a majority of Senecas sided with the British, which brought brutal retaliatory raids by troops under the command of General **John Sullivan** in 1779. Sullivan's march left a path of scorched earth in at least thirty Seneca villages. Some of Sullivan's field commanders also left behind reports characterized by a degree of amazement at the size of the Seneca food stores that they destroyed. Between 2,000 and 3,000 Senecas spent the winter of 1779–1780 in British forts that did not have the space or supplies to house and feed them. Several hundred—no one knows exactly how many—died of starvation, exposure, and various diseases. After yet another very hard winter in 1780–1781, the Senecas returned home to try to reestablish their lives, only to be hit by a new epidemic of smallpox.

After the American Revolution, the Senecas sank into despair as the combined effects of disease, an economy devastated by Sullivan's raids, alcohol, and general lassitude reduced their population by half in one generation, from roughly 1780 to 1800. Large tracts of Seneca lands were usurped by several non-Indian land companies with the connivance of New York State. Anthony F. C. Wallace described the European-Americans who moved to Seneca country as "the ragged conquerers," who bore

a peculiarly dilapidated and discouraged brand of European culture brought by hopeful speculators, by hungry farmers fleeing the cold and rocky hillsides of New England, and by hard-drinking Scotch-Irish weavers driven from Ulster by high taxes and the new weaving machines. The men came with golden dreams, but the dreams quickly faded. . . . These pioneers were almost a lost legion, more primitive in material standard of living, and perhaps socially as well, than the Indians on their reservations. (Wallace, 208–209)

Many thousands of acres were shaved off Seneca holdings in treaties signed at **Buffalo Creek**, the largest and most fraudulent of which was initialled after an alcohol-lubricated "treaty conference" in 1838 that eradicated, for a time, all Seneca landholdings. Some of the land was restored in the "compromise treaty" of 1842.

At roughly the same time, the Code of **Handsome Lake** was spreading among the Senecas and other Haudenosaunee after the prophet experienced a series of visions at the turn of the century. Handsome Lake sought to bring the Senecas out of their despair by opposing the use of alcohol and reconstructing an Iroquois social and political life that was a combination of traditional and imported (mainly Quaker) precepts.

In 1848, the **Cattaraugus** and **Allegany** Senecas withdrew from the Iroquois

Confederacy and established a government modeled on that of the United States, with a written constitution that was passed at a convention and written in Seneca by the missionary Asher Wright. The **Tonawanda** Senecas retained their traditional council of chiefs.

As late as 1862, smallpox was still a major killer in Seneca country. That year, Quakers reported that 135 cases of the disease were diagnosed among the Senecas in western New York.

The Senecas resisted non-Indian encroachment on what was left of their lands, one example of which was the town of **Salamanca**, where non-Indians took up residence on Seneca land. Many refused to pay even token rent or lease payments. A large number of Senecas served in the Union army during the Civil War, including **Ely Parker**, who rose to the rank of general and served as U.S. Grant's secretary. Parker also became the first commissioner of Indian affairs of Native American ancestry before he was hounded from office by entrenched special interests.

Pressure on Seneca landholdings continued into the twentieth century with the construction of the **Kinzua Dam**, completed in 1965, which flooded large portions of Seneca lands in violation of the **Canadaigua Treaty** of 1794. In 1972, the Indian Claims Commission awarded the Senecas $5 million to compensate them for some of the unjust takings of their lands during the previous two centuries.

The Senecas retain legal title to the land remaining to them on three New York State reservations (Tonawanda, Allegany, and Cattaraugus); they rejected allotment—which broke up tribal land base—when it was offered as the nineteenth century ended. Plots of land held individually may be sold only to other Senecas, and all leases to non-Indians must be approved by the tribal council. The Seneca Nation also has retained all mineral rights.

Enrollment in the Seneca Nation follows traditional Iroquois matrilineal kinship ties. Blood quantum is not a factor. One becomes a Seneca by having a Seneca mother or wife or by formal **adoption**.

In March 1995, the Seneca reservation at Cattaraugus was wracked by factional violence that left three people dead. The shootings, which involved a battle for control of the Seneca Nation government, took place at the Seneca tribal building on Route 438 on March 24, following the election of William Bowen as tribal president by three votes. Bowen was later impeached by the faction that opposed him. Myron Kettle, Sam Powless, and Patrick Thompson were killed. All had been opponents of Bowen.

FURTHER READING

Abrams, George H. J. *The Seneca People*. Phoenix: Indian Tribal Series, 1976.

Morgan, Lewis Henry. *League of the Iroquois*. 1851. Secaucus, N.J.: Corinth Books, 1962.

Parker, Arthur C. *An Analytical History of the Seneca Indians*. 1926. Researches and Transactions of the New York State Archeological Association, Lewis H. Morgan Chapter. New York: Kraus Reprint Co., 1970.

————. *The History of the Seneca Indians*. Empire State Historical Publications, 43.
    Port Washington, N.Y.: Ira J. Friedman, 1967.
Reaman, G. Elmore. *The Trail of the Iroquois Indians: How the Iroquois Nation Saved
    Canada for the British Empire*. London: Frederick Muller, 1967.
Wallace, Anthony F. C. *The Death and Rebirth of the Seneca*. New York: Knopf, 1970.

Shenandoah, Joanne (Oneida), b. 1957. Late in the twentieth century, Joanne
Shenandoah, a Wolf Clan **Oneida**, became a major presence in Native American
folk music, fusing traditional songs with contemporary styles such as western,
pop, and new age. In 1986, she was honored with two awards, the Native American Woman's Recognition Award and Native American Woman of Hope
Award. In 1994, she was recognized by the First Americans in the Arts Foundation as its Musician of the Year and was listed among *Who's Who among
Native Americans*.

Shenandoah married Mohawk editor and activist **Doug George-Kanentiio**
and with him formed Round Dance Productions, a nonprofit foundation for the
preservation of Native American culture. George-Kanentiio and Shenandoah
produced films, books, and other media that combined entertainment with
themes emphasizing Native American philosophy, culture, music, birthrights,
and history.

Shenandoah is a daughter of Maisie Shenandoah, an Oneida Clan Mother,
and the late Clifford Shenandoah, an Onondaga chief and jazz guitarist. Clifford
Shenandoah was one of a line of Iroquois chiefs reaching back to **Skenandoah**
(or Shenandoah, the two being variants of the same name, meaning "Deer"),
who organized the Oneidas to carry hundreds of bushels of corn to feed General
George Washington's Continental army during a bitter winter at Valley Forge,
Pennsylvania, in the midst of the Revolutionary War.

Before she could talk, Joanne Shenandoah was named Tekaiawahway (pronounced "De-gal-la-wha-wha"), meaning "she sings." She was urged to study
music and to make use of her voice from a young age. For fourteen years, she
made a living as a computer-systems architectural engineer, but a rediscovery
of her people's stories, songs, and respect for the earth prompted Shenandoah
to begin a music career.

By the middle of the 1990s, Shenandoah had released four albums in the
United States, as well as one single ("Nature Dance") in Germany. She also had
been a guest artist on ten albums, including the CD-ROM version of the motion
picture *Indian in the Cupboard*. Most notably, Shenandoah opened the 1994
concert at Woodstock and Earth Day on the Mall in Washington, D.C., before
audiences of more than 250,000 people in each place. She also contributed to
an album in defense of Leonard Peltier, who was convicted of killing two FBI
agents at Pine Ridge in 1975. Her music was featured on documentaries such
as "The War against the Indians," "How the West Was Lost," "Indian Time II—
Fly with Eagles," and several other national public broadcast programs. Her
original compositions were used in the commercial television series *Northern*

Exposure. Cable News Network's *Larry King Live* aired a song she wrote about the **repatriation** of Native American remains four times. "Hopefully", Shenandoah said after the song was played on the talk show, "my listeners, Indian or not, can begin to see the human side of Indian problems" (Shenandoah, interview).

Shenandoah performed at President Bill Clinton's inaugurals in 1993 and 1997 and also sang at a private tea party for Hillary Clinton and Tipper Gore. One of her compositions, "Ganondagan," was nominated for a Pulitzer Prize in music for 1994. She has performed on stage with Neil Young, Willie Nelson, Kris Kristofferson, Jackson Browne, John Denver, Rita Coolidge, Pete Seeger, Richie Havens, and others. The Association for Independent Music awarded her Native American Record of the Year in 1996 for her collection titled *Matriarch*.

FURTHER READING

Kates, William. "Spirits Move Joanne Shenandoah to Sing of Her Native Iroquois World." Associated Press in *Chattanooga Free Press*, June 27, 1997, D-4.
O'Brien, Jill. "Full-time Fun for Shenandoah." *Indian Country Today*, February 9, 1995, C-1.
Shenandoah, Joanne. Interview with Bruce E. Johansen. May 28, 1996.

Shenandoah, Leon (Onondaga), 1915–1996. Leon Shenandoah, a member of the Eel Clan, served as *Tadadaho* (speaker and Fire Keeper) of the Haudenosaunee Confederacy during much of the late twentieth century, from his initiation into the office in 1967 to his death of kidney failure on July 22, 1996. Shenandoah was a great orator who served the people well and preserved the traditions of the people.

Shenandoah was a contemporary occupant of the oldest political office in North America and one of the oldest in the world. The Iroquois Confederacy has seated a *Tadadaho* or speaker since at least about 1150, and perhaps longer. According to Iroquois oral historians, Shenandoah was the 235th *Tadadaho* of the confederacy. As *Tadadaho*, Shenandoah held an office that combines spiritual and political attributes:

In our ways, spiritual consciousness is the highest form of politics. We must live in harmony with the natural world and recognize that excessive exploitation can only lead to our own destruction. We cannot trade the welfare of our future generations for profit . . . We are instructed to carry love for one another, and to show great respect for all beings of the earth. We must stand together, the four sacred colors of man, as the one family that we are, in the interest of peace. . . . Our energy is the combined will of all people with the spirit of the natural world, to be of one body, one heart, and one mind. (Shenandoah, 14)

When Shenandoah was a small child, while he was crawling along the floor, a pot of hot water was accidentally spilled on him, scalding his entire body, which almost killed him. He was taken to a medicine man to be healed. A sacred ceremony was performed for Shenandoah, and during the ceremony a man stood up and said, "You are that Boy!" (Shenandoah, 14). The same healer predicted that someday Shenandoah would hold a special position among his people.

At home, Shenandoah's demeanor belied his international celebrity. He smoked a corncob pipe and drove an old, donated Pontiac. His home was heated with a wood stove. Shenandoah was born on the Onondaga territory on May 18, 1915, and grew up in a cabin on Hemlock Creek, the youngest of five brothers and sisters. His formal education ended at the eighth grade. Shenandoah and his wife Thelma raised seven children. Shenandoah was fluent in the Onondaga language and was a longtime devotee of the Code of **Handsome Lake**.

When he first assumed office, Shenandoah visited the Museum of the American Indian in New York City. When a receptionist asked, "May I help you," he said, "Yes. You can give us back our **wampum** belts" (Johansen, 349). For almost three decades, Shenandoah worked to have Iroquois wampum belts returned from several museums and the state of New York. In his last official act, on July 4, 1996, he presided over the return of over seventy-three wampum strings and belts from the Museum of the American Indian.

Shenandoah was a steadfast opponent of **gambling** on Iroquois land because he maintained that the culture of money and greed had no place among traditional Iroquois. He also was a frequent spokesman for the Haudenosaunee and spoke before the United Nations twice. He spoke at the Earth Summit in Brazil during 1992 and participated in the affairs of the Green Cross, an international environmental group led by Mikhail Gorbachev, the former president of the Soviet Union.

FURTHER READING

Austin, Alberta. *Ne' Ho Niyo' De:No': That's What It Was Like*. Lackawanna, N.Y.: Rebco Enterprises, 1986.
Johansen, Bruce E., and Donald A. Grinde, Jr. *The Encyclopedia of Native American Biography*. New York: Henry Holt, 1997.
Shenandoah, Leon. "Beliefs." *Akwesasne Notes*, n.s. 2:2 (Spring 1997): 14.

                         Barbara A. Gray (Kanatiyosh) and Bruce E. Johansen

Shikellamy ("He Causes It to Be Light for Us" or "The Enlightener") (Oneida), c. 1700–1748. Shikellamy, an **Oneida** statesman, was one of the most visible statesmen of the eighteenth-century Haudenosaunee League as far as the European invaders were concerned. His presence at the hot spots of the Northeast and at the main colonial conferences held in the Northeast between 1727 and 1748, as well as his generally accommodating manner toward the British, made him a pivotal person in European eyes. Among the Haudenosaunee, he was regarded as a clever negotiator and an able point man who, from his dangerous perch along the "borderlands" at Shamokin (near modern-day Sunbury, Pennsylvania), was able to send constant surveillance reports back to Onondaga, the league's capital.

Shikellamy's parentage is uncertain, but persistent reports held that his mother was **Cayuga** while his father was French. As an infant, he was baptized by the Jesuit priests, a fact he later confided to the Moravian missionary David Zeisberger. At the age of two, the Oneidas took him in. Some say that they "kidnapped" him, although it is uncertain why one league nation (the Oneidas) would kidnap the child of another league nation (the Cayugas) unless he had been living entirely among the French. In any case, the Oneidas raised him to be fully Haudenosaunee, for, under league law, the fact that his mother was Cayuga automatically made him Haudenosaunee, regardless of what his father might have been. Consequently, Shikellamy was fully versed in the tradition and precepts of the **Great Law of Peace** and sought to emplace its triad of virtues—*Ne˝ Skĕñ´no^n* (Health), *Ne˝ Gai´i·hwiio* (Righteousness), and *Ne˝ Găshasde^n´˝sä'* (Popular Sovereignty)—in his dealings with the unruly colonists.

In his mature years, he was recognized by the Haudenosaunee *gantowisas* (women in their official capacities) as a leader. (The women alone nominated all men to office.) Although he was not one of the elected sachems of the Grand Council, Shikellamy was a chief. In 1727, he was sent by the league to the Susquehanna Valley as its head liaison with the European colonists, who stirred up trouble among the states of the league whenever they could as part of their land-grabbing strategy.

Of particular difficulty to Shikellamy were the rum traders who attempted, often successfully, to debauch the Natives of the area as the first step in defrauding them of their lands. As would so many other Native leaders from the eighteenth century on, Shikellamy identified the liquor trade as the main danger to the league and worked diligently to counter its incursions. In 1731, alcoholic matters came to a head. Shikellamy threatened the British officials of Pennsylvania, warning them that if the liquor trade were not controlled, he would not guarantee continued peace between Britain and the league.

The British needed to maintain friendly relations with the league or vacate much of their colonial territory. Furthermore, they were worried that French agents had fanned the flames of the disaffection that the Shawnees were already cherishing toward them over the issue of liquor. (Allies of the league, the Shawnees had been pushed west, into league Ohio, by the rum trade.) Trapped between the diplomatic fire on both sides, British colonial officials could not afford to test Shikellamy's resolve. They agreed to a major council to hash out the matter. One council grew into many as the talks dragged on. Knowing the status of Shikellamy at Onondaga, the British governor of Pennsylvania asked him to go to the Grand Council at Onondaga to invite the league to a treaty council in Philadelphia to settle the matter once and for all.

Accordingly, in 1736, Shikellamy organized a delegation of one hundred primary officials—Clan Mothers as well as chiefs—to go to Philadelphia to finalize negotiations in a binding treaty. This full delegation agreed to transfer the former Susquehanna lands south and east of the Blue Mountains to the colonists in return for regulation of the rum dealers and a guarantee that the lands of western

Pennsylvania and Ohio were not to be disturbed by the colonists, a promise broken almost as soon as it was made. The agreement was only made worse by the fact that the Susquehanna lands ceded in the treaty had formerly been the hunting grounds of the Shawnees, heightening their discontent.

However bad it was, the treaty was struck, and all but a handful of the official delegation then departed. Huddling with the few who remained, the colonists managed to cut a further deal that handed over to the colonists yet more land, the basin of the Delaware River that lay south of the lands officially ceded. This land had belonged to the Delaware Nation, an incorporated nation of the league, but it had never before been claimed by the league. This backroom deal sowed dissent within the league.

The minority group involved in this shady deal included a certain number of the *gantowisas*, for, under the Great Law, the women alone owned the land, meaning that the men could not transfer title without the approval of the women. Even though a few *gantowisas* facilitated the transaction, it was nevertheless illegal under the Great Law because it was not conducted through a **consensus** council but by a minority group acting furtively behind the scenes, after the European fashion of wheeling and dealing. The British did not care that the deal was illegal under Haudenosaunee law, however; all they wanted was the piece of paper stating that they now owned the Delaware River drainage plain.

The Delawares and the Shawnees, who bore the brunt of these deals, deeply resented the sales of their lands, while other league peoples were infuriated by the failure of the British to maintain their end of the bargain. The anger of the injured nations boiled over as British backwoodsmen became ever more blood-thirsty and bold in their violation of what many Natives held to have been a bad treaty in the first place. This deal—or rather, its repercussions—is often reputed to have helped bring on the French and Indian War (1754–1763).

The general turmoil occasioned by the foregoing events made Shikellamy's skill as a mediator even more indispensable to both the league and the British. In 1745, the Grand Council of the league appointed Shikellamy to be its lead liaison among the incorporated Susquehanna nations, the Delawares and the Shawnees, and the British. Keeping the peace was a tricky business, given the agitation among some Delawares to secede from the league to return to their old homeland along the mid-Atlantic coast, an ongoing response of the most dissatisfied who had been affronted over an earlier, illegal sale of their lands ten years before. As long as Shikellamy lived, he was able to keep a lid on this heaving cauldron of disaffection, a result as ardently desired by the league as by the British.

The delicacy and astuteness of Shikellamy's abilities as an emissary were never more obvious than during his tumultuous final years in office. Among other things, Shikellamy convinced the British to arm the league by setting up a forge at Shamokin, his base of operations. In supplying weapons, British officials were thinking in terms of the league's eventual aid in fighting the French (a development transparently on the horizon); the league, however, was thinking in terms of defending itself against the ever-encroaching settlers and rum traders who regarded killing Natives as equivalent to killing buffalo, only more meritorious.

Having second thoughts on its arms deal and in an attempt to rebottle the genie, the British asked Shikellamy to allow the Moravian missionaries to set up shop near Shamokin. (The British frequently employed Moravian missionaries, including Frederick Post and **John Heckewelder**, as spies against Native nations.) For his part, regarding the Moravians as a buffer between his people and the marauding backwoodsmen, Shikellamy allowed them to establish a mission near Shamokin. In the process, he became rather good friends with the lead Moravian missionary in Pennsylvania, David Zeisberger, who was studying the **Mohawk** language preparatory to his attempt to missionize the Haudenosaunee.

This friendship cost Shikellamy his life. In the autumn of 1747, Shikellamy made a trip to the Moravian headquarters at Bethlehem, Pennsylvania, where he helped Zeisberger with his studies. According to the missionary records, Shikellamy was intent upon learning more of the Moravian religion, but it is naïve to take the self-interested records of the missionaries—any missionaries— at face value. It is not unlikely that the legaue had dispatched Shikellamy to learn more about this new missionary sect that had made bold to set up shop on league soil since 1743 without so much as a by-your-leave. (The Moravians later claimed that their "invitation" into Iroquoia had been issued by Shikellamy, whom they claimed as a convert.)

Shikellamy stayed all winter in Bethlehem. In March 1748, he appeared in missionary records as helping Zeisberger compose his Mohawk dictionary. The missionaries also "persuaded" him "to throw away the 'manitou' he wore around his neck as a charm to keep off sickness" (Wallace, 174), one of the deeds that convinced the Moravians that he had converted to their brand of Christianity. Manitouless, Shikellamy promptly contracted smallpox from the epidemic then raging in Bethlehem.

Nearing death, he returned home to his family at Shamokin, where he died on December 6, 1748, in the presence of his weeping kinsfolk. Death ceremonies show that it is unlikely that Shikellamy had converted, for he continued to be honored by the league as a chief after death (a recognition not extended to converts) and was buried, not in a Christian cemetery, but with league rites in the traditional burial ground on the Susquehanna River in modern-day Sunbury. A cliff overlooking his burial site is called "Shickellamy's Face," and a statue was erected to his memory near Womelsdorf, Pennsylvania. With his death, the peace that Shikellamy had carefully glued together fell apart, making it readily apparent just how deeply the league and the British had depended upon his services.

FURTHER READING

Grinde, Donald A., Jr., and Bruce E. Johansen. *Exemplar of Liberty: Native America and the Evolution of Democracy.* Los Angeles: UCLA American Indian Studies Center, 1991.

Heckewelder, John. *Narrative of the Mission of the United Brethren among the Delaware and Mohegan Indians from Its Commencement, in the Year 1740, to the Close of the Year 1808.* 1820. New York: Arno Press, 1971.

Wallace, Paul A. W. *Conrad Weiser, 1696–1760: Friend of Colonist and Mohawk.* 1945. New York: Russell & Russell, 1971.

Barbara A. Mann

Shingask ("Boggy Ground Overgrown with Grass," also given as Shingas, Shingess, Stringas, Chingas) (league Delaware), c. 1700–c. 1763. Shingask became the primary sachem of the Haudenosaunee League Delawares in Ohio. After first having served as league speaker, he later became the war chief of the Delawares, in which capacity he was noted for his fierce resistance to the European invasion of Pennsylvania and Ohio.

Practically nothing was recorded of Shingask's birth or youth, although he was a figure of some importance to the Delawares and the league. Given his connections, he most probably sprang from a distinguished lineage. His brother was Tamaqua ("King Beaver"), while his uncle was Olumapies, the Delaware head sachem at Shamokin, a major council site on the "borderlands" of eighteenth-century Pennsylvania. On June 11, 1752, the Grand Council of the league named Shingask the speaker of the Ohio Delawares (a position misconstrued as "king" in colonial records). In this capacity, he appeared at many councils, some of them recorded in Western sources, including the Council of Carlisle (October 4, 1753); the Councils of Loggstown (January 12–February 3, 1754, and February 20, 1754); the long, wartime Council of Pittsburgh (March 15, 1758–April 12, 1760, where he appeared in July 1759 and on August 20, 1759); and the Council of Easton (October 13, 1758), at which he signed a petition for peace as British and French hostilities were spilling over into the French and Indian War (1754–1763).

In 1758, the personal disgust of Shingask with the colonials and their imported wars led him to rebuke Europeans generally for their untoward behavior and their land-grabbing ways. This position angered the British, who had expected to find an ally. No longer welcome at international councils (his brother Tamaqua took his place as speaker), Shingask became a war chief, intruding forcefully upon colonial notice during the French and Indian War when he fought on the Delaware side (so roundly ignored in Western texts) to expel the invading settlers. His brilliant military strategies laid waste to the Cove and many other important colonial beachheads in western Pennsylvania. Soon he was the most feared war chief on the borders and had earned a reputation in colonial consciousness as a bloodthirsty monster whom the settlers had dubbed "Shingas the Terrible."

John Heckewelder, who lived among the Delawares for forty-nine years, painted quite another portrait of his character, however, showing him to have been a tender father, a loving husband, and a generous adversary who never mistreated a prisoner. In one sketch from 1762, a traveler noted several boys at play in a Delaware town. Some were clearly adoptees, being of European extraction. The traveler asked Shingask whether the European boys were well treated given the hard feelings that subsisted between the settlers and the Delawares as the French and Indian War wound down. Shingask conceded that at first, he had regarded the boys as nothing more than the progeny of a hated foe, "but now, they and my children eat their food from the same bowl" (Heckewelder, 269–270, n.1) "Eating from one bowl" was a league metaphor indicating one people; that is, **adoption** had made the European boys as much his sons as birth had made the rest.

In another, deeply moving glimpse of Shingask in 1762, Heckewelder described the funeral of his beloved wife. As the ceremonies drew to a close, Heckewelder spotted "the disconsolate Shingask retired by himself to a spot at some distance, where he was seen weeping, with his head bowed to the ground" (Heckewelder, 272). Within the year, Shingask followed his wife to the grave just as the war he had done so much first to prevent, and then to win, ground down into history.

FURTHER READING

Heckewelder, John. *History, Manners, and Customs of the Indian Nations Who Once Inhabited Pennsylvania and the Neighboring States.* 1820, 1876. The First American Frontier Series. New York: Arno Press and the New York Times, 1971.

Wallace, Paul A. W. "John Heckewelder's Indians and the Fenimore Cooper Tradition." *Proceedings of the American Philosophical Society* 96:4 (1952) 496–504.

Barbara A. Mann

Silverheels, Jay (Harry Smith) (Mohawk), c. 1920–1980. Born as Harry Smith around 1920, the **Mohawk** who acquired the stage name "Jay Silverheels" became well known as the Lone Ranger's "sidekick" Tonto on the long-running television series of the same name. Silverheels, who was a son of A. G. E. Smith, a highly decorated Canadian soldier during World War I, also acted in a film version of the same plot as well as in other films, including *The Prairie* (1947), *Broken Arrow* (1950), and *War Arrow* (1953). He appeared in more than fifty films.

In 1979, Silverheels became the first Native American to have a star set on Hollywood Boulevard's Walk of Fame. In addition to being a well-known actor, Silverheels was also a noted athlete, excelling in **lacrosse**, ice hockey, soccer, and track.

"Mr. Silverheels was not only a star in Hollywood," said Bob Hicks, chairman of First Americans in the Arts. "He was a hero to many in the Native American community. He reached out to aspiring Native American performers by creating the Indian Actors Workshop. His contributions, generosity, and humor have left an indelible stamp on our community" (Robb). Silverheels was inducted into the First Americans in the Arts Hall of Honor in 1998.

FURTHER READING

Corneau, Ernest N. *The Hall of Fame of Western Film Stars.* North Quincey, Mass.: Christopher Publishing, 1969.

Robb, David. "Silverheels to Go into Hall of Honor." *Hollywood Reporter*, December 16, 1997, n.p.

Six Nations Indian Museum (Onchiota, N.Y.). *See* **Fadden, John Kahionhes**, and **Fadden, Ray**.

Skenandoah ("Deer") (Oneida), c. 1710–1816. Skenandoah, who lived at Oneida Castle, New York, supported the British in the French and Indian War (1754–1763), but switched his allegiance to the patriots in the **American Revolution**. Little is known of his early life or the early years of his chieftainship, except that he became a committed campaigner against alcohol after he got drunk and was robbed while sleeping on a street in Albany. As an adult, Skenandoah was exceptionally tall (about six feet, three inches) and known for his grace of manner.

Although Skenandoah asserted the **Oneidas**' official neutrality at the beginning of the American Revolution, he supplied warriors and intelligence to the patriots. When George Washington's army shivered in the snow at Valley Forge, Skenandoah's Oneidas carried baskets of **corn** to the hungry troops. Washington later named the Shenandoah Valley after the Oneida chief in appreciation of his support. Most of the **Mohawks**, Oneidas, **Senecas**, and **Cayugas** sided with the British, causing the Iroquois League to split. During September 1778, Skenandoah supplied a key warning to residents of German Flats that their settlements were about to be raided by the British with their Iroquois allies under **Joseph Brant**. The settlers were thus able to get out of the area in time, but their homes and farms were burned and their livestock was captured.

After the Revolution, Skenandoah continued to serve as a principal chief of the Oneidas and signed several treaties on their behalf. Skenandoah was a close friend of the missionary Samuel Kirkland and was buried, at Skenandoah's request, next to Kirkland at the Hamilton College cemetery in Clinton, New York, after having lived to the extraordinary age of about 110. One of Skenandoah's descendants, the Oneida folksinger **Joanne Shenandoah**, became prominent in the late twentieth century.

FURTHER READING

Grinde, Donald A., Jr. *The Iroquois and the Founding of the American Nation*. San Francisco: Indian Historian Press, 1977.

"Sleep on it." The advice to "sleep on it" when considering something important has been incorporated into American English from the traditions of the Haudenosaunee Grand Council, where no important actions were taken until at least one night had elapsed since the matter's introduction before the council. The passage of time was said to allow the various members of a Haudenosaunee council to attain unanimity—"one mind"—necessary for consensual solution of a problem. The Grand Council also prohibited carrying debate after sunset to avoid hasty decision making caused by stress.

Snowsnake. Snowsnake is a traditional Native American winter sport in the Northeast. The snowsnake is a shaft of wood shaped like a spear that is thrown by members of competing teams along lengthy gutters formed from ice and snow. Competition is based on the length of team members' throws, which can range up to a mile under ideal conditions. At high speed, the thrown spear appears to move like a snake, giving the sport its name.

The gutterlike track of the "snake," called a "pitch hole," is built to a height of about two and a half feet as soon as sufficient snow is available. The gutter itself is about six inches deep. Once a track is built, a game of snowsnake is only very rarely canceled due to stormy weather unless it rains and melts the snow. Inclement weather may add to the challenge of the game, however. Most players carry a number of "snakes" that behave differently under various conditions. Manufacturers of snowsnakes, called "shiners," are adept at figuring which type of snake is best for particular conditions. An expert shiner may bring twenty to thirty snakes to a contest, alternating them as weather and ground conditions change.

"Snakes" are usually made of hardwood, favorites being hickory, maple, ironwood, or juneberry. "Snakes" may be oiled to increase their weight, water repellency, and speed. "Snakes" also may be tipped with lead, waxed, and varnished to increase speed along the pitch hole. Two types of snakes are used: "mudcats," about three feet long, and "long snakes," of roughly seven feet.

In the past, the game was played along roadways and across frozen rivers. The "snake" may be thrown overhand, underhand, or sidearm and may reach the speed of a pitched major-league fastball, or up to about 100 miles an hour. Spectators are warned to stand clear of the track because snakes can jump it and impale shoes or flesh. A player whose "snake" jumps the track is disqualified for that turn.

FURTHER READING

Wall, Steve. "Gallery: Snowsnake." *Northeast Indian Quarterly* 5:4 (Winter 1988): 26–33.

Standing Arrow (Francis Johnson) (Mohawk), born 1933. As a protest of **Mohawk** displacement by construction of the **St. Lawrence Seaway**, Standing Arrow (Francis Johnson), an **Akwesasne Mohawk** and ironworker, organized about 200 Mohawks who, during August 1957, occupied land near Route 5S on Schoharie Creek near Fort Hunter, on fifteen square miles of land they said belonged to the Mohawks under the **Fort Stanwix Treaty of 1784**. The Standing Arrow encampment received international publicity with the publication of articles by Edmund Wilson in the *New Yorker* that later formed the basis of his book *Apologies to the Iroquois*. The protest camp disbanded after court orders evicted the protesters from the land in March 1958, but the model of land occupations was used again by Native American militants during the 1960s and 1970s.

FURTHER READING

Wilson, Edmund. *Apologies to the Iroquois*. New York: Farrar, Straus & Cudahy, 1960.

Stanton, Elizabeth Cady, 1815–1902. Sally Roesch Wagner asserts that "nineteenth-century radical feminist theoreticians, such as Elizabeth Cady Stanton and **Matilda Joslyn Gage**, looked to the Iroquois for their vision of a transformed world" (Grinde and Johansen, 231–232). Stanton quoted the memoirs of the Rev. Asher Wright, who wrote of **Seneca** home life:

Usually the females ruled the house. The stores were in common, but woe to the luckless husband or lover who was too shiftless to do his share of the providing. No matter how many children, or whatever goods he might have in the house, he might at any time be ordered to pick up his blanket and budge; and after such an order it would not be healthful for him to attempt to disobey. The house would be too hot for him, and unless saved by the intercession of some aunt or grandmother he must retreat to his own clan, or go and start a new matrimonial alliance with some other. (Grinde and Johansen, 221)

According to Stanton, Wright also noted that Iroquois women alone could "knock off the horns" of a sachem who had abused his office, as well as make the original nominations for sachemships. In early treaty negotiations, representatives of the United States, all male, often found themselves face-to-face with Iroquois women. Many of the treaties negotiated before 1800 were signed by both male sachems and their female counterparts.

In her 1891 speech before the National Council of Women, Stanton surveyed the research of **Lewis Henry Morgan**, which indicated that "among the greater number of the American aborigines, the descent of property and children were in the female line. Women sat in the councils of war and peace and their opinions had equal weight on all questions" (Grinde and Johansen, 231–232). In this regard, she mentioned the Iroquois' councils specifically. After surveying tribal societies in other parts of the world as well, Stanton closed her speech with a case for sexual equality:

In closing, I would say that every woman present must have a new sense of dignity and self respect, feeling that our mothers, during long periods in the long past, have been the ruling power and that they used that power for the best interests of humanity. As history is said to repeat itself, we have every reason to believe that our turn will come again. It may not be for woman's supremacy, but for the as yet untried experiment of complete equality, when the united thought of man and woman will inaugurate a just government, a pure religion, a happy home, a civilization at last in which ignorance, poverty and crime will exist no more. Those who watch already behold the dawn of the new day. (Grinde and Johansen, 232)

FURTHER READING

Allen, Paula Gunn. *The Sacred Hoop: Recovering the Feminine in American Indian Traditions*. Boston: Beacon Press, 1986.

Brown, Judith K. "Economic Organization and the Position of Women among the Iroquois." *Ethnohistory* 17:3–4 (Summer–Fall 1970): 151–167.

Carr, Lucien. *The Social and Political Position of Women among the Huron-Iroquois Tribes*. Salem, Mass.: Salem Press, 1884.

Gage, Matilda Joslyn. *Woman, Church, and State*. 1893. Watertown, Mass.: Persephone Press, 1980.

Grinde, Donald A., Jr., and Bruce E. Johansen. *Exemplar of Liberty: Native America and the Evolution of Democracy*. Los Angeles: UCLA American Indian Studies Center, 1991.

Stanton, Elizabeth Cady. "The Matriarchate or Mother-Age." *National Bulletin* [National Council of Women] 1:5 (February 1891): 1.

Stanton, Elizabeth Cady, Susan B. Anthony, and Matilda Joslyn Gage, eds. *History of Woman Suffrage*. Salem, N.H.: Ayer Co., 1985.

Wagner, Sally Roesch. *The Untold Story of the Iroquois Influence on Early Feminists*. Aberdeen, S.D.: Sky Carrier Press, 1996.

Sullivan, John, 1740–1795. John Sullivan, a member of George Washington's military command structure during the American Revolutionary War, is best-known to the Haudenosaunee as the leader of an expeditionary force which destroyed much of the **Senecas'** civilian infrastructure during the summer of 1779. As such, Sullivan has been studied in military schools and institutes as one of the earliest practitioners of "total warfare," which targets civilian populations as well as opposing military forces.

During July of 1779, Sullivan, commanding four brigades of Continental regulars, marched north and westward from New Jersey to punish the pro-British Haudenosaunee for raids against frontier settlements the previous year. Sullivan and his troops reached the Haudenosaunee homelands in August, torching about forty villages and destroying at least 160,000 acres of corn (Fisher, 2). Sullivan's forces also girdled thousands of fruit trees, a tactic specifically designed to kill the trees at the first frost of the coming winter. Sullivan's tactics caused widespread hunger among the Haudenosaunee, especially the Seneca and **Cayuga**, during that winter.

Sullivan's military career before the Iroquois campaign had been lackluster. He led the retreat of an American expeditionary force from Canada in 1776, and was himself captured by the British shortly thereafter at Brooklyn Heights, as the Redcoats outflanked his forces.

Sullivan's scorched-earth tactics in Haudenosaunee country were fully approved by George Washington. After the campaign, Sullivan's forces marched into Fort Sullivan, which had been named for him at Tioga, Pennsylvania, greeted by a thirteen-gun salute and a cheering garrison.

FURTHER READING

Fisher, Joseph R. *A Well-executed Failure: The Sullivan Campaign Against the Iroquois, July–September, 1779.* Columbia: University of South Carolina Press, 1997.

Whittemore, Charles Park. *A General of the Revolution, John Sullivan of New Hampshire.* New York: Columbia University Press, 1961.

Swamp, Jake (Tekaronianeken) (Mohawk), b. 1941. Jake Swamp, of the Wolf Clan of the **Mohawks**, has become known to many people around the world as a chief spokesman of the Tree of Peace Society, which has planted **great white pines**, the principal symbol of the Haudenosaunee Confederacy, in public and private places from Australia to France, including many locations in the United States and Canada. Since 1984, Swamp has traveled the world planting trees for peace as well as explaining the history of the Haudenosaunee Confederacy. He has planted a tree in every one of the fifty United States. One of the trees, planted in 1988, stands near Independence Hall in Philadelphia.

Jake Swamp was born at **Akwesasne**. He is married to Judy Swamp, who often travels with him to public appearances around the world. Together they have had seven children. The Swamps also have eleven grandchildren. Jake Swamp has been a subchief of the traditional Mohawk Nation Council at Akwesasne since his late twenties and has long been an active member of the Grand Council at Onondaga. His duties as subchief include conducting **Thanksgiving** ceremonies, as well as ceremonies attending births and weddings and **condolences** having to do with grieving and funeral ceremonies. Swamp is often called on to mediate disputes between Haudenosaunee people. He was awarded a Peacemaker Award by the State of New York Dispute Resolution Association in 1996. At Akwesasne, Swamp has directed the **Akwesasne Freedom School** and CKON, Akwesasne radio. He also has helped to develop school curricula in the Mohawk language.

Swamp has taken part in many pivotal events in recent Native American history, including the 1968 Akwesasne International Bridge blockade, the Trail of Broken Treaties (1972), the Wounded Knee occupation (1973), the Longest Walk (1978), and the Fourth Russell Tribunal in the Netherlands, which, in 1980, took up war crimes against Native Americans. He has represented the Iroquois Confederacy at the United Nations. Swamp also was a principal figure in the crisis at Akwesasne that culminated in the deaths of Mohawks Mathew Pyke and "Junior" Edwards on May 1, 1990. As a member of the traditional Mohawk Nation Council, Swamp stood strongly against commercial **gambling** and **Warrior Society** influence. His family's home was shot at several times during the crisis.

FURTHER READING

Johansen, Bruce E. *Life and Death in Mohawk Country.* Golden, Colo.: North American Press, 1993.

T

Tadadaho Wampum Belt. The Tadadaho Belt symbolizes the role of the **Onondagas** as Firekeepers of the Haudenosaunee Confederacy. *Tadadaho* (also known as *Adodaroh*) was the name of the "Entangled One," the last holdout against the **Peacemaker**'s message of peace. The name ultimately became the name of the office held by the speaker, or presiding officer, of the Grand Council. The belt measures twenty-seven inches by fourteen inches; the design is comprised of large triangles of purple wampum. A chain of diamonds across the center of the belt represents a covenant or chain of friendship (see **Covenant Chain**).

The Tadadaho (Todadaho) Wampum Belt. © Elizabeth Quintana/Akwe:kon Press.

Taxation disputes, late twentieth century. In New York State, controversy arose in 1997 when Governor George Pataki proposed that state sales tax be collected on purchases of cigarettes and gasoline previously sold tax-free on Indian reservations within the state. Pataki initially negotiated a pact with the Iroquois Grand Council at Onondaga under which the money would not go to the state, but would be used to create infrastructure on the reservations.

During 1996 and early 1997, traditional Haudenosaunee governments, coordinated by the Iroquois Grand Council at Onondaga, had negotiated with Governor Pataki a pact that would have provided something of an indigenous tax base, by which the governments would control the importation of goods to their territories and derive a tax from doing so, to provide, in John C. Mohawk's words, "the things that governments do . . . [such as] improve housing, deliver potable water, provide jobs" (Mohawk, 2-C). The businesspeople who refused to pay taxes even to their own tribal governments seemed to prefer the greatest profit possible instead of reservation development.

During the late winter and spring of 1997, mercantile interests at the **Onondaga** territory, near Syracuse, and on **Seneca** land near Buffalo blocked highways to protest the tax plan. In one incident, state troopers arrested several people at Onondaga territory using forceful tactics as local television-news cameras recorded the clash. After that, facing road closures over a Memorial Day weekend, Pataki on May 22, 1997, withdrew from the tax agreement with the Grand Council and referred the issue to the New York State legislature. Thus a plan that would have recognized traditional Native American governments as having an economic role (such as that of licensing vendors and collecting taxes) was abandoned when factions of the Iroquois Confederacy clashed.

"Most New Yorkers realize that there is a history of struggle by Indian nations against taxation," commented Mohawk, a Seneca who is an associate professor of Native American studies at the State University of New York at Buffalo. "But what's not often understood off the reservations is the conflict within the Indian groups themselves—especially between Indian entrepreneurs . . . and Indian governments" (Mohawk, 2-C).

For many years, for example, disputes simmered between retailers of cut-rate cigarettes and gasoline on Onondaga territory and the Onondaga Nation Council. In 1993, the Grand Council banished three retailers from Onondaga after they refused to pay taxes to the confederacy. One shop later was razed by arson after protesters tried to put it out of business. In 1997, four smoke shops were reopened by the merchants who had been banished in 1993. This time the owners pledged to share their profits with Onondaga residents on a per capita basis, but not with the Onondaga Nation Council. They proposed that $1 per carton sold be returned to a fund to be distributed among enrolled Onondagas; the merchants' proposal indicated that a second $1 would be withheld from the sale of each carton of cigarettes for general programs on the Onondaga territory.

"The Papineaus and their children, Kent and Michelle [smoke-shop operators], have continually tried to disrupt and obstruct the Onondaga Nation's efforts to regulate commerce on its territories," said Chief Sid Hill, *Tadadaho* (**Adodaroh**) of the Grand Council at Onondaga. "Their present activity is a reactivation of several years of turmoil on the territory" (Grau). The renewed conflict at Onondaga arose just as one smoke-shop operator, Kevin Bucktooth, turned his business over to the Onondaga Nation Council.

Other smoke-shop owners were not as cooperative with the Council of Chiefs. On February 12, 1998, a ninety-foot electrical transmission tower that supplies 5,700 households on and near the Onondaga territory with power was toppled. The Council of Chiefs and Clan Mothers issued a statement the next day accusing the smoke-shop owners (whose businesses are located near the tower) of denying access to Niagara-Mohawk Power repair crews. The tower was toppled after the chiefs refused to allow electrical connections to the renegade smoke shops, which were operating with generators. On March 2, a crowd supporting the traditional council burned and bulldozed the renegade smoke shops, aggravating a bitter debate between the council and the freebooting capitalists.

The Indian Law Resource Center Annual Report (1993) stated:

One of the most pressing problems facing the Six Nations Confederacy concerns unlawful and unregulated businesses on their reservations. Tribal efforts have been stymied by state criminal prosecutions of chiefs, lack of resources and lack of cooperation and assistance from state and federal authorities. The operation of business in open defiance of Indian law and the Council of Chiefs threatens the peace and security of reservation residents and threatens the institutions of Indian governments. ("Conspiracy," Kahnawake Web site)

The report elaborated:

[The State of] New York has greatly complicated these negotiations by insisting that extraneous issues be considered, such as resolution of State demands for tax revenues from Mohawk fuel and cigarette sales. . . . Racketeer businessmen have attempted to overthrow or displace the sovereign Indian governments. Some have instigated violence and other criminal activities and refuse to submit to legal controls and taxation by the Indian governments. ("Conspiracy," Kahnawake Web site)

In 1994, in *Department of Taxation and Finance of the State of New York v. Milhelm Attea and Bros., Inc.*, the U.S. Supreme Court upheld the state's right to collect taxes on goods sold to non-Indians by Native American retailers on reservations. The issue then became collection of the taxes, a move that was resisted, at times forcefully (sometimes through blockades of highways), by reservation retailers who, at the same time, were resisting attempts by reservation governments to impose taxes.

New York State has been trying to impose its taxes on reservation retailers for several decades. In 1956, the Grand Council repudiated an attempt to levy taxes, based in part on the **Canandaigua Treaty** of 1794, which recognizes Haudenosaunee sovereignty. The **Buffalo Creek Treaty** of 1842 also specifically exempts the **Allegany** and **Cattaraugus** Senecas from state taxation.

The Internal Revenue Service also has sued several reservation retailers for uncollected federal excise taxes. By the middle 1990s, reservations in New York State hosted almost fifty discount gas stations and smoke shops. These businesses have become major factors in reservation economies. According to Mohawk, such retailing in the middle 1990s supported between 400 and 700 Seneca jobs out of a total working population of about 2,000 people (Kallen, 16). A number of Haudenosaunee also have refused to pay income taxes, placing them in continuous conflict with the Internal Revenue Service. On the subject of taxation, according to Akwesasne Mohawk author and activist **Doug George-Kanentiio**, "New York will have to concede that the Confederacy has the unilateral right to control its internal affairs; whatever agreement is reached on the taxation issue will strengthen the power of Iroquois sovereignty" (Kallen, 24).

FURTHER READING

"Conspiracy: Indian Law Resource Centre, N[ew] Y[ork] S[tate] & Onondaga Chiefs." Mohawk Nation News Service, Kahnawake Mohawk Territory, Quebec. [mohawkns@cyberglobe.net] March 7, 1998. [http://kafka.uvic.ca/~vipirg/SISIS/6nations/mar0798a.html]

Grau, John. "Dispute Simmers As Smoke Shops Open." *Syracuse Post-Standard*, November 18, 1997, n.p.

Martin, Kallen. "Indians Not Taxed: Will Sovereignty Survive?" *Native Americas* 13:2 (Summer 1996): 14–25.

Mohawk, John C. "In the Indian Taxing Conflict, There Is More Than One Kind of 'Us' Against 'Them.' " *Buffalo News*, April 26, 1997, 2-C.

Thanksgiving, Haudenosaunee traditions. Among the Haudenosaunee, Thanksgiving is not a single holiday, but a yearlong seasonal cycle. The **Senecas**, for example, observe six major ceremonies, all of which give thanks to the Creator for natural bounty. During the early spring, "Maple Doings," is observed to give thanks to the maple tree for its sweet sap. The next ceremony in the cycle accompanies spring planting. A third, "Strawberry Doings," takes place when wild strawberries ripen. "Green Corn Doings" are observed when **corn** is mature enough to eat. "Harvest Doings" are observed when the entire harvest is completed. The "Midwinter Doings" usher in the New Year at roughly late January or early February on the Roman calendar.

According to Seneca elder Corbett Sundown, who died in 1992, the elements of the Thanksgiving Address "correspond to an order observable in nature, and represent the sequence of creation" (Chafe, 1). The word "Thanksgiving" in English does not fully convey the meaning of the ritual:

The word "thanksgiving" seems no worse a choice than any other and has been used by most previous writers. When confronted with the Seneca words involved, some speakers balk at any attempt to give an English equivalent. Others translate, to some extent according to context, as "thank, be grateful to or for, rejoice in, bless, greet." The trouble is that the Seneca concept is broader than that expressed in any simple English term, and covers not only the conventionalized amenities of both thanking and greeting, but also a more general feeling of happiness over the existence of something or someone. (Chafe, 6)

A Thanksgiving Address is usually recited at the beginning of all Haudenosaunee formal occasions except funerals. The address is usually arranged in sections in which all parts of the natural world (animate and inanimate) are thanked for their contribution to human life and welfare. The address is also recited to set the mood for ritual observation or decision making. The general outline of the address is traditional, but each speaker chooses his or her own specific words. Usually, thanks are pronounced for the people, the Earth Mother, the waters, the fish, the plants, the food plants, medicine herbs, animals, trees, birds, the four winds, the Thunderers, the sun, the moon, the stars, the teachers of tradition, and the Creator.

A spirit of thanksgiving to the natural world is common in many Native American cultures. In addition to their Thanksgiving Address, the people of the various Haudenosaunee nations also observe a seasonal cycle of thanksgiving celebrations, one of which (the harvest, or fall seasonal thanksgiving) has been adopted in general culture throughout North America.

Mohawk Nation Council subchief **Tom Porter** offered a section of the traditional Mohawk thanksgiving prayer, which in Mohawk is called *Ohen:ton Karihwatehkwen* ("Words before All Else"):

[Before] our great-great-grandfathers were first born and given the breath of life, our Creator at that time said the earth will be your mother. And the Creator said to the deer, and the animals and the birds, the earth will be your mother, too. And I have instructed the earth to give food and nourishment and medicine and quenching of thirst to all life. . . . We, the people, humbly thank you today, mother earth.

Our Creator spoke to the rivers and our Creator made the rivers not just as water, but he made the rivers a living entity. . . . You must have a reverence and great respect for your mother the earth. . . . You must each day say "thank you" [for] every gift that contributes to your life. If you follow this pattern, it will be like a circle with no end. Your life will be as everlasting, as your children will carry on your flesh, your blood, and your heartbeat. (Grinde and Johansen, 35)

Most Thanksgiving Addresses are ended with some version of the following:

We have now arrived at the place where we can end our words. Of all things we have named, it is not our intention to leave anything out. If someone was forgotten, we leave it to each individual to send such greetings and thanks in their own way. Now our minds are one.

A tribute to the Creator and a reverence for the natural world are reflected in many Native American greetings throughout the span of the North American continent. More than 2,500 miles from the homeland of the Mohawks, the Lummis of the Pacific Northwest Coast often begin public meetings this way: "To the Creator, Great Spirit, Holy Father: may the words that we share here today give the people and [generations] to come the understanding of the sacredness of all life and creation" (Russo, ii).

Mohawk author and activist **Doug George-Kanentiio** observes that

in traditional Iroquois society there are a number of sacred rituals developed to bind humans with nature. The more engaging the ritual, the less likely that humans would act contrary to nature or violate her rules. . . . Central to Iroquois beliefs is the idea that no human activity of any importance should be free from the rituals of thanksgiving. Humility before the forces of nature is simple acknowledgement of the ultimate insignificance of intellectual endeavor. (George-Kanentiio, "Iroquois Thanksgiving," AA-5)

Many of the ceremonies are keyed to specific events in the natural cycle of the Haudenosaunee homeland in upstate New York, such as the flowing of maple syrup in late winter, the coming of thunder in the spring, the ripening of strawberries, and the maturity of the "**Three Sisters**" (**corn**, beans, and squash) that form the basis of the Iroquois diet. Iroquois personal names also reflect specific acts of nature, often those occurring at or near the time of a person's birth. Names also may describe a plant, an animal, or a phase of day or season.

Haudenosaunee rituals often are pervaded with a spirit of thanksgiving to the earth and natural forces, as in this excerpt from the Ganeowo ritual of the Senecas related by **Arthur C. Parker**:

> Now the whole assemblage is offering thanks!
> He [the Creator] thought that there should be a world and that people should be upon that world,
> That they should draw their sustenance from the world.
> So we thank the Creator that what he thought has come to pass.
>
> Now the whole assemblage is offering thanks!
> He thought there would be things in the world for sustenance
> And that people should labor for the sustenance.
> Now we petition the Creator that we may again see the season of things growing from which our living is. (Parker, 96)

During the ceremony of the Thunderers, spring storms are recognized as a form of sentient intelligence that has its own society and follows specific rituals related to the natural cycle that renews the cycle of growth in the spring with warming temperatures and soaking rainfall. These sky dwellers are said to travel on the winds to deliver the first true sign that the growing season has come. The ritual is meant as a message from the people on the earth to the sky-dwelling Thunder Beings. Far from dreading the coming of thunder and lightning, Iroquois children are taught to welcome the advent of spring storms, since, according to George-Kanentiio, "We are told that without the spring thunder nothing on earth could grow. Thunder, through lightning, joins with the earth to make it fertile and able to receive the seeds of plants" (George-Kanentiio, "To Iroquois," n.p.). The Haudenosaunee people considered themselves only one part of nature and observed their surroundings from the smallest unseen living organism to the cosmos in order to gain intense understanding of the natural world.

FURTHER READING

Chafe, Wallace. *Seneca Thanksgiving Rituals*. Bureau of American Ethnology Bulletin No. 183. Washington, D.C.: Smithsonian Institution, 1961.

Cornelius, Carol. "The Thanksgiving Address: An Expression of Haudenosaunee Worldview." *Akwe:kon Journal* 9:3 (Fall 1992): 14–25.

Fenton, William N. "The Requickening Address of the Iroquois Condolence Council by J. N. B. Hewitt." *Journal of the Washington Academy of Sciences* 34:3 (1944): 65–85.

George-Kanentiio, Doug. "Iroquois Thanksgiving Is Rooted in Ritual." *Syracuse Herald-American*, July 17, 1994, AA-5.

———. "To Iroquois, Thunder Is Most Welcome Sound." *Syracuse Herald-American*, April 25, 1993, n.p.

Grinde, Donald A., Jr., and Bruce E. Johansen. *Ecocide of Native America: Environmental Destruction of Indian Lands and Peoples*. Santa Fe, N.M.: Clear Light, 1995.

Morgan, Lewis Henry. *League of the Iroquois*. 1851. Secaucus, N.J.: Corinth Books, 1962.

Parker, Arthur C. *The Code of Handsome Lake, the Seneca Prophet*. New York State Museum Bulletin No. 163, Education Department Bulletin No. 530, November 1, 1912. Albany: University of the State of New York, 1913.

Russo, Kurt, ed. *Our People/Our Land: Reflections on Common Ground: 500 Years*. Bellingham, Wash.: Lummi Tribe, 1992.

Stokes, John D., ed. *Thanksgiving Address: Greetings to the Natural World*. Corrales, N.M.: Tracking Project, n.d.

Tooker, Elisabeth. *The Iroquois Ceremonial of Midwinter*. Syracuse,: N.Y. Syracuse University Press, 1970.

The Third Epoch of Time: The *Gaiwí:yo* of Sganyadaí:yoh. Iroquoian history falls into three main epochs: Creation, in the **First Epoch**; the **Great Law of Peace**, in the **Second Epoch**; and the *Gaiwí:yo* (Code) of the **Seneca** Sganyadaí:yoh (**Handsome Lake**), in the Third and Present Epoch of Time. The Third Epoch's primary actors, so far, have been Sganyadaí:yoh (Handsome Lake), the "Seneca Prophet," who helped revive Haudenosaunee culture in New York during the early onslaught by assimilationist forces of the United States; his (half-) brother, Hosanowanna, Shinnewaunah, or Gaiant'waka ("Exalted Name," also called **Cornplanter**); and the Clan Mothers of his time and their speaker, Sagoyewatha (**Red Jacket**).

The *Gaiwí:yo* was revealed to Sganyadaí:yoh between 1799 and 1804 in a series of visions brought by the Four Messengers, traditional spirits connected with the Four Winds (cardinal directions). The tradition begins with Sganyadaí:yoh falling gravely ill after many years of heavy drinking and eventually lapsing into a coma. As Sganyadaí:yoh told his experiences later, when he lay recuperating in his daughter's **longhouse**, a strange man appeared in his doorway and beckoned him to follow. Although barely able to stand, Sganyadaí:yoh staggered to the door and encountered three men who caught him in their arms as he collapsed.

Each man was shining white and carried branches of multicolored fruits, which the Messengers offered him to eat. The men claimed that they were, and had always been, the guardians of the Earth, sent just then to Sganyadaí:yoh by the Creator (Sapling) to help the people through the perilous turmoil caused by the European invaders (Parker, "Religion," 253). There were four guardians, the men said, but only three stood before him since one had hurried back with the news that Sganyadaí:yoh had responded to the vision (Parker, *Code*, 25).

The remaining three guardians gave Sganyadaí:yoh their initial messages, laying out codes of conduct and belief and means of conserving the old ways of life, including the **Great Feather Dance** and the Strawberry Festival. Sganyadaí:yoh accepted the charge and immediately began to spread the words of the Messengers to the people. This was the first in a series of promised celestial visions that collectively became known as the *Gaiwí:yo*, or "Good Message." Thereafter, Sganyadaí:yoh was periodically visited by the Messengers.

The "Four Matters"

Primary among Sganyadaí:yoh's visions were the Four Matters outlawing *one´ga'* (alcohol, which **Jake Thomas** referred to as *deganigohhadé:nyons*, "the mind-changer"); *got´go^n´* ("witchcraft"); (ono´itiyi´yende. ("witch poison," or secret medicine bundles some refer to as "love medicine"); and *yondwi´nias swa´yas* (abortion) (Parker, *Code*, 27–30; Thomas, 29–35). Although traditionally acceptable, all four practices contributed to the high mortality and low birth rates among the Haudenosaunee in Sganyadaí:yoh's time.

During the next sixteen years, numerous lesser prohibitions were added, along with codes regulating social and domestic behavior. Christian precepts were incorporated into the preachments, including monotheism, sin, confession, heaven, and hell. In addition, the code accepted Western contempt for such "sins" as traditional Iroquoian sexual mores ("promiscuity") and **gambling**, despite traditional sexual freedom and gambling's long-standing status as a sacred activity. In addition, cultural habits copied from Europeans—including wife beating, alcoholism, greed, and dysfunctional family relations—were defined as "sins." A special hell, described in lurid detail, awaited each sort of transgression. Some modern adherents of the Longhouse Religion resist the description of such elements as Christian, but as **J. N. B. Hewitt** correctly observed, none of them were traditional Iroquoian beliefs, nor did they enter the culture until they had been brought in by Christian missionaries (Hewitt, "Field Studies," 84).

Although he imposed Christianized social regulations, Sganyadaí:yoh also preserved some very traditional elements of Faithkeeping, including seven-generation prognostication and dream work. He also perpetuated the celebration of the seasonal round of festivals as well as the clan systems of identity and naming that were necessary to performing the **Longhouse** rituals. Finally, he retained the reverence for the earth as "Our Mother" and the triple principles of the Great Law *Ne´´ Skě ñ´no^n* (Health), *Ne´´ Gai´í·hwiio* (Righteousness), and *Ne´´ Găshasde^n´´sä'* (Popular Sovereignty). In this regard, Sganyadaí:yoh is honored as having conserved traditional culture.

Tension between Handsome Lake and the Clan Mothers

When Sganyadaí:yoh attempted to institute Western-style patriarchy with male control of resources, he ran into staunch resistance. The Clan Mothers deeply resented his efforts to disempower the *gantowisas* (woman acting in their official capacities) and displace them from their traditional roles as heads of households in favor of men, European-style. They also resisted his attempt to outlaw abortion. Traditionally, Iroquoian women had always controlled their own fertility, skillfully using abortifacients for the purpose. In addition, they disliked being excluded from major Faithkeeping roles, since women traditionally had constituted better than half of the league's Faithkeepers.

Most important, the women firmly resisted Sganyadaí:yoh's attempt to usurp their traditional ownership and control over the land, a constitutionally guaranteed right of women. At the time, forced land sales were a hot political issue. Because women alone owned the land under the Great Law, they were blamed every time new acreage passed into European-American hands. In fact, most of these "sales" were land frauds perpetrated by dishonest land speculators.

When Sganyadaí:yoh pushed for male rights over the disposal of the land, a power struggle ensued, one largely centered on land deals. The displeasure of the Clan Mothers at Sganyadaí:yoh's interference in their affairs was frequently expressed through their speaker, Sagoyewatha ("He Causes Them to Be Awake," also called Red Jacket). In 1801, Sganyadaí:yoh accused Sagoyewatha of witchcraft because, speaking for the Clan Mothers and fighting a little dirty, he had advocated the sale of favorite fishing lands of Sganyadaí:yoh's followers. On the basis of primary sources, which only recorded men's names, Western commentators have mistakenly assumed that this dispute was between Sganyadaí: yoh and Sagoyewatha, whereas it was really a power struggle between Sganyadaí:yoh and the Clan Mothers.

Part of Sganyadaí:yoh's strategy in this power struggle was to denounce important *gantowisas* as witches on one hand while simultaneously announcing on the other that the Maize Maiden herself (the spirit of the Lynx, or Mother Earth) had spoken to him, embracing his mission (Parker, *Code*, 47). (Traditionally, the Spirit of Corn only spoke to the women in their fields.) The Clan Mothers impatiently rejected his vision.

Tensions boiled over one day when Sganyadaí:yoh's followers ran amuck, rounding up and flogging those women who opposed the *Gaiwí:yo*, using a much-despised European style of corporal punishment, the whip (Parker, *Code*, 46, Plate 12). These actions met with fierce condemnation on all sides, for the Haudenosaunee had always opposed slavery and censured its use of the whip. Sagoyewatha promptly denounced Sganyadaí:yoh as a false prophet.

Although heated accusations flew fairly regularly between these two camps, the heavy backlash caused by the whippings forced Sganyadaí:yoh to back away from his positions against women and "witchcraft." Sensing that he had gone too far, Sganyadaí:yoh claimed to have had no prior knowledge of what his disciples had planned and to have been blameless in the scourgings. (The Clan Mothers did not believe him.) In the end, he recanted and reaffirmed the older cultural codes that flatly outlawed corporal punishment, saying, "The Creator did not intend that you would punish your people" (Thomas, 80).

Sganyadaí:yoh's brother, Gaiant´waka (Cornplanter), also opposed his efforts. Gaiant´waka ridiculed the *Gaiwí:yo* and harassed his sibling at every step.

He alleged that Sganyadaí:yoh's visions were nothing but a montage of Christian concepts he had picked up from his nephew, Henry O'Bail (also spelled Abeel and O'Bayle), who had attended a missionary school in Philadelphia and had introduced Sganyadaí:yoh to the Christian Bible and its precepts.

Handsome Lake's Later Years

As the years passed and resistance remained steady, Sganyadaí:yoh became ever more reluctant to preach his *Gaiwí:yo*. Thus, ironically, as belief in his visions caught on, the prophet became ever more unwilling to expound upon them. In fact, Sganyadaí:yoh told his followers that he had not spoken all of the messages he had been given, and that he regretted not having had the courage to tell all of his visions. No one knows what those untold visions were (Parker, "Religion," 250). Soon after making this confession to his inner circle, Sganyadaí:yoh died, passing along responsibility for the *Gaiwí:yo* to his grandson, Sos´h'owl (Parker, *Code*, 12).

In his lifetime, Sganyadaí:yoh had always been scrupulous about the recitation of the *Gaiwí:yo*, often becoming angry with disciples who, he felt, had misconstrued elements of it. Before his death, he therefore had it committed to **wampum** writing. At first, transmission of the *Gaiwí:yo* was entrusted only to Soseha´wä, but soon other Faithkeepers (all male) took up the *Gaiwí:yo*, reading it from the original wampum. Soon, however, under the pressure of forced assimilation, most of the people lost their ability to read ceremonial wampum. The last two men known to have been able actually to read the *Gaiwí:yo* from the original wampum, Henan Scrogg and Solon Skye, died early in the twentieth century. Thereafter, the *Gaiwí:yo* was passed along from memory (Mann, 44–45).

Development of the Longhouse Religion

Although the Longhouse Religion is usually portrayed as spreading rapidly immediately upon the death of Sganyadaí:yoh, it did not. The Clan Mothers he had so angered in life did not put aside their misgivings that easily. The women's councils did not even consider the matter of the *Gaiwí:yo* for discussion until 1824, nine years after his death, and they did not allow it to go forward to the men's Grand Council until around 1861 (Parker, *Code*, 7; Thomas, 125). Thus they held up the *Gaiwí:yo* for forty-six years, most probably until every last Clan Mother of Sganyadaí:yoh's generation had died.

Even after the *Gaiwí:yo* was recognized, the Senecas remained hotly divided on the issue, but for new reasons. Those who had been "Christianized" disdained the *Gaiwí:yo* as primitive heathenism, while those who attended Longhouse rites reviled the Christian Senecas as imitation Euros "ashamed of [their] ancestors" (Parker, *Code*, 14). In the fight against assimilation, what was essentially the new way of Sganyadaí:yoh came to be called "the Old Way." Belonging to the Longhouse Religion became an act of political resistance. This did not mean that people were strongly aware of the contents of the *Gaiwí:yo*, however.

In 1928 on the Canadian reservations, J. N. B. Hewitt found the *Gaiwí:yo* and

Sganyadaí:yoh to be frustratingly confused in the popular imagination with the *Kayánerénhkowa* (Great Law) and **Deganawida**, especially among the Christianized group. The people had "unwittingly . . . confused the ethical principles of civil government" of the **Peacemaker** "with the religious teachings" of Sganyadaí:yoh. The two sets of teachings having been "thus erroneously coupled," Christian Iroquois "lightly repudiated" both "as the futile expression of rank heathenism" (Hewitt, "Culture," 179, 180). Ten years later, Hewitt found the same problem on the American reservations of New York, with "at least 70 percent of the Iroquois acting under the erroneous impression that the Handsome Lake teachings are merely an extension of the precepts and ordinances of the League of the Iroquois" (Hewitt, "Field Studies," 84). Hewitt's 70 percent accords with the estimate that about one-third of the turn-of-the-century Iroquois were Longhouse Religion adherents, a percentage that remains about the same today on the reservations. This does not mean that the remaining two-thirds are Christian, however, nor does it consider the beliefs of nonreservation Iroquois.

The *Gaiwí:yo* never caught on among the league peoples in Ohio. There were several reasons for this. First, the Ohio and New York Iroquois were growing more distant after the **American Revolution**, a process reinforced by the failure of the Ohio resistance in 1794 and completed with Ohio removal in 1845, at about the same time that Sganyadaí:yoh and his immediate followers were promulgating his *Gaiwí:yo*. Second, unlike New York Natives, who were almost instantaneously targeted for forced assimilation, Ohio Natives remained self-directed for another generation and a half. Christian missionaries entered Ohio at the risk of their lives, while Sganyadaí:yoh did not enter it at all. Third, the successful "prophet" in Ohio during this era was Tenskwatawa, the "Shawnee Prophet," who urged an unmitigated return to the oldest known traditions and cultural habits. As a result, the Iroquois of Ohio who follow tradition today tend to recall beliefs that retain all the old "heathen" elements of the pre-Sganyadaí: yoh traditions.

Today, there is no one standard version of the *Gaiwí:yo*, although the Faithkeepers who are allowed to present it are well known and carefully scrutinized. Foremost among modern Faithkeepers was Chief Jacob (Jake) Thomas (**Cayuga**), who committed his version to paper just four years before his death in 1998. The other major written source from the twentieth century was Edward Cornplanter, whose 1903 version of the *Gaiwí:yo* was published by **Arthur C. Parker** in 1913 as *The Code of Handsome Lake*. The earliest complete version of the *Gaiwí:yo* came from Sganyadaí:yoh's grandson, Sos´h'owl, himself the grandfather of Donehogä´wa (**Ely S. Parker**), the coauthor, along with **Lewis Henry Morgan**, of *The League of the Haudenosaunee*. Soseha´wä's full recital of the *Gaiwí:yo*, taken from Sganyadaí:yoh's own wampum and delivered in 1848, was reproduced verbatim by Donehogä´wa and Morgan (Morgan, 1:223–248).

The *Gaiwí:yo* has been a large element of the Third Epoch of Time, but it should not be confused with the Third Epoch itself, for this epoch is not over, nor have all its stories yet been told. An ancient tradition prophesied the end of the Third Epoch and the beginning of the Fourth Epoch of Time as occurring very traumatically. The people will notice the change when the Great Turtle who bears us all on his back rolls and dives deep, back into the ocean, drowning all but a handful of those standing on his back. Out of this cataclysm, Native America will rise again, once more the sole possessors of **Turtle Island**. (A version of this tradition may be found in Heckewelder, 345.) Some believe that the women's portion of this epoch must be told before the Great Turtle dives.

FURTHER READING

Deardorff, Merle H. *The Religion of Handsome Lake: Its Origin and Development.* Bureau of American Ethnology Bulletin No. 149. Washington, D.C.: Bureau of American Ethnology, 1951.

Heckewelder, John. *History, Manners, and Customs of the Indian Nations Who Once Inhabited Pennsylvania and the Neighboring States.* 1820, 1876. The First American Frontier Series. New York: Arno Press and the New York Times, 1971.

Hewitt, J[ohn] N[apoleon] B[rinton]. "The Culture of the Indians of Eastern Canada." *Explorations and Field-work of the Smithsonian Institution for 1928* (1929): 179–182.

———. "Field Studies of the Iroquois in New York State and in Ontario, Canada." *Explorations and Field-work of the Smithsonian Institution for 1936* (1937): 83–86.

Mann, Barbara A. "The Fire at Onondaga: Wampum as Proto-writing." *Akwesasne Notes*, 26th Anniversary Issue, n.s. 1:1 (Spring 1995): 40–48.

Morgan, Lewis Henry. *League of the Haudenosaunee, or Iroquois.* 1851. 2 vols. New York: Burt Franklin, 1964.

Parker, Arthur C. *The Code of Handsome Lake, the Seneca Prophet.* New York State Museum Bulletin 163, Education Department Bulletin No. 530, November 1, 1912. Albany: University of the State of New York, 1913.

———. *Notes on the Ancestry of Cornplanter.* 1927. Researches and Transactions of the New York State Archaeological Association, Lewis H. Morgan Chapter. New York: Times Presses, 1970.

———. "The Religion of Handsome Lake." Recital by Jimmy Johnson at Tonawanda, October 2–3, 1845. In *The Life of General Ely S. Parker, Last Grand Sachem of the Iroquois and General Grant's Military Secretary.* Buffalo: Buffalo Historical Society, 1919: 251–261.

Shimony, Annemarie Anrod. *Conservatism among the Iroquois at the Six Nations Reserve.* 1961. Syracuse,: N.Y. Syracuse University Press, 1994.

Thomas, Chief Jacob, with Terry Boyle. *Teachings from the Longhouse.* Toronto: Stoddart, 1994.

Wallace, Anthony F. C. *The Death and Rebirth of the Seneca.* New York: Knopf, 1970.

———. ed. "Halliday Jackson's Journey to the Seneca Indians, 1798–1800." Parts 1 and 2. *Pennsylvania History* 19:2–3 (1952): 117–147, 325–349.

Barbara A. Mann

Thomas, Jacob/Jake (Cayuga), 1922–1998. In the late twentieth century, Jacob (Jake) Thomas was the only living person who could recite the entire Haudenosaunee **Great Law of Peace** in all five Iroquois languages. To maintain the oral tradition, Thomas, during the late twentieth century, recited the entire Great Law to the Iroquois Grand Council at Onondaga once every five years. These recitations ended with Thomas's death on August 17, 1998.

Thomas, of the **Cayuga** Snipe Clan, lived in Canada (the Cayugas today have no land in New York State). He was condoled onto the Grand Council at Grand River in 1974 with the title Dawenhethon, replacing Augustus Williams, who had died in 1972.

The Great Law of Peace is available in English translation, but often in vastly condensed versions that lead many to forget that a complete oral recitation of the tradition can take as long as a week. A complete written version was not published until the early 1990s. Thomas's recitation of the Great Law usually took three to four eight-hours days. The recitations usually took place in a simple log building that today functions as the heart of the traditional confederacy on the **Onondaga** Nation, near Nedrow, New York, a few miles south of Syracuse.

Thomas utilized **wampum** belts, some of which were returned to the Haudenosaunee in 1989 after a century of possession by the state of New York. Thomas deciphered the symbols on the ancient beaded belts and recited the law, tenet by tenet, until his feet ached and his voice cracked, recalling the ancient story of the Iroquois League's founding as a union of Native nations that previously had waged vicious war against each other, in part:

I am going to uproot the tree which is a symbol of life and peace. And when I uproot the tree there is a cavity that goes deep into the earth. And at the bottom of that tree there is a swift river. All the generations that you have cried because of the war clubs, the spears and the weapons that killed and injured your fellow men left you in grief. So, therefore, it has been proven that that is not the answer to peace. . . . Now I call upon all the men. All the war leaders come forth and bring your spears and your clubs and all your weapons of war. . . . And I ask you now to throw them in that hole. . . . And they all put their weapons of war [into] that swift water that took the weapons to the unknown regions. . . . There can be no peace unless there is logic and there is reason. Peace cannot be attained through intimidation. Peace cannot be attained with fear and threats. (Thomas, 13)

FURTHER READING

Thomas, Jake. "The Great Law Takes a Long Time to Learn." *Northeast Indian Quarterly* 4:4 (Winter 1987): 13–17.

The Three Sisters (Dyõnhe´hgõ, "Our Life Supporters," "Our Sustenance"). Dyõnhe´hgõ, commonly rendered as "the Three Sisters," indicates the primary food sources of the old Iroquois: the elder sister, **corn**, and her two younger sisters, beans and squash. Of the three, corn was by far the most important crop.

All Iroquoian peoples were farmers and sustained their cultures through massive agriculture organized, managed, and worked by the women. Despite the continuing and inaccurate depiction in Western literature of Iroquoian farming as "horticulture," it was agriculture on a grand scale, with fields averaging several hundred acres per town (Stites, 25). At the beginning of European contact, 65 percent of foodstuffs were produced in the women's fields, with the remaining 35 percent contributed by male and female fishing and by the men's hunting (Delâge, 62). The yields sustained by the women per acre exceeded contemporary European yields (Delâge, 58).

Productivity continued to be high well after contact. For example, in July 1687, when the Marquis de Denonville sacked the **Seneca**'s territory (a league breadbasket), he found towns housing between fourteen and fifteen thousand citizens, six or seven times the population supported by farming towns in Europe. As part of his unsuccessful war effort against the league, Denonville destroyed 1.2 million bushels of corn at one granary (O'Callaghan, 1:147). This was not atypical, as George Washington found out almost a century later when his men sacked Seneca and **Onondaga** territory during the **American Revolution** and found warehouses containing similar stores (Parker, 19).

During the first half of the nineteenth century, in the government-sponsored attempt to forcibly assimilate the Haudenosaunee, the Quakers were unable to push the men into the fields and the women into patriarchal households (Rothenberg). Women continued to be the farmers in the family. To this day, Iroquoian women continue to farm.

Numerous seasonal **ceremonies**, songs, and dances are connected to Dyõnhe´hgõ in the annual round of festivals, including the all-important Midwinter Ceremony, which recognizes the various spirit powers of trees and bushes. Although frequently overlooked in anthropological literature, there is a female presence in this ceremony that was once quite strong. Even today, despite assimilationist pressures, the women's agricultural element remains, and the ceremony is recognized as honoring Dyõhe´hgõ (Shimony, 142–143).

Numerous additional ceremonies recognize Dyõnhe´hgõ in whole or in part. The Seed Planting Ceremony straddling April and May is unquestionably a women's event, once run by a women's society that has since been allowed to lapse in most places. The Corn Sprouting Ceremony toward the end of May honors the tender young shoots. The Corn Testing Ceremony (also called the Little Green Corn) occurs early in September, just before the corn is harvestable. The **Green Corn Ceremony**, the annual harvest festival that follows, is second in importance only to the Midwinter Festival and may at one time have eclipsed it in importance. The Green Corn Ceremony is followed by the Harvest Ceremony in late October, signaling that all three sisters have been properly stored. In addition to these corn ceremonies, there is the annual Green Bean Ceremony, which occurs early in August when the green beans ripen.

The seasonal festivals are quite old. Today's versions on Haudenosaunee reservations of New York and Canada continue largely because the *Gaiwí:yo* of Sganyadaí:yoh (the Code of **Handsome Lake**) sanctioned them in the early nineteenth century. The content of the ceremonies, however, was reworked to fit the precepts of the *Gaiwí:yo*, for example, by recognizing a solitary, male

"Creator" or "Great Spirit" in the Thanksgiving Address. This had not always been the focus. In older times, the spirits of Dyõhe´hgõ and the women of the First Family were given central attention.

FURTHER READING

Delâge, Denys. *Le pays renversé: Amérindiens et européens en Amérique du nord-est, 1600–1664.* Montréal: Boréal Express, 1985.

Lewendowski, Stephen. "Three Sisters: A Iroquoian Cultural Complex." In "Cultural Encounter II, 'Indian Corn of the Americas: Gift to the World.' " *Northeast Indian Quarterly* 6:1–2 (Spring–Summer 1989): 41–45.

Mann, Barbara A. *Iroquoian Women: Gantowisas of the Haudenosaunee League.* New York: Peter Lang, 2000.

O'Callaghan, E. B., ed. *The Documentary History of the State of New York.* 4 vols. Albany: Weed, Parsons & Co., 1849–1851.

Parker, Arthur C. *The Iroquois Uses of Maize and Other Food Plants.* 1913. In William N. Fenton, ed., *Parker on the Iroquois.* Syracuse, N.Y.: Syracuse University Press, 1968: 5–119.

Rothenberg, Diane. "The Mothers of the Nation: Seneca Resistance to Quaker Intervention." In M. Etienne and E. Leacock, eds., *Women and Colonization.* New York: Praeger, 1980: 63–87.

Shimony, Annemarie Anrod. *Conservatism among the Iroquois at the Six Nations Reserve.* 1961. Syracuse, N.Y.: Syracuse University Press, 1994.

Stites, Sara Henry. *Economics of the Iroquois.* Dissertation Monograph Series, vol. 1, no. 3. Bryn Mawr, Penn.: Bryn Mawr College Monographs, 1905.

Barbara A. Mann

Tonawanda Seneca Reservation. The Tonawanda Seneca Reservation, east of Buffalo, New York, occupies 7,549 acres, all of which are tribally owned. The reservation, with a population of 448 in 1990, maintains a traditional council form of government and is a member of the Haudenosaunee (Iroquois) Confederacy. The reservation was formed in 1857 after the **Senecas** relinquished rights to lands granted them by the United States west of the Missouri River.

Treaty diplomacy. Between the mid-seventeenth century and the end of the nineteenth century, the Haudenosaunee negotiated more than one hundred treaties with English and later with U.S. representatives. Until about 1800 C.E., most of these treaties were negotiated according to Haudenosaunee protocol. By the mid-eighteenth century, this protocol was well established as the lingua franca of diplomacy in eastern North America. According to this protocol, an alliance was adopted and maintained using certain rituals. Regarding treaties, Michael D. Green wrote:

Treaties are the acts of sovereigns. By engaging in treating relations with native nations, Europeans recognized the actuality of sovereignty even as they frequently rejected its legality. Autonomy, or self-government free from outside control, is central to the definition of sovereignty. When the United States embraced the treaty system as the mechanism for conducting its relations with native nations, it learned that it must also extend the recognition of sovereignty that underlay the colonial treaties. Congress's Indian policy in the 1780s, shaped largely by its revolutionary experience, rejected such recognition and the results were disastrous. (Green, 462)

Initial contacts between negotiating parties usually were made "at the edge of the forest," on neutral ground, where an agenda and a meeting place and time could be agreed upon. Following the "approach to the council fire," the place of negotiation, a **Condolence Ceremony** was recited to remember those who had died on both sides since the last meeting. A designated party kindled the council fire at the beginning of negotiations and covered it at the end. A council was called for a specific purpose (such as the making of peace) that could not be changed once convened. Representatives from both sides spoke in a specified order. No important actions were taken until at least one night had elapsed since the matter's introduction before the council. The passage of time was said to allow the various members of the council to attain unanimity—"one mind"— necessary for consensual solution of a problem.

Wampum belts or strings were exchanged when an important point was made or an agreement was reached. Acceptance of a belt was taken to mean agreement on an issue. A belt also could be refused or thrown aside to indicate rejection. Another metaphor that was used throughout many of the councils was that of the **Covenant Chain**, a symbol of alliance. If proceedings were going well and **consensus** was being reached on major issues, the chain (which was often characterized as being made of silver) was being "polished" or "shined." If agreement was not being reached, the chain was said to be "rusting."

During treaty negotiations, a speaker was generally allowed to complete a statement without interruption, according to Haudenosaunee protocol, which differs markedly from the cacophony of debate in European forums such as the British House of Commons. Often European representatives expressed consternation when carefully planned schedules were cast aside so that everyone (warriors as well as chiefs) could express an opinion on an important issue. Many treaties were attended by large parties of Iroquois, each of whom could, in theory, claim a right to speak.

The host of a treaty council was expected to supply tobacco for the common pipe, as well as refreshments (usually alcoholic in nature) to extinguish the sour taste of tobacco smoking. Gifts often were exchanged, and great feasts were held during the proceedings, which sometimes were attended by entire Haudenosaunee families. A treaty council could last several days under the most agreeable of circumstances. If major obstacles were encountered in negotiations, a council could extend for two weeks or longer, sometimes as long as a month. The main conference often was accompanied by several smaller ones during which delegates with common interests met to discuss problems that concerned them alone. Usually, historical accounts record only the proceedings of the main body, leaving out the many important side conferences, which, in the diplomatic language of the time, were often said to have been held "in the bushes."

Treaty councils were carried on in a ritualistic manner in part to provide common points of understanding between representatives who were otherwise separated by barriers of language and interpretation based on differing cultural orientations. The abilities of a good interpreter who was trusted by both sides (an example was **Conrad Weiser** in the mid-eighteenth century) could greatly influence the course of negotiations. Whether they knew the Iroquois and Algonquian languages or not, Anglo-American negotiators had to be on speaking terms with the metaphors of Iroquois protocol, such as the council fire, condolence, the tree of peace, and many others.

To the Haudenosaunee, treaty relations, like trading relationships, were characterized in terms of kinship, hospitality, and reciprocity, over and above commercial or diplomatic interests. The Dutch, in particular, seemed to be easily annoyed when they were forced to deal with trade relationships based on anything other than commerce. The **Mohawks** seemed to resent their attitude. During September 1659, a party of Mohawks complained that "the Dutch, indeed, say we are brothers and are joined together with chains, but that lasts only as long as we have beavers. After that, we are no longer thought of, but much will depend on it [alliance] when we shall need each other" (Dennis, 171).

From the first sustained contact with Europeans, shortly after 1600, until the end of the French and Indian War (1763), the Haudenosaunee Confederacy utilized diplomacy to maintain a balance of power in northeastern North America between the colonizing British and French. This use of diplomacy and alliances to play one side off against the other reached its height shortly after 1700, during the period that Richard Aquila calls the "Iroquois Restoration" (Aquila, 16–17).

This period was followed by the eventual alliance of most Haudenosaunee with the British and the eventual defeat of the French. According to Aquila, the Iroquois' power had declined dangerously by about 1700, to a point where they had only about 1,200 warriors, requiring a concerted effort on the part of the Grand Council to minimize warfare and build peaceful relations with the Haudenosaunee's neighbors. By 1712, Haudenosaunee military resources amounted to about 1,800 men. Disease as well as incessant warfare also caused declines in Haudenosaunee populations at about this time; major outbreaks of smallpox swept through Iroquoia in 1696 and 1717. At the same time, sizable numbers of Haudenosaunee, especially Mohawks, moved to Canada and cast their lots with the French.

Alcohol also was devastating the Haudenosaunee at this time, a fact emphasized by the many requests of Haudenosaunee leaders at treaty councils and other meetings that the liquor trade be curtailed. Aquila writes that "sachems complained that alcohol deprived the Iroquois people of their senses, was ruining their lives . . . and was used by traders to cheat them out of their furs and lands. The Iroquois were not exaggerating. The French priest Lafitau reported in 1718 that when the Iroquois and other Indians became intoxicated they went completely berserk, screaming like madmen and smashing everything in their homes" (Aquila, 115).

The English realized the value of an alliance with the Haudenosaunee. On

April 20, 1700, for example, Governor Bellomont wrote to the Board of Trade that if the Iroquois were to defect to the French, the English would be forced out of North America within two months (Aquila, 47).

By the 1740s, England's developing industrial base had become much better at supplying trade goods to the Haudenosaunee and other Native American peoples; the balance of alliance was shifting. After 1763, the Haudenosaunee were no longer able to play the French and the English against each other. Instead, the Haudenosaunee faced pressure to ally with Native peoples to their west against the English. Many **Senecas** sided with Pontiac against the English in 1763 and 1764.

Today, some members of the Iroquois Grand Council travel the world on their own national passports. The passport states that it has been issued by the Grand Council of the League of the Haudenosaunee, and that "the Haudenosaunee continues as a sovereign people on the soil it has occupied on Turtle Island since time immemorial, and we extend friendship to all who recognize our constitutional government and who desire peaceful relations" (Hill, 12). The passports were first issued in 1977 to Haudenosaunee delegates who attended a meeting of the United Nations in Switzerland. Since then, the United States, Canada, Switzerland, Holland, France, Belgium, Germany, Denmark, Italy, Libya, Turkey, Australia, Great Britain, New Zealand, Iran, and Colombia have been among the nations recognizing the Haudenosaunee documents. Even so, it takes a talented travel agent to get a visa on an Iroquois passport, because formal diplomatic relations often do not exist between the country recognizing the document and the Grand Council.

FURTHER READING

Aquila, Richard. *The Iroquois Restoration: Iroquois Diplomacy on the Colonial Frontier, 1701–1754*. Detroit: Wayne State University Press, 1983.

Dennis, Matthew. *Cultivating a Landscape of Peace*. Ithaca, N.Y.: Cornell University Press, 1993.

Green, Michael D. "The Expansion of European Colonization to the Mississippi Valley, 1780–1880." In Bruce G. Trigger and Wilcomb E. Washburn, eds., *The Cambridge History of the Native Peoples of the Americas. North America*, vol. 1. Cambridge, England: Cambridge University Press, 1996: 461–538.

Hill, Richard (Rick). "Continuity of Haudenosaunee Government: Political Reality of the Grand Council." *Northeast Indian Quarterly* 4:3 (Autumn 1987): 10–14.

Jacobs, Wilbur. *Diplomacy and Indian Gifts: Anglo-French Rivalry Along the Ohio and Northwest Frontiers, 1748–1763*. Stanford, Calif.: Stanford University Press, 1950.

Trelease, Allen W. *Indian Affairs in Colonial New York: The Seventeenth Century*. Ithaca, N.Y.: Cornell University Press, 1960.

Van Doren, Carl, and Julian P. Boyd, eds. *Indian Treaties Printed by Benjamin Franklin, 1736–1762*. Philadelphia: Historical Society of Pennsylvania, 1938.

Turtle Island, as reference to North America. In the Haudenosaunee creation story, life on earth takes shape on the back of a giant turtle. To this day, many

Iroquois call North America "Turtle Island." During the late twentieth century, the idea of Turtle Island often was used as an environmental idea by social activists. The idea is not new. **Handsome Lake**, the Iroquois prophet, used it almost two hundred years ago when he urged people to think of how their actions would affect their descendants seven generations into the future.

On Earth Day 1992, several thousand participants in Kansas City's Earth Day decided to unite historical and ecological themes to look at the consequences of 500 years since the first voyage of Columbus. Among other activities, they assembled a design of a turtle from recyclable materials that was larger than a football field in a Kansas City park.

Tuscaroras, historical sketch. The name "Tuscarora" is an anglicized version of their own name, *Dus-ga-o-weh*, meaning "Shirt-wearing people," a name adopted before their emigration from the Carolina country but after their first contact with European-Americans. During the spring of 1712, the Tuscaroras, an Iroquoian-speaking people located in present-day western North Carolina, sent **wampum** belts to the Haudenosaunee Grand Council requesting aid against the Catawbas and English colonists who were impinging on their lands. One of the major causes for friction between the Tuscaroras and their non-Indian neighbors in North Carolina was frequent kidnappings of Tuscarora children, who were sold into slavery (Graymont, 102).

The government of New York interceded with the Haudenosaunee, warning them not to take up the hatchet against the English in the Carolinas or against the Catawbas (who were allies of the English) but to work to solve the problem by diplomatic means. As a result, following several months of hostilities, the Tuscaroras were invited to migrate to Haudenosaunee country and become the sixth nation of the confederacy.

The Grand Council approved the Tusacaroras' admittance in 1722, but the actual migration took almost a century. Because the **Peacemaker** had decreed that the Grand Council could have only fifty positions, Tuscarora representatives were not added as voting members. A representative of the Tuscaroras attended council meetings, but was required to ask permission to speak. The Tuscaroras often were represented by the **Senecas**, from whose land their reservation was carved.

During the late 1950s, New York State power officials (the same people and agencies who were advocating flooding of Seneca land by the **Kinzua Dam**) requisitioned 1,383 acres of Tuscarora land, about one-fifth of the reservation, to serve as a reservoir for expanded power production at Niagara Falls. The Tuscaroras resisted the taking of this land to the point of lying down in front of police and earth-moving equipment, as described by Edmund Wilson:

[T]hey were wise enough to fix on a policy of Gandhian passive resistance, and when the surveyors arrived in the morning, accompanied by no less than ten carloads of State Troopers, plainclothesmen and Niagara County sheriffs—estimated at more than a hundred—armed with tear-gas, submachine guns and revolvers, they were met by placards and signs saying, "Warning. No Trespassing. Indian Reserve," "Must You Take Everything the Indians Own?," and "United States Help Us. We Helped You in 1776 and 1812, 1918 and 1941." About two hundred Tuscaroras stood in the way of the trucks. (Wilson, 144–145)

After a protracted court battle, 550 acres were ceded, 495 for a reservoir and 55 acres for high-power lines that would cross reservation lands.

In the late twentieth century, the Tuscarora Nation's reservation occupies 5,778 acres nine miles northeast of Niagara Falls, near the southern shore of Lake Ontario, at Lewiston, New York. Title to this land was secured by the Tuscaroras by treaty in 1784, after their migration from North Carolina to join the Haudenosaunee Confederacy early in the eighteenth century. Since that time, the Tuscarora Nation has been governed by a traditional council consisting of thirteen chiefs chosen by Clan Mothers with the consent of their nine families. Many Tuscaroras work in the Buffalo and Niagara urban areas. The tribe earns a small amount of money from timber sales.

In August 1997, more than 500 people, nearly the entire population of the Tuscarora Reservation, filed a class-action lawsuit against fourteen chemical companies for more than $1 billion in damages to personal property and personal injury. The suit originates from areas near the Love Canal, near Niagara Falls, which earlier had been a site of much-publicized pollution.

FURTHER READING

Graymont, Barbara, ed. *Fighting Tuscarora: The Autobiography of Chief Clinton Rickard*. Syracuse, N.Y.: Syracuse University Press, 1973.
Wilson, Edmund. *Apologies to the Iroquois*. New York: Vintage Books, 1960.

Two Row Wampum. The Two Row Wampum (Kas-wen-tha) is among the oldest of Haudenosaunee **wampum** belts used in diplomacy. It depicts two parallel rows of purple wampum against a background of white. The two lines depict Haudenosaunee and non-Iroquois living different but mutually respectful lives. Three rows of white beads between the two purple rows represent friendship, peace, and respect. The background itself symbolizes the purity (good faith) of the agreement recognized by the belt.

Tyendinaga Mohawk Reserve (Ontario). The Tyendinaga Mohawk Reserve on the northeastern shore of Lake Ontario was settled by **Mohawks** who had emigrated to Canada after the **American Revolution**. They had factional differences with **Joseph Brant**'s party at **Grand River** that required a separate settlement. This reserve has not been part of the Grand River Iroquois council. Tyendinaga, with approximately 3,000 Mohawk residents living on 17,000 acres, is located near Picton, Ontario, on the Bay of Quinte. The renowned Mohawk chief **Oronhyatekha** is buried at Tyendinaga in the cemetery of Anglican Christ Church, overlooking the Bay of Quinte.

The Tyendinaga Mohawks, who were loyal to the British in the Revolution, migrated to Ontario in 1784, along with a large number of non-Indian loyalists, to escape retribution by the victorious patriots. A tower at All Saints Church on the Tyendinaga Reserve observes:

Fear God and Honor the Queen. This tower was erected Dec. 15, 1884 by the Mohawks of the Bay of Quinte, in grateful memory of Captain John Deserontyou, formerly of the Mohawks of the Mohawk River, in the State of New York, who led his people to abandon their property in support of the British cause and led them and his warriors to follow the British flag to Canada and landed on the Tyendinaga Reserve in May A.D. 1784. (Barnes, 12)

The Tyendinaga Mohawks became so closely identified with the British cause that they formed the only American Indian Lodge of the Orange Order (Loyal Orange Lodge Number 99) as protectors of English Protestantism. In 1995, a delegation of six Tyendinaga Mohawks traveled to Belfast, Northern Ireland, to take part in a march that celebrated the 200th anniversary of the Battle of the Boyne, at which the forces of the Roman Catholic King Charles II were defeated. The Mohawks wore ceremonial headdresses and buckskin tunics in the anniversary march, which drew a crowd variously estimated at between 50,000 and 100,000 people and included several hundred marching bands. "Our hearts go out to our brothers in Northern Ireland," said Albert Maracle, one of the Mohawks who marched in the parade (Ball).

In the middle 1990s, the Tyendinaga Mohawks engaged in a number of business ventures on and off the reserve, including purchase of the Deerhurst Resort in Huntsville, one of the largest and best-known vacation destinations in the province. The resort had piled up more than $31 million in debt, including $8 million in loans from the governments of Ontario and Canada, and probably would close without the Mohawk buyout. In exchange, the Mohawks were asking for permission to open a casino at the resort. Deerhurst, which was one hundred years old in 1996, has a guest capacity of 1,200 people. The Tyendinaga Mohawks operate several businesses, including Peace Tree Technologies, AirDirect/First Nations Air Service, and First Nations Technical Institute. Mohawks at Tyendinaga formed a committee to establish a radio station and in 1994 obtained $28,540 from the provincial government to start a temporary station, with plans to make it permanent. The Tyendinaga Mohawks also have experienced some turbulence in their tribal government. In June 1994, several dozen Mohawks occupied the band council's offices and accused the council's members of spending thousands of dollars on fancy lunches and gifts for each other.

FURTHER READING

Ball, Steve. "Orangemen March to New World Order." *The Times* (London), August 18, 1996, n.p.

Barnes, Sally. "A Double Loss for Canada's Native People." *Toronto Sun*, March 20, 1995, p 12.

U

United Nations, the Haudenosaunee and. For decades, Native American leaders have been knocking at the doors of the United Nations, trying to get in so they can make their arguments for admission as sovereign states, an idea to which the United States is adamantly opposed. This is ironic because the Haudensaunee were called to consult on the organization of the United Nations in the late 1940s, just as, almost two centuries earlier, they had been involved in the evolution of a federal structure of government in the United States.

Several Native nations, such as the Hopi, the Shoshones, and the Haudenosaunee Confederacy, maintain that they have never ceded their independence to the United States. They point to a long history as nations, a tradition that the United States recognized when it entered into treaty relationships with their governments.

Instead, U.S. courts have declared Indians to be members of "dependent" nations who occupy their lands at the pleasure of the United States (under the "plenary power" of Congress), which may at any time elect to abrogate Native status altogether, contrary to international law respecting treaties between nations. In other words, Indians have no rights Congress is legally bound to respect.

Having opposed this concept for generations, the leaders of the Haudenosaunee have tried to have their case heard before the United Nations. In 1977, the confederacy succeeded in gaining recognition as a "nongovernment organization" (NGO) at the UN human-rights assembly in Geneva, Switzerland, but this action was without teeth.

Still, the Haudenosaunee did not give up the fight, which they believe will one day have Iroquois delegates take their rightful place among the community of nations. Iroquois leaders can point to some successes in the last eighteen years that give them considerable cause for hope. The Haudenosaunee and other Native peoples were granted standing before the Fourth Russell International

Tribunal held in Holland during 1988. This entity was composed of judges and legal scholars from throughout the world and provided a forum for disadvantaged peoples to plead their cases. The Iroquois did so, presenting a long list of human-rights abuses suffered at the hands of the United States. Given the strength of the Iroquois case, the tribunal found it relatively simple to condemn the American government for its long-standing policy of suppressing indigenous peoples.

In 1984, the confederacy participated in an international assembly of Native peoples in Panama and while there helped draft a Declaration of Principles of Indigenous Rights. Iroquois delegates returned to Geneva in 1989 to persuade the General Conference of the International Labour Organization of the United Nations to move to protect Native societies against being exploited by land- and resource-hungry governments and corporations. Confederacy speakers were also present at the Earth Environmental Summit in Rio de Janeiro, Brazil, in 1992 and lobbied for the decision by the United Nations to declare 1993 as the "International Year for the Indigenous Peoples."

The hard work of the Haudenosaunee on behalf of the world's Native populations have won for them many friends at the United Nations. Therefore, it came as no surprise when the United Nations Environmental Programme agreed to hold a one-day session at UN headquarters in New York City to listen to the Iroquois concerns about the ongoing contamination of their ancestral homelands.

The confederacy has sent official representatives from all six nations (with the exception of the **Oneidas** of New York, who elected not to participate) to the United Nations to give testimony about conditions on Iroquois territory. The Iroquois pointed to environmental degradation and territorial displacement as the primary cause of the internal tensions that have plagued the confederacy for the past ten years.

Removed from their lands by force and fraud, the Iroquois were compelled to suffer through adverse economic and social conditions that resulted in social chaos and political unrest. From the industrial pollutants that have destroyed farming and fishing at **Akwesasne** to the inundation of the **Allegany Reservation** by the **Kinzua Dam**, the Iroquois have come perilously close to extinction as a distinct people because their traditional economies based on their natural resources have been undermined. It should shock no one, the Haudenosaunee argued, that given poverty and lack of viable economic opportunities, many Iroquois have turned to criminal activities to make a living, with subsequent adverse effects on the environment.

The Haudenosaunee are not ones to simply complain. Working in conjunction with Cambridge University in England, the Environmental Protection Agency, and Indigenous Development International, as well as the United Nations itself, the confederacy submitted a report entitled "Haudenosaunee: Environmental Restoration—An Indigenous Strategy for Sustainability." This document summarizes the current conditions on Iroquois lands and offers concrete solutions to return Mother Earth to her former state. It proposes the creation of an indigenous environmental learning center to study problem areas and offer solutions. This center would also coordinate information, define economic development strategies, and assist in the preservation of culture. The confederacy pledged itself to raise at least $26 million over five years for the project while seeking the assistance of the United Nations, which in turn might use this concept for Native peoples worldwide.

Haudenosaunee representatives such as **Oren Lyons**, Henry Lickers, Dennis Bowen, Leo Henry, Audrey Shenandoah, **Jake Swamp, Leon Shenandoah**, Charles Wheelock, Clint Halftown, Carol Jacobs, and Bernie Parker were applauded by UN Under Secretaries Richard Butler and Keith Johnson for their perseverance, dedication, and creativity in arriving at an equitable solution to a very difficult problem. While the Haudenosaunee Confederacy might be years away from entering the United Nations as a nation, its presence there as the conscience of indigenous peoples from throughout the hemisphere before environmental and human-rights forums makes admission a strong possibility in the future.

Doug George-Kanentiio

W

Wampum. Physically, wampum is a bead carved out of shell. Practically, wampum was a means of recording historical documents and relaying messages; that is, it was a Native American writing system. Wampum was also used ceremonially to facilitate contact with spirits and generally to make and keep pledges. Wampum, in beads, strings, or belts, was and is sacred.

Wampum was fashioned from the shells of whelk (*Buccinum undatum*) or of quahog clams (*Mercenaria mercenaria*), with whelk producing white wampum and quahog clams producing "black" wampum. (In fact, black wampum is really a deep, iridescent purple). Often barrel or oblong in shape and varying in size from 4 mm × 2 mm to 17 mm × 5 mm, wampum beads were carefully bored through the center and strung ("knotted") on threads made of deer sinews or bark (Mann, 40). In belts, the knotting method used intricate interlacings to produce a wide variety of patterns. Some belts, such as the great war belt of the league, which oral tradition states was given by the **Ohio League** to Tecumseh in 1794, were as much as five feet long and three feet wide.

Origins of Wampum

Western scholars long attempted to insist that Europeans inspired wampum with their own bead industry, and even that they had taught Native Americans how to make wampum in the first place. Although this reckless claim still appears from time to time in Western texts, it was discredited in 1949 when Slotkin and Schmitt documented the archaeological existence of wampum slag heaps—dumps containing both wampum beads and materials left over from the manufacture of wampum—all up and down the eastern coast of America. These artifacts predated European contact by centuries, reaching back into the Archaic period of eastern Native history. International communication routes disseminated wampum well into the interior of **Turtle Island** (North America), reaching Tennessee and Ohio. In fact, wampum beads were associated with Adena com-

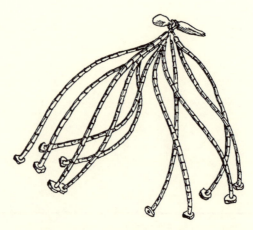

A string of wampum. Courtesy of John Kahionhes Fadden.

plexes in Ohio. Wampum was, therefore, indisputably a Native idea, of Native manufacture (Slotkin and Schmitt, 223–225).

What Europeans did do was subvert the original meaning of wampum from a writing and sacred system into a money system. The Dutch, especially, promoted this false concept around 1610. Not only did the Dutch import glass beads from Europe, as did France and England, but they began to manufacture faux wampum from conch shells, flooding Native cultures with it and even setting distinct trade values for white and black wampum. The British later set an exact 2:1 ratio (white to black) for valuing wampum, as well as exchange rates for wampum in terms of both European forms of cash and skins. In 1770, the British set up a wampum mint in America. The last American wampum mint closed in 1899 (Mann, 41).

Despite this intense effort to commodify and commercialize wampum, its original purpose continued to be honored by the Native nations of the East. It was used ceremonially for spirit work, plighting pledges, and sealing promises. It was also used extensively as a writing system to record documents of the league.

Wampum as Writing

Wampum writing consisted of a set of symbols whose meanings remained consistent from nation to nation despite linguistic differences, much as Chinese characters are recognized and understood by speakers of mutually unintelligible Asian languages: the Han dialects, Mandarin, Ch'eng-tu, Japanese, and others. By the same token, Cherokees, **Senecas**, Mahicans, Choctaws, and others, although they spoke different languages, all could read and comprehend wampum writing. As Daniel Brinton documented in 1876, when many wampum readers were still living, wampum "Designs and figures had definite meanings, recognized over wide areas" (Brinton, 16).

Wampum writers were said to be "talking" their thoughts into the wampum (Palmer, 4:92), as did **Hiawatha**, the inventor of Condolence Wampum and the knotter of the **Hiawatha Belt** symbolizing the league. On a practical level, wampum writers "talked" messages into wampum using a clever combination of white and black characters. The availability of two possible expressions for every character, white and black, effectively doubled the number of available symbols while altering meanings depending on a character's context and whether it was presented in black or white. For example, a fully white belt was a peace token, but a fully black belt meant war. Not all characters were so easily reversed, however. Meanings could vary quite subtly, depending on surrounding fields and characters.

Once "talked" into wampum, the message could be read back out of it with considerable confidence as to its accuracy (Converse, 140). **John Heckewelder**, an eighteenth-century Moravian missionary who lived with the league, stated that a good messenger was "able to point out the exact place on a [wampum] belt which is to answer to each particular sentence, the same as we can point out a passage in a book" (Heckewelder, 108).

In addition to characters, wampum belts themselves were often reversible; that is, they could be figured on both sides, yielding "double wampum." A form used on governmental occasions, it featured two speakers, both "sides" of the clans and/or nations, addressing two audiences, again, the "sides" of the clans and/or nations (Hewitt, "Wampum," 904–990). Heckewelder frequently heard double-wampum addresses. He recorded that "much depends" on the "*turning* of the belt which takes place when [a speaker] has finished one half of his speech. . . . it may be as well known by it how far the speaker has advanced in his speech, as with us on taking a glance at the pages of a book or pamphlet while reading" (Heckewelder, 108; italics in the original).

Because *uki/otkon* (white/black) spirit forces were involved in the creation of the messages talked into wampum, strings and belts of wampum were (and are) held sacred, and knotting wampum is a spiritual activity (Mann, 43–44, 45). Hiawatha's Condolence Wampum is part of a sacred mourning and healing ceremony, while white wampum became part of the confessional rites of the Longhouse Religion in the nineteenth century. The sacral view of wampum is ancient, however, antedating both the **Condolence Ceremony** and the Longhouse Religion. Loose beads of wampum were thrown into sacred water sites by the ancient Senecas (Snyderman, "Function," 590).

Many documents of the league—the *Kayaněñsäko´ ně* (**Great Law of Peace**, or Constitution), the *Gaiwí:yo* of Sganyadaí:yoh (Code of **Handsome Lake**), nomination belts, lineage wampum, treaties, minutes of meetings, and so on— were preserved in wampum writing. The sophisticated recordkeeping of the league, which allowed officials to recall treaty conditions and pledges quite accurately even a century and a half later, dismayed the Europeans. The evidentiary nature of wampum writing was the main reason that colonial governments and later the U.S. government sought to destroy or "collect" wampum, hoping to break down the league by destroying its main administrative tool. Indian agents did their best to acquire wampum belts, while in the nineteenth century, traders unstrung the messages and sold ancient documents, bead by bead, to tourists as "souvenirs."

It was only through great effort that the elders managed to save some of the wampum of the *Kayaněňsäko'ně* and all of the *Gaiwí:yo*. In 1891, the state of New York began its "Indian museum," and in 1898, Yaiéwanoh (**Harriet Maxwell Converse**) persuaded the Grand Council at Onondaga to deposit the wampum of the Great Law there for safekeeping, given its possible fate should traders get ahold of it. Around the turn of the twentieth century, **J. N. B. Hewitt** acquired various wampums of the league, including the wampum of the Condolence Council (Hewitt, " 'League,' " 203; "Requickening Address," 79) and the "Mace" (symbol of the Six Nations) of the Men's Grand Council (Hewitt, " 'League,' " 203; "Requickening Address," 79; "Culture," 181–182; photos inclusive).

The adherents of the Longhouse Religion never relinquished control of the wampum of the *Gaiwí:yo*, however. Unfortunately, the wampum knotted by Sganyadaí:yoh can no longer be read. The last two league wampum readers of the twentieth century, Henan Scrogg and Solon Skye (Snyderman, "Function," 604), are now deceased. With them went the ability to read the original wampum of the *Gaiwí:yo*. It is now recited by Faithkeepers from memory. Modern Haudenosaunee are now attempting to revive both the languages of the league and wampum literacy.

FURTHER READING

Brinton, Daniel G. *The Myths of the New World: A Treatise on the Symbolism and Mythology of the Red Race of America*. 2nd ed., rev. New York: Henry Holt and Company, 1876.

Converse, Harriet Maxwell [Ya-ie-wa-noh]. "Origin of the Wampum Belt" and "The Legendary Origin of Wampum." In *Myths and Legends of the New York State Iroquois*. Ed. Arthur Caswell Parker. New York State Museum Bulletin 125. Education Department Bulletin No. 437. Albany: University of the State of New York, 1908: 138–145; 187–190.

Heckewelder, John. *History, Manners, and Customs of the Indian Nations Who Once Inhabited Pennsylvania and the Neighboring States*. 1820, 1876. The First American Frontier Series. New York: Arno Press and the New York Times, 1971.

Hewitt, J[ohn] N[apoleon] B[rinton]. "The Culture of the Indians of Eastern Canada." *Explorations and Field-work of the Smithsonian Institution for 1928* (1929): 179–182.

———. "The 'League of Nations' of the Iroquois Indians in Canada." *Explorations and Field-work of the Smithsonian Institution for 1929* (1930): 201–206.

———. "Requickening Address of the Iroquois Condolence Council." Ed. William N. Fenton. *Journal of the Washington Academy of Sciences* 34 (1944): 65–79.

———. "Wampum." In Frederick Webb Hodge, ed., *Handbook of American Indians North of Mexico*. New York: Rowman and Littlefield, 1965: 904–909.

Jacobs, Wilbur R. "Wampum: The Protocol of Indian Diplomacy." *William and Mary Quarterly*, 3rd ser. 4:3 (October 1949): 596–604.

Mann, Barbara A. "The Fire at Onondaga: Wampum as Proto-writing." *Akwesasne Notes*, 26th Anniversary Issue, n.s. 1:1 (Spring 1995): 40–48.

Murray, David. *Forked Tongues: Speech, Writing, and Representation in North American Indian Texts*. Bloomington: Indiana University Press, 1991.

Palmer, Rose A. *The North American Indians: An Account of the American Indians North of Mexico, Compiled from the Original Sources*. Smithsonian Scientific Series, vol. 4. Washington, D.C.: Smithsonian Institution, 1929.

Slotkin, J. S., and Karl Schmitt. "Studies of Wampum." *American Anthropologist* 51 (1949): 223–236.

Snyderman, George S. "The Function of Wampum in Iroquois Religion." *Proceedings of the American Philosophical Society* 105:6 (1961): 571–608.

———. "The Functions of Wampum." *Proceedings of the American Philosophical Society* 98.6 (December 1954): 469–494.

Speck, Frank G. "The Functions of Wampum among the Eastern Algonkian." *Memoirs of the American Anthropological Association* 6 (1919): 3–71.

Vidler, Virginia. *American Indian Antiques: Arts and Artifacts of the Northeast*. South Brunswick and New York: A. S. Barnes and Company, 1976.

Barbara A. Mann and Bruce E. Johansen

Warrior Society (Mohawk Warriors). The strife that paralyzed **Mohawk** country in 1990 was not a series of events isolated in time, but the violent culmination of many events and issues growing out of the ruination of the traditional way of life. The nationalistic, paramilitary Warrior Society might never have arisen without construction of the **St. Lawrence Seaway** shortly after World War II. Construction of the seaway and industrialization of the area destroyed traditional ways of making a living in Mohawk country. **Gambling** and smuggling then emerged as ways to make money, sometimes under Warrior Society claims of "sovereignty."

Seeds of Frustration

The seeds of frustration among Mohawks and other Iroquois that gave rise to the Warrior Societies were sown during the 1950s, when the governments of the United States and Canada ignored native protests against construction of the St. Lawrence Seaway. John C. Mohawk, who is a **Seneca**, traces frustrations from the time of first contact with Europeans intent on imposing their languages, cultures, and religions as they acquired Native American lands. Ignoring Native complaints about the seaway during the 1950s fit into an official policy of "termination," under which Native reservations were to be broken down as Indians were absorbed into the "American mainstream" in both the United States and Canada.

At the same time, the events in Mohawk country were accompanied by a rising, often-emotional, debate over the future of the Iroquois Confederacy as a whole. At the heart of this debate were two interpretations of history. One was that of the Iroquois Grand Council at Onondaga, the Mohawk Nation Council,

and many of the other national councils that make up the Iroquois' original
political structure. All reject violence and look at the Warriors as illegitimate.
The other interpretation, synthesized by **Kahnawake** Mohawk **Louis Hall**, the
Warrior Society's ideological founder, and espoused by the Warriors, rejects the
governing structure as a creation of white-influenced religion (especially the
Quakers) and advocates a revolution from within to overthrow it.

These elements combined to produce the Mohawk Warrior Society, perhaps
the most prominent of several revitalization movements among North American
Indians during the second half of the twentieth century. The Warrior Society
was founded in 1971 at Kahnawake, Québec. Its initial activity was to drive all
non-Indians—many of them spouses of Mohawk members—from Kahnawake
territory.

Ganienkeh Established

This effort produced powerful tensions within Kahnawake that helped to mo-
tivate a plan to expand Mohawk territory outside the boundaries of the Mohawk
reservations. On May 13, 1974, a group of Mohawk warriors led by Arthur
Montour, Louis Hall, and Paul Delaronde began an occupation of a former Girl
Scout camp at Moss Lake in the Adirondack Park near Eagle Bay, New York.
They renamed the camp Ganienkeh, a Mohawk word meaning "Land of the
Flint." This designation recalled ancient Mohawk origins because the Mohawk
word for themselves—*Ganienkeh*—translates as "People of the Flint."

During the Warrior Society's occupation of Moss Lake, the occupiers found
themselves isolated and marginalized. The Ganienkeh Council Fire (as they
called themselves) negotiated a move to an area of 5,000 acres at Miner Lake
near Plattsburgh, New York in 1977 (Campbell, 68). They also designated this
new area as Ganienkeh. Miner Lake placed them in the Champlain Valley on a
route between the Mohawk communities of **Akwesasne** and Kahnawake.

In 1979, Akwesasne came under siege after traditional Mohawk chief Loran
Thompson was arrested in a dispute with the rival elected system, which was
trying to build a fence around the Akwesasne territory. Thompson resisted arrest
and was joined by hundreds of supporters in a standoff at his home on Raquette
Point on the western border of Akwesasne. Warrior Society members, led by
Montour, joined the standoff.

The standoff at Raquette Point continued for approximately thirteen months.
During that time, New York State police surrounded the Mohawk enclave and
its varying number of occupants, who were able to ferry supplies into their camp
because it was located adjacent to the St. Lawrence River, which serves as the
U.S.-Canadian border. On several occasions, New York officials threatened invasion, but the Mohawks, including the Mohawk Warrior Society, held their
ground. The Raquette Point standoff was to be the last time the Mohawk traditionalists and the Mohawk Warrior Society would work together.

The standoff was fueled in part by New York State's support of an Akwesasne
police force and the elected-system faction's use of that police force to arrest

its political enemy, Loran Thompson. A vigilante group led by Bill Sears was organized to pressure the state police into taking more direct action against the encampment surrounding the Thompson home. During the course of the stand-off, it was revealed that the state police had supported and even armed members of the elected-system faction, and this and other information, including the cost of the siege, eventually led Governor Mario Cuomo to abandon both the siege and the day-to-day patrolling of Akwesasne.

The Warrior Society had inherited a similar situation in Kahnawake. In the early 1980s, the Sûreté du Québec (SQ), the provincial police, chased a Mohawk man, Richard Cross, across the Mercier Bridge to his home in Kahnawake, where, in a confrontation, he was shot and killed. This led to riots during which police cars were destroyed and the SQ was forced to abandon patrols of Kahnawake. As soon as police enforcement was no longer possible, individuals within Kahnawake began opening smoke shops. Canadian cigarettes are exported tax-free to the United States. Because of the high taxes on retail sales of cigarettes, there were significant profits involved in purchasing this product in the United States and transporting it back into Canada. The cigarette trade grew into a major element of the Kahnawake Mohawk economy, and while members of the Mohawk Warrior Society took advantage of this situation, they were not re-sponsible for creating it.

Casinos Rise at Akwesasne

As soon as New York State forces withdrew from Akwesasne, some former supporters of the elected system began building privately owned commercial bingo halls and within a short time progressed to gambling casinos. These op-erations were illegal under New York and federal laws, but because New York state had assumed jurisdiction over criminal and civil Indian matters it was a state legal concern. This was to prove to be a critical element in the potential success of the Warrior Society movement because in issues of enforcement of a variety of laws, they would face New York State police and not U.S. federal police. New York State police were unwilling to enter Akwesasne to enforce gambling laws, and an underground economy quickly grew that included gam-bling and smuggling cigarettes across the border. "The '**buttlegging**' [cigarette-smuggling] trade followed, beginning in the early 1980s, as Canada's national government imposed high luxury taxes on tobacco products, making untaxed cigarettes purchased on U.S. or Canadian Indian reservations much cheaper. . . . Once the cigarette pipeline got underway, other illegal or illicit goods were added, such as liquor, drugs, and weapons, including AK-47s and other semi-automatics" (Johansen, 23).

Bill Sears had organized a vigilante posse to pursue traditionalists during the siege at Raquette Point. He and a few armed men had threatened to do the violence the state police seemed unwilling to undertake, much as private militias were organized to follow the U.S. military into African-American communities during the urban riots in the late 1960s. Sears built a bingo hall under an agreement with the St. Regis Tribal Council. In 1984, Mohawks Guilford White and Buddy Cook undertook construction of a much-better-financed, larger, and more modern enterprise, the Mohawk Bingo Palace. High-stakes commercial bingo had arrived, and soon gambling machines appeared in these bingo halls.

Akwesasne was already a community that felt under siege. In addition to the long police action, the Mohawk community had felt the impact of a declining building-trades industry that threw hundreds out of work and made entry into these professions by young people very difficult. In addition, Akwesasne was the focus of a series of studies of the environmental impacts of the industries— including aluminum and paper mills and a General Motors factory—that offered the Mohawks more pollution than employment. Economic pressure, ecological devastation, and internal political dysfunction combined to create a sense of hopelessness, especially among the young males.

The Warrior Society first emerged as a player in the gambling dispute at Akwesasne in a statement from Billy's (Bill Sears's) Bingo Hall by Francis Boots, formerly a traditionalist, in 1987: "Any attempt taken by outside police forces will be considered as a military expedition against a people at peace with the United States" (Johansen, 25). This is arguably the first evidence that the Warrior Society, which had been Sears's bitter enemy during the Raquette Point standoff, had changed sides and had joined with members of the former vigilantes who had previously insisted that state law must prevail on Akwesasne. It contains elements of future Warrior rhetoric: the claim that gambling is an exercise of Mohawk sovereignty and the assertion that the Warrior Society represents the interests of "the Mohawk people." The rhetoric of this and the body of Warrior Society statements does not recognize the possibility that there may be Mohawk people who dissent from its views. Loran Thompson, the chief at the center of the Raquette Point standoff, was removed from office ("dehorned," in Iroquois parlance) for allegedly borrowing money in the name of the Akwesasne Longhouse to construct a "Bingo Jack" hall without obtaining the permission of the Longhouse. In a strange twist of events, Sears and Thompson, leaders of opposing factions at Raquette Point, found themselves allies in a rapidly emerging economy that included gambling, smuggling, cigarettes, and motor fuels.

Early on the morning of December 16, 1987, New York State police raided six of these establishments and seized 293 machines that the state estimated provided a total of about $7 million in untaxed profits to their owners. The next day, the casino owners ordered new machines. The St. Regis Tribal Council and the traditional Mohawk Nation Council considered commercial casino gambling illegal at Akwesasne, but more casinos were quickly built, including Hart's Palace and Tony Vegas International. The latter was equipped with armed guards to protect against robberies and to resist police raids that seemed inevitable because although Congress had passed the Indian Gaming Regulatory Act, individual Indians were forbidden to own commercial gambling casinos under the act or under New York State laws.

In June 1988, some 200 Royal Canadian Mounted Police raided Kahnawake, arrested 17 Mohawks, and seized $400,000 in contraband cigarettes and $284,000 in cash. That month the casinos on the American side at Akwesasne unseated antigambling tribal officials and installed progambling "chiefs." Meanwhile, non-Indians invested heavily in some of the "Indian" casinos along Route 37. Widespread community opposition to casinos simmered over the next year until, on June 6, 1989, 400 people were involved in a brawl at Tony Vegas International in which state police finally intervened. The police arrested **Tony Laughing** and seized one slot machine, but Laughing was released on bail, and the gambling continued with little interruption.

"Civil War" at Akwesasne

More raids followed, and both gambling supporters and opponents set up barricades on roads. Groups of armed masked men, supporters of the casinos, patrolled the roads at night and harassed gambling opponents. There was a report of a public referendum in which the progambling forces claimed to have won by a margin of nine to one, but this report is not credible because most of the Mohawk people declined to participate in the referendum (Hornung, 283). The home of traditional chief Ron La France was burned to the ground, and other opponents' windows were shot out.

By late August, Akwesasne was in a state of civil war. Gambling opponents set up roadblocks to keep non-Indian customers away, and a crowd set fire to the Lucky Knight Casino. The Warrior Society issued press releases reiterating its defense of Mohawk sovereignty and the **Great Law of Peace**, and more skirmishes and assaults broke out. Laughing used press conferences to defend the casinos as a source of much-needed employment, claiming that blackjack dealers earned up to $1,200 a week, but gambling opponents reported that most of the jobs went to non-Indians and that Mohawks were left with menial jobs (Johansen, 41).

In January 1990, gambling opponent Jerry McDonald entered Tony Vegas International and sprayed the room with a shotgun. A few days later, five Mohawks received jail terms of up to two years in a federal court for gambling-related crimes, and six other Mohawks were indicted. In February, Laughing was sentenced to twenty-seven months in prison for gambling offenses. At the same time, violence at Akwesasne continued to escalate as more homes were riddled with bullets and more assaults were recorded (Johansen, 57).

In March, on the Canadian side of Akwesasne, the Mohawk Council of Akwesasne began to evacuate residents because of the rising violence. Arthur Montour, the Warrior Society leader at Ganienkeh, went on trial for interfering in a state police raid the previous July. On March 29, a military medical helicopter was hit by gunfire while flying over Ganienkeh, and a doctor was wounded. That day there were more fistfights at Akwesasne between antigambling forces and Warrior Society members.

Antigambling forces erected more sophisticated barricades to keep non-Indian gamblers away from the casinos as the level of violence escalated throughout April. Warriors complained of assaults by "antis" and claimed that these actions "provoked" them to a massive action to trash the barricades during the last week of April (Johansen, 69–70). On April 23, the North American Indian Travelling College, associated with the antigambling forces, was firebombed. A live hand grenade launched by Warriors injured three people in the Akwesasne police station (Johansen, 77). Three days later, the Canadian-side Mohawk Council of Akwesasne asked people to evacuate the territory. More houses were riddled with bullets, and by April 28 at least 2,000 people—more than one-quarter of Akwesasne's population—were refugees.

People fled to Cornwall, Ontario. Despite pleas from anxious Akwesasne residents, Governor Cuomo of New York refused to intervene and responded that the problem was not as serious as the antigambling forces were reporting. At the center of the resistance to the Warriors were **Doug George-Kanentiio**, editor of the nationally distributed publication *Akwesasne Notes*, and his brother David George. By 9 P.M. on the evening of April 30, the shooting intensified. It would not end until the next morning. During that time, two men, "Junior" Edwards and Mathew Pyke, were killed in what can only be described as a major firefight during which thousands of rounds were fired. Diane Lazore, a Warrior Society leader and sometime spokeswoman, owned a dwelling that had provided shelter for snipers who poured fire into antigambler David George's home. On May 1, the Lazore home was burned. New York State police finally entered Akwesasne and brought order. They closed the gambling casinos and patrolled the roads. Akwesasne was now an occupied territory. On July 10, Montour was sentenced to ten months in prison for obstruction of a federal search warrant.

The Warriors' Justification of Violence

The use of violence is justified by the Warriors: "The Mohawk Warrior Movement has an ideology that espouses violence within a specific context. Specifically, members embrace violent self-defense in pursuit of its nationalist political and economic agenda" (Pertusati, 52). Three high-ranking female members of the movement, Dale Dion, Diane Lazore, and Minnie Garrow, are quoted in support of this use of violence:

Violence has given us bargaining power. (Pertusati, 55)

We have accomplished many things through violence. (Pertusati, 54)

[W]e will never be able to achieve legal recognition of Mohawk nationhood through negotiation. (Pertusati, 55)

The combination of an offer of power, nationalism, action, and plunder proved virtually irresistible to alienated, acculturated young people, especially young men. Hall couched his rhetoric in an appeal to tradition, albeit a false one. There is no precedent in Iroquois history or tradition for a paramilitary warrior force maintained to defend economic interests of some Iroquois against others within the Iroquois Confederacy.

By early May 1990, thousands of terrorized Mohawks had become refugees in Cornwall. Many of their Akwesasne homes and cars had been burned or riddled with bullet holes, and two young Mohawk men were dead, not to mention dozens of assaults, more than a dozen Mohawks facing prison terms for gambling offenses, a police occupation of Akwesasne, and numerous charges from assault to property damage. Summer would prove to be equally trying, with confrontations at Akwesasne, Kanesatake (**Oka**), and Kahnawake.

Warrior Activities after 1990

After 1990, the center of Warrior Society action moved to New York State's Seneca, **Onondaga**, and **Tuscarora** reservations. In the Seneca country, a number of privately owned cigarette shops were selling tax-free cigarettes at considerable profit while cases wound through state and federal courts to determine whether state taxation strategies were legal. In 1992, a state court determined that the state was within its legal powers to collect sales taxes on sales to non-Indian customers in the Indian country. The state took moves to collect the tax. On the Seneca Nation, protesters blocked the New York State Thruway near Silver Creek and Route 17 at Salamanca (see **Taxation disputes**). After a short confrontation, the state agreed to delay collection of these taxes pending a ruling by the U.S. Supreme Court. That ruling came in 1994 in an opinion by Chief Justice William Rehnquist giving New York State full authority to collect the tax.

In December 1996, Governor George Pataki announced plans to collect the tax from non-Indian distributors of motor fuels and tobacco products by April 1 on those Indian territories that did not have a tax agreement with the state. The traditional governments at Onondaga, **Tonawanda**, Tuscarora, and Akwesasne formed a negotiating team and reached a tentative agreement whereby the state would collect no taxes and the Indian governments would regulate all sales to non-Indians within their territories. During May 1997, individual Indian retailers on the Seneca Nation and other territories organized opposition to this proposed agreement that culminated in a demonstration at Route 81 at Onondaga in May 1997, resulting in injuries to state police and protesters that caused Pataki to abandon attempts to obtain tax agreements with Indian governments or to collect taxes on sales to non-Indians of motor fuel and tobacco products.

FURTHER READING

Burns, M. C. "Warrior's Words Call for Execution." *Syracuse Herald-Journal*, July 4, 1990, A1, A4.

Campbell, Richard Dean. *The People of the Land of Flint*. Lanham, Md.: University Press of America, 1985.

Hornung, Rick. *One Nation under the Gun: Inside the Mohawk Civil War*. Toronto: Stoddart, 1991.

Johansen, Bruce E. *Life and Death in Mohawk Country*. Golden, Colo.: North American Press/Fulcrum, 1993.

Landsman, Gail. *Sovereignty and Symbol: Indian-White Conflict at Ganienkeh*. Albuquerque: University of New Mexico Press, 1988.

Mohawk, John C. "Echoes of a Native American Revitalization Movement in Some Recent Indian Law Cases in New York State." *Buffalo Law Review* 46 (1998): 1061.

Pertusati, Linda. *In Defense of Mohawk Land: Ethnopolitical Conflict in Native North America*. Albany: State University of New York Press, 1997.

John C. Mohawk and Bruce E. Johansen

Washington Covenant Belt. The two central figures on each side of the house depicted on the Washington Covenant Belt represent the doorkeepers of the Haudenosaunee Confederacy (**Mohawks** at the Eastern Door on the right and **Senecas** at the Western Door on the left). The belt is the largest treaty **wampum** belt known to historical records at 1.92 meters in length and 13.3 centimeters in width. The thirteen other figures represent the thirteen colonies in rebellion against Great Britain. The belt was used at one or more treaty councils during the middle 1770s as representatives of the colonies tried to negotiate Haudenosaunee neutrality during the **American Revolution**.

Weiser, Conrad, 1696–1760. As an interpreter at treaty councils between the Haudenosaunee and Pennsylvania, Conrad Weiser was one of the primary architects, in practical terms, of the **Covenant Chain** alliance between the Iroquois and England during the first half of the eighteenth century. A Palatine German, Weiser had lived with Mohawks in his youth and had learned their language before moving to Pennsylvania, where he was a soldier and government official as well as an interpreter.

FURTHER READING

Wallace, Paul A. W. *Conrad Weiser, 1696–1760: Friend of Colonist and Mohawk*. New York: Russell, & Russell, 1971.

White Dog Sacrifice. On the fifth morning of the Midwinter Ceremony, until the late nineteenth century, the Haudenosaunee engaged in a white-dog sacrifice of a type described by Anthony F. C. Wallace in *The Death and Rebirth of the Seneca*:

This dog, a spotless animal, had been strangled (its blood could not be shed) on the day of the Big Heads [the first day of the Haudenosaunee new year], and its body, garlanded with ribbons, beads, and metallic ornaments, hung on the wooden statue of Tarachiawagon, the Creator, before the longhouse. Now it was burned in the longhouse as an offering to the Creator, and the Thanksgiving dance was performed, and people sang their personal chants. On this day also the medicine societies continued their curing rites in the longhouse, and in the afternoon and evening, in private homes. (Wallace, 53)

The White Dog Sacrifice has been part of the Midwinter Ceremony for a long time. John Adams knew of it, and **Lewis Henry Morgan** described it in his *League of the Iroquois* (1851).

In modern times, at **Akwesasne**, the ceremony is still performed, but the White Dog is no longer used because this type of dog has been interbred out of existence. Instead of a live animal, the White Dog is symbolized by an undyed black-ash splint basket that is strung with colorful ribbons. After a lengthy prayer and offerings of tobacco, the basket is burned.

FURTHER READING

Wallace, Anthony F. C. *The Death and Rebirth of the Seneca.* New York: Knopf, 1970.

Wing (or Dust Fan) Wampum Belt. The Wing (also called "Dust Fan") Wampum Belt depicts an endless white pine tree, so tall that all nations can find shelter under it, provided they bury their weapons beneath the tree. This belt was maintained to remind the chiefs of the Iroquois League to guard against harmful thoughts. The belt is also called a dust fan because it is said to sweep away dust that might cloud the visions of the chiefs. This belt is shown when the **Great Law of Peace** is recited.

Wing (or Dust Fan) Wampum Belt. ©
Elizabeth Quintana/Akwe:kon Press.

Wyandot, name derivation. William N. Fenton says that "Wyandot" is derived from a reference to homeland as "Wendat Ehen," meaning "This Old Island," as in the **Turtle Island** origin story that the Wyandots share in some degree with the Haudenosaunee (Fenton, 3).

FURTHER READING

Fenton, William N. *The Great Law and the Longhouse: A Political History of the Iroquois Confederacy.* Norman: University of Oklahoma Press, 1998.

Selected Bibliography

Abler, Thomas S., ed. *Chainbreaker: The Revolutionary War Memoirs of Governor Blacksnake As Told to Benjamin Williams*. Lincoln: University of Nebraska Press, 1989.

Abrams, George H. J. *The Seneca People*. Phoenix: Indian Tribal Series, 1976.

Aldridge, Alfred O. *Benjamin Franklin: Philosopher and Man*. Philadelphia: J. B. Lippincott, 1965.

———. "Franklin's Deistical Indians." *Proceedings of the American Philosophical Society* 4 (August 1950): 398–410.

Alfred, Gerald R. *Heeding the Voices of Our Ancestors: Kahnawake Mohawk Politics and the Rise of Native Nationalism*. Toronto: Oxford University Press, 1995.

Allen, Paula Gunn. *The Sacred Hoop: Recovering the Feminine in American Indian Traditions*. Boston: Beacon Press, 1986.

Andersen, Diana. "Toxics in the St. Lawrence: An Examination of the Problem." *Northeast Indian Quarterly* 5:3 (Autumn 1988): 16–18.

Anderson, Wallace (Mad Bear). "The Lost Brother: An Iroquois Prophecy of Serpents." In Shirley Hill Witt and Stan Steiner, eds., *The Way: An Anthology of American Indian Literature*. New York: Vintage, 1972.

Aquila, Richard. *The Iroquois Restoration: Iroquios Diplomacy on the Colonial Frontier, 1701–1754*. Detroit: Wayne State University Press, 1983.

Arden, Harvey. "The Fire That Never Dies." *National Geographic*, September 1987, 374–403.

Armstrong, Virginia Irving, comp. *I Have Spoken: American History through the Voices of the Indians*. Chicago: Sage Books, 1971.

Armstrong, William. *Warrior in Two Camps: Ely S. Parker, Union General and Seneca Chief*. Syracuse, N.Y. University Press, 1978.

Austin, Alberta. *Ne'Ho Niyo' De:No': That's What It Was Like*. Lackawanna, N.Y.: Rebco Enterprises, 1986.

Axtell, James. "The Ethnohistory of Native America." In Donald L. Fixico, ed., *Rethinking American Indian History*. Albuquerque: University of New Mexico Press, 1997: 11–28.

Ball, Steve. "Orangemen March to New World Order." *The Times* (London), August 18, 1996, n.p.

Ballantine, Betty, and Ian Ballantine. *The Native Americans Today*. Atlanta: Turner Publishing, 1993.

Barnes, Sally. "A Double Loss for Canada's Native People." *Toronto Sun*, March 20, 1995, 12.

Barreiro, José. "Chief Jacob Thomas and the Condolence Cane." *Northeast Indian Quarterly* 7:4 (Winter 1990): 77–85.

———. "Return of the Wampum." *Northeast Indian Quarterly* 7:1 (Spring 1990):8–20.

Barreiro, José, and Carol Cornelius. *Knowledge of the Elders: The Iroquois Condolence Cane Tradition*. Ithaca, N.Y.: Northeast Indian Quarterly, 1991.

Beauchamp, William M. *Civil, Religious, and Mourning Councils and Ceremonies of Adoption of the New York Indians*. New York State Museum Bulletin No. 113. Albany, N.Y.: New York State Education Department, June 1907.

———. *A History of the New York Iroquois, Now Commonly Called the Six Nations*. New York State Museum Bulletin No. 78. Albany, N.Y.: State of New York, 1905.

———. *The Iroquois Trail, or Footprints of the Six Nations, in Customs, Traditions, and History*. Including David Cusick's "Sketches of Ancient History of the Six Nations." 1825. Fayetteville, N.Y.: H. C. Beauchamp, 1892.

Berkey, Curtis. "The Legal Basis for Iroquois Land Claims." *Akwe:kon Journal* 10:1 (Spring 1993): 23–25.

Bilharz, Joy A. *The Allegany Senecas and Kinzua Dam: Forced Relocation through Two Generations*. Lincoln: University of Nebraska Press, 1998.

Blanchard, David. "High Steel! The Kahnawake Mohawk and the High Construction Trade." *Journal of Ethnic Studies* 11:2 (1983): 41–60.

Bond, Richmond P. *Queen Anne's American Kings*. Oxford: Clarendon Press, 1952.

Bonvillain, Nancy. "Gender Relations in Native North America." *American Indian Culture and Research Journal* 13:2 (1989): 1–28.

Boorstin, Daniel. *The Lost World of Thomas Jefferson*. New York: Henry Holt, 1948.

Boyd, Julian P. "Dr. Franklin, Friend of the Indian." In Roy N. Lokken, ed., *Meet Dr. Franklin*. Philadelphia: Franklin Institute Press, 1981: 237–245.

Bradley, James W. *Evolution of the Onondaga Iroquois: Accommodating Change, 1500–1655*. Syracuse, N.Y.: Syracuse University Press, 1987.

Brandão, José António. *"Your Fyre Shall Burn No More": Iroquois Policy toward New France and its Native Allies to 1701*. Lincoln: University of Nebraska Press, 1997.

Brixey, Elizabeth. "Laugh It Up for Indians." *Wisconsin State Journal* (Madison), February 26, 1993, 1-F.

Brown, Judith K. "Economic Organization and the Position of Women among the Iroquois." *Ethnohistory* 17:3–4 (Summer–Fall 1970): 151–167.

Bruchac, Joseph. *Iroquois Stories*. Trumansburg, N.Y.: Crossing Press, 1985.

———, ed. *New Voices from the Longhouse*. Greenfield Center, N.Y.: Greenfield Review Press, 1989.

Burns, M. C. "Warrior's Words Call for Execution." *Syracuse Herald-Journal*, July 4, 1990, A1, A4.

Butterfield, Consul Willshire. *History of the Girtys, Being a Concise Account of the Girty Brothers—Thomas, Simon, James and George, and Their Half-Brother John Turner—Also of the Part Taken by Them in Lord Dunmore's War, in the Western*

Border War of the Revolution, and in the Indian War of 1790–95. Cincinnati: Robert Clarke & Co., 1890.

Caduto, Michael J., and Joseph Bruchac. *Keepers of the Earth: Native American Stories and Environmental Activities for Children.* Golden, Colo.: Fulcrum, 1988.

Calloway, Colin, ed. *The World Turned Upside Down: Indian Voices from Early America.* Boston: Bedford Books/St. Martin's Press, 1994.

Campbell, Richard Dean. *The People of the Land of Flint.* Lanham, Md.: University Press of America, 1985.

Carr, Lucien. *The Social and Political Position of Women among the Huron-Iroquois Tribes.* Salem, Mass.: Salem Press, 1884.

Carter, Diane Louise. "Preserving the Language." Gannett News Service, October 9, 1995 (in LEXIS).

"Cartier (Jacques)." *Grand Dictionarie Encyclopédique Larousse.* Vol. 2. Paris: Librarie Larousse, 1982: 1829–30.

Chafe, Wallace. *Handbook of the Seneca Language.* New York State Museum and Science Service. Bulletin No. 388. Albany: University of the State of New York, State Education Department, 1963.

———. *Seneca Thanksgiving Rituals.* Bureau of American Ethnology Bulletin No. 183. Washington, D.C.: Smithsonian Institution, 1961.

Champlain, Samuel de. *Works of Samuel de Champlain.* Ed. H. P. Biggar. Trans. W. D. LeSuer and H. H. Langton. 7 vols. Toronto: Champlain Society, 1922–1936.

Child, Lydia Maria. *Hobomok and Other Writings on Indians.* Ed. Carolyn L. Karcher. New Brunswick, N.J.: Rutgers University Press, 1986.

———. *Selected Letters, 1817–1880.* Ed. Milton Meltzer and Patricia G. Holland. Amherst: University of Massachusetts Press, 1982.

Colden, Cadwallader. *The History of the Five Indian Nations Depending on the Province of New-York in America.* 1747. Ithaca, N.Y.: Great Seal Books, 1958.

Converse, Harriet Maxwell [Ya-ie-wa-noh]. *Myths and Legends of the New York State Iroquois*, Ed. Arthur Caswell Parker. New York State Museum Bulletin 125. Education Department Bulletin No. 437. Albany: University of the State of New York, 1908.

Conway, Moncure Daniel. *The Life of Thomas Paine.* 2 vols. New York: J. P. Putnam's Sons, 1908.

Cook, Ramsay, ed. *The Voyages of Jacques Cartier.* Toronto: University of Toronto Press, 1993.

Cornelius, Carol. "The Thanksgiving Address: An Expression of Haudenosaunee Worldview." *Akwe:kon Journal* 9:3 (Fall 1992): 14–25.

Cornplanter, Jesse J. *Legends of the Longhouse.* 1938. Ed. William G. Spittal. Illust. J. J. Cornplanter. Ohsweken, Ontario: Irocrafts, Ltd., 1992.

Crevecoeur, J. Hector St. Jean de. *Letters from an American Farmer.* New York: E. P. Dutton, 1926.

Crowe, Kenneth C. "Museums Work to Restore Tribal Heritage." *Albany Times Union*, December 10, 1995, A-3.

Cusick, David. *Sketches of Ancient History of the Six Nations.* 1827. Second ed. Lockport, N.Y.: Conley & Lathrop, 1828.

Deardorff, Merle H. *The Religion of Handsome Lake: Its Origin and Development.* Bureau of American Ethnology Bulletin No. 149. Washington, D.C.: Bureau of American Ethnology, 1951.

Deer, Kenneth. "RCMP Carry Out Sting Operation." *Eastern Door* (Kahnawake), September 19, 1997, 1.

Dennis, Matthew. *Cultivating a Landscape of Peace*. Ithaca, N.Y.: Cornell University Press, 1993.

Dixon, Susan. "A Voice Coming towards Us: A Tribute to Mohawk Basketmaker Mary Adams." *Akwe:kon Journal* 11:1 (Spring 1994): 28–29.

Dockstader, Frederick J. *Great North American Indians: Profiles in Life and Leadership*. New York: Van Nostrand Reinhold, 1977.

Dwight, Timothy. *Travels in New-England and New-York*. 4 vols. New Haven, Conn.: T. Dwight, 1821–1822.

Eccles, William John. *The Canadian Frontier, 1534–1760*. 1969. Albuquerque: University of New Mexico Press, 1983.

Edmunds, R. David, ed. *American Indian Leaders: Studies in Diversity*. Lincoln: University of Nebraska Press, 1980.

Edwards, Samuel. *Rebel! A Biography of Tom Paine*. New York: Praeger, 1974.

The Encyclopaedia Britannica. 11th ed. Vol. 13/14. New York: Encyclopaedia Britannica, 1911.

Engels, Friedrich. *The Origin of the Family, Private Property, and the State, in the Light of the Researches of Lewis H. Morgan*. In *Karl Marx and Friedrich Engels: Selected Works*. London: Lawrence and Wishart, 1968.

Faber, Harold. "Indian History Alive at New York Site." *New York Times*, July 26, 1987, sec. 1, pt. 2, 36.

Fadden, Stephen. "Beaded History: The Hiawatha Belt Is the Founding Document and Symbolizes the 'Constitution' of the Iroquois Confederacy." *Northeast Indian Quarterly* 4:3 (Autumn 1987): 17–20.

———. "Response." *Northeast Indian Quarterly* 7:1 (Spring 1990): 43–44.

Fenton, William N. "Contacts between Iroquois Herbalism and Colonial Medicine." *Annual Report of the Smithsonian Institution for 1941*, 503–526.

———. *The False Faces of the Iroquois*. Norman: University of Oklahoma Press, 1987.

———. *The Great Law and the Longhouse: A Political History of the Iroquois Confederacy*. Norman: University of Oklahoma Press, 1998.

———. "The Hiawatha Wampum Belt of the Iroquois League for Peace." In *Men and Cultures: Selected Papers of the Fifth International Congress of Anthropological and Ethnological Sciences, Philadelphia, September 1–9, 1956*. Philadelphia: University of Pennsylvania Press, 1960.

———. "An Iroquois Condolence Council for Installing Cayuga Chiefs in 1945." *Journal of the Washington Academy of Sciences* 36:4 (1946): 110–127.

———. "The New York State Wampum Collection: The Case for the Integrity of Cultural Treasures." *Proceedings of the American Philosophical Society* 115:6 (1971): 437–461.

———. *An Outline of Seneca Ceremonies at Coldspring Longhouse*. Yale University Publications in Anthropology, No. 9. New Haven, Conn.: Yale University Press, 1936.

———. "The Requickening Address of the Iroquois Condolence Council by J. N. B. Hewitt." *Journal of the Washington Academy of Sciences* 34:3 (1944): 65–85.

———. [Review of *New Voices from the Longhouse*, by Joseph Bruchac.] *Northeast Indian Quarterly* 6:4 (Winter 1989): 59.

———. *Roll Call of the Iroquois Chiefs: A Study of a Mnemonic Cane from the Six*

Nations Reserve. Washington, D.C.: *Smithsonian Miscellaneous Collections* 111: 15 (1950): 1–73.

———. "Seth Newhouse's Traditional History and Constitution of the Iroquois Confederacy." *Proceedings of the American Philosophical Society* 93:2 (1949): 141–158.

Fenton, William N., and John Gulick, eds. *Symposium on Cherokee and Iroquois Culture*. Bureau of American Ethnology Bulletin 180. Washington, D.C.: Smithsonian Institution, 1961.

Flexner, James Thomas. *Mohawk Baronet*. New York: Harper & Row, 1959.

Foner, Philip S., ed. *The Complete Writings of Thomas Paine*. New York: Citadel Press, 1945.

Foster, Michael K. [Review of *Concerning the League: The Iroquois League Tradition As Dictated in Onondaga by John Arthur Gibson*, comp. Hanni Woodbury, Reg Henry, and Harry Webster on the basis of A. A. Goldenweiser's manuscript.] *American Anthropologist* 97:3 (1995): 582–583.

———. [Review of *Concerning the League: The Iroquois League Tradition As Dictated in Onondaga by John Arthur Gibson*, comp. Hanni Woodbury, Reg Henry, and Harry Webster on the basis of A. A. Goldenweiser's manuscript.] *International Journal of American Linguistics* 62:1 (1996): 117–120.

Foster, Michael K., Jack Campisi, and Marianne Mithun, eds. *Extending the Rafters: Interdisciplinary Approaches to Iroquois Studies*. Albany: State University of New York Press, 1984.

Franklin, Benjamin. *Autobiography of Benjamin Franklin*. Ed. John Bigelow. Philadelphia: J. B. Lippincott, 1868.

———. *The Papers of Benjamin Franklin*. Ed. Leonard W. Labaree and Whitfield J. Bell. New Haven: Yale University Press, 1959.

———. "Remarks Concerning the Savages of North America." In Chester Jorgenson and Frank L. Mott, eds., *Benjamin Franklin: Representative Selections*. New York: Hill & Wang, 1962.

Gage, Matilda Joslyn. *Woman, Church, and State*. 1893. Watertown, Mass.: Persephone Press, 1980.

Gefell, Ann M. "River Recollections: Portraits of Life along the St. Lawrence River in the Twentieth Century." *Northeast Indian Quarterly* 5:3 (Fall 1988): 4–15.

Gehring, Charles T., and William A. Starna, trans. and eds. *A Journey into Mohawk and Oneida Country, 1634–1635: The Journal of Harmen Meyndertsz van den Bogaert*. Syracuse, N.Y.: Syracuse University Press, 1988.

George-Kanentiio, Doug. "How Much Land Did the Iroquois Possess?" *Akwesasne Notes*, n.s. 1:3–4 (Fall 1995): 60.

———. "The Iroquois Nationals: Creating a Sports Revolution for American Indians." *Akwesasne Notes*, n.s. 1:2 (Summer 1995): 94–95.

———. "Iroquois Seek to End Outrage of Sacred Objects Being Sold." *Syracuse Herald-American*, September 17, 1995, C-3.

———. "Iroquois Thanksgiving Is Rooted in Ritual." *Syracuse Herald-American*, July 17, 1994, AA-5.

———. "To Iroquois, Thunder Is Most Welcome Sound." *Syracuse Herald-American*, April 25, 1993, n.p.

Ghobashy, Omar Z. *The Caughnawaga Indians and the St. Lawrence Seaway*. New York: Devin-Adair, 1961.

Glaberson, William. " 'Indian Gold' Splits Tribe; Casinos Have Made One Native American Tribe Rich But the Fight for Spoils Has Divided Families." *Guardian* (London), June 18, 1996, 12.

———. "Struggle for Oneidas' Leadership Grows Bitter As Casino Succeeds." *New York Times*, June 17, 1996, A-1.

Gomez-Géraud, Marie-Christine. "Taignoagny et Dom Agaya: Portrait de deux truchements." In *La renaissance et le nouveau monde*, by Alain Parent. Québec: Musée de Québec, 1984: 52–54.

Grau, John. "Dispute Simmers As Smoke Shops Open." *Syracuse Post-Standard*, November 18, 1997, n.p.

Graymont, Barbara. *The Iroquois in the American Revolution*. Syracuse, N.Y.: Syracuse University Press, 1972.

———, ed. *Fighting Tuscarora: The Autobiography of Chief Clinton Rickard*. Syracuse, N.Y. Syracuse: Syracuse University Press, 1973.

Green, Michael D. "The Expansion of European Colonization to the Mississippi Valley, 1780–1880." In Bruce G. Trigger and Wilcomb E. Washburn, eds., *The Cambridge History of the Native Peoples of the Americas. North America*, vol. 1. Cambridge, England: Cambridge University Press, 1996: 461–538.

Griffin, Robert, and Donald A. Grinde, Jr. *Apocalyspe of Chiokoyhikoy, Chief of the Iroquois*. Laval, Québec: Les Presses de l'Université Laval, 1998.

Grinde, Donald A., Jr. *The Iroquois and the Founding of the American Nation*. San Francisco: Indian Historian Press, 1977.

———. [Review of *Concerning the League*, Hanni Woodbury, comp.] *American Indian Culture and Research Journal* 18:1 (1994): 175–177.

Grinde, Donald A., Jr., and Bruce E. Johansen. *Ecocide of Native America: Environmental Destruction of Indian Lands and Peoples*. Santa Fe, N.M.: Clear Light, 1995.

———. *Exemplar of Liberty: Native America and the Evolution of Democracy*. Los Angeles: UCLA American Indian Studies Center, 1991.

Haga, Chuck. "How Many Comedians Does It Take to Battle Oppression?" *Minneapolis Star-Tribune*, February 26, 1993, 1-R.

Hale, Horatio, ed. *The Iroquois Book of Rites*. Philadelphia: D. G. Brinton, 1883.

Hamilton, Charles, ed. *Cry of the Thunderbird*. Norman: University of Oklahoma Press, 1972.

Hamilton, Milton W. *Sir William Johnson: Colonial American, 1715–1763*. Port Washington, N.Y.: Kennikat Press, 1976.

"Haudenosaunee Confederacy Announces Policy on False Face Masks." *Akwesasne Notes* 1:1 (Spring 1995): 39.

Hauptman, Laurence M. "Iroquois in Blue: From Reservation to Civil War Battlefield." *Northeast Indian Quarterly* 5:3 (Autumn 1988): 35–39.

———. *The Iroquois in the Civil War: From Battlefield to Reservation*. Syracuse, N.Y.: Syracuse University Press, 1993.

———. *The Iroquois Struggle for Survival: World War II to Red Power*. Syracuse, N.Y.: Syracuse University Press, 1986.

Heard, J. Norman. *Handbook of the American Frontier*. Vol. 2, *The Northeastern Woodlands*. Metuchen, N.J.: Scarecrow Press, 1990.

Heckewelder, John. *History, Manners, and Customs of the Indian Nations Who Once Inhabited Pennsylvania and the Neighboring States*. 1820, 1876. The First American Frontier Series. New York: Arno Press and The New York Times, 1971.

————. *Narrative of the Mission of the United Brethren among the Delaware and Mohegan Indians from Its Commencement, in the Year 1740, to the Close of the Year 1808.* 1820. New York: Arno Press, 1971.

Henry, Thomas R. *Wilderness Messiah: The Story of Hiawatha and the Iroquois.* New York: Bonanza Books, 1995.

Hertzberg, Hazel W. *The Great Tree and the Longhouse: The Culture of the Iroquois.* New York: Macmillan, 1966.

Hewitt, J[ohn] N[apoleon] B[rinton]. "A Constitutional League of Peace in the Stone Age of America: The League of the Iroquois and Its Constitution." *Smithsonian Institution Series* (1920): 527–545.

————. "The Culture of the Indians of Eastern Canada." *Explorations and Field-work of the Smithsonian Institution for 1928* (1929): 179–182.

————. *Iroquois Cosmology.* Annual Report of the American Bureau of Ethnology 21. Washington, D.C.: Smithsonian, 1903.

————. "Iroquoian Cosmology, First Part." *Twenty-first Annual Report of the Bureau of American Ethnology to the Secretary of the Smithsonian Institution, 1899–1900.* Washington, D.C.: Government Printing Office, 1903: 127–339.

————. "Iroquoian Cosmology, Second Part." *Forty-third Annual Report of the Bureau of American Ethnology to the Secretary of the Smithsonian Institution, 1925–1926.* Washington, D.C.: Government Printing Office, 1928: 453–819.

————. "*Legend of the Founding of the Iroquois League.*" American Anthropologist (old series) 5 (April 1892): 131–148.

————. "New Fire among the Iroquois." *American Anthropologist* 2 (1889): 319.

————. "Wampum." In *Handbook of American Indians North of Mexico,* ed. Frederick W. Hodge. 2 vols. Washington, D.C.: Bureau of American Ethnology, 1910: 2:904–909.

Hill, Richard (Rick). "Continuity of Haudenosaunee Government: Political Reality of the Grand Council." *Northeast Indian Quarterly* 4:3 (Autumn 1987): 10–14.

————. "Rattling the Rafters: High Stakes Gambling Threatens the Peace of the Longhouse." *Northeast Indian Quarterly* 6:3 (Fall 1989): 4–11.

————. *Skywalkers: The History of Indian Ironworkers.* Brantford, Ontario. Woodland Indian Cultural Educational Centre, 1987.

Hornung, Rick. *One Nation under the Gun: Inside the Mohawk Civil War.* Toronto: Stoddart, 1991; New York: Pantheon, 1992.

Howard, Helen A. "Hiawatha: Co-founder of an Indian United Nations." *Journal of the West* 10:3 (1971): 428–438.

Hunt, George T. *The Wars of the Iroquois: A Study in Intertribal Trade Relations.* Madison: University of Wisconsin Press, 1940.

Jacobs, Renée. "Iroquois Great Law of Peace and the United States Constitution: How the Founding Fathers Ignored the Clan Mothers." Notes. *American Indian Law Review* 16.2 (1991): 497–531.

Jacobs, Wilbur. *Diplomacy and Indian Gifts: Anglo-French Rivalry along the Ohio and Northwest Frontiers, 1748–1763.* Stanford, Calif.: Stanford University Press, 1950.

————. "Wampum: The Protocol of Indian Diplomacy." *William and Mary Quarterly,* 3rd ser. 4:3 (October 1949): 596–604.

Jefferson, Thomas. *Notes on the State of Virginia.* 1784. Ed. William Peden. Chapel Hill: University of North Carolina Press, 1955.

Jemison, G. Peter. "Sovereignty and Treaty Rights: We Remember." *Akwesasne Notes*, n.s. 1:3–4 (Fall 1995): 10–15.

Jennings, Francis. *The Ambiguous Iroquois Empire: The Covenant Chain Confederation of Indian Tribes with English Colonies from Its Beginnings to the Lancaster Treaty of 1744*. New York: W.W. Norton, 1984.

Jennings, Francis, ed.; William N. Fenton, joint ed.; Mary A. Druke, associate ed.; David R. Miller, research ed. *The History and Culture of Iroquois Diplomacy: An Interdisciplinary Guide to the Treaties of the Six Nations and Their League*. Syracuse, N.Y.: Syracuse University Press, 1985.

Johannsen, Christina B., and John P. Ferguson, eds. *Iroquois Arts: A Directory of a People and Their Work*. Warnerville, N.Y.: Association for the Advancement of Native North American Arts and Crafts, 1983.

Johansen, Bruce E. *Forgotten Founders: Benjamin Franklin, the Iroquois, and the Rationale for the American Revolution*. Ipswich/Boston: Gambit/Harvard Common Press, 1982.

———. *Life and Death in Mohawk Country*. Golden, Colo.: North American Press/ Fulcrum, 1993.

Johansen, Bruce E., and Donald A. Grinde, Jr. *The Encyclopedia of Native American Biography*. New York: Henry Holt, 1997.

Johansen, Bruce E., and Roberto F. Maestas. *Wasi´chu: The Continuing Indian Wars*. New York: Monthly Review Press, 1979.

Johnson, Brian D. "Dances with Oscar: Canadian Actor Graham Greene Tastes Stardom." *Maclean's*, March 25, 1991, 60–61.

Johnson, Chief Elias. *Legends, Traditions and Laws, of the Iroquois, Or Six Nations*. 1881. New York: AMS Press, 1978.

Johnson, E. Pauline. *Flint and Feather: The Complete Poems of E. Pauline Johnson (Tekahionwake)*. Toronto: Musson Book Co., 1969.

———. *Legends of Vancouver*. 1911. Toronto: McClelland & Stewart, 1922.

Johnson, Tim. "The Dealer's Edge: Gaming in the Path of Native America." *Native Americas* 12:2 (Spring/Summer 1995): 16–25.

Kahnawake, Mohawk Nation at. "Crimes against the Confederacy: New York State and Oren Lyons Conspired against the Iroquois since 1988." June 15, 1997. http:// kafka.uvic.ca/~vipirg/SISIS/Mohawk/jun15ore.html.

Kates, William. "Oneidas' Enterprises Bolster Struggling Central New York." Associated Press in *Omaha World-Herald*, November 5, 1997, 22, 25.

———. "Spirits Move Joanne Shenandoah to Sing of Her Native Iroquois World." Associated Press in *Chattanooga Free Press*, June 27, 1997, D-4.

Katzer, Bruce. "The Caughnawaga Mohawks: The Other Side of Ironwork." *Journal of Ethnic Studies*, 15:4 (1988): 39–55.

Kelsay, Isabel Thompson. *Joseph Brant, 1743–1807, Man of Two Worlds*. Syracuse, N.Y.: Syracuse University Press, 1984.

Kenny, Maurice. *On Second Thought: A Compilation*. Norman: University of Oklahoma Press, 1995.

Koch, John. "Comic Stands Up for Native Americans." *Boston Globe*, November 21, 1990, 39-P.

LaDuke, Winona. "Breastmilk, PCBs, and Motherhood: An Interview With Katsi Cook, Mohawk." *Cultural Survival Quarterly* 17:4 (Winter 1994): 43–45.

Lafitau, Joseph-François. *Customs of the American Indians Compared with the Customs of Primitive Times.* 1724. Ed. and trans. William N. Fenton and Elizabeth L. Moore. 2 vols. Toronto: Champlain Society, 1974–1977.

Lancelle, Mark. "American Indians in New York State: A Demographic Profile." *Northeast Indian Quarterly* 3:4 (Winter 1986): 4–11.

Landsman, Gail. "Portrayals of the Iroquois in the Woman Suffrage Movement." Paper presented at the Annual Conference on Iroquois Research, Rensselaerville, N.Y., October 8, 1988.

————. *Sovereignty and Symbol: Indian-White Conflict at Ganienkeh.* Albuquerque: University of New Mexico Press, 1988.

Lipsyte, Robert. "Lacrosse: All-American Game." *New York Times Sunday Magazine,* June 15, 1986, 28.

Lyons, Oren, John Mohawk, Vine Deloria, Jr., Laurence Hauptman, Howard Berman, Donald A. Grinde, Jr., Curtis Berkey, and Robert Venables. *Exiled in the Land of the Free: Democracy, Indian Nations, and the Constitution.* Santa Fe, N.M.: Clear Light Publishers, 1992.

Mann, Barbara A. "The Fire at Onondaga: Wampum as Proto-writing." *Akwesasne Notes,* n.s. 1:1 (Spring 1995): 40–48.

————. "Haudenosaunee (Iroquois) Women, Legal and Political Status." *The Encyclopedia of Native American Legal Tradition.* Ed. Bruce Elliott Johansen. Westport, Conn.: Greenwood Press, 1998: 112–131.

————. "The Lynx in Time: Haudenosaunee Women's Traditions and History." *American Indian Quarterly* 21:3 (Summer 1997): 423–450.

Mann, Barbara A., and Jerry L. Fields. "A Sign in the Sky: Dating the League of the Haudenosaunee." *American Indian Culture and Research Journal* 21:2 (1997): 105–163.

Marshe, Witham. *Lancaster in 1744: Journal of the Treaty at Lancaster in 1744, with the Six Nations.* Annotated by William H. Egle, M.D. Lancaster, Penn.: New Era Steam and Job Print Press, 1884.

Martin, Kallen. "Indians Not Taxed: Will Sovereignty Survive?" *Native Americas* 13:2 (Summer 1996): 14–25.

Marx, Karl, and Friedrich Engels. *Selected Works.* New York: International Publishers, 1968.

Matthiessen, Peter. *Indian Country.* New York: Viking Press, 1984.

Mohawk, John C. "Echoes of a Native American Revitalization Movement in Some Recent Indian Law Cases in New York State." *Buffalo Law Review* 46 (1998): 1061–1080.

————. "Economic Motivations: An Iroquoian Perspective." *Northeast Indian Quarterly* 6:1–2 (Spring/Summer 1989): 56–63.

————. "In the Indian Taxing Conflict, There Is More Than One Kind of 'Us' against 'Them.' " *Buffalo News,* April 26, 1997, 2-C.

————. "The Indian Way Is a Thinking Tradition." *Northeast Indian Quarterly* 4:4 (Winter 1987): 13–17.

"Molly Brant—Loyalist." *Ontario History* 45:3 (Summer 1953).

Morgan, Lewis Henry. *Ancient Society.* New York: Henry Holt, 1877.

————. *Houses and House-life of the American Aborigines.* With an introduction by Paul Bohannan. Chicago: University of Chicago Press, 1965.

————. *League of the Ho-de-no-sau-nee, or Iroquois* [1851]. New York: Dodd, Mead & Co., 1922.

———. *League of the Iroquois*. 1851. Secaucus, N.J.: Citadel Press, 1962.

———. *Systems of Consanguinity and Affinity of the Human Family*. Washington, D.C.: Smithsonian Institution, 1870.

Morison, Samuel Eliot. *Samuel de Champlain: Father of New France*. Boston: Little, Brown, 1972.

Morrison, Andrea P., and Irwin Cotler, eds. *Justice for Natives: Searching for Common Ground*. Montréal: McGill–Queen's University Press, 1997: 298–312.

Mt. Pleasant, Jane. "The Iroquois Sustainers: Practices of a Longterm Agriculture in the Northeast." *Northeast Indian Quarterly* 6:1–2 (Spring/Summer 1989); 33–39.

Nabokov, Peter, ed. *Native American Testimony*. New York: Viking, 1991.

Norton, A. Tiffany. *History of Sullivan's Campaign against the Iroquois*. Lima, N.Y.: A. T. Norton, 1879.

Oakes, Richard. "Alcatraz Is Not an Island." *Ramparts*, December 1972, 35–38.

O'Brien, Jill. "Full-time Fun for Shenandoah." *Indian Country Today*, February 9, 1995, C-1.

O'Callaghan, Edmund B., ed. *The Documentary History of the State of New-York*. 4 vols. Albany: Weed, Parsons, 1849–1851.

O'Callaghan, Edmund B., and Berthold Fernow, eds. *Documents Relative to the Colonial History of the State of New-York*. Vol. 6. Albany: Weed, Parsons & Co., 1853–1887.

Paine, Thomas. "Common Sense." In *The Complete Political Works of Thomas Paine*. New York: Peter Eckler, 1892.

Parker, Arthur C. *An Analytical History of the Seneca Indians*. 1926. Researches and Transactions of the New York State Archeological Association, Lewis H. Morgan Chapter. New York: Kraus Reprint Co., 1970.

———. *The Code of Handsome Lake, the Seneca Prophet*. New York State Museum Bulletin No. 163, Education Department Bulletin No. 530, November 1, 1912. Albany: University of the State of New York.

———. *The Constitution of the Five Nations, or The Iroquois Book of the Great Law*. Albany: The University of the State of New York, 1916.

———. "The Constitution of the Five Nations: A Reply." *American Anthropologist* 20:1 (1918): 479–507.

———. "Handsome Lake The Peace Prophet." Speech, 1916. *The Life of Ely S. Parker, Last Grand Sachem of the Iroquois and General Grant's Military Secretary*. Buffalo: Buffalo Historical Society, 1919: 244–251.

———. *The History of the Seneca Indians*. Empire State Historical Publications, 43. Port Washington, N.Y.: Ira J. Friedman, 1967.

———. "Iroquois Adoption." *The Life of General Ely S. Parker: Last Grand Sachem of the Iroquois and General Grant's Military Secretary*. Buffalo: Buffalo Historical Society, 1919: 329–333.

———. *Iroquois Uses of Maize and Other Food Plants*. Albany: University of the State of New York, 1910.

———. *The Life of General Ely S. Parker, Last Grand Sachem of the Iroquois and General Grant's Military Secretary*. Buffalo Historical Society Publications 23. Buffalo, N.Y.: Buffalo Historical Society, 1919.

———. *Notes on the Ancestry of Cornplanter*. Rochester, N.Y.: Lewis H. Morgan Chapter, 1927.

————. *Parker on the Iroquois*. Ed. William Fenton. Syracuse, N.Y.: Syracuse University Press, 1968.

————. *Seneca Myths and Folk Tales*. 1923. Lincoln: University of Nebraska Press, 1989.

Parker, Ely S. "Address to the New York State Historical Society, May 27, 1847." Ely S. Parker Papers, Reel 1, American Philosophical Society.

Pertusati, Linda. *In Defense of Mohawk Land: Ethnopolitical Conflict in Native North America*. Albany: State University of New York Press, 1997.

Powell, J. W. "Wyandot Government: A Short Study of Tribal Society." *Annual Report of the Bureau of Ethnology to the Secretary of the Smithsonian Institution* 1 (1879–1880) : 57–69.

"Proceedings of the Commissioners Appointed by the Continental Congress to Negotiate a Treaty with the Six Nations, 1775." Papers of the Continental Congress, 1774–89. National Archives, M247, Roll 144, Item No. 134. See Treaty Council at German Flats, New York, August 15, 1775.

Prucha, Francis Paul, ed. *Documents of United States Indian Policy*. Lincoln: University of Nebraska Press, 1975.

Quintana, Jorge. "Agricultural Survey of New York State Iroquois Reservations, 1990." *Northeast Indian Quarterly* 8:1 (Spring 1991): 32–36.

Ramsay, Allan. "Thoughts on the Origin and Nature of Government." Cited in Staughton Lynd, *Intellectual Origins of American Radicalism*. New York: Pantheon Books, 1968.

Ransom, James, and Henry Lickers. "Appraisals of Toxic Contamination at the St. Regis Mohawk Reservation." *Northeast Indian Quarterly* 5:3 (Fall 1988): 22–34.

Reaman, G. Elmore. *The Trail of the Iroquois Indians: How the Iroquois Nation Saved Canada for the British Empire*. London: Frederick Muller, 1967.

Red Jacket. *A Long-Lost Speech of Red Jacket*. Ed. J. W. Sanborn. Friendship, N.Y.: N.p., 1912.

Reif, Rita. "Museum Displays Indian Artifacts." *New York Times*, November 15, 1992, 43.

Reilly, Jim. "Group from St. Regis to Return to Land of Mohawk Ancestors; Indians Buy 322 Acres of Land for a Fresh Start." *Syracuse Herald-Journal*, September 12, 1993, n.p.

Resek, Carl. *Lewis Henry Morgan: American Scholar*. Chicago: University of Chicago Press, 1960.

Richards, Cara E. *The Oneida People*. Phoenix: Indian Tribal Series, 1974.

Richter, Daniel K. *The Ordeal of the Longhouse: The Peoples of the Iroquois League in the Era of European Colonization*. Chapel Hill: University of North Carolina Press, 1992.

Richter, Daniel K., and James H. Merrell, eds. *Beyond the Covenant Chain: The Iroquois and Their Neighbors in Indian North America, 1600–1800*. Syracuse, N.Y.: Syracuse University Press, 1987.

Rickard, Jolene. "The Indian Defense League of America." *Akwesasne Notes*, n.s. 1:2 (Summer 1995): 48–53.

Robb, David. "Silverheels to Go into Hall of Honor." *Hollywood Reporter*, December 16, 1997, n.p.

Russo, Kurt, ed. *Our People/Our Land: Reflections on Common Ground: 500 Years*. Bellingham, Wash.: Lummi Tribe, 1992.

Sagard, Fr. Gabriel. *The Long Journey to the Country of the Hurons.* 1632. Ed. George M. Wrong, with Introduction and Notes. Trans. H. H. Langton. Toronto: The Champlain Society, 1939.

Saul, Stephanie. "Oneida Casino a Boon, But Not to the Tax Base." *Newsday,* September 24, 1996, A-6.

Schoolcraft, Henry R. *Notes on the Iroquois, or, Contributions to American History, Antiquities, and General Ethnology.* Albany, N.Y.: Erastus H. Pease, 1847.

Seaver, James. *A Narrative of the Life of Mrs. Mary Jemison.* 1823. Foreward by George Abrams. Syracuse, N.Y.: Syracuse University Press, 1990.

Seeber, Edward D. "Critical Views on Logan's Speech." *Journal of American Folklore* 60 (1947): 130–146.

Shebbeare, John. *Lydia, or Filial Piety.* 1755. New York: Garland Publishing, 1974.

Shimony, Annemarie Anrod. *Conservatism among the Iroquois at the Six Nations Reserve.* 1961. Syracuse: Syracuse University Press, 1994.

Siegel, Beatrice. *Fur Trappers and Traders.* New York: Walker & Co., 1981.

Snow, Dean. "Dating the Emergence of the League of the Iroquois: A Reconsideration of the Documentary Evidence." In Nancy Anne McClure Zeller, ed., *A Beautiful and Fruitful Place: Selected Rensselaerswijck Seminar Papers.* Albany, N.Y.: New Netherland Publishing, 1991: 139–143.

Snow, Dean R., Charles T. Gehring, and William A. Starna, eds. *In Mohawk Country: Early Narratives about a Native People.* Syracuse, N.Y.: Syracuse University Press, 1996.

Speck, Frank Gouldsmith. *The Iroquois: A Study in Cultural Evolution.* Cranbrook Institute of Science Bulletin No. 2. Bloomfield, Mich.: Cranbrook Press, 1945.

Stanton, Elizabeth Cady. "The Matriarchate or Mother-Age." *National Bulletin* [National Council of Women] 1:5 (February 1891): 1.

Stites, Sara Henry. *Economics of the Iroquois.* Lancaster, Penn.: New Era Printing Co., 1905.

Stokes, John D., ed. *Thanksgiving Address: Greetings to the Natural World.* Corrales, N.M.: Tracking Project, n.d.

Stone, William L. (William Leete). *Life and Times of Red-Jacket, or Sa-go-ye-wat-ha: Being the Sequel to the History of the Six Nations.* New York: Wiley and Putnam, 1841.

Sullivan, James, ed. *The Papers of Sir William Johnson.* Albany, N.Y.: University of the State of New York, 1921–1965.

Swanton, John R. "John Napoleon Brinton Hewitt." *American Anthropologist* 40:2 (1938): 286–290.

Stanton, Elizabeth Cady, Susan B. Anthony, and Matilda Joslyn Gage, eds. *History of Woman Suffrage.* Salem, N.H.: Ayer Co., 1985.

Swezey, Carl. "For Iroquois Nation, Lacrosse Is Spiritual." *Washington Post,* July 20, 1998, D-12.

Sword, Wiley. *President Washington's Indian War: The Struggle for the Old Northwest, 1790–1795.* Norman: University of Oklahoma Press, 1985.

Tehanetorens [Ray Fadden]. *A Basic Call to Consciousness.* Rooseveltown, N.Y.: Akwesasne Notes, 1986.

———. *Tales of the Iroquois.* Rooseveltown, N.Y.: Akwesasne Notes, 1976.

———. *Wampum Belts.* Onchiota, N.Y.: Six Nations Indian Museum, 1972.

Thomas, Chief Jacob, with Terry Boyle. *Teachings from the Longhouse*. Toronto: Stoddart Publishing Co., Ltd., 1994.

Thwaites, Reuben Gold, ed. and trans. *The Jesuit Relations and Allied Documents: Travels and Explorations of the Jesuit Missionaries in New France, 1610–1791*. New York: Pageant Book Company, 1959.

Tiller, Veronica E. Velarde, ed. *Tiller's Guide to Indian Country: Economic Profiles of American Indian Reservations*. Albuquerque: BowArrow Publishing, 1996.

Tomsho, Rupert. "Reservations Bear the Brunt of New Pollution." *Wall Street Journal*, November 29, 1990, 1.

Tooker, Elizabeth. *The Indians of the Northeast: A Critical Bibliography*. Bloomington: Indiana University Press, 1978.

———. *The Iroquois Ceremonial of Midwinter*. Syracuse, N.Y.: Syracuse University Press, 1970.

———. "The League of the Iroquois: Its History, Politics, and Ritual." In *Handbook of the North American Indians*. Vol. 15, *Northeast*. Washington, D.C.: Smithsonian Institution, 1978: 418–441.

———. *Lewis H. Morgan on Iroquois Material Culture*. Tucson: University of Arizona Press, 1994.

———. [Review of *Exemplar of the Liberty*, by Donald A. Grinde, Jr., and Bruce C. Johansen.] *Northeast Anthropology* 46 (Fall 1993): 103–107.

Trautmann, Thomas R. *Lewis Henry Morgan and the Invention of Kinship*. Berkeley: University of California Press, 1987.

Trelease, Allen W. *Indian Affairs in Colonial New York: The Seventeenth Century*. Ithaca, N.Y.: Cornell University Press, 1960.

Trigger, Bruce G. *The Children of Aataentsic: A History of the Huron People to 1660*. Montréal: McGill–Queen's University Press, 1976.

———. *Natives and Newcomers: Canada's "Heroic Age" Reconsidered*. Kingston and Montréal: McGill-Queen's University Press, 1985.

———. ed *Handbook of North American Indians*. Vol. 15, *Northeast*. Washington, D.C.: Smithsonian Institution, 1978.

Trigger, Bruce G., and Wilcomb E. Washburn, eds. *The Cambridge History of the Native Peoples of the Americas. North America*. 2 Vols. Cambridge, England: Cambridge University Press, 1996.

Tuck, James A. *Onondaga Iroquois Prehistory*. Syracuse, N.Y.: Syracuse University Press, 1971.

Tucker, Robert C., ed. *The Marx-Engels Reader*. New York: W. W. Norton, 1972.

Van Doren, Carl, and Julian P. Boyd, eds. *Indian Treaties Printed by Benjamin Franklin, 1736–1762*. Philadelphia: Historical Society of Pennsylvania, 1938.

Vecsey, Christopher, and William A. Starna, eds. *Iroquois Land Claims*. Syracuse, N.Y.: Syracuse University Press, 1988.

Venables, Robert W. "The Founding Fathers: Choosing to Be Romans." *Northeast Indian Quarterly* 6:4 (Winter 1989): 30–55.

———. "More Than a Game." *Northeast Indian Quarterly* 6:3 (Fall 1989): 12–15.

———. ed. *The Six Nations of New York: The 1892 United States Extra Census Bulletin*. Ithaca, N.Y.: Cornell University Press, 1995.

Vennum, Thomas, Jr. *American Indian Lacrosse: Little Brother of War*. Washington, D.C.: Smithsonian Institution Press, 1994.

Wagner, Sally Roesch. "The Iroquois Confederacy: A Native American Model for Non-sexist Men." *Changing Men* (Spring–Summer 1988): 32–33.

———. *The Untold Story of the Iroquois Influence on Early Feminists*. Aberdeen, S.D.: Sky Carrier Press, 1996.

Wall, Steve. "Gallery: Snowsnake." *Northeast Indian Quarterly* 5:4 (Winter 1988): 26–33.

Wallace, Anthony F. C. *The Death and Rebirth of the Seneca*. New York: Knopf, 1970.

———. "The Dekanawideh Myth Analyzed as the Record of a Revitalization Movement." *Ethnohistory* 5:2 (1958): 118–130.

———. "Political Organization and Land Tenure among the Northeastern Indians, 1600–1830." *Southwestern Journal of Anthropology* 13 (1957): 301–321.

Wallace, Paul A. W. *Conrad Weiser, 1696–1760: Friend of Colonist and Mohawk*. New York: Russell & Russell, 1971.

———. *Indians in Pennsylvania*. Harrisburg: Pennsylvania Historical and Museum Commission, 1961.

———. "John Heckewelder's Indians and the Fenimore Cooper Tradition." *Proceedings of the American Philosophical Society* 96.4 (August 1952): 496–504.

———. "The Return of Hiawatha." *New York History: Quarterly Journal of the New York State Historical Association* 29:4 (1948): 385–403.

———. *The White Roots of Peace*. Philadelphia: University of Pennsylvania Press, 1946; Reprint, Santa Fe, N.M.: Clear Light Publishers, 1994.

———. ed. *Thirty Thousand Miles with John Heckewelder*. Pittsburgh: University of Pittsburgh Press, 1958.

Washburn, Wilcomb E., and Bruce G. Trigger. "Native Peoples in Euro-American Historiography." In Bruce G. Trigger and Wilcomb E. Washburn, eds., *The Cambridge History of the Native Peoples of the Americas. North America*, Vol. 2. Cambridge, England: Cambridge University Press, 1996: 61–124.

Waters, Frank. *Brave Are My People*. Santa Fe, N.M.: Clear Light, 1993.

Waugh, F. W. *Iroquois Foods and Food Preparation*. 1916. Ottawa: National Museum of Canada, 1973.

Weaver, Sally M. "Seth Newhouse and the Grand River Confederacy in the Mid-Nineteenth Century." In Michael K. Foster, Jack Campisi, and Marianne Mithun, eds. *Extending the Rafters: Interdisciplinary Approaches to Iroquoian Studies*. Albany: State University of New York Press, 1984: 165–182.

Whitaker, Robert. "Akwesasne Seek to Rebuild a Nation." *Plattsburgh* [New York] *Press-Republican*, January 15, 1989, 1.

White Roots of Peace. *The Great Law of Peace of the Longhouse People*. Rooseveltown, N.Y.: Akwesasne Notes, 1977.

Wickens, Barbara, ed. "On the Case with Greene." *Maclean's*, October 20, 1997, 74.

Wilson, Edmund. *Apologies to the Iroquois*. New York: Farrar, Straus & Cudahy, 1960; Vintage Books, 1960.

Womack, Craig. "The Spirit of Independence: Maurice Kenny's *Tekonwatonti/Molly Brant: Poems of War.*" *American Indian Culture and Research Journal* 18:4 (1994): 95–118.

Woodbury, Hanni, comp. *Concerning the League: The Iroquois League Tradition As Dictated in Onondaga by John Arthur Gibson*. Comp. Hanni Woodbury, Reg Henry, and Harry Webster on the basis of A. A. Goldenweiser's manuscript.

Algonquian and Iroquoian Linguistics, Memoir No. 9. Winnipeg, Manitoba: University of Manitoba Press, 1992.

Wraxall, Peter. *An Abridgment of the Indian Affairs in the Colony of New York, 1678–1751*. Ed. C. H. McIlwain. Cambridge, Mass.: Harvard University Press, 1915.

Wright, Ronald. *Stolen Continents*. Boston: Houghton Mifflin, 1992.

York, Geoffrey, and Loreen Pindera. *People of the Pines*. Toronto: Little, Brown, 1991.

Index

Page numbers in **bold type** refer to main entries in the encyclopedia.

About the Contributors

JOHN KAHIONHES FADDEN is associate curator of the Six Nations Indian Museum in Onchiota, New York. He is also a noted artist who has illustrated more than sixty books.

DOUG GEORGE-KANENTIIO has established Round Dance Productions with his wife, the noted Indian singer Joanne Shenandoah. He also has written a weekly opinion column for the *Syracuse Herald-American* and is a member of a number of Haudenosaunee policy committees.

BARBARA A. GRAY (KANATIYOSH) is pursuing a doctorate in justice studies at Arizona State University.

BRUCE E. JOHANSEN is Robert T. Reilly Professor of Communication and coordinator of the Native American Studies Program at the University of Nebraska at Omaha. He has written fifteen books and numerous magazine articles.

BRENDA LAFRANCE has served as a tribal trustee for the St. Regis Mohawk Tribal Council. LaFrance holds academic degrees in biology and chemistry, as well as industrial management with an emphasis in computer-based information systems.

BARBARA A. MANN teaches in the English Department at the University of Toledo (Ohio). She is the author of *Iroquoian Women: Gantowisas of the Haudenosaunee League* (2000).

KALLEN MARTIN is a frequent contributor to *Native Americas*, a national news magazine published at Cornell University. Martin freelances from Syracuse, where she also is working on her Doctorate at Syracuse University. She also has worked as general manager of CKON radio at Akwesasne and in several professional positions on the reservation.

JOHN C. MOHAWK is an associate professor of Native American Studies at the State University of New York at Buffalo. He is a coauthor of *Exiled in the Land of the Free* (1992) and is a frequent contributor to *Native Americas* magazine.

ISBN 0-313-30880-2